BERENIKE
1999/2000

BERENIKE

1999/2000

REPORT ON THE EXCAVATIONS AT BERENIKE,

INCLUDING EXCAVATIONS IN WADI KALALAT

AND SIKET, AND THE SURVEY OF THE

MONS SMARAGDUS REGION

EDITORS:
STEVEN E. SIDEBOTHAM
WILLEKE WENDRICH

COTSEN INSTITUTE OF ARCHAEOLOGY · UNIVERSITY OF CALIFORNIA, LOS ANGELES

THE COTSEN INSTITUTE OF ARCHAEOLOGY at UCLA is a research unit at the University of California, Los Angeles that promotes the comprehensive and interdisciplinary study of the human past. Established in 1973, the Cotsen Institute is a unique resource that provides an opportunity for faculty, staff, graduate students, research associates, volunteers and the general public to gather together in their explorations of ancient human societies.

Former President and CEO of Neutrogena Corporation Lloyd E. Cotsen has been associated with UCLA for more than 30 years as a volunteer and donor and maintains a special interest in archaeology. Lloyd E. Cotsen has been an advisor and supporter of the Institute since 1980. In 1999, The UCLA Institute of Archaeology changed its name to the Cotsen Institute of Archaeology at UCLA to honor the longtime support of Lloyd E. Cotsen.

Cotsen Institute Publications specializes in producing high-quality data monographs in several different series, including Monumenta Archaeologica, Monographs, and Perspectives in California Archaeology, as well as innovative ideas in the Cotsen Advanced Seminar Series and the Ideas, Debates and Perspectives Series. Through the generosity of Lloyd E. Cotsen, our publications are subsidized, producing superb volumes at an affordable price.

THE COTSEN INSTITUTE OF ARCHAEOLOGY AT UCLA
Charles Stanish, Director
Shauna K. Mecartea, Executive Editor & Media Relations Officer
Eric C. Gardner, Publications Coordinator

EDITORIAL BOARD OF THE COTSEN INSTITUTE OF ARCHAEOLOGY
Jeanne E. Arnold, Christopher B. Donnan, Shauna K. Mecartea, John K. Papadopoulos, James Sackett, and Charles Stanish

EDITORIAL ADVISORY BOARD
Chapurukha Kusimba, Joyce Marcus, Colin Renfrew, and John Yellen

This book is set in 10-point Janson Text, with titles in 29-point OPTI Forquet Oldstyle.
Edited by Rena Copperman
Designed by William Morosi
Index by Robert and Cynthia Swanson

Library of Congress Cataloging-in-Publication Data
Berenike 1999/2000 : report on the excavations at Berenike, including excavations in Wadi Kalalat and Siket, and the survey of the Mons Smaragdus Region / editors, Willeke Wendrich, Steven E. Sidebotham.
    p. cm. -- (Monograph ; 56)
  Includes bibliographical references and index.
  ISBN 978-1-931745-28-4 (pbk. : alk. paper) -- ISBN 978-1-931745-29-1 (cloth : alk. paper)
  1. Baranis (Egypt)--Antiquities. 2. Egypt--Antiquities. 3. Excavations (Archaeology)--Egypt. I. Wendrich, Willemina. II. Sidebotham, Steven E.
III. Cotsen Institute of Archaeology at UCLA. IV. Title. V. Series.

DT73.B375B48 2007
932--dc22

2007014234

CONTENTS

TABLES, FIGURES, AND PLATES

PLATES

CHAPTER 1

INTRODUCTION

S. E. SIDEBOTHAM AND W. Z. WENDRICH

The fifth and sixth excavation seasons at Berenike, on the Red Sea coast of Egypt, were conducted by the University of Delaware and Leiden University from December 1998 to March 1999 and from December 1999 through March 2000 respectively. The primary focus of these seasons was continued excavations at Berenike (23° 54.62' N / 35° 28.42' E), about 825 km south of Suez and approximately 260 km east of Aswan. The previous excavation seasons, starting in 1994, have been published in five volumes of reports on the archaeology, survey, and finds analysis in a special series of Leiden University's CNWS publications (Sidebotham and Wendrich 1995–2000). The Berenike publications have found a new home in the Monographs Series of the Cotsen Institute of Archaeology at the University of California in Los Angeles.

After seven years of work, we have reached a suitable moment to look back on previous excavation reports. The chapter on the Berenike Survey (Chapter 2) gives a convenient overview of the trenches excavated to date. Here, the reader can find references to the maps and plans published in the earlier volumes. At the back of the volume a list of errata for the first five volumes has been incorporated. The interpretative summary and conclusion give an overview of the information available from the past seven excavation seasons and thus rounds off what could be considered the first phase of the Berenike project, during which the main research questions focused on the international trade in the early and late Roman periods.

During the 1999 and 2000 seasons, the project concentrated excavations on the eastern parts of the site, specifically the area due east of the Serapis temple. This involved excavations in whole or part of 18 trenches, including one begun in the 1996 season and two started during the 1998 season. The main research focus this season was the function of the two rings of buildings east of the town's center. The easternmost ring borders the ancient shoreline. Here work was continued on a large building where trenches BE96-8, BE96/97/98-12, and BE98-22 had been excavated in previous seasons. During the 1999 and 2000 seasons trenches BE98/99-22, BE99/00-30, and BE00-39 were excavated here, and just to the north of this building a separate trench was started (BE99-26).

The second semicircle lies two cross streets inland (west) of the outer ring of buildings. A number of trenches were placed or continued in an area dubbed the "late Roman quarter," the remains between the eastern edge of the site and the town's center near the Serapis temple. Trenches here in previous seasons included BE98-20, BE98-21, and BE98-23. During the 1999 and 2000 seasons, the trenches excavated were BE98/99-23, BE99/00-32, BE99-27, BE99-28, and adjacent BE00-38, BE00-34, BE00-37, and BE00-41. Excavation here aimed to shed additional light on the "international" commerce that passed through Berenike, but also was preparation for the second phase of research in Berenike, concentrating on the Ptolemaic habitation of the town, because the position of these trenches would help determine the eastern limits of the Ptolemaic settlement.

In the central part of town, excavations continued in trench BE96/97/98/99/00-10. Work in this large trench at the highest point of the site, just north of the Serapis temple, aimed at as complete a recovery as possible of a continuous stratigraphic record of activity at Berenike from the latest until the earliest period of its history.

Excavations in the early Roman trash dump at the northern edge of the city continued to provide a wealth of material, including ostraka, papyri, textiles, basketry, leather, wood, and faunal and botanical remains. In previous seasons trenches BE96/97-13 and BE97/98-19 were excavated in this area, and work continued in trenches BE99-29, BE99-31, and BE00-33.

For the first time during the 2000 season, trenches in the extreme western part of the site in the Ptolemaic industrial quarter, south of trench BE96-11, were excavated; their placement was based upon a magnetic survey conducted in 1999. These included BE00-35, BE00-36, and BE00-40. In addition to excavations at Berenike, there were small-scale excavations at two nearby sites, the small fort in Wadi Kalalat and the small *praesidium* at Siket.

There was no survey during the 1999 season; that undertaken during the 2000 season comprised both site-extensive and site-intensive fieldwork. The former included the recording of a number of sites—road stations, gold and beryl mines, and a settlement site of unknown function—continued survey and recording the course of the Via Hadriana, and a site-intensive survey of the beryl-mining settlement at Sikait. Excavations at Berenike are planned for a number of seasons to come.

The 1999 and 2000 seasons of fieldwork at Berenike were possible due to the collaboration of many individuals from the United States, the Netherlands, the United Kingdom, Belgium, Australia, Italy, Poland, and Egypt and the financial support of numerous granting agencies and private donors. The team, consisting of people both in the field and those who were not actually at Berenike, included Steven E. Sidebotham (co-director, numismatist, surveyor, and photographer), Willemina Z. Wendrich (co-director and basketry specialist) and (in alphabetical order) Roger S. Bagnall (papyrologist, ostrakologist, epigrapher), Ronald Bakker (photographer), Hans Barnard (medical doctor, architect, and surveyor), Heather Beckman (trench supervisor), Jolanda E. M. F. Bos (trench supervisor and draftsperson), Rebecca Bridgman (pottery specialist), Lauren (M.) T. Bruning (trench supervisor), Paola Buzi (trench supervisor), Millie C. Cassidy (general assistant), R. C. (Christine) Dijkstra (artist), Crystal D. Fritz (trench supervisor), Brandon C. Foster (surveyor), Zadia A. Green (artist), Anne E. Haeckl (trench supervisor and sculpture specialist), James A. Harrell (geologist), C. C. (Christina) Helms (papyrologist, ostrakologist, epigrapher), A. Martin Hense (metal specialist, architect, and artist), Tomasz M. Herbich (geophysicist), Bahaa S. Labib (pottery assistant), Stephennie Mulder (trench supervisor), Paul T. Nicholson (glass specialist), Hendrikje M. Nouwens (registrar and camp manager), David K. Pearce (pottery specialist), Fabienne Pigière (assistant archaeozoologist), Lisa A. Pintozzi (trench supervisor and surveyor), Jennifer A. Price (glass specialist), Gillian Pyke (pottery specialist), Jean-Louis G. Rivard (surveyor and architect), Wayne Sawtell (trench supervisor), Ilka Schacht (trench supervisor and surveyor), Bastiaan J. Seldenthuis (photographer), Veerasamy M. Selvakumar (trench supervisor), Ashraf al-Senousi (pottery specialist), Roberta S. Tomber (pottery specialist), Barbara J. M. Tratsaert (trench supervisor and draftsperson), Wim J. Van Neer (archaeozoologist), André J. Veldmeijer (cordage specialist), Arthur M. F. W. Verhoogt (papyrologist, ostrakologist, epigrapher), Caroline Vermeeren (wood and charcoal specialist), Felicity C. Wild (textile specialist), John P. Wild (textile specialist), Ingrid Ystgaard (trench supervisor), and Ronald E. Zitterkopf (surveyor). We are thankful to Dr. Nabil Swelim, who prepared several of the illustrations for Chapter 3, to Jean De Angelis for proofreading, to Zoe Borovsky for many hours of document reformatting, and to Hans Barnard, who spent days redrawing, lettering, scanning, and updating the many maps, plans, and photographs in this volume.

Success was due to our hardworking support staff: Dessouki Saad Dawud (cook), Salaam Abd el-Harris Ibrahim/Awad (steward), Adel Abd el-Harris Ibrahim (steward), Redah Sayed Hassan/Hamam (liaison officer). The backbone of our excavations was, as always, the hardworking and good-humored team of Ababda workmen who labored tirelessly, even during the month of Ramadan.

Our sincerest thanks go to Dr. Gaballa Ali Gaballa, Secretary-General of the Supreme Council of Antiquities (SCA), members of the Permanent Committee of the SCA, Mr. Husein Afyuni, chief of the SCA Inspectorate of Qena and the Rea Sea area and the representatives of the SCA at the excavations; in 1999 they were Mr. Mohammed Gamal Saad el-Din and Mr. Mohammed Abbas Ahmed, in 2000 Mr. Mohsen Lamey Reaad and Mr. Mohammed Abbas Ahmed.

The following agencies and individuals provided financial support or donations in kind for the 1999 and 2000 seasons: the National Geographic Society, the Royal Netherlands Embassy in Cairo, the University of

Delaware (office of the Dean of the College of Arts and Science), Leiden University Department of Languages and Cultures of the Ancient Near East, Columbia University, the American Philosophical Society, the Dorot Foundation, the Gratama Foundation, Mallinson Architects of London, Philips Egypt, Organon Egypt, 3-Com computer (Mr. T. Hudnall and Mr. F. Prunesti), Dionysos Systems (Mr. Nico Remiens and Ms. Denise Schmidt), the Lotus Hotel, Cairo (Mr. Wasfi Doss), the private donors of the Berenike Foundation and in the United States (in alphabetical order): Ms. Millie C. Cassidy, Mr. Bruce R. Gould, Ms. Norma Kershaw, and Ms. Carol R. Maltenfort. In addition we would like to thank Prof. C. C. Balascio, University of Delaware for loan of equipment and Mr. W. Weissman of Instrument Sales and Service, Inc., in Wilmington, Delaware, for his advice and expertise.

We dedicate this volume to two dear friends and colleagues who both sadly succumbed to illness in the past two years. Our dear friend and longtime survey guide, (Hagg) Tawfiq Ali Mohammed, passed away in August 1999 (Plate 1-1), and our friend and colleague, Dr. Vimala Begley (Plate 1-2), died in March 2000. They are sorely missed.

Plate 1-1 (Hagg) Tawfik Ali Mohammed

Plate 1-2 Dr. Vimala Begley

CHAPTER 2 ～

SURVEY OF BERENIKE

H. BARNARD AND W.Z. WENDRICH

The purpose of this chapter is to give a tabular overview of the excavations at Berenike from 1994 to 2000, organized by distinctive areas of the site, which will enable the reader to trace information in earlier reports and locate the different maps and plans published over the years. During the Berenike 2000 season, the authors checked the Berenike site grid and coordinates of the excavation trenches using a Wild T16 theodolite and attached Wild DI4 EDM (electronic distance measuring device). The Berenike site grid had been laid out in 1994, using the same theodolite and steel-tape measures to facilitate survey of the ancient city and its environs (Aldsworth et al. 1995). During the following seven excavation seasons, 41 trenches were laid out with the aid of steel tape measures and the 50-m grid markers placed during the 1994–1996 site survey (Aldsworth and Barnard 1996a; Aldsworth and Barnard 1998a). Given the sometimes-awkward position of these trenches in relation to the markers, the locally rough terrain and the often-difficult conditions, such as extremely strong winds, these measurements could not always be taken with maximum accuracy. As soon as a more accurate survey method became available, the above-mentioned EDM system with sufficient electric power to run it, it was decided to check the accuracy of the site grid (both angle and distance), followed by a survey of the existing trenches.

In the course of this survey a number of new markers were installed to allow for the future planning and excavation of more-distant areas. All except one of the previously installed survey markers appeared to be placed with sufficient accuracy (less than 0.05 m deviation). This single inaccurately located marker was moved to the correct position, less than 0.15 m toward the north.

2.1 OVERVIEW OF TRENCHES 1994-2000

A new survey of the existing trenches was done by placing the theodolite with EDM over one of the survey markers and measuring distance and angle (both horizontal and vertical) to the southwest and northeast corners of nearby trenches. Grid coordinates and dimensions of all trenches were then calculated using trigonometry. Dimensions of the trenches could be easily checked against plans drawn during excavation. Over the years the original corners of most trenches had collapsed, due to wind and water erosion. Because of this and the aforementioned problems with the original positioning of the trenches, it was decided to round off all grid coordinates to the nearest 0.5 m. Table 2-1 records the results of this survey, along with information on the season, or seasons, in which the trench was excavated, as well as the person, or persons, responsible for the excavation and recording. For the convenience of the reader, the dimensions of each trench (NS x EW) and, where relevant, its association to other trenches or previously identified structures are given. More important, the quarter of Berenike in which the trench was opened is provided. Maps of these areas are shown in Figures 2-3 through 2-10. An updated overall plan of the site can be found at the back of this book (Figure 2-15). Finally, there are references to a more detailed description of each trench. The archaeology of each trench and the unearthed materials are described in one of the Berenike reports, or in separate volumes, some of which are still in preparation, since the full reports on trenches are published after excavation has been finished.

Trench	Year	Grid Coordinates and Size	Supervisor	Description
1	1994 1995	555-560 NS / 1995-2000 EW 5 x 5 m	Dori Gould	leveled area (Fig. 2-3) **94**: 21-23, 33-36 **95**: 8-25, 271-287
2	1994 1995	425-430 NS / 2170-2175 EW 5 x 5 m	Paul Haanen	SE quarter (Fig. 2-6) **94**: 23-27, 36-37 **95**: 25-42
3	1995	579-584 NS / 1916-1921 EW 5 x 5 m in Structure N	Heather Beckman	trash dump (Fig. 2-9) **95**: 43-52, 287-289
4	1995	630-635 NS / 2123-2128 EW 5 x 5 m in Structure F	Lenny Sundelin	NE quarter (Fig. 2-7) associated with 7 and 17 **95**: 53-76, 205-208, 315-317
5	1995 1996 1997	384.5-389.5 NS / 2127-2132 EW 5 x 5 m in Structure D	Shinu Abraham	SE quarter (Fig. 2-8) **95**: 76-82, 209-211 **96**: 13-20 **97**: 5-13, 124-136, 219-222, 258-259, 277
6	1995 1996	527-532 NS / 1906-1911 EW 5 x 5 m in Structure H	Heather Beckman	western quarter (Fig. 2-4) associated with 16 (West Shrine) **95**: 82-93, 229-243 **96**: 20-45, 238-240 **97**: 207-213, 222-223
7	1995 1996	637-642 NS / 2118-2123 EW 5 x 5 m in Structure F	Jolanda Bos	NE quarter (Fig. 2-7) associated with 4 and 17 **95**: 53-76 **96**: 46-62
8	1996	552-559 NS / 2161-2165 EW 7 x 4 m	Lisa Pintozzi	NE quarter (Fig. 2-7) associated with 12, 22, 30 and 39 **96**: 63-79
9	1996	451-456 NS / 2112-2118 EW 5 x 6 m in Structure A	Laurent Tholbecq	SE quarter (Fig. 2-8) **96**: 79-96, 240-241
10	1996 1997 1998 1999 2000	516-526 NS / 1988-1998 EW 10 x 10 m 516.5-525.5 NS / 1988.5-1997.5 EW 9 x 9 m 517-525 NS / 1989-1997 EW 8 x 8 m 517.5-524.5 NS / 1989.5-1996.5 EW 7 x 7 m 518-524 NS / 1990-1996 EW 6 x 6 m	Jeroen van Eijk Jeroen van Eijk / Lauren Bruning Lauren Bruning	leveled area (Fig. 2-3) originally 10 x 10 m, steps in 0.5 m each season **96**: 97-101 **97**: 13-29, 243-255, 279 **98**: 3-24, 172-173, 192-195 (this volume)
11	1996	545-550 NS / 1603-1608 EW 5 x 5 m in Structure R	Anne Haeckl	Ptolemaic area (Fig. 2-10) **96**: 101-118, 163-196
12	1996 1997 1998	559-566 NS / 2167-2171 EW 7 x 4 m	Lisa Pintozzi	NE quarter (Fig. 2-6) associated with 8, 22, 30 and 39 **96**: 63-79 **97**: 29-46 **98**: 25-28, 174
13	1996 1997	614-615 NS / 1931-1932 EW 1 x 1 m *sondage* 614-619 NS / 1927-1932 EW 5 x 5 m	Dori Gould Jenny Cashman	trash dump (Fig. 2-9) originally a 1 x 1 m *sondage*, extended to 5 x 5 m trench **96**: 242-243, 290-305 **97**: 46-57, 137-143, 201-205, 259-274, 279-282
14	1996	578-579 NS / 1961-1962 EW 1 x 1 m *sondage*	Dori Gould	trash dump (Fig. 2-9) **96**: 244-246, 290-305

15	1996	400-401 NS / 2072-2073 EW 1 x 1 m *sondage*	Dori Gould	southern quarter (no map) **96**: 246-248, 290-305
16	1997 1998	527-532 NS / 1899-1906 EW 5 x 7 m in Structure H	Anne Haeckl	western quarter (Fig. 2-4) associated with 6 (West Shrine) **97**: 57-80, 144-145, 222-223, 283-284 **98**: 44-73, 174
17	1997 1998	635-638 NS / 2108.5-2117.5 EW 3 x 9 m in Structure F	Jolanda Bos	NE quarter (Fig. 2-7) associated with 4 and 7 **97**: 80-87, 224 **98**: 73-88, 174
18	1997 1998	479-483 NS / 2163-2171 EW 4 x 8 m	Shinu Abraham	SE quarter (Fig. 2-8) **97**: 87-90 **98**: 88-100, 174
19	1997 1998	618.5-621.5 NS / 1910-1913 EW 3 x 3 m	Jolanda Bos/Barbara Tratsaert	trash dump (Fig. 2-9) associated with 29, 31 and 33 **97**: 90-91, 201-205 **98**: 100-107, 174-176, 179-181, 230-241
20	1998	541-545 NS / 2071-2078 EW 4 x 7 m	Heather Beckman	central quarter (Fig. 2-6) associated with 27 **98**: 107-120, 176
21	1998	519-523 NS / 2107-2113 EW 4 x 6 m	Geoff Compton	central quarter (Fig. 2-6), trash dump **98**: 120-134, 176, 183-189, 241-250
22	1998 1999	546-555 NS / 2178-2182 EW 9 x 4 m	Lisa Pintozzi	NE quarter (Fig. 2-7) associated with 8, 12, 30 and 39 **98**: 29-44 (this volume)
23	1998 1999	614-619 NS / 2031-2036 EW 5 x 5 m	Barbara Tratsaert	northern quarter (Fig. 2-5) associated with 32 (North Shrine) **98**: 134-144, 178, 195-197 (this volume)
24	1998	662-663 NS / 1919-1920 EW 1 x 1 m *sondage*	Dori Gould	trash dump (Fig. 2-9) **98**: 144
25	1998	613.5-614.5 NS / 1949-1950 EW 1 x 1 m *sondage*	Dori Gould	trash dump (Fig. 2-9) **98**: 145, 230-233
26	1999	622.5-631.5 NS / 2158.5-2162.5 EW 9 x 4 m in Structure B	Jolanda Bos	NE quarter (Fig. 2-7) (this volume)
27	1999	545-549 NS / 2071-2078 EW 4 x 7 m	Heather Beckman	central quarter (Fig. 2-6) associated with 20 (this volume)
28	1999	569-578 NS / 2066.5-2070.5 EW 9 x 4 m	Anne Haeckl	central quarter (Fig. 2-6) associated with 38 (this volume)
29	1999	619-624 NS / 1916-1919 EW 5 x 3 m	Ilka Schacht	trash dump (Fig. 2-9) associated with 19, 31 and 33 (this volume)
30	1999 2000	554-566 NS / 2178-2183.5 EW 12 x 5.5 m	Lisa Pintozzi	NE quarter (Fig. 2-7) associated with 8, 12, 22 and 39 (this volume)
31	1999	604.5-609.5 NS / 1909.5-1913.5 EW 5 x 4 m	Ilka Schacht	trash dump (Fig. 2-9) associated with 19, 29 and 33 (this volume)
32	1999 2000	614-619 NS / 2036-2039 EW 5 x 3 m	Barbara Tratsaert	northern quarter (Fig. 2-5) associated with 23 (North Shrine) (this volume)

33	2000	611.5-616.5 NS / 1909-1914 EW 5 x 5 m	Stephennie Mulder	trash dump (Fig. 2-9) associated with 19, 29 and 31 (this volume)
34	2000	537-543.5 NS / 2101.5-2107.5 EW 6.5 x 6 m	Barbara Tratsaert	central quarter (Fig. 2-6) (this volume)
35	2000	464-470 NS / 1544-1550 EW 6 x 6 m	Wayne Sawtell	Ptolemaic area (Fig. 2-10) associated with 36 (this volume)
36	2000	455.5-463 NS / 1550-1556 EW 7.5 x 6 m	Veerasamy Selvakumar	Ptolemaic area (Fig. 2-10) associated with 35 (this volume)
37	2000	507-514 NS / 2041-2049 EW 7 x 8 m	Ingrid Ystgaard	central quarter (Fig. 2-6) (this volume)
38	2000	569-579 NS / 2070.5-2074.5 EW 10 x 4 m	Anne Haeckl	central quarter (Fig. 2-6) associated with 28 (this volume)
39	2000	548-558 NS / 2165-2170 EW 10 x 5 m	Lisa Pintozzi	NE quarter (Fig. 2-7) associated with 8, 12, 22 and 30 (this volume)
40	2000	396.5-404.5 NS / 1532.5-1538.5 EW 8 x 6 m	Wayne Sawtell	Ptolemaic area (Fig. 2-10) (this volume)
41	2000	556-562 NS / 2057.5-2064 EW 6 x 6.5 m	Crystal Fritz	central quarter (Fig. 2-6) (this volume)
mag. survey	1999	340-540 NS / 1520-1600 EW 200 x 80 m	Tomasz Herbich	Ptolemaic area (Fig. 2-10) area of magnetometric survey (this volume)
SM-1	1996	594-596 NS / 1848-1850 EW 2 x 2 m	Anton Ervynck	shell midden on trash dump (west of Fig. 2-9) 96: 360

Table 2-1 Trenches excavated at Berenike between 1994 and 2000.
Trench: trench number without the usual prefixes indicating the year of excavation;
Year: year(s) of excavation;
Grid coordinates and size: location of the trench on the Berenike site grid, dimensions of the trench (NS x EW) and, where applicable, position of the trench in relation to structures identified on the Berenike Site Survey 1994–1996 as published in the report on the 1996 season (Sidebotham and Wendrich 1998a);
Supervisor: person(s) primarily responsible for the excavation and recording of the trench;
Description: identification of the part of Berenike in which the trench was excavated. Figures 2-3 through 2-10 show maps of the areas mentioned. Where relevant, an association with other trenches is mentioned and, finally, references (volume, in bold, with page numbers) to a more detailed description of the results are given. The relevant volumes are:
94: report on the 1994 season (Sidebotham and Wendrich 1995);
95: report on the 1995 season (Sidebotham and Wendrich 1996a);
96: report on the 1996 season (Sidebotham and Wendrich 1998a);
97: report on the 1997 season (Sidebotham and Wendrich 1999a);
98: report on the 1998 season (Sidebotham and Wendrich 2000a).

2.2 TRENCHES IN THE HINTERLAND

From 1996 onward the survey of the hinterland of Berenike included excavations in certain areas of special interest. These include the desert settlement in Wadi Shenshef (about 21 km SW of Berenike), the large fort (*praesidium*) and the small fort in Wadi Kalalat (about 8 km SW of Berenike), and the *praesidium* at Siket ("Murray's fort," about 7 km WNW of Berenike (Sidebotham and Wendrich 1999b: 446; Sidebotham and Wendrich 2000b, 420). With the relatively large distances to Berenike, the trenches in these areas were not oriented to the Berenike site grid but were laid out in relation to the local structures visible on the surface. The characteristics of these trenches appear in Table 2-2.

Trench	Year	Supervisor	Description
BE96 501	1996	Hans Barnard, René Cappers	Shenshef (south side of wadi), section through midden M7 **96**: 170-179, 211, 290-305, 368
BE96 502	1996	Hans Barnard, René Cappers	Shenshef (north side of wadi), section through midden M29 **96**: 170-179, 211, 290-305, 368
BE96 503	1996	Hans Barnard, René Cappers	Shenshef (south side of wadi), section through midden M10 **96**: 170-179, 211, 290-305, 368
Ka.01	1997	Dori Gould	Kalalat, large fort (*praesidium*), 5 x 5 m trench in gate area **97**: 145, 319, 443-444; **98**: 340, 381-387, 403-413
Ka.02	1998	Dori Gould	Kalalat, large fort (*praesidium*), 5 x 5 m trench in blocked portal **98**: 340, 387-391
Ka.03	1998	Dori Gould	Kalalat, large fort (*praesidium*), 5 x 6 m trench inside east wall **98**: 340, 392-395, 403-413
Kl.01	2000	Anne Haeckl	Kalalat, small fort, 4 x 6 m trench in gate area (this volume)
Sh.01	1997	Dori Gould	Shenshef (north side of wadi), 2 x 2 m trench in M20 (area 5) **97**: 146-151, 372-373; **98**: 251
Sh.02	1997	Dori Gould	Shenshef (south side of wadi), 1 x 4 m trench in M4 **97**:146-151, 373; **98**: 251
Sh.03	1997	Dori Gould	Shenshef (north side of wadi), 1 x 4 m trench in M53 **97**: 373-374; **98**: 251
Sh.04	1997	Dori Gould	Shenshef (north side of wadi), 4 x 1 m trench in M54 **97**: 374; **98**: 251
Sh.05	1997	Dori Gould	Shenshef (north side of wadi), 4 x 1 m trench in M21 **97**: 274, 374; **98**: 251
Sh.06	1997	Dori Gould	Shenshef (south side of wadi), 4 x 1 m trench in M55 (area 2) **97**: 374-375; **98**: 251
Sh.07	1997	Dori Gould	Shenshef (south side of wadi), 4 x 1 m trench in M56 (area 3) **97**:146-151, 375; **98**: 251
Sh.8a	1997	René Cappers	Shenshef (north side of wadi), 1 x 1 m *sondage* through M29 **97**: 420-426
Sh.8b	1997	René Cappers	Shenshef (north side of wadi), 1 x 1 m *sondage* through M29 **97**: 420-426
Sk.01	2000	Lisa Pintozzi	Siket *praesidium*, 4 x 3 m trench in gate area (this volume)

Table 2-2: Trenches excavated in the environs of Berenike between 1996 and 2000.
Trench: trench number without the usual prefixes;
Year: year of excavation
Supervisor: person(s) primarily responsible for the excavation and recording of the trench
Description: location and, where relevant, dimensions of the trench (NS x EW) followed by references (volume, in bold, with page numbers) to a more detailed description of the results
The relevant volumes are:
96: report of the 1996 season (Sidebotham and Wendrich 1998a)
97: report of the 1997 season (Sidebotham and Wendrich 1999a)
98: report of the 1998 season (Sidebotham and Wendrich 2000a)

2.3 AREA DIVISION OF BERENIKE

Distribution of the trenches over the site, combined with results from the excavation of these trenches, allows for a division of ancient Berenike into several areas. This division is primarily based upon the present topography and the remains of human activity visible on the surface. This, and the fact that this human activity includes recent leveling with a bulldozer or front-end loader of part of the site, make it unlikely that this division reflects the original layout of Berenike. It is intended as an aid to visualize the relative positions of the trenches. For these reasons, the names given to the areas are rather descriptive and only serve to identify them. With this in mind, the areas are described as follows.

2.3.1 THE LEVELED AREA (Figure 2-3)

This irregular and obviously disturbed area is located around, but mostly north and west of, the large Serapis temple, which must have been the center of the town for most of the period it existed. It includes Structure M as well as trenches BE94/95-1 and BE96/97/98/99/00-10.

Leveling of this area most likely took place in or shortly after 1973 as a part of the defensive efforts by the Arab Republic of Egypt. It was performed by pushing the soil and ancient remains that made up the highest part of the site just north of the main Serapis temple, over the lower-lying areas. This was done with large earth-moving equipment, probably to ensure a clear view and line of fire from the bunkers about a

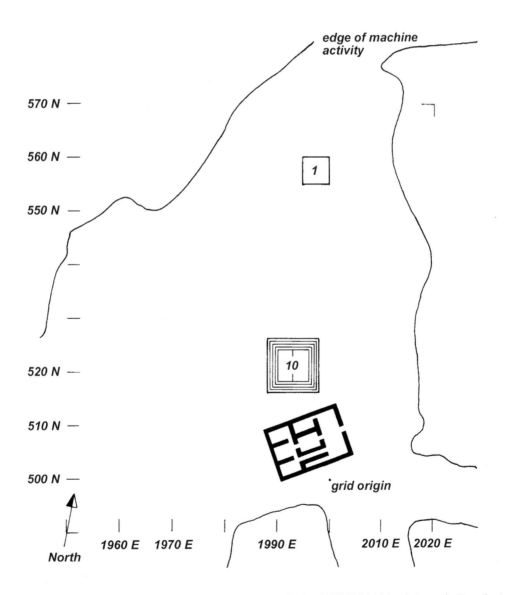

Figure 2-3   Part of the *leveled area* showing the position of trenches BE94/95-1 and BE96/97/98/99/00-10 in relation to the Berenike site-grid (note the grid origin) and the Serapis temple.

kilometer inland. There is no information available on how high the remains were standing before the leveling took place. At present the level of this area, which is still the highest of the site, is about 6.5–6.6 m above sea level (asl).

Trench BE94/95-1 was opened in this area to determine the downward extent of the damage. After removal of the debris, excavation and coring indicated at least 7 m of undisturbed remains under the surface. It soon became clear that it would be impossible to excavate trench BE94/95-1 down to natural layers without serious danger of collapse and contamination. The loose composition of the surrounding soil makes the trenches in Berenike prone to wind and water erosion, which undercuts their balks. It was, therefore, decided to open a much larger trench, BE96/97/98/99/00-10, which would be decreased in size by stepping it in whenever necessary to keep the sides stable. Trench BE96/97/98/99/00-10 showed a thick deposit of late Roman date (fourth to sixth centuries AD), which included several building phases and small industrial areas. The late Roman deposits overlay earlier Roman remains (first to third centuries AD), which possibly related to the sanctuary of the nearby Serapis temple. The earliest remains found in trench BE96/97/98/99/00-10 are Ptolemaic.

The Serapis temple of Berenike was cleared and studied by several nineteenth-century travelers, including Belzoni, Wilkinson, Wellsted, and Golénischeff (cf. Sidebotham 1995a). Given these studies and the fact that Wellsted reported as early as

1838 that many of the reliefs were weathered to a point that they could be removed from the walls of the temple merely by passing a hand over them, it was decided not to clear the temple again, but instead to cover it completely with sieved sand from the excavation of trench 10 in order to protect it. The 1973 leveling of the site seems not to have affected the temple, and it can now safely await future conservation. The origin of the Berenike grid (which was given the coordinates 500 N/2000 E) is just south of the temple and a temporary benchmark (7.18 m asl) has been inserted into the top of a north wall of the temple (cf. Sidebotham and Wendrich 1995, Appendix A)

2.3.2 THE WESTERN QUARTER (Figure 2-4)

This area, with obvious surface traces of the ancient settlement, is directly west of the Serapis temple and the leveled area surrounding it. It includes Structures H, J, K and L as well as trenches BE95/96-6 and BE97/98-16 (in the Western Shrine). The ancient remains are mostly located on and south of a ridge extending westward from the center of the settlement. Further west, this ridge curves toward the south, and the finds on the surface are more industrial in appearance.

Trenches BE95/96-6 and BE97/98-16 revealed the walls of a building as well as a number of religious objects, including offering tables, parts of bronze statues, and two inscriptions. The latter date to the late second to early third centuries AD and indicate the presence of a contingent of Palmyrene archers. The

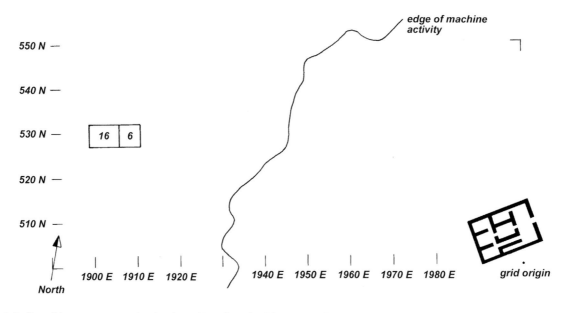

Figure 2-4   Part of the *western quarter* showing the position of trenches BE95/96-6 and BE97/98-16 (in the Western Shrine) in relation to the Berenike site grid (note the grid origin) and the Serapis temple.

third-century AD building was, therefore, identified as a (Palmyrene) shrine or *schola* west of the main Serapis temple. The later phase of the Western Shrine showed that it maintained a religious function in the fourth to fifth centuries AD. Samples taken with a geological hand auger within trench BE97/98-16 revealed Ptolemaic remains, but the condition of the sides of the trench made further excavation impossible.

2.3.3 THE NORTHERN QUARTER (Figure 2-5)
The region north of the leveled area also preserves traces of the ancient settlement on the surface. It includes trenches BE98/99-23 and BE99/00-32 (comprising the Northern Shrine). The ancient remains are mostly

located on and east of a ridge extending northward from the center of the settlement. This ridge disappears under the *sabkha* beach farther north of the site. Trenches BE98/99-23 and BE99/00-32 revealed the walls of a building and a number of religious objects, including offering tables, a stone altar, and a painted ostrich egg. The building in which these trenches were opened was, therefore, identified as a shrine north of the Serapis temple. Activity in this area dates to the late Roman period (fourth to fifth centuries AD).

2.3.4 THE CENTRAL QUARTER (Figure 2-6)
Located east of the leveled area, this region was probably once part of the center of the settlement, most

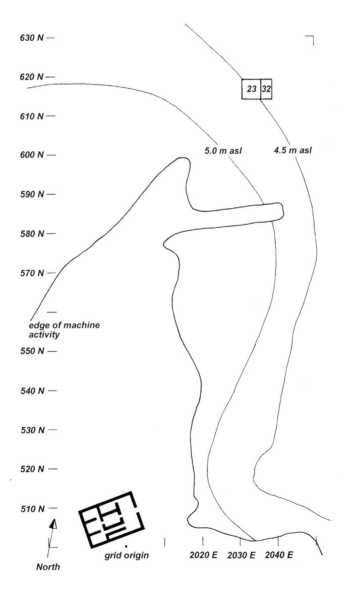

Figure 2-5   Part of the *northern quarter* showing the position of trenches BE98/99-23 and BE99/00-32 in relation to the Berenike site grid (note the grid origin) and the Serapis temple.

of which must now be under the "leveled area" north of the Serapis temple. The surface still shows clear traces of the latest phase of the settlement, including the possible street pattern. The area (3.5–4.5 m asl) seems to be crossed by a number of streets running north-south and one larger street running east-west (tentatively identified as the *decumanus maximus*), from the Serapis temple toward the Red Sea. It includes trenches BE98-20, BE98-21, BE99-27, BE99-28, BE00-34, BE00-37, BE00-38, and BE00-41. The trenches, except BE98-21, which was excavated in a trash dump, revealed edifices with niches, courtyards, and staircases suggesting a layout of buildings common to the Mediterranean area, with room for industry

and trade on the ground floor and living quarters on a higher level. Activity in this area dates to the late Roman period (fourth to fifth centuries AD). The buildings show extensive re-use of materials from earlier structures, including blocks with dedicatory inscriptions from the first and second centuries AD. At this point, it is not known when building activity in the central quarter started, but it is likely that early Roman and Ptolemaic remains underlie the later structures.

2.3.5 THE NORTHEAST QUARTER (Figure 2-7)
Northeast of the Serapis temple and the leveled area surrounding it is another region with obvious traces of buildings. This area, between the central quarter

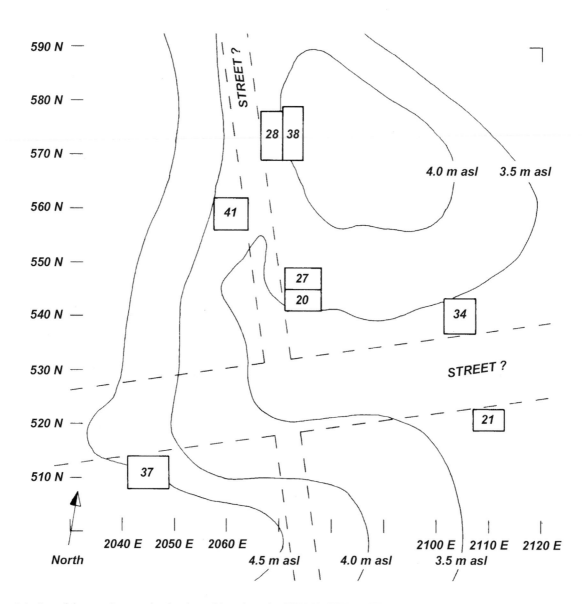

Figure 2-6   Part of the *central quarter* showing the position of trenches BE98-20, BE98-21, BE99-27, BE99-28, BE00-34, BE00-37, BE00-38 and BE00-41 in relation to the Berenike site-grid and the tentatively located streets in this area.

and the *sabkha* beach north and east of the ancient city, includes Structures B and F as well as trenches BE95-4, BE95/96-7, BE96-8, BE96/97/98-12, BE 97/98-17, BE98/99-22, BE99-26, BE99/00-30, and BE00-39. This quarter of the city (3.0–1.0 m asl) seems to contain a number of large and, most likely, public buildings. The remains of Structure F suggested a temple or possibly another public building. No conclusive evidence, however, could be inferred from the three trenches excavated in this area.

Excavation of a second large public building to the southeast of Structure F revealed two clearly discernable parts: a domestic, "dirty" area to the north and a public, "clean" area to the south. The present supposition is that this structure at some point in its history was transformed into a Christian ecclesiastical establishment.

It appears that the topography in this area has been subject to extensive remodeling in the fourth century AD through a massive redeposition of early and late Roman (first-fourth centuries AD) debris. This may well be directly related to the fact that the sea has effectively retreated over the centuries, forcing the settlement to follow it and move or expand from west to east. It is, therefore, unlikely that substantial Ptolemaic remains will be found here.

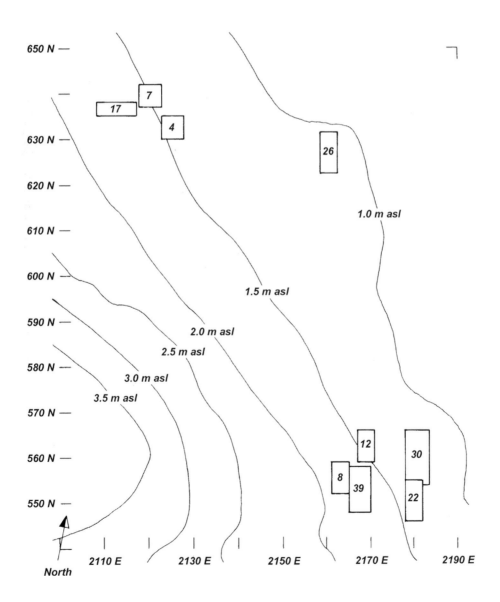

Figure 2-7   Part of the *NE quarter* showing the position of trenches BE95-4, BE95/96-7, BE96-8, BE96/97/98-12, BE97/98-17, BE98/99-22, BE98-26, BE99/00-30 and BE00-39 in relation to the Berenike site-grid.

2.3.6 THE SOUTHEAST QUARTER (Figure 2-8)
This area, with obvious traces of the ancient settlement on the surface, is southeast of the Serapis temple and the leveled area surrounding it, between the central quarter and the *sabkha* beach east and south of the ancient town. It includes Structures A, C, D, and G, as well as trenches BE94/95-2, BE95/96/97-5, BE96-9, and BE97/98-18. This area (3.0–1.0 m asl) seems to contain a number of public or semipublic buildings most likely related to the long-distance trade. A massive stone wall, found in trench 94/95-2, was possibly the demarcation between land and sea in the early Roman period. It appears that, much like the northeast quarter, in the fourth century AD, part of the area was leveled before the buildings were constructed. Excavations in trench BE95/96/97-5 revealed a warehouse that was in use from the fourth century AD until the latest phase of occupation at Berenike in the sixth century AD. Trench BE96-9 was excavated in the highest mound ("A") in the southeastern quarter and revealed extensive walls, probably forming foundation cells for a high-standing structure.

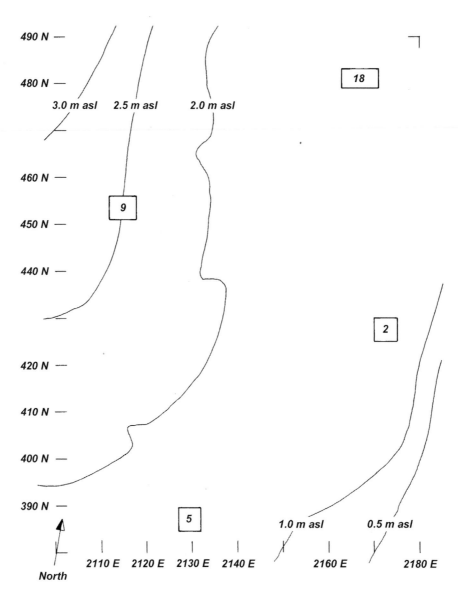

Figure 2-8   Part of the *SE quarter* showing the position of trenches BE94/95-2, BE95/96/97-5, BE96-9 and BE97/98-18 in relation to the Berenike site-grid.

2.3.7 THE TRASH DUMP (Figure 2-9)

This area, littered with ancient refuse, is northwest of the Serapis temple and the leveled area surrounding it. It includes Structure N, as well as trenches BE95-3, BE96/97-13, BE96-14, BE97/98-19, BE98-24, BE98-25, BE99-29, BE99-31, BE00-33, and shell midden SM-1. This area is a large, early Roman (first-century AD) trash dump, that is, at least in some places, on top of the remains of Ptolemaic structures built of unfired sand brick. Excavations here unearthed very little architecture, but yielded numerous finds, including many organic materials, as well as a substantial number of ostraka and some papyri. The early Roman trash completely conceals all underlying, earlier structures. It is, therefore, impossible to understand the extent of the town during the Ptolemaic period in this area.

2.3.8 THE PTOLEMAIC AREA (Figure 2-10)

This area, which on the surface appears almost devoid of ancient remains, is west of the Serapis temple and the leveled area surrounding it, between the western quarter and the sandy desert and modern military bunkers west of the ancient city. It includes Structure

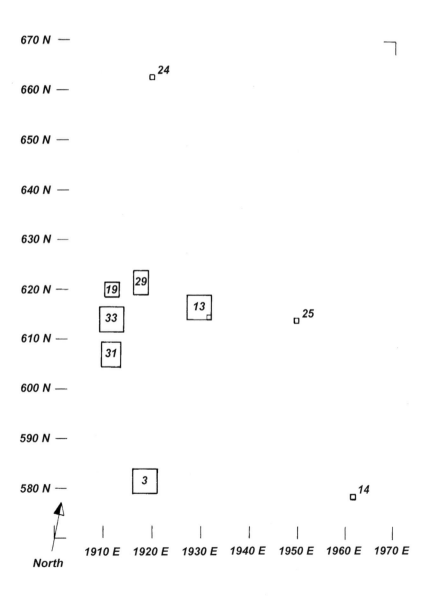

Figure 2-9 Part of the *trash dump* showing the position of trenches BE95-3, BE96/97-13, BE96-14, BE97/98-19, BE98-24, BE98-25, BE99-29, BE99-31 and BE00-33 in relation to the Berenike site-grid (SM-1 is towards the west of this map in the same area).

R, as well as trenches BE96-11, BE00-35, BE00-36, and BE00-40. Trench BE96-11 was opened in the only obvious feature in the area, Mound R, and revealed little architecture but many finds dating to the early Ptolemaic period. Trenches BE00-35, BE00-36, and BE00-40, opened after a magnetic survey of the area in 1999 (see Chapter 3), indicated the remains of walls and possible kilns. Only then could it be confirmed that the Ptolemaic phases of Berenike lay west of the Roman town, which is concordant with the fact that the sea has effectively retreated over the centuries, forcing the settlement to follow it eastward.

2.3.9 THE SOUTHERN QUARTER (no map)

This area, with clear lines of coral blocks, indicating the wall lines of the latest phase of occupation, shows obvious traces of the ancient settlement. It is south of the Serapis temple, between the central quarter and the *sabkha* beach south of the ancient city. It includes Structures E and P. So far, only 1 x 1 m *sondage* BE96-15 has been opened here, which appears on the large map at the back of this volume (Figure 2-15).

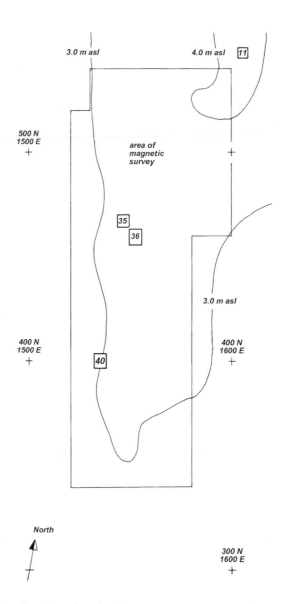

Figure 2-10   Part of the *Ptolemaic Area* showing the position of trenches BE96-11, BE00-35, BE00-36 and BE00-40 in relation to the Berenike site-grid and the area in which the magnetic survey took place in 1999 (Chapter 3).

2.3.10 THE MODERN CAMP SITE (Figure 2-11)

The region between the trash dump and the Ptolemaic area west of the site appears devoid of ancient remains. Perhaps in antiquity this area was a small inlet or a swamp, unsuited for habitation and at the same time too shallow for ships to enter. This area was chosen to pitch the camp of the expedition. The newly constructed museum, which houses a collection of contemporary artifacts of the Ababda nomads, with temporary storerooms and work areas for the expedition, was also built here. This building was financed by the Netherlands Ministry of Foreign Affairs through the Local Cultural Fund of the Royal Netherlands Embassy in Cairo. Since this edifice is likely to remain in place for the duration

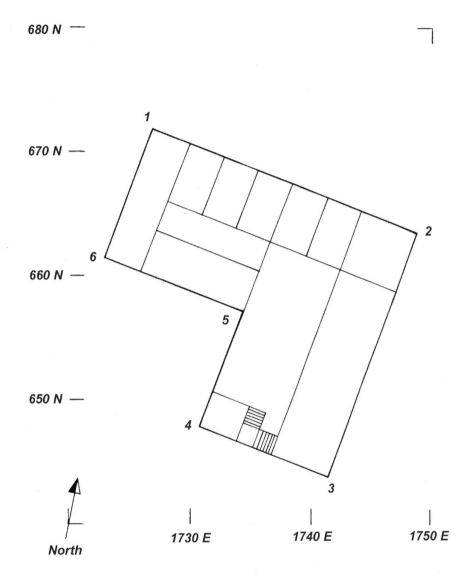

Figure 2-11   Part of the *modern campsite* showing the position of the modern building at Berenike in relation to the Berenike site-grid (cf. Table 2-12).

Corner	Grid-coordinates
1. NW corner	671.8 N / 1726.7 E
2. NE corner	664.6 N / 1748.6 E
3. SE corner	643.8 N / 1741.4 E
4. Southern concave corner	647.9 N / 1730.8 E
5. Internal (convex) corner	657.5 N / 1734.6 E
6. Northern concave corner	661.3 N / 1723.2 E

Table 2-12   Grid-coordinates of the modern building at Berenike (cf. Figure 2-11).

of the excavations, it was carefully surveyed in relation to the Berenike site grid in order to serve as a backup in case all or most grid markers are lost. Table 2-12 lists grid-coordinates for the six corners of the modern building at Berenike.

2.4 OVERVIEW OF PUBLISHED PLANS AND MAPS

A large number of maps and plans showing Berenike, its environs or details of the site have been published.

The detailed, measured plans of the excavation trenches can be found with the description of each trench, as indicated in Tables 2-1 and 2-2.

Table 2-13 shows the page number and caption of each of the additional plans and maps published in previous Berenike volumes, including the large maps that have been published in association with each volume. Table 2-14 gives a cross-reference between the subject and type of each plan or map ("classification") and the volume and page number where it was published.

Volume	Page	Caption	Classification
94	3	Egypt and the location of Berenike on the Red Sea coast, just south of Ras Benas.	**Tl**
	4	Map of Berenike, associated sites and road networks.	**Rr**
	16	J.G. Wilkinson's plan of the central area of ruins of Berenike drawn in 1826.	**Be-Th**
	18	J.G. Wilkinson's plan of Berenike and harbor drawn in 1826.	**Be-Th**, printed upside down in this volume
	88	Plan of the small fort in Wadi Kalalat.	**Ka**
	89	J. G. Wilkinson's plans of the large fort and the small forts in Wadi Kalalat drawn in 1826.	**Ka-Th**, original north arrows point south
	100	Three-dimensional reconstruction of the fort at Abraq.	**Ba-Ai**
	107	Sketch plan of the Serapis temple with triangulation points for establishing the grid origin.	**Be-Th**
	(113) 126	Plan of the central town of Berenike. Berenike site survey 1994.	**Be**
	(113) 127	Plan of Berenike. Berenike site survey 1994.	**Be**
95	vii	Map of Egypt showing location of important ports on the Nile and on the Red Sea coast.	**Tl**
	3	Map of the Berenike-Nile road and associated sites.	**Rr**
	4	Map of the region of Berenike and to the south, between the Nile and the Red Sea coast.	**Rr**
	(5)	Detailed map of Berenike (red and black, scale 1: 500) Berenike site survey 1994–96.	**Be**, separate foldout map
	29	Trench BE94/95-2, artist impression looking southeast.	**Be-Ai**
	54	Building F (trenches BE95-4 and 7).	**Be**
	79	Trench BE95-5, artist impression looking northeast.	**Be-Ai**
	87	Trench BE95-6, artist impression looking southeast.	**Be-Ai**

	100	Geological map of the Berenike area.	**Th**
	113	Map of the eastern part of Berenike ruins showing locations of traverses and cores on *sabkha*.	**Th**
	373	Abraq fort (overall).	**Ba**
	374	Abraq fort (small enclosure).	**Ba-Th**
	385	Map of Berenike regional road network.	**Rr**
	386	Map of Kalalat-Berenike road.	**Rr**
	388	Plan of the large fort (*praesidium*) in Wadi Kalalat.	**Ka**
	390	The large fort in Wadi Kalalat with surrounding hydraulic remains.	**Ka**
	392	Elevational difference between Wadi Kalalat and Berenike.	**Ka**
	395	Plan of the hilltop fort in Wadi Shenshef.	**Sh**
	400	Plan of two graves at the cemetery east of Hitan Rayan.	**Hr-Th**
	401	Map of Hitan Rayan-Shenshef road.	**Rr**
	404	Map of putative route Kalalat-Shenshef/Hitan Rayan.	**Rr**
	407	Map of route just north of Kalalat to Vetus Hydreuma (Wadi Abu Greiya) route.	**Rr**
	412	Hitan Rayan, regional location map.	**Tl**
	413	Hitan Rayan, location plan showing the settlement and the cemetery.	**Tl-Hr**
	-416	Detailed plan of Hitan Rayan (scale 1:750) Hitan Rayan site survey.	**Hr**, separate foldout map
	424	Hitan Rayan, distribution of Type 1 structures.	**Hr-Th**
	427	Hitan Rayan, distribution of Type 2 structures.	**Hr-Th**
	431	Hitan Rayan, distribution of Type 3 structures.	**Hr-Th**
	435	Hitan Rayan, distribution of Type 4 structures.	**Hr-Th**
	438	Hitan Rayan, sketch plan of ring-cairn cemetery.	**Hr-Th**
96	vii	Map of the Egyptian Eastern desert showing the location of Berenike.	**Tl**
	-3	Overview of Berenike (red and black, scale 1:962) Berenike site survey 1995 and 1996.	**Be**, separate foldout map
	4	Map of the wider environs of Berenike.	**Tl**
	9	The position of SM-1, PQ-2, and the points where the level of the groundwater table was measured.	**Be-Th**
	33	Trench BE95/96-6, artist impression of the statue base, inscription, and statue.	**Be-Ai**

	47	Building F (trenches BE95-4 and BE95/96-7).	**Be**
	122	Map of the coastal zone near Berenike.	**Th**
	126-127	Topographic map of the Wadi Kalalat-Berenike area.	**Tl**
	128	Map of the Berenike site.	**Th**
	132	Map of Shenshef area.	**Tl-Sh**
	134	Map of Hitan Rayan area.	**Tl-Hr**
	398	Sketch map of grave concentrations around Berenike.	**Tl-Ai**
	399	Sketch map of a modern Ababda Bedouin grave.	**Ai-Th**
	400	Sketch map of a number of Bedouin graves in Wadi Shenshef.	**Ai-Th**
	416	Overall map of routes in the Berenike area.	**Rr**
	418	Map of route from Vetus Hydreuma (Wadi Abu Greiya) to Wadi Kansisrub.	**Rr**
	422	Map of route from large *praesidium* in Wadi Kalalat to Hitan Rayan.	**Rr**
	425	Map of route from Vetus Hydreuma (Wadi Abu Greiya) to the fort in Wadi Lahma.	**Rr**
	(428)	Plan of Hitan Senshef (scale 1:2500) Shenshef site survey 1996.	**Hr**, seperate foldout map
	444	Map of the Indian Ocean basin.	**Tl**
97	ix	Berenike in the context of the Roman Empire.	**Tl**, revised version published in **98**: xi
	108	Map of ancient ports, mentioned in the *Periplus*, involved in the rock and mineral trade.	**Tl-Th**
	350	Map of the ancient roads and settlements in the direct vicinity of Berenike.	**Rr**
	362	Sketch plan of Qariya Ali Mohamed Hussein.	**Ai-Th**
	366	Map showing the Marsa Nakari (Nechesia?)—Edfu (Apollinopolis Magna) route.	**Rr**
	(387)	Detailed plan of Hitan Shenshef (red and black, scale 1:1000) Shenshef site survey 1996.	**Sh**, separate foldout map
	387	Plan of Shenshef area 1.	**Sh**
	389	Plan of Shenshef area 2.	**Sh**
	391	Plan of Shenshef area 3.	**Sh**
	393	Plan of Shenshef area 4.	**Sh**
	395	Plan of Shenshef area 5.	**Sh**

98	xi	Berenike in the context of the Roman Empire (revised).	**Tl**, revised version of **97**: ix
	139	Trench BE98-23, artist impression looking west.	**Ai**
	(355)	Roads and settlements in the vicinity of Berenike (red and black, scale 1:112 500)	**Tl-Be**, separate foldout map
	360	Plan of the fort (*praesidium*) at Siket.	**Sk**
	361	Plan of the environs of the fort (*praesidium*) at Siket.	**Sk**
	380	Plan of the *praesidium* in Wadi Kalalat, showing the location of the excavation trenches.	**Ka**
	420	Map of the environs of Berenike.	**Tl**

Table 2-13 List of plans and maps published in the Berenike volumes, not including the detailed plans of the trenches.
Volume (in Tables 2-13 and 2-14 following):
94: report of the 1994 season (Sidebotham and Wendrich 1995)
95: report of the 1995 season (Sidebotham and Wendrich 1996a)
96: report of the 1996 season (Sidebotham and Wendrich 1998a)
97: report of the 1997 season (Sidebotham and Wendrich 1999a)
98: report of the 1998 season (Sidebotham and Wendrich 2000a)
Page: Pages numbered with Roman numerals can be found at the beginning of each volume. Page numbers in parenthesis refer to the place of the caption of the drawing where this is different from the page of the drawing.
Captions: The captions have sometimes been shortened or changed for the sake of clarity
Classification (indication of types of maps for Tables 2-13 and 2-14 following):
Tl: Topographic maps or location maps covering a large area
Rr: Maps showing ancient road systems or routes
Be: Detailed, measured plans of (structures in) Berenike
Sk: Detailed, measured plans of (structures in) Siket
Ka: Detailed, measured plans of (structures in) Wadi Kalalat
Hr: Detailed, measured plans of (structures in) Hitan Rayan
Sh: Detailed, measured plans of (structures in) Wadi Shenshef
Ba: Detailed, measured plans of (structures in) Bir Abraq
Ai: Artist impressions and sketch maps
Th: Thematic maps and miscellaneous plans and maps

	94	95	96	97	98
Tl	3	vii, 412, 413	vii, 4, 126-127, 132, 134, 398, 444	ix, 108	xi, (355), 420
Rr	4	3, 4, 385, 386, 401, 404, 407	416, 418, 422, 425	350, 366	(355)
Be	16, 18, 107, 126, 127	(5), 29, 54, 79, 87	(3), 9, 33, 47		
Sk					360, 361
Ka	88, 89	388, 390			380
Hr		400, 413, (416), 424, 427, 431, 435, 438	134		
Sh		395	132, (428)	(387), 387, 389, 391, 393, 395	
Ba	100	373, 374			
Ai	100	29, 79, 87	33, 398, 399, 400	362	139
Th	16, 18, 89, 107	100, 113, 374, 392, 400, 424, 427, 431, 435, 438	9, 122, 128, 399, 400	108, 362	

Table 2-14 References to the maps and plans in the previous Berenike volumes. For a legend and remarks, see the caption of Table 2-13 preceding.

Figure 2-15 Foldout map of Berenike showing the position of all trenches excavated between 1994 and 2000 (included with this book as separate plan).

CHAPTER 3 ～

MAGNETIC SURVEY

T. M. HERBICH

From 1994 to 1996, a surface survey of Berenike recorded all traces of buildings visible on the surface. The maps published of this survey clearly reveal the extent of the area of densest occupation on the site. This surface survey also provides data to establish the approximate extent of the whole site. On the map showing the dense area of occupation (Aldsworth and Barnard 1998a), it is clear that building traces are not distributed regularly; there are also areas in which no surface remains are visible. The map of the entire site shows few traces of buildings in the western part where the surface remains indicate the area was once occupied.

3.1 METHOD AND MATERIALS

The goal of the geophysical survey conducted at Berenike at the very start of the 1999 excavation season (December 17–21, 1998) was to identify buildings in areas that were probably occupied in the past, but which preserve few visible surface remains. The survey was also a test of the efficiency of the geophysical method as applied to specific conditions at Berenike: its geological setting and construction materials (cf. Hasek 1999; Scollar, *et al.* 1990).

The magnetic method was chosen to enable a survey of a relatively large area (1/4 to 1/2 hectare per day) in a short time. The resistivity method—another technique widely used in archaeology—in the case of Berenike seemed to be less useful due to poor conductivity of the very dry surface layer. Use of this method at Berenike would have made surveying much more time consuming. Considering the dimensions of the site (i.e.,

the areas to be surveyed) the time factor was of critical importance. The radar method, also frequently used in studying archaeological sites, is usually only considered if magnetic and resistivity surveying prove ineffective, due to its high costs.

Anticipation of negative results from a magnetic survey of Berenike resulted from our knowledge of the geological setting of the site and the construction materials in general use in antiquity, namely, walls built primarily of coral heads. Most walls were founded on sand and the ruins are covered with sand. Both materials, that is, sand and coral heads, have no magnetic properties. To obtain positive results, the magnetic properties of structures (e.g., walls) should differ from the properties of the matrix (e.g., sand). This was not the case at Berenike. Therefore, the survey was to be a test to determine if there was a factor that could make at least parts of the walls visible on a magnetic map. We knew that magnetometry would allow the registration of remains of an industrial nature: traces of pottery and metal production, since kilns and concentrations of ash and fired material produce strong magnetic anomalies and there was surface evidence of both in the areas chosen for survey. One of the areas chosen for surveying lay at the western edge of the site, the other at the northeastern edge of the site just beyond an area of dense occupation.

The survey instrument used was the fluxgate magnetometer FM36 (Plate 3-1). The instrument has two sensors placed vertically at the distance of 0.4 m. The instrument observes changes in the intensity of a magnetic field simultaneously at two different heights and registers the difference between readings of the two sensors. This gradient method also allows the elimination of any effect of the general changes of the Earth's magnetic field. It traces the objects that cause local change in the magnetic field and are situated close to the surface.

The 0.5-m measurement grid was applied, that is the measurements were taken along lines 0.5 m apart every 0.5 m on the line. The measurements were taken within rectangles measuring 20 x 10 m. The sensors were aligned at a reference point after completing every rectangular grid. The readings were taken in the parallel mode (the instrument was moved only in one direction along traverses). Both functions considerably lengthen the survey time, but are vital to obtaining the best possible results.

The data were processed initially using Geoplot 2.03 software (Geoscan Research). The final maps, which illustrate changes in intensity of the magnetic field, were created with Surfer 6.0 software.

3.2 AREA 1 (PTOLEMAIC INDUSTRIAL AREA)

Area 1, with a size of 13,400 m², was located at the western edge of the site. In contrast to the coral lines littering the surface of most of the site, this area showed very few surface remains: some ash, slag, pottery, and randomly distributed pieces of coral (Figure 3-2). Excavations in 1996 had revealed that trench BE96-11 in this area could be firmly dated to the early Ptolemaic period. Ancient activity in this area was related to industrial rather than domestic use (most probably the production of fired brick). The western area was, therefore, dubbed the "Ptolemaic industrial area."

Anomalies of high amplitude, registered in the southern part of the survey area and marked with arrows on Figure 3-5, may correspond to industrial traces; the high amplitude of values is typical for kilns and concentrations of ash and slag. In the area of surface anomalies, there were no traces that might indicate the presence of kilns or ash concentrations (Figure 3-2).

In spite of doubts caused by theoretical assessment of the efficiency of the magnetic method in Berenike, the results indicate that the method seems to be very useful in recording building remains (Figures 3-3 to 3-6).

Regular linear anomalies of minus values visible in most of the survey area (grid squares A3–B9) would

Figure 3-1   Magnetic surveying in Area 2 using the fluxgate-magnetometer FM36. Photograph by W. Z. Wendrich.

Figure 3-2
Area 1 of the magnetic survey. Elements of
surface relief after the map by Aldsworth
and Barnard 1998a.

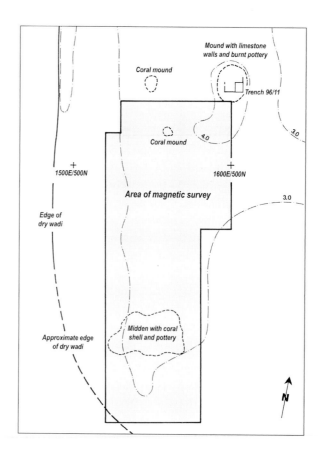

Figure 3-3 (below, left)
Magnetic map of Area 1 (white corresponds to
maximum, black to minimum values).

Figure 3-4 (below, right)
Magnetic map of Area 1 (black corresponds to
maximum, white to minimum values).

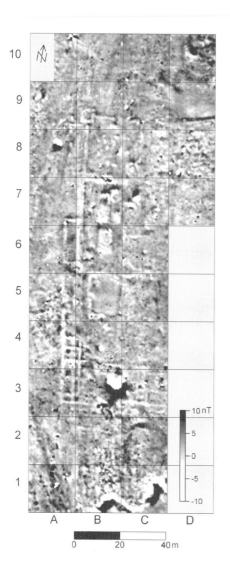

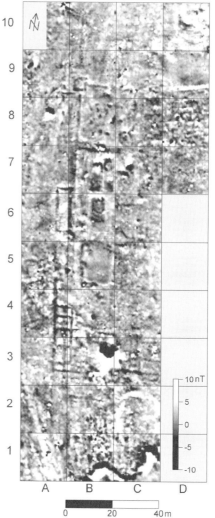

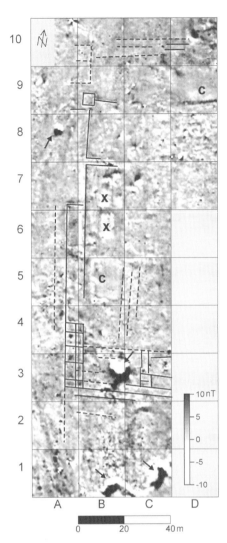

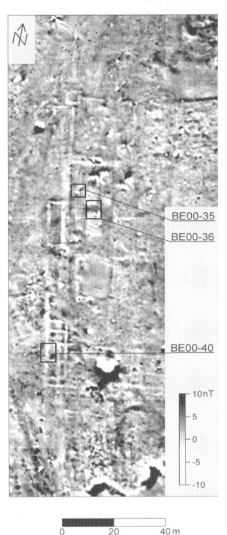

Figure 3-5
Magnetic map of Area 1 with a preliminary archaeological interpretation. Solid lines indicate remains of walls; dashed lines indicate possible remains; arrows indicate industrial traces.

Figure 3-6
Magnetic map of Area 1 with the location of the trenches excavated in 2000.

correspond to walls. In some areas the map allows reconstruction of dimensions of individual rooms (grid squares A3–B4, see Figure 3-5).

Comparison with photographs of the surface relief (Plates 3-7 and 3-8) shows that the areas that stand out most in the magnetic map have no particular surface features. The key for proper interpretation of the anomalies should be provided by excavation. However, both shape and perpendicular arrangement of the anomalies allow one to interpret them with a very high probability as wall remains. Also, the excavation and analysis of soil samples explain why the walls are seen as negative anomalies. A slight admixture of highly magnetic material (ashes, pottery sherds, and possibly slag) to the sand matrix seems to be the reason for the phenomenon. Due to this addition, the walls

of nonmagnetic coral heads are seen as negatives, surrounded by materials characterized by slightly higher values of the magnetic field.

It is difficult to explain what kind of structures correspond to the low-value anomalies of rectangular shape registered in squares B6–B7, marked X (Figure 3-5). Lower values might suggest a concentration of coral-head blocks. It is also not clear what structures might correspond to the areas marked C, having distinctive borders on all sides (square B 5) or at least on one side (Figure 3-5, square D 9), characterized by very low amplitude changes. Homogeneity of materials in this area and their shape might suggest that they reflect areas without buildings, filled with sand (without admixture of ash, etc).

Plate 3-7
Area 1—Surface relief of the Ptolemaic industrial area (squares B1–C1) from the west. Photograph by T. M. Herbich.

Plate 3-8
Area 1—Surface relief of the area of anomalies interpreted as traces of walls. Only coral-head fragments are visible on the surface. The notebook marks the intersection of squares A4–B5, from the north. Photograph by T. M. Herbich.

3.3 AREA 2 (PUTATIVE HARBOR AREA)

The goal of the survey in Area 2 was to register remains of harbor-related structures, such as quays, or buildings to the north of the town. In this low-lying area that was considered one of the possible locations for a sheltered mooring place, no traces of structures were visible on the surface (Figure 3-9). However, the area was surrounded by surface remains of buildings and excavations resulted in the discovery of the North Shrine (see Figure 2-5, trenches 23/32). The area in its lowest, flattest part was covered by *sabkha* with no coral-head fragments on the surface; the survey at its western side reached low sandy mounds with coral-head fragments (Plate 3-10). An area of 2,400 m² was surveyed.

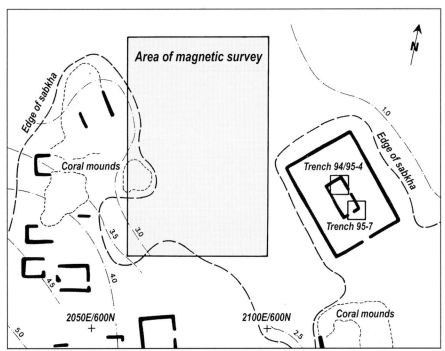

Figure 3-9　Area 2 of the magnetic survey with elements of surface relief. After the map in Aldsworth and Barnard 1998a.

Plate 3-10
Area 2, view from the south.
Photo by T. M. Herbich.

The magnetic map shows low amplitude of values; for the majority of the survey area the readings range between +5 an -5 nT (Figure 3-11). The only traces that can be interpreted as possible wall remains are situated at the western and southern edges of the area (squares B1–C1 and A5–A6; Figure 3-12). The linear structure in squares A1–A3 (Plate 3-13) constitutes a border between areas of lower and higher changes. Also the area of squares C1–D3 is characterized by a low amplitude of changes; the borders of this area are not distinctive. The goal of the survey—to register traces of buildings that could be interpreted as remains in the harbor area—was not achieved. In this case, either the magnetic method seems to have been useless or there were no structures in this area. If the former, it remains to be determined which survey technique would be best applied here. If the latter, this suggests that this area may have been a bay or inlet in antiquity that silted up at some point in the history of Berenike.

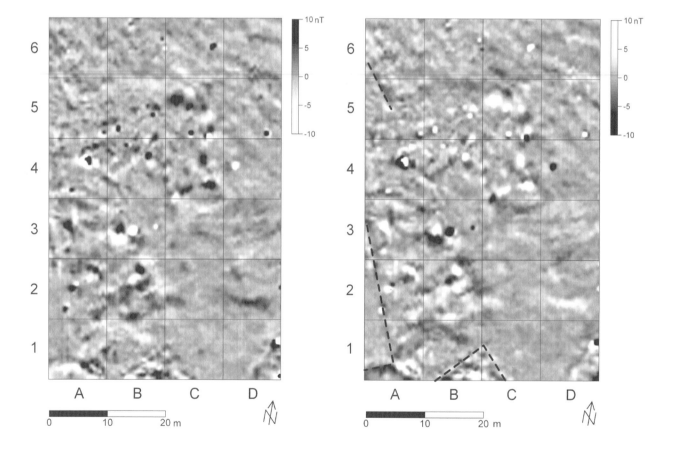

Figure 3-11
Magnetic map of Area 2 (black corresponds to maximum values).

Figure 3-12
Magnetic map of Area 2 with a preliminary interpretation. Dashed lines indicate possible remains of walls.

Plate 3-13   Area 2, western edge of the survey area. The tape marks the western edge of squares A1—A4, from the south. Photograph by T. M. Herbich.

3.4 CONCLUSION

The survey proved the efficiency of the magnetic method in recording the remains of buildings in some areas of the site. No doubt continuing the survey in the western part of the site—where there are few visible surface remains—will provide additional data to create a map of the city. Close cooperation between geophysical and archaeological teams is crucial for better understanding the geophysical results: verification by excavation of selected structures found by the survey would provide a key to interpreting the magnetic map of Berenike.

CHAPTER 4 ～

EXCAVATIONS

S. E. SIDEBOTHAM

During the sixth and seventh seasons of fieldwork at Berenike (December 1998–March 1999 and December 1999–March 2000) the project excavated in whole or in part 19 trenches encompassing a surface area of 748 m². Excavations in three of these trenches continued from previous seasons: BE96/97/98/99/00-10, BE98/99-22, and BE98/99-23. Others were begun, and some completed, during these two seasons: BE99-26, BE99-27, BE99-29, BE99-30/BE99-39, BE99-31, BE00-33, BE99/00-32, BE00-35, BE00-36, BE00-40, BE99-28/BE00-38, BE00-34, BE00-37, and BE00-41.

Trenches excavated on the western part of the site in an early Ptolemaic industrial area included 35, 36, and 40. Excavations continued in the early Roman trash dump at the northern edge of the city, with newly opened trenches 29, 31, and 33 where, in previous seasons, numerous papyri, ostraka, and other inorganic and organic remains had been recovered. Excavations carried on in trench 10 (just north of the Serapis temple) and in the center of the site in trenches 23/32 (a late Roman shrine), and 27, 28/38, 34, 37, and 41 (all late Roman buildings). Finally, excavations continued on the eastern edge of the site in trenches 22, 30, and 39 in a possible Christian ecclesiastical building, and were begun in 26, a late Roman public building of unknown function immediately north of trenches 22, 30, and 39. This report will describe results of excavations beginning in the western part of the site and proceeding east.

4.1 THE PTOLEMAIC INDUSTRIAL AREA
Trenches BE00-35, BE00-36, BE00-40

4.1.1 TRENCH BE00-35
Trench supervisor: W. Sawtell

BE00-35 was a 6 x 6 m trench with grid coordinates 470–464 N-S/1544–1550 E-W located on the extreme western side of the site, near the edge of Wadi Umm Salim (see Aldsworth and Barnard 1998a: 4 and Fig. 2-2). The choice of its placement was based on a 1999 magnetic survey of the western area of Berenike (see Chapter 3) and on the presence of copious surface finds, including industrial metal waste and pottery. The results of the magnetic survey indicated several possible structures in the area, including rectilinear features possibly implying two long, parallel, north-south walls connected by short east-west walls. Near the northern limit of these features and immediately east of them, the magnetic survey recorded two truncated, juxtaposed rectangular features. Trenches BE00-35 and BE00-36 were placed to expose these.

Although excavations in BE00-36, which was almost adjacent to BE00-35, encountered two large structures (see following), the latter trench was largely devoid of archaeological remains. Excavation penetrated as deep as the natural bedrock (locus *017*): fossilized coral reef, at 2.26–2.43 m above sea level (asl). The fossilized coral-reef bedrock had a very undulating surface, and initially it seemed that two channels, one roughly east-west and another roughly north-south, had been cut into this layer, suggesting possible archaeological remains within this locus. Comparison with the bedrock in BE96-11, particularly inclusions of small, rounded pebbles and shells, however, confirmed that *017* was, indeed, part of an extinct coral reef. There was no indication whatsoever that it had been quarried for building material. No coral heads were present. It was a solid layer, as hard as concrete, and a massive effort with heavy tools would have been required to dislodge any usable blocks.

Above bedrock were several layers of water-deposited and windblown sand, varying from fine to coarse grained, and containing occasional small stone inclusions and almost no finds. Locus *014*, a windblown sand layer with no finds or inclusions, accounted for most of the material in the trench and was up to 1.25 m thick. In the upper layers, there was a little pottery, shell, charcoal, iron, bronze, seeds, bone, insects, and botanical remains, including wood.

On the surface was a roughly north-south linear arrangement of sporadic, badly decomposed rock anhydrite (*004*), which may have been intended as a retaining wall for rubbish dumping. Excavation, however, recovered very few finds; so perhaps BE00-35 was in a marginal, barely used part of the western zone of industrial activity and dumping, the existence of which was confirmed by BE00-36, BE96-11 (indirectly), and BE00-40. The stone of *004* was anhydrite (Harrell 1996:106–107). The stones comprising *004* had melted down to a maximum thickness of 0.06 m and were placed one course high, or in a few places, two courses high, although some robbing probably occurred during the post-abandonment phase. This type of construction paralleled that in BE00-40 (see following). So, although none of the pottery from BE00-35 was datable, this ephemeral structure could possibly be Ptolemaic based on similarity of architecture and its proximity to the Ptolemaic industrial dump/working area in BE00-36.

East of *004*, along the eastern balk, was pit *006*, 2.80 m N-S x 0.60 m E-W. It was truncated by the balk and was sublinear in plan, concave in section, and was cut to a maximum depth of 0.07 m through sand locus *003*. This pit was the only locus that contained copper-alloy fragments and a significant quantity of pottery. It may have been related to activity taking place in the area of BE00-36 since there was a structure in the northern half of the latter trench that extended north beyond the balk. No indication of archaeological activity was visible between *004* and *006*. West of *004* was a sand layer with a denser-than-normal concentration of small, black, rounded pebbles. A similar layer was found in the western area of BE00-36 and provisionally identified as a pathway leading to and between the two structures of that trench, yet stopping halfway through the trench. It did not seem likely that these two loci were connected because the deposit in BE00-36 was linear in plan and ran east-west, although it may have branched out to the north close to wall BE00-35.*004*. This possibility was remote because there was nothing else in BE00-35 to which people would have walked.

Thus, BE00-35 appeared to have been in a marginal, unused area of the Ptolemaic industrial zone. Approximately 20 m to the west, based on the magnetic survey results, there may be the remains of the continuation of wall BE00-40.*039*, which may have enclosed the whole industrial zone.

4.1.2 Trench BE00-36
Trench supervisor: V. Selvakumar
Figures/Plates 4-1 to 4-4

BE00-36 measured 7.5 m N-S x 6 m E-W with grid coordinates of 455.5–463 N-S/1550–1556 E-W and trench datum at 3.55 asl (Figure 4-1 and Plates 4-2 and 4-3). The trench was placed in the southwestern part of the site in order to recover evidence for Ptolemaic activity and to expose possible architectural remains identified by the magnetic survey undertaken in 1999 (see Chapter 3). Although the trench could not be completely excavated due to lack of time, the excavated area did reveal evidence mostly datable to the Ptolemaic period; this included pottery for which no further refinement of date was possible. Based on stratigraphic information, however, the features found in this trench can be assigned to four periods:

Phase I: Ptolemaic
Phase II: Post-Ptolemaic a
Phase III: Post-Ptolemaic b
Phase IV: Post-Ptolemaic c

Trench 36, Phase I
Most of the evidence from this trench, except burial *024* in pit *032* and the associated loci (*005/015/019* and *027*), belonged to the Ptolemaic period. Evidence recovered from the trench indicated that structure *022*, remains of a possible hydraulic structure or cistern *029*, and installation *020*, which was probably meant for storage purposes, formed the earliest subphase.

Since all three features were in different parts of the trench and had no direct physical relationship with one another, it was not possible to establish their internal

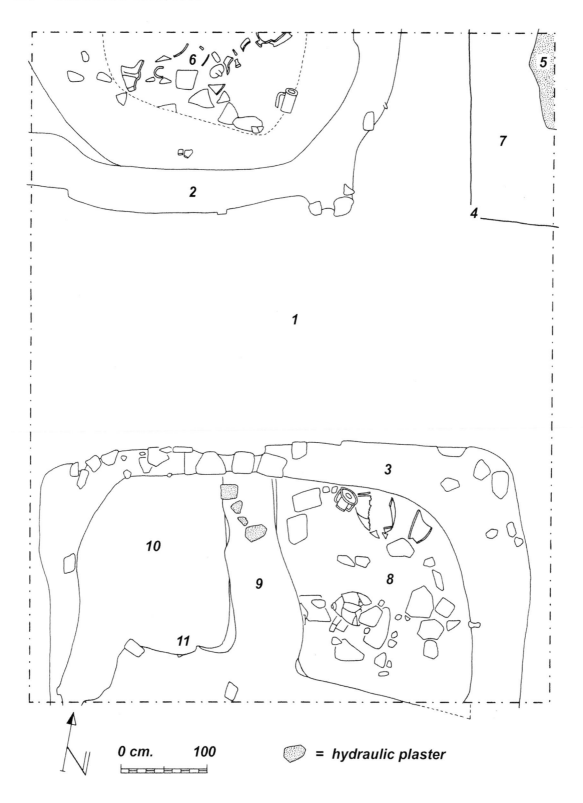

Figure 4-1   Plan of trench BE00-36. Drawing by H. Barnard.

1.=*018*	4.=*035* (cut)	7.=*025/032/069*	10.=*057/066*
2.=*020*	5.=*029*	8.=*033/033a/059/061/062–063/064–065*	11.=*060*
3.=*022*	6.=*031*	9.=*037*	

0 cm.   100

= hydraulic plaster

Plate 4-2
Trench BE00-36. Loci *025/032/069* in pit to upper left in photo, northeastern corner of the trench. Hydraulic installation *024/029* is in the bottom of the pit. Installation *020/031* in the bottom left of the photo (to the north), installations *022/037* in upper right part of the photo (to the south), looking southeast. Scale=1 m. Photograph by S. E. Sidebotham.

Plate 4-3
Trench BE00-36. Loci *025/032/069* in pit to upper right in photo, northeastern corner of the trench. Hydraulic installation *024/029* is in the bottom of the pit. Installation *020/031* in the top left in the photo (left of the pit), installations *022/037* in bottom right in the photo (to the south), looking northeast. Scale=1 m. Photograph by S. E. Sidebotham.

chronology. From the stratigraphic evidence, however, it was clear that they were earlier than most of the loci excavated to date. Interestingly, all these installations were subsurface features, that is, built below the ancient surface level. The ancient natural surface level in this area lay at approximately 3.32 m asl. It should be noted that trench BE00-35, immediately northwest of this trench, yielded no substantial occupational evidence. The southern part of the trench revealed the northern part of a rectilinear structure. It had an east-west wall measuring 5.5 m long, and two parallel north-south walls, each measuring 2.25 m long, which extended farther outside the trench toward the south. The structure was not completely excavated. In the eastern part of the trench, it was exposed to a maximum height of 1.57 m. Its minimum height, in the northwestern corner, was 1.12 m. It was not a well-built structure. Its width varied from 0.3 m to 1.15 m. In the southwestern part, the bottom of the wall was broader than the top. In several places the structure was not well preserved, especially in the southwestern corner where the upper part was damaged.

This structure was built of undressed blocks of, possibly, sandstone, limestone, coral heads, and anhydrites. In several places the binding material was a pale olive-brown clay. It also contained pottery fragments, gravel, pebbles, and complete shells. This installation was constructed against the outer limits of the trench dug into the natural sand deposit (locus *018*). The loci excavated within the area enclosed by the structure belonged to Phase II, when this structure was abandoned and used as a dump. Excavations did not encounter the working floors or the activity areas of the structure. Locus *072* might have belonged to the period when the structure was in use. As this locus had not been completely excavated, however, it was difficult to draw conclusions about its nature and date. Only when this structure is completely excavated can its function be determined. Nevertheless, since it was a subsurface feature it was probably not used for living purposes, but more likely for industrial activities.

The northeastern corner of the trench had part of a pit (*025*) containing the remains of a floor, which was intact and *in situ* only in an area measuring 0.3 m N-S x 0.15 m E-W. The remainder of the pit lay outside the trench. The rest of the area of the pit had only the bottom part of the floor, which consisted of a densely packed/rammed mixture of sand, gravel, pebbles, stones, and some other binding material. The extant part of the floor measured about 0.27 m thick. The top of the floor had two layers of plaster and its surface was smooth. The topmost layer was 0.03 m thick, while the next layer measured 0.04 m thick. As samples from the floor have not been studied systematically, its composition was not known. It appeared that the floor at the bottom comprised mortar or concrete prepared using crushed pebbles and gravel mixed with sand and possibly lime. The topmost layers had only sand particles and possibly lime as inclusions. The color of the floor was 5YR 6/4 light yellowish brown. It appeared that a particular variety of stone, perhaps sandstone, was crushed to obtain material for making the floor. Fragments of this (sand)stone, having the same color as the floor, were found in the trench and similar stone fragments were also used to construct wall *020*.

Sections of *025* preserved remains of plaster. Moreover, plaster fragments with curved surfaces, which most probably came from floor *029*, were also found in

locus *031*. Therefore, it is clear that *029* was actually the remaining part of a hydraulic feature, perhaps a cistern. The two layers of plaster found in the floor suggested a hydraulic purpose. Plaster lining very similar to this can be seen in hydraulic features at *praesidia* elsewhere in the Eastern Desert. The actual size of the hydraulic tank could not be determined as it was robbed and besides only a small portion of it lay within the trench. Moreover, making an approximate calculation of the size of the cistern was also not feasible, since pit *025* was also disturbed when the plaster of the cistern was ripped out, and again when burial pit *032* was dug. Pit *025* measured 2.25 m N-S x 1.02 m E-W on top and 2.10 m N-S x 0.82 m E-W at the bottom. The natural surface level lay at about 3.32 m asl in this area, and the floor surface of the cistern was at 1.69 m asl. Hence it could be suggested that the tank was at least 1.5 m deep.

In the northwestern part of the trench, excavations unearthed part of an installation enclosed by wall *020*. It was subrectangular in plan with its northern part beyond the limits of the trench. The low wall was built of clay, mixed with gravel, pebbles, and stone fragments. The wall, though not completely excavated, was 0.4–0.78 m wide x 0.75 m exposed height. The entire feature covered an area approximately 4.15 m E-W x 2.12 m N-S. Immediately next to the wall, was raised platformlike feature *070*, measuring about 0.25 to 0.30 m wide, consisting of sand and gravel particles, and in the middle of the platform was a concave surface or a pitlike feature. Though not completely excavated, this installation was clearly used as a dumping area during Phase II. Hence, it was not known whether these characteristics belonged to the original feature or were created when it was subsequently used as a dumping area. Only when it is completely excavated might the purpose of this feature be determined. Considering its shape it may have been used as a storage facility.

Trench 36, Phase II
During Phase II (post-Ptolemaic a), structure *022* was abandoned, and used as a dumping area. It appeared, however, that cistern *029* and storage facility *020* continued in use. Phase II could be distinguished from Phase III on the basis of the occurrence of plaster fragments, which most probably came from hydraulic tank *029*. The loci preceding the loci that yielded the plaster fragments dated to Phase II.

Most of the loci belonging to Phase II were in the area enclosed by structure *022*. Although structure *022* was excavated to a depth of about 1.85–2 m asl, the area, which lay below wall *037* of Phase III, was unexcavated. This wall arbitrarily divided the structure into two halves: the eastern and the western. Throughout Phase II, structure *022* was used as a dump, where stones, pottery, lead waste, charcoal, and other materials were discarded. Moreover, structure *022* preserved charring and burnt marks at several places in both the parts. Large amounts of charcoal and ash were also found in the loci from both parts of the structure. Therefore, it is certain that some organic materials were dumped within the structure and burned. The materials dumped into the eastern and western parts of the building were, however, of different kinds. Loci in the eastern part of the building had large quantities of pottery, scrap lead, and slag, while those in the western part mostly had charcoal and bones without much pottery and lead.

About 95 kg of lead was found in this trench (from all the three phases). Of this, 85 kg came from the eastern part of the structure. About 70 kg came from Phase II. Locus *066*—lying in the eastern part of the structure—alone yielded about 40 kg of lead. Other loci in this area also contained quantities of lead. Clearly, leadworking took place in the area lying east of structure *022*. Most of the lead found in this phase was slag. A few flat pieces were also found. In loci *071* and *074* lead slag was found inside hearthlike features with substantial quantities of charcoal and ash. It is not known, however, whether they were in a primary or secondary context as a part of the dumped material.

In the middle part of the trench, in the area lying between structure *022* and storage facility *020*, there was little evidence for occupation. The loci in the middle of the trench, in an east-west orientation (*003*, *006*, and *008*), preserved very little evidence for occupation. Stratigraphically, locus *003* belonged to Phase II. The chronology of the other loci is not known. It appeared that this area was used as a pathway. Hence, it is possible that it contained evidence belonging to Phases I through III. The topmost loci in this area were *003*, which had a thin layer of decayed anhydrite, and locus *006*, comprising gravels and pebbles. Locus *003* appeared to have been remnants of a decayed wall built of anhydrite blocks. It is not clear whether *006* was deliberately deposited or a naturally occurring gravel deposit.

Trench 36, Phase III

During Phase III (post-Ptolemaic b), portions of hydraulic tank *029* were ripped out and the large plaster fragments were used to build structure *037*. Plaster fragments were also found within feature *020*, which suggests that it was abandoned and functioned as a dumping locale.

Locus *037* was entirely built of plaster fragments ripped from *029* with clay as binding material. Since structure *022* was used as a dump during Phase II, by the beginning of Phase III, it had steeply sloping surfaces on the eastern and western parts, which met at a depth of about 2.5 m asl in the middle. In order to level this depression, large amounts of pottery, stones, and plaster fragments were dumped here, and structure *037* was built above. Structure *037* had a wall about 2.5 m long N-S x 0.65–0.87 m wide. It was not excavated this season. However, study of the exposed sections on the eastern and western sides of the wall suggests that it was 0.15–0.42 m high. It was joined by another east-west running wall near the southern balk. Only the western part of the east-west wall lay within the trench. Its eastern part extended beyond the southern balk. The nature of wall *037* was not clear. No working floor associated with this structure could be clearly identified. Even after wall *037* was built, the eastern part of structure *022* was used as a dump. Perhaps some industrial activities took place in the area lying west of the north-south wall of structure *037*.

During this phase storage facility *020* was abandoned and used as a dump. The bottom-most part of *031* contained large quantities of plaster fragments. Loci *017* and *007* formed due to dumping activities in this phase. These loci also had numerous amphora fragments, bones, and metal objects. They did not yield much lead, as did those in the eastern part of structure *022*. Loci lying above walls *037* and *007* did not provide any significant information about the activities conducted in this area.

Trench 36, Phase IV

In Phase IV (post-Ptolemaic c), a human burial was interred in the northeastern corner of the trench, in pit *032*, which cut pit *025*, and which contained the remains of robbed hydraulic tank *029*. This burial stratigraphically belonged to the latest period of occupation. Moreover, as burials would not normally have been made in residential or industrial areas in the Ptolemaic or Roman periods, one must assume that the burial postdated abandonment of the area. Excavations uncovered a human burial in pit *032*, in the northeastern corner of the trench.

Part of pit *032*, dug into earlier pit *025*, measured 2.2 m N-S x 1.32 m E-W. Pit *025* had a hydraulic tank (*029*) that was robbed subsequently. The pit fills above (*005/015/019*) and below (*027*) the skeleton (*024*) contained charcoal and pottery. It appeared that the pit was partly covered with windblown sand when the burial was made. It seems that since the natural sand in this area was very hard to dig, the burial was made in the already existing pit.

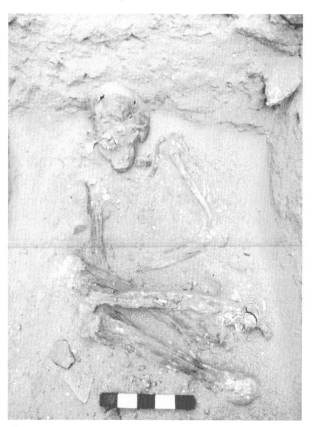

Plate 4-4   Trench BE00-36 Burial *024* in pit *032* in the northeastern corner of the trench, view looking north. Scale=20 cm. Photograph by S. E. Sidebotham.

Skeleton *024* lay in a crouched position on its right side, with the head on the north and the limbs and the face on the west (Plate 4-4). The head rested on an undressed sandstone slab and the face was tilted approximately 45 degrees towards the west. The left upper arm was on the body, the lower-left arm was folded at a right angle, and the hand was on the knee of the left leg. The upper right arm and most of the ribs and the pelvic bones were missing. Given the extremely friable condition of the surviving bones, the ribs and pelvic area had decayed. The lower right arm was parallel to the body and the right hand was folded and lying just below the mandible. The legs were folded at an angle of less than 45 degrees. The left leg was not exactly resting on the right leg. The knee of the folded right leg was slightly above the knee of the left leg.

Since only part of pit *032* was within the trench, nothing could be definitely stated about the nature of the burial. The burial had only a shell on the pelvic area. It was not clear whether it was part of the grave goods or naturally deposited material. The location and nature of the burial combined with very little or no grave goods suggest that the individual did not enjoy a high socioeconomic status.

As mentioned previously, it is clear that the burial belonged to the period following abandonment of this area. The posture of the skeleton suggests that it did not belong to the Islamic period. Hence, it could tentatively be placed between the end of the Ptolemaic and the beginning of the Islamic eras. The trench yielded no significant evidence for occupation during the Roman period. Since this area did not appear to have been occupied during Roman times, it may at that time have been used occasionally as an informal cemetery and the burial may well have been Roman in date.

The skeleton could not be studied systematically since it decayed badly when exposed to the air. Based on preliminary observations, Dr. H. Barnard indicated that it could belong to an adult. Since most of the bones were badly decayed, identifying the gender was not possible. The skeleton measured about 1.35 m long.

Discussion

Trench BE00-36 revealed clear evidence for Ptolemaic occupation. Since the trench was not completely excavated, nothing much could be determined about the function of structure *022* and feature *020* in Phase I. During the second phase, there was a shift in the type of activities undertaken in this area. While feature *020* and cistern *029* continued in use, structure *022* was abandoned and used as a dump. The amount of lead found in structure *022* indicated that metalworking took place in the vicinity of the trench. In Phase III, hydraulic tank *029* was abandoned, robbed, and used to build structure *037*. This area was deserted at the end of Phase III. In Period IV this area was unoccupied and burial *024* was deposited.

Although excavations recovered about 95 kg of lead from this trench, no definitive evidence for lead smelting was found. It is not clear whether there was ever any proper installation for smelting lead. Since melting lead does not require a very high temperature, it could have been smelted without any significant installation. More excavation in this area might reveal the furnaces used for smelting lead. From the available evidence, however, it is clear that leadworking took place in this part of the site during the Ptolemaic period. Questions including the source(s) of the lead and the purposes for which it was used must be explored further. Thin sheets of lead were normally fixed to the exterior of ancient merchant ships in order to protect the wooden hulls from natural elements (Casson 1971:214–216; Casson 1994:106), and examples have been found in excavations at Quseir al-Qadim about 300 km north of Berenike (Thomas and Whitewright 2001:39, 40, Fig. 9.5; Thomas, Whitewright and Blue 2002:82). The sheets found in trench BE00-36, however, seemed too thick for such a use. Clearly, the question requires further research.

The architectural remains identified by the magnetic survey were not found in the trench. It appears that the architectural remains identified through the magnetic survey could not be exposed because of the problems in superimposing the site map on the magnetic survey map. The reworked magnetic survey map seems to indicate structure *022*, hydraulic tank *029*, and storage feature *020* as white or gray areas.

4.1.3 TRENCH BE00-40
Trench supervisor: W. Sawtell
Figures/Plates 4-5 to 4-10

Trench BE00-40 was an 8 m N-S x 6 m E-W trench with grid co-ordinates 396.5–404.5 N-S/1532.5–1538.5 E-W (Plates 4-5, 4-7 and 4-8, Figure 4-6). Excavation of BE00-40 uncovered a massive north-south stone wall (*039*) resting in a foundation trench. Along part of its length, this trench cut through a raised ridge of possible coral reef covered by a salt layer, which had concreted before the ditch was dug. Several east-west walls were built abutting wall *039* on its eastern side: two contemporary with it (*026* along the southern balk and *108* along the northern balk) and two later than it (*027* midway along *039* and *103* along the northern balk). All archaeological activity within BE00-40 centered on these walls, yet no occupation structure could be discerned. Most loci produced industrial by-products including iron slag, copper-alloy fragments (including nails), and charcoal; some contained lead, crucible fragments, and a spindle whorl.

All activity took place within a short chronological period, similar to BE96-11 and, unlike most of the trenches excavated at Berenike thus far, within the Ptolemaic era. This activity was dated from ceramic evidence, all of which was Ptolemaic, except for a few sherds from loci on the exposed surface. Unlike the

Plate 4-5
Trench BE00-40. Large north-south wall *039*, wall *108* in bottom left in photo (in the northeastern part of the trench), wall *026* in top left in photo (in the southeastern part of the trench, looking south. Scale=1m. Photograph by S. E. Sidebotham.

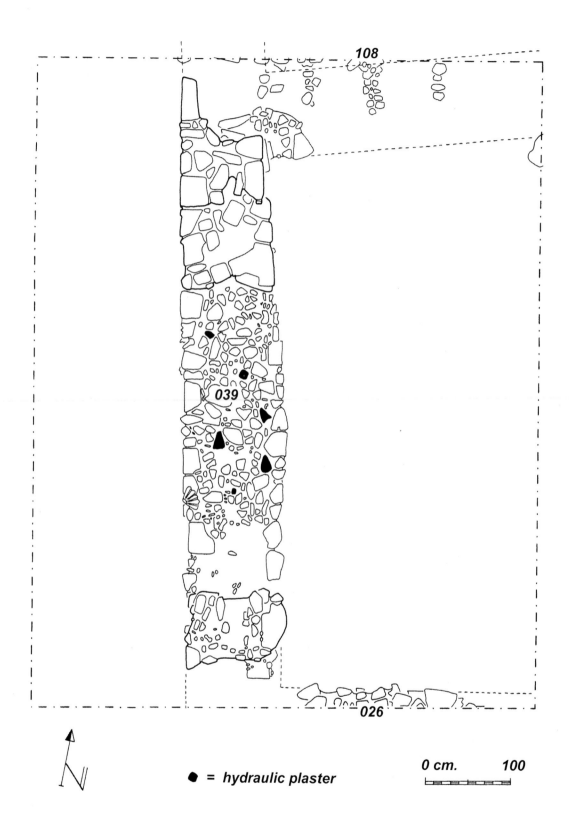

0 cm. 100

● = hydraulic plaster

Figure 4-6   Plan of trench BE00-40. Drawing by H. Barnard.

Plate 4-7
Trench BE00-40. Large north-south wall *039* in center of photo, wall *108* (in the northeastern part of the trench) is not visible, wall *026* is in the upper right of the photo (in the southeastern part of the trench), looking southeast. Scale=1 m. Photograph by S. E. Sidebotham.

Plate 4-8
Trench BE00-40. Large north-south wall *039*, wall *108* in the top right in the photo (in the northeastern part of the trench), wall *026* is barely visible in the right in the photo (in the southeastern part of the trench, looking northeast. Scale=1 m. Photograph by S. E. Sidebotham.

rest of Roman-period Berenike, very few coral heads were used in the construction of any of the walls. In the earlier phases, the fine-grained, undecayed stone (possibly gypsum) predominated and, in the latter phases, anhydrite.

The earliest archaeological levels reached (*084* and *096*) were fine, windblown sand layers dated to the Ptolemaic period, probably second century BC or earlier. A 1.25 x 1.25 m probe dug into the sand below *084* penetrated sterile sand strata down to an obviously sea-deposited pebbly sand layer (*104*) at 1.20 m asl, in contrast to BE00-35, where limestone coral reef was encountered just below a similar layer.

Trench 40, Phase I

Based on architectural and stratigraphic evidence, one phase (Ptolemaic) with eight subphases (Ia–h) was identified.

Subphase Ia

In Subphase Ia, no occupation activity was encountered. The gradual deposition of finds and windblown sand (up to 0.75 m deep) suggested that this location was on the fringe of a larger area of industrial and dumping activity over an extended period of time up to the second century BC or earlier. It comprised loci *084*, *096*, *092*, and *059*.

Subphase Ib

Subphase Ib, dated to the second century BC, saw the construction of a massive north-south wall (*039*) placed in a deep foundation trench (*090–091*) down the middle of the trench. Underneath the wall, the bottom part of this trench was filled with sand (*096*, *095*, *094*, and *093*) containing moderate amounts of archaeological material, including charcoal, pottery, and iron, upon which the massive ashlars of the wall rested. Notably, excavations recovered a fragment of an iron bloom in *094*, thus confirming that industrial activity took place somewhere in the western area by the time the walls in BE00-40 were built. At the southern end of BE00-40, up to 2.20 m from the southern balk, the trench cut through natural rock/concreted salt where an outcrop rose above the ancient surface. At the southern extremity of the wall, a robber cut extended down to the base of the wall, but at the northern end, wall *039* extended farther north beyond BE00-40. The foundation trench was very wide (up to 0.80 m) on the western side, but only 0.13 m wide on the eastern side. The ditch was probably dug first along the entire planned length of the wall, without too much care given to accuracy. The wall was built along a straight line and fitted to the trench. The coursing, however, was relatively sloppy; there was no plaster facing, and no mortar was used to bond the ashlar blocks. The outer edges of wall *039* comprised large, roughly squared, fine-grained, undecayed ashlar blocks made of gypsum or anhydrite (cf. Harrell 1996:106–107) and a few coral heads. These were probably re-used from elsewhere since some have chisel marks on them, and one has remnants of thin plaster facing. The interior consisted of small- to medium-sized stones, pieces of pottery, and fragments of hydraulic flooring material, which may have been robbed from hydraulic tank *029* in BE00-36 located 60 m to the north. A visual comparison with the hydraulic plaster from BE00-36 revealed close similarity of fabric

and thickness. Furthermore, the robbed material from *029* was re-used in wall *037* of Phase III in BE00-36 (see preceding). Therefore, Subphase Ib of BE00-40 may correspond to Phase III in BE00-36.

In BE00-40, two east-west abutting walls (*026* along the southern balk and *108* along the northern balk) were built at the same time atop *084*, 6.05 m apart, wall *108* being integrated into the fabric of *039*. Neither of these walls, nor wall *039*, however, was very high. They survived to a maximum height of 1.20 m (five courses). The tops of the walls almost reached the modern ground surface (minimum depth 0.27 m), and no tumble, except a small amount in *108*, was found, indicating that the walls were probably never much higher. Their purpose was, therefore, not entirely clear. They do not seem to have formed an occupation structure. There were no surfaces, installations, pits, or structures east of *039* or associated with the walls; only an accumulation of sand containing moderate amounts of finds, including industrial by-products, and three very small possible dumps (*081*, *082*, and *085*), no more than 0.07 m deep, were noted. Narrow ditch *091* along wall *039* was either allowed to fill up with debris or else was deliberately filled soon after the construction of the wall, before much windblown sand could accumulate. There were no features west of *039*, and foundation trench *090* seemed to have filled with windblown sand to the top of the cut. Therefore, north-south wall *039* may have been an enclosure around the settlement or, more likely, just around the industrial area, and, again, the subarea represented by BE00-40 was marginal to the main dumping/industrial activity zone, but saw slightly more activity. Further investigation of the wall would be required in order to ascertain the validity of these conclusions.

Subphase Ic

At some point, *039* must have fallen into disrepair and been neglected since the top two courses were severely robbed in the middle 3.30 m (along the north-south axis) of the wall. Then, still during a phase of neglect or abandonment, another, more focused robber cut (*072*) penetrated the top of wall *039* near the southern end.

Subphase Id

Slightly later, in the late second century BC, in Subphase Id, the top of the wall, in the area where it had been robbed, was leveled and used as a domestic occupation surface (*038–054*) which extended out 1.40 m to the east of wall *039*. The eastern ditch was also leveled (fill *044–077*). Large amounts of domestic remains, including bones, as well as industrial by-products were embedded in the occupation surface. This was a *de facto* surface; it had not been deliberately built. Excavations found several delicate objects, for example, a soapstone dish fragment, a long bronze pin or fibula, a pair of bronze tweezers, a bronze door from a model of a temple or shrine, and another, smaller bronze pin in the form of a snake (see Chapter 9). Locus *044–077* produced a small, thin, rectangular piece of faience with serrated edges and a large chi character or *X* inscribed on both of the flat faces (see Chapter 21). Almost identical pieces, but with varying numbers of serrated notches, were found in loci *066* and *006* (the fills of pits *067* and *058*, respectively). All were pierced by two very small holes in both of their long ends, strongly suggesting that all were beads or parts of necklaces, thus implying that the pit cuts to the west of the wall were contemporary with the upper dumping fill of *091*, the eastern part of the foundation ditch. In addition, two jar stoppers, one with rope impressions (see Chapter 15), and a large amount of fine, decorated second-century BC tableware were among the ceramics from locus *054*. No superstructure was evident above this surface, so it was probably a temporary living area, perhaps used during the day by people working nearby.

Also, lying on sand layer *014*, just east of *038–054*, were several small subcircular industrial hearths and a deposit of lead. All the hearths (*040, 049, 071, 074,* and *109*) contained significant amounts of charcoal, and many contained iron slag, copper-alloy fragments, including nails, bone, and burned stone. Locus *040* was largely an ash deposit; clearly a large amount of burning, most probably metalworking activity, took place here. It seemed, however, that no metal smelting occurred within the area of BE00-40. There were no structures that resembled furnaces found, and only one bloom fragment was retrieved. The latter emerged from a leveling deposit below wall *039*, was clearly residual, and predated the subphase of major industrial activity within BE00-40. Excavations recovered a large amount of iron slag, which could have originated from either metalworking or metal smelting, but absolutely no copper slag (personal communication from A. M. Hense); so certainly no copper smelting for bronze production took place within the area of BE00-40. It is interesting that there was no iron stock available to be made into finished products. The only tool found in BE00-40 was an iron blade from one of the lower fills (*089*) of *090*. Secondary-use material from *089* also included a fragment of a ceramic crucible with vitrification on the exterior surface, indicating that it was

probably used for metalworking. Locus *089* seemed to date to Subphase Ib since the base of *089* was level with the base of wall *039*. If *089* and cuts *058, 050,* and *067* were later than Subphase Ib, however, then the blade may have been deposited during Subphase Id and may have been used in the activity indicated by the industrial hearths on the other side of the wall.

The lead deposit contained a medium-sized ring of rolled or folded lead, possibly used as a brailing ring for sailing or a lead line or net-freeing ring, although the sheet from which it was rolled was very thin and, thus, not very strong (cf. Oleson 1994:73, M28, M29, and Plate 10). Another large, but equally thin, sheet fragment of lead was found bonded to the putative brailing ring/lead line/net-freeing ring noted previously, probably due to corrosion in the soil. This fragment had been pierced three times, twice from the outer face and once from the inner face, then folded over once and shaped slightly. Unlike the more-massive and numerous fragments of lead from BE00-36, which may have been used for sheathing the hulls of ships, this thin fragment may have been destined to line a stone or wooden basin. The lead itself may also possibly have originally been a waste fragment from another area where the fabrication of pieces for ship-hull repair took place. Since the melting temperature of lead is very low, the small industrial hearths of BE00-40 would have been sufficient. If all this industrial activity was associated with ship repair, then the interpretation of Berenike as a significant port during the Ptolemaic period would be further strengthened.

West of wall *039*, foundation trench *090* was recut three different times, by loci *058, 050,* and *067*. These cuts were pits and went through *062*, a relatively sterile sand deposit, implying that the cuts were made after a period of time during which the ditch had filled with windblown sand up to the base of the wall. The earliest pit, *058*, was limited to the southernmost 2.5 m of the ditch and its fill. Locus *006* was densely packed with waste material, particularly cooking and tablewares from the second century BC.

Although the western edge of the pit corresponded to the western limit of the ditch, it was probably not dug to maintain the ditch because of several factors. First, it left the rest of the ditch filled with sand. Second, rubbish was deposited immediately after it was dug. Third, that part of foundation trench *090* had been cut through concreted salt on rock, so it would have been easiest to dig through the accumulated sand only and incidentally follow the original ditch limit. Therefore, locus *058* could be dated to Subphase Id, the period after which main wall *039* had been abandoned and severely robbed. Also, the amount and nature of material in the locus implies that it must have come from relatively intense occupational activity, but none occurred in BE00-40 until Subphase Id. There could have been activity outside BE00-40 and nearby, but if the wall had been intact and the area to the east of it within BE00-40 was not being used, then it is unlikely that anyone would have made the extra and unnecessary effort of climbing the wall to dump garbage. After this dumping took place, sand layer *007*, which contained occasional finds, accumulated over the western part of BE00-40. On this basis the two later cuts, *050* and *067*, were attributed to Subphase Ie, making it late second century BC.

Probably also during Subphase Id, two shallow ditches, *051* and *069*, were cut parallel to wall *039* along the eastern and western balks respectively, not coming close to the foundation trench ditch that lay more than 2.5 m away. Their fills (*045* and *012* respectively) contained small amounts of pottery, shell, bone, charcoal, iron slag, and copper-alloy fragments and may or may not have been contemporary with each other. Their purpose remains unknown. They probably dated to Subphase Id on the basis of the layers, which they cut, but since they were not close to any of the other features of that subphase, they might also have belonged to Subphase Ie.

Subphase Ie
During Subphase Ie, still in the late second century BC, a leveling operation took place atop and along the eastern side of wall *039* and an attempt was made to build up wall *039*. A layer of sand rich in finds, *033*, was laid atop *038*, respecting the limits of wall *039*, and *037* and *053*, also rich in finds, were deposited in two separate depressions in *054* leading down to the wall, with part of *037* covering a small portion of surface *054*. Again, there was a phase of occupation, probably roughly contemporary with Subphase Id because the broad pottery dating was the same, and there was no discernable buildup of windblown sand between *054* and either *037* or *053*. During this occupation, layers *034* and *030*, rich in finds, were laid down within the same limits as *033*, stopping short of wall *036*; additionally, another compacted *de facto* surface, *032*, developed on top of *034* and *030*. All these leveling dumps and the new surface contained a wide variety and large amount of domestic material. From the dumps and the new surface, there were ceramic cooking and tablewares (among which was an import from Rhodes), bone, a

bronze *ankh* from *053*, and an oil lamp from *030* with evidence of burning on the spout. Mixed with this evidence was industrial waste, including charcoal, iron slag, and copper-alloy fragments. So, clearly, dumping material was taken from an area close to this zone of mixed industrial and domestic occupation, and the industrial hearths of Subphase Id most likely continued in use, although hearth *047* replaced *049*. Also, a new ash deposit, locus *046*, appeared. On the western side of wall *039*, there seems to have been little activity, only dumping of pottery, represented by locus *017*, but this may have occurred in Subphase Id.

There were two additional pit cuts within western foundation trench *090*: *050* and, slightly later, *067*, which cut into the former. It could not be explained why these cuts followed the western edge of *090*, despite the fact that there was only sand farther to the west, through which it would have been easy to dig. Given the discussion of pit *058* and the robbing of wall *039*, it was unlikely that ditch *090* was being maintained. It is likely that pits *050* and *067* were also dug for rubbish disposal, although they only contained moderate amounts of archaeological material.

Subphase If
After a brief period of activity, the area was, once again, abandoned in Subphase If, and the stones of the main wall were partially robbed. A very deep cut (*065*) was the result of robbing the southernmost 0.40–0.60 m of walls *036* and *039* within BE00-40 down to the base of *039*. Locus *065* completely destroyed any possible relationship between wall *026* and wall *039*, which might have been visible; so *026* and *039* may have been roughly contemporary based on the common layer stratigraphically beneath both of them. A second robber cut (*111*) penetrated the northernmost 1.0 m of wall *039* within the trench. During this subphase there was a gradual accumulation of windblown sand mixed with occasional archaeological material, represented by loci *003*, *013*, and *002*. The area was probably again on the margins of a larger dumping area, so that only a small amount of archaeological material trickled in, and a large amount of sand built up. All pottery from this subphase was second century BC; however, these layers were still dated to the late second century BC, since they were stratigraphically above the loci of Subphases Ib and Id, the latest pottery of which dated to the late second century BC.

Subphase Ig
In Subphase Ig, walls *039*, *108*, and *026*, most likely, still protruded from the sand. Being visible, they were probably covered with some soil containing trash,

and very low, makeshift walls (*004, 103, and 027*), primarily made of low-grade anhydrite stones, were laid on top. Locus *004* covered *039* and *026*, while *103* covered *108*, and *027* had no earlier wall below it. Two possible, shallow cuts (*029* and *113*), visible in section, may have been dug in order to lay walls *104* and *108* respectively. The pottery from these walls was mostly Ptolemaic mixed with a small amount of early and late Roman wares. Excavations recovered two fragments of a Ptolemaic frog lamp in locus *010*, the tumble from *004*. The Roman pottery was probably residual since these walls were still exposed on the surface when excavation began; so this subphase probably still dates to the late second century BC or slightly later. The purpose of the new walls was to contain the spread of trash (locus *001*) from the industrial area, since the area east of *004* within BE00-40 contained a dense concentration of very mixed finds, including industrial material. No structures, surfaces, or installations were associated with these walls or the trash layer. Clearly, the zone represented by the trench was a major dumping area. However, the walls were not effective since there was also a large amount of trash west of *004*.

Subphase Ih

Finally, after the total abandonment of the western area as an industrial zone, sporadic activity took place in the vicinity of BE00-40 in Subphase Ih. In the southeastern corner of BE00-40, a small pit (*019*) was dug into *001*, which, by then, had become compacted. This locus was only identified in section, so no finds were recovered. Large amounts of pottery and charcoal and some metal, however, were visible. The pit was recut twice (represented by loci *021* and *023*), each time completely within the fill of the previous cut. Only windblown sand filled locus *021*.

Trench 40, Discussion

Despite the large number of small loci, the ancient activity that took place within the confines of BE00-40 was limited to a short chronological period. Much of the pottery, however, was severely abraded by salt corrosion and undatable, which compounded the problem that not much is known about Ptolemaic pottery from this region of Egypt. Further excavation in this area of the site may recover more ceramic evidence that will allow a more precise dating of the sequences found in BE00-40. In trench BE00-36, only tumble layers were excavated this season, and occupation layers may be reached in future excavations.

Since trench BE96-11 showed that the western part of Berenike was an industrial zone in the early Ptolemaic period, BE00-40 has proven that the area continued in the same function in the middle Ptolemaic era as well. The posited brick-making activity implied by the waste material discovered in BE96-11, however, was not found in BE00-40. There was limited evidence for iron- and leadworking. The only tool discovered was an iron blade, so, perhaps the area of most intense metalworking activity lay outside BE00-40.

There were moderate amounts of finds from BE00-40, which clearly originated from much farther afield and were probably trade objects: imported pottery from almost half the loci, carnelian beads, a spherical gypsum gaming piece or bead, and a Nubian-style statuette head made of local gypsum/anhydrite (Figure 4-9). In addition, there were two unstratified amphora handles with stamped Greek characters on them (Plate 4-10). These handles were from amphorae that may have originated from the Mediterranean and probably contained trade goods. The purpose of the leadworking activity could have been related to ship repair, a hypothesis further supported by the pervasive presence of copper-alloy nails (cf. Hense 2000:191–193).

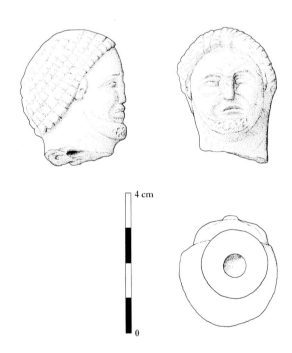

Figure 4-9   Head of a small statue of a man with Nubian features. Gypsum or anhydrite. BE00-40.*002* (1602-tt). Drawing by A. M. Hense.

Plate 4-10 Detail of stamped amphora handle with two lines of Greek:
ЕΠΙΑ[?] ΡΙΣΤ[A?]. Photograph by S. E. Sidebotham.

The most interesting discovery was massive north-south wall *039*, which clearly continued farther north and possibly south of BE00-40 and probably functioned as a demarcation boundary of the industrial zone. The industrial activity that began in the early stages of the western part of the settlement probably spread out too much, and waste dumping spread with it, so it had to be contained. Since BE00-40 was situated at the western extremity of the site, this wall could easily have surrounded most of the industrial zone. Alternatively, perhaps there was a higher degree of specialization among the people working in the industrial zone or a distinction made between them and the residents of the putative occupation area. If so, then a definition of space was deemed necessary or appropriate by those who controlled or administered the port of Berenike. Only further research can answer these questions. Nevertheless, several conclusions can be drawn. First, there was continuous settlement and industrial activity throughout at least the early and middle Ptolemaic periods. Second, there was commercial contact with the Mediterranean (based on pottery finds), perhaps India or Phoenicia (based on the design on a spherical gypsum bead found while trimming the east balk: personal communication from P. Francis, Jr.) and sub-Saharan Africa (find of an elephant tooth west of wall *039*). Third, the inhabitants of Berenike, or at least a portion of the population, must have enjoyed a relatively high level of wealth, since luxury items such as carnelian beads, worked bronze objects (a shrine, two pins, and an *ankh*), a soapstone dish, worked ostrich eggshell (from *003*), and faience, as well as trade objects from the Mediterranean and possibly India or Phoenicia

were found not only in a working area, but in a marginal section of a working area. Further excavation will, hopefully, fill out the picture of the range of industrial activity and provide a more precise dating sequence for the phasing encountered thus far.

4.2 EARLY ROMAN TRASH DUMP
Trenches BE99-29, BE99-31, BE00-33

4.2.1 TRENCHES BE99-29 AND BE99-31
Trench Supervisor: I. Schacht
Figures/Plates 4-11 to 4-19

Trenches BE99-29 and BE99-31 were laid out in the northern area of the site, in the vicinity of two trash dump trenches excavated in previous seasons (BE96/97-13 and BE97/98-19). Trench BE99-29 was 5 m N-S x 3 m E-W while BE99-31 measured 5 m N-S x 4 m E-W. The coordinates of trenches 29 and 31 were 619–624 N/1916–1919 E and 604.5–609.5 N/1909.5–1913.5 E, respectively, at heights of 4.29 m and 4.61 m asl.

The two earlier trenches (BE96/97-13 and BE97/98-19) excavated first-century AD Roman trash. This coupled with evidence of copious ostraka, some papyri (Bagnall, Helms, and Verhoogt 2000), surface pottery and organic finds, such as textiles and basketry (Chapters 11 and 12), wood, and floral, and faunal remains, suggested that locating two new trenches here would allow exploration of this large dumping area in more detail and, in particular, add to the body of textual material (papyri and ostraka) recovered from the earlier trenches. Furthermore, a Ptolemaic sand-brick structure in trench 13 (Sidebotham 1999b: 46–57) and sand bricks recovered from trench BE97/98-19 (Sidebotham 2000b: 100–101) indicated the presence of Ptolemaic architecture beneath the early Roman dumping phases (Figure 4-11).

Pottery and glass recovered from trenches BE99-29 and BE99-31 dated all loci mid- to late first century AD, comparable with dating for trenches BE96/97-13 and BE97/98-19. This and the similarity in characteristics of all four trenches suggested they were all areas of one large dump.

Excavation of trenches 29 and 31 revealed a definite pattern of soil types and associated finds and the quantities of finds and the depth of individual phases. The most concentrated phase of trash occurred in the latest period of dumping. In both trenches the loci in this phase (BE99-29.*002, 006*, BE99-31.*006/007*) were a dusty gray silt with finds making up a large bulk of the soil (up to 80 percent in some areas). Finds consisted of large quantities of textiles, rope, basketry, wood, leather, and ostraka, and papyri. Most of the notable finds recovered from the two trenches (carved gems, brailing rings, reed pens, amphora stoppers, carved wood, stone and bone, metal objects, painted glass, coins, etc.) came from this phase of dumping.

The next heaviest period of dumping occurred just before the latest phase and consisted of a reddish loamy soil (i.e., BE99-29.*007, 009,* BE99-31.*018-020*). Again, a large quantity of rope, textiles, wood, and some notable finds including an ostrakon in Demotic (Plate 4-12) and a broken figurine of the goddess Aphrodite/Venus made of local gypsum/anhydrite (Figures/Plates 4-13 to 4-16) were recovered from the loci in this phase.

Plate 4-12   Ostrakon in Demotic from 31.*019* (4646-A-068). Scale=10 cm. Photograph by S. E. Sidebotham.

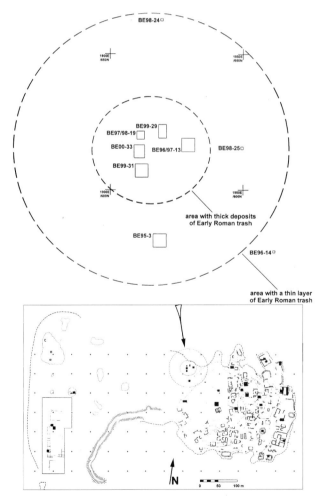

Figure 4-11   Concentration of trash layers in the early Roman trash dump. Drawing by A. M. Hense.

Page 46:   Plates 4-13 and 4-14; Figures 4-15 and 4-16
Front and back of gypsum statuette of Aphrodite/Venus (BE99 31.*018* 3491-tt). Scale=10 cm. Photographs by S. E. Sidebotham, drawings by C. E. Dijkstra.

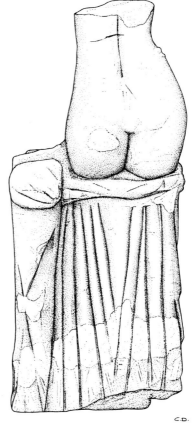

Below these rich phases of dumping, the soil was progressively sandier and the finds (organic phase of sandy loamy loci (i.e., BE99-29.*010, 012-013*, and BE99-31.*012, 014, 017*) still contained rope, textiles, basketry, wood, and some other notable artifacts, but there was a definite decrease in the concentration of finds.

By the earliest Roman phase of dumping, the soil was very sandy, sometimes slightly gravely, very clean, and devoid of organic material (BE99-29.*022*, BE99-31.*019*). Large quantities of pottery were recovered from this early phase (significantly more than in later phases), as well as a lot of shell and bone, but textiles, rope, basketry, wood, and individual noteworthy finds were almost nonexistent in this phase. In the deeper levels of these loci the sand became sterile.

Approximately 1.5 m of clean sand separated the earliest phase in Trench 31.*021* from the later Roman phases. Although not completely excavated, this locus seems to have been a small trash dump (or the edge of a larger one) and was dated to the Ptolemaic period by a Demotic ostrakon (Plate 4-17). Trench BE99-29 was, due to lack of time, not excavated beyond the Roman phases so it is unknown whether Ptolemaic remains might have been present there also.

Excavation of these two trenches raised many questions about the process and psychology of dumping in particular and, on a broader level, about the relationship of this trash dump to the settlement.

Plate 4-17   Ostrakon in Demotic from the late Ptolemaic period, discussing wine. Trench BE99-31 south balk trim (4423-A-082). Scale=10 cm. Photograph by S. E. Sidebotham.

An important question about the dump is why organic materials (textiles, rope, basketry, wood, etc.) became scarcer in the earlier phases. Was the dump (or newer areas of the dump) used less heavily in the beginning (possibly while simultaneously still using older ones) and then more heavily later (maybe when older ones were completely full)? Or is there another reason? For example, did organic materials decay more quickly at deeper levels due to natural conditions that did not affect the higher elevations? On the other hand, what role did rain and other weather conditions play, which one would expect to affect levels closer to the surface? Did seawater or salt adversely impact lower strata more than higher strata?

Another factor that raised questions about the use of the dump was the layers of cleaner sand in the trenches (i.e. BE99-29.*014, 017*, and BE99-31.*007a, 012a, 014, 017a, 019*), which often separated strata of organic material. Did users of the dump seal it with clean sand (to reduce smell and deter rodents and insects), or were these layers deliberate dumps of sand from a particular location (e.g., from a building site, clearance of an area, etc.)? Were areas of the dump out of use at particular times when they became covered with windblown sand (or were covered during use due to a particularly bad sandstorm)? Or was it a combination of two or more of these factors? Some areas (as opposed to levels) of clean sand may have been clean, unused areas of the dump.

This leads to the question of how these dumps were created. Were large pits dug in which trash was subsequently deposited over a long period of time, or were more temporary smaller areas dug for particular dumps of trash (which later may have merged to form one larger dump)? Were pits dug at all, or was trash dumped at ground level, piling up, in an area set aside for trash? Maybe advantage was taken of a natural ditch or slope for disposing of refuse. Evidence from trench balks seems to suggest that the dump in these areas followed the natural slope of the ground from south down toward the north, and there seems to be no indication of an artificial cut. It was, therefore, likely that this dump accumulated at ground level.

The location of this large dump prompts questions about how it related to the settlement. To date there is no evidence for where the first-century buildings/houses that may have utilized this dump were located. They may have been situated around the edge of the dump, but are unlikely to have been within the area of the dump as it did not (from the evidence of excavations to date) seem to have utilized abandoned buildings of the same or earlier date. It was also not subsequently built upon. The dump seems to be located in what was an empty area outside of the Roman habitation/industrial zone. Ptolemaic finds from trenches 19 and 31 may indicate that the dump was located over an earlier Ptolemaic area of the settlement, but there was no evidence to suggest that trash was dumped in abandoned Ptolemaic structures.

Houses and other buildings probably utilized individual rubbish piles locally, but excess trash may have been deposited farther away. It is possible that trash was collected, in part, from buildings in the settlement by some agent (private or civic) and removed to the dump. The evidence from some of the finds so far may indicate this; for example, of all the glass recovered, not very much material from the heavy bases of vessels has been found. Jennifer Price (personal communication) has commented that glass in the Roman period, as a valuable commodity, was definitely recycled. Since we are missing more recyclable pieces of glass, it is possible that collection of refuse glass occurred. Maybe other rubbish was also collected and eventually disposed of at the main dump.

Other questions about who used the dump (private individuals, public/civic groups, both) may be answered eventually by the categories of finds recovered and their distribution within the dump. Papyri from trenches 29 and 31 were recovered only from the latest phase (i.e., BE99-29.*002* and BE99-31.*006/007*). Ostraka were distributed seemingly randomly throughout seven different loci in each of the two trenches. There does not seem to be a pattern in the deposition of these textual finds, and the contents seem to be mixed official and ordinary documents. Specialist work on these and other finds, however, has been limited to date, and further information will almost definitely be revealed in time. Nevertheless, evidence suggests that material that may have originated from private households, offices, and industrial/maritime sources seems to have been deposited indiscriminately together into the dump.

Ash deposits (BE99-31.*005, 008–010*) also raise a question about the use of the dump. Was ash brought from houses or industrial/market areas and discarded at the dump or was rubbish burned on-site at the dump? Some of the ash deposits contained unburned material, suggesting they were burned elsewhere, mixed with other trash, and brought to the dump. Other deposits contained nothing but ash and charcoal with some burned stone/shell beneath, suggesting that they may have been burned on the site. It was likely both methods were represented in the dump.

A study of the finds recovered from trenches 29 and 31 will obviously reveal much about the everyday life and major activities of the first century AD inhabitants of Berenike. Only a few points can be made at this stage. One theme raised by trench 31, which was not as prevalent in trench 29, is that of fishing and other maritime activities. Excavations have recovered fishing hooks of various sizes, cork floats for fishing nets, nets that could have been used for fishing, and remains of fish. On a broader scale there seems to be evidence of maritime activity at Berenike. In the past, excavations recovered sailcloth (Wild and Wild 2000:265–269; Wild and Wild 2001) and ropes from trench 31 that were too large to have been utilized for ordinary household activity. An industrial, heavy work activity seems more likely, and it is possible that these large ropes were used on ships.

Many brailing rings were recovered from trench 31 (for examples, from trench 33; see Plate 4-22, below; cf. Thomas and Whitewright 2001: 38, 40, Fig. 9.4; Thomas, Whitewright and Blue 2002: 81, 83, Fig. 58). Mats of a very large weave of stiff reed have also been recovered and may have been used as screens or shade structures, possibly in a shipping-related capacity (see Chapter 12). A large, heavy, rope net (Plate 4-18) was used to carry amphorae. That these finds plus some very large ropes were all found together, the net and ropes on top of the mats, seems to suggest they originated from the same location and possibly from the same activity. Other finds recovered from trench 31, triangular leather pieces, pierced with a finished hole in the bottommost corner (Plate 4-19), remained unidentified. Local workmen suggested they were the ends of saddle girth-straps, but another possibility may be corner reinforcing for sails or tents (cf. Brun and Leguilloux 2003:540–542, nos. 3, 13–15).

A question first raised during work in trench 29 was the use of mica. Mica was recovered from both trenches 29 and 31, which had been worked (cut into square/rectangular shapes) 0.01 to 0.05 m thick. Is it possible that mica was used as windows/skylights to light a room? It seems too fragile to have been used as flooring or wall material, but maybe it was strong enough to be used in some decorative fashion (e.g., to decorate walls). A piece (from BE99-29.*028*) in the shape of a handle (?) suggested that mica may also have been used to cut household items.

Apart from these finds, which have raised particular questions, other interesting finds included ostraka and papyri (see preceding) and reed pens. Excavations in trench 31.*007* and *016* unearthed two billion

Plate 4-18   Fragment of an amphora-carrying net (trench BE99-31, south balk trim, 3957-h-3891). Scale=10 cm. Photograph by S. E. Sidebotham.

Plate 4-19   Pierced leather triangular pieces, perhaps ends of saddle girths or corner reinforcements for tents or sails (BE99-31.*006*, 3057-J). Scale=10 cm. Photograph by S. E. Sidebotham.

tetradrachms struck during the reign of Tiberius in 20/21 AD at the Alexandria mint (see Chapter 8, catalogue numbers 5–6). Both were in very good condition, suggesting that they may not have been in circulation long before being lost. These coins were earlier than the dates suggested by most other finds from this trench.

Quantities of textiles recovered from trenches 29 and 31 included some interesting pieces dyed in stripes of green and yellow and others dyed in single colors of bright green, yellow, orange, and natural brown. Some pieces are very fine and others coarser (the coarsest: a rough sackcloth material; see Chapter 11).

Leather was much more prolific in trench 31 than in 29. To date, a large quantity of leather has been recovered, including what seem to be shoes, some almost whole and only parts of others. One shoe was very small, possibly a child's, providing information about the presence of women and children at the site. A large piece of tanned leather with fur was recovered as well as the triangular pierced pieces of leather discussed previously.

Excavations unearthed large varieties of glass of different vessel shapes and decoration (gilded, painted, applied, molded). Particular pieces raised interest, for example, fragments of a bowl decorated with painted marine scenes (see Chapter 10). Metal included fishhooks, an arrowhead, nails, a belt buckle, and a key (see Chapter 10). Worked wood or reeds included pens, a comb, cork stoppers (see Chapter 14), a gaming piece, pieces of wooden bowls, a spindle, and other small pieces. Many beads were recovered, mostly small orange ones (cf. Francis 2000).

With regard to floral finds, quantities of seeds came to light, including coconut shell, peppercorns, olive pips, hazelnuts, walnuts, date seeds, palm nuts, and other smaller edible seeds and grains. Faunal remains include a quantity of bone, some found scattered and others that were almost complete remains of one animal. Quantities of small animals, fish, and birds were present (some probably scavengers of the refuse) as well as bones from much larger animals (probably camel, buffalo, cow, donkey). One interesting find, suggesting animals may have been kept as pets, was a small skeleton (cat or small dog) found in the neck of a large pottery jar with a handful of faience beads, possibly the animal's collar.

4.2.2 TRENCH BE 00-33
Trench Supervisor: S.F. Mulder
Figures/Plates 4-11 and 4-20 to 4-22

BE00-33 was the fifth trench excavated in the early Roman trash deposit located at the northern side of Berenike. BE00-33 was a 5 x 5 m trench with grid coordinates 611.5–616.5 N-S/1909–1914 E-W; trench datum was 4.48 m asl (Figure 4-11). BE00-33 lay between two trenches excavated in previous seasons, BE97/98-19 to the north, and BE99-31 to the south. Two other previously excavated trenches (BE96/97-13 and BE99-29) lay northeast of BE00-33. These trenches were located on a slight incline that sloped downward from south toward the north from the main area of occupation at Berenike. A dense scatter of potsherds and other organic and inorganic remains covered much of the surface of this area. The removal of a few cm of soil often revealed trash deposits just below ground surface. The virtual absence of architecture indicated that in the early Roman period this area was probably exclusively reserved for trash, which was apparently piled in heaps still extant on the surface. Excavation also suggested that deposits tended to follow the natural, ancient surface topography of this area of the site (cf. trenches BE99-29 and BE99-31 preceding).

The excavation of trench BE00-33 had two goals. The first was the recovery of ostraka from an area near the extensive ostraka archives discovered in excavations of trenches 13, 19, 29, and 31 (Bagnall, Helms, and Verhoogt 2000). Thus, it seemed likely that a trench situated between trenches 19 and 31 would produce similar numbers of texts. The second goal was the recovery of various artifacts and floral and faunal material from these middens. This has been a critical part of the reconstruction of ancient life at Berenike in the early Roman period, and the careful sieving and sorting of a wide range of materials for specialist study has proven invaluable for broader understanding of many aspects of the city's function.

Though the number of ostraka excavated from BE00-33 was somewhat less than had been expected, the amount of papyri and papyrus fragments was greater than other trenches in this area had produced. Many of the ostraka were well preserved, several longer than eight lines, with the longest preserving 19 lines of easily legible Greek script. Papyrus fragments were numerous and included several larger, folded pieces and one rolled text tied with string.

Excavation of trench BE00-33 did not reach sterile sand. The phasing of the trench to the level at which excavation halted (ca. 3.40 m asl), however, closely paralleled that in previously excavated trash deposits. The phases include:

Phase I: Great deal of pottery, metal, and glass with little botanical material: first century AD

Phase II: Rich with botanical matter, rope and other artifacts: first ccenturyAD

Trench 33, Phase I: early Roman pottery dump

Phase I was likely an early Roman pottery dump and comprised locus *011* and loci *022* through *042*. These loci were primarily deposits of windblown sand and trash with a heavy concentration of pottery. Previous excavations in the early Roman trash dump had designated this as a period of abandonment, but excavation of trench BE00-33 indicated that a more accurate understanding of this phase might be as one of pottery dumping or industrial waste, as opposed to a later phase of concentrated household waste deposit. Though loci in this phase were virtually devoid of botanical material, dung, and textiles, there remained a significant concentration of bone, wood, and rope, with certain categories of artifacts in even higher concentrations than in Phase II, such as metal and glass. The excavator of trenches BE99-29 and 31 speculated that loci in later phases tended to preserve botanical material better, being near the surface. But the presence of easily degradable finds, such as wood and rope, in Phase I, would seem to rule out such a thesis. Additionally, the loci in later phases continued to produce finds such as cork stoppers (see Chapter 15), brailing rings, leather objects such as shoes, a bronze ring, an agate cameo blank, coins (see Chapter 8), worked wood and sticks with rope wrapped around them, painted glass, and other objects not consistent with this thesis of a phase of abandonment. The presence, however, of windblown sand interspersed with loci *022* through *042*, and the very sandy consistency of the soil matrix itself in these loci, did suggest a different pattern of deposition than that of Phase II. It was likely that Phase I was deposited over a longer period of time than Phase II. Such a scenario would have been likely to produce the pattern of deposition exhibited in Phase I, with periods of slow deposition of pottery and trash, allowing time for the accumulation of windblown sand. Another likely thesis, also proposed by the excavator of trenches BE99-29 and 31, was that trash deposits might have been covered with layers of sand to control odor and animal scavenging.

It is interesting to note that the small amount of dung recovered from Phase I was almost exclusively canine, suggesting animal scavenging.

The final locus (*040*) excavated in Phase I was a layer of clayey, loamy sand. This locus was begun on the last day of excavation in trench BE00-33 and was only cleared a few cm along the eastern balk. Above locus *040* was locus *041*, a layer of coarse, pale sand. This pattern of layers of sandy, relatively sterile deposits, interspersed with often equally sandy strata containing denser concentrations of finds, characterized many of the loci in Phase I. All loci had high concentrations of pottery. The most significant loci in Phase I were *037/039*, *033*, *026*, *025*, and *011*.

Loci *037/039* appeared as a possible surface. This raises the issue of secondary use of the trash-dumping area. Loci *037/039* appeared to be a packed-earth surface of clay and small pieces of decayed white gypsum, next to a concentration of charcoal, pottery, and other trash, including a paddle-impressed sherd. Though impossible to prove conclusively, it is likely that this locus represented an area of ephemeral secondary use of the trash dump area, perhaps for some sort of activity generating too much debris to be taken elsewhere. Three ostraka, a large rope, a large piece of cork, a piece of bronze, and a sherd from a storage jar emerged from this locus. One of these ostraka preserved 12 lines of text. Secondary use of the trash deposit (though of a different nature) was clearly attested from excavation of Phase II (see following).

Locus *033* was interesting for a concentration of lithic artifacts, including a basalt-grinding stone, a small, perfectly round worked stone, and a probable stone weight (of about five Roman pounds) with inscriptions on both ends (see Chapter 5). This locus was also representative of many of the loci in Phase I, a layer of fine, loamy sand with small pebbles and pottery. In addition to the stone artifacts mentioned previously, the locus produced four ostraka and a dipinto, a significant quantity of metal and rope, several glass handles, a piece of worked and polished shell, and a large piece of turtle shell. Finds such as these were typical of most loci in Phase I. Also typical was a large proportion of mother-of-pearl fragments in many Phase I loci. The presence of mother-of-pearl and turtle shell in appreciable quantities suggests some sort of manufacture of decorative objects or their importation, a possibility raised by excavation of trench BE00-30, though the shells found there were in a later, fifth century AD, context (on which, see following).

Above locus *033* was locus *025*. Two ash layers separated these loci, but they were otherwise similar in terms of composition of the soil matrix: fine, loamy sand with a large amount of pottery. Locus *025* was, perhaps, the most significant locus in Phase I, both in terms of stratigraphic depth and quantity of finds. Several decayed gypsum blocks appeared in this locus. Consistent with earlier loci in Phase I, *025* had little botanical material and abundant pottery and shell, especially mother-of-pearl. Metal, particularly iron, was also found in quantity. The appearance in this locus of a large amount of burned wheat among the sparse botanical matter was also of interest. Other botanical finds were unburned, but wheat from this locus consistently appeared blackened by fire.

Locus *025* was most interesting for its pottery, which included complete or nearly complete vessels, as well as several partial lamps and lamp fragments. An interesting sherd of coarse-grained, brown-slipped pottery with incised slashes and a zigzag design, and several sherds of green and yellow glazed pottery with molded vine leaves, probably from Tarsus in Cilicia (personal communication R. S. Tomber), were also found. Preliminary pottery dates from locus *025* were mid- to late first century AD, consistent with dates from most loci in trench BE00-33.

Locus *026* in Phase I also deserves mention, as it was something of an anomaly in Phase I. It was a typical trash layer of the sort that was common in Phase II. This locus consisted of fine sand and densely packed wood mixed with debris including cloth, rope, and pottery. Fragments of a nearly complete blue faience bowl emerged from this locus, as well as one ostrakon, a piece of worked wood, a fragment of inscribed eggshell, and a scrap of inscribed turtle shell. That a dense trash deposit should appear in this phase lent credence to the theory that Phase I could not represent a period of abandonment.

Locus *011* marked the boundary between Phase I and Phase II. It was this locus that first indicated the phasing of an early pottery dump with later deposition of dense household trash. Pottery dates and numismatic evidence seem to support this, for preliminary readings of pottery from locus *011* provide dates of mixed Ptolemaic and early Roman, with several residual sherds of Hellenistic gray ware and heavy, bead-rimmed amphorae. This strongly suggests that during Phase I the trash area was used for secondary dumping of pottery from other areas of the site. It is likely that earlier loci containing high concentrations of pottery were deposited similarly, and that Phase I represented a pattern of differing deposition, rather than a period of abandonment or decomposition of botanical matter. In addition to concentrations of wood, metal and rope, other interesting finds from this locus were a sherd of painted glass from a "fish bowl," previously excavated from trench BE99-31 (see Chapter 10), a large glass bead still attached to a string, and a tablet, perhaps made of leather or bone.

Trench 33, Phase II: early Roman trash deposit

Phase II was characterized by a series of thick, densely packed trash layers interspersed with strata of sandy loam and windblown sand. This phase represented a period of intensive use of the trash dump, with heavy concentrations of rubbish being deposited, most likely, within a short period of time. In addition, a large quantity of botanical matter, insects, and dung characterize loci in Phase II. It is likely that these deposits represent the dumping of household waste, indicated by the presence of large quantities of seeds from dates, olives, wheat, fruit, coconut shells, and other food matter. Quantities of insects and animal dung could also indicate that this dumping of household waste, with its concentration of food matter, attracted scavenging animals. There was little pottery, metal or glass from Phase II loci. This phase, however, produced a large number of interesting finds, many of which could easily have come from household contexts. These include balls of human hair and small wooden combs (Plate 4-20), reed pens made from sorghum, small leather or fur bags tied with string, leather belts, belt buckles, and shoes, quantities of light textile likely from clothing, a brilliant, rainbow-hued glove finger (which may be modern), pieces of uncut gemstones and agate cameo blanks, terracotta oil lamps (Plate 4-21), matting and basketry, and considerable amounts of cordage. In addition to a number of ostraka, Phase II loci also produced virtually all of the papyri recovered from trench BE00-33.

The most significant loci in Phase II were *017, 018, 009,* and *008.* Loci *017, 018,* and *009* were levels of sandy trash, while locus *008* formed the densest substantial layer of trash deposition in trench BE00-33. Loci *006* and *007a* were interesting as evidence for secondary use of the trash dump.

Situated on either side of locus *013,* they were excavated separately and, together with loci *013* and *022* formed the earliest boundary of Phase II. Both represented trash deposits mixed with windblown sand or

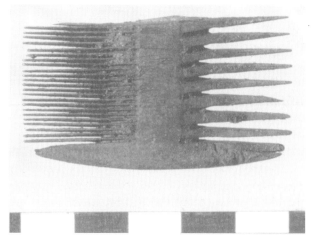

Plate 4-20   Wooden comb (BE00-33.*003* 1076-pp). Each black-and-white increment on the scale=1 cm. Photograph by S. E. Sidebotham.

Plate 4-21   Tops of terracotta oil lamps of the "frog" style (left: BE00-33.*038,* 5020-gg-24; right: BE00-33.*027,* 2678-gg-69). Scale=10 cm. Photograph by S. E. Sidebotham.

Plate 4-22   Bone brailing rings (trench BE00-33.*018,* 1672-11). Scale=10 cm. Photograph by S. E. Sidebotham.

sandy fill. Together they produced a significant number of finds. In addition to wood, charcoal, botanical matter, textile, and cordage, these loci produced five ostraka, 40 fragments of papyrus, two leather bags tied with string, a leather belt buckle, a well-preserved amphora stopper made of plaster with coarse grass and a rope attached, a nearly complete coconut shell, the top of a woven bag tied with string, and basketry including the top of a small round basket and a complete basketry bag (see Chapter 12). Other finds were a reed pen, the neck and handle of a pitcher with stopper in place and leather around the neck, a jar handle wrapped with rope, a coin, brailing rings (Plate 4-22) and a rolled papyrus tied with string.

Locus *008* was, without doubt, the richest in trench BE 00-33 in terms quantity of finds. Located approximately 0.20 m below surface level in the west, it sloped downward in the trench toward the east, and consisted of a densely packed reddish-brown trash layer, comprising approximately 70 percent wood. This locus produced 31 fragments of papyrus and 10 ostraka, one of which preserved 18 lines of text. Several other ostraka preserved at least five to six lines. Other interesting finds were a brown and yellow fur bag tied with string, a small twig brush and a wooden comb fragment, coins, one of which survived cleaning (Chapter 8, catalogue no. 20, a pre-296 AD reform *aes* issue), two agate cameo blanks, a reed pen, a bronze ring, a wooden tag tied with string and marked with the letter *B* (possibly representing a quantity of two), various pieces of worked wood, three cat (?) claws with fur still attached, a stamped plaster jar stopper (see Chapter 15, Plate 15-28), two small baskets, seven rough semi-precious gemstones, and a bit of bright red textile tied in a ball with string. In addition, there were copious quantities of wood, leather, turtle and eggshell, botanical matter, bone, and shell. The quantity of pottery, metal and glass remained rather low.

Locus *009*, though generally similar to loci *017* and *018*, was interesting for the inclusion of shiny black soil that protruded from the eastern balk. Within this inclusion was a very high quantity of small, translucent yellow stones and a bright, crumbly substance that had the appearance of red ochre. In addition, this inclusion produced a number of flat stones with a bright yellow pigment adhering to their surfaces. Though not yet studied by the geologist, it is possible that these inclusions represented waste from some sort of industrial activity, possibly cloth dyeing.

Finally, as in Phase I, Phase II produced evidence for secondary use of the trash dump. Loci *006* and *007a*

were two pits of sterile, coarse, green sand lined with plaster or crushed gypsum and pottery. It is unclear precisely what role these installations played. Both were found near the surface, with locus *006* protruding from the western balk and locus *007a* cut into locus *004* in the northeastern corner of the trench. Locus *007a* was almost perfectly round, 0.26 m in diameter, with a central area of green sand bordered by white plaster/gypsum mixed with small sherds of pottery. It was 0.05 m directly south of another small circular pit installation (*007b*), this one reddish brown in color with a darker brown central area. Locus *007b* seemed likely to be a posthole. Locus *006* was virtually identical to *007a* but was larger, with a more irregular boundary both vertically and horizontally. Two other loci may have represented similar installations, namely loci *012* and *030*. It is possible that these installations represent some sort of mixing pits, with the green sand being deteriorated mortar or concrete. If so, it is not clear why the mortar or concrete would have been left in the pit after mixing. A better explanation is clearly necessary. Whatever their precise function, these loci provide evidence of some sort of secondary activity in the vicinity of the early Roman trash dump.

Trench 33, ash and charcoal layers
Ash and charcoal layers in trench BE00-33 exhibited a consistent pattern of deposition. Of 10 ash and charcoal layers, all but locus *010* showed clear evidence of having been burned elsewhere and deposited in the trash dump after cooling. Most were about 0.50 m in diameter and quite shallow; some only a few cm deep. Many contained a large amount of unburned material, and several were deposited directly over fragile objects such as cordage, basketry, and matting, which also appeared unburned. There were often quantities of botanical material, rope, and textile within these loci as well. It was likely that these ash layers represented the remains of small household fires that were gathered elsewhere, along with unburned material from that location, and deposited in the trash dumps after they cooled. Locus *010* was the only departure from this pattern, and the hardened earth below this locus suggested that the ash was either burned *in situ* or thrown there while still extremely hot.

4.2.3 DISCUSSION
Trenches BE99-29, BE99-31, and BE00-33 produced nine Greek papyri, one Latin papyrus, 46 ostraka with enough text to warrant study (two written in Demotic),

and 10 jar-stopper inscriptions in Greek (see Chapters 14 and 15). Documents from the dump, aside from the late Ptolemaic ostraka, ranged in date from 1 BC to AD 73 (See Bagnall, Helms, and Verhoogt 2000). Unlike trenches 13 and 19, except for possible surface BE00-33.*037/039*, no additional architecture or evidence of architecture in the trash dump came to light during these two seasons.

Patterns of deposition in the trash dump trenches suggest dumping on the existing ground surface; no special trash pits seem to have been dug. Deposition included both industrial and household waste, which contained both official and private written documents, the former usually ostraka and the latter usually papyri.

Many questions remain about the nature and utilization of this first-century-AD Roman dump. Study of the finds recovered so far, future excavation in this area and investigation into similar dumps excavated at other sites should provide some answers.

4.3 THE LEVELED AREA
Trench BE96/97/98/99/00-10
Trench Supervisor: M.T. Bruning
assisted (in 1999) by P. Buzi
Figures/Plates 4-23 to 4-45

4.3.1 INTRODUCTION: OUTLINE OF PHASING
1999 and 2000 were the fourth and fifth seasons of excavations in 10 x 10 m trench 10, grid coordinates 516–526 N-S/1988–1998 E-W (the 1996 coordinates of the original 10 x 10 m trench). The trench lay immediately north of the Serapis temple in the center of ancient Berenike. At the start of the 1999 season, trench 10 was narrowed to an 8 x 8 m square, to diminish the danger of balk collapse. As stated in previous reports, the purpose of excavating trench 10 was to provide as complete a sequence of occupational levels and ceramic chronology as possible at Berenike.

At the beginning of the 1999 season the trench had heavily eroded balks, but after removal of balk collapse, it became apparent that the lower 8 x 8 m balks were fairly well preserved. The architectural structures in the trench appeared to be in relatively good condition due to architectural consolidation activities undertaken during the 1998 season (cf. Roby 2000), as well as protection provided by backfilling; only wall *036A* in the northeastern corner of the trench suffered some collapse.

Excavations in 2000 yielded 18 distinct phases. Phases BE00-VIII to BE00-XIV represented the most recent

periods that partly overlapped BE99 phasing. Below Phase BE00-VIII loci, the trench was divided in a northern and a southern area by wall *557* crossing the trench from west to east. North of wall *557*, Phases BE00-I to BE00-VII were excavated. South of wall *557*, four more phases were encountered, comprising a total of 18 phases. The relation between the phases excavated north of wall *557* and those revealed south of the wall could not be established stratigraphically. The phases south of the wall, therefore, were lettered separately, A to D, A being the earliest phase, and D that prior to Phase BE00-VIII.

Apart from these 18 phases numerous subphases were identified and generated the following phasing in the various parts of the trench:

North of Wall 557:

I	Architectural debris and sand layers (*632, 646, 647, 648*) over architectural structures (*609, 610, 645, 649*). Largely unexcavated: late Ptolemaic
II	Small-scale industrial activities involving the processing of clay (*de facto* surfaces *613/618, 621, 628, 642, 637*, and *644*, and clay, ash, and sand dumps *620, 631, 633, 635, 638, 639, 640, 641*): early Roman
III	Erection of wall *557*. North of wall *557* no occupational levels associated with this phase were encountered. Excavation south of the wall did not reach this level: early Roman
IV	Erection of wall *612* and subsequent occupation (surfaces *616, 623, 624*): early Roman
V	Construction and use of a large stone structure (*614*) that was dug into Phase II and IV occupation levels. The complete state of collapse of this structure made interpretation difficult: early Roman
VI	Short period of abandonment, resulting in accumulation of windblown sand and architectural debris (loci *593, 596, 600–603*, and *605–606*): early Roman
VII	Return to the area north of wall *557*; by a sequence of walking surfaces (*576, 570/573*), *de facto* surfaces (*562/563, 568*) and small-scale activities: early Roman
VIIa	Minor trash dumping and small firing activities
VIIb	*De facto* surface *568*, representing iron-working (not production) activities
VIIc	Surface *562/563* with amphorae *560, 561*, and *582*, associated activities not clear

South of Wall 557:

A   *De facto* surface *589/598/599* functioning in phase with wall *557*. Small firing activities (*588*) in a courtyard area. Not excavated: early Roman

B   Period of intense transitory use (*584*, *587*) and some trash dumping (*585*): early Roman

C   Construction and use of small firing installation *552* and associated *de facto* surfaces *555*, *575*, and *577*, functioning in phase with wall *557*: early Roman

D   Abandonment of installation *552*, followed by another period of intense transitory use (*551*, *559*) of the area south of wall *557*: early Roman

Entire 7 x 4 meter trench:

VIII   Domestic phase, subsequent to both Phase A and Phase VII.
Erection of walls *529* and *530*, establishment of floors *528/550* and *531/537*: early Roman
Construction of small firing installation *524* in courtyard area. Domestic occupation of the building, small firing activities on *de facto* surface *527* in courtyard area (*525*, *532–534*, *538*, *544*): early Roman

IX   Abandonment of the domestic building and courtyard, followed by a period of substantive trash dumping: early Roman

X   Erection of walls *269* and *507* and subsequent occupation. Trash dumping west of wall *269* continued: early Roman

XI   Erection of walls *242* and *488*. Associated occupational levels were located outside of the boundaries of the trench. Trash dumping west of walls *242* and *488* continued: early Roman

XII   Equals BE99 Phase II: major trash- and pottery-dumping activities: first century BC to first century AD

XIII   Equals BE99 Subphase III: courtyard phase that included major building activities in the whole trench, i.e., the erection of walls *236*, *238*, and *485* and the establishment of floors *387*, *389*, *438*, *350*, *351/352*, and *357*: early Roman period?

XIV   Equals BE99 Phase IV: industrial metalworking activities west of walls *236*, *015*, and *093* that included significant remodeling of the earlier architectural structures as well as the erection

of walls *102*, *175*, and *176* and installations *140* and *153*: second and third centuries AD.

Schematically:

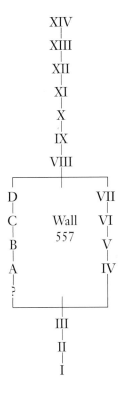

For later phasing and loci see the Berenike 1996, 1997, and 1998 reports (Sidebotham 1998:97–101; Sidebotham 1999:13-29; Sidebotham 2000b: 3–24).

A major operation undertaken during the 2000 season was the dismantling and removal of all the pedestaled architecture, including foundation structures and sediments. This architecture comprised walls *015*, *036A*, *072*, *093*, *187*, *236*, *238*, and *485*, which together functioned in a (long) sequence of phases, starting with BE99 Subphase IIIa/BE00 Subphase XIIIa, excavated in previous seasons (Sidebotham 1998:97–101; Sidebotham 1999:13–29; Sidebotham 2000b: 3–24).

Still present in the trench following the dismantling of the previously mentioned architecture were wall *442*, along the western balk, and walls *242*, *488*, and *269* along the eastern balk in the northeastern corner of the trench. Given the extent of the area to be excavated, and the absence of any substantial architecture, the working space was reduced to the eastern 7 m N-S x 4 m E-W portion of the trench only; excavation of the remaining western section depended upon results obtained in this eastern part. In the course of five weeks, excavations lowered the 7 x 4 m area from about 3.30 m asl to 1.50–1.60 m asl.

Excavations revealed an almost-uninterrupted sequence of rapidly changing activities dated to the late Ptolemaic and early Roman periods. Compared with the results of excavation of the mid- and late Roman strata, it is clear that the height of activity in this part of Berenike must be placed in the early Roman period. In previous seasons huge fourth- and fifth-century AD windblown sand layers were excavated in trench 10, but there were no indications during the early Roman period that this part of the town was abandoned for any significant period of time. Striking was the large variety of activities and their rapid succession. Within a very short period, there was evidence for various construction and occupational phases (Phases BE00-III, IV, V, A, C, VIII, X, XI, XIII), various periods of small-scale industrial activities (Phases BE00-II, VIIb, VIIc), and minor trash dumping (Phases BE00-VIIa, B, IX, X, XI, XII).

In addition to the amount and variety of activities apparent from the 2000 excavations, a third remarkable aspect is the small scale of these activities. Excavations generated no evidence at all for a large public building or publicly used areas, as one would expect in the center of town. A tentative explanation for this could be that the excavated area was part of the temple domain and, therefore, a restricted zone where temple duties and small daily tasks were performed. This explanation, however, is highly speculative, and must be tested by further excavation.

4.3.2　STRATIGRAPHIC REPORT AND INTERPRETATION

Trench 10, Phase I

Phase I comprised walls *609*, *610*, *645* (Figures and Plates 4-23 to 4-28) and architectural structure *649* as well as architectural debris and sand layers *632* and *646-648* that were deposited in this area prior to Phase II clay-processing activities.

None of the architectural structures of this phase was fully exposed, nor was the earliest occupation associated with this architecture found, so for a solid understanding of their functioning and stratigraphic relationships further excavation is necessary.

Wall *610* measured 1.20 m long x 0.50-0.60 m (three rows) wide x 0.47 m (two courses) exposed height. Wall-building material comprised rather large coral heads, which had been used to construct the two outer rows, and smooth, longitudinal, blue-gray stones that made up the middle row in a mixture of sandy mortar and stones.

Wall *609* had the same north-northwest-east-southeast orientation as wall *610*, but differed completely from *610* in building materials and construction techniques. Wall *609* measured 1.70 x 0.52 x 0.30 m exposed height. It comprised rather small coral heads and stones embedded in a thick, strong mortar of (possibly marine) clay. It bonded with much less well-preserved wall *645* in the north, the poor remnants of which were found at the bottom of pit *619/643* and along the edge of the ditch for architectural structure *614* (both Phase V).

Wall *645*, built in the same manner as *609*, measured 1.85 m long x 0.75 m wide. Wall *645* was barely exposed by excavations during the 2000 season, but it might very well have run up to wall *610*. Walls *609* and *610* both continued to function during Phase II clay-processing activities and were later used as foundations for wall *557* (Phase III). Wall *645* was abandoned earlier, possibly deliberately leveled to prepare the area for the clay-processing activities, and further largely destroyed by digging pit *619/643* and the foundations for structure *614* (Phase V).

Loci *632* and *646-648* were all similar small architectural debris layers, overlaying sand and tumble loci. These produced little pottery and were, therefore, difficult to date, but *632* had only Ptolemaic sherds and the assemblages of *646* and *648* were also, in all likelihood, dated to the Ptolemaic period. The pottery dates for these sediment loci tentatively suggested that stratigraphically underlying walls *609*, *610*, and *645* represented Ptolemaic occupation preceding Phase II early Roman occupation. This is important, because excavations in trench 10 would then, indeed, cover a full sequence of occupation at Berenike and, as such, meet the primary goals of excavations in the trench.

Locus *648* revealed a coral structure in the extreme northeastern corner of the trench (locus *649*) with an east-west orientation measuring 1.0 m N-S x 1.2 m E-W. Not much of this structure has been exposed, so its function is unclear.

Trench 10, Phase II

Phase II included a series of floors and surfaces (*613/618*, *621*, *628*, *642*, *637*, and *644*), and clay, ash, and sand dumps (*631*, *633*, *635*, and *638–641*) that may have been remnants of small industrial activities involving clay processing.

Phase I walls *609* and *610* functioned respectively as eastern and western architectural boundaries to the

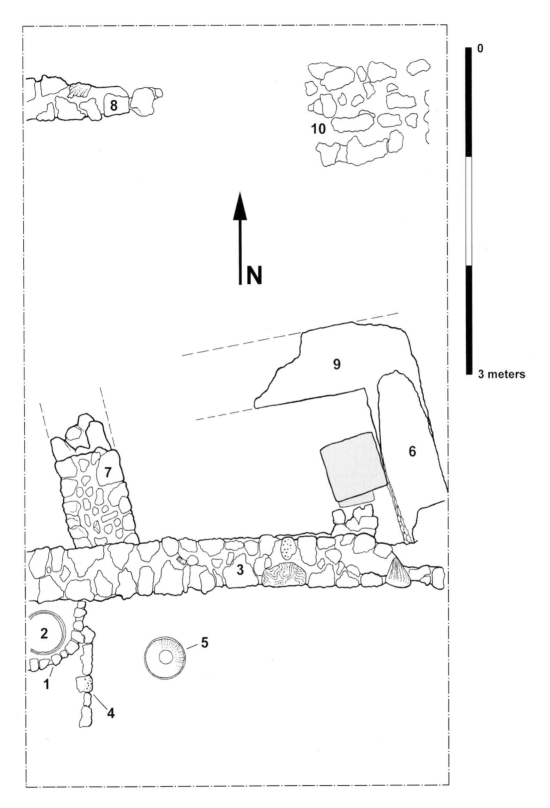

Figure 4-23. Plan of trench BE96/97/98/99/00-10 earliest phase reached in the BE00 season. Drawing by A. M. Hense.

1=552   6=609
2=554   7=610
3=557   8=612
4=567   9=645
5=590   10=649

Plate 4-24   Trench 10 earliest phase, looking north. E-W wall *557* runs across entire trench. Southwest of *557* is amphora *554* encircled by coral-head wall *552*, immediately east of and abutting wall *552* is wall *567*, east of wall *567* is amphora installation *590*. Wall *610* extends from the western end of *557* toward the northwest; walls *609/645* extend from the eastern end of *557* toward the northwest; wall *612* is at the northern end of the trench extending from the western balk; the stone feature in the northeastern corner is *649*. Scale=1 m. Photograph by S. E. Sidebotham.

Plate 4-25   Right column, top: trench 10 earliest phase, looking southwest. Scale=1 m. Photograph by S. E. Sidebotham.

Plate 4-26   Right column, bottom: trench 10 earliest phase, looking northwest. Scale=1 m. Photograph by S. E. Sidebotham.

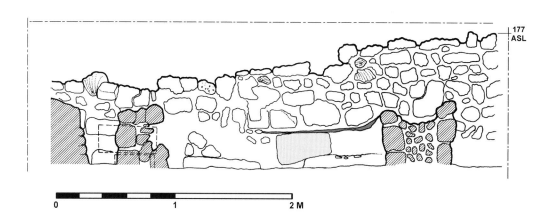

Figure 4-27   Trench 10, north face of wall *557*. Drawing by A. M. Hense.

Plate 4-28   Detail of trench 10 earliest phase, looking west. West end of wall *557* (to the right/north), amphora installation *554* and enclosing coral wall *552* (to the left/south) of *557*. Wall *567* extends south of encircling coral-head wall *552*. At bottom of photo (east) is amphora installation *590*. Scale-=20 cm. Photograph by S. E. Sidebotham.

clay-processing area. The southern part of the clay-processing area underlay wall *557* and has not yet been excavated. It was not clear whether the northern part of the area was originally enclosed as well because it was cut by construction activities for structure *614* and associated pits (*619/643, 636:* Phase V).

Phase II comprised Subphases IIa and IIb. The distinction between the two was based upon a change toward increasingly random trash dumping in Subphase IIb, as well as the introduction of large amounts of shells and copper in the finds' assemblage.

Subphase IIa.
The earliest Subphase IIa surface was floor *644*, a firm, 0.05–0.14 m thick layer of sandy clay with charcoal and gypsum inclusions, overlaying the sand and tumble underneath. Locus *644* was clearly a deliberate, well-made beaten-earth floor with a regular, even surface, unlike some of the subsequent surfaces. *De facto* surface *637*, a very hard 0.05 m thick layer consisting of clayey sand and tamped-down debris originating from the clay-processing activities, covered floor *644*. The debris in surface *637* included charcoal, gypsum flecks, coral pebbles, clay lumps, fragments of baked bricks, and a single mud brick. Surface *637* was, in turn, covered by a thin layer of ash (locus *642*) turned into a new *de facto* surface by continuous use of the area.

A series of dumps was subsequently deposited upon surface *637/642*, all associated with clay-processing and firing activities. Loci *633, 638,* and *641* were small ash dumps. Loci *631, 635,* and *639* contained a mixture of clay, sand, ash, and charcoal, and were probably dumps

of clay containing too many other materials to be used for whatever clay-processing and firing activities took place here. Locus *640* was a thin layer of sand, possibly meant to temper the clay.

Some coral tumble (locus *634*) lay amid all of these dumps, concentrated in a very small area immediately below and north of wall *557* and almost directly upon surface *642*. Since this tumble could not be associated with any of the standing architectural structures, (it should have included the blue-green natural stones if it had come from wall *610*, and the stones were too big to have come from wall *609*), it might have represented the remains of a small installation upon surface *642*. Possibly excavation of the area south of wall *557* and wall *557* itself will reveal further information about this putative installation.

Subphase IIb
Beaten-earth floor *628* marked the beginning of Subphase IIb. It clearly covered the clay, ash, and sand dumps and the collapsed putative installation underneath. It consisted of loamy sand with numerous inclusions, such as charcoal, gypsum flecks, and pottery sherds. It had a maximum thickness of 0.09 m and had a regular and rather smooth surface. Subsequent locus *621* was a *de facto* surface, up to 0.13 m thick, composed of a trashy layer of sandy clay mixed with substantial amounts of ash and charcoal.

Deposited immediately atop *621*, was huge trash dump locus *620*, a mixture of sand, clay, and ash with charcoal, gypsum flecks, coral pebbles, and cobbles. This trash dump did not differ much from *de facto* surface *621* underneath, except that it was less compact and had a higher percentage of trash and other inclusions. Sandy ash layer *613/618*, tamped down to form a *de facto* surface, covered locus *620*. Surfaces *613/618* was the last of the surfaces of the clay-processing area that was subsequently abandoned.

Surfaces *613/618, 621,* and *628* and trash dump *620* produced large amounts of broken and complete seashells and copper objects, which were virtually absent in Subphase IIa loci. The copper objects included several nails. The shells were *Strombus tricornis*, an edible species, which had to be broken open in order to eat the contents.

The excavated loci may have represented small industrial clay-processing activities. The enormous amounts of waste in all loci suggested that the excavated area covered the periphery of the clay-processing zone rather than the center of activities itself. The virtual absence of any objects or products for which the clay was processed supports this argument. The purpose of the processed clay is not clear. The fragmentary baked bricks and mud brick debris in locus *637* might have indicated that the clay was used to make bricks that were subsequently fired. The bricks, however, were found in locus *637* only, which made this interpretation somewhat speculative.

The link between the clay-processing activities and the appearance of seashells and copper nails in Subphase IIb is not clear. The shells, the contents of which were presumably eaten, were subsequently dumped in the clay-processing area. This mixture of food and industrial waste seems strange, but supports the idea that the excavated area was merely a dump. The nails may have reflected a slight change, adding possibly small-scale construction activities that required nails.

The great similarity of the excavated loci and of the finds assemblages especially of Subphase IIb loci suggests that they were deposited in a very short period, possibly within a few days. There was no evidence for any long-term use of the area for clay-processing activities. It could be that the excavated loci were the remnants of some sort of temporary work area that was arranged for one specific task and that was abandoned immediately after termination of that job.

Excavation of the area south of wall *557* and the removal of *557* during the next excavation season will, hopefully, provide better insights into the clay-processing activities that took place here.

Trench 10, Phase III

Phase III saw the erection of wall *557*. Walls *609* and *610* were leveled to provide a solid foundation for wall *557* that was built directly upon them and directly upon surface *613/618*. Wall *557* had an east-west orientation perpendicular to walls *609* and *610*, crossing the trench from the western to the eastern balk. Wall *557* measured 4.00 m long x 0.57 m wide x 0.39–0.74 m (two–six courses) high and comprised large coral heads that were occasionally cut to fit into the wall and that were constructed in such a way that the stones of its two rows meshed into each other. Sandy mortar bonded the stones. There were no traces of plaster on either side of the wall, not even in the form of wall slump layers, so the wall was either never plastered, or its plaster had eroded off before *de facto* surface *589/598/599* (Phase A) was laid down.

A few coral heads at the northeastern side of the wall that were slightly out of line with the rows of the

wall tentatively suggested the presence of a side wall immediately west or, more logically, partly upon wall *609*. Excavations north of wall *557*, however, did not provide conclusive evidence for this, especially because wall *557* was slightly damaged on its northeastern side.

No occupational levels associated with wall *557* were excavated north of it. This does not necessarily mean that they were never there. The huge construction efforts associated with structure *614* and the apparent digging (trench for *614*, pits *619/643*, and *636*) that was involved may have destroyed the occupational levels related to wall *557*.

Four phases of occupation were encountered south of the wall and are described separately following (Phases A–D). Phase A represented the earliest of these, but could not be assigned to Phase III, because it could not be shown to be the earliest occupation related to wall *557*.

Trench 10, Phase IV

Phase IV included the construction of coral-head wall *612* and subsequent occupation. There is not much information on this phase. Wall *612* was preserved over a length of 1.23 m (continuing into the western balk) x 0.44 m (two rows) wide x 0.10–0.15 m (two courses) high.

Sand layers *623* and *624* were, possibly, a surface and foundation that went with wall *612*, but this is not at all clear. Excavations did not generate data that provided information on the function of wall *612* and the associated occupation. It seems likely, however, that wall *612* functioned partly in phase with wall *557*, though activities associated with these respective walls were not necessarily related.

Some information concerning the abandonment of wall *612* could be deduced from loci abutting and overlaying it (*607*, *622/625*). Almost no tumble was found in these loci, suggesting that the stones of wall *612* were taken away shortly after its abandonment, to be reused elsewhere. By Phase V, sand layers *607* and *622/625* had already covered the remnants of *612* completely, which indicated that wall *612* was used only for a very short period.

Trench 10, Phase V

Extensive building activities took place during Phase V. These included construction of a long, shallow trench to contain architectural structure *614* and the excavation of pit *619/643* and small trench 636. These trenches and pit destroyed much of the earlier architecture and occupation by cutting deep into walls *609*, *610*, and *645* and into the surfaces of the clay-processing area (Phases I and II).

The largest trench (*614a*) cut from west to east and was filled with a mixture of rather coarse, brown sand and about 30 percent cobble-sized architectural debris. This fill had also spread out over the area north of *614*. Approximately 95 percent of the architectural debris consisted of gray, rather soft and coarse, natural stones, which remain to be identified. Small coral heads made up 4 percent of the total, and fragments of pink, sandy plaster with 1cm wide incised stripes accounted for the remaining 1 percent.

None of the architectural structures in the trench contained natural stones or plaster resembling those of locus *614*. This, and the fact that *614* was found in a restricted area, that is, in trench *614a* and just outside of *614a*, led to the interpretation that *614* comprised the remnants of an architectural structure that had been built in the trench and that had collapsed *in situ*.

Pit *619/643* functioned in phase with *614a* and the architectural structure, but it is not clear how and why. Pit *619/643* was a 0.44 m deep oval cut into the corner between walls *609* and *645*. It had a fill of rather hard, compact loamy sand with charcoal, gypsum flecks, and coral pebbles. Possibly this pit originally held a construction that was intended to support the architectural structure (*614*) in trench *614a*, but this cannot be proven.

A third feature associated with this phase was a small curved channel (*636*), starting at the southern edge of trench *614*, cutting through the surfaces of the clay-processing area and then turning westward to disappear into the sandy deposits of loci *622/625* below. The fill of *636* consisted of olive-brown, rather coarse sand, different from the sand in the ditch and from that of *622/625*, without inclusions or finds. Again, the function of *636* is not clear.

Both pit *619/643* and channel *636* were dug after the construction of trench *614a*, but not necessarily after construction of architectural feature *614* in trench *614a*. There were a few clues as to what architectural structure *614* in the large trench might have been. The plaster fragments in between the tumble suggested that the feature must have been at least partly waterproofed. Sand deposit *622/625* underneath *614a* was clearly a water deposit, indicating that at some point there was water present in this area. These two arguments suggested that structure *614*, pit *619/643*, and small trench *636* might have functioned as part of a hydraulic

system. This interpretation, however, is highly speculative. Comparison with other hydraulic installations in Roman times as well as identification of the stones in the debris of *614/614a* are necessary before anything conclusive can be said. The recovery of bath flasks from trench 10 during the 1998 season (Nicholson 2000:203–205) may suggest that this structure was affiliated with a putative small bathing facility (cf. Sidebotham 2000b: 146) in the area.

Structure *614* did not operate very long. It either collapsed shortly after it was abandoned, or it was abandoned because it collapsed, ushering in a short period of abandonment of the area north of wall *557* (Phase VI, see following).

Trench 10, Phase VI

Phase VI witnessed the only episode of abandonment encountered in the trench in the early Roman period thus far, represented by sand and tumble loci *593*, *596*, *600–603*, and *605–606*. After collapse and abandonment of the putative hydraulic system/bath, the area north of wall *557* remained unoccupied for a short period, allowing accumulation of tumble and windblown sand. Loci *600* and *605* were both substantial windblown-sand strata stretching over the entire area north of wall *557*, covering the debris of *614* as well as walls *609–610* and *645*. Upon these layers some tumble accumulated (*596*, *601*, *602*) and more windblown sand (*593*, *603*).

Tumble loci *596*, *601* consisted solely of cobble-sized coral heads and in tumble locus *602* mostly boulders up to 0.45 m in diameter. The tumble could not be associated with any specific architectural structures in the trench. Between the tumble two small fires had been kindled (*594*, *597*), probably by passers-by who undertook no further activities in this area. These small fires mark the end of the abandonment phase north of wall *557*.

Trench 10, Phase VII

Phase VII comprised a sequence of sandy trash layers in the area north of wall *557* that were probably used as walking surfaces. These were loci *562/563*, *564*, *566*, *570/573*, *575*, and *583* that exhibited a great range of activities. This sequence also included *de facto* surface *568*. None of these surfaces came with any new architecture, but all functioned in phase with wall *557*. The amounts, and especially the kinds of finds, from these surfaces varied greatly, sometimes allowing and sometimes limiting understanding of the activities occurring. Excavations proved, however, that after a short period of abandonment, the area north of wall 557 was, again, intensively used.

Three subphases could be distinguished. This division was mainly based upon the presence of *de facto* surface 568 and was somewhat arbitrary for the other loci.

Subphase VIIa

All of the sand strata in this subphase covered almost the entire area north of wall 557. Trashy sand layer 583 marked the return of activity to the area north of wall 557 with some minor trash dumping combined with further accumulation of windblown sand. Trash dumping slightly increased in locus 576, another trashy sand layer similar to 583. Locus 576 must have been exposed just long enough for some small firing activities (578, 579) to occur on its surface. Minor trash dumping and combined accumulation of windblown sand continued in loci 570/573, which preceded Subphase VIIb *de facto* surface 568.

Finds from Subphase VIIa loci included large amounts of pottery, amphora stoppers (573, 576; see Chapter 15) and numerous beads. Locus 570 alone generated at least 323 beads, mostly small, white specimens pierced in the middle, but also some large beads, one of which was made of mother-of-pearl. It is not clear whether the large amounts of beads reflected activities associated with beadmaking in this area of the trench, or whether these beads were dumped or lost here.

Subphase VIIb

De facto surface 568 consisted of rather fine sand with so much iron in it that the entire area had been turned into a substantial crust overlaying sand locus 570. Surface 568 clearly reflected ironworking activities (not production: no slag finds) that occurred either on the surface or in the vicinity. No installations were found on the surface, no tools, and the iron finds were either too small or too decayed to be identified, so what these activities were remains unclear.

Subphase VIIc

Minor trash dumping combined with the accumulation of windblown sand continued in loci 562–564 and 566. Two larger trash dumps (556/558 and 565) appeared in the eastern part of the area north of wall 557. Locus 565 was a genuine pottery dump, with pottery sherds accounting for 30 to 40 percent of the total deposit. It contained mainly sizable sherds of large vessels like amphorae and storage jars, and also produced several amphora stoppers (see Chapter 15). Loci 556/558 formed a shallow pit, which produced a variety of trash, including massive amounts of pottery and bones, predominantly of large animals (camel).

Loci 562/563 formed a *de facto* surface that covered almost the entire area north of wall 557, consisting of tamped-down trashy sand. Its presence could be discerned from two concentrations of broken amphorae (560 and 561) and pit 580 that had been dug into 562 to contain amphora 582. The northernmost concentration of amphorae (560) lay just north of pit 580, and had one amphora base and three necks, lying on their sides, with the rims pointed toward the east-northeast. The second concentration (561), south of pit 580, had three bases and five necks, with the rims facing toward the west. Pit 580 was about 0.60 m deep. Amphora 582, lacking both rim and handles, was found still standing in pit 580, slightly tilted towards the northeast. The contents (581) of the amphora showed numerous thin, black fragments of an unknown substance (too thin for bitumen), which remain to be identified by the paleobotanist.

Neither the amphorae themselves, nor other items recovered from loci 562/563, provide any clues as to what activities took place on this surface involving the amphorae. It seems clear, however, immediately after abandonment of these activities that the area was reused for construction associated with the erection of walls 529 and 530 for the domestic phase (Phase VIII).

Trench 10, Phase A

De facto surface 589/598/599 represents the earliest occupation associated with wall 557 on its southern side. This surface was only exposed in 2000 and will be excavated in a future season. Surface 589/598/599 was about 0.30 m above the lower end of wall 557 (as measured from its northern side). Further excavation here might reveal more occupation related to wall 557 that predates surface 589/598/599.

Surface 589/598/599 covered about half of the area south of wall 557 but did not touch the wall itself. It consisted of a layer of loamy sand mixed with tamped-down trash, pottery sherds, ash, and charcoal. It was best preserved in the center, where it was very dark and ashy (locus 589). Loci 598 and 599 made up the rest of the less-ashy northeastern and eastern parts of the surface, but they were clearly contemporary with 589.

Standing upside down on surface 589 was the lower half of broken storage jar 590. The jar stood with its flat base straight up. It seemed plausible that it was put there deliberately after being broken, to serve as a seat or some sort of table. No installations were found on the surface.

The high percentage of ash and charcoal in surface 589/598/599 and the presence of ash spot 588 on surface

589 indicate that small scale firing activities took place here. These were clearly concentrated in the center area (*589*). The small scale of the firing activities might have indicated domestic use of the area. The absence of any architectural boundaries other than wall *557* suggests that surface *589/598/599* functioned in a largely open, possibly a domestic, courtyard area.

Trench 10, Phase B

Phase B loci *584–585* and *587* proved that abandonment of *de facto* surface *589/598/599* did not mean abandonment of the area south of wall *557*. This zone continued to be used intensively. Locus *587* was a trashy sand layer covering almost the entire area south of wall *557* including *de facto* surface *589/598/599*. Deposited upon *587* and against amphora *590* was highly organic trash dump *585* that produced a large quantity of pottery. Of the organic remains in the dump, only the animal bones could be recovered, but it is clear that the dump also originally held substantial amounts of wood. Locus *584* was deposited over *585* and *587*, and was, again, an extended trashy sand layer. Loci *584* and *587* were clearly formed in an area where a great deal of activity had taken place, presumably not any restricted or specific activities, but perhaps substantial pedestrian traffic combined with minor trash dumping. Locus *587* produced a Ptolemaic silver tetradrachm dating to year 10 of an unidentified ruler from Ptolemy VI Philometor to Ptolemy XII Neo Dionysos/Cleopatra VII (about 170–51 BC; see Chapter 8, catalogue no. 32).

Trench 10, Phase C

During Phase C, not much changed for most of the area south of wall *557*; transitory use continued with the same intensity (Figures and Plates 4-23 to 4-28). An area in the northwesternmost part of the trench, however, was prepared for the erection of small firing installation *552*. A maximum 0.13 m thick sand deposit (*586*) supported installation *552* and its wall *567*. Wall *567* was constructed first, a single row of coral heads with a straight north-south orientation that abutted wall *557*. The wall was 0.90 m long x 0.15 m wide x 0.30 m (one course) preserved height. Wall *567* was probably not originally much higher. It supported the eastern part of installation *552* and also functioned as an enclosure for the area to the south, because surfaces *555*, *575*, and *577* were located in this region only.

Installation *552* was built directly against wall *557* in the north and directly against supportive wall *567* in the east (Figure 4-23 and Plate 4-27). It could not be fully exposed, because it extended partly into the western balk. Installation *552* was round to oval in plan and made of small coral heads, measuring 0.56–0.70 m N-S x 0.40–0.57 m E-W. It contained the upper part of a large, secondarily used, storage jar (*554*, maximum diameter 0.36 m), which had been placed in the installation upside down.

The packing fill of the jar consisted of a rather homogenous ash deposit (*553*). The jar itself was filled with ash (*574*), again a homogenous deposit, with large chunks of charcoal and burned soil (*572*). Traces of burning on the inside of the jar suggested that fires were kindled there.

Three consecutive surfaces, which differed greatly from one another, functioned in phase with the installation. All of these surfaces were excavated in a very limited area only, so description and interpretation might change when excavations are conducted in the western portion of the trench.

Surface *577* was a 0.01–0.06 m thick beaten-earth floor comprising loamy sand with gypsum flecks, laid out immediately over foundation fill *586*. Remarkably, this floor preserved no traces of ash and produced only small amounts of charcoal.

While installation *552* continued to function, some trash and sand (*575*) accumulated on floor *577*, tamped down to become a 0.02–0.03 m thick *de facto* surface. This surface had neither ash nor significant amounts of charcoal. Finally locus *555*, a 0.03–0.04 m thick layer of sandy ash, was deposited accounting for the last *de facto* surface associated with installation *552*.

The differences between these surfaces must have reflected changes in activities related to installation *552*. The absence of ash and significant amounts of charcoal in and upon surfaces *575* and *577* suggests that installation *552* was only converted into a firing installation in its latest stage of use (associated with surface *555*). Before, it possibly served as some sort of pot stand. Installation *552* was abandoned after a relatively short period of use and covered by trashy sand layers *551* and *559*.

Trench 10, Phase D

Transitory use of the area south of wall *557* continued during Phase D, resulting in trashy sand layers *551* and *559*, which slowly covered installation *552* and wall *557*. These layers were similar to *584* and *587* underneath in soil type, extent, and assemblage of finds, suggesting that Phases B–D covered a relatively short time span.

Significant remodeling of the whole area to prepare for the domestic building and courtyard of Phase VIII followed the phases of transitory use of the area south of wall 557 (Phases B–D) and the sequence of the small-scale activities on walking and *de facto* surfaces north of wall 557 (Phase VII).

Trench 10, Phase VIII
Phase VIII saw huge leveling and building efforts all across trench BE00-10 preceding occupation that comprised a building of at least two rooms and a courtyard. Two connected foundation trenches (549a, b) were dug perpendicular to each other: one running east-west to found north wall 530, and the other one running north-south to found wall 529, separating the two rooms of the building. East-west trench 549a was 2.85 m long x 0.75 m wide x 0.20–0.57 m deep. North-south trench 549b was 5.05 m long x 0.65–0.75 m wide x 0.44–0.57 m deep. These foundation trenches cut deep into the *de facto* and walking surfaces of Phase VII and also hit the northern side of wall 557. The foundation trenches were filled with a thick layer of rather coarse olive-brown sand (549) that had almost no inclusions and no finds except for a surprising amount of large amphora sherds spread throughout the entire deposit. This same fill was used to level areas west and east of the foundation trenches and was deposited immediately upon Subphase VIIc surface 562/563. The amphorae (560, 561) on this surface were possibly smashed deliberately, which would explain the number of sherds in the foundation fills. Amphora 582 in pot 580 might have suffered from the leveling actions as well, by being pushed sideward forcefully, losing rim and handles, and thus acquiring the tilted position in which it was found.

Walls 529 and 530 were subsequently constructed upon sand in the foundation trenches. Wall 529 separated the two rooms of the building. It comprised coral heads and a single natural stone. It preserved a length of 1.54 m x 0.48 m wide x 0.20–0.23 m (one course) high, but its original length could be quite accurately deduced from the length of the foundation trench, that is, about 3.80 m.

Three gypsum blocks, bonded with wall 529, were all that survived of wall 530. This wall had originally enclosed the building on its northern side, as could be reconstructed from the foundation trench, but had been preserved in the eastern room only. Its extant length was 0.85 m, reconstructed length (for the two rooms) at least 2.25 m x 0.38 m wide x 0.14–0.34 m high.

Excavation revealed neither a southern wall nor its foundation trench. The location of the southern wall, however, could be quite accurately derived from the length of the north-south foundation trench. The division between the sandy floors in the building and the courtyard area, though disturbed by huge trash pit 519/548, was about 3.80 m south of the north wall.

The western and eastern walls of the building were not located within the 7 x 4 m excavated area, since the floors (550/528, 531, 537) of both western and eastern rooms continued into the respective trench balks.

Measurements for the eastern room were 3.80 N-S x at least 2.10 E-W. The western room measured 3.80 N-S and must have been at least 1.80 m E-W. Sand deposits 550 in the western room and 537 in the eastern room were either floors or foundations for floors 528 and 531 respectively. Both were layers of compact fine sand with few inclusions and few finds, and would not have been recognized as floors if it were not for the presence of the foundation trenches and walls 529 and 530. Locus 528, which hardly qualified as a floor, covered deposit 550. The only substantial surface in the building was beaten-earth floor 531 in the eastern room, which had been laid on the sand of 537. Floor 531 (thickness of 0.04–0.09 m) consisted of loamy sand with numerous gypsum flecks and had a very smooth and regular surface. It was best preserved in the corner between walls 529 and 530 and less so toward the southern part of the building. All the floors inside the building were devoid of finds.

South of the building, a courtyard area was organized to prepare for the household's small firing activities. Installation 524 was built directly atop the sand (551). A frame of coral heads was constructed, which was consolidated with two varieties of mud brick: a majority of bright green bricks of sandy clay and a single, light-brown clayish mud brick. A double circle of small coral heads (543), consolidated with mud brick, was constructed in the eastern part of the installation to support the first pottery vessel (535), the rim and shoulder of a large jar that were placed upside down on the sand in the circle of stones. The maximum diameter of this jar was 0.30 cm. A second pottery vessel was placed in the western part of the installation. This was the neck and rim of a Nile silt Roman amphora 0.23 m high x 0.11 m in diameter. This vessel was also put upside down with its rim on the sand (551) and filled with a layer of plain sand (539) to prepare for firing activities. Some coral heads—most of which had disappeared—lying next to 535 could have indicated that they originally formed a circle around the amphora. Both pottery vessels had a fill of ash and charcoal (*538* in *536* and *541* in *535*). Jar *535* preserved traces of fire, which could not be discovered on amphora neck *536*; still it seemed likely that fires were set in both vessels.

Installation *524* measured 0.65 m N-S x 1.02 m E-W, but was clearly incompletely preserved. A line of crystallized salt and minerals north of the installation probably delineated its original dimensions, which would have added 0.13 m to its north-south measurements.

De facto surface *527*, in the courtyard area, ran up against installation *524*. This surface, up to 0.10 m thick, was a firm layer of loamy sand with gypsum flecks, ash, and charcoal. Five fireplaces were preserved on *527*. Loci *525*, *534*, and *544* were fireplaces with very thick layers of ash and charcoal, clearly the result of substantial and repeated use. Two curious features were small and shallow fire pits *532* and *533* (0.17 x 0.15 x 0.02 m deep and 0.15 x 0.14m x 0.02 m deep respectively) that contained almost entirely charcoal and virtually no ash, as if something had been burned *in situ*. The function of these pits was not evident. They were definitely too shallow to be postholes.

Another remarkable feature on surface *527* was a rectangular layer of 75 percent gypsum/coral gravel and 25 percent loamy sand intermixed with substantial quantities of charcoal (*445*) in the southeasternmost corner of the trench. This layer was clearly a deliberate deposit, but it is difficult to say anything about its function and even its appearance since it ran into the southern and eastern trench balks, and its extent could not be estimated. It might have been some sort of platform, possibly for another installation.

The small scale of the architecture and the firing activities associated with this phase suggest that the building and the courtyard were used for domestic occupation. The building and the courtyard were abandoned after a relatively short period of use. The fact that so little had been left of walls *529* and *530* and almost no tumble was found that could be associated with them, except in loci *616* and *495*, might indicate that the walls were at least partly broken down for the materials to be reused elsewhere. Installation *524* was left untouched and was slowly covered by the trashy sand deposits that followed domestic occupation (Phase IX).

Trench 10, Phase IX
A period of intensified rubbish dumping in the whole trench followed abandonment of the domestic building and courtyard. First, however, a thick layer of almost-sterile light olive-brown sand (*517*) was deposited on floor *528*. This must have happened immediately after abandonment of the floor, because there was no evidence of any trash or windblown sand or other deposits accumulating upon floor *528* prior to the deposit of *517*. Locus *517* was clearly not a natural accumulation, because it would have been impossible for such a thick (up to 0.13 m), regular, and almost-sterile sand layer to be deposited by natural processes in an area that showed evidence of so much human activity. Given its similarity to foundation fill *549* (Phase VIII), *517* might also have been foundation fill. Neither architectural structures nor occupational levels that could be linked to *517* were, however, found in the trench, so these had either disappeared, were not recognized by the excavators, or must have been located largely outside the boundaries of the trench. Sand layer *516*, deposited over floor *531* and the remnants of walls *529* and *530*, did not seem to be a natural deposit either, although it was much less sterile than *517*. Its function, however, was not at all clear.

Trashy sand layer *503/514/515* covered both *516* and *517*, and ushered in a period of minor trash dumping combined with the accumulation of windblown sand. A larger trash dump deposited in shallow pit *502/506* comprised quantities of pottery and animal bones. Minor trash dumping continued and produced trashy sand strata *494* and *495*. The regularly aligned tumble in *494* suggests that wall *529* was at that time at least partly still standing.

Some small firing activities took place on *495* (*496*–*498*). These were all insignificant fires, which were probably set by passersby. At the same time, trash dumping intensified in the southern area, accounting for the large and highly organic trash layer *504*. Trashy sand layers *520* and *521* had already buried most of decaying installation *524*, which was now covered completely.

Finally, a large pit was dug in the eastern part of the area that contained two major trash dumps (*519*, *548*) and two small fire pits (*522*, *523*), dug into the lowest of these trash dumps (*548*) and later covered by a second trash dump (*519*). This pit was dug deep into the floors and surfaces of the domestic phase (Phase VIII), possibly destroying (the remnants of) the southern wall of the domestic building, and even touched some of the surfaces underneath domestic occupation (*563*, *564*). Finds from the pit were especially abundant in pottery and animal bones.

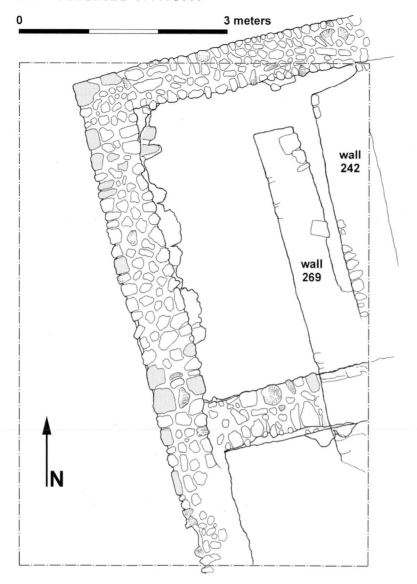

Figure 4-29   Plan of northwest quadrant of trench 10. Drawing by A. M. Hense (see Figure 4-34).

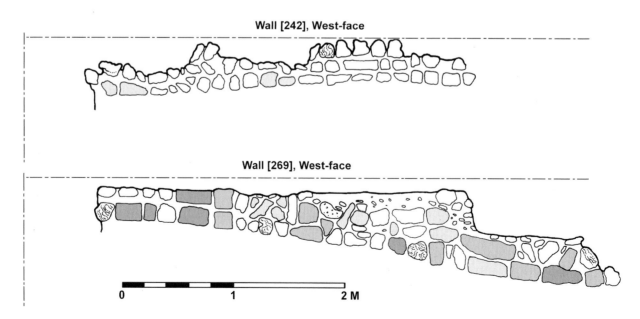

Figure 4-30   Trench 10, elevations of the west faces of walls 242 and 269. Drawing by A. M. Hense.

Plate 4-31
Trench 10, looking northwest. Long diagonal N-S wall is *236*, at top right/north and abutting is *236* is E-W wall *238*; at *236* mid-wall and perpendicular to it is wall *485*; inside the northeastern room formed by walls *236/238/485* are walls *269* (to left/west) and *242* (to right/east). Scale=1 m.
Photograph by S. E. Sidebotham.

Plate 4-32
Trench 10, looking southwest. E-W wall to the right (northeastern corner of the trench) is *238*; parallel to it on the left (south) is wall *485*; large diagonal N-S wall in the middle is *236*. Enclosed by these are walls *269* (top/west) and *242* (bottom/east). Scale=1 m.
Photograph by S. E. Sidebotham.

Trench 10, Phase X

Phase X saw a continuation of trash-dumping activities for the main part of the trench, and the construction and subsequent occupation of a new building in the north-easternmost corner of the trench (Figures 4.29–4.32). Only small portions of the occupational levels associated with this building were located within the boundaries of the trench. These were, where present, largely destroyed by foundation pit *510/513* for wall *242*, which significantly limited understanding of this phase.

Wall *269* was erected upon foundation layer *493/505* in the north and trash layers, including *504*, in the south. The latter also provided foundation for wall *507*. Wall *269* had a total length of 6.05 m x 0.70 m (two–three rows) wide x 0.40–0.70 m (two/three–five courses) high; two extra courses in the south made up for the height difference between the northern and southern area. The building materials were mainly coral heads and ashlar blocks, some gypsum blocks, and some natural stones, embedded in compact sandy clay.

Wall *507* abutted approximately the middle of the eastern side of wall *269*, suggesting that it was an inside wall separating a northern and a southern room in the building. This might explain the slightly

Plate 4-33 Trench 10, looking south-east. Large diagonal N-S wall is *236*, E-W wall at left that intersects *236* at its northern end is *238*, wall *242* is visible to the left/east of wall *236* and south of wall *238*. Scale = 1 m. Photograph by S. E. Sidebotham.

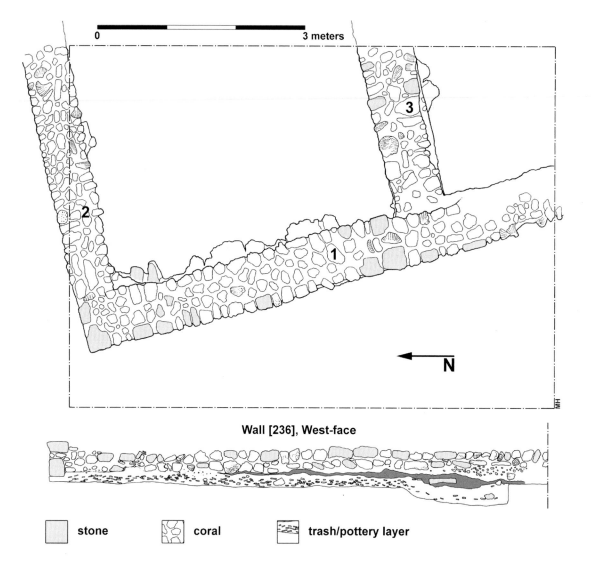

Wall [236], West-face

stone coral trash/pottery layer

Figure 4-34 Plan of northwest quadrant of Trench 10 and elevation of the west-face of wall *236*.
Please note that north is to the left. Drawing by A. M. Hense.
1 = *236* 2 = *238* 3 = *485*

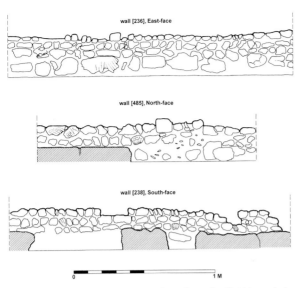

wall [236], East-face

wall [485], North-face

wall [238], South-face

0   1 M

Figure 4-35   Trench 10, elevations of east face of wall *236*, north face of wall *485*, and south face of wall *238*. Drawing by A. M. Hense.

inferior construction technique used for this wall, which comprised a mixture of clay and large coral pebbles. Wall *507* had a length of 0.30 m in the trench x 0.67 m wide x 0.33 m preserved height.

Walls *269* and *507* were similar to Ptolemaic walls *609* and *645* (preliminary date), and also Ptolemaic wall *022* in trench BE00-36 in the use of clay as mortar.

Not much Ptolemaic architecture has been exposed in excavations at Berenike yet, but clay was used in the construction of the vast majority of the Ptolemaic architecture that has been found. Thus, the use of clay and clay mortar in the construction of walls was definitely not an exceptional and probably even a common technique during the Ptolemaic period. None of the other early Roman walls encountered in the trench used clay mortar, but not enough early Roman architecture has been exposed in the trench or on the site as a whole to say whether clay mortar was still common in the early Roman period.

The foundation for floor *509* in the putative northern room of the building comprised a very hard 0.03–0.4 m thick layer of bright red sand intermixed with 30 percent chunks of concreted sand (*511*). It is not clear whether pottery dump *512* underneath was a foundation deposit as well or just a trash dump. The floor of *509* was 0.03–0.04 m thick, beaten earth, of loamy sand with an irregular ashy and patchy surface. The whitish ash and charcoal found on the surface provided a minor clue as to what occurred in the building; this must have included firing activities. Covering floor *509* was a layer

of yellow clay with gypsum spots and charcoal (*508*), the same clay that was used in the construction of walls *269* and *507*. Thus, *508* was either a repair of floor *509* or slump coming from walls *269* and *507* after abandonment of the building.

While the building was occupied, rubbish dumping in the area to the west continued, producing trash layers *489*, *491*, and *492/501*. These strata were clearly deposited in a large open area that was publicly accessible and were not specifically related to whatever activities took place inside the building. Loci *491*, *492/501*, and especially *489* were large rubbish deposits containing a wide variety of trash intermixed with some architectural debris (pebble-sized pieces of coral, cobbles, and mud brick). Finds were abundant, especially in pottery and animal bones, and included several ostraka (on potsherds and on ostrich eggshell), a graffito, 50 to 60 beads, a ring bezel, some cloth (a rare find at this level in the trench), and part of the coiffure of a terracotta figurine of a human female.

Building *269/507* was abandoned after a relatively short period of use. This was immediately followed by the erection of new architectural structures (*242*, *488* in Phase XI).

Trench 10, Phase XI

Phase XI included the construction of walls *242* and *488* (Plate 4-33). These walls were part of a building whose inner space was located completely outside the boundaries of the trench, so no occupational levels connected with it were excavated. Wall *242* was built almost immediately east and partly directly against wall *269*, which at that time had not suffered much decay, and directly upon wall *507*, which was leveled for this purpose. Wall *242* had a preserved length of 3.85 m (being cut both in the north and in the south by activities involved in the construction of walls *238* and *485* (in Phase XIII) x 0.70 m (four rows) wide x 0.22–0.37 m (two courses) high. It comprised coral heads and also had some natural stones and *Tridacna squamosa* shells. Wall *242* came with a huge foundation pit (*510/513*) that destroyed most of the occupational levels related to walls *269* and *507* and cut into various trash layers underneath (*512*, *495*, *503/514/515*), even hitting the floors of the Phase VIII domestic building (*531/537*). An unidentifiable billon tetradrachm of the mid- to late third century AD (see Chapter 8, catalogue no. 40) from foundation pit *513* must be an anomaly, perhaps fallen from the balk of a later locus into this otherwise—based on the pottery—early Roman subphase (see following for a similar occurrence in Subphase XIIa).

Sidewall *488* cornering wall *242* in the northeast was only visible in the trench for 0.18 x 0.18 x 0.16 m. It comprised coral heads and a fragment of a worked gypsum stone secondarily used here as building material. Excavation generated no information on the function of building *242/488*.

Trench 10, Phase XII (= BE99 Phase II)
There were four subphases of BE00 Phase XII/BE99 Phase II. Only after complete removal of all Phase XI loci was the trench narrowed to 7 x 4 m.
Sub-phase XIIa
Phase XIIa comprised huge early Roman trash and pottery dumps that had been partly excavated in BE99 and completed during the BE00 season. The loci excavated were *423, 443, 453, 464, 465, 468/482, 469, 473, 474, 483, 486,* and *490*. At this point, excavations were still conducted in the 7 x 7 m trench.

Excavations revealed that small firing activities taking place on the trashy layers below (*489*, others not excavated) predated the massive rubbish and pottery dumps. These were loci *475, 476* and *477/478* in the western portion of the trench and *479–481* overlaying locus *489*. Because the western half of the trench was not excavated further, the stratigraphic relationship between fireplaces *475, 476,* and *477/478* on the one side and *479–481* on the other could not be established. All these fires predated the huge trash- and pottery-dumping activities.

Locus *475* was a small fireplace filled with ashes, suggesting repeated use. Four square holes (0.02 m x 0.02 m), that were only visible in the burned soil below the ashes, suggested, possibly, that some sort of small brazier (metal or stone) had been put over the fire and was later removed. Dug into the sand underneath the trash and pottery dumps was oval fire pit *477/478*, containing a thick layer of dark-brown burned soil mixed with ash and charcoal (*478*) with a stratum of homogenous bluish-gray ash (*477*) atop it. Given the homogeneity of both *478* and especially *477*, it appears that this extensive firepot was used only once. Fireplace *476* preserved only a very thin deposit of mixed ashes.

Three more fires were kindled upon the surface of trash layer *489*. Unlike fireplaces *475* and *477/478*, these fires involved little effort and were clearly unique events. The presence of these small fires upon the underlying rubbish layers suggests that trash dumping in the area

ceased for a short period to be replaced by small and repeated firing activities of little significance.

A period of massive trash and pottery dumping followed abandonment of the small-scale firing activities. A sequence of sandy trash and pottery dumps was deposited (loci *423, 443, 453, 464, 465, 468/482, 469, 473, 474, 483, 486, 490*), each producing huge amounts and many varieties of finds. Pottery included vast amounts of sherds, several ostraka and dipinti (*423, 482*), numerous lamp fragments and EDW sherds (see Chapter 7). Other finds were amphora stoppers, dozens of beads, and gemstone ring bezels. The most remarkable find came from locus *423:* a small stone-cut statuette in Pharaonic style representing a baboon. Suggestions put forward were that it was either Hapy, one of the four sons of Horus, or the Greek god Hermes of the Ptolemaic period (personal communication from H. M. Nouwens). There were a few arguments to suggest that these dumping activities were purposeful actions as opposed to the more-random trash dumping in the earlier phases (Phases IX, X, XI), and that the area in which they occurred was possibly even selected and restricted deliberately for the purpose of trash and pottery dumping. These arguments included: the sudden appearance and the extent of the dumps that marked a clear break in density of trash as well as in find assemblages with the earlier trash deposits; the very high density of trash and especially pottery—in some deposits up to 40 percent of the total deposit—and the continuity of the dumping activities. There were no indications of any other occupation taking place in this area in this period nor was there evidence of temporary abandonment.

The question arises whether these were simply dumps or possibly foundations for the courtyard phase (BE99 Phase III/BE00 Phase XIII); this could not be answered easily. On the one hand, it seems highly unlikely that such a large area in the center of the town was suddenly transformed into a garbage dump. If these dumps were foundations, however, then it seems strange that they followed rather than leveled the height difference of 0.80 m in the area. Further research is necessary before this question can be answered.

The earliest phase encountered by the end of the 1999 season had been windblown sand layer *426*, found in the northern and northwesternmost parts of the trench. It lay immediately below trash dump *424, 409, 417, 423* in Subphase XIIb, which dated first century BC/early first century AD (see following). Abandonment and accumulation of windblown sand represented by locus *426* was not found in the 7 x 4 m eastern part of trench 10.

One stratigraphic anomaly in this early Roman subphase was the find in locus *463* of a mid-third-century AD-billon tetradrachm of either Philip I or II (cf. Chapter 8, catalogue number 39) dating AD 244–249. The fact that middle-Roman BE00-Phase XIV architectural structures and installations were built directly upon this and other early Roman subphases (cf. mid-third-century AD tetradrachm, catalogue number 40 found in Subphase XI) may explain this. The coin may, during the course of excavations, have fallen from a balk into this otherwise early Roman subphase.

Subphase XIIb
Subphase XIIb comprised various types of trash dumps. Dump *424*, probably kitchen refuse, was deposited immediately upon windblown sand locus *426*. Locus *424* produced several worked stones, that is, a rubbing/grinding stone and a fragment of a grinding slab, as well as quantities of pottery and charcoal and small concentrations of fish sauce (*garum*), sometimes still adhering to pottery vessels. A small trash pit (*420*) south of this kitchen dump showed signs of small firing activities, possibly the burning of trash. Study of the sample taken could shed further light on the function of this pit. Trash layer *417/423*, consisting of brown sandy loam, covered almost the entire western half of the trench, generating enormous amounts of small pottery sherds, with relatively few diagnostics. Atop of *417/423*, in the westernmost part of the trench, some tumble accumulated, presumably coming from architectural structures outside the boundaries of the trench, while trash dumping in the more central areas continued. Loci *409* and *418* each generated huge amounts of pottery. Locus *409* produced a graffito, but relatively few other finds.

Subphase XIIc
Subphase XIIc preserved *de facto* surface *416*, running up against tumble in the western area (*400*), and cut by the BE99 Phase III/BE00 Phase XIII foundation trench (loci *390*, *399*, *405*, *412*, and *414*) for wall *236* in the east. This surface consisted of brown sand with some sort of white coating; it decayed quickly after exposure to sun and wind. Surface *416* averaged 10–30 mm, and at some spots 50 mm thick, and produced a large amount of pottery.

Subphase XIId
Trash dumping, as well as the accumulation of tumble in the western area, continued in Subphase XIId, producing sandy sediments in the northern area and loamy sand layers in the more-southerly areas. Loamy sand stratum *408* generated massive amounts of pottery, mostly large, sherds many of which were diagnostics. These were poorly dated, possibly early Roman. Finds from *408* included a dipinto in black paint on a brown Nile silt body sherd, a coin (disintegrated on cleaning), some sulfur, and some red ocher. Sand layer *392* also had a large volume of finds, especially animal bones (mainly sheep/goat and fish) and pottery. From the pottery came an almost complete Italian *sigillata* cup with a stamp on the bottom. Of particular interest was the presence of EDW sherds. The so-called EDW ware in Berenike has so far only been found in fourth-century-AD layers at its earliest, whereas *392* dated to the first century AD. EDW sherds were also present in trash layer *404*, which covered roughly the same area as *408* and had a similar assemblage of finds.

Trench 10, Phase XIII
(= BE99 Phase IIIa-c, the courtyard phase):
BE00 Phase XIII/BE99 Phase III consisted of three subphases, dated early Roman or perhaps somewhat later. These comprised the construction of walls *236*, *238*, and *485* in the courtyard (Plate 4.33 and Figures 4.35–36). Wall *485* abutted wall *236* and functioned in phase with *236* and *238*. Wall *485* had been broken down to its two foundation courses to prepare for the construction of wall *072* (cf. Sidebotham 2000b: 12–13). It comprised four rows of coral heads, natural stones, ashlar blocks, and some *Tridacna squamosa* shells and was 0.70–0.78 m wide. Wall *485* had no foundation trench, but it was founded, instead, upon *457/462*. Some of this architecture was described and interpreted in a previous report (Sidebotham 2000b: 4, 11, 22–23) and will not be repeated here. Excavations in 1999 and 2000 focused upon the foundations of walls *236*, *238*, and 485. BE00 Subphase XIIIa saw major leveling and building activities in the whole trench. A foundation trench for the northern part of wall *236* was dug into the sandy sediments of Phase BE00 XII/BE99 II trash deposits. Dates for this phase could be early to mid/late Roman; the find in the matrix of wall *236* of a sherd of an Aksumite bowl (see Chapter 6, catalogue number 2) of the second to fourth century AD leads to some uncertainty about the dating of this phase.

The foundation trench for wall *236* was excavated in the 1999 season in loci *390*, *399*, *405*, *412*, and *414*, and in the 2000 season finished in loci *405* and *449*. Only the northern part of wall *236* was excavated;

the southern portion was not. The southern one-third of the wall rested upon thick foundation layer *448/557/562* that consisted of 50 percent sand and 50 percent gravel comprising gypsum and coral. Wall *236* had two foundation courses that consisted of large coral heads, large natural stones, and a large rounded reused gypsum column fragment at the northern end. The space between the stones had been filled with smaller stones and sandy mortar. The width of the foundation courses totaled 0.72–0.76 m, that is, about 0.10 m wider than the wall itself. The southern part of wall *236* was not dug in. The reason for this was not revealed by this year's excavations, but it could be that the lower, more-compact and firmer sediments in the southern area as compared to the sand in the higher northern area made a stable enough foundation for the wall, or that the southern part of wall *236* was built upon an earlier architectural structure, thus making a foundation trench superfluous. The foundation trench on the north included loci *390, 399, 405, 412,* and *414* and varied in width, depth (leveling the natural slope of the area), and backfill material. Since it was decided not to remove wall *236,* the foundation trench was not completely excavated in order not to undermine the wall. Three foundation courses of large fossilized coral heads and chunks were constructed over the full length of the wall. These were covered by the backfill of the foundation trench (loci *390, 399, 405, 412,* and *414*). Wall *236* was erected, as well as wall *238* that was bonded with *236* at its northern side.

Wall *238* also had a foundation trench with fill *447* covering the two lowermost courses. The lowest of these courses consisted of large gypsum blocks and natural stones neatly aligned in two rows. The second foundation course consisted of four rows of cobble-sized coral heads. The width of the foundation courses was 0.60–0.68 m, that is, the same as the wall itself. The foundation trench was only a few cm wider than the foundation courses.

The area west of wall *236* was leveled with firm sandy loam layers *385, 393,* and *419* to prepare for courtyard surfaces *387* and *389.* The area east of *236* still must be excavated. Surface *389* covered the northern and central parts of the section west of wall *236.* Surface *389* was in the southern part of this section where it was preserved only along wall *236.* It consisted of white to almost pink-gray, very fine gravel, determined by J. A. Harrell as 95 percent gypsum and 5 percent sand. The northern/center part, excavated as locus *389,* had a thickness of 20–110 mm; the southern part, locus

387, was 80–150 mm thick. Surfaces *387* and *389* had no boundaries in the trench other than wall *236.* They were completely devoid of finds, so their interpretation as a possible temple courtyard can only be deduced from data available from Subphases XIIIb/IIIb and XIIIc/IIIc (see following).

Subphase XIIIa (BE99 IIIa)

Subphase XIIIa/IIIa saw the repair of surfaces *387* and *389* by backfill layers *375, 377,* and *378,* and surfaces *350, 351/352,* and *357,* as well as the erection of several new architectural structures; wooden fences *160, 237,* and *288;* and installation *329.*

Backfill layer *375* covered approximately the northern half of the area west of wall *235* and derived its importance mainly from the fact that it produced six ostraka, one of which preserved 16 lines in Latin. Loci *377* and *378* provided the necessary raising and leveling of the area in the northwest corner.

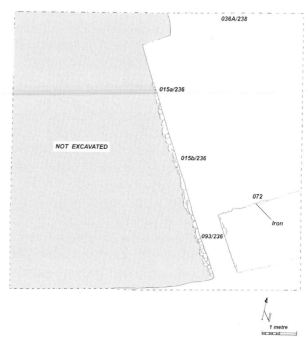

Figure 4-36   Plan of trench 10 at the end of the 1999 excavation season, indicating the wall line of *236* and walls *015a/015b/093* built on top of it. Drawing by H. Barnard.

Subphase XIIIb (BE99 IIIb)

At this point the courtyard area was subdivided into three smaller areas by the erection of wooden fences (visible on Plates 4-37 and 4-40). The best preserved of these fences was *288* in the south, with a length of 2.55 m x 0.05 m wide x 0.08 to 0.13 m high, running up against wall *236* in the east and wooden beam *237* in the southwest. Fence *288* had a doorway with a width of 0.80 m immediately west of wall *236*. Enclosing the area north of *288* and west of wall *236* was wooden fence *160*, that was preserved only for a length of 0.76 m x 0.03 m wide x 0.45 m high (preserved so high because it was protected from decay by Phase XIV/IV wall *175*) in the northwesternmost part of the trench. Fence *160* may have been connected originally to beam *237*, its presence being deduced merely from the sharp line visible in the trench that separated floor *350* from floor *351/352*. No northern enclosure for this area was found in the trench. Wooden beam *237* was dug into pit *306*, and was preserved to a height of 0.69 m with a thickness between 0.22 m and 0.26 m.

In the southern area, surface *357* was laid down immediately upon surface *387*, and consisted of 95 percent gypsum gravel and 5 percent sand, with a thickness of 0.03–0.16 m. Surface *350* comprised a similar mixture of gravel and sand, with a thickness of 0.05–0.15 m. Backfill layers *375*, *377*. and *378* in the north and surface *389* in the south covered earlier surface *350*. Surface *351/352* covered the western area; it differed from *350* and *357* in that it was much thinner, only 0.01–0.02 m, and consisted of 85 percent sandy loam and only 15 percent gypsum gravel. Surfaces *351/352*

and *357* were devoid of associated architecture as was *350* in this subphase, except for installation *329* and pivot construction *382* at the doorway in fence *288*.

Installation *329* was built upon 0.02 m thick foundation layer *381*, which was, in turn, atop floor *350*. Installation *329* consisted of three one-row-wide walls made up of small coral heads and pottery sherds covered with a thick layer of mortar; the northern and southern walls of the installation abutted wall *236*. Installation *329* was 0.93 m N-S x 0.59 m E-W x 0.20–0.22 m high. The interior rectangular part of the installation measured 0.67 m N-S x 0.35 m E-W, and produced huge amounts of iron, including a fragmented iron ax with the remnants of its wooden shaft still attached. Study of the iron finds so far has not provided conclusive evidence about the function of installation *329*, which continued in use during Subphase BE99 IIIc/BE00 XIIIc.

Subphase XIIIc (BE99 IIIc)
In Subphase XIIIc/IIIc the courtyard area was significantly remodeled. The doorway in fence *288* was closed by covering pivot construction *382* with dirt (*376*) and at least one ashlar, thus blocking the entrance from the southern area toward the center area. It was not clear where or even if a new doorway was constructed.

Plate 4-37
Trench 10, looking east. Scale=1 m. Large wall is *015a/015b/093* built on top of wall *236*. The two holes on the right are the tops of Indian-made storage jars *361* (west/bottom) and *362* (east/top). To the right of these are remains of wooden fence *288*. Photograph by S. E. Sidebotham.

In the southeast corner of the center area, along fence *288*, were two large pits (*358* and *359*) that contained one storage jar each, *361* and *362* (Plates 4-37 to 4-40). The first and westernmost pit (*358*) measured 1.20 m N-S x 0.80 m E-W x 0.68 m deep. It was dug immediately north of fence *288* and contained a complete storage jar *361*, which had been placed in the pit standing upright with its rim just above floor level. Storage jar *361*, made in India, had a height of 0.65 m and a rim diameter of 0.355 m. Several damaged spots on its body, which must be assigned to an earlier period of use, had been repaired with matting and bitumen. The bottom quarter of the storage jar contained 7.55 kg of unburned black peppercorns. This comprises the largest single cache of peppercorns ever recovered anywhere in the Roman Empire. Storage jar *361* must have had a cover, since its contents were not contaminated. Small fragments of wood around the rim could point to a wooden lid, like the one on storage jar *362* (see following). The fill in pit *358* around storage jar *361* consisted of compact sandy loam with gypsum specks as inclusions.

Plate 4-39   Detail of the wooden lid atop storage jar *362*. Scale=20 cm. Photograph by S. E. Sidebotham.

Plate 4-38   Detail of the two Indian-made storage jars *362* with remains of wooden lid and *361* with complete rim, containing 7.55 kg of black peppercorns. Scale=20 cm. Photograph by S. E. Sidebotham.

Plate 4-40   The two pits dug in the courtyard to contain storage jars *361* and *362*. To the right, wooden fence *288*. Scale=50 cm. Photograph by S. E. Sidebotham.

Pit *359*, which lay immediately west of wall *236*, measured 0.72 m N-S x 1.20 m E-W x 0.65 m deep. Pit *359* contained storage jar *362*, which also had an Indian provenance, with a height of 0.65 m. Its rim was missing, a clear indication that it was reused. A 0.01–0.02 m thick wooden lid with a diameter of 0.36 m covered the neck of the storage jar. The remains of a 0.16–022 m long handle were still visible on the upper side of the lid. The storage jar was empty, and there were no indications as to what it originally might have contained. The packing fill around storage jar *362* was similar to that around storage jar *361*, consisting of compact sandy loam with inclusions of gypsum specks.

Important finds on surface *350* in this subphase were two positively identified wooden bowls. The first and best-preserved wooden bowl, *360*, was found on the northern part of *350*. It consisted of a small oval of decayed wood with some charcoal and was surrounded by the characteristic white circle of salt, which, according to wood specialist C. E. Vermeeren, forms when the salt withdraws from the wood while it decays. Excavations unearthed a second bowl (locus *360 bis*), also with a white circle around it, immediately west of wall *236*, on a heap of dark-brown soil (*363*).

Thus far, wooden bowls in Berenike have been found only in religious contexts. In trench BE97/98-16 they came from the late phase of the sanctuary dating from the fourth and fifth centuries AD and were interpreted as offerings (Sidebotham 1999:70–74). The shrine in trench BE98/99-23 also had several wooden bowls (see following). The presence of the wooden bowls on surface *350*, therefore, suggests that the courtyard area served a religious context as well, possibly as part of the precinct of the adjacent temple of Serapis. The peppercorns in storage jar *361* might well have been intended as votive offerings. An analogy for use of peppercorns in religious contexts can also be found in trench BE97/98-16 (Sidebotham 1999:70–78).

Trench 10, Phase XIV
(= BE99-Phase IV, industrial metalworking phase) BE00 Phase XIV equaled BE99 Phase IV and overlapped BE9810 Phase V (cf. Sidebotham 2000b: 22–23). Phase XIV represented industrial metalworking activities that took place west of wall *236* as well as the associated remodeling of existing architecture and the erection of walls *102*, *175*, and *176* and installations *140* and *153*: second and third centuries AD (see Sidebotham 2000b: 4–12); (Plates 4-41 to 4-44). Most of the sediment loci

associated with the metalworking phase, including the floors, were excavated during the 1998 season, except for *290*, *296*, and *334*; they will be described below. For subphasing of the metalworking phase see the 1998 report (Sidebotham 2000b: 23). Loci excavated during the 1999 season dated second century AD, suggesting that the metalworking area was established in this period, and, as proven in the 1998 season, was consequently in use well into the third and early fourth centuries AD.

The architectural structures and installations of the metalworking phase were built directly upon or almost directly upon the structures of the courtyard phase; this may explain the presence of third-century AD coins in those earlier phases (see previous Subphases XI and XIIa), the intermediate areas slightly backfilled and leveled by sand layers *340/341* and *347/348*, and

Plate 4-41 Trench 10, looking northeast, with installation *140* backed by wall *236* and installation *153* just behind the 1 m scale. Photograph by S. E. Sidebotham.

Plate 4-42 Trench 10, looking northeast. Installations *140* and *153*. Scale=1 m. Photograph by S. E. Sidebotham.

by sandy loam layers *290*, *296* and *334*. The BE99 Subphase IIIa/BE00 XIIIa wall *236* in the east, and the newly erected walls *102* and *175* in the south and west respectively defined the metalworking area.

Wall *102*, founded on loci *290* and *296*, was 3.55 m long x 0.55 m (four rows) wide x 0.54–0.61 m (six courses preserved) high. The wall, which showed very regular coursing, comprised coral heads and chunks and shells including some *Tridacna squamosa*, with sandy mortar as bonding. It abutted wall *236* in the east. Locus *295* produced a sherd of an Aksumite bowl of the second to fourth century AD (see Chapter 6, catalogue number 1).

In sharp contrast to the regular construction of wall *102* was the haphazard manner in which wall *175* was built. Founded upon the compact sandy loam of locus *334*, it had one course of mainly reused ashlar stones topped by various building materials, including coral heads and chunks, shells, *Tridacna squamosa* shells, natural stones and reused fired bricks, loosely piled up. This poorly built structure could not have been very high and probably merely served as an enclosure for metalworking rather than as a permanent wall.

Installation *140* (see Sidebotham 2000b: 8 Pl. 2-4, 9 and Pl. 2–5, 11, Pl. 2-7, see Plates 4-41 to 4-43 this chapter) was built directly upon BE00 Phase XIII/BE99 Phase III installation *329*, though slightly farther to the north, and upon sand layer *319*. It was 1.07 m long N-S x 0.68 m wide E-W, and consisted of three small one-row-wide walls with heights varying from 0.37 to 0.59 m (maximum four courses), enclosing a rectangular area with a pottery vessel in it. The building material for the installation consisted of coral heads and chunks, some fossilized shell, and some reused ashlar stones in the lowest courses. The pot (*320*) in the rectangular area preserved only the rim and the upper part of the body, and had been placed in the installation upside down, with its rim in the sand of locus *319*. Bitumen on the inside of the pot, which originally must have been a large and heavy vessel, clearly indicated that it was reused. Built into the western wall of the installation, directly on the lowest course, was the upper part of another pottery vessel, a Nile silt Roman amphora (*323*), lying on its side with a pottery plug still sticking in the rim. Both pots contained ash with charcoal, mixed with sand (loci *318* and *324* respectively). No packing fill for pot *320* was encountered in the installation.

Finds from installation *140* included large amounts of metal, metal slag, and crucibles. It is obvious that installation *140* had some as yet undetermined function

in the metalworking process. Despite all of the burned material that was found in the installation (ash, charcoal, slag, crucibles), neither the installation itself nor the pottery vessels in it preserved any traces of fire, which rules out any function for *140*'s association with firing, and, consequently, quite a number of stages of the metalworking process. To understand fully the function of installation *140*, expert advice and a search of the literature for parallels are necessary.

Installation *153* functioned in phase with installation *140* and walls *102* and *175* (Plate 4-44). It was founded upon thick, sandy loam layer *290*. Installation *153* was 1.21 m long N-S x 1.12 m wide E-W x 0.36 m maximum preserved height. As building material it had reused ashlars, mud brick, reused fired bricks, coral heads, and chunks. For a detailed description of the construction of *153*, see Sidebotham 2000b: 10. The northern part

Plate 4-43   Installation *140*, looking southeast. Scale=50 cm. Photograph by S. E. Sidebotham.

Plate 4-44   Installation *153*, looking southeast. Scale=50 cm. Photograph by S. E. Sidebotham.

of the installation had an opening at its southeastern side at the bottom. This opening was no more than a hole in the eastern side of the structure and certainly not an architectural feature. The lowest fill layer in the northern part of the installation, 0.03–0.04 m thick ash layer *304*, was found not only in the installation but also in this opening and outside the installation (where it was excavated as locus *291*). The body of a brown Nile silt amphora (*300*) with its base cut off (height 0.19 m, maximum diameter 0.20 m) was standing in the ash of *304* in the northeastern corner of the northern part of installation *153*. Lying on the northern enclosure of the installation was the neck of the amphora, which apparently had broken off after abandonment of the installation. Both the body and the neck of the amphora contained a mixture of ash, charcoal, and sand (loci *299a* and *299b* respectively).

The fill of *153* consisted of ash and sand layers. Two thin sand layers—*302* in the square area around the amphora, and *303* west of *302*, separated from one another by a thin straight ridge in *304*—covered ash layer *304*. Ashy layers *298a* in the square area around the amphora and *298b* for the remaining part of the installation covered *302* and *303* as well as the top of the southern part of *153*. Since the ash and sand layers in *153* were sharply defined and not at all mixed, they were interpreted as the result of short-term activity in the metalworking process. Bearing in mind that installation *153* must have been in use for a considerable period of time, there must have been a repeated action, where the installation was cleaned out every time and then filled again with ash, sand, ash, and sand again, until it was necessary to clean it out. Unfortunately, it is difficult to say more about the function of *153*. Abundant finds in metal objects, metal slag, and crucibles coming from all fill layers from *153* except for *299a* and *299b* were clear indications that *153* was, indeed, a metalworking installation, but *153* showed no traces of fire and, therefore, cannot have been used for firing activities itself.

No loci excavated in the area east of wall *236* could be assigned to the second or third century AD in general or to the metalworking phase in particular. For later phasing and loci see the earlier Berenike volumes for the 1996–1998 seasons.

4.3.3 DISCUSSION

Excavations in 1999 and 2000 in trench 10 indicated extensive and diverse activities in this part of Berenike in the early Roman period. These included industrial (possibly brickmaking and metalworking), domestic, religious, other public (bathing?) and trash-dumping activities conducted in relatively short periods of time, suggesting a vibrant ebb and flow of people in the city during this period. This area adjacent to the Serapis temple must have been one of the major focal points of life in the early Roman city and, thus, witnessed a great diversity of building within a short span of time.

The latest recorded inscriptions from the Serapis temple are from the later second century AD (Meredith 1957:61), but it is uncertain if these texts reflect merely the latest dedications/repairs or the latest use. It may well be that the temple continued to operate for centuries after the latest temple texts and that many of the activities taking place in the adjacent area to the north (in trench 10), which at present appear to be secular in nature, may, in fact, be in some way associated with religious functions of the temple itself.

The stratigraphy thus far reveals fairly continuous occupation interspersed with some periods of trash deposition and abandonment in portions of the trench spanning over five centuries from the late Ptolemaic period until the sixth century AD. Phases II to XIII and A to D contained early Roman period and latter pottery as well as third-century AD coins. More detailed study of the pottery in a future season should provide more accurate dates. At this point, too little of the Ptolemaic period has been documented in trench 10 to determine what type of activities took place here.

4.4 THE NORTHERN QUARTER—NORTH SHRINE

Trenches BE98/99–23 and BE99/00–32
Trench Supervisor: B. Tratsaert
Figures/Plates 4-46 to 4-60

4.4.1 STRATIGRAPHIC REPORT

Excavation of the building in trench BE98–23 continued in the 1999 and 2000 seasons as trenches BE98/99–23 and BE99/00–32. Grid coordinates for the former were 614–619 N and 2031–2036 E. Excavations reached the bottom of walls *005*, *007*, and *009/010*, which were founded on sand. The highest wall, north wall *005*, was preserved to a height of 1.69 m (14 courses), the lowest, *007* west wall, preserved a height of 1.47 m (12 courses). The trench was extended toward the east for another 3 m as BE99/00–32 in order to excavate the entire interior of the building. The overall external dimensions of the building were 7.80 m long E-W x ca. 4.60 m wide N-S. With the 3.0 m extension, grid coordinates for BE98/99-23/BE99/00-32 were 614–619 N/2031–2039 E.

The building had four phases:

Phase I: Prebuilding occupation/use: before the late fourth century AD

Phase II: Backfill/foundation for the building: late fourth century AD, construction of building

Phase III: Building in use: late fourth to fifth century AD

Phase IV: Abandonment and decay: sometime in the fifth century AD

Only the stratigraphy, which suggested a rather short period of occupation in the late fourth to fifth century AD, revealed chronological sequences; the pottery helped little in this regard.

Trench 23/32, Phase I

Earliest pre-building occupation/use: before the late fourth century AD. The earliest phase found thus far may be trash and windblown ash, in loci *065*, *066*, and *067* in trench BE98/99-23. Locus *065* was a reddish-brown sand deposit with quantities of sherds, wood, bone, and coral fragments of various sizes. Locus *065* ran under walls *005* and *007* in the northwestern corner of the trench. Locus *066* was an ash layer, sloping steeply north-south under west wall *007*. Locus *067* was another sand locus. None of these loci was dated, but had to be pre-late fourth century AD, the period of the following phase.

These loci piled up in the northwestern corner of the trench, but not within the limits of walls *005*, *007*, and *009/010*. The loci, especially *065*, less so *066*, sloped steeply toward the south and east. At least two other trenches (aside from those in the early Roman trash dump comprising trenches BE96/97-13, BE97/98-19, BE99-29, BE99-31, and BE00-33), BE96/97/98/99-10 and BE97/98-16 also revealed traces of trash dumps either beneath or postdating building phases.

Roman trash dumps were known from the early and late Roman periods west of BE98/99-23/BE99/00-32. South of BE98/99-23/BE99/00-32 late Roman refuse deposits were known in areas east (unexcavated) of BE99-28 and in BE98-21. There was also late Roman rubbish found on the southeastern part of the site just west of trench BE95/96/97-5 in 1 x 1 m sondage BE96-15 (Sidebotham 1998a: 109; Cappers 1998:291). It was, therefore, possible that loci *065* and *066* in BE98/99-23 were also trash deposits. The presence of ash locus

066 within *067*, however, suggested that the latter was a windblown locus rather than a deliberate deposition. Locus *066* separated *067* from *060* and sloped down from north to south, as did *065*. It must be remembered, however, that only the western portion of the trench reached this depth. Thus, a balanced evaluation of the data revealed in loci *065–067* cannot be made at this time.

Trench 23/32, Phase II

Backfill, foundation and construction of building, late fourth century AD. Phase II had two subphases:

Subphase IIa: backfill/foundation

This "earlier occupation" phase (loci *065–067*) had been covered by sand loci (*034–037, 053, 056–057, 059–060, 062–064*) that were intentionally deposited backfill to support the walls of the building. This construction deposition probably had a two-fold purpose. First, it covered over an earlier layer of rubbish which, by its steeply sloping nature, seems to have been deposited on sloping ground and second, *060* and the associated sand loci were also designed to level the area for subsequent construction of a building.

Subphase IIb, construction of building.

During this phase, a rectangular, possibly vaulted, building was erected. This comprised walls BE98/99-23.*005* (=BE99/00-32.*006*), BE98/99-23.*007*, BE98/99-23.*009/010* (=BE99/00-32.*004*), and BE99/00-32.*014–015/023/023*bis.

The walls of this edifice were made of coral heads with gypsum blocks as quoins/corner posts for support. The entrance (BE99/00-32.*023*) with a wooden threshold (BE99/00-32.*023*bis) faced east; this threshold was, apparently, not an original part of the door, but a later addition made during Subphase IIIc (see following). The edifice's external measurements were 4.55 m N-S x 7.60 m E-W (internal 3.70 m N-S x 6.50 m E-W). Possible vaulted courses were visible along a small part of north wall *005* toward its eastern end and on south wall *009/010*. West wall *007* leaned toward the inside perhaps because of pressure; no wooden roof support was found or was there any evidence of windows or light wells.

There were no traces of foundation trenches. The same type of sand that comprised locus *060* was then deposited (at least inside the structure), for the lowest two to three courses of the walls themselves, undoubtedly to stabilize them. Nevertheless, the bottoms of the walls were not horizontally level. The bottom of

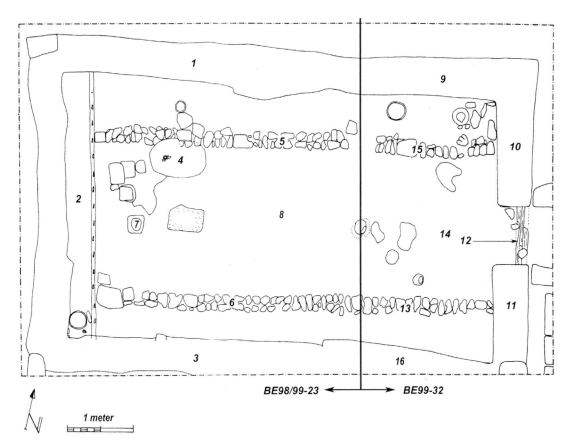

Figure 4-45   Trenches BE98/99-23 and BE99/00-32, subphases IIIa–b. Drawing by B. Tratsaert and H. Barnard.

Key:
1=23.005	5=23.021b	9=32.006	13=32.026
2=23.020	6=23.033	10=32.014	14=32.028b
3=23.009	7=23.032a	11=32.015	15=32.031
4=23.018	8=23.051	12=32.028	16=32.004

Plate 4-46
Trench BE98/99-23 looking northwest. Outer walls *009/010* to the south (left), *007* to the west (upper left) and *005* to the north (right). Columnar altar *032a* with burning on the top sits between parallel benches *033* on the south side (left) and *021b* on the north side (right). Teakwood beam *032g* extends between the N and S walls behind the altar. The round, pedestaled features are remains of wooden bowls. Scale=50 cm. Photograph by S. E. Sidebotham.

north wall BE98/99-23.*005*/BE99/00-32.*006* sloped down from west toward the east with maximum differences in the elevations of the bottoms of the wall varying as much as about 0.16 m. The bottom of south wall BE98/99-23.*009/010*/BE99/00-32.*004* also had maximum differences in elevations between its eastern and western ends of approximately 0.10 m. The bottoms of the northern and southern ends of west wall BE98/99-23.*007* were at approximately the same level. These variations in elevations of the bottoms of the northern and southern east-west running walls suggest that the building had been erected on ground that sloped down toward the east and that the earlier sand fill/leveling loci above the preoccupation "trash" were not that carefully deposited.

Plate 4-47   Trench 23, looking west. Columnar altar *032a* in the center. Amphora installation *019*bis is located in the southwest corner of the building (top left). Scale=50 cm. Photograph by S. E. Sidebotham.

Trench 23/32, Phase III

Building in use: late fourth to fifth century AD. Phase III had four subphases, IIIa–d, all based on floors found in this building. The structure had been in use for some indeterminate period during the late fourth and fifth centuries AD. The excavation of BE99/00-32 uncovered the same floors and some of the same installations as appeared in BE98/99-23. The following table associates the loci of these abutting trenches:

Subphase	BE98/99-23		BE99/00-32
IIIa	floor *051*	=	?
IIIb	floor *041*	=	floor *028*
IIIc	floor *027*	=	floor *025*
IIId	floor *016*	=	floor *019*

Subphase IIIa

Earliest floor: late fourth to fifth century AD. BE98/99-23.*051* was a beaten gray surface associated with a number of internal architectural features and installations (Figure 4-45, Plates 4-46 and 4-47). These installations were BE98/99-23.*032a*, a columnar shaped altar made of local gypsum 0.60 m high x 0.32 m in diameter; remains of what appeared to be a wooden bowl with burning inside appeared on the top of this altar. *032a* lay south of a series of stone temple pools (BE98/99-23.*013a–e*, see following; cf. Sidebotham 2000b: 136–142). Around the base of the altar were seven ash lenses (BE98/99-23.*017, 021, 028, 029a, 029b, 040,* and *042*) indicating, most likely, that burned offerings were made here. Ash lens BE98/99-23.*029b*

was associated with altar *032a* as well as with temple pool *013b* and pedestal stones *032e–f.* There was a large ashlar (*032h*) in front of altar *032a*. The ashlar, 0.50 m x 0.30 m x 0.07 m, had one nicely worked side with chisel marks that was face up; the other side was smooth and unworked. Both ashlar *032h* and the very gray surface suggested some kind of cultic activity in front (east) of columnar altar *032a*.

There were two benches (Figures and Plates 4-45 to 4-50) that ran parallel to the northern and southern external walls of the building. Northern bench BE98/99-23.*021b*/BE99/00-32.*031* was built of coral heads, ashlars, some type of igneous bluish-colored cobbles, and a large shell. Southern bench BE98/99-23.*033*/BE99/00-32.*026* was built only of coral heads. Both the northern and southern benches abutted walls BE99/00-32.*014* and BE99/00-32.*015* in the east respectively and a long wooden beam *032g* (see following) in the west (Figure 4-45 and Plates 4-46 and 4-47). Floor BE98/99-23.*051* had the large ashlar *032h* noted previously. Here excavations also unearthed two amphora toes and a bronze artifact that may be an earring.

During Subphase IIIa only altar BE98/99-23.*032a* and one temple pool, BE98/99-23.*013d*, were in use; the latter pedestaled on stones BE98/99-23.*032e–f.* Stone *032f* lay atop *032e* and probably slid off it at some point, because *032f* was laying partly on *032e* and partly on the floor. BE98/99-23.*032b* was a large square stone embedded in the floor. It appeared to be a pedestal stone, but it lacked a temple pool so its function could not be determined.

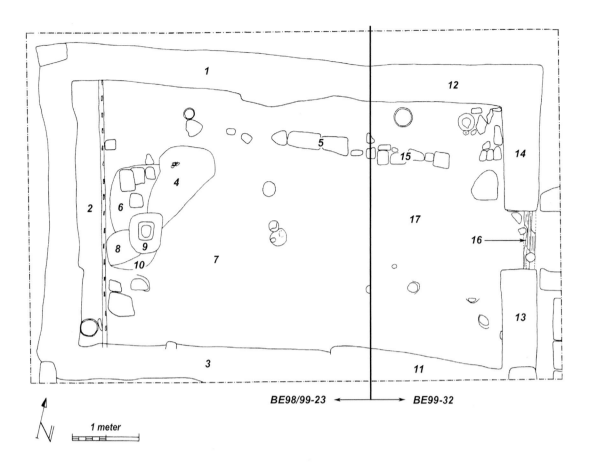

BE98/99-23 ←→ BE99-32

N

1 meter

Figure 4-48   Trenches 23 and 32, plan of Subphase IIIc. Drawing by B. Tratsaert and H. Barnard.

1=23.005	4=23.018	7=23.027	11=32.004	15=32.031
2=23.020	5=23.021a	8=23.028	12=32.006	16=32.023
3=23.009	6=23.024	9=23.032a	13=32.015	17=32.025
		10=23.040	14=32.014	

Plate 4-49
Trench 32, looking north. Walls 32.014 (top right) and 015 (bottom right) are interrupted by entrance 32.023/023bis. The southern bench 32.026 (not on plan above) is just visible north of wall 32.004, while the line of the northern bench 32.031 runs parallel to wall 32.006. Two amphora installations are visible against north wall 028: installation 32.020 to the left and 016 to the right. Scale=1 m. Photo by S. E. Sidebotham.

Soil loci BE98/99-23.*048/058* lay atop floor *051* around pedestal stones BE98/99-23.*032e–f.* This soil, 0.08–0.12 m thick, was colored by what may have been some spilled liquid. Ash lens BE98/99-23.*029b* had 17 alternating layers of light-brown sand and ashes within a depth of only 0.06 m. This suggests frequent and rapid use of altar BE98/99.23.*032a* alternating with periods when the ash residue was covered up. Although floor *051* soon fell out of use, the installations built on it continued to function until abandonment of the building. These included the parallel set of one-course-high benches that ran east-west inside the building: BE98/99-23.*021b*/BE99/00-32.*031*, the northern benches, and BE98/99-23.*033*/BE99/00-32.*026*, their southern counterparts. Other features originally built on this earliest floor BE98/99-23.*051* included BE98/99-23.*018*, a locus comprising hard, compact sand that sloped down around an approximately 0.50 m high wooden beam dug into the floor. Stones and coral heads held the beam in place. The beam rested against the southern face of benches BE98/99-23.*021b*. A heap of extremely compact soil rose around the beam during its use that eventually covered these benches. This compact locus contained only a few small pieces of bone, some small pieces of bronze and very little pottery. Part of this locus may have been remnants of spilled liquids. Floor BE98/99-23.*051* lay between the northern and southern benches, the altar and temple pools in the west, and the eastern end of the building.

Subphase IIIb
Second floor, repair of earlier floor in subphase IIIa, late fourth to fifth centuries AD.
BE98/99-23.*041*/BE99/00-32.*028* was a beaten-earth surface that completely covered floor BE98/99-23.*051*. It lay between the northern and southern benches, west up to altar *032a* and the temple pools, and stretched east up to the inside face of the eastern walls (BE99/00-32.*014–015*) and to the entrance (BE99/00-32.*023/023*bis) of the building. No new installations or features were added at this time, suggesting that floor *041* was only a repair to floor *051* and that there was no need for other alterations of the cultic paraphernalia inside the edifice. The installations found on floor *051* continued in use during the floor *041* Subphase IIIb as did the ash lenses around altar *032a* and the soil locus around temple pool *013b* above pedestal stones *032e–f.*

Subphase IIIc
Third floor, late fourth to fifth century AD.
Beaten-earth surface BE98/99-23.*027*/BE99/00-32.*025*

lay atop surface BE98/99-23.*041*/BE99/00-32.*028*. It almost completely covered the northern and southern benches indicating an important phase change in the internal use of the building. At this time another temple pool appeared (BE98/99-23.*013c*) that rested atop pedestal stone BE98/99-23.*032c*. Another pedestal stone (BE98/99-023.*032d*) also appeared on this surface, but had no associated temple pool. This new temple pool and pedestal stones were placed north of Subphase IIIa temple pool BE98/99-23.*013b* and pedestal stones *032e–f.* Behind (west of) columnar altar BE98/99-23.*032a* and behind the pedestal stones and temple pools was a 3.68 m long x 0.07–0.08 m wide x 0.06 m high wooden beam made of teak that was embedded 0.09 m into northern wall BE98/99-23.*005* and 0.09 m into southern wall BE98/99-23.*009*. Teakwood beam *032g* preserved 17 notches (0.08 x 0.015 m) spaced at regular intervals; the notches did not penetrate the entire width of the beam.

Plate 4-50   Trench 32 looking west. The two east-west running lines of stones, 32.*026* left and 32.*022* right link up with 23.*033* and 23.*021b* (see Figure 4-45 and Plate 4-46). The opening of pot 32.*020* is visible between the wall and the line of stones to the right. Scale=1 m. Photograph by S. E. Sidebotham.

Plate 4-51   Detail of pot 32.*020* and face of wall 32.*006*, looking north. Scale=20 cm. Photograph by S. E. Sidebotham.

Clearly, this beam was in a secondary use in this position and may have been part of a dismantled ship (Vermeeren 1999:319; Vermeeren 2000:340–342) or perhaps a large packing crate. In its position in the trench beam 23.*032g* defined and separated the strip along the interior face of west wall BE98/99-23.*007* of the building from the religious paraphernalia to the east. It could not be determined if wooden beam *032g* had been placed during Subphase IIIa or IIIc (Figures 4-45 and 4-48, Plates 4-46 and 4-47). The sand west of beam 23.*032g* (BE98/99-23.*020*) and flush with the northern (BE98/99-23.*005*/BE99/00-32.*006*) and southern (BE98/99-23.*009/010*/BE99/00-32.*004*) interior walls of the building was fine and had some charcoal (BE98/99-23.*039*), but was otherwise devoid of any inclusions, similar to that in the foundation fill of Phase II. In sand locus BE98/99-23.*034*, south of the southern benches, excavations recovered a piece of a bronze protome. Excavations also uncovered, in the sand locus under BE98/99-23.*021b*, some beads (one group of five and another group of 21 (stuck together). This sand stratum was sealed with a more compact sand layer containing inclusions of small coral fragments (BE98/99-23.*020/022/030*/BE99/00-32.*027*).

The northern benches received another course comprising reused and broken blocks including the fragment of a relief (see following and Plate 4-53 and Figure 4-54). Associated with this surface were some wooden bowls. Such bowls have been found in other religious contexts at Berenike in trench BE97/98-16 (Sidebotham 1999b:70–78) and on surface BE96/97/98/99/00-10.*350* (one as *360* and the other as *360*bis; see preceding).

During Subphase IIIc loci around altar BE98/99-23.*032a* and temple pools BE98/99-23.*013c–d* may have seen less-intensive use than in earlier subphases. Ash lens *029a*, near columnar altar *032a*, for example, had only four alternating layers of sand and ash compared to earlier locus *029b* (in Subphase IIIa) that had 17 such alternating layers. Each ash layer in *029a*, however, was somewhat thicker than any found in *029b*. The sand strata perhaps represented periods of noncultic activity at the altar. Locus *029a* associated with temple pools *013b–c* was only 0.03 m thick and situated farther east of the altar and temple pools whereas during Subphases IIIa–b alternating ash/sand loci were found on both sides of the temple pools. The discovery in BE98/99-23.*027* of the remains of at least six wooden bowls (*027a–f*), plus five others in BE99/00-32.*025* (*025a–e*) containing charred remains (perhaps of offerings) may explain the decreased use of the stone installations; perhaps cultic sacrifices in this subphase centered more on the wooden bowls than on the stone installations, which appear to have been more heavily used in the earlier subphases (cf. Sidebotham 1999b: 70–78). These wooden bowls lay spread across surface BE98/99-23.*027*/BE99/00-32.*025* between the northern and southern benches. The bowls were in a very deteriorated state of preservation, and the species of wood from which they were made could not be identified. As in the case of similar bowls found in trench BE97/98-16 (Sidebotham 1999b: 70–78) and on surface BE96/97/98/99/00-10.*350* (*360* and *360*bis), the bowls were also marked with an accompanying circle of white salt that had leached from the wood. It is unclear at this point whether the decreased use of stone temple pools and introduction of wooden bowls signaled a change of cult worshiped in the building or if this had some other significance. Perhaps this apparent change in types of equipment signaled reduced economic circumstances of the cult and its adherents. This would be odd given the relative economic prosperity at Berenike at this time. Perhaps antipagan and pro-Christian legislation promulgated throughout the Roman Empire in this period (cf. *Codex Theodosianus* 16.10.1–16.11.3 in Pharr 1952:472–476) played a role. Much of this legislation economically punished pagan and rewarded Christian places of worship.

Subphase IIIc floor almost completely covered the two benches, BE98/99-023.*021b*/BE99/00-032.*031* on the north and BE98/99-023.*033*/BE99/00-32.*026* on the south. Some traces of the southern benches survived in the eastern end of BE99/00-32. During this subphase, 15 approximately rectangular-shaped ashlar blocks (BE98/99-23.*021a*/BE99/00-32.*022*) were placed atop the northern benches (Figure 4-48 and Plates 4-46, 4-47, 4-50, and 4-51). These ashlars were in a secondary use; one was a stone box (found in BE99/00-32) that measured 0.40 m x 0.28 m x 0.12 m x 0.09 m deep (Plate 4-52).

Plate 4-52
Stone box found reused as part of the northern row of stone seats 32.*022*. Looking north toward wall 32.*006*. Photograph by S. E. Sidebotham.

Plate 4-53   Relief fragment (BE99 1487-tt), made of local gypsum/
anhydrite, reused as part of locus 23.02la. Scale=10 cm.
Photograph by S. E. Sidebotham.

Figure 4-54   Relief fragment (BE99 1487-tt), made of local gypsum/
anhydrite, reused as part of locus 23.021a. Drawing by C.
E. Dijkstra.

The box had a notch at the top suggesting that
it had originally been associated with liquids. The
box contained remains of an unidentifiable residue
comprising brownish-yellow sand and a few seeds
(BE99/00-32.024). An oblong hollow gouge on the
bottom interior of the stone box suggested extensive
use, perhaps the result of scraping out over a long period
of time. The presence of seeds suggested a connection
with plants. Plants and gardens were frequently associated with cult temples in ancient Egypt (Wilkinson
1998:119–144). The original provenance of this stone
box could not be determined, but its shape and contents
indicated that it might have originally been associated
with plants and gardening, perhaps as an offering tank
or planter (cf. Wilkinson 1998:81–82) and perhaps in
connection with a necessarily small garden in the immediate environs of the cult venerated in this building.

Another bench top comprising BE98/99-23.021a/
BE99/00-32.022 was a fragment of the bottom left
corner of a relief made of local gypsum (found in
BE98/99-23.021a, site ID 1487tt, and noted briefly
previously). The anepigraphic stone measured 0.22 m
x 0.14 m x 0.06 m thick (Plate 4-53, Figure 4-54). An
undecorated border that was wider at the bottom than at
the extant left side framed the relief. There were portions
of two figures on the relief. One on the left was the lower
part of a draped figure, of undetermined gender, facing
right. The left leg stepped forward and bore most of
the figure's weight. There is a faint indication that this
figure holds something in his/her right hand. This figure
stands immediately in front of another draped image atop
a base, podium, or elevated dais. This second human
representation is preserved from just above the knees
down and projects his/her left leg forward toward the
figure standing on lower ground. That the relief is carved
from local stone suggests the activity of a local sculpture
school in the city. It could not be determined if this relief
was related to the cult practiced inside the building or
was secondarily used from elsewhere. Both the stone box
and the relief had been placed upside down to provide
seating atop the benches.

Excavations recovered approximately 50 amphora
toes heaped together in the southwestern corner of the
building west of altar 032a, temple pools 013b–c, and
pedestal stones 032d–f. These were deposited during
Subphases IIIc–d. The toes were very worn and made
of a coarse fabric. Similar amphora toes were recovered
in other loci inside the building and in all subphases.
Each toe was broken off immediately above the base
of the body of the amphora. The shallow hollow spot

at the top of some of the toes preserves a black shiny material, which may be the resinous coating found inside many amphorae or the remains of deliberately burned material. The large number of toes lacking any associated vessels suggests that the toes themselves may have been used inside the building. As the structure was probably vaulted, apparently had few if any windows or light wells and preserved only a very narrow door, the interior must have been quite dark, requiring artificial illumination. Perhaps these toes served as torches for lighting. Terracotta oil lamps, including the "frog" type, remains of which were recovered inside the building, would have supplemented illumination provided by the amphora toes.

The presence of installations comprising broken amphorae in the northeastern interior corner of the building combined with fire pit BE99/00-32.021, which lay only about 0.10 m from wall BE99/00-32.015, suggests that charcoal was kept warm here for lighting lamps or torches or for some other use in ceremonies adjacent to the altar farther west. That the walls adjacent to these installations and charcoal lens were not blackened by fire/flame suggests low-intensity flames or embers.

Wooden threshold BE99/00-32.023bis within door 023 lay about midway along the eastern side of the structure (eastern walls BE99/00-32.014–015). The threshold comprised two planks and a pivot hole. By the end of the 2000 season, this had been uncovered, but the species of wood had not been identified.

Subphase IIId
Fourth (latest) floor of building, late fourth to fifth century AD.

The latest floor of the building was in Subphase IIId, loci BE98/99-23.016/BE99/00-32.019. This floor, made with much more care than its three beaten-earth predecessors, signaled a significant rearrangement of the structure's interior. This Subphase IIId floor completely covered the earlier benches and most of the later bench ashlars and covered the entire interior (including west of the various stone installations described in earlier subphases, Figure 4-55 cf. Sidebotham 2000b: 136–142).

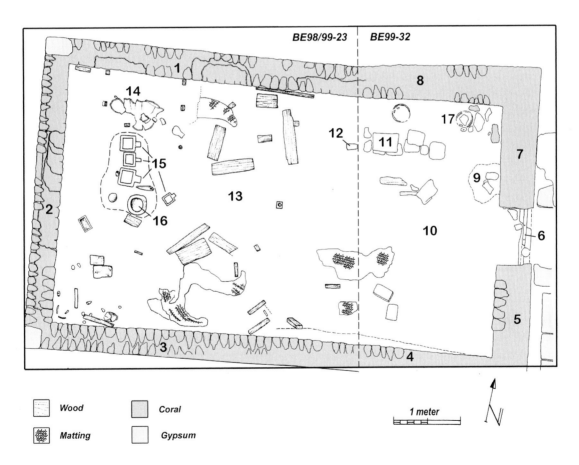

Figure 4-55   Trenches 23 and 32, latest occupational phase. Drawing by A. M. Hense.

1=23.005	5=32.014	9=32.021	13=23.016	17=32.016bis
2=23.007	6=32.023/bis	10=32.019	14=23.014	
3=23.009	7=32.015	11=32.022	15=23.013a-d	
4=32.004	8=32.006	12=23.021a	16=23.032a	

During this phase, two stone temple pools (BE98/99-23.*013d-e*) were added, three amphorae were dug into the floor and a new feature, teakwood installation BE98/99-23.*014* (cf. Sidebotham 2000b: 141 and 143, Plates 2–97), built in the northwestern corner of the building.

Floor BE98/99-23.*016*/BE99/00-32.*019* comprised three construction layers. First, the entire area was leveled and small coral chunks laid down. Atop this was woven grass matting to act as a stabilizer; matting was not a single large unit, but smaller standardized pieces (Plate 4–56, see Chapter 12). These were laid down atop one another with no particular orientation. Five separate pieces of matting were preserved in the eastern part of the building. A third construction layer covered the matting with a thin beaten-earth surface. Directly atop the surface, and not atop the pedestal stones, as was the case with earlier temple pools, were added the last two temple pools (BE98/99-23.*013d–e*). Temple pool *013d* was on the same north-south alignment as temple pools *013a–c*, while temple pool *013e* lay somewhat east of this alignment. All temple pools were in use during Subphase IIId. Also on floor BE98/99-23.*016*/BE99/00-32.*019* were four complete cowrie shells.

In the southwestern corner of the building and along northern wall BE99/00-32.*006*, excavations uncovered three amphorae. These were either dug into the floor or had earth heaped up around them. One of these amphorae (BE98/99-23.*019*bis), in the southwestern corner of the building, rested upside down and had been dug into surfaces BE98/99-23.*020/022*. The bottom was broken and missing, but the neck and handles remained *in situ*. This contained a mud jar stopper (see Chapter 14, catalogue number 21) and two handfuls of charcoal. Its contents dated late fourth to fifth century AD. The main concentration of amphora toes noted previously lay around installation *019*bis. Another amphora was *in situ* (BE99-32.*016*bis) in the northeastern interior corner of the building. It rested right side up, but lacked a rim and handles. A pottery lid topped the amphora. Amphora *016*bis contained a cowrie shell, two amphora toes, and pieces of bone, shell, and charcoal. The third amphora/installation (BE99/00-32.*020*), also still *in situ*, lay immediately west of installation *016*bis (Figure 4-51). Amphora *020* was a poorly preserved oblong pointed jar resting right side up; only the bottom half was preserved. It contained one amphora toe, placed in another amphora bottom, a piece of ostrich eggshell, glass fragments, charcoal, and bits of bone and seashell.

Plate 4-56　Matting and wood next to northern wall 23.*005*/32.*006* (to the right) of the North Shrine. Looking northwest. Scale=50 cm. Photograph by S. E. Sidebotham.

All the amphora installations (BE98/99-23.*019*bis, BE99/00-32.*016*bis, and BE99/00-32.*020*) were secondary, reused as storage facilities, with bases or necks deliberately removed. Installation BE98/99-23.*019*bis was probably associated with stone installations BE98/99-23.*032a–f* and temple pools *013b–c*. The other two amphorae (BE99/00-32.*016*bis and *020*) in the northeastern interior of the building must have been associated with activities near the entrance. At this point, 15 ashlars of various sizes (BE98/99-23.*021a*/BE99/00-32.*022*) that capped the northern bench (BE98/99-23.*021b*/BE99/00-32.*031*) were partly covered and separated installations BE99/00-32.*016*bis and *020* from the rest of the building interior. The feature in the northwestern corner of the building, the amphora and wooden framework BE98/99-23.*014* that covered the amphora, were described in the 1998 excavation report (Sidebotham 2000b: 141). This western interior end of the building preserved a fair quantity of wood, much of it teak.

Installation BE99/00-32.*021*, near building entrance BE99/00-32.*023/023*bis, was still in use at this time. It contained a piece of iron slag. Excavations recovered an additional chunk of iron slag immediately east of (outside) the east wall of the building. There was, however, no evidence that the slag was produced inside the structure.

All subphases used the same cult objects (temple pools *013b–e* and columnar altar and pedestal stones *032a–f*). Each temple pool was square/rectangular in shape with a grooved handle 0.06–0.08 m long. The center of each temple pool was a hollow square decorated with staircases along each of the four sides. These temple pools are reminiscent of the sacred temple pools

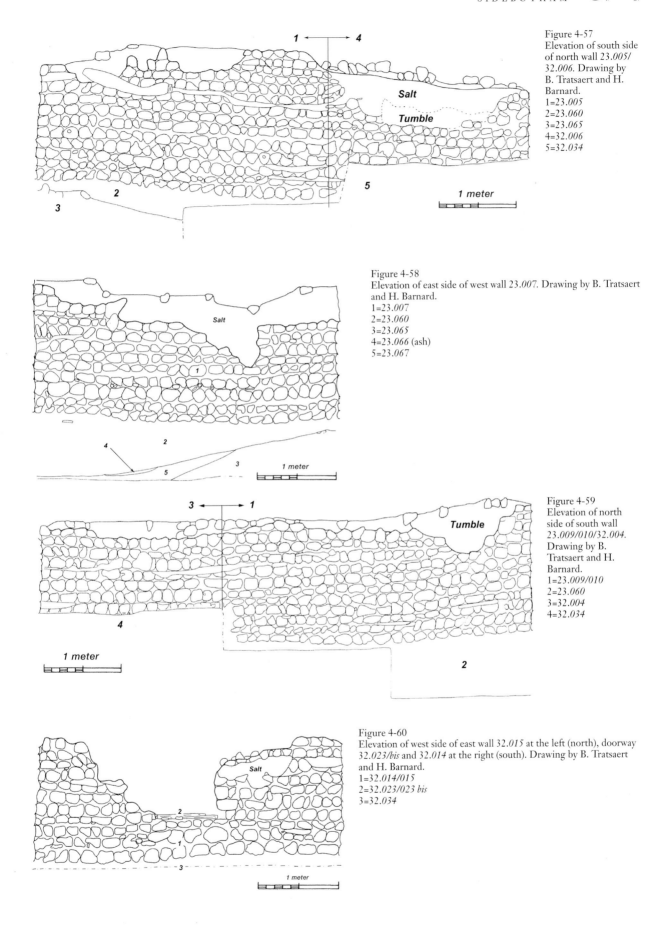

Figure 4-57
Elevation of south side
of north wall 23.*005*/
32.*006*. Drawing by
B. Tratsaert and H.
Barnard.
1=23.*005*
2=23.*060*
3=23.*065*
4=32.*006*
5=32.*034*

Figure 4-58
Elevation of east side of west wall 23.*007*. Drawing by B. Tratsaert
and H. Barnard.
1=23.*007*
2=23.*060*
3=23.*065*
4=23.*066* (ash)
5=23.*067*

Figure 4-59
Elevation of north
side of south wall
23.*009/010*/32.*004*.
Drawing by B.
Tratsaert and H.
Barnard.
1=23.*009/010*
2=23.*060*
3=32.*004*
4=32.*034*

Figure 4-60
Elevation of west side of east wall 32.*015* at the left (north), doorway
32.*023/bis* and 32.*014* at the right (south). Drawing by B. Tratsaert
and H. Barnard.
1=32.*014/015*
2=32.*023/023 bis*
3=32.*034*

of the Pharaonic period (Kuenz 1981). Pools *013b–c* were large, approximately 0.28 m x 0.25 m x 0.15 m, and were placed in a row facing east toward the entrance to the building and were north of altar *032a*. Pool *013d* was the smallest temple pool, measuring 0.15 m x 0.15 m x 0.10 m, and was set somewhat east of the others. Pool *013b* was covered by two sherds; another temple pool contained an *aes* coin of the second half of the fourth century (Sidebotham 2000a: 178, catalogue no. 75, C7365) which was, perhaps, an offering.

Stones *032c–f* were square/rectangular-shaped, measuring 0.30 x 0.22 x 0.10 m, placed beneath the temple pools. Temple pool *013d* rested upon stones *032e–f*, while *013b* had no stone underneath it, though all temple pools were at the same level. Evidence suggests that the different religious apparatus were used with varying degrees of intensity over time. Thicknesses of ash lenses around altar *032a* and temple pools *013b–e* varied during their use. Ash lenses in the earlier periods of use of the temple pools occurred on both sides of the pools while in the later periods of use they occurred only east of the temple pools.

Trench 23/32, Phase IV
Abandonment and decay (inside the building): sometime in the fifth century AD

Prior to abandonment of the building, sometime after Subphase IIId, many of the ritual objects were left behind. There were several possible explanations for this. First, the cult worshiped here was no longer viable, and the associated religious paraphernalia were, therefore, no longer needed and abandoned or the cult moved to a new location where it may have had new cultic equipment.

After abandonment, only slight amounts of windblown sand accumulated before the roof and walls collapsed, shattering the wooden shelter above BE98/99-23.*014* all over the room. There were planks and pieces of wooden beams concentrated along south wall BE98/99-23.*009/010*/BE99/00-32.*004*. That phase was found and excavated during the 1998 season (Sidebotham 2000b: 143–144).

The resulting wall and roof tumble (BE98/99-23.*012* and BE99/00-32.*013*) mixed with windblown sand. In tumble BE99/00-32.*013* there was a large fragment of Proconnesian marble measuring 0.35 x 0.25 x 0.05 m (3775-R, cf. Chapter 5, section 5.3.1, in this volume). It appears to have been floor or wall revetment, but there was little to suggest that it was part of the original

interior decoration of this building. Wall tumble loci BE98/99-23.*012* and BE99/00-32.*013* also contained a large number of iron nails and a small *situla*. There was also an iron rod with a hook broken in four pieces. The overall measurements were 0.40 m long x about 5–6 mm in diameter; the hook was about 25 mm long (See Chapter 9, section 9.3, in this volume). Eventually, very fine textured light- to dark-brown windblown sand (BE98/99–23.*001/002/008* and BE99/00–32.*001–003* and *007–012*) completely covered the building except for the very top portions of the extant northern, western, and southern walls.

Although seashells were found throughout the trench, excavations uncovered two middens of cowrie shells, one of eight shells in the northeastern corner and one in the southeastern corner of 37 shells. Lengths varied between 0.05–0.09 m and they were all pale in color. Each had a small round hole near the narrowest end. These shells were recovered in this tumble and above Subphase IIId floor BE98/99-23.*016*/BE99/00-32.*019*.

The only areas excavated outside the building were north of wall BE98/99-23.*005*/BE99/00-32.*006* and east of walls BE99/00-32.*014–015*; the western and southern walls of the structure lay in their respective balks. These exposed areas were very narrow—about 0.40–0.50 m wide—and did not allow any deep excavation. They were filled with wall tumble and windblown sand.

Loci BE98/99-23.*004*/BE99/00-32.*005* lay north of the building and were, compared to loci inside the structure, rich in pottery finds. Excavations also recovered basalt fragments here. East of entrance BE99/00-32.*023/023bis* excavations recovered granite and basalt fragments and a quarter of a frog-style lamp. BE99/00-32.*017/018* lay outside and east of the building adjacent to walls BE99/00-32.*014* and *015* respectively. They were actually the same loci, but were separated at first by wall tumble and salt locus BE99/00-32.*013*. This lay inside the building and also protruded toward the east outside entrance *023/023*bis. Beneath this was locus BE99/00-32.*032*. Loci *32.013* and *032* were separated from adjacent loci *018* (to the north) and *017* (to the south) by two large gypsum ashlars east of each side of the doorway. There was some wall tumble and later windblown sand on top. BE99/00-32.*017* had a gypsum ashlar aligned with the southern doorway face/northern exterior side wall of BE99/00-32.*014*. South of it lay three ashlars (rectangular and in the balk) aligned, running north-south. The eastern balk at its southern end in locus BE99/00-32.*017* preserved a brown line that may be the remnants of wood or matting laying atop three ashlars.

The ashlars could have collapsed in a line. Or they could have been a feature forming, perhaps, a sunscreen with matting. BE99/00-32.*018*. Northeast of the building was one gypsum ashlar (in the balk as well) aligned with the northern end of door *023/023*bis on the outer face/southern exterior face of wall BE99/00-32.*015*. There was some matting in the tumble atop the stone and more to the north. The grass matting in BE99/00-32.*018* was not the type used in wall construction (personal communication from W. Z. Wendrich). It was folded and lay near the building and under wall tumble. These may have been floor mats or the remnants of awnings.

Pottery dating for both BE98/99-23 and BE99/00-32 was difficult because each subphase inside the building had been cleared in antiquity. Most pottery (aside from the amphorae) came from outside (BE98/99-23.*004*/BE99/00-32.*005* north of the building and BE99/00-32.*017/018*, east of the building). The dates for all phases of the edifice were late fourth to fifth century AD. There were dates available neither for earlier occupation *065* nor for sand locus *060*.

4.4.2 DISCUSSION

The rectangular-shaped, probably barrel-vaulted, building clearly rested atop an earlier area of activity (likely trash dumping; Phase I) that had been covered over and leveled off sometime in the fourth century to allow for its construction (Phase II/Subphases IIa–b). There followed several periods in the late fourth and early fifth centuries of intensive use and remodeling including four surfaces (Subphases IIIa–d). Aside from the benches and wooden bowls, the other religious paraphernalia including a columnar altar and some of the temple pools were used throughout the cult life of the building. Sometime in the fifth century the building was abandoned, and it decayed and collapsed (Phase IV). All the excavated evidence suggests that the edifice formed within walls BE98/99-23.*005*/BE99/00-32.*006*, BE98/99-23.*007*, BE98/99-23.*009/010*/BE99/00-32.*004*, and BE99/00-32.*014/015* and *023/023*bis (Figures 4-57 to 4-60) was used for religious purposes only.

While the cult worshiped here could not be identified with certainty, the enclosed nature of the sanctuary suggests that it was a mystery religion. That of Isis in her many syncretized forms and, less likely, Mithras, are possible candidates (cf. Sidebotham and Wendrich 2001–2002:30–31). The cult was conducted in a relatively small, constricted structure requiring artificial illumination. Other than the narrow entrance on the

east, there was no evidence of other sources of natural lighting inside the edifice though the presence of a light well cannot be ruled out.

4.5   THE CENTRAL QUARTER (LATE ROMAN BERENIKE)

Trenches BE99-27, BE99-28/BE00-38, BE00-34, BE00-37, BE00-41

4.5.1   TRENCH BE99-27
Trench Supervisor: H. Beckman
Figures/Plates 4-61 to 4-70

BE99-27 was a 4 m N-S x 7 m E-W trench with grid coordinates 546–550 N/2071–2078 E. The datum point was 4.82 m asl (Figure 4-61 and Plates 4-62 to 4-65). Trench BE99-27 was directly north of trench BE98-20, which had the same dimensions as BE99-27, effectively creating a balkless 4 m trench extension in a northward direction. BE98-20 preserved a structure at the intersection of two streets: a major east-west thoroughfare (possibly the *decumanus maximus*) and a secondary north-south running street (*kardo*). Excavations here aimed to provide information on the function(s) of the building itself, as well as facilitate a better understanding of its broader context in the municipal organization and urban development of Berenike in late antiquity.

Excavation in BE98-20 exposed a number of architectural features in which the function and structural relationships were not clear, largely due to the limitations of the lateral exposure and, additionally, to the handicap of small ceramic assemblages from occupational loci. A substantial expansion northward, as well as 0.50-m eastern and western balk extensions, were recommended for the 1999 season. Upon return at that time, it was discovered that balk collapse in the eastern portion of BE98-20 had exposed a north-south running eastern wall, which tied wall BE98-20.*019* with BE98-20.*006*. This section of wall appeared to have had a doorway, blocked either intentionally or by collapse, and it was this blockage that had been noted in BE98-20 eastern balk as locus *060*.

This confirmation that wall BE98-20.*019* was not the southernmost wall of a building extending north, but an interior wall of a structure including BE98-20.*006*, *026*, and *033*, suggested that the best way to achieve BE98-20's research goals would be to excavate a northern extension (BE99-27) down to the same phase as was reached in BE98-20 and then excavate the two areas in tandem. This was partially successful, but unfortunately

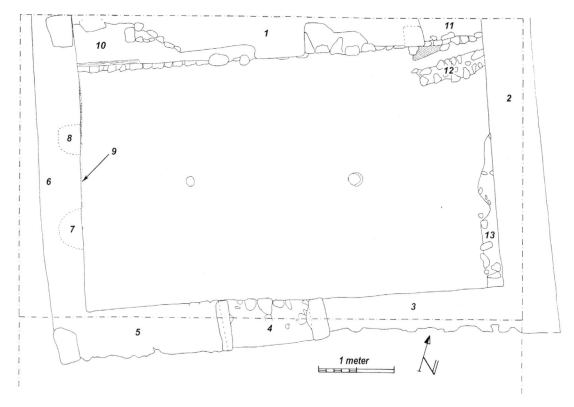

Figure 4-61 Plan of trench BE99-27. Drawing by B. Tratsaert and H. Barnard.

1=*010*	4=*012*bis/*045*	7=*014*bis	10=*028/010*
2=*011/041*	5=*013/045*	8=*014*tris	11=*039/010*
3=*012/045*	6=*014*	9=*027*	12=*041*
			13=*042*

the collapse loci of BE99-27 were substantial and with a shorter field season, excavation of occupational debris had only just begun when the season came to a conclusion. Consequently, phasing in this report is tentative and will change with further excavation and analysis. It should be noted, however, that phasing of BE99-27 seemed to reflect the same patterns of activity suggested by excavations in BE98-20. This assumption will be tested by simultaneous excavation of the two areas in a future season. Loci in BE99-27 could be organized into three phases:

Phase I: Use of early wall/installations *041*, *042*, and *045*. Use of walls *014* and *010* with their associated features *028* and *039*. Deposition of occupational debris surface *038* (corresponded to BE98-20 Phase II): late fourth century AD.

Phase II: Continued use of wall *014* and *010/028/039*. Construction and use of walls *012/013* and *011*. Deposition of occupational debris

surface *035* (corresponded to BE98-20 Phase III) fifth century AD.

Phase III: Abandonment and architectural collapse (corresponded to BE98-20 Phase IV): fifth century AD and later.

Trench 27, Phase I
Use of early walls/installations, occupational surface: late fourth century AD.

Architectural loci *041*, *042* and *045* primarily defined the earliest phase of BE99-27, reached since only one small and localized occupational debris locus of this phase, *036*, was excavated during the 1999 season. Exposed with the removal of later Phase II surface *035*, was locus *045*, a wall that ran east-west along the southern boundary of BE99-27. Measuring 5.5 m long E-W x 0.78 m (three rows) wide N-S, only one coral course (0.12 m maximum extant height) of wall *045* was exposed in 1999. Later Phase II walls *012/013* were constructed atop *045* at approximately the same alignment, thereby creating the feature referred to in BE98-20 excavations as locus *019*. The uppermost preserved course of *045* was visible laterally in an area 1.27 m N-S that also functioned as a Phase II threshold (*012*bis/*045*) between walls *012* and *013*. This exposed area revealed that early wall *045* was preserved at an average depth of 2.61 m asl.

Loci *041* and *042* were walls/installations found respectively in the northeastern and southeastern sections of trench BE99-27. Removal of Phase II fill locus *040* exposed both of these features. Locus *041* measured 1.10 m long E-W x 0.47 m (three rows) wide N-S x 0.15 m (one course) preserved height at an average depth of 2.60 m asl. Locus *041* comprised both coral heads and anhydrite gypsum ashlars. Phase II wall *011* appeared to be constructed atop *041*, although it is difficult to say with certainty. Likewise, *041* may have run underneath wall *010* and associated feature *039* as well; future excavation in this area should provide conclusive evidence.

Plate 4-62
Trench 27 during Phase I, looking southwest. To the south (top left) part of trench BE98-20 is visible behind doorway *012*bis in walls *012*/*045* to the east (left) and *013*/*045* to the west (right). The N-S running wall with the two niches is *014*. Scale=1 m. Photograph by S. E. Sidebotham.

Plate 4-63
Trench 27, niches *014*bis (to the left and *014*tris (to the right). The north wall perpendicular to wall *014* is *028*/*010* (upper right). Looking northwest. Scale=1 m. Photograph by S. E. Sidebotham.

By the end of the 1999 season, *010/028/039* was in Phase I. Locus *042* measured 1.90 m N-S x 0.27 m E-W; it ran under Phase II wall *011*, which obscured from view all but two rows of this feature. Wall *011* had a maximum extant height of 0.10 m (one course) and was preserved at an average depth of 2.61 m asl.

Walls *014* and *010* also seem to have been in use during this phase. Locus *014* was a north-south running west wall preserved at an average depth of 4.03 m asl. It was 3.85 m long x 0.75 m (three rows) wide x 1.75 m (13 courses) high. Wall *014* exhibited "normal" coral course construction of medium-sized coral heads in mud mortar. The northern end of this wall was finished with gypsum/anhydrite ashlars. Wall *014* preserved two niches (*014*bis to the south and *014*tris to the north) spaced 0.70 m apart, set into its interior face at a depth of 3.23 meters asl. These shared the same dimensions and were about 0.30 m high x 0.40 m wide x 0.20 m deep. Upright gypsum blocks formed the sides of these niches, and both appeared to have had wooden interior surfaces (Figure 4-61 and Plates 4-62 and 4-63). A piece of worked bone, possibly a pendant, was recovered from southern-most niche *014*bis when cleaning out wall collapse (*034*, pottery bucket number 73). Wall *014* was plastered (locus *027*) along its lower courses and, consequently, its designation as Phase I architecture was somewhat tentative. Later excavation of Phase I occupational loci may prove to run under *027* and excavation of *027* may reveal that *014*, like *012/013/045* and *011*, was built atop an earlier structure.

Wall *010* was a poorly preserved east-west running wall along the northern balk. It had a maximum extant length of 5.60 m and a minimum length of 2.41 m. It appeared to have been built of coral heads and gypsum/anhydrite ashlars, though it was in such a poor state of preservation that it was difficult to speculate on construction techniques. Wall *010* ranged from 0.15 m (one course) high in the west to 1.5 m (approximately 13 courses) high in the east. Its width varied from 0.36–0.80 m. In this report possible thresholds *028* and *039* will be dealt with as features of wall *010*. As previously mentioned, subsequent excavations may prove that these loci were actually part of an earlier wall, atop which *010* was constructed later during Phase II.

Excavation of Phase II surface *035* exposed occupational debris layer *036*, fill *040*, charcoal lense *037UNEX*, and ceramic installations *043UNEX* and *044UNEX*, all atop *038UNEX*. Stratigraphically, the debris and installation loci were earlier than surface *035* and later than or set into earliest surface *038UNEX*, but unfortunately unrelated to fill *040*, which marked the end of Phase I architecture and the beginning of Phase II. Consequently, this, and the fact that most of these sediments remained unexcavated, made their phasing somewhat subjective, since *038UNEX* seemed to stretch across the entire trench, abutting earlier *041*, *042*, and *045*. Additionally, on the basis of comparison with BE98-20 stratigraphy and phasing, these occupational debris loci were considered as use of Phase I architecture. Thus, they appeared before leveling the east with *040* in order for Phase II construction to take place. Of Phase I loci, only *036*—a fine sand mixed with swirled ash and charcoal—has been excavated. Three separate, circular charcoal impressions, each 0.14 m in diameter, appeared within this locus. Possibly these were caused either from overturning the contents of a vessel or, in light of *043* and *044*, may have been a similar ceramic installation in which the vessel has since decayed. Locus *043* was a 0.20 m diameter broken ceramic vessel with ash and charcoal, which appeared to be set into surface *038UNEX*. Locus *044UNEX* was the same, but 0.14 m in diameter. Both of these loci lay beneath earlier charcoal deposits (*031* and *032* respectively) found on surface *035*. Locus *037UNEX* was a 0.14 m in diameter charcoal deposit, which, with excavation, may also expose a vessel. Trench BE99-28, located about 21.5 m north of BE99-27, had similar loci (*054*, *058*, and *066*, see following) which, in two instances, were also found below charcoal/debris deposits *046* and *047* on a later surface. The function and the nature of these installations were uncertain. It seems that vessels already set into the floor were utilized, and possibly broken, to create these charcoal-debris-related installations. It can be hypothesized that these Phase I occupational debris loci in some way correspond to BE98-20 ash and charcoal lenses *046* and *047*, but there is no conclusive evidence. Locus *036* produced minimal finds and a small assemblage of pottery, but was dated to the late fourth century AD. This is compatible with BE98-20 Phase II, late fourth to fifth century AD dates.

Trench 27, Phase II
Continued use of wall 014, etc. deposition of occupation surface 035: fifth century AD.
Like BE98-20 Phase III, this period of activity in BE99-27 seems particularly marked by a flurry of construction. It began with locus *040*, interpreted as a construction fill, laid in the east over *041* and *042* in order to create a level area on which to build wall

011. Wall *011* ran north-south along the eastern balk of the trench and measured 3.75 m long x maximum extant height of 1.90 m (13 courses) x 0.75 m (three rows) wide. Wall *011*, preserved at an average depth of 4.10 m asl, was of "normal" construction, utilizing medium-large coral heads and mud mortar. This wall had a wooden beam with a square cut, much like those found on ashlars used in doorways, protruding from the northern section of the wall, 10 courses up. It is possible that this wood had some functional connection with threshold *039* of wall *010*.

Walls *012* and *013* (atop *045*), the upper sections of the feature shared with trench BE98-20-*019*, were also constructed during this phase. The unusual construction technique of these walls utilized gypsum/anhydrite ashlars in order to frame or box loose smaller-sized coral cobbles in a mud-mortar matrix. This technique used upright ashlars set at regular intervals to reinforce wall segments composed of rubble. In this case, boxed units forming rectilinear frames of gypsum ashlars enclosed cobble-sized coral-head fill; these alternated with stretches of coursed coral heads. This technique had been noted during the 1998 season as a variant of *opus Africanum* style construction termed *opus Berenikeum* (cf. Adam 1994:120–124; Sidebotham 2000b: 108–109). It has since also come to light in trench BE99-28.*020/030* and, likely, in BE99-26.*012* (see following).

The construction break suspected last season, that plaster BE98-20.*037* found along the exterior face actually ran between the normal coral courses (BE99-27.*045*) and the upper *opus Berenikeum* style components (BE99-27.*012/013*), was verified with the excavation of *035* from the threshold area. Both *012* and *013* ran east-west along the extreme southernmost part of the trench. Wall *012* was in the east and measured 2.70 m long x 1.45 m high x 0.60 m wide. It was preserved at an average elevation of 3.74 m asl. Wall *013* was in the west and measured 1.88 m long x 1.30 m maximum extant height x 0.75 m wide. Entrance *012*bis/*045* separated wall *012/045* from *013/045*. Wall *013/045* was preserved at an elevation of 3.77 m asl. Characteristic of *opus Berenikeum* construction, in both walls were wooden beams, which may have been used to level and strengthen the overall construction.

This phase of activity had several associated occupational debris loci. Removal of the latest tumble locus exposed Phase II occupational surface *035* and four ash/charcoal debris loci atop this surface: *029–032*. Unfortunately, finds and pottery assemblages were minimal. All four of the ash/charcoal deposits were bagged and sent for botanical analysis. Pottery dates may be forthcoming if there is enough material. Locus *035* was a fine swirled sand and occupational debris locus with a thin clayey skin. This locus was interpreted as a surface due to all the flat-lying sherds and ashlars found atop it, but it was probably not an intentionally laid floor; more likely, it became a compacted surface through use. Excavation of *035* pottery bucket number 66 produced one mid–late fourth century AD coin (see Chapter 8, catalogue no. 64, C4586). Otherwise finds were minimal. Pottery from this locus dated fifth century AD and produced one handmade EDW sherd from pottery bucket number 66.

BE99-27 Phase II was fifth century AD on the basis of its one securely dated sediment locus *035*. Consultation with the pottery specialists confirmed that there was no problem in considering this phase to correspond, on the basis of stratigraphy and architecture, with BE98-20 Phase III, which dated late fourth to early fifth century AD. The nature of ceramic analysis was somewhat subjective, and BE98-20 Phase III's shift into the late fourth century AD is an observation based on a change noted in the ratio of LRA1 (late Roman Amphora I) which peaked in the late fourth to fifth century AD, to LRA3 (late Roman Amphora III) which peaked in the fourth century AD. Furthermore, this change was noted specifically in BE98-20.*039*, a construction fill that preceded the use of related phase architecture. The corresponding fill for BE99-27's construction only produced 139 g of poorly dated late Roman pottery. It would stand to reason that construction fills might have a higher percentage of residual earlier material.

Trench 27, Phase III

Abandonment and architectural collapse defined the final phase (III) of BE99-27. Dates for this phase were fifth century AD and later with several loci exhibiting a high (75 percent or more of the sherds) occurrence of residual early Roman material. Again, this is not unusual for tumble loci, which constituted the collapse of architecture that may have been constructed partially of earlier "robbed out" materials. Tumble loci *023*, *024*, and *026* produced some of the best material culture found in BE99-27. Locus *026* was a combination of occupational debris left behind at the time of abandonment of the structure and architectural debris of the earliest decay and collapse.

This locus produced some interesting finds (pottery bucket numbers 55, 57), many of which paralleled

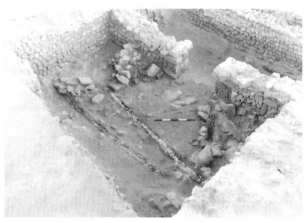

Plate 4-64 Trench 27, Phase III, looking southwest. Note the fallen wooden roof beams. Scale=1 m. Photograph by S. E. Sidebotham.

Plate 4-65 Trench 27, Phase III, looking southeast. Note the fallen wooden roof beams. East-west running wall *012/045* (with entrance *012*bis*/045*) abuts east wall *011/041* (top left of photo). Scale=1 m. Photograph by S. E. Sidebotham.

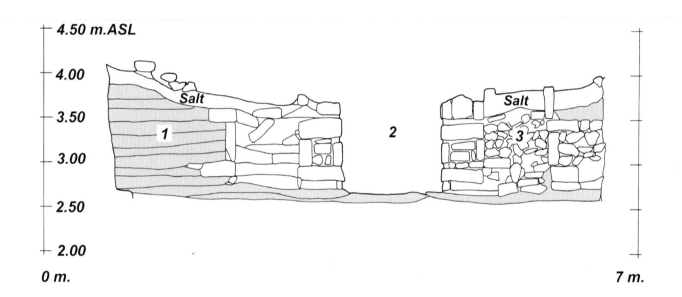

Figure 4-66 Trench BE99-27, south balk. Drawing by H. Beckman and H. Barnard.
1=*012/045*
2=*012*bis*/045*
3=*013/045*

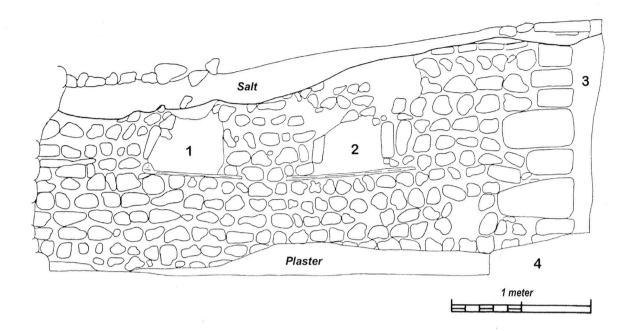

Figure 4-67   Trench BE99-27, north balk. Drawing by H. Beckman and H. Barnard.
    1=*014*bis   3=*019-022*
    2=*014*tris   4=*028*

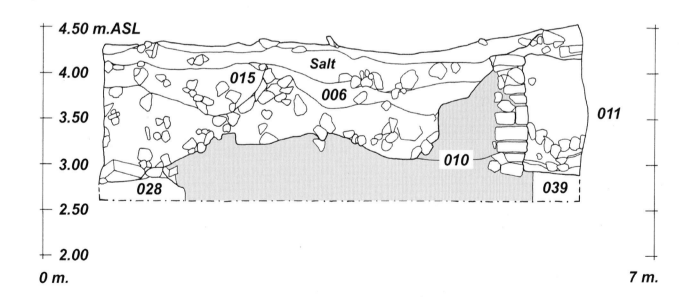

Figure 4-68   Trench BE99-27, west balk. Drawing by H. Beckman and H. Barnard.

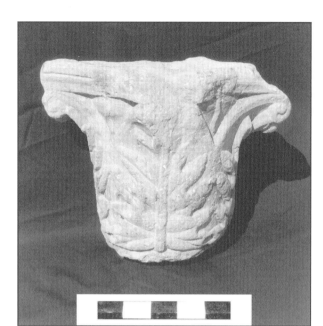

Plate 4-69 Corinthian/composite column capital from locus *023*. Scale=20 cm. Photograph by S. E. Sidebotham.

Figure 4-70 Corinthian/composite column capital from locus *023*. Drawing by A. M. Hense.

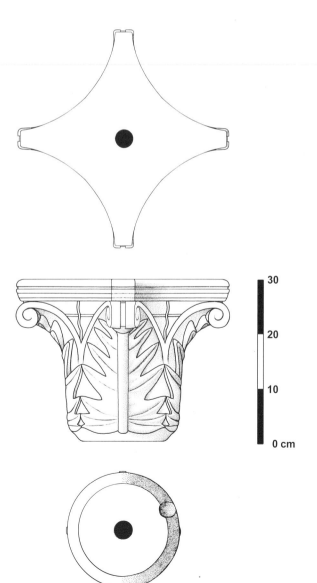

those found in BE99-28/BE00-38 (see following). One octagonal bronze and lead weight of 30 g was recovered (cf. BE99-27.*038* pottery bucket number 74), a small bronze hinge possibly from a box, bronze and iron fish hooks, bronze knife fragments, large iron rings, and a possible iron locking mechanism (see Chapter 9). This locus also produced a considerable array of personal ornaments, beads, and gemstones of jewelry quality. Several bases of glass perfume/essence bottles were also recovered. Two large fallen roof beams (Plates 4-64 and 4-65) and three pieces of Proconnesian marble revetment were found at this level, but it is doubtful with such a small quantity of marble that the building was reveted and more likely this material was robbed from some earlier structure possibly for its aesthetic quality. Tumble *023* also produced a large quantity of material culture, including a large *dolium* and several transport amphorae. A late Roman Corinthian/composite column capital was found (Plate 4-69, Figure 4-70), but it most likely had a secondary use within BE99-27. Locus *023* also produced several different fragments of small bronze balance scales, including a length of chain with a hook still attached; excavations in trench BE99-28.*037* recovered a similar balance (see following and Chapter 9). Locus *018* produced an Aksumite sherd (Chapter 6, catalogue number 3).

Discussion
It is interesting to note that trenches BE98-20/BE99-27 and BE99-28/BE00-38 shared more than just a similarity of small finds and stratigraphy. It appears that the architecture itself is actually a reverse or mirror image, each with an entrance or exit onto an adjacent street, a *kardo* in the case of BE99-28/BE00-38 and a *decumanus* in the case of BE98-20/BE99-27. Each also has an *opus Berenikeum* interior wall as its axis. The approximately 21.5 m space that separated the two trenches may have been some sort of courtyard, thus designating half of an entire *insula* (city

block) for a specific function that required cooperation between several "offices" (Figure 4-71). This seems to be supported by the small and possibly more easily controlled thresholds to the street (i.e., public access) and the seemingly large and open interior thresholds. Excavations recovered several locking mechanisms (locus *024*, pottery bucket number 51 and *026*, pottery bucket number 57; cf. Hense 2000:201) and many ashlar blocks that had been worked possibly for locking or threshold purposes in the northwestern quadrant of the trench near threshold *028*. The locking mechanisms and narrow entrance suggest that security was a paramount consideration.

The purpose of the structure brought to light in trenches BE98-20/BE99-27 has not been securely identified. Several factors suggest, however, that it served a commercial function. These include its location on a major east-west street between the Serapis temple and the easternmost region of the city. The find of small bronze scales and weights and a single small entrance, possibly one that could be locked, implying restricted access, suggest that small valuable objects were stored, traded, or otherwise handled inside this edifice.

Its proximity and similarity of construction to the structure in trenches BE99-28/BE00-38, taken together with the restricted access into the structure found in BE99-28/BE00-38 and discovery of small bronze scale, suggest that whatever activity took place in BE98-20/BE99-27 also occurred in BE99-28/BE00-38.

4.5.2   Trenches BE99-28 / BE00-38
         Trench Supervisor: A.E. Haeckl
         Figures/Plates 4-71 to 4-82

Trench BE99-28 measured 9.00 m N-S X 4.00 m E-W with grid coordinates 569–578 N/2066.5–2070.5 E (Figures 4-71 to 4-73, Plates 4-74 and 4-75). The trench investigated a late Roman building that lay between the Serapis temple and the eastern edge of Berenike, approximately two to three "city blocks" west of the late Roman shoreline. The exposed walls, all built of coral heads that were characteristic of fourth- to fifth-century AD construction at Berenike, indicated that the BE99-28/BE00-38 building measured 9.00 m N-S x ca. 8.00 m E-W. Comparable to the building excavated in the same area (trenches BE98-20 and BE99-27), it occupied the corner of two streets. Figure 4-71 shows the relation of the streets and the two buildings, that may have belonged to the same commercial complex.

Although separated by a seemingly empty area that measured about 21.50 m N-S, the two buildings were essentially mirror images of each other.

The principal western façade of the building and its single western-facing entrance lay along the *kardo*. A sizeable mound of trash, apparently of late antique date, lay northeast of the trench. The building in trenches 20/27 also stood at a street corner; its western side had the same *kardo* frontage as the BE99-28/BE00-38 building, while its southern facade opened onto a large thoroughfare, leading to the shore, which may have been the *decumanus maximus*. In fact, when viewed together as pendant structures flanking a shared open area, the buildings may have been a single architectural complex that occupied one-half of an entire *insula* in late Roman Berenike. Given its location on prime urban real estate in direct street communication with the harbor, this "complex" may have been a late Roman commercial establishment, one perhaps composed of two office suites, warehouses, or workshops functionally connected by a common courtyard. Testing this hypothesis was a primary goal of excavation in trenches BE99-27 and 28/BE00-38 (Figure 4-71).

Trench BE99-28 was laid out just within the *kardo* façade of the building and oriented to uncover its northern, southern, and western exterior walls. Most of the 1999 season entailed excavation of abandonment-phase windblown sand and architectural tumble. The tumble layers were unexpectedly heavy and thick, indicating that the BE99-28/BE00-38 building was originally at least two stories high (see following). Occupational levels were not encountered until the end of the season, and only the latest of three exposed floors was actually excavated in 1999. Pending further excavation, therefore, the stratigraphy of trench BE99-28 comprised only two major phases each with three subphases:

Phase I: Occupation: fifth century AD
    Subphase Ia: Occupational sequence
    Subphase Ib: Occupational sequence
    Subphase Ic: Occupational sequence
Phase II: Post-occupation abandonment and architectural decay: fifth century AD and later
    Subphase IIa: Abandonment
    Subphase IIb: Decay
    Subphase IIc: Decay

Trench 28, Phase I
Occupation: fifth century AD.

The architectural plan of the latest phase of the western, *kardo*-facing half of building BE99-28/BE00-38 emerged clearly during its first season of excavation. All walls and architectural features uncovered in 1999 were in use during the final occupation phase of the building. Since excavation did not reach the foundation levels of these features, it is unclear whether the major interior and exterior walls of the building belong to a single phase of initial construction. All that is known is that the excavated architecture of building BE99-28/ BE00-38 functioned in tandem with its latest subphases of flooring.

The northern, southern, and western exterior walls of the building were exposed along the respective lengths of the northern, southern, and western balks of trench BE99-28. Western wall *019* defined the principal *kardo* façade of the building. Northern wall *022* lined the small *decumanus* harbor street. Southern wall *004* demarcated the northern side of the possible courtyard between buildings BE99-28/BE00-38 and BE98-20/BE99-27. The only excavated entrance to the building lay in its southwestern corner. Here a 1.20 m wide doorway, defined by gypsum ashlar door-jambs bonded into wall faces *004* and *019* and three subphases of threshold installations, led from the *kardo* down steps into the building (Plate 4-76). The exterior walls of the building were all constructed of coral heads laid in regular courses. The full 0.60 m width of only one external wall, southern wall *004*, was exposed. The walls of building BE99-28 were preserved to a considerable height. At the end of the 1999 season, 11 courses of wall *019* had been uncovered, to a height of 1.50 m; 12 courses of northern wall *022*, to a height of 1.78 m and ten courses of southern wall *004*, to a height of 1.42 m.

Building BE99-28 measured 8.00 m N-S in interior dimensions. An internal cross wall 0.60 m wide subdivided the space into two rooms of roughly equal size (3.80 m N-S for the southern room and 3.60 m. N-S for the northern room). The two rooms communicated through a 1.00 m wide interior doorway. Fully exposed cross wall *020* (Plates 4-77 and 4-78) formed its western side; cross wall *030* defined its eastern side and continued into the eastern balk of the trench. Although no formal threshold appeared in the internal doorway in the 1999 season, unexcavated subphases of late flooring still concealed a primary installation found the following season (see following). Wall *020*

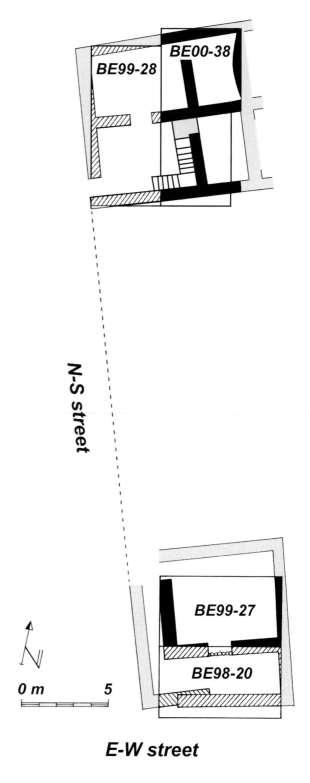

Figure 4-71 The relation between trenches BE98-20/BE99-27 and BE99-28/BE00-38, along a N-S oriented street (*kardo*), that opens onto a major E-W street (perhaps the *decumanus maximus* of Berenike). Drawing by H. Beckman and H. Barnard.

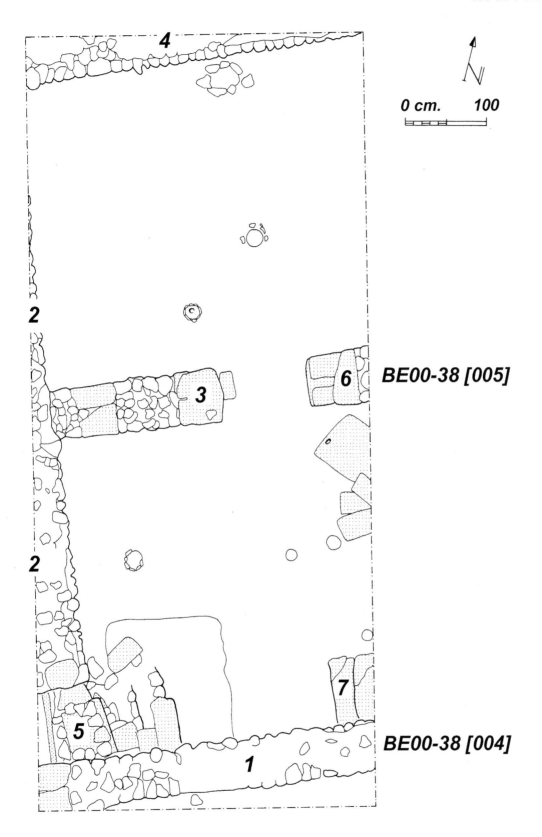

0 cm.   100

BE00-38 [005]

BE00-38 [004]

Figure 4-72   Plan of trench BE99-28. Drawing by J. E. M. F. Bos
1=28.004   3=28.020   5=28.026/049/048   7=28.043
2=28.019   4=28.022   6=28.030

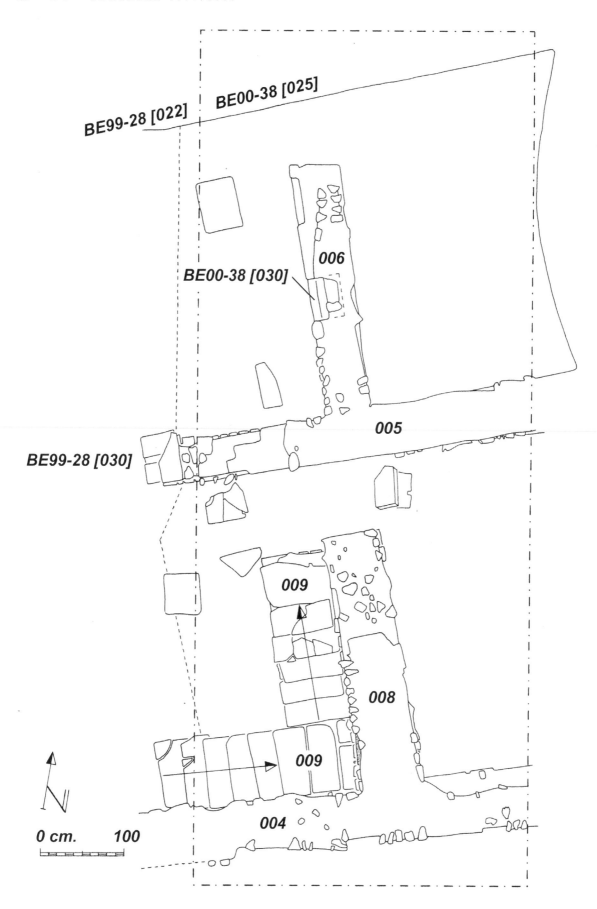

Figure 4-73   Plan of trench BE00-38. Drawing by H. Barnard.

Plate 4-74
Trenches BE99-28 and BE00-38 looking east. The E-W running wall in the north balk (left on photo) is 28.*022*/38.*025*. The N-S running wall (with niche 38.*030*) is 38.*006*. This wall intersects the E-W wall in the middle of the photo (38.*005*/28.*030*). The wall at the bottom center of the photo is 28.*020*. Wall 28.*004*/38.*004* runs in the south balk (right of photo), with wall 38.*008* perpendicular to it. The staircase (28.*043*/38.*009*) abuts both walls. Scale=1 m. Photograph by S. E. Sidebotham.

Plate 4-75
Trenches BE99-28 and BE00-38 looking southeast. Walls 28.*030* and 28.*020* on both sides of the door opening in the center of the photo are *opus Berenikeum*. The photo also gives a clear view of coral-head wall 28.*004*/38.*004* in the south balk (top right of photo). Scale=1 m. Photograph by S. E. Sidebotham.

was excavated to a height of 1.57 m (11 courses) in 1999, and *030* to a height of 1.00 m (nine courses). It is unclear whether interior cross wall *020* was built against or bonded into the interior face of *019*, the western exterior wall of the building.

Any eastern interior wall(s) of the two rooms inside building BE99-28 lay beyond the eastern balk of the trench (on which, see following). There was an especially heavy concentration of architectural tumble in the southern half of the eastern balk, suggesting that a major north-south cross wall may have lain in close proximity; this wall was uncovered during the following season (see following). There was, however, another explanation for this localized agglomeration, which included gypsum ashlar blocks as well as coral heads. Two 0.20 m high steps of a gypsum ashlar staircase came to light in the southeastern corner of the trench, directly across from the southwestern entrance to the building. Staircase *043* (Plate 4-79) was built against the interior face of southern wall *004* and ascended into the eastern balk. Staircase *043* was 0.80 m wide and aligned with three-1.25 m wide entryway steps (*026/048/049*) that led down into the building from its southwestern entrance off the *kardo*. Excavations in 2000 determined that the heavy coral and ashlar tumble in the eastern side of the southern room of building BE99-28 derived from staircase BE99-28.*043*/BE00-38.*009* and from an eastern wall of the room (see following).

Plate 4-76 Entrance of building with threshold 28.*026/049/048* at the southwestern corner of the trench (intersection of walls 28.*004* and 28.*019*). Looking southwest. Scale=20 cm. Photograph by S. E. Sidebotham.

Plate 4-77 *Opus Berenikeum* construction style (south face of wall 28.*020*). Note the remains of grass floor mats lying on floor 28.*038*. Looking north. Scale=50 cm. Photograph by S. E. Sidebotham.

Building BE99-28/BE00-38 combined a uniformity in the dimensions of its architectural features with an attention to the design of its interior appointments that suggested a single phase of construction. Interior and exterior walls had a consistent width of 0.60 m; the exterior entrance was only approximately 0.20 m wider than the internal doorway, and the north-south lengths of both northern and southern rooms were essentially identical. Although interior staircase *043* was 0.45 m narrower than the building's entryway steps, the two staircases in the southern room were aligned with each other.

There were different masonry styles between some interior and exterior walls of building BE99-28/BE00-38. While exterior walls BE99-28.*004*, BE99-28.*019*, and BE99-28.*022*/BE00-38.*025* and interior walls BE00-38.*006*, BE00-38.*005*, and BE00-38.*008* were built of coral heads laid in courses, interior cross wall *020* (and *030*) displayed a distinctive local construction technique designated *opus Berenikeum* (described previously in trench BE99-27; cf. Adam 1994:120–122; Plates 4-77 and 4-78). The *020 opus Berenikeum* wall had a coat of render, indicating that its attractive masonry pattern was functional rather than decorative, never intended to be seen once construction of the wall had been finished.

Other examples of *opus Berenikeum* masonry have appeared at Berenike and, significantly, one of these may form part of the same complex as building BE99-28/BE00-38.

Opus Berenikeum wall BE98-20.*019*/BE99-27.*012/013/045* in trench BE98-20/BE99-27 seemed to mirror the BE99-28/BE00-38 structure across an open courtyard. Like BE99-28.*020*, *opus Berenikeum* wall BE98-20.*019*/BE99-27.*012/013/045* was an interior wall fitted with a doorway. The two *opus Berenikeum* walls also revealed evidence of standardized workmanship: segments of coursed coral heads consistently measured about 0.85 m long; the ashlar boxed units, about 0.50 m square.

There were three subphases in a single major phase (Phase I) of occupation in building BE99-28. Each subphase comprised a floor or surface of compacted sandy clay and a new, progressively raised threshold/step installation in the southwestern entrance to the building (Plate 4-76). In Subphases Ib and Ic, whose strata were excavated or fully exposed across the building, a series of small cobble and pottery installations also dotted the interiors of both rooms. Subphase Ib and Ic floors seem to have maintained an unchanging functional relationship to the major architectural features of building BE99-28: the *004*, *019*, and *022* exterior walls, the southwestern entryway, the *020/030* cross walls and internal doorway, and the *043* staircase. There was insufficient exposure to say the same about emerging Subphase Ia strata.

Plate 4-78 *Opus Berenikeum* construction style (north face of wall 28.*020*). Looking south. Scale=50 cm. Photograph by S. E. Sidebotham.

Sub-phase Ia
Occupational sequence.

Evidence for Subphase Ia was restricted to the southwestern corner of the southern room of the building in BE99-28. Here, in an area that measured approximately 1.50 m square, a patch of clayey surface and two 0.10 m high cobblestone steps leading up from the interior of the room to the southwestern entrance of the building began to emerge at the very end of the 1999 season. Surface *065* was compacted against *049* steps, and together they represented the earliest occupational subphase encountered in the 1999 season. Until the overlying Subphase Ib *050* floor and *026* threshold/step installation are excavated, it is impossible to determine whether *065* was a localized surface or fill deposit connected with construction of the *049* entryway steps or a floor that extended across the south room to staircase *043*.

Sub-phase Ib
Occupational sequence.

Although no strata that defined Subphase Ib have actually been excavated, their complete exposure and articulation allow some observations about the use of building BE99-28/BE00-38 in this period. Locus *050* was a substantial floor composed of compacted sandy clay and render laid upon Subphase Ia *065* surface. It extended without interruption through the doorway between the northern and southern rooms of the building to pave its entire excavated interior. Floor *050* ran up to the lowest exposed step of ashlar staircase *043* in the southeastern corner of the trench.

In the *kardo* entrance to the building, a new Subphase Ib threshold/step installation was constructed in conjunction with floor *050*. Entryway *026* combined a wooden doorstop and two stone threshold pavers with two or three bonded gypsum ashlar steps (0.15 m high) down into the building. Only one block of entry staircase *026* remained securely in situ, stabilized against the interior face of south wall *004* (Plate 4-76). Other blocks that once formed part of the 1.00-m wide staircase were partially dislodged or had shifted out of position. Locus *026* steps were founded directly upon their worn and damaged Subphase Ia *049* cobble predecessors.

The *026* ashlar refit of entryway stairs suggested that foot traffic into the building must have been fairly heavy over time. The necessity of funneling all access to the *kardo* through a single, relatively narrow, doorway undoubtedly increased wear and tear on its threshold installations. Indeed, it seems legitimate to ask why there was only one small and off-axis entrance in the *kardo* façade of the building. Although situated on a major north-south street, the building did not exploit its communication with the *kardo*. Instead, its only streetside doorway was tucked inconspicuously into a corner. In commercial warehouses, like the *horrea* of Ostia, such restricted access was often interpreted as a security measure (Meiggs 1973:163). If this did, indeed, reflect evidence of security consciousness, a desire to control and monitor access in the design of building BE99-28/BE00-38, then the theory that important trade and business dealings took place there gains plausibility.

Plate 4-79 Detail of westernmost part of staircase 28.*043* against interior face of southern wall 28.*004*. The black remains to the left are fires 28.*052–063*. Looking southeast. Scale=50 cm. Photograph by S. E. Sidebotham.

The new *026* entryway installation is not the only evidence of heavy Subphase Ib use of building BE99-28/BE00-38. An array of small fires and installations upon floor *050* also attests intensive activity. One cluster of 12 small circular (about 0.13 to 0.28 m in diameter) fires (loci *052–063*) defined the surface of *050* in the southern room (Plate 4-79). These fires concentrated in a 1.60 m N-S x 1.80 m area in the center of the eastern side of the room, between ashlar staircase *043* and the doorway into the northern room. A black smear of charcoal ash about 1.20 m in diameter outlined the densest cluster of nine fires (*054–059; 061–063*). Only two of these fires, *054* (0.15 m in diameter) and *058* (0.20 m in diameter), were excavated in the 1999 season. Each had been kindled in the base of a broken pottery vessel embedded in floor *050*. The ten other fires in the southern room may also overlay ceramic containers, but this can only be determined by future excavation.

Two non–fire-related installations in the southern room of building BE99-28/BE00-38 also belonged to Subphase Ib. Installation *051* was aligned with the cluster of fires, but located in the western side of the room. Locus *051* was a circular hole (approximately 0.30 m in exterior diameter x 0.20 m interior diameter x 0.13 m deep) cut into floor *050* and lined with cobbles. Based on parallels from trenches BE96/97/98/99/00-10, BE96/97/98-12, and BE97/98-18, installation *051* probably served as a pot stand. Locus *064* was the broken base (0.13 m in diameter) of a late Roman Nile-silt amphora embedded in floor *050* next to staircase *043*. Noting its position next to a staircase, the function of amphora *064* may have been as a *zir* (water jar).

Three Subphase Ib installations (*066, 067,* and *068*) were preserved on floor *050*, all oriented in a north-south line down the center of the northern room. The only one excavated in the 1999 season was *066*. Like its *054* and *058* counterparts in the southern room, installation *066* was a fire kindled in the base of a broken ceramic vessel. The *066* base, like the southern room's *064* "*zir*," belonged to a late Roman Nile silt amphora. The *067* cobble-rimmed fire lay about 0.80 m north of *066*. The cobble border of this feature was approximately 0.50 m in diameter; the *067* fire itself was about 0.20 m in diameter. Installation *068*, located near *022* northern wall of the room, resembled *051* in the southern room. Like *051*, *068* was an empty ring of cobblestones (0.50 in exterior diameter x about 0.20 m in interior diameter) that could have functioned as a pot stand. Possible pot stand *051*, however, was dug into floor *050*, while cobble circle *068* was freestanding upon it.

Floor *050* surfaced both the northern and southern rooms of the western side of building BE99-28/BE00-38; the same types of installations, broken amphorae reused as fireboxes and cobble pot stands, appeared in both rooms. The distribution of these installations (three in the northern room versus 14 in the southern), however, suggested that the latter received heavier use during Subphase Ib. The many fires kindled in front of the doorway to the northern room must have interfered, at least occasionally, with the flow of traffic between the rooms. At this point we can say nothing definitive about the purpose of this array of Subphase Ib installations in building BE99-28/BE00-38. Similar installations were encountered in stratigraphically equivalent layers of neighboring building BE98-20/BE99-27 (see preceding), bolstering the theory that the two structures formed functionally related areas.

Subphase Ic

Subphase Ic was the latest occupation in building BE99-28/BE00-38 and the only one completely excavated in the 1999 season. Subphase Ic comprised a 0.10 m thick floor (*038*) composed of compacted sandy clay and render. Floor *038* extended across the entire excavated interior of the building and obliterated the underlying Subphase Ib installations. Floor *038* also resurfaced, in ramplike fashion, the battered Subphase Ib *026* entryway stairs; it filled in gaps where *026* blocks had presumably been removed and was packed up against those that remained *in situ*. At the same time, a third subphase of threshold installation, the *048* cobblestones, was set directly upon the preexisting *026* ashlar pavers to raise the level of the *kardo* entrance to the building.

The necessity for frequent remodeling of thresholds to keep pace with a rapid rise in street level is attested archaeologically in the Eastern Desert in the Roman period at the quarry site of Mons Claudianus (cf. Bingen 1996:33 and n. 5). It is interesting to note that while the entryway stairs into building BE99-28/BE00-38 were renovated every time a new Phase I floor was laid, interior staircase *043* apparently required no similar attention. Although staircase *043* seems to have been in use throughout Phase I, there is no evidence that it was ever repaired or rebuilt. This suggests that traffic between stories of the BE99-28/BE00-38 building was considerably lighter than that from the *kardo* into its ground floor.

In the southern room of building BE99-28/BE00-38, two flat-lying woven grass mats positioned in the northwestern corner of the room defined the surface of floor *038* (Plate 4-77). The smaller mat lay next to west wall *019* and measured 1.17 m long x 0.53 m wide; the larger one lay alongside cross wall *020* and measured 1.24 m long x 0.75 m wide. The panels were so well preserved that they could be identified as a type of floor mat still manufactured today in Middle Egypt (personal communication from W. Z. Wendrich). It is, therefore, possible, that the grass mats on floor *038* were intentionally placed there. They could have represented comfortable workstations, where one had walls to lean against and would not disturb traffic patterns between the doors and staircases in the southern room.

Aside from the grass mats, the Subphase Ic *038* floor preserved little evidence of occupational use, especially in comparison to the numerous installations atop the Subphase Ib floor *050*. In several spots, special "pothole" patches were applied to floor *038* to cover Subphase Ib installations. In the southern room, sealing patch *046* overlay both floor *038* and the earlier Subphase Ib *058* ceramic firebox. The same was true in the northern room, where patch *047* added extra coverage to floor *038* and the underlying Subphase Ib *066* feature. Otherwise, Subphase Ic occupation comprised only two small fires in the northeastern quadrant of the northern room, where fires *039* (about 0.25 m in diameter) and *040* (approximately 0.30 m in diameter) overlay floor *038*.

Floor *038* produced a considerable quantity of solidly fifth-century AD pottery (including one dipinto) and five badly worn coins, one of the fourth century AD (see Chapter 8, catalogue numbers 70–74). Metal objects (iron, copper alloy, and lead) were the most abundant small finds, the most significant being an octagonal bronze or lead weight of 28 g (25 scruples). (See Chapter 9, subsection 9.4.) Trench BE99-27 produced a weight of exactly the same size and heft, suggesting that small expensive objects like jewelry and gemstones may routinely have been weighed in both BE99-28/BE00-38 and BE98-20/BE99-27 buildings. Overlying Phase II abandonment-phase strata shared the fifth-century AD date of the Subphase Ic *038* floor. In view of this uniform fifth-century AD stratigraphic history, all three subphases of Phase I occupation in the western portion of building BE99-28/BE00-38 can be provisionally ascribed to the fifth century AD, pending further excavation.

Trench 28, Phase II
Post-occupational abandonment and architectural decay: fifth century AD and later.

There was stratigraphic documentation for three distinct episodes in the Phase II desuetude of building BE99-28. Following abandonment were windblown sand and architectural debris layers that contained high percentages of occupation-related artifacts dating to the fifth century AD. Weathering and neglect gradually took its toll, producing strata of heavy architectural tumble as the upper story (ies) of the building collapsed. These windblown sand and heavy tumble layers yielded decreasing quantities of pottery and occupational material. Semisterile deposits of stratified sand with a few tiny windborne flecks of pottery characterized the final phase of abandonment.

Subphase IIa
Loose windblown sand layer *034=042* marked the initial abandonment of building BE99-28. This deposit was localized in the southern room of the building, where it swirled through the southwestern entrance and covered the unswept threshold, stairs, and *038* floor. Along with a considerable amount of fifth-century AD pottery, windblown sand layer *034=042* contained the fragment of another possible metal weight. A substantial layer of compact architectural and occupational debris, *036=037*, subsequently accumulated over *034* and throughout the north room as well.

Ironically, the *036=037* stratum of abandonment-related debris proved, in terms of artifacts, to be the richest layer excavated in trench BE99-28. It produced substantial quantities of pottery; 22 round-cut sherds; two whole lamps (one a frog lamp); 10 coins (seven of which survived cleaning; see Chapter 8, catalogue numbers 75–81); worked bone and stone; and a varied group of high-quality metal objects, including an iron ring and knife blade, a copper-alloy fibula fragment, a *situla* handle, a bell, and the balance of a small scale (see Chapter 9). A similar scale fragment came to light in a contemporary tumble layer in trench BE99-27.*023* (see preceding). The fifth-century AD pottery included a shattered, but potentially reconstructable, Aqaba amphora. One sherd of this amphora bore a scrawled dipinto that may read *oinos* (wine). Stratum *036=037* also yielded two joining fragments of a pink-slipped terra-cotta figurine, a saddled camel detailed in black paint. The figurine is a late Roman type manufactured in Aswan, a less-well-preserved example of which was recovered from fourth- to fifth-century AD trash in trench BE94-1 (cf. Hayes 1995:36).

The other strata that can be assigned to Subphase IIa were, from earliest to latest, *032=033*, *035*, and *031*, *028*, *027*, *029*, and *025*. Locus *028* produced a copper-alloy key and decorative box mounting (see Chapter 9). Layer *025*, which extended across the entire building, defined the stratigraphic boundary between Subphase IIa architectural and occupational debris layers and Subphase IIb windblown sand and heavy tumble strata. While *025* still produced a considerable quantity of fifth-century AD pottery, it also displayed a zone of aligned tumble arrayed around the doorway between the northern and southern rooms of the building. Embedded in *025* were three quadrilateral clusters of gypsum ashlars, each measuring about 0.50 m square. This patterned collapse undoubtedly represents "boxed units" that fell, as coherent chunks of masonry, from the adjacent *020* *opus Berenikeum* wall.

Sub-phase IIb

The pace of structural deterioration in building BE99-28 accelerated during abandonment in Subphase IIb (phase of decay). Whereas only interior cross walls crumbled in the first stage of architectural decay in building BE99-28, the superstructure of its exterior walls began to collapse in Subphase IIb. Sloping heaps of coral-head masonry gradually accumulated along southern wall *004*, western wall *019*, and northern wall *022* of the building, creating the heavy *021=024*, *018*, *012=013*, and *010* architectural tumble layers. Loose deposits of windblown sand and waterborne washdown, *023*, *017*, and *011*, accumulated across the trench in the intervals between episodes of catastrophic wall collapse. In contrast to Subphase IIa architectural and occupational debris layers, which contained a high proportion of clay and render, the soil matrix of Subphase IIb tumble strata was mostly composed of windblown sand. Although the quantity of pottery in Subphase IIb layers declined noticeably from that in Subphase IIa strata, it remained fifth century AD in date.

Subphase IIc

Approximately 1m of stratified windblown sand accumulated in trench BE99-28 during the final subphase in its stratigraphic history. Excavations recovered few artifacts from windblown sand layers *016*, *015*, *014*, *009*, *008*, *007*, *005*, and *006*, *002=003*, and *001*; the pottery was not datable.

Discussion

At the end of the 1999 season of excavation in trench BE99-28, the theory that the BE99-28 and BE98-20/ BE99-27 buildings formed part of a single commercial complex remained viable. The two buildings exhibited significant similarities in location, orientation, plan, and construction technique. Each occupied a street corner at opposite ends of a shared city block; each had only one known entrance, BE98-20/BE99-27 onto the *decumanus maximus* and BE99-28 onto an adjacent *kardo*. The two buildings effectively bracketed or framed a central open area that could have served as a common courtyard, physically separating but functionally connecting the mirror-reverse structures to each side (Figure 4-71). Both buildings contained interior walls and doorways of *opus Berenikeum* style masonry, the only securely identified examples of this distinctive coral-head and ashlar construction technique thus far encountered on site (cf. following, however, trench BE99-26).

A busy period of fifth-century AD use that created several subphases of flooring marked the final phase of occupation in both buildings. In both cases, the predominant pottery types recovered from fifth-century AD floors and occupational debris layers were late Roman Nile silt and imported amphorae. An unusually high quantity of elite small finds also came to light in these strata, including light weights made of metal and delicate scale fragments that imply the processing of small but costly commodities like jewelry and gemstones (which were, indeed, found in building BE99-27) and, possibly, precious metals. When coupled with evidence for security consciousness in the design of this possible complex, such as restricted access from adjacent streets, door-locking mechanisms (from BE99-27), the types of artifacts found therein—small luxury goods and the storage vessels, weights, and measures for handling them—these certainly seem appropriate to some late Roman trading concern: a shipping office or import/export business, for example.

More excavation will be devoted to this putative commercial complex in the future. During the 2000 season architectural exposure took precedence over stratigraphy. Instead of continuing to excavate earlier phases of occupation in trench BE99-28, a new trench (BE00-38) was opened immediately to its east in order to clarify the overall plan of the building. Once accomplished, excavation of occupational strata can then proceed simultaneously in both trenches.

Trench BE00-38, introduction

In order to expand the area of excavation in a substantial fifth-century AD building first investigated in 1999, trench BE00-38 was opened immediately east of and abutting trench BE99-28. Trench BE00-38 measured 9.00 m N-S x 4.00 m E-W (Figures 4-71 and 4-73,

Plates 4-74 and 4-75). As there was no balk between the two trenches, the total combined excavated area of BE99-28 and BE00-38 was 9 m N-S x 8 m E-W. Trench BE99-28 had grid coordinates of 569–578 N/2066.5-2070.5 E while those of trench BE00-38 were 569–578 N/2070.5-2074.5 E. Several days before the end of the 2000 season, trench BE00-38 was expanded 1 m to the north, to regularize the effects of a major balk collapse that exposed two new walls in the northeast quadrant of the trench. By the end of the season, therefore, trench BE00-38 measured 10 m N-S and occupied grid coordinates 569–579 N. Only the original 9 m N-S area of the trench, however, was actually excavated stratigraphically; the northeastern corner of both trench BE00-38 and its building was revealed by collapse of overlying north and east balks.

Since trench BE00-38 was not opened until halfway through the 2000 season, when only three weeks of excavation remained, its goals were limited to exposure of as much of the architectural plan of the BE99-28/BE00-38 building as possible, and to make as much progress as possible toward bringing trench BE00-38 into phase with contiguous trench BE99-28. Excavation revealed the entire northern half of the building, and, although the two trenches were not completely in phase, their respective stratigraphies could easily be correlated.

Excavation in trench BE00-38 encountered only the two latest phases in the history of the building. Phase I—fifth-century AD architecture was exposed, and Phase II—sediment and debris strata from the post–fifth-century AD abandonment of the building were excavated. Although excavation did not reach occupation levels in trench BE00-38, architectural debris layers created by the collapse of its Phase I walls and features yielded dates consistent with those of floor BE99-28.*038*. This was the latest floor in the western half of the building, and dated to the fifth century AD or later. The earliest structural debris strata excavated in trench BE00-38, in the eastern half of the building, produced pottery from the same period (i.e., fifth century AD on).

Trench 38, Phase I
Architectural plan of the fifth century AD building.
The urban quarter of Berenike in which building BE99-28/BE00-38 stood has been a strategic focus of excavation since 1998. The area spanned two city blocks, as defined by one major north-south *kardo*-like avenue and two east-west *decumanus*-like streets that led

to the harbor. The Serapis temple lay about one and a half blocks west of the sector, and the ancient shoreline two or three blocks to the east.

Five buildings in this quarter have now been partially excavated. Building BE99-28/BE00-38 occupied the same block as its southern neighbor, the building in BE98-20/BE99-27; both lay on the eastern side of the main north-south avenue. Two contiguous trenches and two seasons of excavation have been devoted to each of these structures, with more work planned in the future. Three additional edifices in the quarter were investigated this season. The BE00-41 building stood on the west side of the *kardo*, across the street from trenches 20/27 and 28/38. The building in trench BE00-34 shared its block with the BE98-20/99-27 structure; both lay on the northern side of one east-west street. The BE00-37 building stood one block to the west, on the south side of the main east-west street.

The first two buildings excavated in this quarter, in BE98-20/BE99-27 and BE99-28/BE00-38, shared many similarities, in date (late fifth century AD), orientation, design, construction materials, and techniques. In fact, as noted previously (under BE99-28), they paralleled each other so closely that they were interpreted as belonging to the same single, large-scale architectural complex. Excavations in 2000, however, broadened the picture of this quarter to the point that one can reconstruct an entire bustling neighborhood of late fourth- to early fifth-century-AD buildings, all of which shared equally close architectural affinities.

The plan of the fifth century AD architectural phase of building BE99-28/BE00-38 emerged; the building was almost square, measuring about 8.20 m N-S x approximately 8.40 m E-W in interior dimensions. Its exterior walls were all built of coral heads, laid in courses, bonded with clayey sand mortar and faced with silty render. Here, gypsum ashlar masonry was restricted to the building's single entrance. This ashlar-lined doorway, excavated in 1999 (see preceding under BE99-28), stood in the southwestern corner of the building and opened onto the major north-south avenue of the neighborhood.

Three of the exterior walls of the building were excavated in trench BE00-38. Trench BE99-28.*004* southern east-west exterior wall traced continuously along the southern balk of trench BE00-38 and preserved a maximum height of 1.51 m (11 courses).

Almost the entire interior face of BE99-28.*022* northern east-west exterior wall, unfortunately, collapsed between the 1999 and 2000 seasons. For conservation reasons there was a concerted effort not to expose the eastern continuation of this unstable wall in trench BE00-38. The northern boundary of the new trench was designed to leave a sediment balk along the threatened southern wall face. This measure, however, proved ineffective. The northern balk collapsed, exposing the BE00-38.*025* segment of the BE99-28.*022* northern exterior wall of the building. The new *025* northern wall face survived to a maximum height of 1.68 m (10 courses; Figure 4-73 and Plate 4-74).

Within a day of the northern balk collapse, the contiguous northern half of the eastern balk also fell, shearing off against another wall face. The new wall was the *026* eastern north-south exterior wall of the building, whose interior face lay just beyond the eastern balk of trench BE00-38. These balk collapses made an important contribution to our understanding of the plan of the building. By exposing the northeastern interior corner of the edifice, they allowed its overall interior dimensions to be calculated. Wall *026* survived to a maximum height of 1.63 m (12 courses).

A system of internal cross and spine walls articulated four rooms in the interior of building BE99-28/BE00-38. Space was apportioned symmetrically north-south, but unequally east-west. Two central east-west cross walls divided the interior into northern and southern halves of equal size, while two north-south spine walls accorded twice as much space to the western rooms as to the eastern rooms. The spacious northern and southern rooms at the front of the building measured approximately 3.80 m N-S x 5.50 m E-W; their smaller eastern annexes measured about 3.80 m N-S x only approximately 2.30 m E-W.

Two symmetrical cross walls formed an east-west partition between the two large front rooms. Western cross wall BE99-28.*020* measured 2.20 m long E-W x 0.60 m wide N-S (Plates 4-77 and 4-78). The segment of eastern cross wall BE99-28.*030*=BE00-38.*005* that defined the western sides of the anterior rooms also measured 2.20 m E-W x 0.60 m N-S. These two symmetrical cross walls also articulated a central 1.10 m wide doorway between the western rooms.

The BE99-28.*020* western segment of this cross wall was confined to the western rooms of the building. Eastern cross wall BE99-28.*030*=BE0038.*005*, however, extended about 5.10 m E-W across the building to form a corner with eastern exterior wall *026*. This wall, therefore, divided northern rooms from southern in both the eastern and western sections of the building. Cross wall BE99-28.*030*=BE00-38.*005* displayed two

different masonry styles. The 2.20-m-long segment that defined the large western rooms was built in the *opus Berenikeum* technique (see preceding under BE99-28), while the segment that articulated the smaller eastern rooms was made only of coral heads.

Western cross wall BE99-28.*020* of the front rooms was also an *opus Berenikeum* feature. This distinctive combination of gypsum ashlar and coral-head masonry, therefore, appeared exclusively in the east-west cross walls of the large anterior rooms of the building. The newly exposed western segment of eastern cross wall BE99-28.*030*=BE00-38.*005* preserved two "boxed units" of *opus Berenikeum* masonry, each about 0.50 m square. This segment of the wall was about 1.10 m high. The eastern coral portion of the wall had a maximum height of 1.90 m (12 courses).

The reasons for the differing masonry styles in the western and eastern segments of the major east-west internal cross wall of the building remain elusive. At the current level of exposure, the entire 5.10 m E-W length of wall BE99-28.*030*=BE00-38.*005* seems to belong to a single period of construction. The transition from *opus Berenikeum* and to wholly coral masonry was handled fluidly; the construction break in this section of the wall was no more pronounced than those between the alternating ashlar and coral units of *opus Berenikeum* proper. The *opus Berenikeum* walls appear to be contemporary with the coral-head walls. Aesthetic appeal was also not a factor as a thick coat of render, the same treatment accorded coral-head walls, originally masked the *opus Berenikeum* masonry. Finally, the architect identified no structural value in incorporating ashlar blocks into a single stretch of internal cross wall (personal communication from J.-L. Rivard). Trench BE00-38 failed to resolve the problem of the function of *opus Berenikeum* masonry.

Two north-south spine walls articulated the final spatial divisions within the building. Both measured 3.00 m N-S x 0.60 m E-W, and both were constructed of coral heads. In the southern half of the building, southern spine wall *008* formed a corner with southern exterior wall *004*, from which it extended 3 m toward the north. Wall *008* divided the southwestern anterior room from a smaller southeastern chamber. The two southern rooms of the building communicated through a 0.80-m-wide doorway at the northern end of wall *008*. Wall *008* itself formed the southern side of the doorway, while the southern face of cross wall BE99-28.*030*=BE00-38.*005* served the same purpose on the north. Cross wall *005* received no special architectural treatment on the northern side of the doorway; its coral-head masonry extended uninterrupted through the passage. In contrast, the doorway end of spine wall *008* terminated in nine courses of gypsum ashlars that stood to a height of 1.50 m. Wall *008*, however, had only a single row of ashlar blocks, all confined to the doorway. The coral-head masonry of this wall preserved a maximum height of 1.56 m (10 courses).

In the northern half of the building, spine wall *006* duplicated the function and configuration of southern spine wall *008*. Wall *006* formed its southern corner with cross wall *005*, to divide the large northwestern room from its smaller northeastern counterpart. The ashlar-faced northern end of wall *006* articulated the southern side of an 0.80-m-wide doorway between the two rooms, while northern exterior wall *025* articulated its northern side. Six courses of gypsum ashlar blocks, laid header/stretcher fashion, survived at the doorway end of wall *006*. The coral heads of the northern spine wall stood to a maximum height of 1.69 m (10 courses).

The western anterior faces of both spine walls in the building were associated with special architectural features. Impressive staircase BE99-28.*043*=BE00-38.*009* was built against southern wall BE99-28.*004*, and a rectangular niche was built into northern wall *006*. The staircase, however, was the premier architectural feature of the building. Excavations in 1999 exposed its two lowest treads (Plate 4-79) and the rest of its surviving superstructure was revealed in trench BE00-38 (Plate 4-80). The two-flight *009* staircase stood in the southeastern quadrant of the large southwestern room of the building. Its lower east-west flight

Plate 4-80 Trenches BE99-28/BE00-38 staircase 28.*043*/ 38.009 abutting the interior face of south wall 38.*008*. The large slabs making up tumble 38.*023* have fallen from the upper part of the staircase. Looking east. Scale=1 m. Photograph by S. E. Sidebotham.

was built against southern exterior wall *004* and its upper north-south flight against spine wall *008*. An intermediate landing between the pivoting flights of steps occupied the southeastern corner of the room and was built against both walls *004* and *008*. The northern, rear end of the staircase was aligned with door *008* between the southwestern and southeastern rooms of the building.

A substructure of coral heads with five courses of gypsum ashlar quoins at its outer northwestern corner carried staircase *009*, which rose to a maximum height of 1.47 m. The three lower ashlar blocks were laid stretcher-wise, while the two uppermost courses were set vertically, to serve as facing blocks for the northern back wall of the substructure. Eight courses of coral-head masonry were exposed in the interior, western face, of the installation.

Each flight of the staircase was about 0.80 m wide; the intermediate landing measured approximately 0.80 m N-S x 0.86 m E-W. A total of 11 steps survived, five in each flight and an additional step up to the landing. The treads and landing were constructed of gypsum ashlar masonry. Each tread comprised a single ashlar block, 0.80 m long x 0.30–0.35 m wide x 0.13–0.18 m high. Three such blocks were laid side by side in the landing to create a level flagstone pavement.

Collapsed gypsum ashlar blocks were uncovered alongside the northern half of the staircase, immediately west of doorway *008*. This *023* tumble layer (Plate 4-80) contained 12 whole and broken ashlar blocks, whose dimensions conformed to those still *in situ* in staircase *009* and its substructure. Two intact *023* blocks (0.80 m x 0.30 m x 0.09 m and 0.80 m x 0.35 m x 0.10 m, respectively) fit the parameters of size for ashlar treads in staircase *009*. Another block, which measured 0.77 m long x 0.57 m wide x 0.08 m thick, was virtually the same size as an ashlar landing paver in the very similar BE00-37.*009* staircase (see following). Architectural tumble *023* contained another possible landing paver; it was smaller and measured 0.48 m long x 0.44 m wide x 0.06 m thick.

The location, configuration. and contents of ashlar tumble layer *023* argued strongly that it derived from contiguous staircase *009*. The pile of ashlars can be reconstructed as fallen treads and a second-story landing. Numerous coral heads also appeared in tumble *023*, equally distributed throughout the layer. The project architect suggested that a coral-head arch may once have spanned the 1 m N-S distance between staircase *009* and cross wall *005*, supporting the upper landing and forming an attractive arched ceiling for doorway *008* (personal communication from J.-L. Rivard; cf. under BE00-37.*009* following).

There is evidence that staircase *009* was originally equipped with some type of wooden railing. The outer walls of its substructure contained two fragments of bronze nails, both driven horizontally into the wall face. One was located 0.40 m below the uppermost surviving tread. Another appeared in the lower flight of the staircase, 0.10 m below its fourth tread from the bottom. These nails may once have affixed the struts of a wooden railing to the outer face of the substructure. The two possible landing pavers in tumble *023* each contained an intriguing pair of shallow rectangular cuttings that might also have been connected with wooden fixtures. The notches in the larger block were set 0.10 m apart and measured 0.10 m long x 0.05 m wide x 0.06 m deep and 0.06 m long x 0.04 m wide x 0.06 m deep, respectively. The cuttings in the smaller block were also 0.10 m apart and measured 0.08 m long x 0.05 m wide x 0.03 m deep and 0.01 m long x 0.03 m wide x 0.01 m deep, respectively. Perhaps these cuttings functioned together somehow to anchor a railing to the upper landing of staircase *009*.

When the BE99-28.*043* steps were exposed in the 1999 season, they represented only the second staircase ever discovered at Berenike and, as such, seemed to be of special importance. Excavations in 2000, however, revealed that staircases and two-story buildings were, in fact, standard features in the architecture of late Roman Berenike at least in this quarter of the city. Five of the late fourth- to early fifth-century AD buildings excavated last season had staircases. In addition to staircase BE00-38.*009*, there were BE00-30.*013*, BE00-34.*015*, BE00-37.*009*, and BE00-41.*013*. Three of these staircases (BE00-34.*015*, BE00-37.*009*, and BE00-41.*013*) appeared in the immediate neighborhood of trench BE00-38, a thriving late fourth-to early-fifth-century AD quarter whose character clarified dramatically during this season. The fourth staircase (BE00-30.*013*) belonged to the putative fifth-century AD church (see following).

The closest contemporary parallel for staircase BE00-38.*009* was BE00-37.*009*, which also comprised two flights and 11 steps, and pivoted at an intermediate landing. It was also built of ashlar treads supported by a coral-head substructure. Staircase BE00-37.*009*, however, stood in what appeared to be a forecourt, rather than in an interior room, as the BE00-38.*009* staircase did.

Plate 4-81   Detail of niche 38.*030* in the upper portion of N-S spine wall 38.*006* (cf. Figures 4.74 and 4.75). For a drawing of this niche in comparison to those found in trench BE00-37, see Figure 4.115, p. 137. Scale=20 cm. Photograph by S. E. Sidebotham.

Staircase BE00-38.*009* dominated the southeastern quadrant of the large anterior southwestern room of the building. The same sector of the anterior northwestern room also received special treatment. Here, rectilinear niche *030* was built into the western face of spine wall *006* (Plate 4-81). The niche, which measured 0.45–0.50 m in N-S width, was roughly centered in wall face *006*. It was located 1.35 m south of the northern doorway end of the wall, and 1.15 m north of the southeastern corner of the room, where spine wall *006* intersected with the *opus Berenikeum* segment of cross wall *005*. The niche was about 0.35 m deep; its back wall survived to a height of approximately 0.55 m, while its anterior *006* face was preserved only to a height of about 0.40 m.

Niche *030* stood 0.85 m above the earliest stratum of Phase II architectural debris excavated below it. This *029* layer (see following) stratigraphically equated with BE99-28.*036*, the earliest architectural debris layer excavated inside the northwestern room in the 1999 season. Floor BE99-28.*036* directly overlay BE99-28.*038*, the latest floor of the room, which presumably also underlay unexcavated BE00-38.*029*. To judge from the top levels of floor BE99-28.*038*, niche *030* stood about 1 m above the latest floor of the northwestern room.

In the western face of coral-head wall *006*, one row of small gypsum ashlars defined each side of niche *030*. Two courses of this ashlar frame remained *in situ*. The blocks were laid header fashion, so that their long sides formed the interior sidewalls of the niche. In exposed dimensions, the *030* ashlars ranged in size from 0.19 and 0.26 m in N-S width x 0.35 m in E-W length x 0.06

m–0.09 m in height. The back wall and portions of the base of the niche comprised roughly coursed cobbles faced with render.

Traces of two extremely decayed wooden fixtures appeared in niche *030*. A wooden beam that measured about 0.05 m wide N-S x at least 0.35 m long E-W x 0.07 m high was built header-fashion into the base of the southern side wall of the niche, to form its lowest course. A fragment of decayed wood, measuring 0.13 m wide E-W x 0.03 m high, was still visible in section in the northern side wall of the niche, 0.38 m above its interior surface. Another piece of wood, about 0.40 m long N-S x 0.08 m wide E-W, lay flat upon this render at the back of the niche. These two fragments of wood probably represented the remains of a collapsed wooden shelf similar to those preserved in other trenches nearby.

Other artifacts uncovered near niche *030* in adjacent architectural debris layers may also have been associated with the feature. Directly below the niche, a decayed wooden board lay flat upon debris layer *029*. This board measured about 0.35 m long x 0.15 m wide, and had a 0.05 m square notch cut in the center of one end. Since the length of board *029* was identical to the depth of the niche, it probably once formed part of a wooden fitting in the cupboard.

Excavation of architectural tumble *018*, which directly overlay niche *030*, produced finds that could have fallen out of the cupboard. In the southeastern corner of the room, a decayed wooden box that still contained four large copper-alloy nails appeared in *018*. The little box, which did not survive excavation, measured 0.18 m long x 0.10 m wide x 0.06 m high. A degraded slat of wood, 0.35 m long x 0.04 m wide x 0.02 m thick, lay beside the box. Since the length of this slat conformed to the depth of niche *030*, it may have belonged to that installation. Perhaps the box of nails was at one time stored in the niche.

As was the case with late fourth- to early fifth-century AD staircases, this season revealed that built-in niches furnished with wooden shelves and fixtures were standard features in the late Roman buildings of Berenike. The best preserved and most numerous series of such features came to light in the building partially revealed in BE00-41, located just across the *kardo* from building BE99-28/BE00-38. Here, one room contained six niches (see following). Niche *030* in building BE00-38, although its wooden fixtures were less well preserved, conformed in every sense—location in wall, dimensions, and construction technique—to

those in BE00-41. Similar built-in niches have also been identified in three other contemporary late fourth- to early fifth-century structures, the neighboring BE98-20/BE99-27 building, in trench BE98/99-22, and in trench BE00-37 (see following).

Building BE99-28/BE00-38 contained two additional candidates for niches, but confirmation awaits further excavation. One appeared in north wall *025* of the northeastern room, where a rectilinear gap in the interior wall face approximated standard niche dimensions. This possible niche was located in wall face *025*, about 1.25 m west of the northeastern corner of the room. It measured approximately 0.50 m in E-W width x about 0.40 m high. Feature *025*, however, lacked the ashlar framing courses of the niches in *030* and in trench BE00-41; its sidewalls, if so they were, were built solely of coral heads.

The other possible niche appeared in the western face of spine wall *008*, directly above the intermediate landing of staircase *009*. Here a piece of wood that measured 0.38 m long N-S x 0.04 m wide E-W x 0.03 m thick still adhered to the uppermost edge of the wall, 0.85 m (seven courses) above the surface of the landing. It is conceivable that this piece of wood represented the dislodged wooden lip of a collapsed niche. As A. M. Hense pointed out, a stairwell niche would have been a practical convenience; lamps stored there could have illuminated a dark corner staircase day and night.

Trench 38, Phase II
Post-fifth century AD abandonment and architectural decay.

The stratigraphy of the massive windblown sand, architectural tumble, and debris layers excavated within the building in trench BE00-38 mirrored those excavated in contiguous trench BE99-28 (see preceding). In trench BE00-38, which comprised the eastern half of the BE99-28/BE00-38 building, excavation terminated at the level of two loci that can be equated with BE99-28.*036*, the earliest architectural debris layer excavated in the western half of the building during the 1999 season. In trench BE00-38, the exposed but unexcavated *022*=BE99-28.*036* architectural debris layer extended across the entire southern half of the building. Its stratigraphic equivalent in the northern half of the building was *029*=BE99-28.*036*, which was exposed but not excavated in the northwestern room. Time did not permit coral-head tumble layer *024*, which directly overlay *029*, to be cleared from the northeastern room of the building. Architectural debris stratum *024* in the northeastern room will, therefore, be the first layer excavated in any future work conducted in trench BE99-28/BE00-38.

As was the case for abandonment-era strata excavated during the 1999 season, the architectural tumble and debris layers excavated in trench BE00-38 produced significant quantities of pottery dating to the fifth century AD or later. The trench BE00-38 ceramic assemblage, however, provided an important new insight into the use of the building. The existence of the ground floor *009* staircase allowed one confidently to interpret a number of the architectural tumble strata excavated in trench BE00-38 (*021*, *020*, and *023* in the southern rooms of the building and *019*, *024*, *027*, and *028* in the northern rooms) as a mixture of architectural and occupational debris from the second storey of the edifice.

The pottery from these layers was a homogeneous corpus consistent with a domestic context. With the exception of Aqaba amphorae, whose fabric deteriorated badly in the salty soil of Berenike, the sherds were in good condition. From a ceramic standpoint, this absence of wear, abrasion, and encrustation argued for a primary context rather than redeposition. Storage vessels used in daily life and fine tablewares (ESA, Aswan white slip cups, glazed wares, and flangeless bowls) predominated. A sherd of a Hayes LRP Form 82 plate from locus *019* was particularly interesting, as a better-preserved example of the same type was recovered from BE00-37.*008* tumble. This was the building whose staircase most closely paralleled the one in trench BE99-28/BE00-38. There was an Aksumite body sherd from locus *017*.

The high proportion of tablewares and quotidian storage jars in second-story debris layers suggests that the upper floor of the BE99-28/BE00-38 building comprised living quarters. It was certainly common in Roman Egypt (cf. Karanis) and in the Roman world in general (Rome itself, Ostia, Pompeii, and Herculaneum) to consign business and working areas to the ground floors of multistoried buildings, with dwelling units relegated to the upper floors (Boëthius and Ward-Perkins 1970:288-289; Meiggs 1973:272-273). The omnipresence of staircases in late fourth- to early fifth-century AD buildings at Berenike and analysis of pottery from these locales, suggest that finds from contemporary architectural debris layers in the neighborhood conformed to this pattern as well.

These same second-storey architectural and occupational debris layers produced almost all the coins excavated in trench BE00-38: one from *019* (disinte-grated) one from *023* (Chapter 8, catalogue number 82, a small concave/convex aes issue, possibly from southern Arabia, that disintegrated during a second cleaning) seven from *024* (Chapter 8, catalogue numbers 85–90 plus one disintegrated) and two from *028* (Chapter 8, catalogue numbers 83–84).

Discussion

Now that it is almost completely exposed architecturally and almost completely in phase stratigraphically, future excavation is planned for the BE99-28/BE00-38 building. However, the precarious state of its architecture poses a serious problem. Tentative plans, dependent upon funding, are to devote next season to architectural consolidation and conservation in the building and to recommence excavation sometime thereafter. The building in trench BE99-28/BE00-38 was clearly part of a larger late Roman neighborhood that lay between the Serapis temple and the coast. This quarter of the city, at least in the later fourth and fifth centuries AD, functioned as both a commercial and residential area for some of Berenike's inhabitants.

4.5.3 TRENCH BE00-34
Trench supervisor: B. Tratsaert
Figures/Plates 4-82 to 4-92

Trench BE00-34, 6.5 m N-S x 6 m E-W with grid coordinates of 537–543.5 m N/2101.5–2107.5 m E, lay immediately north of and across the *decumanus maximus* from BE98-21 (a late Roman trash dump) and east of BE98-20/BE99-27 (a late Roman commercial-residential edifice). Trench BE00-34 was placed in this area to investigate a large rectangular building with a doorway facing south, toward the *decumanus maximus*. Trench BE98-21may have been the trash dump used by those living and working in the building now partly excavated in BE00-34. Excavations in BE00-34, not completed during the 2000 season, yielded three phases:

Phase I: Possible foundation fill of the building: pre-late fourth to fifth century AD

Phase II: With two subphases of occupation: late fourth to fifth century AD
             Sub-phase IIa: First group of *de facto* surfaces
             Sub-phase IIb: Second cluster of *de facto* surfaces

Phase III: Abandonment, decay and building collapse during and after the fifth century AD occupation

Trench 34, Phase I

Phase I, pre–late fourth to fifth century AD, comprised a dark brown, very loose, loamy sand layer, which was, most likely, only used as a foundation or construction fill. Locus *027* ended at the same level where, in western wall *006*, the courses veered inward for 0.10 m, where southern wall *012* and *013* joined, and where the lowest step of staircase *015* started. Locus *027* was not sterile; there was some coral tumble along wall *003* containing pottery, a few pieces of iron slag. and a fragment of a stone vessel. Excavation of the trench halted at the end of the 2000 season in this locus. Locus *027* may well have been a major leveling fill associated with the putative earlier walls beneath walls *003/012/013*that is, the phase immediately preceding the earliest phase (I) excavated this season.

The walls of the room appearing in BE00-34 comprised the southwestern corner of an edifice. The structure was probably built or remodeled during this phase, perhaps, atop earlier walls; not all its walls were within the trench. Traces of these walls extended an additional approximately 3 m to the east and approximately 6 m to the north, outside the trench. Overall measurements of the building were approximately 12.10 m N-S x 9.70–9.90 m E-W.

Excavations uncovered north-south running western wall *006*. Made of coral heads, *006* was 1.74 m (nine courses) high x about 0.64 m (three rows) wide. Doorway *021/021a* divided the east-west running southern wall in two; the wall east of *021/021a* (see Subphase IIa following) was locus *012*; the wall west of *021* was *013*. Wall *012/013* varied from 1.14–1.25 m (seven courses) high x approximately 0.68 m (three rows) wide.

Two cross walls in the northeastern part of the trench formed an internal division in the building and may have postdated the more-substantial coral-head walls that formed the boundaries of this room. Wall *002* ran north-south for about 2 m and wall *003* ran east-west also for 2 m. Wall *003* ran up against another doorway (*003a*) that was not completely excavated; approximately three-quarters of it lay beyond the eastern balk. Walls *002* and *003* were 1.30 m (nine courses) high x 0.28–0.32 m (three rows) wide.

Only one corner of the room was exposed inside the trench created by walls *002* and *003*. It was made of gypsum/anhydrite ashlar blocks, which was, most likely, the case for all corners of the building. The doorposts also comprised gypsum/anhydrite ashlar blocks, which stood upright with the short sides resting vertical to the threshold; they were preserved to a height of 1.14–1.25 m; the width of these ashlars varied from 0.38–0.56 m. Remains of many ashlar blocks and fragments in the wall tumble near the doorway suggested that the doorposts were primarily or entirely built of them. This was the case for doorway *021/021a* in southern wall *012/013* and that (*003a*) in wall *003*. Doorway *021*comprised a wooden threshold (*021a*) consisting of five wooden planks that filled the entire exposed entrance, 1.0 m E-W wide x 0.50 m N-S deep (Figures 4-82 and 4-84; Plates 4-85 and 4-87). The northernmost plank continued into the adjacent walls for about 0.60 m. It was clearly visible in wall *012*. The extension of the wooden plank into wall *013* was more difficult to discern due to the presence of installation *020/026/028/029/030/011* in front of *013* (Plate 4-87). The width of the planks varied 0.08–0.14 m x about 0.02 m (laid flat). In the southern balk, just outside the doorway that lead to the *decumanus maximus*, was a 0.12 m high plank standing on its shortest side. Its purpose is not clear; it may have been a step up to a higher street level. This doorway lay, by the end of the excavation season, atop two courses of coral heads that connected walls *012* and *013*. Wooden threshold *021a* lay on the same level as *de facto* surface *019c*. Both appeared to have been built and used simultaneously. The coral-head courses beneath *021/021a* were either foundations for wall *012/013* or earlier parts of walls (associated with a pre-Phase I—as yet unexcavated—period in the history of the structure; noted previously) atop which these later walls and door were erected. Two other features might confirm this hypothesis: west wall *006* and staircase *015* (see Subphase IIa following). As noted previously, the two lowest courses of wall *006* lay about 0.10 m inward in the wall. These lower courses were, perhaps, part of an older wall (slightly) offset from the later one. Additionally, staircase *015* ran north-south and had four steps and a little platform on top.

The lowest step of staircase *015* (Plates 4-83 and 4-86) lay directly upon *019c*. Whether it made a turn or ran farther north is difficult to discern because it lay outside the trench.

The rectangular-shaped platform atop the extant staircase measured 0.80 m x 1.0 m and consisted of several blocks of varying sizes. The steps themselves comprised large ashlar blocks, which overlapped each other; coral heads filled spaces in between. The ashlars appeared to have been reused from an earlier context. Measurements for each step were 0.80 m long x 0.45–0.50 m wide x 0.16–0.20 m high. Immediately east was

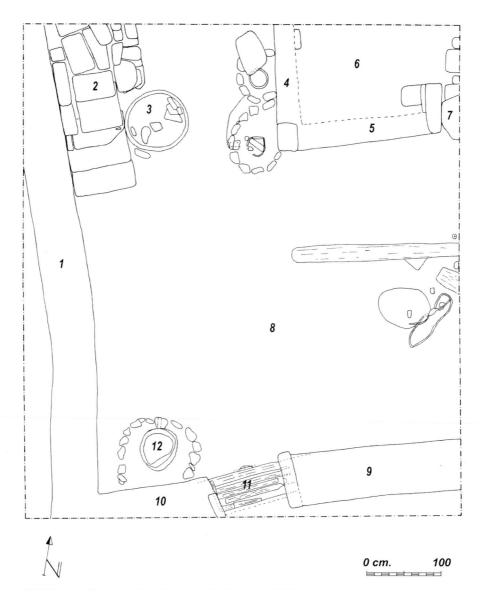

0 cm. 100

Figure 4-82   Trench BE0034 plan of Subphases IIa–b. Drawing by B. Tratsaert and H. Barnard.

1=006	4=002	7=003a	10=013
2=015	5=003	8=019c	11=021/021a
3=031	6=004	9=012	12=020/026/028/029/030/011

Plate 4-83
Trench BE00-34 in Subphases IIa-b. Looking northwest. Note staircase *015* in the northwestern part of the trench (top center in photo), abutting N-S wall *006*. This wall intersects with E-W wall *013* with entrance *021/021a* (bottom left of photo). The top of wall *012* is visible in the bottom center of the photo. To the north (upper right) are walls *002* and *003*. Parallel to these is a fallen wooden roof beam. Scale=1 m. Photograph by S. E. Sidebotham.

another group of stones (*015a*) abutting the platform of staircase *015*. It was approximately at the same level of the lowest step of staircase *015*. *015a* comprised ashlars (not as large as the steps in *015* staircase) built on coral heads. The group of stones (*015a*) may have been part of the support for staircase *015* when it turned east; alternatively, it may have been a bench. There were two installations about 2 m east of staircase *015* and one south of *015a* (discussed under Subphase IIb: *009/017/025* and *016/023/024*).

In later phases when the floor level rose, this lowest step was gradually covered over. This suggests that floor *019c* and staircase *015* were, indeed, originally contemporary. Door/threshold *021/021a* in wall *012/013* was undoubtedly constructed at this time as well (Figure 4-84, Plate 4-85).

Trench 34, Phase II: occupation

Phase II, dated to the late fourth to fifth century AD had two subphases (IIa and IIb). Phase II included installations in the northwestern and north central parts of the trench (*009/017/025* and *016/023/024*) installation *020/026/028/029/030/011* in the south western part of the trench and de facto surfaces *019a-c*.

Sub-phase IIa

To this subphase belongs *de facto* surface *019c*, staircase *015*, and *dolium 031* (Figure 4-82 and Plate 4-83). Surface *019c* was the only surface in this subphase. as well as the earliest excavated in the trench and the first surface directly atop locus *027* (from Phase I). Surface *019c* was contemporary with staircase *015* and was the surface onto/into which *dolium 031* was placed. *Dolium 031*, in the northwestern corner of the trench immediately east of staircase *015*, had an outside diameter of 0.84 m with its opening covered by sherds from other vessels. Surface *019c* comprised a dark loamy soil with charcoal and gypsum flecks embedded in it, possibly an indication of intense use. The flecks may have derived from eroded ashlars, a possible indication that during this subphase this area either lacked a roof or had one made of very lightweight materials that did not completely protect it from the elements.

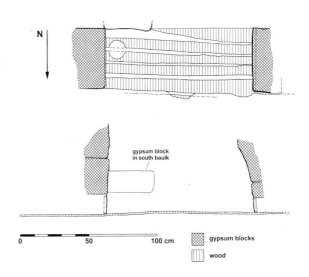

Figure 4-84
Threshold 34.*021a* (in doorway *021*). BE00-34 Subphase IIb. Drawing by A. M. Hense.

Plate 4-85   Threshold 34.*021a* (in doorway *021*). BE00-34 Subphase IIb. Looking south. Scale=50 cm. Photograph by S. E. Sidebotham.

Finds included copper-alloy nails, a bracelet, and another copper-alloy fragment decorated with a cobra. Ceramic dating of this subphase was late fourth to fifth century AD.

Sub-phase IIb

In this subphase belong *019b* (an approximately 0.01 m thick fill of brown sand) topped by another new floor *019a* (a patchy, loamy soil with ash rather than charcoal about 0.11 m thick), which together eventually covered surface *019c*. *Dolium 031* also fell out of use with the reflooring of *019c* by *019b* and *019a*. This new floor (*019b* and *019a*) also covered the lowest step of staircase *015* (Plate 4-86). Three installations were associated with this subphase. They included pot stand/storage container *009* (with ash fill *017* and retaining coral wall *025*), pot stand/storage container *016* (with ash fill *023* and retaining coral wall *024*) and another storage container *020/030*, also with windblown fill *029*, an ash fill (*011*), wooden pipe *028*, and accompanying coral retaining wall *026*.

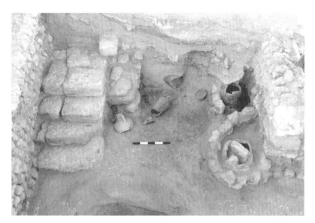

Plate 4-86   Trench BE00-34, northwestern corner with staircase *015* abutting wall *006* (to the left/west). Installations *016/023/024* and *009/010/017/025* to the right (east) abut N-S wall *002*. Looking north. Scale=50 cm. Photograph by S. E. Sidebotham.

Plate 4-87   Trench BE00-34, installation *020/026/028/ 029/030/011* at the interior junction of walls *013* and *006* and threshold *021a*. Looking southwest. Scale=50 cm. Photograph by S. E. Sidebotham.

Pot stand installation *009/017/025* comprised a Late Roman I amphora placed upside down with its bottom cut off. Deliberately placed ash locus *017* was packed between the outer wall of *009* and the inner face of retaining wall *025*. The latter comprised three courses of coral heads 0.50-0.53 m high. *009/017/025* was at a higher elevation than, but was contemporary in date with, storage container/pot stand/installation *016/023/024*, which also lay in the northern part of the trench along the west side of wall *002* and immediately east of staircase *015*. Ash fill *023* was packed between the outer walls of ceramic vessel *016* and the inside face of retaining wall *024*. The latter preserved two–three to four courses of coral heads varying in height from 0.21/0.30–0.51 m (Plate 4-86).

In the vicinity of these installations were three amphorae and one bowl, which appear to have fallen onto surface *019a*. Storage container/installation *020/026/028/029/030/011* lay in the southwestern part of the trench/room near walls *013* and *006* (Plate 4-87). This comprised a large *dolium* lacking a rim with dimensions of 0.44 m high x 0.50 in diameter. The bottom appeared to be of unfired clay (*030*) and sloped down toward the inner sides approximately 0.04 m. It was filled with what appeared to be windblown sand with some charcoal (*029*). A small wooden pipe (*028*) pierced the bottom of the northern side of *dolium 020*. The resulting hole in *020* was about 0.10 m in diameter; pipe *028* was 0.05 m in diameter x 0.07 m long; the interior of the pipe appeared to be burned, but whether deliberately or accidentally could not be determined. Pipe *028* was contemporary with *020* though its function could not be determined; perhaps, if the *dolium* contained grain, the pipe was for ventilation purposes. The pipe's extremely close proximity to the ground ruled out its use as a spigot for pouring liquids as there would have been no way to place a container beneath the pipe. A piece of marble revetment (probably Proconnesian), approximately 0.07 m thick, covered/protected that part of pipe *028* protruding outward from *dolium 020*. The space over the pipe and marble revetment and between the outer wall of *dolium 020* and coral-head retaining wall *026* was deliberately filled with ash (*011*). Some of this ash spilled out over wall *026* toward the west and north. The ash contained charcoal, sherds, including a dipinto, animal bones, and sheep or goat dung. Besides the ashes there was no evidence of any burning.

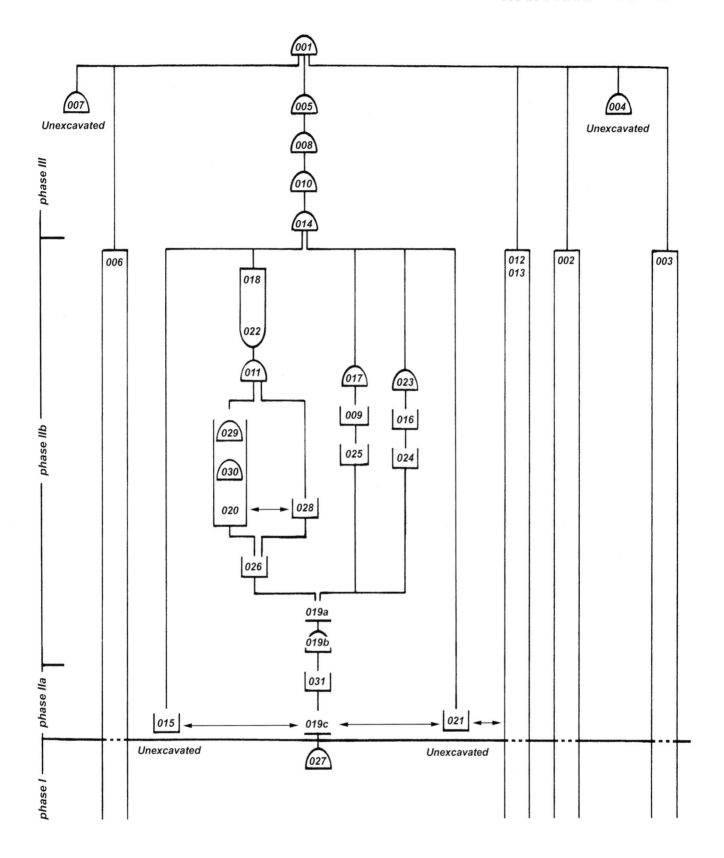

Figure 4-88   Matrix for trench BE00-34.

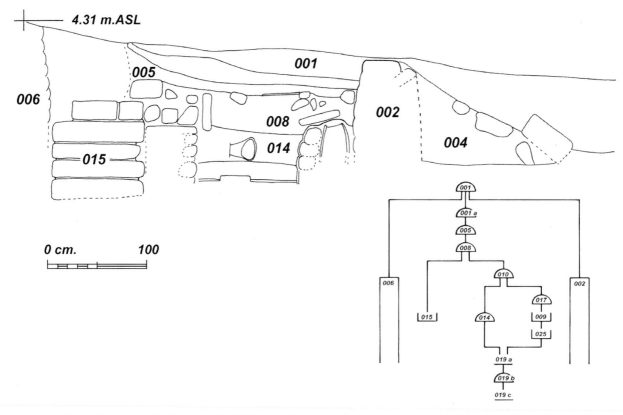

Figure 4-89   Trench BE00-34 north balk. Drawing by B. Tratsaert and H. Barnard.

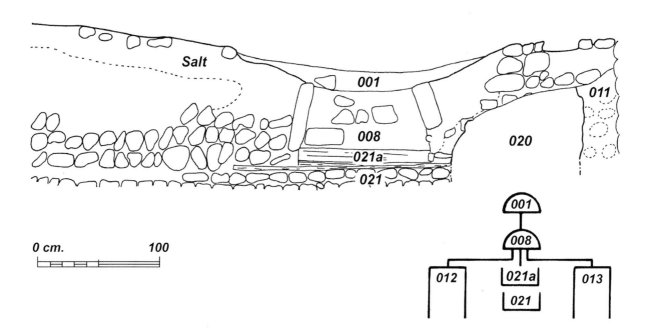

Figure 4-90   Trench BE00-34 south balk. Drawing by B. Tratsaert and H. Barnard.

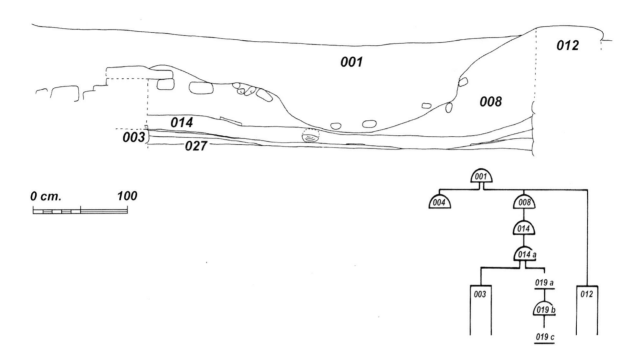

Figure 4-91   Trench BE00-34 east balk. Drawing by B. Tratsaert and H. Barnard.

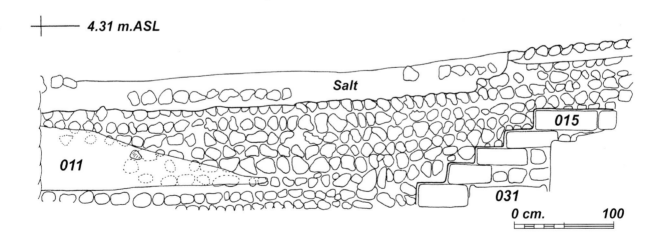

Figure 4-92   Trench BE00-34 west balk. Drawing by B. Tratsaert and H. Barnard.

This was also the case with ash deposit *017*, associated with installation *009/025* and ash deposit *023*, affiliated with installation *016/024*. This would suggest that in all three cases (and as other examples found elsewhere on site) the ashes served some utilitarian function, perhaps as insulation or insect and rodent repellents. This later theory would be especially attractive if these various containers had, indeed, been used to store grains or other perishable foods.

During Subphase IIb, this area seems to have been roofed as a large wooden beam 2.50 m long (minimally, an additionally 0.20 m could be traced into the eastern balk) x 0.15–0.17 m in diameter was found upon surface *019a*. The presence in the beam of three iron nails spaced 0.35 m apart and the find nearby of matting lying too flat to have derived from wall tumble (personal communication from W. Z. Wendrich) reinforced the interpretation that this beam was, most likely, used for roofing.

Other small finds from this subphase included a terracotta oil lamp, another ceramic object that could be hung by a string, and three stone objects. One of the latter appeared to be a hammer or pounder, while two others looked like sharpening or polishing stones.

Trench 34, Phase III

After abandonment the building began to decay. The walls collapsed and windblown sand covered the room. Locus *001* was a major windblown sand locus and *005*, *007*, *008*, *010*, and *014* were wall-tumble loci containing a fair amount of iron slag. Tumble locus *010*, situated in the northern part of the trench, was particularly interesting since it consisted only of ashlars. There were about 12 ashlar blocks grouped together that collapsed from some installation, probably not a wall, from outside the trench. The blocks were substantial, measuring between 0.36–0.89 m long x 0.27–0.57 m wide x 0.10–0.16 m high. They fell with sufficient force that the southern part of the tumble lay deeper than the northern part by almost 0.50 m. The northern highest part must have been exposed for some time because there were traces of erosion. The top part of at least one of the stones eroded flat to the same level as the surrounding surface. This might indicate that this part of the building lacked a permanent roof. There may have been a sun screen here since some matting fragments were found lying flat on and in the wall tumble. Little coral-head tumble appeared in the locus.

Wall tumble locus *007* lay outside and west of the building and was barely excavated; just enough of its sand was removed to articulate the face of wall *006*. Tumble locus *004* lay north of walls *002* and *003*, which formed a small room in the northeastern corner of the trench. The small space inside the room formed by walls *002* and *003* did not allow excavations to continue for any great depth.

Locus *014* comprised more windblown sand than tumble and must have filled this part of the building before any substantial collapse had taken place. There was coral tumble along south wall *012/013*, but not as much as in later loci. Locus *014* lay atop the Subphase IIb occupation level.

Discussion

The building appearing in trench BE00-34 lay in the same late Roman commercial-residential quarter as trenches 21, 20/27, 28/38, 37, and 41. It had the same general appearance as the structures that appeared in those trenches, including a narrow, and seemingly single, entrance onto a main street, the *decumanus maximus*, an internal staircase to a now-missing upper storey, and the same dates of use in its latest period of occupation. During one period, at least, of its existence (Subphase IIb) it appears to have been fully or partially roofed. The pot stands/installations appearing in trench 34, however, seemed to be for food rather than for industrial purposes. The proximity of the fifth-century AD trash dump in trench BE98-20 to trench 34 may indicate that at least some of the discarded rubbish found in trench 20 derived from the neighborhood around and including trench 34.

4.5.4   TRENCH BE00-37
         Trench supervisor: Ingrid Ystgaard.
         Figures/Plates 4-93 to 4-109

Trench BE00-37 was located in a building on the southern side of the *decumanus maximus*, which extended from the Serapis temple east toward the Red Sea. The building is about one city block east of the temple and appears to have had a function similar to those in trenches BE98-20/BE99-27, BE99-28/BE00-38, BE00-34, and BE00-41, that is, with commercial activities on the ground floor and residential/domestic on the upper floor(s). Excavations this season removed collapse from the interior of the northern room; occupational levels were uncovered, but not excavated.

After some alterations to accommodate the northern wall and entrance and the southern wall of the large open area at the northern end of this building, dimensions of the trench were 7 m N-S x 8 m E-W with grid coordinates of 507–514 N/2041–2049 E (Figures and Plates 4.93–4.97). There were two phases each having two subphases:

Phase I: Late occupation
                   (late fourth into the fifth century AD)
                   Phase Ia: Late surfaces
                   Phase Ib: Storage of stone blocks
Phase II: Abandonment and collapse
                   (after fifth century AD)
                   Phase IIa: Wall collapse
                   Phase IIb: Windblown sand deposition

Mainly on the basis of the architectural features found within it, the uncovered area was tentatively interpreted as a courtyard, which measured 4.5 m N-S x 7.0 m E-W. This courtyard had two entrances, one in the north (on the eastern end of an exterior wall) from the street (Figure 4-93, number 6: locus *022*), and a second from the unexcavated room to the south (Figure 4-93, numbers 12–13: loci *043/044*). Furthermore, it had two staircases, one wide "grand," leading to the threshold between the northern and the southern room (Figure 4-93, number 9: locus *035*), which was probably also the main entrance to the interior of the building from the courtyard; while wide, this staircase was not high (only two steps). The other staircase led to an upper floor or a roof over the southern (unexcavated) room.

Excavations in 2000 uncovered two main phases, each with two subphases. The first phase represented the latest occupation of the courtyard. Its first subphase included the latest occupational surfaces. These were uncovered but not excavated in 2000. The second subphase represented a stage when the room was used for the storage of gypsum ashlars of various types and sizes, all of them from another context, in one case clearly from the early second century AD. Among these blocks were two column capitals, a large basin, and an ashlar with an inscription in Greek from the period of Trajan (AD 98–117) dedicated to Isis (Plate 4-100 and Figure 4-101). This phase dated late fourth into the fifth century AD.

The second main phase represented the abandonment and collapse of the building. In the first subphase, the walls of the building collapsed. Remarkable finds in the wall collapse included two other inscribed gypsum ashlars, one a duplicate of the other, in Greek, from the reign of Nero (AD 54–68) dedicated to Zeus by a woman named Philotera (Plates 4-102 and 4-103). In the last subphase, which occurred sometime in the fifth century AD, the collapsed building filled with windblown sand.

Architecture

The exposed courtyard preserved extensive architecture. This included *002*, the eastern wall of the room (perhaps the building); *003*, the northern wall of both the courtyard and the building that fronted the *decumanus maximus*; *010*, which was the western wall of the building; and walls *027* and *032*, which together with threshold *043* formed the southern wall of the courtyard. All the walls were built of coral heads reinforced with gypsum blocks as quoins and at doorways. Judging by the material in the tumble, the walls also seem to have contained bone, shell, and pottery in addition to pieces of wood as binding material.

The southern end of the eastern wall of the building (*002*) joined wall *027* in the southeastern corner, where it preserved a height of 1.63 m (12 courses) x 4.80 m long x 0.65 m wide. Render covered most of the wall's interior (western) face. Wall *027* was less well preserved toward the north, where it formed the eastern part of the northern doorway. Here it was 0.90 m high. There is no evidence of gypsum quoin blocks towards the northern end of wall *002*, which is peculiar, considering that all wall ends and doorways uncovered in the rest of the room were strengthened with quoins. Wall *003*, the northern wall of the building facing the street, was also built of coral heads. Its greatest preserved height was toward the west, where staircase *009*'s lowest flight ascended along the wall from east up toward the west. Here the wall was uncovered to a height of 1.55 m (11 courses). The wall was less well preserved towards the northern doorway, where it was only 0.75 m high. In this section, gypsum quoins strengthened the wall.

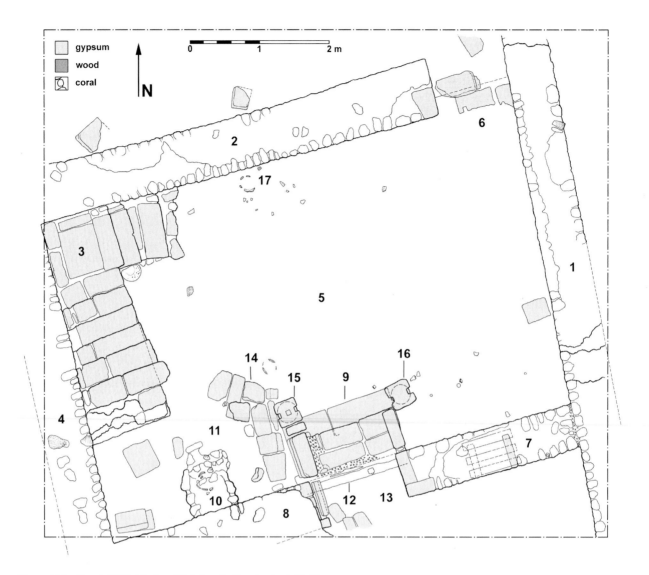

Figure 4-93   Trench BE00-37, plan of Subphase Ia. Drawing by A. M. Hense.

1=*002*	4=*010*	7=*027*	10=*037*	13=*044*	16=*047*
2=*003*	5=*013*	8=*032*	11=*038*	14=*045*	17=*048*
3=*009*	6=*022*	9=*035*	12=*043*	15=*046*	

Plate 4-94
Trench BE00-37 looking south. The entrance to the courtyard is in the left bottom corner of the photo adjacent to E-W wall *003*. In the middle of the photo are steps leading into the building *(035/043/044*, the "grand staircase" flanked by column capitals *047* to the left and *048* to the right), with E-W walls *027* to the east (left) and *032* to the west (right). Wall *032* intersects N-S wall *010* (in the western balk, right on the photo). Staircase *009* abuts wall *010*. Scale=1 m. Photograph by S. E. Sidebotham.

Plate 4-95   Trench BE00-37 looking southeast. To the north (left) is outer E-W wall *003* with entrance *022*, with N-S wall *002* at the top of the photo (east). It intersects at the southern end with E-W wall *027*. The "grand staircase" *035/043/044* is visible to the right. The top of staircase *009* is visible at the bottom left of the photo. Scale=1 m. Photograph by S. E. Sidebotham.

Plate 4-96   Western part of trench BE00-37, looking west-northwest. Staircase *009* at the top abutting N-S wall *010* and E-W wall *003*. The "grand staircase" *035/043/044* is visible to the left at the entrance of the building. Scale=1 m. Photograph by S. E. Sidebotham.

Wall *003* was 5.90 m long x 0.80 m wide adjacent to the doorway, while the rest of it was 0.65 m wide. Patchy remnants of render adhered to the wall's interior (southern) face.

Wall *010* was the building's western wall. It was built entirely of coral heads, and its interior (eastern) face was partially concealed by staircase *009*, which turned at the intersection of walls *010* and *003* and rose from the north up toward the south. Wall *010* was 4.50 m long x 1.60 m (12 courses) extant height. The width could not be determined because the trench did not extend to the outer (western) face of the wall; it would, most likely, have been about 0.65 m wide as were the other exposed walls in the building. Render coated portions of the wall's interior both north and south of the staircase.

Locus *027* was the eastern part of the southern wall, which marked the division between the excavated courtyard and the unexcavated room to the south. It was built of coral heads, and strengthened with gypsum blocks adjacent to the southern doorway (*035/043*, see following). Its greatest preserved height was at the eastern end where it formed the southeastern corner of the courtyard with wall *002*. Wall *027* was 2.5 m long. At its eastern end it was 1.45 m (11 courses) high. Towards the southern doorway it was 1.20 m high x 0.65 m wide. The southern face of wall *027* facing the unexcavated room to the south was damaged in ancient times and it did not appear to have been properly repaired.

This suggests that the damage occurred during a late occupational phase.

Locus *032* was that part of the southern wall west of the doorway. It was built of coral heads and strengthened with gypsum blocks adjacent to the doorway with the "grand staircase," although the gypsum part of the wall collapsed except for one block that remained *in situ*. It was 2.90 m long x 1.35 m maximum preserved height at the western end, where it formed the southwestern corner with wall *010*. At the eastern end, next to the collapsed gypsum portions near the staircase/entrance joining the courtyard to the room to the south, it was 0.90 m high. The width could not be determined, as the wall was not completely within the trench. Remains of render covered the northern wall face. The southern face of this wall preserved remains of two niches, but these were not completely exposed since that part of wall *032* in which they were located lay outside the boundaries of the trench.

There were two doorways in the courtyard. Northern doorway *022* was 1.17 m wide x 0.50 m deep. The threshold, built of several reused ashlar blocks, connected the courtyard and building to the adjacent *decumanus maximus* immediately to the north. The 1.10 m wide southern doorway *043* was on a higher level, as staircase *035* lead up to it. It had a wooden threshold consisting of two beams. The lower beam continued into wall *032*; the upper beam was probably a later addition to the threshold as the lower beam wore out due to traffic between the courtyard and the unexcavated room to the south.

In the northwestern corner of the courtyard, staircase *009* led up to an upper floor or roof, presumably over the unexcavated southern room. It was built directly against walls *003* and *010*. It had two flights of stairs; the lower along wall *003* comprised four steps and ascended toward the west to a landing in the corner, and the higher flight, which preserved six steps, ascended toward the south along wall *010*. This upper flight of stairs was undoubtedly higher since four gypsum blocks, which must have been steps, had fallen into the nearby tumble—altogether 10 steps. An ashlar, probably another landing on top of the stairs, had fallen in the corner between walls *010* and *032* (dimensions 0.60 m x 0.55 m x 0.10 m). The landing in the corner between walls *003* and *010* was on the same level as the lowest step of the higher flight of stairs. The steps comprised gypsum ashlars of various dimensions, the average full-step ashlar measuring 0.80 m x 0.30 m x 0.10 m. The third step from surface *013*, however, measuring 0.77 m x 0.28 m x 0.23 m, was of especially good quality. None of the blocks in the staircase had exactly the same dimensions; thus, smaller blocks were fit in between the larger ashlars and the walls. This was also true for the landing, where three smaller blocks flanked the middle ashlar, 0.65 m x 0.54 m x 0.09 m. Some of the blocks in the staircase were trapezoidal in shape. All these ashlars were probably reused from earlier contexts. The core of the staircase was built of coral heads. The upper flight, thus, rested on a coral-head "wall" facing east into the courtyard. The preserved part of the core was 1.30 m (nine courses) high. The staircase core also formed a wall facing south, at a 90 degree angle to wall *010*. The lowest two courses of this wall were built of gypsum blocks. On top of these were six additional preserved courses of coral heads. The corner of the staircase core was built of gypsum ashlars, altogether eight preserved courses. It is not clear how the upper part of the staircase was constructed. It originally had four more steps and a landing, all of which have collapsed. The architect suggested for *009* in trench BE00-38 that the upper part of that staircase rested on a coral-head arch (personal communication J. -L. Rivard). There is no extant evidence for such a construction in trench 37; there was a span of 1.3 m between the southern wall of staircase *009* and wall *032*, and it would have been possible to construct a coral-head arch over this rather short distance (cf. BE99-28.*043*/BE00-38.*009*). In any

case, the final interpretation of the upper construction of the staircase should be based on information on the floor level and calculations of the height of the walls in the unexcavated southern room.

There were staircases also in trenches BE99-28.*043*/BE00-38.*009*, BE00-34.*015*, BE00-41.*013*, and BE00-30.*013*. The closest parallel to staircase BE00-37.*009* was BE99-28.*043*/BE00-38.*009* mentioned previously. This staircase also had two flights of stairs with a landing in the southeastern corner, and an ashlar had fallen from what was probably another landing on the floor above. This was reflected in staircase BE00-37.*009*; even the dimensions of the intermediate floor landing blocks were similar (0.60 m x 0.55 m x 0.10 m in trench *37* and 0.64 m x 0.56 m x 0.08 m in trench *38*). This suggests that some of the reused material in the two trenches may have derived from the same source and that the buildings were constructed in the same period and perhaps by the same builders. This was confirmed by similar techniques and materials used, and by contemporary pottery dates.

A "grand staircase" (*035*) led up to the southern doorway and threshold *043* between walls *027* and *032*. It was entirely built of gypsum blocks comparable to those used in staircase *009* and in the ends of the walls adjacent to the doorway. No coral-head core could be seen. The staircase, comprising two steps, was 1.50 m wide; thus, it extended 0.20 m on either side of the doorway. It was 0.80 m broad; the lower step was 0.30 m wide; the higher step, more like a landing or a platform, was 0.54 m broad. A gypsum block formed a low railing or balustrade on each side. Threshold *043* was contemporary with walls *032* and *027* and lay atop staircase *035*. Thus, staircase *035* was also constructed simultaneously with the walls separating the courtyard from the room to the south. Staircase *035* made a monumental impression, and it probably lead into the main room of the building. The wooden beam in threshold *043* showed that there had been considerable traffic, not surprising since it was the main entrance to the building from the courtyard. The monumentality of the staircase adds to the impression that this was the main, and only, entrance to the building from the courtyard. This further suggests that the main activities in this building took place in the southern room. In the late occupational phase, two column capitals (*046* and *047*) were added to the staircase to make it appear even more impressive (see following). Figure 4-97 presents an artist's reconstruction of the building and courtyard.

Semicircular shaped installation *041* was constructed against wall *032*, in the corner space between staircase *009* and walls *010* and *032*. Built of coral heads, it measured 0.72 m E-W x 0.90 m N-S x 0.30 m high from surface 013. It was covered with a layer of matting mixed with charcoal and ash. Inside it was a pottery vessel, surrounded by a layer of light-gray ash. The installation, which remained unexcavated, was similar to those revealed in trenches BE00-30.*008* and BE00-34.*011/020/026/028/029/030* and was probably used for food storage.

The uniformity in dimensions and construction of the walls and stairs suggest that the visible architecture was built at one time, except perhaps for installation *041*, which might be a later addition to the existing ensemble. All the architecture uncovered during the 2000 season was in use in the late occupational phase (late fourth to fifth century AD). The earliest occupation levels, however, have not been uncovered, and it is still unknown whether there was more than one occupational phase associated with the architecture thus far uncovered.

Trench 37, Phase I
Late occupation: late fourth to fifth century AD
Subphase Ia
The latest occupation surfaces in the building were *013* and *038*. Surface *013* covered most of the courtyard except in the southwestern corner. It consisted of dark grayish-brown soil with specks of charcoal, ash, and decayed gypsum, in addition to pottery spread throughout the surface. It contained no coral-head tumble. Near wall *003* was a possible pot stand or a ceramic vessel (*048*) with evidence of burning embedded in locus *013*. Neither installation *048* nor surface *013* were excavated during the 2000 season. The surface in the southwestern corner of the courtyard (*038*) had a somewhat different composition; the soil was darker than that of surface *013* and it contained a greater concentration of ash and charcoal. Surface *038* lay west of installation *041*, and it was likely that this surface provided a working space connected to the activities associated with installation *041*. Embedded in surface *038* was a square gypsum ashlar, 0.50 x 050 x 0.10 m, which may have served as a platform for storing objects or as a working surface. East and northwest of installation *041* were two basalt stones with average dimensions of 0.25 x 0.15 x 0.10 m.

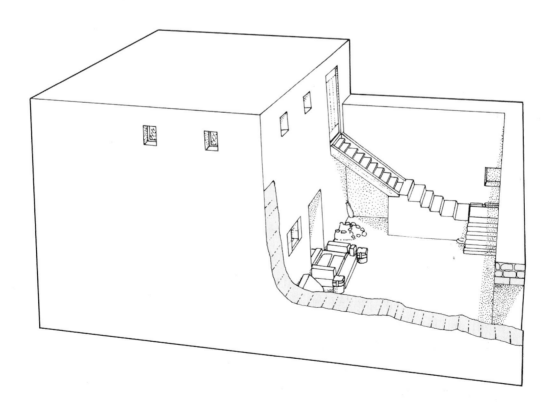

Figure 4-97   Artist's reconstruction of the courtyard and building in trench BE00-37. Drawing by A. M. Hense.

Plate 4-98   Ashlars *014* in front of wall *002* in trench BE00-37, Subphases Ib/IIa, looking east. Scale=50 cm. Photograph by S. E. Sidebotham.

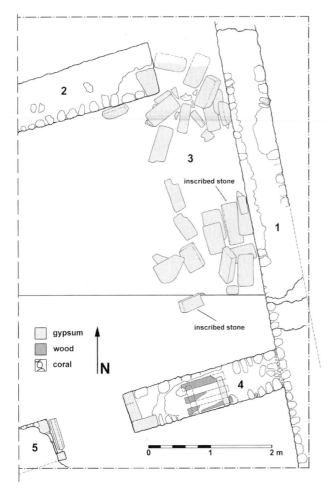

Figure 4-99   Plan of eastern part of trench BE00-37 during Subphases Ib/IIa showing ashlars (3) and the location of two inscribed blocks (the northern one cf. Figure 4.101, the southern one cf. Figure 4.102). Drawing by A. M. Hense.

1=002   3=014   5=032
2=003   4=027

The eastern one rested on surface *013*, the northwestern one on surface *038*. Such stones were unknown from the tumble in the rest of the trench. They might have had some function in connection with the installation, but this is uncertain. The stratigraphic relationship between surfaces *013* and *038* is also unknown.

A layer of matting mixed with ash and charcoal covered installation *041* and part of surface *038*. The matting was probably not tumble from a roof construction but had been deliberately placed over the installation to cover it. The ash and charcoal may also have had a protective function, since ash repels insects and small animals from stored food. Installation *041* seems to have been used in the late occupational phase, but surfaces *013* and *038* were built up against it, so the installation was older than the latest occupational surfaces.

Between installation *041* and staircase *035* was a low wall or row of nine gypsum ashlars of various sizes and shapes (*045*) embedded in surface *013*. The gypsum ashlars might have been put there for storage, somewhat earlier than the rest of the blocks that were stored here, or they might have acted as a low wall, sheltering installation *041* from the rest of the room. Of course, the stones could both have been stored and have been placed in exactly this spot to provide a division between installation *041* and the rest of the room.

Ash layer *011* also represented a late occupational stage. It did not preserve signs of a proper fire but rather seems to have been deposited or dumped in the building. It also might have had some connection with putative pot stand *048*; the ash may have been placed around it to keep insects away from the contents of the pot.

Sub-phase Ib

In the second occupation phase, the courtyard was used for the storage of architectural blocks (Plate 4-98, Figure 4-99), some of which had inscriptions or other features that gave an indication of their previous use (Plate 4-100 and 4-102 to 4-105, Figure 4-101). Two column capitals of pinkish gypsum (*046* and *047*), which flanked staircase *035*, were both from a monumental context, and perhaps a public one (Plates 4-104 and 4-105). They both rested on surface *013*. Thus, they were added to staircase *035* in the late occupational phase.

Plate 4-100
Inscription dedicated to Isis by the son of Papiris during the reign of Trajan (sometime between AD 113–117). Inscription found in trench BE00-37 Subphase Ib. Each black and white increment on the scale=20 cm. Photograph by S. E. Sidebotham.

Figure 4-101
Inscription dedicated to Isis by the son of Papiris during the reign of Trajan (sometime between AD 113–117). Inscription found in trench BE00-37 Subphase Ib. Drawing by A. M. Hense.

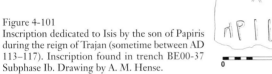

Plates 4-102/103
Duplicate Inscriptions dedicated to Zeus by Philotera during the reign of Nero. From trench BE00-37 Subphase IIa. Each increment on the scale=20 cm. Photograph by S. E. Sidebotham.

Plate 4-104   Trench BE00-37, "grand staircase" *035*. Column capital *047* is left (east) and *048* is on the right (west). Looking south. Scale = 1 m. Photograph by S. E. Sidebotham.

Plate 4-105   Trench BE00-37, "grand staircase" *035*. Stone basin *026* is leaning against wall *027* to the left (east). Looking south. Scale = 1 m. Photograph by S. E. Sidebotham.

Plate 4-106   Stone basin *026* from trench BE00-37 Subphase IIa. Scale = 50 cm. Photograph by S. E. Sidebotham.

Capital *047* flanked the lower step of the staircase to the east, while capital *046* stood in front of the western end of the lower step, probably because installation *045* was already there and the capitals could not be placed symmetrically on each side of the staircase. An additional effect of placing capitals was that a visitor entering the courtyard through the northern doorway would be led toward staircase *035* and from there over threshold *043* and into the southern room. The position of the column capitals underlined that the really important entrance was the one into the southern room.

Immediately west of staircase *035*, atop locus *045*, were three stacks of gypsum ashlars of various shapes and dimensions (*042*). The stacks were deposited later than column capital *046*, as one of the ashlars rested atop it. The stacks were all on top of the blocks in locus *045*, stored here for some unfulfilled purpose. An additional function may have been that the stacks added height to the division of the room already marked by locus *045*.

Leaning against wall *027* was a large gypsum basin *026*, with a semicircular front and a straight back (Figure 4-107 and Plates 4-105 and 4-106). Overall it measured 0.68 x 0.67 x 0.24 m; the circular basin itself measured 0.55–0.58 m in diameter, and was 0.15 m deep. The basin rested on its rounded side on surface *013*. It was, thus, an architectural feature from another context, perhaps lustral and, therefore, likely religious, which had been stored in this room. It may have come from the nearby temple area that had fallen out of use (as had the previously mentioned inscriptions dedicated to Zeus and another, which follows, dedicated to Isis), but it is also an intriguing thought that it might have come from a church in Berenike. A cross-shaped piece of copper found in the tumble layer (locus *008*) just south of wall *027* may hint at a Christian origin.

In the eastern part of the courtyard were two large piles of gypsum blocks, much less organized in their structure than stacks *015* and *016* on locus *042*. Their proximity to the northern doorway suggests that these were the latest gypsum ashlars deposited in the courtyard.

Locus *016* comprised nine high-quality gypsum ashlars, with dimensions ranging from 0.62 x 0.27 x 0.10 m to 0.42 x 0.24 x 0.9 m. One of the blocks preserved cuts suggesting that it came from a doorway. Another block had traces of green paint on it in addition to a pivot hole on its narrow long side, which indicated that the block derived from a doorway. In fact some of the stones in locus *016* might have come from the collapsed doorway part of wall *003*, but it is not possible to determine which stones were piled for storage and which were tumble from the doorway, as the blocks left in the standing part of the doorway had dimensions similar to those of the ashlars in locus *016*. Excavated as part of locus *008*, but clearly associated with locus *016*, was a finely cut block—possibly a base for a statue—that measured 0.52 m x 0.34 m x 0.13 m.

Locus *015* consisted of 13 gypsum ashlars with dimensions ranging from 0.68 x 0.225 x 0.26 m to 0.40 x 0.26 x 0.12 m. The blocks seemed to be piled up toward wall *002*, and were, most likely, put there for storage purposes. The largest of the blocks had an inscription in Greek on one of its long sides, covering parts of four lines. Broken at both ends, the block's extant dimensions were 0.68 m x 0.225 m x 0.26 m. The inscription dated from the reign of Trajan (AD 98–117) when Rutilius Lupus was prefect of Egypt (AD 113–117) and its four lines recorded a dedication to Isis by the son of Papiris who was an interpreter and secretary.

This inscription was obviously put into the building along with the other blocks in locus *016* by someone who had a later use in mind. The blocks were obviously from another, religious, context—they may even have been reused before they ended up in this building. This accords well with the pattern of extensive reuse of building material, especially gypsum ashlars, apparent in much of the late fourth- to fifth-century architecture of Berenike.

Thus, during the late occupational phase in the courtyard, gypsum ashlars and finer architectural features such as the stone basin, two column capitals, and part of an inscribed stone dedication to Isis of the early second century AD were taken from other contexts and placed here partially as additions to the already existing architecture (column capitals *046* and *047* to staircase *035*) or simply for storage (loci *045* and *015*, maybe also part of locus *016*). This building was probably chosen as a storage place because of its proximity to the temple areas, whence most of the blocks probably derived or because the convenient open courtyard was near where the blocks were to be used. There is no evidence of similar storing of gypsum blocks in trenches in the immediate vicinity of trench 37 (BE99/00-28/38, BE00-41, BE98/99-20/27, and BE00-34), perhaps because evidence from these edifices suggests that they were entirely roofed. However, there is evidence for storing similar blocks in trench BE96/97/98-12.*046/167* (see following and Sidebotham 1999:44), located closer to the harbor area.

Trench 38, Phase II: abandonment and collapse
Subphase IIa

The walls collapsed on top of the surfaces and installations described above and covered the entire interior of the courtyard, sloping somewhat from south down toward the north. This collapse locus (*008*) attained a maximum thickness of 0.65 m and consisted mainly of coral heads, bone, shell, and pottery. In the tumble, close to wall *027*, were two more inscribed gypsum blocks (Plates 4-102 and 4-103).

The first inscription measured 0.68 m x 0.18 m x 0.11 m. 0.125 m from the top, the stone narrowed from 0.18 m to 0.145 m at the very top, so that it formed a slightly trapezoidal end. All four surfaces preserved shallow chisel marks, up to 0.09 m long (Plate 4-102). Along the inscribed side was a shallow line in the middle of the stone, possibly intended to center the letters in the inscription. A 25 mm x 35 mm square hole, 0.180 mm from the bottom of the stone, indicated secondary use of the block possibly in a doorway or wall prior to its deposition in trench 37. Thus, the stone may have been taken from a secondary context before it was stored in the building in trench 37. The inscription itself covered 0.41 m of the length of the stone, measured from the top. The lower 0.25 m was anepighraphic. The inscription preserved 12 lines in Greek. On the sixth and seventh lines a name or a title has been chiseled away.

The text on the second inscribed ashlar, smaller than the first, was a duplicate of that on the first one (Plate 4-103). The spelling of one of the words, however, was incorrect in both inscriptions, but they both exhibited different misspellings of the same word. The dimensions of the second stone were 0.44 m x 0.18 m x 0.12 m. It was broken just below the eleventh line of the inscription.

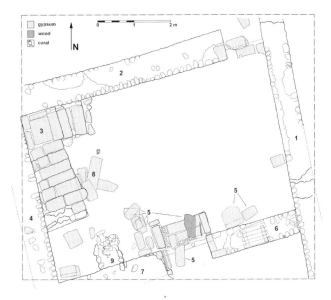

1 = 002   4 = 010   7 = 032
2 = 003   5 = 026   8 = 034
3 = 009   6 = 027   9 = 037

Figure 4-107
Trench BE00-37 plan of Subphases Ib/IIa. Drawing by A. M. Hense.

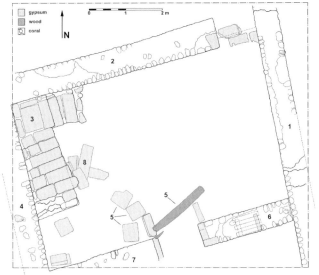

1=002   4=010   7=032
2=003   5=026   8=034
3=009   6=027

Figure 4-108
Trench BE00-37 plan of Subphase IIa. Drawing by A. M. Hense.

The second stone had the same type of trapezoidal tapering of the upper part of the block as did the first block. There was a mid-line also on this block. The text was partially chiseled out, most efficiently toward the bottom, and was, thus, more difficult to read than the text on the first inscription. The name or the title had been chiseled out as well. This text dates to the reign of Nero and, like the one noted preceding, a woman named Philotera dedicated it to Zeus.

These two blocks may have fallen from wall *027* since this was a logical explanation for their presence in the middle of wall tumble. This indicated that they were part of an architectural feature in wall *027* that required gypsum ashlars. Such a feature might have been a niche like those in trenches BE00-38.*030*, BE00-41.*017-022*, and trench BE98/99-22 in the western face of wall *005*. That there was wood preserved in wall *027* might support this interpretation. This is, however, less likely, since the niches known from the other buildings tended to be built of smaller blocks than these two ashlars. Another possibility is that the blocks were part of an *opus Berenikeum* "box" in wall *027*. Judging from the size of the blocks, this is a more likely option. A gypsum ashlar was left in wall *027*, which might have been the lower part of an *opus Berenikeum* feature. This might have been a bit high in the wall for an *opus Berenikeum* feature, but on the other hand we still do not know the floor level of the unexcavated southern room. There is no evidence of niches or of *opus Berenikeum* in wall *032* west of the southern doorway, but this wall was not preserved any higher than wall *027*.

In front of the southern doorway, in the tumble atop staircase *035*, was a large wooden plank, 1.90 m long x 0.27 m wide x 0.10 m thick. This must have been the lintel over the southern doorway. In the same area, in the tumble atop and in front of staircase *035*, was evidence of very decayed matting. This appeared as 20 mm thick sheets of reddish sand at 50-200 mm intervals in the tumble. A 0.50 m broad piece of matting stretched across the room from staircase *035* to wall *003* in the very lowest part of the tumble. This may have been roofing or floor matting. There was similar matting in trenches BE00-41, BE98-20/BE99-27, and in trench BE00-34 (see preceding).

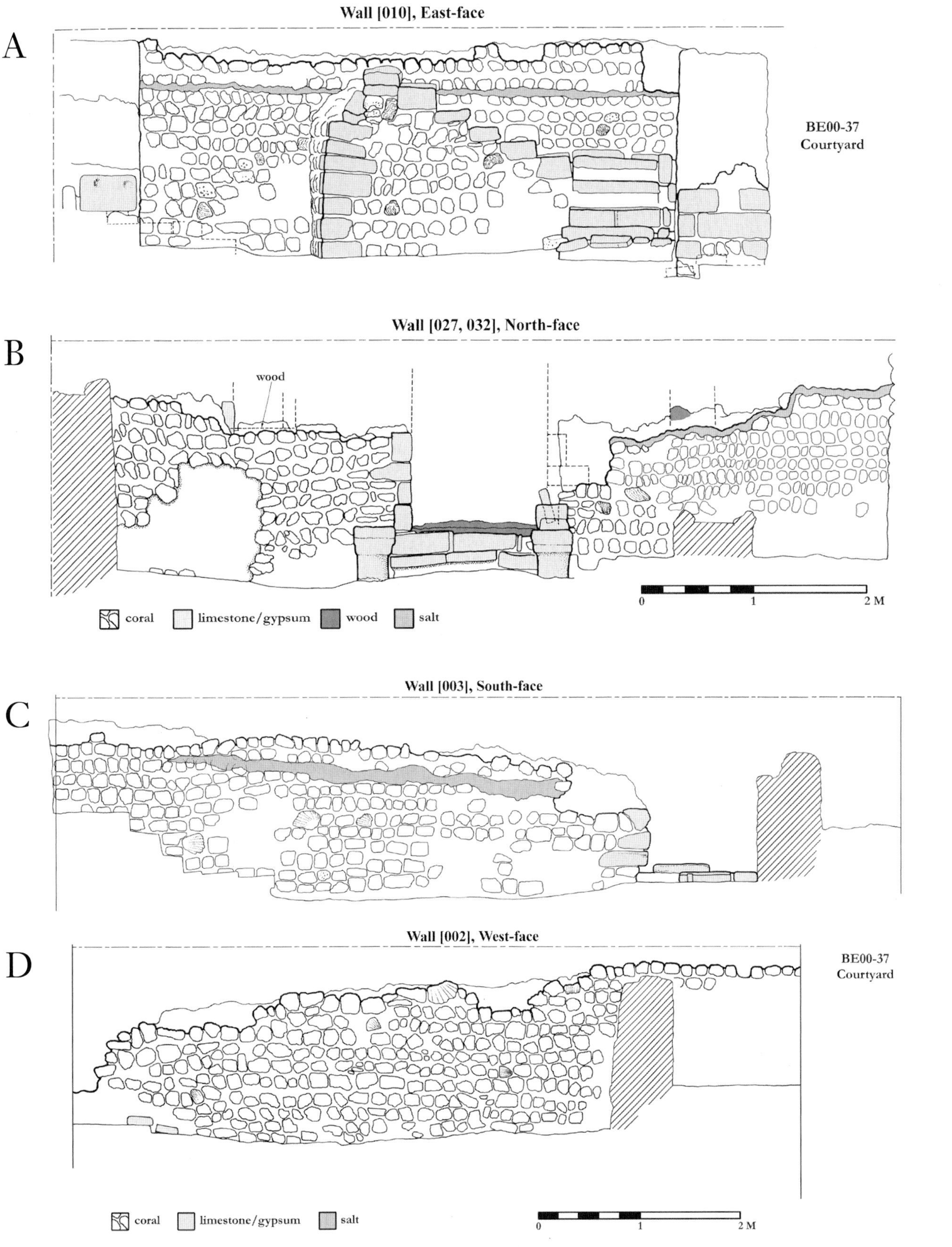

Figure 4-109   Trench BE00-37 wall elevations. A: east (interior) face of wall *010* and staircase *009*; B: north face of wall 027 (left/east) "grand staircase" *035* (center) and wall *032* (right/west); C: south face of northern wall *003* and entrance *022* (to the right/east); D: western (interior) face of wall *002*. Drawing by A. M. Hense.

The matting seemed to be found in areas that may have had light roofing and, thus, such areas in which they have been recovered might be interpreted as courtyards or hallways.

Small finds in tumble *008* included several fine pieces of pottery. Resting on top of staircase *035* was an almost complete ribbed Nile silt amphora, only lacking its base. It dated from the fifth century AD. Close to the large gypsum basin, almost on top of surface *013*, was an Aila/Aqaba amphora, also almost complete, but lacking its base. This amphora also dated to the fifth century AD. Sherds of a large open African Red Slipped (ARS) ware plate with decorated stamps were found scattered in the lower parts of tumble locus *008*. This vessel dated from late fifth to early sixth century AD; a similar fragment of ARS ware was also found in Phase II in trench BE00-38 (see preceding). In the tumble in the area around and over staircase *035* were additional noteworthy shards: an EDW vessel (Chapter 7), Indian fine ware, and Aksumite pottery (Chapter 6).

Five *aes* coins were found in the lower parts of the tumble in loci *006*, *008*, *018*, and *026* (see Chapter 8, catalogue numbers 97–101). One was an unidentifiable late fourth-century specimen (catalogue number 98) and the other a mid to second half of the first century AD *aes* (catalogue number 97); the remaining coins were unidentifiable, although one of these had been halved (catalogue number 101), suggesting a lengthy circulation life.

Staircase *009* collapsed after most of the walls had fallen into the building. The gypsum blocks forming the upper four steps and the upper three corner ashlars in the staircase core collapsed and landed in a somewhat odd position east of the staircase. The only reasonable explanation is that they slid on top of other tumble, probably the coral heads and windblown sand in locus *031*. Locus *031* probably represented late coral-head tumble, containing less wall material and more windblown sand. Excavations documented pieces of wood in locus *008* close to staircase *009*. These might have derived from a wooden staircase railing similar to one postulated in trench BE00-38.*009*, where there were bronze nails that might have supported a railing.

There was also wall collapse outside the excavated room. North of wall *003* was wall tumble in partially excavated locus *017*. The tumble consisted of coral heads and wall material such as sand, bone, and pottery. East of wall *002* was wall tumble in locus *018*, which had the same composition as loci *008* and *017*.

Loci *025* and *029* were the crumbled top parts of walls *027* and *032* respectively. They consisted of coral heads and wall binding material.

Sub-phase IIb

After the walls had collapsed, the building was filled with fine, windblown sand (locus *006*). In the southern part of the trench were traces of decayed matting, which may have either been for roofing or flooring similar to those found in locus *008*.

During the period when the sand blew into the ruined structure, two occupational fires were kindled in the shelter of the courtyard. Nondiagnostic pottery was associated with one of the campfires.

Excavations in *006* recovered two pieces of early Roman glass. A similar piece was found in trench BE00-34.*008*. These pieces were obviously residual and somehow must have been deposited in the deserted building.

Loci *023* and *028* represented wall collapse atop the windblown sand in locus *006*. They were both located south of the courtyard, locus *023* in the west and locus *028* in the east. The wall tumble atop the windblown sand indicated that walls *002* and *010* were higher in the southern part of the courtyard than in the northern part. The matting in locus *006* suggested, possibly, that the roofing here was also preserved for a longer period of time than in the rest of the room. The taller walls of the building's upper floor may have supported the putative roof over the unexcavated southern room. The courtyard was most likely open and had no upper floor and perhaps no roof or one made only of light materials. There was no evidence of wooden beams that might have carried a floor, but instead there was plenty of matting that might have indicated light roofing.

On top of the windblown sand were layers of decayed gypsum and sand, which dominated the surface layers in the area. There was also windblown sand outside the courtyard and in the partially excavated southern room, loci *005* and *030*, respectively. Excavations recovered part of a stone figurine in locus *005* outside wall *003*.

Discussion

Trench BE00-37 uncovered a courtyard in a building located close to and east of the Serapis temple. Proximity to the latter or to other, as yet unlocated, cult centers, may be part of the reason why two inscribed blocks were apparently incorporated into the building itself;

blocks stored and most likely intended for reuse seem to have stemmed from a monumental and, at least in some cases, religious contexts. Many of the stones appear to have been reused at least once prior to deposition in this structure.

The courtyard may have had a light mat roof. Staircase *009* led either to a solid roof or to an upper floor over the unexcavated southern room. Staircase *035* marked the entrance from the courtyard into the main building, which was probably located in the southern unexcavated room. Staircase *035* led to a level 0.53 m higher than the top level of locus *013*, the latest occupational surface in the courtyard. This explains why there had to be four more steps on staircase *009* so that it could reach the roof or the upper floor of the building, which must have been quite high above the floor level of the courtyard.

Future excavation of the occupational layers in the courtyard should determine whether the preliminary interpretation of the room as a courtyard is correct. Furthermore, the southern room should be excavated in order to examine the true floor level there in order to calculate the height of the walls in the building's ground floor and of staircase *009*, and to establish the building's function in the larger environment of late Roman Berenike.

4.5.5   TRENCH BE00-41
Trench supervisor: C. Fritz
Figures/Plates 4-110 to 4-116

Trench BE00-41 measured 6.00 m N-S x 6.50 m E-W with grid coordinates 556–562 m N/2057.5–2064 m E (Figure 4-110 and Plates 4-111 to 4-113). It was positioned approximately 80 m north of the *decumanus maximus* on the western side of a secondary *kardo* and across the street from the buildings exposed in trenches BE98-20/BE99-27 and BE99-28/BE00-38. Its position was determined according to surface coral mounds, which formed a roughly rectangular shape, suggesting a building in this area.

The immediate goals of this trench were the identification of the dates and function of this structure, which will be completed only with future excavations. The long-term goals include the possible identification of the Ptolemaic period shoreline and a further understanding of the municipal plan and economic function of this area of ancient Berenike in the fourth and fifth centuries AD. Excavations in 2000 produced two phases, one of which had five subphases. No occupation levels were reached and all phases/subphases were late fourth to fifth century AD.

Phase I: Primary architecture (before late fourth century AD)

Phase II: Abandonment, architectural decay and collapse (fifth century AD)

Subphase IIa: earliest decay and collapse

Subphase IIb: More architectural collapse

Subphase IIc: Windblown sand

Subphase IId: Wall render and decayed organic material

Subphase IIe: Topsoil

Trench 41, Phase I
Primary architecture (before late fourth century AD)

Although excavations were not completed this season, Phase I contained a substantial amount of architecture, primarily comprising a small, niche-lined room. The walls within BE00-41 comprised primarily coral heads bonded with a mortar of light gray-brown clay containing 15 percent inclusions, including small coral pieces, shell, bone, and pottery (cf. walls in BE00-37 preceding). Gypsum ashlars appeared as quoins and stairs. Where both faces were exposed, the walls were 0.45–0.60 m wide. Walls survived at elevations of 4.00–4.15 m asl. The construction technique, materials, and position above sea level were comparable to those in other structures in this area, which were identified as late fourth- to fifth-century AD commercial and domestic edifices.

Most of the trench consisted of a room with internal dimensions 5.35 m E-W x 2.90 m N-S; the northeastern corner of the room was in the northeastern corner of the trench. At the end of the excavation season, the walls were exposed to a height of 1.00 to 1.50 m. The entrance to the room was in the southwest corner. The southern end of the eastern face of the room's west wall (*007*) formed the western edge of the doorway.

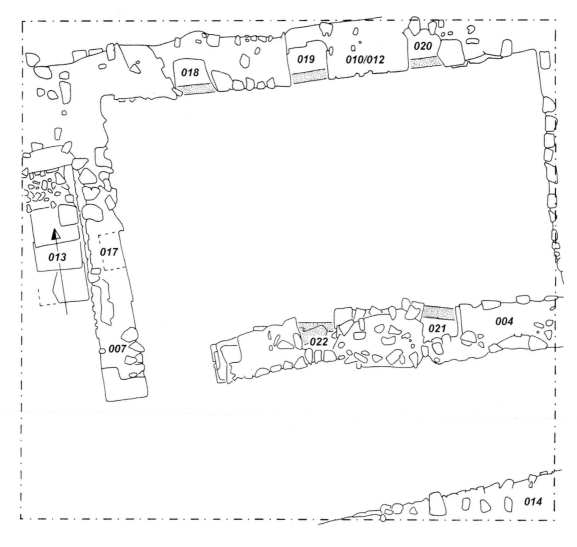

Figure 4-110 Trench BE00-41 plan. Drawing by H. Barnard.

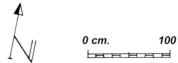

0 cm. 100

Plate 4-111
Trench BE00-41, looking northeast. Staircase *013* is
visible in front (west) of N-S wall *017* (left on photo).
Top left is E-W wall (*010/012*) with niches *018*, *019*
and *020*. Wall *011* in the east balk has no niches. For
a view of the inside face of wall *004* (with niche *017*)
see Plates 4-112 and 4-113. For a view of wall *007*
(with niches *021* and *022*) see Plate 4-113. Scale = 1
m. Photograph by S. E. Sidebotham.

Plate 4-112   Trench BE00-41, looking northwest. N-S wall at the top with niche *017* is *007*. The E-W wall to the right (*010/012*) contains niches *018*, *019* and *020*. E-W wall *004* in the middle of the photo contains niches *021* and *022*. Wall *011* in the east balk (to the right) has no niches. Scale = 1 m. Photograph by S. E. Sidebotham.

Plate 4-113   Trench BE00-41, looking southwest. N-S wall at the top with niche *017* is *007*. The E-W wall to the left contains niches *021* and *022*. Wall *010/012* in the north balk (to the right) contains niches *018*, *019* and *020*. Wall *011* in the east balk (to the bottom left) has no niches. Scale=1 m. Photograph by S. E. Sidebotham.

The eastern face of this wall measured 3.50 m N-S with gypsum ashlar quoins at the southern end. Niche *017* was centered in the eastern face, 1.50 m from either end. At its northern end *007* met the southern face of wall *010/012*, which formed the northern side of the room and was 5.35 m E-W. This face contained three niches of similar construction to *017*, spaced evenly in it. The northern face of *010/012* was unexcavated due to its proximity to the northern balk, which it met 2 m from the northeastern corner of the trench. At its eastern end *010/012* met wall *011*, which formed the eastern side of the room and measured 2.90 m N-S; only the western face of this wall was within the trench. The southern end of *011* met wall *004*, which measured 4.10 m E-W and contained two niches similar to others in the room. Gypsum ashlars with wooden leveling courses formed quoins at the western end of *004;* they also comprised the eastern edge of the doorway.

On both the eastern and western sides of the doorway the ashlars preserved holes approximately 0.10 x 0.10 m at 3.60 m asl, presumably for some portion of a door mechanism. Excavations recovered a worked gypsum block with a cone-shaped indentation in the doorway; this may also have been part of a door mechanism, perhaps a door pivot.

Parallel to the southern face of *004*, coral-head wall *014* ran along the southern balk. These walls together formed a corridor 1.60 m wide N-S, which presumably

opened onto the *kardo* immediately to the east. Wall *014* and tumble loci north of it ended 3 m from the eastern balk, adjacent to the western end of *004* and the doorway, suggesting that *014* and the corridor ended at this point.

Six niches adorned three of the four wall faces within the small room (Figure 4-110 and Plates 4-111 to 4-116). Niche *017* in wall *007* was the best preserved (Figure 4-114, top, niche 1 and Plates 4-111, 4-112, and 4-116). Its discussion will serve as the model for the other five, as they seem to have originally been identical. Niche *017* was centered in the eastern face of wall *007*, 1.50 m from either end, and the bottom was 3.66 m asl. The base of the niche comprised wooden slats, approximately 0.10 x 0.10 x 0.30 m long, that extended into the wall, lining the base of the niche on both sides. A wooden ledge 0.10–0.20 m wide with a lip approximately 0.05 m high ran between the beams and flush with the wall face to form the eastern edge of the bottom of the niche. The lip was centered on the ledge lengthwise. Within the bottom of the niche was surface (*023*) made of unidentified material, which although unexcavated, contained fragments of iron and bronze. Above the beams were three courses of gypsum ashlars approximately 0.20 m wide x 0.10 m thick, and of varying lengths placed horizontally with the short side flush with the wall face. The longer edge of these formed the eastern and western sides of the niches.

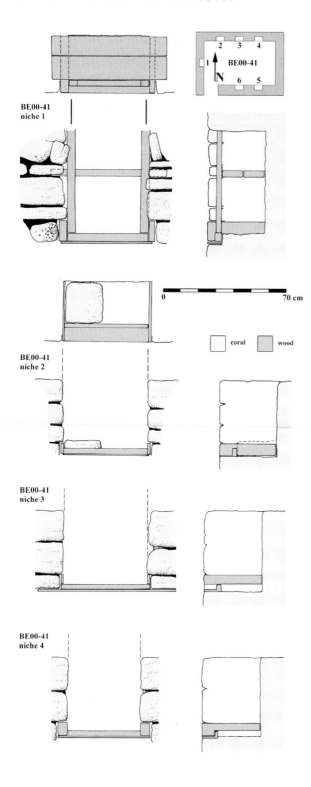

Figure 4-114   Location of four of the six niches in trench BE00-41. Elevations and sections of niches 1=*017*, 2=*018*, 3=*019* and 4=*020*. Drawing by A. M. Hense.

Above the horizontal ashlars, 0.30 m above the bottom of the niche, was a wooden shelf constructed with two planks, each 0.13 m wide x 0.04 m thick and of an unknown length. These extended beyond the sides of the niche into the walls between the third and fourth ashlar courses. On the shelf was a surface (*024*) identical to the one in the bottom of the niche; this remained unexcavated. In the southwestern corner of the shelf was a mound of resinous substance approximately 250 mm x 250 mm and 30 mm high. Some traces of plaster survived in the areas where the shelf met the side of the niche. Above the shelf the niche was constructed of single ashlars placed vertically on either side. Only the bottom portion of these survived. The niche, 0.20 m above the shelf, and the wall around it were only preserved as a layer of wall tumble and decay. In the ceiling area of the niche were fibers within the wall matrix. Whether this represented the original ceiling of the niche or was part of wall decay is unclear. The tops were not preserved in any of the other five niches within the room. The rear face of the niche was not well preserved and may originally have consisted of wall matrix material; the seemingly intact sides of the niche showed no signs of any surfacing besides the matrix used in the walls, which may also have served as wall render. Some of wall *007* may have collapsed into the niche, since one large coral head and wall matrix were excavated from the bottom of the niche.

Excavations recovered badly deteriorated wooden planks with maximum extant widths of 0.07 m along the northern and southern front edges of the niche. These together with the bottom wooden ledge originally formed a wooden frame around the niche.

The other five niches in the room were less well preserved, but seem to have originally been identical to *017*. Locus *018*, the easternmost niche in the southern face of wall *010/012* began 0.90 m from the western end of the inner wall face and 4.10 m from the eastern end. At its lowest point, *018* was 3.69 m asl and preserved for a height of 3–3.5 ashlar courses. The wooden beams were partially preserved along either edge, as were the front ledge and lip. Surface *025*, similar to loci *023* and *024*, also survived in the bottom of *018*; it was also unexcavated. Niche *018* had a depth of 0.36 cm.

Central niche *019* in the southern face of wall *010/012* was 2.40 m from the western end, 2.50 m from the eastern end of the wall, and was 0.45 m wide E-W. The bottom of *019* was 3.62 m asl. Only remnants of the wooden side beams and the front ledge survived in this niche. It was excavated to a depth of 0.42 m N-S.

Niche *020* was 3.85 m from the eastern end and 1.05 m from the western end of the southern face of wall *010/012* This niche contained tumble and, as a result, remained unexcavated because the tumble seemed to be collapse from the unexcavated northern face of the wall (behind the niche). In *020* the wooden ledge, lip, and western side beam were especially well preserved. In the western side beam, 0.05 m from the end flush with the wall face, a notch cut in the bottom of the beam fit the lip of the niche. The lip in this niche was preserved 0.05 m wide N-S. This feature was not preserved in the other five niches, but this technique was presumably used in their construction as well. In abandonment locus *009*, a wooden plank 0.60 m long x 0.10 m wide x 0.03–0.04 m thick was found directly south of and beneath niche *020*. This was probably originally part of the niche, possibly the shelf, as the dimensions correspond to shelves in niches *017* and *022* (see following). In the area immediately surrounding the plank were a few coral cobbles and two gypsum ashlars. These, together with the plank, presumably represent a small episode of tumble from the niche area.

Eastern niche *021* in the northern face of wall *004* was 2.70 m from the western end of the wall and 1.15 m from the eastern end. Its bottom was 3.48 m asl. It seemed to be of identical construction to the others. The wooden ledge, lip, and side beams were partially preserved.

Niche *022* was the western one of two in the northern face of *004*. Its western edge was 1.10 m from the wall's western end, its eastern edge 2.90 m from the eastern end and separated from the western edge of *021* by 1.15 m. The bottom of niche *022* was 3.48 m asl. Wooden side beams, ledge, lip, side framing, and shelf were partially preserved in this niche. The side framing was preserved as wood decayed to powder in the sand along the sides of the niche. The wooden shelf was preserved 0.30 m above the bottom of the niche, broken by the collapse of the vertical ashlar that formed the eastern side of the niche above the shelf. Because this shelf was partially broken, the construction technique could be seen. The 0.04 m thick plank was visible between the coral courses in the southern face of wall *004* adjacent to where it protruded into the niche on the southern side; clearly, the shelf was built into the wall.

All six niches received first-aid conservation of 15 percent Paraloid B72 in acetone and 10–20 percent PVA in water until they could be photographed and drawn.

Between the western face of *007* and the western balk were remains of a staircase (*013*) 0.60 m wide E-W

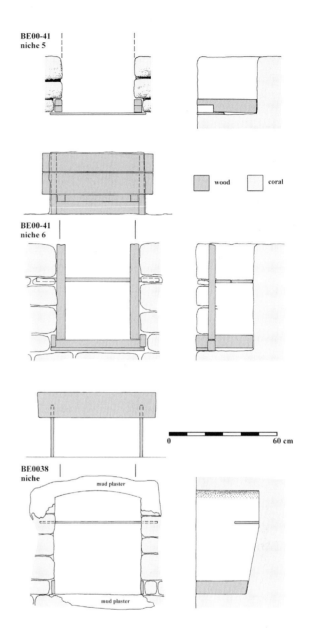

Figure 4-115   Elevations and sections of niches 5=*021* and 6=*022* in trench BE00-41, in comparison to the construction of the niche in trench BE00-38 (Plate 4-81). Drawing by A. M. Hense.

(Plate 4-111). Staircase *013* was constructed of gypsum ashlars. The highest stair was 3.87 m asl, and was 0.60 m E-W x 0.45 m N-S x 0.10 m thick. South of the first stair was a second 3.68 m asl, which was 0.60 m E-W x 0.35 m N-S. A third, partially broken stair was 3.54 m asl and was 0.51 m E-W x 0.38 m N-S. Excavation of the staircase was not completed this season, but, presumably, it continued down toward the south. North of the uppermost-preserved stair was a fill section 1.0 m high containing wall render, shell, pottery, and ashlar blocks; the same fill appeared among the three preserved stairs. There did not appear to be a wall west of the staircase, suggesting that another room opened to the west, beyond the trench balk, similar to the staircase in trench BE99-28/BE00-38, which was located on the eastern side of the same *kardo* as BE00-41. A construction parallel between the staircase in trench BE99-28.*043*/BE00-38.*009* and BE00-41.*013* seems likely, as the trench 28/38 building contained walls of identical construction to those in the small room of trench 41.

In the midst of architectural collapse three small fires (loci *028–030*) separated compositionally identical architectural tumble loci *027* and *031*. These fires and the resulting ash debris represented a brief period of transitory use of the building during the abandonment phase. Locus *031* continued over the entire trench, and its excavation was not completed this season.

Plate 4-116   Niche *017* (1 in Figure 114). Scale 20 cm. Photograph by S. E. Sidebotham.

Trench 41, Phase II
Abandonment and architectural decay and collapse (fifth century AD).

Phase II had five subphases:

Subphase IIa

This season excavations recovered approximately 1.50 m of architectural and windblown debris from BE 00-41. Subphase IIa in the earliest levels of loose sand excavations uncovered substantial amounts of decayed matting concentrated in the lowest 0.05–0.10 m of locus *009* and the upper 0.05 m of loci *015* and *027*. The matting had deteriorated to a reddish powder, but in areas the layers were thick enough to be identified.

Decayed matting was found in the corridor between the southern face of wall *004* and the northern face of wall *014*, sloping toward the north and continuing over the top of *004*, 0.75 m west of the eastern balk. Concentrations continued north of *004* in the area west of wall *011*. The position of the matting remained directly above and within late architectural tumble loci, suggesting that it may have been part of the construction of the building, possibly part of the roof.

Subphase IIb

Below windblown sand were layers of architectural collapse, primarily composed of 40 percent coral-head cobbles; 20 percent bone, shell, and pottery inclusions; and the rest a red-brown clayey sand matrix.

Sub-phase IIc

Beneath subsoil was approximately 1.00 m of windblown sand (loci *005* and *009*), interrupted by two late tumble episodes, loci *006* and *008*, along eastern wall *011* and western wall *007*.

Subphase IId

Earlier than this was a subsoil layer of decayed gypsum, wall render and sand containing decayed organic material 0.05 m thick in the areas above the walls, to 0.10 m thick toward the center of the trench.

Subphase IIe

Topsoil was a layer of windblown sand approximately 0.05 m thick.

Discussion

Although excavations were not completed in BE00-41 during the 2000 season, some conclusions can be made about its contents. The presence of a staircase signaled that this building was originally at least two stories high. There was no structure abutting the western side of the staircase, suggesting that, as in BE00-38, an open room lay to the west. This indicated that the room excavated in BE00-41 was part of a larger structure.

The room with niches had no door leading from the *kardo*; rather, it was accessed via a corridor. The door leading from the corridor into the room with multiple niches possibly had a locking mechanism. This suggested while the corridor itself had no commercial function that the multiniched room did. Though little evidence was forthcoming from the corridor or the multiniched room, the presence of a stone staircase west of the corridor and room indicated an upper storey, probably over the still unexcavated room west of the corridor and multiniched room. By analogy with other edifices in the neighborhood, it could be postulated that this upper floor probably, like its contemporaries elsewhere in this late Roman quarter, also served a domestic-residential function.

4.6   THE NORTHEAST QUARTER
Late Roman Building, Trench BE99-26;
Basilica (Putative Ecclesiastical Building),
Trenches BE98/99-22, BE99/00-30, and
BE00-39

4.6.1   TRENCH BE99-26
Trench supervisor: J.E.M.F. Bos
Figures/Plates 4-117 to 4-122

This late Roman building of unknown function was excavated on the northeastern side of the site. Trench BE99-26 was a 9 m N-S x 4 m E-W trench with grid coordinates 622.5-631.5 N/2158.5–2162.5 E. The height of the trench datum was 2.04 m asl. BE99-26 was situated in the northeastern corner of one of the larger buildings on the northeastern part of the site, marked as Mound B on the 1996 site survey plan. The structure was erected close to the sea just southeast of Building F (trenches BE95-4, BE95/96-7, and BE97/98-17). The wall outlines, as they appeared from the surface, suggested the presence of several large rooms along the north-south axis of the building (Figure 4-117 and Plates 4-118 and 4-119).

The aim during the 1999 season was to excavate at least two rooms and expose both the northern and eastern outer walls of the building to determine its function and its relationship to the surrounding area. Excavations exposed eight phases of activity, including three building phases. The latter comprised two large buildings in the area and one modification of the latest building. The phasing at the end of the 1999 season (excavations did not continue here in 2000) was as follows:

Phase I: Dumping: (fourth possibly to late fourth century AD)
Phase II: Earliest "conglomerate" building (late fourth to early fifth century AD)
Phase III: Dumping layers (fourth to fifth century AD)
Phase IV: Building B earliest phase (late fourth to fifth century AD and later)
Phase V: Fill deposits (fifth century AD)
Phase VI: Building phase (fifth century AD)
Phase VII: Abandonment and collapse (later fifth century AD)
Phase VIII: Washed/blown-in sand (after late fifth century AD)

The results of the 1999 season excavations revealed a significant amount of activity in this area of Berenike in late antiquity. Walls were often broken down, building blocks reused in the next building phase and, in a short period of time, several changes in use of the area occurred. Building F also exhibited this type of remodeling. Building F was a series of edifices whose specific functions remain enigmatic, but which are believed to have been public in nature. The stratification in both areas (Building F and Building B in Mound B) was very similar; in the upper strata excavations revealed several layers of architectural debris coming down on the floors of virtually empty buildings, beneath which were several rapidly changing phases of occupation. Building B in Mound B was situated approximately 10 m southeast of Building F. One of the questions posed by excavation was the relationship between activities taking place here and in Building F.

Trench 26, Phase I
The earliest phase excavated (fourth possibly to late fourth century AD) comprised layers of a large dump or fill mainly of pottery and some pieces of bone of the fourth, possibly late fourth century AD. The loci excavated included *041*, *042*, *049*, and *052*, all dark-brown sediments with a high density of finds and loosely compacted soil. This phase will be examined more fully in the future since this season only a maximum of about 10 cm of it were excavated.

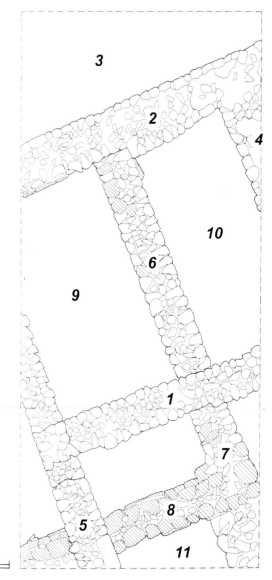

Figure 4-117
Trench BE99-26 plan of all phases. Drawing by J. E. M. F. Bos.

1=*010*	6=*032a*
2=*012*	7=*032b*
3=*014*	8=*036*
4=*018*	9=*051*
5=*020*	10=*053*
	11=*055*

Plate 4-118
Trench BE99-26, looking north. Small boxed walls in foreground (southern end of trench) are clockwise from bottom: *036*, *020*, *010*, and *032b*, northern extension of *032b* (beneath wall *010*) is *032a*, which intersects EW wall *012* (at top of photo/northern end of trench). Wall *018* intersects the eastern end of *012* and continues into the eastern balk. Scale=1 m. Photograph by S. E. Sidebotham.

Plate 4-119   Trench BE99-26, looking south. E-W wall in the foreground (northern end of trench) is *012*. To its left and intersecting with it is N-S wall *018* (continues in balk). Parallel to *018* to its right (west) is N-S wall *032a*, which intersects wall *010* at the top of the photo. Scale=1 m. Photograph by S. E. Sidebotham.

By the end of the 1999 season, excavations reached approximately 0.70 m asl in the southern area of the trench.

The loose compaction of these sediments made the layers above very unstable, and holes approximately 10 cm in diameter formed when walking on its surface, showing the sherds of pottery in the dump below that were stacked on top of each other. These loci will be newly exposed in some future season.

Trench 26, Phase II

The earliest building found thus far was constructed atop the Phase I dump apparently sometime in the late fourth to early fifth century AD (Figure 4-120). The outlines of this edifice differed from the configurations of the walls seen on the present ground surface. Its walls were in a different position than the walls of later Building B. The bottoms of the walls were not fully exposed as their foundations continued down into the Phase I dump beneath. Phase II included walls *032* and *036* in the southern and central parts and *012* in the western half of the trench together with surfaces *051*, *053*, *050*, *048*, and *055*.

The largest wall uncovered was *032*, running roughly southeast to northwest in the trench. Two other walls crossed this one from northeast to southwest: *036* in the southern area and *012* in the northern part of the trench. The position of surface *053* on the eastern side of the wall *032a* (the northern end of wall *032*)

suggested that walls *012* and *036* continued toward the east creating another room for this building, but excavations in 1999 could not confirm this. Wall *036*'s eastward continuation fell outside the area covered by the trench; wall *012* was reused in a later construction phase and was built over with different blocks covering up the putative older wall.

The walls were built of two different types of stones: coral heads and a conglomerate type of stone of a bluish color found in the vicinity of Berenike. This stone was in very poor condition when uncovered, but seemed to have formed strong blocks when used in antiquity since it had primarily been found atop sea wall BE98-17.*110/116/125* and wall BE99-22.*083*. The blocks used in this building in BE99-26 may well have been reused from one or both of those structures. Evidence from trenches BE97/98-17 and BE95/96-7 showed that these walls were sometimes robbed out and building stones removed, possibly for use elsewhere on site.

Excavations revealed foundations on the southern side of wall *032* made of large coral chunks randomly thrown into the area to harden the surface. A mortar-like material formed a matrix among the coral chunks. These foundations appeared to be approximately 0.90 m wide while wall *032* itself was 0.60 m wide. The wide foundation prevented the wall from sinking into the soil below.

Wall *036* was about 0.60 m wide supported by foundations approximately 0.80 m wide made of conglomerate stones. In fact, *036* had many more conglomerate stones in it than *032* and *012* and seems to have been filled in the center with small coral heads. Wall *032* was mostly built of coral heads although it also contained quantities of building blocks made of conglomerate "stone." Wall *012*, or at least the western part of that wall in the trench, preserved what appears to be a horizontal variation of *opus Berenikeum* that was also attested in trenches BE98-20.*019* (Sidebotham 2000b: 108-109), BE99-27.*012/013*, and BE99-28.*020/030*/BE00-38.*005* (see preceding). At other places the wall comprised flat conglomerate slabs stacked atop one another with a mortar-like bonding substance a few centimeters thick. This technique was attested in the center of wall *012*.

Wall *032* seems to have been constructed first with wall *012* built up against it. This could be surmised from the fact that part of wall *032* was incorporated inside wall *012*'s reuse (in the later building B), showing a clear construction break in the later wall.

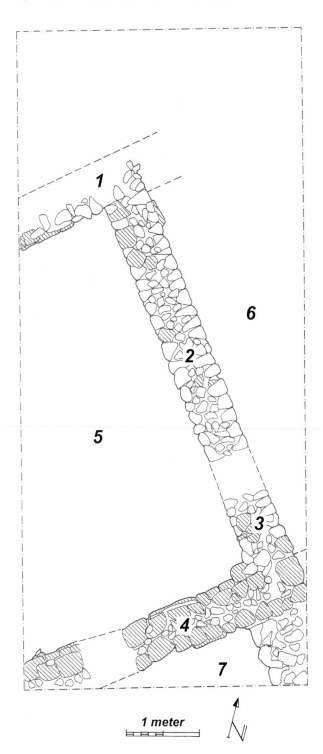

1 = 012   3 = 032b   5 = 051   7 = 055
2 = 032a   4 = 036   6 = 053

Figure 4-120   Trench BE99-26 plan of Phase II. Drawing by J.E.M.F. Bos.

The coarse surfaces associated with this building were made of a soft light light-gray mortar-like substance also found in the packing of the walls. The surfaces had small coral chunks as inclusions, were often uneven, and preserved evidence of having been repaired several times. The use layers inside this building were *043, 045, 038, 039, 054, 046, 047,* and *037.* These loci preserved various small ash deposits, but no other finds were uncovered from these thin strata that might have revealed the function of the building. Bone and pottery were the best represented finds in these layers. Strata *046* and *047* will be excavated in some future season. The thickness of the layers and repairs of the surfaces indicate that most activity occurred in the southern room of this building, which fell almost completely outside the trench.

Trench 26, Phase III
This phase revealed dumping activity in the area after the previous conglomerate building phase had ended with the partial collapse of the structure (fourth to fifth century AD). Most dump layers occurred atop surfaces *051* and *053* in the center of the trench in order to level the area for subsequent building. Inside the loosely compacted layers of this phase (*035, 033, 034, 044,* and *040*) were some building blocks; the finds were mostly pottery and bone. Building B, as discerned from present-day ground level, lay atop these fill and use layers of the conglomerate structure.

Trench 26, Phase IV
The earliest construction phase of Building B (late fourth to fifth century AD and later) in the trench preserved two rooms along the north-south axis of the edifice. In the northeastern corner, the northern doorway was just outside the trench; the entrance to the southern room also lay outside the trench. On the western side of the trench, the sediment layers sloped down slightly, and wall *012* was damaged as well in that area, indicating that the position of the doorway was in the northwestern corner of the room just outside the area encompassed by the trench.

The walls associated with this building phase were *010, 012, 018,* and *020.* Walls *010* and *012* were oriented east northeast-west southwest while *018* and *020* ran northwest to southeast and were perpendicular to walls *010* and *012* (Figure 4-121). Walls *012* and *018* were the two outer walls of the building, and *010* and *020* were interior walls separating different areas or

1 meter

N

rooms. Although *018* was only partially exposed in the eastern part of the trench, it could be discerned that this was unusually thick as was *012*. Wall *012* was almost 0.90 m wide at some points whereas walls *010* and *020* had average widths of about 0.60 m.

Wall *012* clearly showed several modifications including the reuse of other walls. As in the previous building in the area, the conglomerate building phase (Phase II) was broken down to prepare the area for a different structure and, as a result, several parts of the earlier walls were reused. The western part of wall *012* functioned in Phase II completely and was modified in this phase with the addition of coral heads on the top. In the center of *012* the northern part of earlier wall *032* (*032a*; Phase II) was also left standing, while the rest of this wall running roughly north-south was broken down. The eastern face of *012* was then added to the remains of the earlier walls forming the outer wall of the building. The southern face of *012* revealed construction breaks of different wall parts used in its erection while coral heads completely covered the northern face; no construction breaks could be seen there. This northern wall face, however, formed the outer face of the building and was, thus, strengthened by an extra row of coral heads as this side of the edifice suffered most from the powerful and prevailing northerly winds at Berenike.

Most parts of walls *012* and *032* comprised coral heads with some ashlars inside; they appeared to lack foundations. Over time they sank approximately 0.20 m. Wall *020* was built first, and *010* was built abutting *020*. That may be the reason why parts of *032* were not reused inside wall *010* as was the case with *032* in wall *012*. Wall *010* may have been planned later.

Surfaces associated with this phase (*025, 028, 030, 026,* and *031*) comprised fine, white, beaten plaster with some coral inclusions, potsherds, and bone. These surfaces were much finer than those in the previous building phase and after deposition of some use layers, like *027*, mostly in the center area of the trench, surface *025* was repaired up against the walls where most use-sediment was deposited as surfaces *026* and *031*.

Phase IV occupation layers were all brown sand loci *022, 024, 027,* and *029*. Surface *025* had some ashy spots mostly in the center of the northern room. The area was very clean and, apart from approximately 0.05 m of soil, not much was left indicating this phase's use. Excavation in loci *022, 024, 027,* and *029* produced quantities of glass, stone beads, and gemstones, and, in *022*, an Aksumite-style pot handle (cf. Chapter 6,

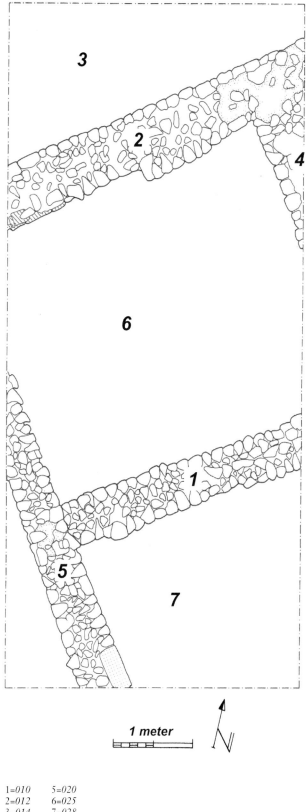

1 meter

1=*010*	5=*020*
2=*012*	6=*025*
3=*014*	7=*028*
4=*018*	

Figure 4-121   Trench BE99-26 plan of Phase IV. Drawing by J. E. M. F. Bos.

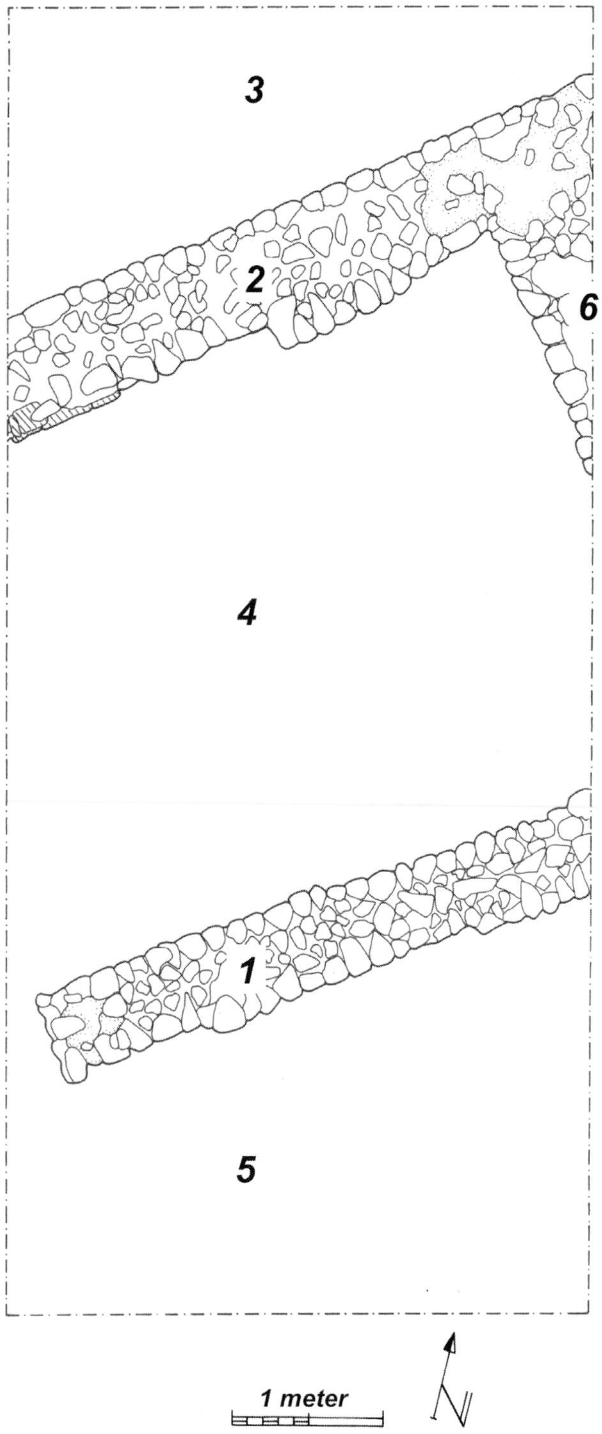

1=*010*   4=*015*
2=*012*   5=*017*
3=*014*   6=*018*

Figure 4-122   Trench BE99-26 plan of Phase IV. Drawing by J. E. M. F. Bos.

catalogue number 6). There was, however, no clear indication that jewelrymaking took place here. Most activity, whatever it may have entailed, went on in the center of the trench between walls *012* and *010* in the northeastern room of building B.

Trench 26, Phase V
Fill loci *019*, *021*, and *023* comprised the next phase of deposition in the area south of wall *010* (fifth century AD). These loci raised the area to the height of the central zone before the surfaces of the next building phase were put down and the building was remodeled. The fill layers contained some coral blocks and quantities of bone and pottery.

Trench 26, Phase VI
This latest building phase (fifth century AD), which included walls *010*, *012*, and *018*, was remodeled at this time. The entrances to the two rooms in the northeastern corner of the building were enlarged due to almost complete demolition of wall *020* on the northern and the southern side of wall *010*. Only a small part of wall *020* remained, forming a face on the western end of wall *010* (Figure 4-122).

Methods used to remodel coral-head walls *010* and *020* revealed how they were constructed. First, the wall faces seemed to have been erected using triangular-shaped coral heads; the interiors of the walls were then filled with a rubble core of smaller-shaped coral pieces. Wall *010* postdated wall *020* and abutted wall *020*. When at a later date wall *020* was broken down, that part remaining formed a face at the end of wall *010* on the western side, but not at the northern or southern sides of wall *010*. There the faces of the wall were improvised: coral heads covered with plaster.

The entrance to the northern room, and probably also to the southern room, was enlarged considerably, leaving only a cross wall parallel to wall *012* to differentiate between both areas. There was no doorway in this new wall *012*.

The surfaces associated with remodeled Building B were *015* and *017*, two light yellowish-brown layers of a beaten-down mortarlike material. Excavation of these surfaces recovered only sherds from vessels that seem to have been crushed by the collapsing walls. No other finds associated with these surfaces provided any information on the use or function of these rooms.

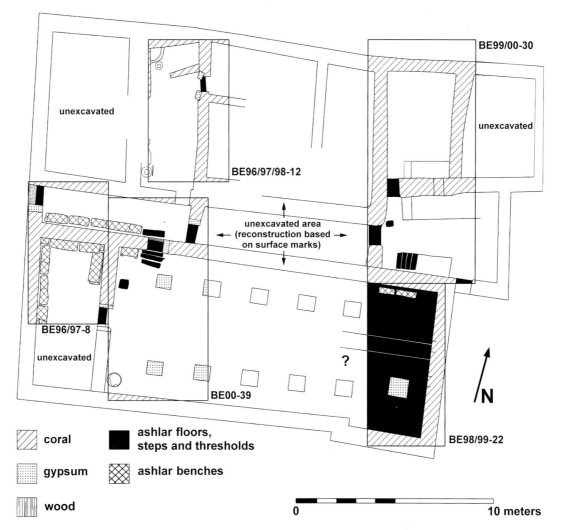

Figure 4-123   Plan of the trenches excavated in the basilica or putative Christian ecclesiastical area (BE96-8, BE96/97/98-12, BE98/99-22, BE99/00-30, and BE00-39). Drawing by A. M. Hense.

Trench 26, Phase VII
Atop this collapse phase of the building were a few salt-concreted loci (*001, 003, 004, 008,* and *TC*) of washed-in and windblown sand (deposited after the late fifth century AD). These layers were almost sterile and contained only some pottery flakes.

Discussion
Excavations in trench BE99-26 exposed two separate buildings close to the sea on the northeastern part of the site. In approximately 0.20 m deposited before the buildings collapsed or were reused, sediments revealed several modifications and reuse of walls or parts of walls.

Excavations uncovered no finds on surfaces associated with these building phases that shed light on their use or function. Of course, this is to be expected in an area that was remodeled several times. As the walls

were removed or broken down and the area leveled for a different building or modification, objects, or installations that related to the previous activity in the area would have been cleared away.

The position of Building B, close to building F, and the layout of the walls in the latest construction phase of Building B suggested a public use for that part of the edifice. The walls of that latest building, and the last modification in particular, revealed a very open plan. Walls closing off the rooms along the north-south axis were broken down in order to open or enlarge the rooms. Perhaps these rooms were used as storage or working areas where little privacy was needed thereby contributing to the interpretation of the building as a public one.

Of the building phase underneath Building B very little was left to indicate its use; most parts of the walls were broken down and very few use layers were uncovered. Excavation in this area, however, has only just begun. In future seasons several more trenches may be opened inside Building B to determine its function.

Although little specific information came to light about the function of this building, it was clear that the northeastern area of the town (where over the years trenches BE95-4, BE95/96-7, BE96/97-17, and BE99-26 were excavated) witnessed a great deal of activity in the fourth and fifth centuries AD. This accords well with the site-wide phenomenon of a major urban renewal beginning sometime in the second half of the fourth century AD. Substantial modifications of the large buildings and reuse of walls or wall parts in new buildings or foundations were common at that time.

4.6.2   TRENCH BE98/99-22
Trench Supervisor: L.A. Pintozzi
Figures/Plates 4-123 to 4-125

Trench BE98/99-22 was one of five trenches excavated in an area that is now thought to be a basilica with a putative Christian ecclesiastical function (Figure 4-123). Trench BE98/99-22, begun in 1998 (Sidebotham 2000b: 29–44) encompassed the southeastern sector of a large building on the northeastern part of the site whose western portions were explored in the 1996 and 1997 seasons with trenches BE96-8 and BE96/97/98-12 (see Sidebotham 1998:63–79; Sidebotham 1999:29–46; Sidebotham 2000b: 25–28). Trench BE98/99-22 measured 9 m N-S x 4 m E-W with grid coordinates 556–555 N / 2178–2182 E. Excavation in trench 22 begun during the 1998 season and completed during the 1999 season sought to understand fully its complete stratigraphic history. Additional goals were to comprehend putative pier structure *083* that had been revealed at the end of the 1998 season and to explore further the extent of the huge late Roman pottery dump, which had been found in trenches along the easternmost limits of the site.

At the end of the 1998 season, three phases, two of which were architectural, had been revealed within the trench. These architectural phases included: (1) the later phase—the courtyard of a late Roman edifice, paved with gypsum flagstones, and dated to the fifth century AD, and (2) the earlier phase, beneath the gypsum flagstones—putative pier *083*. Pier *083*, which extended east-west through the sectioned portion of the trench along the southern balk inside the late Roman building with the flagstone floor, was not fully revealed during the 1998 season. The fills abutting the structure dated to the late fourth century AD.

The 1999 excavation season allowed reinterpretation of locus *083* not as a pier, but as a wall constructed in conjunction with newly exposed wall *105* to form the corner of a late fourth-century-AD building. In addition, further evidence for the Roman pottery dump, which had been excavated in other trenches along the ancient coastline, was revealed. And finally, an earlier structure, *106/116*, was exposed. This structure, constructed upon sterile marine sediments, was perhaps, an early Roman pier or seawall. Excavations in the 1998/1999 season in this trench revealed six distinct phases:

Phase I: Sterile marine sediments

Phase II: Early Roman structure *106/116* (early first century AD)

Phase III: Roman pottery dump (mid-late fourth century AD)

Phase IV: Late Roman structure *083/105* (late fourth to fifth century AD) subphases:

    Subphase IVa: See the 1998 report

    Subphase IVb: See the 1998 report

Phase V—Fill-in preparation for construction (fifth century AD); construction of structure and occupation (fifth century AD)

    Subphase Va: See the 1998 report

    Subphase Vb: See the 1998 report

Phase VI: Decay and abandonment of late Roman structure; see the 1998 report.

Trench 22, Phase I

Phase I comprised sterile marine sediments and included loci *119–121*, which were excavated to approximately 0.40 m below present sea level. These sediments were devoid of all cultural material. For further discussion of marine sediments see Harrell (1996:114–126).

Plate 4-124   Probe in southern part of trench BE98/99-22 beneath flagstone floor *023* looking east. Walls *083/105* are to the right of the scale, rubble *106/116* of the first century AD structure in the deepest part of the probe. Flagstones of floor *023* are to the left and lower left of the photo while wall *020* is to the right (south of) walls *083/105* and wall *005* is at the top (east) of the photo. Scale=50 cm. Photograph by S. E. Sidebotham.

Trench 22, Phase II
Early Roman structure: early first century AD.
Although geological analysis suggested that locus *118* was naturally deposited *sabkha* along the coastline, it seems, rather, to have been intentionally deposited upon the sterile marine sediments of Phase I to create a stable environment upon which to construct early Roman structure *106/116* revealed within this phase. Although *118* was only 0.10 m³ in volume, half a *guffa* of large seashells and half a *guffa* of pottery were embedded

within the sediment; the latter included a high concentration of Ptolemaic sherds intermixed with a small number of early Roman sherds. Dumps resembling this exact assemblage have been found elsewhere in Berenike in BE97/98-16.*172* and *176*, which were not associated with *sabkha* sediments. It is very likely that fill *118* and the natural *sabkha* sediment were removed as one locus. When working below sea level excavating water-soaked sediments, stratigraphic control is difficult to maintain. Fill *118* provided a *terminus post quem* date for structure *106/116* of the early first century AD. The core of early Roman structure *106/116* arose on construction fill *118*. This structure, interpreted as the rubble core for an early pier or seawall erected along the edge of the harbor, consisted of two features: (1) the *116* non-concreted rubble core and (2) the *106* rubble core, concreted together by natural processes.

Non-concreted rubble core *116*, which lacked regular coursing, extended 1.20 m east-west, beneath the eastern and western trench balks and 1.70 m north-south beneath the southern and northern trench balks. The rubble-core structure sloped downhill from west toward the east where it terminated, leaving an 0.80 m x 0.20 m section along the eastern balk devoid of coral heads, presumably where erosion had completely destroyed the structure. The greatest extant height of rubble core *116* was 0.25 m. Rubble core *116* comprised cobble and small boulder-sized coral heads and large seashells embedded in construction fill *118*. The entire structure was not bonded together, but simply embedded in a loamy sand sediment identical to that of construction fill *118*.

Rising 0.54 m above *116* and extending beneath later structure *083* was concreted rubble core *106*. This structure was also composed of boulder and cobble-sized coral heads, all with irregular coursing. Geological analysis confirmed that natural processes concreted together this structure. It is clear that *106* and *116* were merely one architectural feature, with the upper stratum affected by the natural concretion processes and the lower standing unaffected. Most likely, lower stratum *116* remained unaffected due to its relative proximity to the water table or sea level, which did not allow moisture present in the loamy sand sediments to evaporate and the natural concretion process to occur.

Feature *106/116* was probably the rubble-core foundation of an early pier or seawall. A parallel for such construction appeared in trench BE98-17.*110/116/125*, a structure built directly upon marine sediments and which was, most likely, a protective seawall rather than

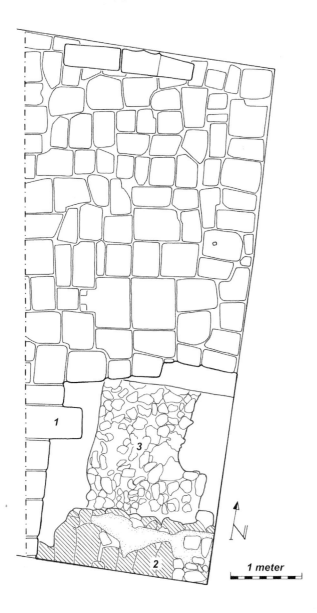

1=*023*
2=*083/105*
3=*106/116*

Figure 4-125   Probe beneath the flagstone floor in trench BE98/99-22.
Drawing by H. Barnard.

a pier of the first century AD (see Sidebotham 2000b: 74–75, 88). Both structures in trenches 17 and 22 had identical stratigraphic sequences. Each was constructed upon sterile marine sediments in the early first century AD and subsequent to the harbor receding due to natural sedimentation processes, each was also covered by a pottery dump during an episode of mid- to late fourth-century-AD raising and leveling of the coastal zone.

Trench 22, Phase III
Roman pottery dump: mid to late fourth century AD.

Due to natural sedimentation processes, the harbor receded (Harrell 1996:103–105). This led Roman builders to deposit a large leveling fill with the intent of reclaiming the recently exposed *sabkha* sediments along the coastline. This fill lay atop feature *106/116*, which had, by that time, clearly fallen out of use. The large quantity of diagnostic material dated this fill deposit to the mid- to late fourth century AD with a large component of residual early Roman pottery. This massive dump was similar in date to dense pottery deposits found in trenches BE95-4, BE95/96-7, BE97/98-17, and BE96/97/98-12 at the northeastern and eastern parts of the site and BE95/96/97-5 at the southeastern end of the site. It is apparent that these fills were part of a large-scale leveling project during the late Roman period in preparation for subsequent occupation all along the eastern side of Berenike. This fourth-century AD pottery dump comprised huge amounts of large pottery sherds and a high concentration of iron objects. A thin (0.05 m) deposit of beach sand, *102*, extended over and essentially capped the entire pottery dump. Aksumite sherds were found in locus *104*, pb # 119 (see Chapter 6, catalogue no. 14).

Trench 22, Phase IV
Construction of the late Roman structure and associated fills: late fourth to fifth century AD.

Phase IV had two subphases.

Subphase IVa

Following early Roman leveling of the area, a later structure was built, consisting of wall *083*, tentatively identified as a pier at the end of last season, and newly revealed wall *105*. The two features, no longer believed to be a pier, are now interpreted as a single installation constructed during a mid- to late fourth-century building phase.

Wall *105* was the earlier of the two and was built directly upon sand locus *102*, which capped the earlier

pottery dump. Sand locus *102* extended 1.40 m N-S x 0.54 m E-W x 0.37 m extant height. The structure extended beneath the northern, southern, and western trench balks. Wall *105* consisted, possibly, of a lower course of flat-lying ashlar blocks over which sand had naturally concreted. Although the concreted sand over the blocks remained *in situ* and flat-lying ashlars had not been exposed, it is clear that the sand had concreted over an extensive level area, over 1.40 m in length. The conglomerate ashlar blocks present in wall *083* of this structure were probably also utilized in the lowest course of wall *105*. The concreted sand extended up against the upper course of wall *105*, which was composed of two large boulder-sized coral-head blocks. The concreted sand also extended partially over the flat-lying sherds that were a feature of wall *083*.

Wall *083* extended 2.50 m E-W x 0.75 m N-S and ran beneath the eastern, western, and southern section balks. Where the two walls joined to form a corner, it was clear that *083* was erected upon the lowest course of wall *105*. Wall *083* was constructed as follows: (1) a single layer of large pottery sherds was deposited over structure *105*, presumably marking out the area of construction; (2) leveling fills were deposited to raise the eastern portion of the section in anticipation of construction. These leveling fills were all *in situ* and unexcavated; (3) *083* superstructure was constructed. The extant structure consisted of four irregular courses of a locally quarried conglomerate stone (personal communication from J. A. Harrell) intermixed with coral heads. These conglomerate stones were adjacent to one another, never overlapping, creating a level surface for subsequent coursing. Placement of the lowest course of wall *105* used a similar construction technique.

Subphase IVb

The sediments within Subphase IVb consisted of silty loam deposits or loamy sand deposits *089–093*, *095–096*, and *09–101*. All of these had an average thickness of 0.05 m, which suggests that they were not fills intended to raise and level the area, but rather naturally deposited during use of the structure. Also one locus, *094*, consisted of a trash deposit up against wall *083*. Associated ceramics dated these to late fourth to fifth century AD.

This late fourth-century building was torn down to its lowest courses in order to clear the area for the subsequent fifth-century structure. This pattern of late fourth- and fifth-century construction has been revealed in many other trenches at Berenike in the central and eastern parts of the site (e.g., BE94/95-2, BE95/96/97-5, BE95/96-6/BE97/98-16, BE96-9, BE96/97/98/99/00-10, BE95-4, BE95/96-7, BE97/98-17, BE97-18, BE98-20/BE99-27, BE98/99-23/BE99-00-32, BE99-28/BE99-38, BE00-34, BE00-37, BE00-41). In trench BE97/98-17 a late fourth-century building phase was followed by the subsequent construction of a fifth-century putative *temenos* temple wall (locus *010*; Sidebotham 1999:85–86; Sidebotham 2000b: 79). Also, in trench BE99-26 (see preceding), another late fourth-century building was removed down to its lowest courses in anticipation of the later fifth-century construction. It is interesting to note that within the earlier fourth-century phase in BE99-26, the walls of the structure were constructed of the identical conglomerate ashlar stones found in BE98/99-22.*083*. Aksumite sherds were found in locus *091* Pb 106 and in *trench clean* Pb 101. Chapter 6, on the Aksumite pottery, does not include the finds from the trench clean, because these are, technically, out of context.

Discussion

Excavations in BE98/99-22 revealed three important phases. First, the rubble core of an early Roman pier or seawall (locus *106/116*) was constructed directly upon sterile marine sediments. A parallel for such a structure at Berenike was BE97/98-17.*110/116/125*. Second, the mid-fourth-century-AD pottery dump, evident elsewhere in trenches along this side of the site, appeared in this trench, thereby providing further evidence for the phenomenon of raising and leveling the coastline along the eastern edge of the city to reclaim the newly exposed *sabkha* sediments following recession of the harbor due to natural sedimentation processes. Finally, the presence of structure *083/105* brought to light a late fourth-century building phase along the northeastern section of the coast. This widespread mid- to late fourth-century construction activity has also been attested in trenches BE94/95-2, BE95/96/97-5, BE96-9, BE96/97/98-12, BE97/98-17, and BE99-26 along the eastern side of the site. It has also been noted farther inland in the late Roman commercial and residential quarter in trenches BE98-20/BE99-27, BE99-28/BE00-38, BE00-34, BE00-37, and BE00-41, near the Serapis temple in trench BE96/97/98/99/00-10 and in the cult sanctuary in BE95/96-6/BE97/98-16.

4.6.3   TRENCH BE99/00-30
Trench Supervisor: L.A. Pintozzi
Figure/Plates 4-126 to 4-132

The stratigraphy of trench BE99/00-30 consisted of two major periods: 1) late Roman construction and occupation (Phases II–VI) and (2) abandonment and decay of the building (Phase VII).

Phases revealed during the 1999 and 2000 seasons were:

Phase I: Sterile marine sediments (undatable)
Phase II: Redeposited Roman pottery dump (mid- to late-fourth-century AD fill, included early Roman material)
Phase III: Late Roman structure I (late fourth to fifth century AD)
Phase IV: Late Roman structure II
　Subphase IVa: Construction (late fourth to fifth century AD)
　Subphase IVb: Occupation (fifth century AD)
Phase V: Early occupation of late Roman building (fifth century AD)
　Subphase Va: Remodeling and use
　Subphase Vb: Occupation
　Subphase Vc: Remodeling
Phase VI: Late occupation of late Roman building (fifth century AD)
　Subphase VIa: Construction
　Subphase VIb: Use
Phase VII: Decay and abandonment (fifth century AD)
　Subphase VIIa: Accumulation of debris prior to collapse of structure
　Subphase VIIb: Collapse of structure
　Subphase VIIc: Sand accumulation

Trench BE99/00-30, measuring 12 m N-S x 5.5 m E-W and with grid coordinates of 554–566 N-S x 2178-2183.5 E-W, encompassed the northeastern sector of a large building on the northeastern part of the site south of trenches BE95-4, BE95/96-7, BE97/98-17, BE99-26 (in Mound B) and north of trenches BE94/95-2, BE95/96/97-5, and BE97/98-18. The western portions of this structure were explored in the 1996, 1997, and 1998 seasons with trenches BE96-8 and BE96/97/98-12 and the southeastern part of the building was explored in 1998 and 1999 with trench BE98/99-22 (see preceding).

BE99/00-30 was adjacent to and due north of trench BE98/99-22. Excavation of BE98/99-22 and BE99/00-30 exposed a cross section through the entire eastern portion of the large building. The southern grid coordinates of

BE99/00-30 overlapped with the northern grid coordinates of trench BE98/99-22. This was due to a problem encountered while excavating BE98/99-22: the positioning of the trench in relation to BE98/99-22 wall *003*. Wall *003*, extending east-west through the trench, was about 0.50 m south of the northern balk, leaving too small of an area north of the wall to excavate. In fact, only topsoil was removed north of this wall during its excavation. Thus, it was decided that the southern coordinates of BE99/00-30 would be positioned in such a manner that the new trench would encompass the unexcavated strata north of wall *003*. This resulted in BE98/99-22.*003* physically separating the two trenches. BE98/99-22 wall *003* was then renumbered as a feature within trench BE99/00-30 as wall *017*.

Trench 30, Phase I

Phase I comprised sterile marine sediment locus *179* that was excavated to approximately 0.47 m below sea level. This sediment was devoid of all cultural material (Cf. Harrell 1996:112–125) and was, therefore, undatable.

Trench 30, Phase II
Roman pottery dump: mid to late fourth century AD.

A large land filling operation occurred with the intent of reclaiming the recently exposed *sabkha* sediments. These fills redeposited early Roman mixed with late Roman pottery (loci *163*, *168*, *170*, and *172–176*) to raise and level the area prior to late Roman occupation. Further evidence for a large-scale landfill process was the presence of two retaining walls. Both walls *164* and *169* comprised coral heads. Wall *169* extended into the northern balk and measured 0.65 m x 0.50 m (two rows) wide x 0.15 m (one course) high. Wall *164* was 3.35 m x 0.25 m (one course) high. Because later wall *137* was constructed directly upon *164*, it was impossible to determine the original width of the structure. Also within Phase II was fill locus *167*. Composed of boulder-sized fieldstones, certain stones were deliberately set to form an ephemeral retaining wall for the remaining boulders in the fill. With the deposition of these fills, the *sabkha* sediments were reclaimed and late Roman construction commenced. Locus *174* produced the rim fragment of an Aksumite bowl (see Chapter 6, catalogue number 4).

Trench 30, Phase III
Construction of walls 160 and 166: late fourth–fifth century AD.

Following deposition of the fills within Phase II, two walls were erected that were identical in construction and in phasing to walls found in trench BE98/99-22. These two walls were constructed directly upon the pottery dump; both dated to the mid–late fourth century AD. The walls of this structure were completely broken down to foundation levels in an attempt to clear the area for the subsequent construction of the latter fifth-century structure.

Walls *160* and *166* comprised one-course-high structures composed of field cobbles. Both walls were cleared down to foundation levels in preparation for the construction of the later Roman structure. Wall *160* extended 2.5 m E-W in the trench; it was 0.60 m wide x 0.12 m high. The wall was partially founded upon sand locus *161* and upon leveling fill *163*. Later wall *010* was constructed directly upon earlier wall *160*. Wall *166* extended 2.60 m N-S in the trench x 0.40 m extant width x 0.25 m high. Wall *008* was constructed directly upon earlier wall *166*.

As in trench BE98/99-22, excavations recovered no occupational surfaces or debris associated with wall *166*. Unfortunately, because the walls were broken down to foundations, no interpretation could be made regarding the function of this structure. Nevertheless, this edifice was part of the late fourth- to fifth-century AD construction boom that took place once the *sabkha* sediments had been reclaimed.

Trench 30, Phase IV
Construction of walls 010 and 137, feature 165, associated de facto surfaces and fills: late fourth–fifth century AD.

After leveling the earlier structure, walls *137* and *010* were constructed. Wall *137* extended N-S and was the foundation for later wall *016*. Wall *137* was also founded upon earlier retaining wall *164*. Extant wall *137* was 4.89 m long x 0.26 m high. East-west running wall *010* was founded upon earlier wall *160*. Fully exposed wall *010* was 4.15 m long x 0.75 m wide x 1.14 m high. Two doorways constructed within the wall used a course of the wall as thresholds. Eastern doorway *178* was blocked during a later phase of occupation. In the western doorway, a threshold was constructed by plastering over earlier wall coursing *127*. Measuring 0.78 m x 0.64 m x 0.12 m, threshold *127* was used throughout all occupational phases of the structure.

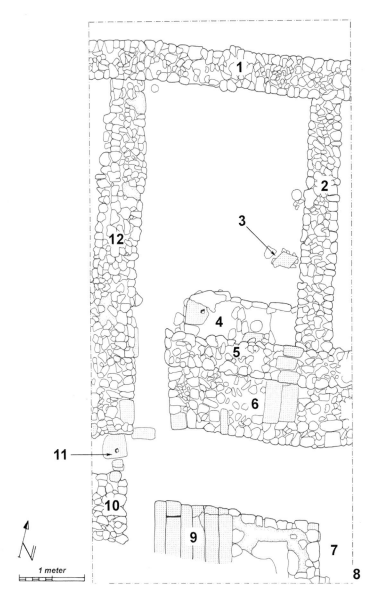

1 = *007*
2 = *016*
3 = *076*
4 = *011*
5 = *010*
6 = *028*
7 = *138*
8 = *017*
9 = *013*
10 = *041*
11 = *075*
12 = *008*

Figure 4-126   Trench BE99/00-30 plan.
Drawing by H. Barnard.

Plate 4-127
Trench BE99/00-30 looking north. Wall *017* (=BE99/00-22 wall *003*) is at the bottom of the photo (southern end of trench); abutting on its north face is staircase *013*. The N-S wall to the left (west) is *008* (at southern end of which is doorway/threshold *075*), with wall *007* perpendicular to *008* at its northern end; wall *016* is parallel to *008* and intersects wall *007*. Wall *041* is the southern continuation of wall *008*, in the middle is installation *028*, which abuts E-W wall *010*. The earliest phases were recorded in the probe in the northern room (top of photo). Scale=1 m. Photograph by S. E. Sidebotham.

Walls *010* and *137* functioned in unison, with the excavated area lying outside the structure. No deliberately laid surfaces associated with this phase were excavated. Instead, excavations revealed an accumulation of tamped-down debris, or *de facto* surfaces (loci *150* and *145*). In many cases this accumulation of debris appeared to be dumped against a possible structure (*165*) found beneath later wall *008*. It is not possible to give a full interpretation of this feature that has extant dimensions of 0.50 m long x 0.30 m (one course) high. Composed of five fieldstone boulders, it is clear that debris, including ash locus *152*, was dumped against it. Also three fires (*151*, *155*, and *156*) were kindled on associated *de facto* surface *150*. Because of the fires and dumps of ash without the presence of deliberately laid surfaces, this area was probably outside the structure formed by walls *137* and *010*.

Additional evidence that the excavated area lay outside the structure was the presence of the two doorways found within wall *010*. Although two doorways less than 1.5 m apart lend credence to such an interpretation, it is the physical evidence that furthered the argument. Built up against the southern face of wall *010* was later installation *028* constructed during Phase V. In 1999, the construction technique was thought to consist of two low-lying perimeter walls. One wall extended south from *011*, and the second, forming a right angle, extended the length of the southern face of installation *028*; a rubble-core foundation was then packed between these perimeter walls. Excavations in the 2000 season suggest that the wall extending south from *010* was, indeed, an earlier structure.

Plate 4-128
Trench BE99/00-30 looking south. Floor surface in the southern room is still intact (cf. probe visible at the top of Plate 4-127). E-W wall 30.*017* (=*22.003*) is at the northern end of the trench (top of photo), with abutting staircase *013*. Parallel E-W wall is *007* with installation *011* abutting it to the north. N-S south walls are *016* to the left (east) and *008* to the right (west). Installation *076* ("table and seat") is north of platform *011*. The E-W wall at the bottom of the photo is *007*. Scale=1 m. Photograph by S. E. Sidebotham.

Plate 4-129
Trench BE99/00-30 looking southeast. At the top left of the photo wall 30.*017* (=*22.003*) with abutting staircase *013* is visible, as well as the flagstone floor in trench 22. Parallel E-W wall is *010* with installation *028* abutting it to the south and *011* abutting it to the north. Scale=1 m. Photograph by S. E. Sidebotham.

This wall, *180*, defined the two interior rooms of this earlier building and was incorporated into later installation *028*. It was in this phase in locus *159* Pb 221 that excavations recovered a silver coin of the West Indian monarch Rudrasena III (reigned AD 348–390). (See Chapter 8, catalogue number 115.)

Trench 30, Phase V
Construction of fifth-century structure and early occupation: fifth century AD.
   Subphase Va
Construction of fifth-century structure.
Following occupation Phase IV, the area underwent a dramatic transition with the entire plan totally changed. First, wall *137* was broken down to foundations, and wall *016* was partially constructed upon it. Although both walls *016* and *137* extended north-south along the eastern balk, the two structures lay at different angles as the new floor plan for the fifth-century structure differed greatly from the earlier phase. Wall *016* formed the eastern border of the newly created room. Wall *016* was 5.10 m long x 0.60 m wide x 1.06 m high. During construction of *016*, a small installation was built up against the wall face; nothing survived of this feature except a "ghost," locus *149*. Consisting of a large hole, 0.21 m in diameter x 0.32 m deep, *149* must have accommodated a beam of wood used during the construction of wall *016*. After the wall was constructed, the beam was no longer used and removed and later leveled with fill *146*. Also, wall *008* was constructed partially upon earlier feature *165* and partially upon wall

010. In addition, the portion of wall *010* extending west of threshold *127* was dismantled. Wall *008* extended along the western balk for 7.70 m x 0.80 m wide x 1.20 m high. Also, wall *180* was partially broken down to foundation levels. Remaining wall *180* extended 1.22 m south of wall *010,* deliberately preserving the corner formed by these walls. Any installation nestled in the corner during this subphase must have been destroyed by the subsequent construction of *028.* Wall *007,* forming the northern border of the room, was also founded on earlier fills. Extending 5.5 m throughout the trench, wall *007* was 0.75 m wide x 1.50 m high. Finally, eastern doorway *178* within wall *010* was blocked though the western doorway with threshold *127* remained functioning.

Following construction of the new structure, leveling fills *146* and *135* were deposited to prepare the area for occupation. Subsequent to this leveling, fill clay, locus *117,* was deposited throughout the room to seal earlier fills. This phenomenon of clay deposition sealing earlier fills prior to occupation of the late structure has been documented elsewhere. In trench BE96/97/98-12, clay fills *265* and *266* were deposited to seal the earlier fills within the courtyard (Sidebotham 1999:36); a similar phenomenon also occurred in the late Roman military installation at Abu Sha'ar where a clay "sealant" separated the earlier late Roman military phase from the later Christian ecclesiastical occupation (cf. Sidebotham 1994:140, 144, 147). Upon these clay fills, a number of small fires were kindled prior to laying the initial floor; there was pitting of this floor. In trench BE98/99-30, this pattern continued. Upon clay sealant *117* a single fire, *135,* was kindled and a single small pit, *134* was cut. Pit *134,* 0.25 m in diameter x 0.25 deep, was filled with a number of small bones, many most likely fish. Perhaps, this pitting activity was a last attempt to clean up the area before use. Capping the pit was a single ashlar block that must have functioned as the precursor to later table installation *076* that was constructed upon it.

Finally, installation *011* was constructed during this subphase. Locus *011* lay in the corner created by walls *016* and *010.* Subsequent construction of installation *148* during late occupational Phase VI destroyed portions of installation *011* rendering it impossible to determine its function within the room.

Subphase Vb

Floors *125* and *129* defined this subphase of occupation. Floor *125,* north of threshold *127,* extended throughout the entire northern room and consisted of fine render

material. Floor *129,* south of threshold *127,* extended throughout the southern corridor and comprised a sandy render. Found lying upon floor *125* were 36 complete and three partial mother-of-pearl bivalve shells; the 39 shells weighed 4.398 kg. Evidence that inlay production may have been associated with this phase included a worked mother-of-pearl inlay from floor *125* and a second mother-of-pearl inlay found in a sweep of the southern corridor. Clearly, production of such inlays took place at Berenike (Plate 4-130).

Subphase Vc

A large remodeling project (Subphase Vc) followed Subphase Vb. In the northern room, floor *104/106* was laid, extending over threshold *127,* which separated the two rooms. Cut into the northwestern corner of the room was simple pot-stand installation *120.* This type of installation has been found throughout Berenike. Excavations in trench BE96/97/98-12 revealed eight of these types of installations (Sidebotham 1999:32–34).

Plate 4-130 Mother-of-pearl and painted bone decorations from trench BE99/00-30, Phase IV and Subphase Vb. Clockwise, starting with moon-shaped mother-of-pearl from locus *159* (3007-mm), *125* (1783-mm), from photo sweep (1569-mm), and two fragments of painted bone also from locus *125* (1784-11). Scale=10 cm. Photograph by S. E. Sidebotham.

A pot stand was a permanent installation that housed temporary vessels. This particular stand was Type A, the simplest form, where a hole was dug to house the installation, an inverted broken amphora was placed within, and packing fill was deposited around the vessel (cf. Sidebotham 1999:32–34). Also, a table, locus *076,* was constructed upon the ashlar block serving as a cap over early pit *134.* Table *076,* constructed of a reused broken ashlar block, measuring 0.35 x 0.33 x 0.10 m, rested upon four coral-head cobbles (Plates 4-128 and 4-131).

Plate 4-131 Closeup of the "table and seat" (30.*076*), west of wall *016* and north of installation platform *011*. Looking southeast. Scale=50 cm. Photograph by S. E. Sidebotham.

Within the southern corridor, staircase *013* and platform *028* were constructed (Plates 4-127 to 4-129). Prior to building the staircase, construction fill *126* was deposited, consisting of an extremely dense, concreted fill that created a firm foundation for the staircase. Fill *126* extended from beneath the foot of the staircase into the corridor. Also, platform *028* was constructed at this time. Utilizing earlier wall *180* and constructing a low lying wall to delineate the southern perimeter, rubble core fill formed a foundation for the installation. Later, a packing fill was deposited over the rubble core, and large ashlar blocks were positioned to form a platform. Although only two blocks remained *in situ*, ashlars probably originally covered the entire length of the rubble core, forming a platform. This installation measured 3.60 x 1.25 m. Also, threshold *128* created within the doorway in wall *008*, was raised with a new threshold block, *075*. Finally, a floor fully covered threshold block *127* and extended throughout the corridor. The construction of platform *028* produced a 2 m long x 0.75 m wide passageway between the corridor and the northern room. At the southern end of this passageway the placement of curb *099* physically divided the southern corridor from the northern room. This curb consisted of one ashlar block 0.45 m x 0.25 m x 0.17 m high. There was fragmentary evidence for more curbing extending eastward suggesting a continuous physical divide between the passageway and the southern corridor.

Loci *104/106* and *105* were the only occupational surfaces excavated in this subphase. During this entire phase of occupation, no debris accumulated within the structure. This, however, was not the case in the next phase.

Trench 30, Phase VI
Late occupation of the fifth-century structure.

An obvious change of conditions within the structure signaled the latest occupational phase. This included a small episode of destruction. Occupation of the structure, possibly by new inhabitants, followed refurbishment of the building. During the early occupation phase, the interior space of the structure was fully respected. During this late occupational phase, however, the occupants appeared to have been squatters. During this phase, large fires were kindled upon the surfaces; ash and occupational debris were also dumped throughout the building (see trench BE00-39 following).

These sediments may now be interpreted as part of the late occupational phase where, as in trenches BE96/97/98-12, BE97/98-22, and BE00-39 (see following), partial collapse of the structure occurred and *de facto* surfaces accumulated. Subsequent to the late occupational phase, the structure collapsed totally. Excavations fully uncovered this late occupational phase in the southern corridor during the 1999 season.

Within the northern room, however, a series of *de facto* surfaces and one late installation defined this late phase. The *de facto* surfaces consisted of dumps of occupational debris, including ash, tamped down by constant use. No longer was the structure used for its original purpose. The floors were kept clean during the earlier occupational phase, and, once again, the pattern continued of different occupants inhabiting the structure. These new inhabitants clearly dumped occupational debris within the structure rather than depositing it outside the building.

Phase VI included installation *148*, which encroached upon earlier installation *011*, destroying its upper portions and all evidence of the initial function of *011*. With a series of gypsum ashlars and coral heads, installation *148* subdivided larger installation *011* into three compartments. Within the central compartment was a pot stand (Type C installation, see Sidebotham 1999:34). Once again, the feature comprised a single inverted broken amphora. Both packing fills *123* and *124* at the bottom of the installation consisted of pure ash, perhaps used as an insect repellent. Installation *148* then reused the base of earlier installation *011* as two working platforms.

As noted, this final phase of occupation included dumping occupational debris, which was tamped down to create *de facto* surfaces *102–103*, *111*, and *114–116*. In one case, *112* was tamped-down ash, which before other sediments could accumulate, was tracked throughout the room. All these *de facto* surfaces concentrated around two installations in the southern portion of the room, *011* and *076* (table installation). In the space between these two installations, up against wall *016*, was a large dump of ash. Also debris accumulated around table *076*. At one point, a second small broken ashlar block, *124*, was added to the installation, creating a larger working surface. This coincided with the buildup of debris *114*, which created a berm around the table. This berm wrapped around two-thirds of the installation, approximately 0.30 m away. This debris accumulated as the working surface was used. The distance between table and berm was suitable for an individual squatting, with the accumulation at the soles of the feet.

All occupational debris that accumulated during this subphase consisted of large quantities of small fish bones. This parallels the late occupational phase in trench BE96/97/98-12 where dumps and an amphora (containing *garum)* including a high quantity of fish bones were present (Sidebotham 1999:30, 32; Sidebotham 2000b: 25–27). In this trench was a broken vessel with numerous fish bones scattered all around on *de facto* surface *107*. Perhaps this vessel contained *garum*, as was found in trench in BE96/97/98-12.*062* (Sidebotham 1998:75-77; Van Neer and Ervynck 1998:363).

Trench 30, Phase VII

Phase VII was the abandonment and decay of the building in the fifth century AD. There were three subphases. These consisted of VIIa, an accumulation of debris before collapse of the building including numerous episodes of sediments washed/blown into the area intermixed with architectural tumble; VIIb, total collapse of the structure; and VIIc, accumulation of windblown sand over collapsed architectural tumble.

Subphase VIIa

Sub-phase VIIa was the largest within this phase and comprised sediments which were washed/blown into the area after abandonment of the structure. Intermixed with these sediments was architectural tumble. As the building slowly decayed, plaster slumped off the walls and installations. The structures then experienced decay with small episodes of fall, resulting in the render eroding from within the newly exposed interior of the walls. The tumble represented small episodes of collapse prior to the destruction the structure. Many

of these sediments were termed "wash-down and bake" debris in that they appeared to have been naturally deposited in the area and then dried by the sun. In some cases, these wash-down sediments worked their way in between and beneath earlier tumble loci, clearly indicating the presence of rainwater associated with their deposition. The small amount of windblown sand and tumble found within this subphase suggested that the walls stood for some time after abandonment of the building.

Most of the sediments exposed in this subphase were found within the southern corridor. This corridor, accessible from the main hallway, allowed direct flow of water or windborne sediments from one area of the building to another. The sediments in the corridor fell into four categories: (1) architectural tumble, (2) windblown sand, (3) wash-down debris, and (4) slump of wall render.

Because the architectural tumble represented small episodes of collapse, each could be correlated with a particular wall, doorway, or installation from which it fell. Locus *066* was tumble from installation *028*. Loci *079/091* fell from the exterior doorway (from the eastern face of the doorway, a structure found outside the trench), loci *065/088* from wall *008*, loci *050/070* from wall *041*, locus *039* from wall *008*, locus *038* from wall *013*, and locus *034* from wall *013*. Render slump from various installations included: *094, 074, 060,* and *034*. Sand loci blown into the area were *090, 037,* and *030*. Finally, the washed/blown in sediment loci included *095, 093, 089, 087, 067, 077-078, 072, 052–054, 062–063, 056, 058, 046–047, 043, 037, 029–033,* and *026*.

Although no discernable pattern could be determined for the loci found within the corridor, on the microlevel, the washed/blown-in sediments did exhibit a pattern. The earlier loci were composed of silty sediments whereas the later loci were intermixed with sand. Clearly, this pattern reflected the preservation of the structure of the building. The taller the walls, the less sand was washed/blown into the area. Once the walls had suffered some damage, the interior of the building was more susceptible to the elements. During this subphase, one small fire, *073*, was kindled within the southern corridor at the foot of staircase *013*, presumably by squatters who were using the building as a windbreak.

In the northern room, the pattern of architectural tumble intermixed with washed/blown in sediments and wall slump was identical. This room was not on the main access of the building so the accumulation was not as great. Architectural tumble *051/059* fell from wall *008* and *055* from wall *016*. The sediments washed/blown into the area included *068, 064, 057, 049, 045,* and *012*. Locus *048* was render that slumped off wall *016*. Squatters most likely kindled small fire *044*, taking advantage of the area as a windbreak.

Finally sediment *064* washed in along the northeastern corner of the room. Here excavations recovered one *aes* Aksumite coin of King Aphilas dating approximately AD 270/290–330 (see Chapter 8, catalogue number 114). This was the first Aksumite coin discovered at Berenike. The coin, along with Aksumite pottery discovered in trench BE98/99-22 (see preceding and Chapter 6, catalogue numbers 8 and 14), provided evidence of contact between the Roman Empire and the Kingdom of Aksum in the later period (cf. Munro-Hay 1996:410–412).

Subphase VIIb

During Subphase VIIb, the building collapsed. The slumping of render occurred first, followed by collapse of the walls in stages, various courses falling at different times or the corners collapsing. The first walls to fall (*007* and *008*) were those facing the prevailing northerly winds. After these, the remaining standing walls were exposed to the same forces of nature and quickly tumbled.

Portions of *007* and *008* fell toward the south into the center of the northern room with associated architectural tumble *005/036/042* and *027*. Outside of the building, north of wall *007*, there was also evidence for architectural collapse. Locus *098* must be the remnants of the northern face of wall *007*. Next, wall *016* fell in two stages with associated architectural tumble *021* and *022*. Wall *010* suffered three separate stages of collapse. First, the northern face of cross wall *010* collapsed as loci *006/020/080*.

Wall collapse in the northern room exposed the southern room to prevailing winds, and it began to degrade. The southern exterior courses of cross wall *010* collapsed southward into the corridor as loci *014* and *024*. Then wall *017*, which divided the corridor from the courtyard in trench BE98/99-22, collapsed. Architectural tumble *009/025* associated with this collapse completely covered the entire courtyard.

Subphase VIIc

Following collapse during Subphase VIIb, the structure was exposed to the elements. Windblown sand accumulated over the architectural tumble. A unique locus found within the windblown sand strata in the north room was *003* where the sand was intermixed with a great quantity of camel dung. Also, a small fire

(*018*) was kindled directly upon sand locus *019* in the southeastern quadrant of the trench. Fire *018*, was most likely set by a bedouin passing through the area and could have been kindled at the time when the camels created *003* in the north.

In its latest major architectural phase, the room in trench BE99/00-30 was subdivided into two rooms, a northern room and a corridor to the south linked by a doorway. The interior dimensions of the northern room were 5.4 m N-S x 3.70 m E-W; it lay completely within the confines of the trench. The interior dimensions of the southern corridor were 4.30 m N-S x 5.5 m E-W; it extended eastward beyond the trench balk.

Walls *007, 008, 010,* and *016* bounded the northern room. Due to remnant wall plaster, it is not possible to determine whether walls *007/008* and *007/016* abutted or were bonded together. It is clear, however, that wall *016* abutted wall *010*.

Wall *007*, forming the northern border of the room and the only exterior wall of the building exposed within this trench, extended east-west for 5.5 m x 0.75 m wide x 1.05 m extant height. Extending south of wall *007* for 7.70 m and forming the western border of the northern room was wall *008*. Wall *008* was 0.80 m wide x 0.70 m extant height. Also extending south of wall *007* for 5.10 m and forming the eastern border of the northern room was wall *016*, which was 0.60 m wide x 0.90 m extant height. Finally, cross wall *010* defined the southern border of the northern room and created the division between the northern room and the southern corridor. The exposed section of wall *010* was 3.70 m long x 0.75 m wide x 1.15 m extant height.

One large installation, *011*, which abutted walls *010* and *016* and measured 2.25 m E-W x 0.70 m N-S x 0.38 m extant height, dominated the southern end of the northern room. It comprised reused gypsum blocks and coral heads and was partitioned into three irregular sections. The western section, measuring 1.05 m wide, consisted of flat-lying reused gypsum and conglomerate ashlars forming a level platform. The middle section, measuring 0.55 m wide, contained a broken pottery vessel framed by cobble-sized fieldstones, anhydrite blocks, and coral heads. This pottery vessel resembled pot stands found within the kitchen in trench BE96/97/98-12 (cf. Sidebotham 1999:32-34, 38–41, 45). The eastern segment, 0.55 m wide, was most likely an additional work surface, pendant to that operating in the west. The presence of the pot stand along with the two working surfaces suggested that the installation was a food preparation area or low counter.

Approximately 0.50 m north of installation *011* was a second installation, *076*. Consisting of two reused gypsum ashlars, *076* functioned as a table and seat. The ashlar forming the table was 0.35 m x 0.33 m x 0.10 m thick and rested upon four cobblestones. The tabletop was 0.20 m above the exposed floor. The ashlar seat was 0.21 m x 0.22 m x 0.05 m high; it was 0.10 m west of the table. The seat, resting upon the exposed surface, would have been moveable, the distance between table and seat being adjusted for comfort.

Other evidence that this room functioned in association with food preparation was the presence of locus *100*, a crushed amphora possibly filled with *garum*. Locus *100* lay 1.50 m north of table/seat *076*. Although the contents of the crushed vessel were removed for future study, the vessel itself remained *in situ*. Without further excavation, it is not possible to determine whether the amphora was an installation or a vessel resting upon the surface. Preliminary analysis suggests that it was similar in fabric to the amphora containing *garum* found within the storeroom directly off of the kitchen in BE96/97/98-12.*062*. That vessel had an Aswani provenance (Sidebotham 1998:75, 76, 77, Figure 3-61; Sidebotham 1999:30, 41).

In the northwestern corner of the room stood the final installation exposed this season, *101*. Although unexcavated, this consisted of a deliberately broken pottery vessel embedded in the surface, which was suggestive of similar types of installations revealed in other trenches at Berenike. Trench BE96/97/98-12 preserved eight similar types of installations (Sidebotham 1999:32, 34) as did trenches BE96/97/98-10, BE97/98-18, and BE99-28 (see Sidebotham 1999:32, 34 for the typology of the installations found within trench BE96/97/98-12). These vessels were interpreted as pot stands, semipermanent structures intended to house secondary vessels. A pot stand provided support to a second temporary vessel inserted inside. When the contents of the temporary vessel were emptied, it could easily be removed from the pot stand and replaced with a new vessel. The presence of both the installations and the vessel containing *garum* suggests that food preparation and/or consumption took place within this room. Questions to be addressed next season will include determining whether this was another kitchen and/or an informal dining area.

Trench 30, Southern Corridor

Walls *010* and *008*, *041*, and *017*, enclosed the southern corridor. The exposed section of wall *017*, extending

Plate 4-132   Door *138* (number 7 in Figure 4-126) in the south balk of trench BE99/00-30, between wall *017* and behind staircase *013*, looking south. Scale=20 cm. Photograph by S. E. Sidebotham.

east-west along the southern balk for 4.60 m, was 0.79 m wide x 1.23 m extant height. Wall *017* terminated with upended gypsum quoin blocks forming an exterior doorway (*138*) of the building located in the southeastern corner of the trench. Doorway *138* faced south away from the prevailing winds (Plate 4-132).

Staircase *013* formed a small vestibule or foyer for this doorway; it ascended along wall *017*, rising from west towards the east, on a platform, 1.05 m wide x 3.20 m long, which consisted of up to five courses of coral heads (Figure 4-126 and Plates 4-127 to 4-129). The first flight of stairs was fully preserved with six steps leading up to a landing. The landing comprised one large gypsum ashlar block with extant dimensions of 0.82 m x 0.60–0.30 m x 0.05 m high. The stairs were also constructed of large gypsum ashlar blocks with average dimensions of 0.94 x 0.27 x 0.12 m high. The average tread length was 0.13 m. East of the landing was evidence for additional courses of coral heads, suggesting that a banister had been present at the eastern edge of the landing as a safety feature.

The landing and the banister at the top of the preserved flight of stairs pivoted in the direction of ascent toward the north; ascent of the staircase would have been within the corridor. Although there is no evidence for an upper flight of stairs, one must have existed and was, most likely, made of wood. Similar staircases appeared in the late Roman commercial-residential quarter (in trenches BE99-28/BE00-38, BE00-34, BE00-37, and BE00-41) east of this possible Christian ecclesiastical structure. This putative wooden flight of stairs must have been constructed upon and most likely functioned in unison with installation *028*.

Installation *028*, constructed 1.50 m due north and roughly parallel to the staircase, consisted of a platform abutting wall 010. Locus *028* measured 3.60 x 1.25 x 0.66 m at its greatest exposed height (Figure 4-126 and Plates 4-127 and 4-129). The platform was constructed in two separate stages. In the first stage, low-lying walls extending out from cross wall *010* delineated the installation. A rubble-core fill was then deposited within the structure to form a foundation for the installation. In the second stage, a packing fill was deposited over the rubble core and large ashlar blocks were positioned to form a platform. Although only two blocks remained *in situ*, ashlars probably originally covered the entire length of the rubble core, forming one large platform. The two *in situ* blocks lay due north of the staircase landing.

This storage platform probably had a two-fold function. First, it was designed to be a foundation on which an upper flight of stairs was constructed. As noted above, the preserved staircase pivoted toward the north during ascent. The upper flight of stairs, possibly constructed of wood, must have traversed the empty space between the extant stone staircase and the platform. Utilizing cross wall *010* for additional structural support, the platform probably functioned as a foundation upon which the putative wooden superstructure was built. It seems probable that once the empty space between the staircase and platform was traversed, a second landing would have been constructed, necessitating a pivot to the west, with additional stairs leading to the roof. Thus, the entire *028* installation would have supported the putative wooden flight of stairs. Secondly, the platform would have functioned as a storage area beneath these stairs. This platform would have then served an additional function, as a cool, dry place to store commodities brought in through the rear door of the building (BE99/00-30.*138*).

The construction of platform *028* and its putative superstructure produced a 2 m long x 0.75 m wide passageway between the corridor and the northern room. At the southern end of this passageway, curb *099* divided the southern corridor from the northern room. This curb consisted of one ashlar block 0.45 x 0.25 x 0.12 m high. There was fragmentary evidence for more curbing extending eastward, suggesting a continuous physical divide between wall *008* and installation *028*. South of the curbstone was a floor. North of the curbstone were *de facto* surfaces, tamped-down occupational debris associated with activities occurring in the room. The curb, like threshold block *076* described below, limited the amount of debris tracked from one area of the building to the next.

Finally, extending north from wall *017* for 1.44 m and forming the western corner of the southern corridor was wall *041*, which measured 0.58 m wide x 0.23 m high. Wall *008*, terminating in gypsum quoins, was aligned with wall *041*, forming a doorway that lead to the western portion of the building. Raised threshold block *075*, which measured 0.66 m x 0.53 m x 0.23 m high, was constructed within this doorway. The threshold stood above the floor to keep sand and occupational debris of the domestic space from entering into the deeper confines of the building. This doorway restricted access from one area of the structure to the next, subdividing the public entrance of the grand hallway in the west from the modest corridor in the east with its private back entrance.

Discussion

Evidence from trench 30 suggests the existence of a late Roman food-preparation area accessed directly by two doorways, one apparently from outside the facility to the east (*138*) and a second (*075*) joining the two rooms in trench 30 with another interior portion of the building to the west. The southern end of the trench preserved evidence of an upper story in the form of stone staircase *013*. The northern room of the trench also provided evidence of mother-of-pearl inlay making. Despite a rather elaborate stratigraphy, which documented phase changes, however, all the pottery recovered here dated to the fifth century. Thus, the ceramic evidence provided no more refined chronological information as to when these various phases occurred.

4.6.4   TRENCH BE00-39
             Supervisor: L.A. Pintozzi
             Figures/Plates 4-123 and 4-133 to 4-137
During the 2000 field season, excavations continued (begun in 1996) in a large structure located on the

Plate 4-134   Trench BE00-39, looking northeast, with piers *012* and *010* (bottom, south) and *014* (top, north), while pier *025* protrudes from the east balk. Scale=1 m. Photograph by S. E. Sidebotham.

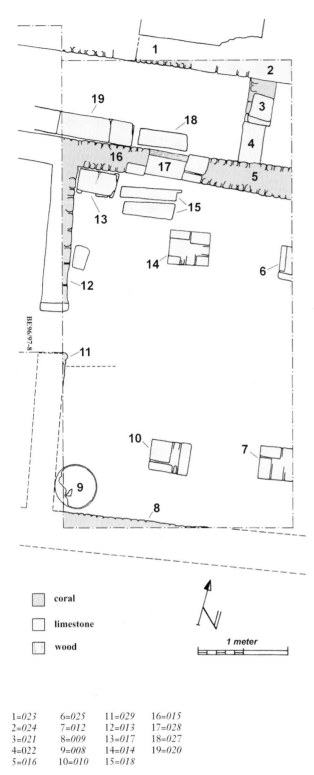

Plate 4-135   Trench BE00-39, looking northwest. Dolium *008* is in the southwest corner of the trench (left in photo). At the far (northern) end of the trench are walls *015* and *016* with threshold *028* and bench *017* abutting the south face of wall *015*. Scale=1 m. Photograph by S. E. Sidebotham.

coral

limestone

wood

1 meter

1=*023*   6=*025*   11=*029*   16=*015*
2=*024*   7=*012*   12=*013*   17=*028*
3=*021*   8=*009*   13=*017*   18=*027*
4=*022*   9=*008*   14=*014*   19=*020*
5=*016*   10=*010*   15=*018*

Figure 4-133   Trench BE00-39 plan. Drawing by A. M. Hense.

Plate 4-136   Trench BE00-39, looking southwest. Wall *023/024* in the foreground, with steps *021* and *022* perpendicular to it. Bench *020* abuts the north face of wall *015*. Scale=1 m. Photograph by S. E. Sidebotham.

northeastern part of the site, south of Mound B. The latest of the trenches here, BE00-39, measured 10 m N-S x 5 m E-W with grid coordinates of 548–558 N and 2165–2170 E. During this and previous seasons, four other trenches had been excavated within this structure: BE96-8, BE96/97/98-12, BE98/99-22 and BE99/00-30. Trench BE00-39 was contiguous to trench 8, lying due east of the former and one meter south of trench BE96/97/98-12.

Trench BE00/39 further explored the fifth-century structure to determine its purpose. Theories regarding the function of this structure varied considerably over previous seasons. The investment of five trenches in a single structure allowed a broader interpretation as the plan of the building continued to emerge. By the close of the 2000 season it appeared to be a single structure devoid of other encroaching buildings. The edifice lay on a central axis, with an east-west breezeway or hallway dividing the building in half. The northern portion of the structure served as the domestic private sphere of the building, while the southern half where trench BE00-39 was located functioned as the public sphere.

Trench BE00-39 had three phases of which one had two subphases. These were:

Phase I: Early occupation (fifth century AD)
Phase II: Later occupation (fifth century AD)
 Subphase IIa: Occupation
 Subphase IIb: Refurbishment
Phase III: Abandonment and decay
 (sometime in the fifth century AD)

Although both trenches 12 and 30 documented the private sphere of the building with the presence of kitchens and storage rooms, the public sphere (trenches 8 and 22) was not fully understood until the excavation of trench 39. Trench 39 revealed the interior portion of the foyer and also part of a colonnaded room south of and connected to the foyer by a door. The relationship between this courtyard and the room lined with benches found within trench BE96-8 can now be fully understood. Also, the function of the flagstone floor and single pillar at the eastern end of the building excavated in BE98/99-22 can be interpreted in a holistic way. Plans for the BE01 season are to expose fully the remaining space between trench 22 and trench 39.

Excavations revealed that the main entrance to the building lay to the west, from a minor *kardo* off the *decumanus maximus*. The doorway opened up onto the foyer in which a series of benches lined the southern portion of a hallway. With excavations in 2000, it was quite clear that this main foyer extended deep into the structure where it terminated with separate doorways allowing access into either the public sphere or private sphere of the building. If one chose to enter the public sphere, a turn to the south (right) led to the large pillared hall. Although excavations have not fully revealed the entire public space, it appears likely that this section of the structure firmly adhered to typical Roman architecture. This consisted of three separate spaces functioning as one, with a focal point at the eastern portion of the pillared hall, the area of the flagstone floor in trench 22.

The least important space at the back of the "public sphere" portion of the structure was the westernmost room lined with stone benches (trench BE96-8), which was connected by a single door to the main pillared hall. The main hall consisted of an unknown number of pillars, four of which (*010, 012, 014,* and *025*) were revealed during the 2000 season. One (missing) column found in trench BE98-22.*087* would have aligned

Plate 4-137   Major part of a bronze cross from *39.007* (4532-D). Each black and white increment on the scale = 1 cm. Photograph by S. E. Sidebotham.

perfectly with those excavated in 2000, suggesting that the courtyard continued as a trabeated feature. Finally, in the eastern portion of the structure, flagstone floor BE98-22.*023* clearly indicated prominence of that space. Unnoticed in previous seasons were two niches in the eastern (interior) face of wall BE98-22.*005*.

Although excavations in 2000 further revealed the plan of the public space, the function of the building is still not fully understood. The building, devoid of other encroaching structures, comprised public and private spaces that functioned as a single complex. Evidence for the purpose of this complex was tied to two artifacts with Christian iconography. In trench BE98-22.*024*, a single lamp found in the fills deposited above the flagstone floor and beneath the southernmost of the niches in wall BE99-22.*005* recorded a Coptic aphorism: "Jesus forgive me" (Sidebotham 2000b: 43–44). Also, in tumble layer BE00-39.*007* excavations recovered a large fragment of a bronze cross (Plate 4-137). Clearly, these two items were insufficient to provide a definitive interpretation of the structure as a Christian ecclesiastical complex, but, together with the orientation of the building, they are compelling. Future excavation of the public sector of the structure will undoubtedly shed additional light on this subject.

Excavations in 2000 revealed a transition zone between the "public" and "private" spheres of the structure. This was the foyer that was initially exposed in BE96-8 with the excavation of the main door to the structure and a series of four gypsum benches lining the southern wall. The interior portion of the foyer comprised two walls framing a doorway. Excavations in trench BE96/97/98-12 indicate that this room north of the foyer was a kitchen. One wall, BE96/97/98-12.*023*, extended east-west along the northern balk and terminated at this doorway. Wall *023*, a continuation of BE96-8 wall *017*, extended 3.10 m from the western balk x 0.85 m (five courses) extant height. The wall extended into the northern balk, preventing measurement of thickness. East of the doorway and framing the eastern limits of the foyer was wall *021*. Extending south from the northern balk for 1.45 m, wall *021* had an extant height of 0.40 m x 0.55 m wide. Wall *021* created a doorway between it and wall *016* with threshold block *022*, a single gypsum ashlar measuring 0.80 x 0.15 m high. This doorway restricted access into the public sphere of the edifice, strongly suggesting that the entire building functioned as one integrated unit.

Framing the southern limits of the foyer were two walls separated by a doorway that opened onto the courtyard. The two doorways exiting the foyer were not aligned. Wall BE96/97/98-12.*015*, a continuation of BE96-8 wall *011*, was 1.40 m long x 0.62 m wide x 0.76 m (three courses) high. East of the doorway was wall *016*. Extending into the eastern balk, wall *016* measured 2.35 m long x 0.60 m wide x 0.80 m (four courses) extant height. Threshold *028*, situated between the two walls, measured 0.70 m long. North of *028*, was a secondary threshold block, *027*, constructed of a single ashlar block, 1.05 m x 0.39 m x 0.09 m.

Within the foyer was a single bench, BE00-39.*020*, that extended eastward along the southern balk. This bench was the fifth of those found in trench BE96-08.*009* extending along the southern limits of the foyer. Bench BE00-39.*020* measured 1.60 m long x 0.50 m wide and was 0.37 m above the exposed surface. Although the western strut support lay within the balk, the eastern support consisted of one ashlar block measuring, 0.45 m long x 0.14 m wide and was raised 0.29 m above the floor.

Walls BE00-39.*015* and *016* framed the courtyard on the north. South of threshold *027* between the doorway, another threshold (*017*) was constructed as a mirror image of *027*; *017* was more substantial than *027*. Composed of two ashlar blocks, the entire installation measured 1.07 m long x 0.66 m wide x 0.12 m high.

Two additional walls framed the pillared hall to the south. Extending south from wall *016* along the western balk for 3.10 m was wall BE00-39.*013*, a continuation of BE96-08 wall *012*. The wall stood 1.10 m (four courses) high and terminated at a doorway that led to the southern bench room excavated in BE96-8. The adjoining wall south of *013* did not appear in the trench. This doorway was centered within the courtyard. Finally, wall *009* extended 5.0 m along the southern balk, framing the southern limits of the colonnaded room. Although only one course of coral-head facing remained, wall *009* had an extant height of 1.10 m and extended into the balk.

Within the large space of trench BE00-39, excavations revealed four rectilinear-shaped pillars, constructed primarily of gypsum ashlar blocks. These formed two rows extending east-west. The nearest pillar face was approximately 1.10 m away from the corresponding wall. Within the rows, the pillars were spaced approximately 1.65 m apart. Measurements of the courtyard suggested that six pillars existed in each row, totaling 12 within the large space. Excavations in trench BE98-22 had revealed a robbed hole of one such pillar (locus *087*). This aligned directly with those found in trench 39 along the southern "colonnade." Along the southern "colonnade," the westernmost pillar, *010*, measured 0.90 x 0.60 x 0.64 m extant height. It was both two courses high x two rows wide. The easternmost pillar, *012*, partially extended into the eastern balk and measured 0.75 m x 0.76 m x 0.82 m high. The remaining structure, *025*, was two rows wide and three courses high. Along the northern "colonnade" the westernmost pillar *014* measured 0.90 x 0.69 x 0.77 m extant height.

There were a number of installations in the large open space. In the southwestern corner was *dolium 008*. This crushed vessel measured 0.90 m in diameter x 0.40 m extant height. An identical configuration was found in trench BE98-22 where a large *dolium* (loci *021/062/063*) was located in the southeastern corner of the room. No distinguishable remains survived in *dolium* BE98-22.*021/062/063*; possibly it functioned as a water container. Although *dolium* BE00-39.*008* was not fully excavated this season, it is likely that it, too, was a water-storage vessel. Also nestled in the corner formed by walls BE00-39.*013* and *015* was a single bench (*017*) that measured 0.80 m x 0.50 m, and stood 0.05 m above the late *de facto* surface of the courtyard. Finally, a single ashlar block functioning as a shelf (*019*) abutted wall *013*. Shelf *019* measured 0.45 m x 0.29 m x 0.13 m high.

Trench 39, Phase I
Early occupation of the structure (fifth century AD).
Due to time constraints, the early occupational phase of the structure was only revealed, but not excavated. At the end of the 2000 season, a single floor, *011*, had been exposed, that extended throughout the courtyard. This floor was later than all other extant installations in the courtyard. Although floor *011* remained unexcavated and no pottery dates were available, all other trenches excavated in this structure suggest that the floor and the occupation dated to the fifth century AD.

Trench 39, Phase II
Later occupation (fifth century AD).
Although this later occupational phase was only first identified in trench 39, it appeared to be a structure-wide phenomenon. This phase of occupation had a small episode of destruction. There was subsequent refurbishment of the building. During the earlier occupation phase, the interior space of the structure was fully respected. However, during the occupation,

the residents appear to have been squatters. This phase witnessed large fires kindled upon surfaces, along with ash and occupational debris dumped throughout the building.

Although the evidence for late occupation occurred throughout the structure, it was not recognized until the 2000 season. In trench BE96/97/98-12, the late occupational phase had been interpreted as a subphase of early occupation. In trench BE96/97/98-12, Phase III there was a change in the pattern of dumping activity subsequent to large-scale destruction and leveling. No longer were small patches of debris building up in the kitchen, but large fills containing ash and fish remains were deposited haphazardly (Sidebotham 1999:43-45).

In trench BE98/99-22, this late occupational phase was a subphase of the earlier occupational phase. During this late phase, destruction occurred outside the western balk, resulting in the deposition of leveling fills extending over flagstone floor *023*. Constructed upon these late fills was wall *004*, which subdivided the courtyard. Subsequent occupational debris accumulated within the newly created northern room; these included dumps and kindled fires (Sidebotham 2000b: 42–43).

Finally, in BE99/00-30, this late occupational phase was recognized, but not interpreted as such. Debris accumulated, following a period of slight destruction in the southern corridor of the building, south of installation *028*. Although there was no massive dumping in this heavily trafficked corridor leading to the external doorway, debris accumulated rapidly (see preceding BE99/00-30). During excavations in BE00-30, however, the late occupational phase was recognized. Dumps of ash and debris accumulated throughout the northern room following use of deliberately laid floors (see preceding).

Within trench BE00-39, this pattern of kindling of fires and not respecting the space for which it was originally intended was common. Upon floor *011* of the earlier phase was a small episode of tumble (*007*), which represented the phase change between early and late occupation. During Subphase IIa, fill *006* was deposited over the earlier tumble, as in trenches BE96/97/98-12 and BE98/99-22. This structure-wide deposition of leveling fills over earlier tumble suggests partial destruction of the building, either due to weathering as a result of abandonment or deliberate destruction. One occupational debris locus appeared atop *006* leveling fill. There were remains of a large fire (*005*) in the center of the courtyard due north of the doorway, which led to the room with the benches. Fire *005* characterized this late occupational phase. Although, the space was occupied, it no longer functioned as originally intended. Pottery dates for these loci cannot be refined any more closely than fifth century AD, identical to the early occupational phase.

Nevertheless, the occupational phase change in the building was significant especially if the structure functioned as an ecclesiastical complex. The archaeological evidence may point to a period when the controlling authority of the building had withdrawn and a new group had arrived. Historically, this might be attributed to the advent of the Blemmyes, a desert group from the south that invaded the area in late antiquity (cf. Sidebotham 1995:8–10).

If this structure was an ecclesiastical complex, late Blemmye occupation of the building was possible. As late as the fifth century AD, the Blemmyes still worshiped at pagan temples at Philae, and the first Blemmyes were Christianized only during the first half of the sixth century, around AD 530 (cf. Altheim and Stiehl 1971:418–419, 532–536). Thus, the pagan Blemmyes would not necessarily have respected a church as a sacred site.

Trench 39, Phase III
Abandonment and decay (later in the fifth century AD).
Following the latest occupation, the building underwent complete and utter collapse. All walls collapsed resulting in architectural tumble *003*. Subsequent to the total collapse of the structure, windblown sand *002* accumulated over the entire trench, including the walls and pillars, sealing it off from view.

4.6.5   DISCUSSION OF THE "BASILICA"

Entrance to the putative Christian structure was from a small *kardo*, which extended off the *decumanus maximus* (Sidebotham 2002:236 and 237–238, Figs. 21–25). This main entrance was 1.10 m wide (Sidebotham 1998:72) and was centered along the western face of the building. Excavations revealed that immediately inside the main entrance was a passageway and to the right (south) was a wall lined with stone benches. Although the entire passageway has not been excavated, the surface topography suggests that it extended west-east through the entire building. The passageway was divided by a doorway that subdivided the more-formal portions of the building (on the south) from the less formal (on the north). Rooms and hallways opened from this main passageway suggesting that it was designed as a

breezeway, allowing air circulation to cool the interior of the building. Placement of the hallway also reduced the amount of sand blown by the prevailing northerly winds into the interior of the building. The presence of the benches also suggests that the passageway was a vestibule or waiting area.

The formal rooms excavated within the building included an area in the southwestern corner where gypsum benches lined the walls (trench BE96-8). Also found within this room was a stone basin with a base and a crushed terracotta vessel. All stone features appear to have been reused. The wear patterns on these benches suggest that they may have originally been paving stones (Sidebotham 1998:63–73). Scratched into one of the stone seats was a simple graffito of seated human figure (Sidebotham 1998:71, Plate 3-56).

Another formal space excavated within the building was a room in the southeastern corner. This room comprised a paved gypsum flagstone floor (BE98/99-22.*023*), two benches constructed of reused gypsum blocks (BE98/99-22.*057*) at the northern end, and a single column (BE98/99-22.*017/066*) in the southeastern corner of the courtyard that may have supported a small roofed area. The paved room was clearly not a utilitarian domestic area. Beneath this putative roofed area was a large storage vessel *in situ* (BE98/99-22.*021/062/063*). There was also evidence for a robbed-out installation (BE98/99-22.*087*) that had originally been defined by a parapet (BE98/99-22.*065*) on its northern side. The grandeur of the paved room suggests that it was designed to receive large numbers of persons and probably operated as a public area within this building.

Rooms classified as the private sphere of the building included a kitchen in trench BE96/97/98-12. Evidence such as fragments of two braziers, numerous small fires, an abundance of animal and fish bones, knife-sharpening stones, pot stands, and mortar and pestle sets led to this interpretation. Also, further evidence for this function was the presence of a storeroom (BE96/97/98-12.*062* within walls *016*, *047*, *053*, and entrance *064*) that contained one amphora of *garum* found *in situ*, propped up against a wall (Sidebotham 1998:75–77; Van Neer and Ervynck 1998:382). Adjacent to the kitchen was a storeroom (BE96/97/98-12.*046* within walls *016*, *015*, and *036*) littered with reused gypsum blocks, similar to those found in the floor in BE98/99-22.*023*.

The large room in the northeastern quadrant of the building seems to belong to the private sphere. Locus *011*, a large installation that contained both a storage vessel and a level work surface, dominated the room.

Near *011* was *076*, a small table and seat constructed of reused gypsum blocks. Also, embedded in the floor in the northwest corner was *101*, a vessel *in situ*, most likely functioning as a pot stand similar to those found in the kitchen in trench BE96/97/98-12 (cf. Sidebotham 1999:32–34, 40, 45). Finally, upon exposed *de facto* surface *102* lay one crushed vessel, probably containing *garum*. The presence of the *garum*, the pot stands, storage vessel, and work surfaces suggests that this room was a food preparation area

Excavations have also revealed the eastern segment of the corridor that led from the western entrance of the building (BE96-8.*024/029*). As noted above, a doorway blocked access from the corridor to the grand entranceway of the building. Found within the corridor was *013*, a staircase to an upper floor/roof and *028*, a large platform. A second exterior doorway (*103*) was tucked behind the staircase to the east, away from the prevailing winds. Although there was access to the interior of the building through this portal, the doorway that separated the corridor from the grand hallway restricted activities undertaken in this area.

The numerous architectural installations taken together with results from trenches BE96-8, BE96/97/98-12, BE98/99-22, and BE99/00-30 indicate the intermixing of private and public spaces within one large building that operated as one unit in the fifth century AD. The find of a terracotta lamp with a Coptic Christian aphorism (Sidebotham 2000b: 43–44) and a large copper-alloy fragment of a clearly Christian cross (see Chapter 9) suggest that this building may have had a Christian ecclesiastical function.

4.7 CONCLUSION

The 1999 and 2000 excavation seasons produced a wealth of data on various aspects of Ptolemaic-Roman Berenike between the third century BC and the sixth century AD. Substantial archaeological evidence indicating activity at Berenike in the third and second centuries BC came to light in the western part of the site in trenches BE00-35, BE00-36, and BE00-40. There, portions of an industrial metalworking area were recorded. Manufacture of iron, copper-alloy, and lead implements added to knowledge acquired in 1996 (in trench BE96-11) of evidence for brickmaking in the earliest history of the site. Some late Ptolemaic material also derived from beneath the early Roman trash dump and the northern end of the site and from the lowest excavated reaches of trench 10.

Additional documents (mainly papyri and ostraka) from the early Roman period continued to appear in quantity in excavations in the trash dump at the northern edge of the site in trenches BE99-29, BE99-31, and BE00-33. This area also produced huge quantities of other organic and inorganic finds that shed light on various facets of life in the early Roman city and of the long distance trade that was its raison d'être. Early Roman and very late Ptolemaic levels were also uncovered in the large trench (BE96/97/98/99/00-10) immediately north of the Serapis temple. There some architectural remains and ostraka from the early Roman city supplemented the plethora of papyri and ostraka revealed in the early Roman trash on the history of Berenike at that time.

Still, the best documented period in the excavations was the late Roman. The massive late Roman pottery dump used to level the eastern edge of the site in preparation for large-scale building from the mid–late fourth century on and which had been noted in earlier seasons, continued to appear in trenches especially in the putative Christian ecclesiastical structure (BE98/99-22 and BE99/00-30/BE00-39). Excavations in numerous trenches in the area between that structure and the Serapis temple documented a structure for an as yet unidentified mystery cult (BE98/99-23/BE99/00-32) and numerous multistoried structures (BE98-20/BE99-27, BE99-28/BE00-38, BE00-34, BE00-37, and BE00-41). The latter appear to have had the dual purpose of commercial functions on the ground floors and domestic/residential purposes on the floors above (cf. Sidebotham 2002).

There is, as yet, no evidence for if or how Berenike was divided into urban districts/regions (*amphoda*) in any period in its history. Elsewhere in Egypt little is known about such urban divisions in the Ptolemaic period, but a fair amount of data is available for cities from the Roman era (cf. Alston 2002: 103–165, 172–174). Continued excavations should document this aspect of the urban history of Berenike.

Knowledge of the social, economic and ethnic backgrounds of the port's residents in all periods also expanded. There is now evidence for 11 different written scripts/languages used at the port from late Ptolemaic to late Roman times. These include Hieroglyphs, Demotic, Greek, Latin, Coptic, Hebrew, Aramaic, Palmyrene, Tamil-Brahmi, a Prakrit-Sanskrit hybrid and one script which has yet to be identified. The religious preferences of Berenike's residents also point to a population from varied origins. Evidence indicates worship of Serapis, Jupiter, Isis, Yarhibol/Hierobol, the Roman imperial cult (Caracalla and Julia Domna), Harpocrates, Aphrodite/Venus, Christianity, possibly Judaism and one other as yet unidentifiable mystery cult. The discovery of the remains of a pet dog or cat, Proconnesian marble floor or wall revetment, escargot from the Nile or Mediterranean, fancy carpets, floor or furniture coverings, carved intaglio bezels from signet rings and a gold and pearl earring provide some indication of the wealthier residents of the port.

Knowledge of the areas with which Berenike was in direct or indirect commercial contact also expanded as a result of excavations in 1999 and 2000. In the Ptolemaic period contact with Rhodes (amphoras), Phoenicia or India (beads) and sub-Saharan Africa (an elephant tooth and ivory) is now known. By early Roman times products from virtually every region of the Roman Empire could be found at Berenike and contacts with other regions of the Red Sea and South Asia (especially India and Sri Lanka) are well documented. These included, by late Roman times, Berenike's contacts with the western Mediterranean which had withered while the bulk of the port's Mediterranean relations, as attested by pottery and numismatic evidence, were confined to the eastern Mediterranean. Extra-imperial contacts in tuhe late period included the Kingdom of Aksum (attested in pottery and a single coin), western India (a single coin), Sri Lanka (numerous beads) and elsewhere in the Indian Ocean basin (teakwood, coconut, sorghum and bamboo). The discovery of beads from Vietnam and/or Thailand and from eastern Java expanded Berenike's known eastern contacts farther afield than had hitherto been possible. These latter finds probably arrived at Berenike second or third hand via contacts in southern India and/or Sri Lanka.

Excavations in future seasons will concentrate on the Ptolemaic industrial area and putative harbor, the early Roman trash dump, the large trench north of the Serapis temple, the late Roman quarter between the Serapis temple and the coast, and buildings along the coast, especially in the putative Christian ecclesiastical structure.

CHAPTER 5 ～

GEOLOGY

J. A. HARRELL

The author examined geological samples from trenches excavated during the 1998 and 1999 seasons at Berenike (in 1999) and those excavated during the 2000 season (in 2001). The 291 items from 1998 excluded most of the worked stone objects, which had been placed in storage at Quft. In contrast, nearly all of the samples collected in 1999 (272 total) and 2000 (408 total) were stored at Berenike and examined there. A visit to the antiquities storage magazine in Quft in 2002 permitted the author to see another 82 samples, consisting mostly of stone beads that were not available previously, and so the inventory of geological materials from 1998 through 2000 is now virtually complete. The majority of the samples from both seasons were unremarkable and included materials such as trench sand, gravel clasts of many rock types from the local wadis, fragments of the rock gypsum and rock anhydrite building stones used on the site, and pieces of selenite and satin spar gypsum, as well as lumps of gypsum paste derived from the aforementioned building stones. There were, however, many rock and mineral specimens that were notable either because they were worked or because they represented valuable trade commodities or utilitarian materials. These are described in section 5.3. Geological identifications for all 563 samples examined are available from the author. Other sections of this chapter record miscellaneous geological observations, including the source of coral used for walls in Berenike (5.1.1), a possible sand plaster on a coral-head wall in trench BE99-27 (5.1.2), a putative quay in trench BE97/98-17 (5.1.3), and the geographic source of bitumen found at Berenike (5.2).

5.1 ASPECTS OF BERENIKE ARCHITECTURE

5.1.1 SOURCE OF CORAL USED FOR WALLS

Berenike's walls are built mostly of "coral heads." These are large (15 40 cm across), somewhat rounded pieces of primarily *Platygyra*, *Leptoria*, and *Favites* corals, all genera of the *Faviidae* family (Harrell 1996:106). Hundreds of thousands of coral heads were used and the question is, where did they all come from? The author has previously hypothesized (Harrell 1996:108; 1998:130–131) that prior to Berenike's settlement loose pieces of coral abundantly littered the tops of the two local reef-limestone terraces: the one on which Berenike was built, and the one forming the "south promontory" on the opposite side of the lagoon. It is to be expected that coral would be plentiful atop these terraces because at about 5,000 to 8,000 years ago, when sea level was 2–3 m higher than present, the ~2 m terraces along the Red Sea coasts, like those at Berenike, originated as wave-cut benches eroded into earlier and more elevated reef deposits (Harrell 1996:102–105; 1998:129–130). These shallowly submerged benches would have accumulated pieces of coral tossed landward by storm waves from the living reefs along their seaward edges. Until now it has not been possible to test this hypothesis because undisturbed reef-limestone terraces do not exist in the immediate vicinity of Berenike, and the neighboring stretches of coast, which may have such terraces, have been off limits due to military restrictions.

In June 1999 the author had the opportunity to visit an undisturbed coastal site at Marsa Tundeba (24° 57.43' N/34° 56.20' E), 13 km south of Marsa Alam, where a reef-limestone terrace is present at about 2 m above sea level. It is covered with a thin layer of windblown sand and large numbers of coral fragments of a size similar to those in Berenike's walls (Plate 5-1). Corals of the *Faviidae* family are not especially common but this may only be a local anomaly. In all other respects, however, the Marsa Tundeba terrace is similar to those of Berenike and the south promontory. These observations, therefore, support the author's original suggestion that the coral used for Berenike's walls came from the tops of the local reef-limestone terraces.

Plate 5-1   Loose pieces of coral on top of the 2 m reef-limestone terrace at Marsa Tundeba. Photograph by J. A. Harrell.

5.1.2   PUTATIVE SAND PLASTER IN TRENCH 27

Berenike's coral-head walls have a sand mortar and, given their exceedingly rough surfaces, may also have been covered with a "sand plaster" (Harrell 1998:141–142; Schijns, *et al.* 1999:95–101). The locally available *sabkha* (salt-flats) and terrace-top, windblown sands would have worked well for these applications because of the minute amounts calcium sulfate (gypsum) and especially sodium chlorite (halite) that occur naturally within them. These salts dissolve when wetted and precipitate as a weak, intergranular cement when the sand dries. Sand plaster would not make a durable surface, but it would have the advantage of being easy to apply and maintain.

Trench supervisors have reported seeing what they believed to be sand plaster on many excavated coral-head walls, but it was always removed when cleaning the walls for photography and drawing. The first opportunity for the author to see a putative sand plaster *in situ* occurred during the 1999 season, and this was in trench BE99-*27.027*. The material covering one wall consisted of very fine to fine-grained sand (grains smaller than 0.25 mm) with common larger bioclasts (coral and mollusk fragments) up to 2 cm in size. There was no clay, and so the sand owed its hardness only to a halite-gypsum cement. It could be *sabkha* sand, but given its fine size, it is more likely to be mostly windblown sand like that accumulating today on top of the Berenike terrace. It is not certain, however, that it is actually an applied plaster. It could just be sand blown into the abandoned building that later hardened and adhered to the walls.

5.1.3   PUTATIVE QUAY IN TRENCH 17

The original limestone surface of the reef terrace on which Berenike was built is about 2 m above current mean sea level (Harrell 1996:102–105 and 112–126; 1998:125–130), and the low, broad and flat *sabkha* that now fringes the terrace on three sides (north, south, and east) is the product of wadi deposition over the millennia. When Berenike was first settled in the early Ptolemaic period there might have been little or no *sabkha*, thus allowing boats to dock on many sides of the terrace. Over time the *sabkha* expanded seaward and rose in elevation with the result that the northern anchorage filled in with sediment first followed by the eastern one. Only a small remnant of the southern anchorage now remains in the form of the lagoon. This pattern of progressive sedimentation is supported, not only by the geological evidence, but is also consistent with the growth of Berenike as it is now understood (Sidebotham and Wendrich 1998:87). In Ptolemaic times the settlement occupied mainly the western and northern portions of the site, perhaps because the northern anchorage was favored, and by Roman times, with the retreat of the sea, the settlement had expanded to the eastern and southern portions of the site, and even extended out onto the *sabkha*.

We should expect to see around the edges of the settlement some massive walls that served as either quays (or piers) for boats. The first structure discovered that might be a quay (but originally was interpreted as a seawall) dates to the first century AD and occurs in trench BE94/95-2.*054a–b* on the southeast side of Berenike (Harrell 1996:107, 124; Sidebotham 1996:25–26). In the 1998 season another possible quay, also dating to the first century AD, was uncovered in trench BE97/98-17 (wall 17.*110/116/125*, Sidebotham and Wendrich 1998:87–88) on the northeast side. Yet another structure in BE98/99-22.*083* on the east side and dating from the fifth century AD was originally thought to be a quay (Sidebotham and Wendrich 1998:87–88) but now appears to be the wall of a building not unlike many others erected on the *sabkha* during the late Roman period.

Wall BE97/98-17.*110/116/125* was constructed mainly from coral heads like most of the rest of the walls in Berenike. Its 1.30 m width, however, is much greater than that typical for the walls of buildings, which have maximum widths of about 0.80 m. At its top, on the west end, there are cut slabs of calcareous pebbly sandstone, a rock occasionally seen in other trenches and coming from outcrops along the west side of Berenike (Harrell 1998:125, Figure 4–4). The slabs are 4–5 cm thick and up to 65 cm across. This wall differs markedly from the one in BE94/95-2, which is 1–1.2 m wide and built with large (25–75 cm across), irregular blocks of algal-coral limestone (Harrell 1996:107–108) that were probably quarried from Berenike's reef-limestone bedrock. In BE97/98-17, the base of the wall has an elevation of 0 to -3 cm (that is, 3 cm below the Berenike zero datum, which corresponds to the average high tide level) and rests on at least 40 cm of medium- to coarse-grained sand (grains mostly between 0.25 and 1.00 mm) with sparse to abundant, larger (up to 2 cm) mollusk shells (mainly pelecypod fragments) plus occasional pottery sherds. Within this layer are thin, discontinuous lenses of finer-grained bluish sand and red clay. This sediment corresponds to the lagoon fill facies of the *sabkha* deposits identified by coring (Harrell 1996:112–126).

Although wall BE97/98-17.*110/116/125* was built atop lagoonal sediment, its base is above current mean sea level, which is at least 1 m higher now that it was at the time of Berenike's founding (Harrell 1996:104). Given this, the wall could not have been a quay with seawater lapping up against it and boats afloat beside it. It does appear, however, that it functioned as a seawall. The term *seawall*, as used here, refers not so much to a protective barrier as to a structure marking the seaward limit of the settlement. On its north side was a sandy beach that sloped down to a lagoon. Boats pulled up onto this beach would have been tied to wooden poles planted in the sand to keep them from being carried off by the high tide. Further supporting the notion of the structure in BE97/98-17 being a seawall is its location at the eastern edge of what is almost certainly an artificial embayment or harbor on the west side of Building F on the site maps attached to the reports for the 1995 and 1996 seasons (Harrell 1996:125).

5.2 BITUMEN ANALYSES

As in other parts of the ancient world, petroleum-derived bitumen may have been used in Greco-Roman Egypt for at least some of the following applications: sealant for ceramic pots, baskets, and boats and ships; adhesive for jewelry and tools; varnish for wood, stone, and metal; fuel; and medicine (Forbes 1964:1–124; Nissenbaum 1978:841–842; Connan, *et al*. 1992:2743–2744). Perhaps its best-known use was as a preservative for mummies (Lucas 1962:271, 303–308; Serpico 2000:454–468). The word *mummy*, in fact, comes from the Persian and later Arabic *mummiya* meaning *bitumen*. Bitumen is a general term that encompasses liquid petroleum, semisolid tar, and solid asphalt or pitch.

At Berenike, bitumen is found in the excavations mainly as small, loose pieces of asphalt where the ancient application is not evident (Harrell 1998:146; and section 5.3.2 in this chapter). A couple of pieces have been carved (BE97 4246-X from Shenshef-05.*002*) and drilled (BE97 4247-X from Shenshef-03.*003*), and some bitumen has been used to seal stoppers and holes in ceramic pots.

It is widely assumed that the bitumen used anciently in Egypt came from the Dead Sea area of Palestine, where petroleum seeps and tar and asphalt deposits are common (Lucas 1962:303; Nissenbaum 1978; Ikram and Dodson 1998:106). This view is based both on a perceived absence of a bitumen source in Egypt and on two texts from the late first century BC that mention the importation of Dead Sea bitumen into Egypt: Diodorus Siculus 19.99, and Strabo, *Geography* 16.2.45. Recent chemical analyses have confirmed that the Dead Sea was, indeed, a source for bitumen used in Egypt during the Greco-Roman period (Rullkötter and Nissenbaum 1988), but there is now new evidence that demonstrates the Egyptians also used bitumen from a source within Egypt proper during the Roman period (Harrell and Lewan 2002). This is a petroleum seep at the southern end of the Gebel Zeit range (27° 51.35' N/33° 34.30' E), which is located on the southwestern shore of the Gulf of Suez, 70 km north of Hurghada. The Arabic name translates as "oil" (*zeit*) "mountain" (*gebel*).

It is of interest to know if the bitumen found at Berenike comes from Gebel Zeit, the Dead Sea, or somewhere else. To find out, the following thirteen bitumen samples (all asphalt) were selected for chemical analysis: BE98 1909-R, BE98 3320-R, BE98 3325-R, BE98 6350-R, BE98 6484-R, BE99 2117-R, and BE99 4812-G from trench BE96/97/98/99-10 (loci *141*, *158*, *184*, *256*, *222*, *374*, and *361* respectively); BE98 2996-R and BE98 5221-R from trench BE97/98-16 (loci *087* and *142*, respectively); BE98 1935-R and BE98 2999-R from trench BE98-19 (loci *006* and *009*, respectively); and BE98 5419-R and an unregistered sample from trench BE98/99-23 (loci *012* and *022A*, respectively). The unregistered sample came from the top of a fifth-century AD amphora toe, and the BE99 4812-G sample came from the outside of a first-century AD jar containing peppercorns, where it was used as a patch to cover a hole. All the other samples were found as loose pieces of asphalt in the trenches.

The bitumen samples were analyzed by gas chromotography–mass spectrometry (GC/MS) in an effort to identify the molecular signatures or biomarkers that uniquely characterize the hydrocarbon source rocks. The analytical work was done by Dr. Michael D. Lewan, a senior research geochemist, and Mr. David King, a GC/MS technician, both of the Petroleum Section of the United States Geological Survey in Denver, Colorado. Lewan compared the sterane and terpane biomarkers of the Berenike samples with those already well established for the Gebel Zeit and Dead Sea sources (Harrell and Lewan 2002). He found that the organic molecules in five of the bitumen samples were too degraded to yield meaningful results (BE98 1935-R, BE98 6350-R, BE98 2999-R, BE99 2117-R, and BE99 4812-G). However, samples BE98 1909-R, BE98 3320-R, and BE98 5419-R are almost certainly from the Dead Sea and 022-A, BE 98 3325-R, and BE98 6484-R may be as well. Samples BE98 2996-R and BE98 5221-R are definitely not from Gebel Zeit, but the results are inconclusive with regard to the Dead Sea. More analyses are needed, but the preliminary indication is that the people of Berenike eschewed the bitumen of Gebel Zeit and imported, instead, bitumen from the much more distant Dead Sea. Perhaps the Dead Sea bitumen, which was abundantly available as semisolid asphalt, was preferred because it was more easily transported or because it could be obtained

in larger quantities. Alternatively, perhaps there was simply more shipborne trade coming south to Berenike through the Gulf of Aqaba (just below the Dead Sea) than through the Gulf of Suez. It is also, of course, possible that Gebel Zeit petroleum was used at Berenike but, being a liquid, either has not been preserved as asphaltic deposits or, if thickened to asphalt by inspissation, has not yet been sampled and tested.

5.3   DISTRIBUTION OF SELECTED ROCKS AND MINERALS (GEOLOGICAL SAMPLES FROM THE 1998–2000 SEASONS)

The compilation that follows is a continuation of section 4.7 in Harrell (1998), which includes samples from the 1995, 1996, and 1997 seasons. In this earlier report, which lists materials by trench and locus, the rocks and minerals are described as are also their probable uses and possible geologic sources. This same detailed information is presented here only for the few materials not previously recorded at Berenike. The specimens identified below are all unworked unless otherwise noted, and site identification numbers are given only for the worked objects. Samples not from excavation loci but rather picked up during trench cleanings are registered variously as *bfw* (balk fall west), *cb* (clean balk), *cbe* (clean balk east), *cbn* (clean balk north), *cbs* (clean balk south), *cbw* (clean balk west), *ct* (clean trench), and *surf* (found on the surface and not associated with any trench). Following, these codes are preceded by the year in which the sample was excavated.

5.3.1   DECORATIVE / (SEMI-)PRECIOUS MATERIALS

Note: numerals in parentheses after some loci are numbers of specimens found, and if no numeral appears then only one specimen was recovered.

Previously reported materials
   Marble, *var. Proconnesian*
Use: Harrell 1996: 111 and 1998: 142
Source: *Idem*
Finds: Fragments of flat slabs. Those cut (sawn) and polished on two sides vary in thickness from 1.8 to 5.0 cm with six of the nine ranging between 2.5 and 3.2 cm. All fragments have two cut sides, except where otherwise noted.
   BE96/97/98/99-10.*127* (BE98 1874-rr). BE97/98-18.*153* (BE98 5647-rr). BE98-21.*003* (BE98 1895-R).

BE99-27.*056* and *057* (no site IDs, both left on spoil pile). BE99-28.*037* (BE99 3610-R), and *038* (BE99 4580-R). BE99-32.*013* (BE99 3775-R). BE00-34.*026* (one cut side). BE00-37.*008* (irregular piece), *030* (2, one irregular piece and another with one cut side).

Alabaster Gypsum
Use: Harrell 1996: 107–108 and 1998: 136–139
Source: *Idem*
Finds: Architectural and sculptural elements from trenches BE96/97/98/99/00-10 (vessel rim, BE00 4097-rr), BE97/98-16 (head from a statuette, BE98 5039-t; carved sphinx, BE98 3927-t), BE98/99-23 (two pedestals, BE99 4608-S and BE99 4611-S; altar, BE99 4609-S; relief, BE99 1487-tt; four offering basins, BE98 7452-rr), BE99-27 (capital, BE99 4614-S), BE99-28 (capital, BE99 4602-S), BE99/00-30 (unusual polygonal block, BE00 3820-rr), BE99/00-32 (platter, BE99 4612-rr), BE00-39 (circular disk with square hole, BE00 4778-rr), BE00-40 (head from statuette, BE00 1602-tt) and BE00-41 (circular ring, BE00 5410-rr). These objects are carved from the same stone used for many of the ashlar blocks found at Berenike. The statuette of a goddess found in trench BE99-31 (BE99 3491-tt) is also carved from alabaster gypsum but is finer grained than the variety used for the aforementioned objects.

Beryl, *var. Emerald*
Use: Harrell 1996:112 and 1998:142–143
Source: *Idem*
Finds: BE96/97/98/99/00–10.*036, 132, 134, 154, 158, 159* (bead BE98 2963-B), *221, 393, 423, 425, 431, 435, 486* (3), *489, 517, 559, 620, 99ct.* BE96/97/98-12: *299* (2), *302, 303.* BE97/98-16.*118, 152, 169, 181.* BE97/98-17.*083, 086* (2), *114, 98ct* (2). BE98-20.*004, 020, 023, 027, 053.* BE98-21.*001* (2), *003, 004, 012, 017, 023* (3), *027, 030* (bead BE98 4121-B), *033, 040.* BE98/99-22.*024, 061, 104, 112, 98ct* (2). BE99-26.*004, 009, 022* (3), *99cbw.* BE99-27.*009, 015, 020* (3), *021, 023, 024, 026.* BE99-28.*021, 028.* BE99-29.*014* (possibly worked BE99 1128-R), *99cbw.* BE99/00-30.*002, 033,* 136, 163, 174, *99cbe, 00ct.* BE99-31.*002.* BE00-33.*004, 013, 00bt.* BE00-34.*008* (2), *011.* BE00-37.*006* (2), *008, 017, 018, 023* (3), *026, 029, 00ct* (2). BE00-38.*002.* BE00-41.*005, 031.* BE99-Surface

Quartz, *var. Rock Crystal*
Use: Harrell 1998:143
Source: *Idem*
Finds: All quartz specimens are colorless unless otherwise indicated. BE96/97/98/99/00-10.*095, 374*

(bead BE99 2135-B), *468* (4), *469, 471, 482* (bead BE00 2982-B), *519.* BE97/98-16.*107, 176.* BE97/98-18.*002, 152* (4, one worked, BE98 5240-rr). BE98-19.*006.* BE98-21.*010* (2), *015* (2), *018* (2), *019, 020* (bead BE98 2961-B), *021, 023, 027, 040* (2). BE98/99-23.*012* (3, one milky-white bead, BE98 5010-B), *033.* BE98-24.*004.* BE99-26.*019, 022.* BE99-27.*004, 005, 006* (2), *021* (2), *024* (2, one pendant BE99 3942-bb), *026* (bead BE99 4407-B), *99cbn.* BE99-28.*017, 032* (2), *036* (2), *038.* BE99-29.*006* (bead on a string BE99 0693-bb). BE99/00-30.*009, 055, 062, 145, 174* (worked BE00 3819-R). BE99-31.*99cbe.* BE99/00-32.*029.* BE00-33.*008, 013* (worked BE00 2153-R), *033* (milky-white pendant BE00 3402-rr). BE00-34.*001.* BE00-37.*003, 026* (2). BE00-40.033 (milky-white pendant BE00 3402-rr). BE98-Surface (bead BE98 2825-B)

Chalcedony, *vars. Carnelian and Sard*
Use: Harrell 1998:143
Source: *Idem*
Finds: BE96/97/98/99/00-10.*036A* (bead BE98 2564-B), *169, 222, 236, 370* (3), *371, 385* (5), *392, 393* (4), *397, 404* (6), *408, 409, 414, 443, 448, 450* (bead BE00 0582-B), *482* (bead BE00 1441-B), *485, 489, 490, 503, 516, 519, 520, 527* (bead BE00 4957-B), *548, 551, 559* (2, one bead BE00 5569-B), *562* (bead BE00 5574-B), *564B, 569, 583, 648* (bead BE00 6714-B), *99ct* (2, one bead BE99 4583-B), *00ct* (6, one bead, BE00 6714-B). BE97/98-18.*057* (bead BE98 2583-B). BE97/98-19.*006* (bead BE98 2536-B), *023* (bead BE98 2576-B). BE98-21.*004* (bead BE98 2570-B), *017* (bead BE98 3336-B), *018* (three beads BE98 2585-B, 2643-B), *020* (bead BE98 2961-B), *025* (bead BE98 3830-B), *030* (bead BE98 4121-B), *033, 98cb* (bead BE98 6883-B), *98cbn* (bead BE98 6887-B). BE98/99-22.*068, 084, 086.* BE98/99-23.*030* (bead BE99 0861-B). BE99-27.*99ct* (engraved disk or cabachon BE99 4234-R). BE99-28.*028.* BE99-29.*011* (engraved disk BE99 0842-bb). BE99/00-30.*163* (2, one cameo blank fragment BE00 2937-R, and one bead BE00 2928-B). BE99-31.*012, 018* (3), *020, 99cbs.* BE99/00-32.*035.* BE00-33.*005, 013, 018, 019* (bead BE00 1502-B), *022* (bead BE00 2519-B). BE00-34.*001.* BE00-37.*005, 00ct* (3, two beads BE00 5870-B). BE00-40.*001* (bead BE00 1570-B). BE00-41.*005, 00ct.*

Chalcedony, *vars. Onyx and Sardonyx Agates*
Use: Harrell 1998:144
Source: *Idem*
Finds: The letter after the locus or site ID numbers

indicates the type of agate: *o* for onyx and *s* for sardonyx. BE96/97/98/99/00-10.*036A*/o (bead BE00 1766-B), *121*/o (bead BE98 2539-B), *236*/s, *269*/s (bead BE00 3481-B), *334*/o, *385*/s (cameo blank BE99 2274-bb), *446*/s, *465*/s, *468*/s, *502*/s, *505*/s, *516*/s (worked BE00 4088-R), *521*/o, *98ct*/o (worked BE98 1938-R), *99cb*/o. BE97/98-16.*059*/o (cameo blank BE98 1879-rr), *087*/o (oval cameo blank BE98 1894-rr). BE97/98-18.*041*/s, *032*/o (2), *062*/s, *063*/o, *074A*/o, *107*/s, *158*/o (bead BE98 4863-B). BE97/98-19.*021*/o, *024*/o (bead BE98 2588-B). BE98-20.*015*/o (bead BE98 2574-B), *053*/s, *98ct*/o (bead BE98 4866-B). BE98-21.*005*/o (bead BE98 2567-B). BE98/99-22.*056*/o (bead BE98 5011-B), *112*/o. BE98/99-23.*033*/o, 051/s (bead BE99 1865-B). BE99-26.*017*/o (worked BE99 4817-R), *99cbw*/s (bead BE99 2608-B). BE99-27.*017*/s, *018*/s (bead BE99 2136-B), *026*/o+s (2, one bead BE99 4411-B/s). BE99-28.*023*/o (worked BE99 4818-rr), *032*/o (bead BE99 3497-B), *036*/s (bead BE99 3486-B). BE99-29.*006* (engraved disk BE99 0548-bb), *014*/o+s (2, cameo blanks BE99 0974-R/o and BE99 1128-R/s). BE99/00-30.*159*/o (bead BE00 2772-B). BE99/00-32.*008*/o (bead BE00 0187-B). BE00-33.*008*/o+s (3, two cameo blanks BE00 1318-R/o), *038*/o+s (2, one cameo blank BE00 4704-R/o). BE00-37.*026*/s (bead BE00 4838-B). BE00-40.*053*/s (bead BE00 3378-B)

Chert, *var. Jasper*
Use: Harrell 1998:144
Source: *Idem*
Finds: BE99-26.*043*, *049*. BE99-28.*038*

Olivine, *var. Peridot*
Use: Harrell 1998:144 and 1999:115–116
Source: *Idem*
Finds: BE96/97/98/99/00-10.*471*. BE97/98-17.*131*. BE98/99-22.*98ct*. BE00-33.*008*. BE00-37.*006*

Obsidian
Use: Harrell 1996:112, 1998:145, and 1999:115
Source: *Idem*
Finds: BE96/97/98/99/00-10.*141*, *151*, *219*, *426*, *526* (4), *00ct*. BE98-20.*98cbe*. BE98-21.*004*, *018* (3), *038*. BE00-37.*026* (2). BE00-40.*054*. BE96/97/98/99-10.*141*, *151*, *219*, *426*. BE98-20.*98cbe*. BE98-21.*004*, *018* (3), *038*.

Newly Encountered Materials
Marble, *var. Lygdos?*
Use: Sculptures and other carved objects
Source: Unknown but this fine-grained, brilliantly white marble may be the "lygdos" mentioned by ancient writers as coming from Arabia Felix, modern Yemen (Harrell 1999:109–110).
Finds: BE96/97/98/99/00-10.*96btn* (decorated platter fragment BE99 5076-X)

Beryl, *var. Aquamarine*
Use: Jewelry
Source: Probably Sri Lanka or, more likely, India (Herath 1975:60–63; Warmington 1974:250–251; Wadia 1975:458; Sinkankas 1989:445–455)
Finds: BE98-21.*023* (bead BE98 3339-B)

Quartz, *var. Amethyst*
Use: Jewelry
Source: Probably the Eastern Desert, where two Roman-period quarries are known: Wadi el-Hudi, 25 km southeast of Aswan (Shaw and Jameson 1993) and Wadi Abu Diyeiba, 25 km southwest of Safaga (Murray 1914; Shaw and Jameson 1993; Aston, *et al.* 2000:50–52). The Romans are also known to have imported amethyst from India (Warmington 1974:245).
Finds: BE99-27.*026*. BE99-29.*002* (carved oval cabachon BE99 0549-bb). BE99/00-30.*159* (oval cabachon BE00 2766-R), *163* (2). BE98-Surface.*98surf* (bead BE98 2644-B)

Garnet
Use: Jewelry
Source: Probably India. Although garnet occurs in many metamorphic rocks in the Eastern Desert, no garnets of gem quality have been reported and no ancient workings are known. India was an important source of garnets during the Roman period, and the principal varieties it produced were the red almandine and the commonly brown to orange grossular and spessartine (Smith 1972:332, 335–336; Warmington 1974:252–253; Wadia 1975:459), examples of which are represented in the finds.
Finds: BE96/97/98/99/00-10.*196* (red), *435* (red, carved tear-shaped cabachon BE99 3961-bb). BE98-21.*037* (brown, 12-sided crystal). BE99-26.*006* (brownish orange). BE00-37.*016* (red), *029* (red 12-sided crystal)

Calcite, *var. Crystal*
Use: Jewelry
Source: Unknown. Calcite is a ubiquitous mineral and colored varieties could occur in many of the areas where the Romans traded.
Finds: BE00-37.*026* (2, one pink bead BE00 5187-B and one white bead BE00 5727-B).

Calcite, *var. Travertine*
Use: Sculptures and other carved objects
Source: This rock, which is often incorrectly referred to as alabaster, was quarried by the Romans at several sites in Middle Egypt (Aston, *et al.* 2000:59–60).
Finds: BE00-33.*025* (possibly travertine, piece with one cut/sawn side BE00 3026-rr). BE00-40.*047* (cylinder with longitudinal hole BE00 6442-rr)

Serpentinite
Use: Jewelry
Source: Unknown but probably the Eastern Desert where outcrops of serpentinite are common (Aston, *et al.* 2000:56–57).
Finds: BE99/00-30.*102* (worked BE00 0750-rr). BE00-34.*008* (bead BE00 0965-B)

Magnetite
Use: Magnetite is not actually a precious stone but it is included here because the one specimen recovered is a perfect octahedral (8-sided) crystal. This may have made it useful as an item of jewelry or a gaming piece.
Source: Unknown but probably the Eastern Desert where magnetite is a common accessory mineral in many igneous and metamorphic rocks. Large, well-formed crystals are, however, highly unusual. They may be associated with some of the iron-ore deposits that are especially rich in magnetite (Hussein 1990:518–519). No ancient workings are known.
Finds: BE98-21.*005* (crystal)

5.3.2   UTILITARIAN MATERIALS
Previously reported materials
Steatite
Use: Harrell 1998:145
Source: *Idem*
Finds: BE96/97/98/99/00-10.*036A* (worked BE98 1891-rr), *132, 140* (worked BE99 1131-R), *141, 327* (bead BE99 1308-B), *423* (bead BE00 0789-bb), *546* (decorated vessel wall+base fragment, BE00 4939-rr), *583* (vessel wall fragment, BE00 6826-rr), *98cb* (vessel fragment BE98 6913-R). BE96/97/98-12.*000* (platter fragment BE98 7275-R). BE97/98-16.*143* (possibly worked BE98 4104-R). BE97/98-17.*082*. BE97/98-18.*030, 046, 057A* (worked BE98 5242-R). BE98-20.*034* (worked BE98 5228-R). BE98-21.*037* (vessel rim fragment BE98 5243-R). BE98/99-23.*027* (worked BE99 0972-R). BE99-26.*033* (worked BE99 3276-rr). BE99-27.*024* (pendant BE99 3940-rr), *026* (two pendants BE99 4227-rr). BE99-28.*018* (pear-

shaped pendant BE99 1731-bb). BE99/00-30.*174, 00ct* (vessel rim+handle fragment BE00 5841-rr). BE99-31.*018*, *98cbs*. BE00-33.*008*. BE00-34.*027* (vessel wall+base fragment BE00 4413-rr), *00ctn* (decorated platter fragment BE00 2231-rr). BE00-36.*031* (rod BE00 6773-rr). BE00-37.*021* (statuette arm and shoulder fragment BE00 3006-tt). BE00-38.*024* (decorated cup BE00 5695-rr). BE00-40.*003* (pendant fragment? BE00 1588-rr), *054* (body and rim fragments from two vessels BE00 4031-rr). BE98-Surface (fragment of statuette head BE98 7212-t)

Tremolite
Use: Harrell 1998:145–146
Source: *Idem*
Finds: BE96/97/98/99-10.*221, 409, 98ct*. BE97/98-16.*081*. BE98-19.*024*. BE00-35.007, *031*

Realgar
Use: Harrell 1998:146 and 1999:116–117
Source: *Idem*
Finds: BE98/99-22.*99cb*

Bitumen, *var. Asphalt*
Use: Harrell 1998:146
Finds: Usually several pieces per locus. BE96/97/98/99/00-10.*036, 134, 141, 158, 164, 169, 182, 184, 193, 221, 222, 228, 230, 234, 241, 256, 374, 98cbs, 98ct, 99ct*. BE97/98-16.*060, 087, 099, 141, 142, 98cb*. BE98-19.*006, 009, 030, 98cbw*. BE98/99-23.*012*. BE00-37.*026*

Sulfur
Use: Harrell 1998:146
Source: *Idem*
Finds: Usually several pieces per locus. BE96/97/98/99/00-10.*119, 358, 404, 408, 516, 00ct*. BE97/98-17.*063*. BE98-19.*011, 014, 98cbe*. BE98-20.*004*. BE98-21.*019*. BE98/99-23.*020, 054*. BE99-26.*043*. BE99-31.007, *018, 019*. BE00-33.013, *008, 025, 026, 038, 039*. BE00-37.*028*

Newly encountered materials
Pumice
Use: Abrasive, possibly for metal or removing rough skin.
Source: Unknown, but not from Egypt. Pumice is a highly vesicular glass associated with geologically recent rhyolitic volcanism. It is common on many of the volcanic islands in the Mediterranean Sea (for example, the Lipari Islands north of Sicily and off the

southwest coast of Italy) and, because it often floats, reportedly washes ashore on the north coast of Egypt (Lucas 1962:73). Although the Mediterranean is the closest source of pumice, it could also come from any of numerous locales south and east of the Red Sea.

Finds: One specimen per locus unless otherwise indicated. BE97/98-17.*086* (carved with red-painted circles BE98 3000-rr), *094.* BE98-19.*008* (several pieces), *99cbn, 99cbw* (several pieces). BE99/00-30.*163* (carved cone BE00 2933-rr)

Malachite

Use: Green colorant for paint and cosmetics, copper metal, and jewelry

Source: Unknown, but probably the Eastern Desert, where malachite is commonly associated with copper deposits (Hussein 1990:515, 518, 550, Aston, *et al.* 2000:43–44), dozens of which have been mined anciently. For example, there are 16 ancient copper mines of indeterminate age within a 100-km radius of Berenike, with the closest being on Ras Banas (EGSMA 1979:14–16, map). Nothing is known about the occurrence of malachite at any of these sites.

Finds: BE97/98–16.*98ct*

5.3.3.   MISCELLANEOUS WORKED STONES

Vesicular Basalt

Use: Grinding querns and ballast.

Source: Harrell 1996:109; 1998:139–140

Finds: All are fragments of rotary grinding querns except where otherwise noted. There is one fragment per locus. BE97/98-18.*048* (BE98 1884-R). BE98-20.*027* (subcylindrical, possibly a weight or pestle BE98 3886-R). BE98/99-23.*004* (BE98 3319-R), *061* (BE99 4605-rr). BE99-27.*026* (BE99 4227-rr). BE99-28.*037* (BE99 3612-rr). BE99-32.*005* (BE99 2732-rr), *023* (BE99 0171-R). BE00-33.*00btw* (flat grinding-stone fragment BE00 5810-rr). BE00-34.*019* (subcylindrical, possibly a weight or pestle BE00 3572-rr). BE00-37.*026* (BE00 6450-rr). BE00-38.*011* (BE00 2877-rr). BE00-41.*009* (BE00 2724-rr). Besides these pieces, there are many more from other loci that are not worked.

Metaconglomerate

Use: Possibly stone vessels

Source: The Eastern Desert, where identical metaconglomerates of the Hammamat Formation occur. These rocks are found mainly in the central and northern parts of the desert, but small outcrops also occur in the south along the coast beginning just north of Marsa Alam.

The Hammamat metaconglomerate was quarried by the Romans in Wadi Hammamat, between Quseir on the Red Sea and Quft on the Nile (Aston, *et al.* 2000:57–58; Harrell, *et al.* 2002), and was referred to by them as *lapis hexecontalithos* or "stone of sixty stones."

Finds: BE99-29.*017* (possible platter fragment BE99 1579-rr).

Gypsum, *var. Selenite*

Use: Harrell 1996:107–108

Source: *Idem*, occurs as thin veins within the rock gypsum used as building stone at Berenike

Finds: BE96/97/98/99/00-10.*122* (cut edge BE98 1886-R), *196* (possible bead BE98 4497-B). BE98-19.*006* (worked BE98 1935-R)

Metadiorite/Metagabbro

Use: Grinding stones, hammer stones, weights, mortars, pestles

Source: Locally derived wadi gravel

Finds: BE96/97/98/99/00-10.*193* (flat grinding stone BE98 3525-R), *222* (probably flat grinding stone BE98 6488-R). BE97/98-18.*052A* (grinding mortar BE98 5247-R), *074A* (flat grinding stone BE98 5236-R), *112* (pestle or weight BE98 3880-R). BE98-20.*027* (macehead or hammer?, notched to take a handle BE98 5239-R). BE00-33.*008* (circular disk BE00 1456-rr)

Milky Vein Quartz

Use: All possibly used as pestles

Source: Locally derived wadi gravel

Finds: BE97/98-18.*025* (BE98 1889-R), *052A* (2 pieces BE98 5247-R)

Granite / Granodiorite, Granite Gneiss, and Aplite

Use: Grinding stones, hammer stones, weights, mortars, pestles

Source: Locally derived wadi gravel, unless otherwise noted.

Finds: BE96/97/98/99/00-10.*424* (flat grinding stone BE99 3479-S), *435* (pestle or weight BE99 3941-rr). BE98/99-22.*004* (flat grinding stone BE98 5648-R). BE99-29.*002* (circular disk BE99 0394-rr). BE99/00-30.*136* (possibly Aswan granite/granodiorite, flat grinding-stone fragment BE00 2087-rr). BE99-31.*99bfw* (circular disk BE99 4525-rr), *99cbn* (circular disk BE99 4525-rr). BE00-36.*063* (flat grinding stone BE99 6774-rr)

Sandstone

Use: Pestle or weight

Source: Unknown but probably the Eastern Desert

where outcrops of the Nubia sandstone are common.
Finds: BE98/99-22.*022* (siliceous sandstone, pestle, or
weight BE98 2947-R). BE99/00-30.*159* (two fragments
from same platter BE00 2616-rr and BE00 2786-rr).
BE00-34.*019* (platter fragment BE00 3674-R)

Limestone and Dolerite Cobbles

Use: For tallies or possibly weights. Each is carved
with a series of short, nearly parallel grooves.

Sources: The dolerite comes from the local wadi gravel,
but the limestone was imported from a distant source,
possibly as ship ballast (see Harrell 1996:109–110)

Finds: One cobble per locus. BE96/97/98/99-10.*184*
(one, dolerite BE98 3331-R), *222* (one, limestone, BE98
6488-R), and *275* (two, limestone BE98 6489-R)

CHAPTER 6 ⌇

AKSUMITE SHERDS FROM BERENIKE 1996–2000

R. S. TOMBER[1]

The purpose of this chapter is to draw attention to and catalogue the pottery in the Aksumite tradition identified at Berenike during the 1996–2000 excavation seasons. More-detailed analysis of this material, and its significance within the wider context, will appear in a future report. At present the most comprehensive and recent ceramic research has been carried out on material from Aksum itself (e.g., Wilding 1989; Phillips 2000a and b) and, thus, most parallels here are drawn primarily from this site. Overviews of the Aksumite Kingdom as a whole have recognized that two somewhat distinctive provincial ceramic traditions, to the east and the west, exist within the region (Kobischanov 1979:26), as reflected in differences in the assemblages at Aksum and farther east at Matara and Adulis (Munro-Hay 1989b: 234). This can be seen from an initial scan of the literature (e.g., compare Phillips 2000b with Anfray 1963, 1966, 1967), where differences in form and decoration can be seen between Aksum and Matara; equally, similarities exist between the sites, although in these cases the execution of the decoration frequently differs for the two areas. Additional comparison of Aksum and other sites with Berenike, both from the literature and particularly side-by-side inspection of sherds, would enhance our understanding of the Berenike material. Nevertheless, unifying features of the Aksumite ceramic repertoire make attribution of the Berenike material to the Aksumite culture relatively secure.

Historically, the *Periplus Maris Erythraei*, a first-century-AD mariner's handbook, documents contact between the two regions (Munro-Hay 1991:69, see also Casson 1989) and, thus, the tangible evidence afforded by these sherds is not surprising. At Berenike a single Aksumite coin of the last pre-Christian emperor, Aphilas (ca. AD 270/290–330, see Chapter 8, catalogue number 114), complements the ceramic corpus. The coin was found in a fifth-century-AD deposit from trench 30; there is also a dipinto of possible Aksumite origin (Gragg 1996) in a late fourth- or early fifth-century AD locus from trench 5.

6.1 AKSUMITE POTTERY: TYPOLOGY AND FABRIC

To date approximately 55 Aksumite sherds have been positively identified at Berenike. This represents the minimum number, since in most cases identification relies heavily upon the presence of characteristic decorative techniques associated, particularly, with the fourth- and fifth-century AD classical Aksumite tradition and to a certain extent the late fifth- through seventh-century AD late Aksumite wares (Phillips 2000b: Figure 401; Phillipson 2000: Figure 415). Additional undecorated sherds are undoubtedly present.

At Berenike the most common indicator is a rounded, horizontal handle with incised decoration on the join between the wall and handle and/or on the handle itself (Wilding 1989: 238; Figure 6.2, catalogue numbers 5–8); similar slashed incising on the wall and handle juncture is also seen on strap handles (Figure 6.3, catalogue number 10), but tends to be associated with the late Aksumite rather than classical tradition (cf. Phillips 2000b: fig. 278b; J. Phillips, personal communication). Another technique represented at Berenike and associated with classical Aksumite pottery is punctate decoration (described as "ovoid walk punctate or

OWP" in the Aksumite literature). Although patterns identical to those recorded at Aksum (Phillips 2000b: fig. 419B–H, 2–6, b–f) are absent, variations on this theme appear in Figure 6.3, catalogue numbers 13–14. The extremely distinctive bowl with vertical ribbed or corrugated decoration and hollow-rod handle (Figure 6.1, catalogue numbers 1–2, possibly representing a single vessel), again conforms in all respects to the classical Aksumite tradition (Phillips 2000b: fig. 491, 1). Ledge-rim bowls, occasionally with a notched rim (Figure 6-1, catalogue numbers 3–4), thought to be inspired by Roman vessels, are another indicator of Aksumite tradition, which in this case appear to be more common during the late than classical Aksumite period (Phillips 2000b: 457). One vessel form, the concave lid (Figure 6-3, catalogue number 12), may predate the remainder of the material, as the type in general, illustrated by both plain vessels and one with wavy-line incision, has elsewhere been associated with pre-Aksumite levels (Phillips 2000b: fig. 270b; Phillipson and Reynolds 1996: fig. 27c). For several reasons the identification of our vessel as pre-Aksumite is tentative. Firstly, it cannot be exactly paralleled with the known pre-Aksumite repertoire, and secondly, although it could be residual it is associated with a well-dated and generally homogeneous fifth-century AD dump deposit. If we follow Phillipson's (2000: fig. 415) terminology and chronology, the earliest Berenike levels fall within his proto-Aksumite period (third through first centuries BC). Bard, *et al.* 1997:387 define the early Aksumite period as beginning in the first century AD, with a pre-Aksumite period incorporating the first millennium BC.

Fabric is another important means by which to identify undecorated sherds. In this case the coarse and variable nature of the aplastic inclusions has made characterization difficult, not only for limited Berenike sherds, but also for the extensive material from Aksum (personal communication from J. Phillips). In publication the Aksum fabric is normally described as variable, occurring as both fine and coarse, and in a variety of colors, which are considered chronologically significant (Wilding 1989).

Assignation of the Berenike sherds to Wilding's categories based initially on color is somewhat problematic, because the Berenike sherds tend to be mottled and discolored from use over the fire. Wilding (1989:236) describes the Red Aksumite ware as a "finely levigated red paste, tempered with crushed limestone or decayed basalt . . . quartz and mica as coarse powders and grog

were also used as tempers, but only in the heavier pieces. Micaceous inclusions are relatively rare. . . ," while noting that the later brown Aksumite fabric is "more finely levigated than that of the RA ware, and . . . lacks the coarse grains and temper" (Wilding 1989:290). In her observations of clay sources local to Aksum, Phillips (2000b: 458) notes the availability of a micaceous clay similar to those seen in brown pre-Aksumite wares.

Macroscopically two main fabric groups can be identified at Berenike. Both are handmade and display a large range of variability in aplastic inclusions. Essentially Group 1 is characterized by a somewhat soft clay, containing silt-sized inclusions, some elongate (possibly chaff) inclusions, obvious gold mica and varying quantities of larger ill-sorted fragments, while Group 2 has a denser (frequently well-sorted) matrix, common, ill-sorted and diverse aplastic inclusions and no obvious mica on the surface. These distinctions roughly correlate with surface treatment and in turn loosely with Wilding's groups: Group 2 normally has well-burnished surfaces and is most similar to Wilding's Red Aksumite ware, while Group 1 has surfaces that are untreated or wiped and is most similar to Wilding's Brown Aksumite ware. More detailed examination of the aplastic inclusions may determine whether these two groups are meaningful in terms of source area or if they reflect functional and/or chronological differences.

Fabric similarities between the Berenike sherds and fabrics excavated by Phillipson at Aksum and exported as small samples to the United Kingdom, where the author examined them, may indicate a shared source. However, the absence of exact parallels for some Berenike forms (e.g., Figure 6–2, catalogue number 5) at Aksum, despite the classical handle decoration, raises the possibility of multiple source areas, as does Figure 6–3, catalogue number 9 whose form is common to Aksum, but decoration is paralleled only at Matara (Anfray 1966: pl. VIII, 163). Also to be considered is the presence of some unified geological tracts on the adjoining Yemeni coast and mainland, which could result in similar fabrics from the two locations. Nevertheless, the distinctive decoration on these sherds would ally them firmly with the Aksumite tradition, although their exact area of production is not known.

That vessels linked by form and decorative techniques were produced in more than one production center can be taken as given, but nevertheless is supported by another group of Aksumite material, comprising complete vessels, examined by the author at the British Museum. Acquired from Tringali, through the intermediary of Munro-Hay, the material is generally unprovenanced from either Ethiopia or Eritrea. Although the fabric cannot be examined in fresh fracture, these vessels seem to differ technologically from the Berenike sherds, with a tendency to be thinner and lacking the glossy burnishing typical of Berenike Fabric Group 2. While the latter difference could result from surface erosion, the presence of external and the lack of internal burnishing on a bowl with vertical corrugation (British Museum registration EA 71772) in contrast to the Berenike vessel (or vessels Figure 6–1, catalogue numbers 1–2) burnished internally and externally suggests a more intentional difference. In some instances differences between the Berenike and British Museum vessels may be due to chronological variation (C. Perlingieri, personal communication), but the possibility of differences in source areas should not be excluded.

The greater reliability in identifying decorated sherds means that the identifiable assemblage from Berenike is biased toward the more heavily decorated classical vessels. At Aksum the classical assemblage primarily derives from funerary contexts, the late assemblage from domestic ones (Phillips 2000b: 456–457); these functional distinctions may result in ceramic definitions that are overly exclusive chronologically and may require readjustment when additional evidence becomes available.

6.2   ROMAN POTTERY: CORRESPONDING EVIDENCE

The artifactual evidence from Berenike presented here comes from the late Roman period, between the fourth and early sixth centuries AD, which falls within the floruit of Aksumite civilization, although there is necessarily the problem of identifying residual material in late Roman loci at Berenike. Late Roman ceramics from Aksum include a range of well-dated African Red Slipware vessels (Phillips 2000b: figs. 170b ARS 52B; 188a ARS 70variant; 283d ARS 72; 283h ARS 52/70; 343g ARS 31/50 or 81B; Wilding 1989:315 including ARS 59, 91A, 72b, 170(?), 50; ARS forms after Hayes 1972) dating especially to the late fourth and early fifth centuries. Recurring amphora types include vessels produced at Aqaba (Melkawi, *et al.* 1994; Phillips 2000b: figs. 283a, 343a; Wilding 1989: figs. 16.468–470, which are sometimes equated with Egyptian amphorae, e.g., Fattovich and Bard 1993:90) and in Cilicia or Cyprus (de Contenson 1963, Williams 2000), both of which are

common at Berenike (Tomber 1998: fig. 6–8) and the latter throughout the eastern Mediterranean during the fifth and sixth centuries.

Although not an exhaustive survey, elsewhere in the region, Aqaba amphorae have been published from Matara (Anfray 1966: fig. 9) and Adulis (e.g. Anfray 1965: fig. 9; Munro-Hay 1989a; Parabeni 1907: figs. 2, 58). An additional red slip ware vessel of ARS 72 is illustrated from Matara (Anfray 1966: fig. 10) and late Roman red slipwares were common at Adulis, where Roman lamps and amphorae stoppers were also recorded (Parabeni 1907). Artifacts with a specifically Egyptian origin are known from Adulis and include an Abu Mena flask (Parabeni 1907: figs. 41, 54) and a faience scarab, albeit pre-Roman (*ibid*, fig. 3). This range of Roman finds at Adulis is not unexpected, since it was the port of contact between Ethiopia and Roman Egypt and Egyptian merchants may have settled there (Casson 1989:112).

6.3   CONCLUSIONS

The evidence presented here documents the contact between Berenike and the Aksumite Kingdom during the classical and the first part of the late Aksumite period. The relationship between the two areas is attested, not only by the presence of Aksumite-style pottery at Berenike, but also by Roman pottery throughout the contact zone. It is not yet clear whether the ceramic material found at Berenike originated in Aksum itself or in an adjoining region, or both. Further analysis of the pottery should allow this question to be addressed.

6.4 CATALOGUE

In the following catalogue, silt-sized inclusions refer to those measuring 0.06 mm or less; multicolored inclusions are primarily white, gray, or red, with occasional darker fragments. Colors are cited both as free descriptive terms and as values from the Munsell Soil Color Charts.

Bowls

1   Bowl with plain, tapered rim and vertical ribbing; a handle scar is visible on the wall. Fabric Group 2. Pink (*10R 5/6*) with dull red-brown (near *10R 5/4*) inside surface, outside more red (near *10R 5/6-4/6*) in color, mottled with gray to black patches from misfiring; surfaces are well burnished to a glossy finish.

BE99 10.*295* 4598-G Locus Date: At least mid-second century AD and more likely at least late fourth.

2   Bowl form as catalogue number 1, but with horizontal, hollow-rod handle below the rim. Three rims, joining. Fabric Group 2. Red-brown (*10R 5/4*), mottled outside, including some darkening on the rim; the inside is a similar color although slightly duller; surfaces are well burnished, but not as glossy as number 1, although this may be due to burial conditions.

BE00 10.*236* Locus Date: At least mid-second century AD, but possibly at least fourth century AD, mixed with first-century AD pottery.

Catalogue Numbers 1 and 2: Sherds illustrated as catalogue numbers 1 and 2 may well belong to one vessel but this cannot be verified. Both are burnished horizontally inside, and on the rim both inside and outside; the external ribs are burnished vertically. They share a fabric with abundant ill-sorted dark and light inclusions to 1 mm. The form equates to Wilding 1989: figs. 16.73–16.74.

3   Bowl with flat- oriented ledge rim, notched on the outside edge. Diameter and orientation uncertain. Near Wilding 1989: fig. 16.141; Phillips 2000b: fig. 43f. Fabric Group 1. Rare ill-sorted angular white and dark inclusions to 1 mm; no obvious mica is visible. Discolored to dark gray (*4/N–3/N*) on the surfaces, from burning (?); gray (*3/N*) break with very thin brown (*10R 4/4*) margins; smooth surfaces with no obvious burnishing.

BE99 27.*018* Locus Date: generally fifth century AD with some earlier pottery.

4   Bowl with slightly upturned, ledge rim. Sooted on the outside of the rim. Cf. Wilding 1989: figs. 16.122,131,133. Fabric Group 2. Very coarse with common ill-sorted multicolored inclusions up to 2 mm (particularly on the surface), but normally < 1 mm. Surfaces red-brown (*10R 5/6*) mottled to brown-gray (*2.5YR 4/1*) on the rim top and slightly more orange (*2.5YR 5/6*) outside and on the break; an irregular core is similar in color to mottling on the rim; surfaces are irregularly burnished resulting in a matte surface.

BE00 30.*174* Locus Date: late fourth or fifth century AD.

Handled bowls or jars
5   Open vessel with beveled rim oriented on the outer surface and horizontal handle arching above the rim; the handle is incised, as is its juncture

with the wall. Rim and handle, joining; second rim, nonjoining. Sooted on the outside wall below the handle. Fabric Group 1. Moderately vesicular with elongate and moderate angular ill-sorted inclusions (< 0.6 mm), mostly light in color. Pale brown (*5YR 5/4*) surfaces with the break generally dark gray (*4/N–3/N*); burnished or wiped resulting in soft, matte surfaces with some organic voids, particularly on the inside.

BE98 17.*088* 7561-G Locus Date: mid–late fourth century AD.

6   Open vessel with incised, horizontal handle and bevel on the inside wall. Sooted outside under the handle. Fabric Group 1. Moderate chaff (?) and ill-sorted larger inclusions, occasionally to ca. 1 mm. The break is black with dull brown (*2.5YR 5/3*) badly abraded surfaces, somewhat encrusted with salt, resulting in rough and soft or powdery surfaces with some organic voids.

BE99 26.*022* 4601-G Locus Date: fifth century AD with rare earlier material.

7   Open vessel with horizontal, incised handle. Sooted outside. Fabric Group 1. Common ill-sorted, subangular inclusions mostly ca. 0.5 mm, but up to 1 mm, and some elongate inclusions of chaff (?) and voids. Inside and outside surfaces are red-brown (*10R 5/4*) where unsooted, with dark gray (*4/N–3/N*) break; generally abraded inside with some salt concretions, but probably originally wiped rather than burnished.

BE98 20.*027* 7564-G Locus Date: undated, but the trench is generally late fourth or fifth century AD.

8   Open vessel with horizontal handle. Handle and sherd, joining. Sooted on the outside and on the handle underside. Fabric Group 2. Fairly fine matrix with larger ill-sorted inclusions to ca. 1 mm; rare silver (?) mica may be visible on the surface. Red-brown (*10R 5/4*) outside and dark red-brown (*10R 4/6*) inside with a gray (*2.5Y 5.1*) core of varying thickness; well burnished, although irregular, to glossy inside, outside wiped around the handle join.

BE98 22.Trench Clean 7567-G Locus Date: undated, but the trench is generally fifth century AD.

Their handles and particularly the decoration on them unite catalogue numbers 5–8. Although they undoubtedly belong to the Aksumite tradition, it is difficult to parallel them to specific types without more of the vessel; catalogue number 5 is without parallel, despite its extant rim.

9   Bag-shaped jar or bowl with sharply everted, grooved rim and horizontal handle incised on the juncture of the wall and handle; flanking the handle are further zig-zag (?) incisions. Three rims, two joining. Sooted under the rim, on, and around the handle, and on the lower wall. Cf. Wilding 1989: fig. 16.222 for form; Anfray 1966: pl. VIII 163 for form and decoration. Fabric Group 2. Common, ill-sorted multicolored inclusions to ca. 1 mm, occasionally to 2 mm. Dull brown-red (*5YR 5/4*) surfaces with dull pink (*10R 6/6-5/6*) break where not discolored from surface sooting, with gray (*5/0*) core of varying thickness, sometimes also as a thick internal margin; outside where unsooted, on the rim, and irregularly inside, burnished to glossy.

BE98 17.*076* 7566-G Locus Date: fourth century AD or possibly later.

10 Strap handle, incised on the juncture with the wall. Orientation uncertain. Cf. Wilding 1989: fig. 16.406; Phillips 2000b: fig. 278b. Variant incorporating features of both Fabric Group 1 and 2, most similar to Fabric Group 1. Moderate-sized well-sorted matrix, fairly vesicular with elongate voids and occasional dark inclusions <0.5 mm; possibly some very fine silver mica on the surface, but this may be concretion. The inner break and margin are dull pale gray (*5/N*), the outer break and margin orange-brown (*2.5YR 5/8*); the outside surface is dull red-brown (*2.5YR 5/6*), inside gray (*4/N*); there is no obvious burnishing, but the surfaces are concreted with salt (?).

BE98 21, dump deposit. Locus Date: late fifth or early sixth century AD.

Shallow dishes and lids

11. Shallow dish or lid with incised crisscross decoration inside. Fabric Group 1. Occasional angular dark inclusions to ca. 0.5 mm. Black break with dull brown (near *7.5YR 5/3-4/3*) surfaces and slightly blacker hue inside; rough, unfinished surfaces.

BE98 21 east balk trim 7569-G Locus date: undated, but the trench is generally late fifth or early sixth century AD.

12. Concave lid, originally with basket-style handle; incised in four bands on the internal surface. Fabric Group 1. Coarse with ill-sorted light and dark inclusions, mostly 0.5 mm, but up to 2 mm on the abraded surface and burnt elongate organic(?) inclusions. Dark gray (*3/N*) break with very thin orange (*10R 5/6*) margins; dull red-brown (near *10R 5/3-4/3*) surfaces, abraded on the underside.

BE98-21.014 Locus Date: late fifth or early sixth century AD.

Other sherds

13. Body sherd from a vessel decorated with punctate decoration enclosed within an incised, diamond-shaped frame, centrally divided. Not belonging to either Fabric Group 1 or 2. Slightly micaceous, sandy fabric containing moderate-sized well-sorted matrix with common ill-sorted larger fragments to *ca.* 1 mm. The inside surface is dull brown (*5Y 5/2*), the outside mottled red-brown (*10R 5/4*) to black with a gray-brown (*5YR 4/1*) core and brown (*5YR 5/4*) inner margin; the inside surface is burnished and fairly smooth.

BE00 38.*017* Locus Date: fifth or early sixth century AD.

14. Body sherd from closed vessel with punctate decoration, punched before firing but after the application of the slip. The inside wall is very uneven and poorly finished. The lower part of the sherd is blackened from use. Fabric Group 1. Vesicular matrix with both narrow and occasional rounded voids; rare light-colored inclusions < 0.5 mm are also present. The outside surface is decorated with red (*5R 4/4*) slip, the inside is dull brown (*7.5YR 5/3*); the inner break and margin are black, the outer break and margin orange-brown (*2.5YR 5/6*).

BE99 22.*104* 4600-G Locus Date: poorly dated, probably mid–late fourth century AD with extensive mid-first-century-AD pottery.

NOTE

1. The author is grateful to the Seven Pillars of Wisdom Trust (UK) for their financial support including airfare and subsistence for Gillian Pyke and myself during the 2000 season. Funding in the final stages was provided by the AHRB (UK). The pottery was drawn by Gillian Pyke, and her illustrations were prepared for publication by Graham Reed. The study was made possible through examination of the Aksum material: for this my thanks go to Professor David Phillipson (Cambridge University) who permitted me to study fabric samples exported from his excavations at Aksum and Dr. Derek Welsby (Department of Ancient Egypt and Sudan, the British Museum) who provided access to the departmental collections. I am particularly grateful to Dr. Jacke Phillips (Cambridge University) for her generosity, guiding me through the Aksumite material and discussing the Berenike sherds with me. Any errors are, of course, my own.

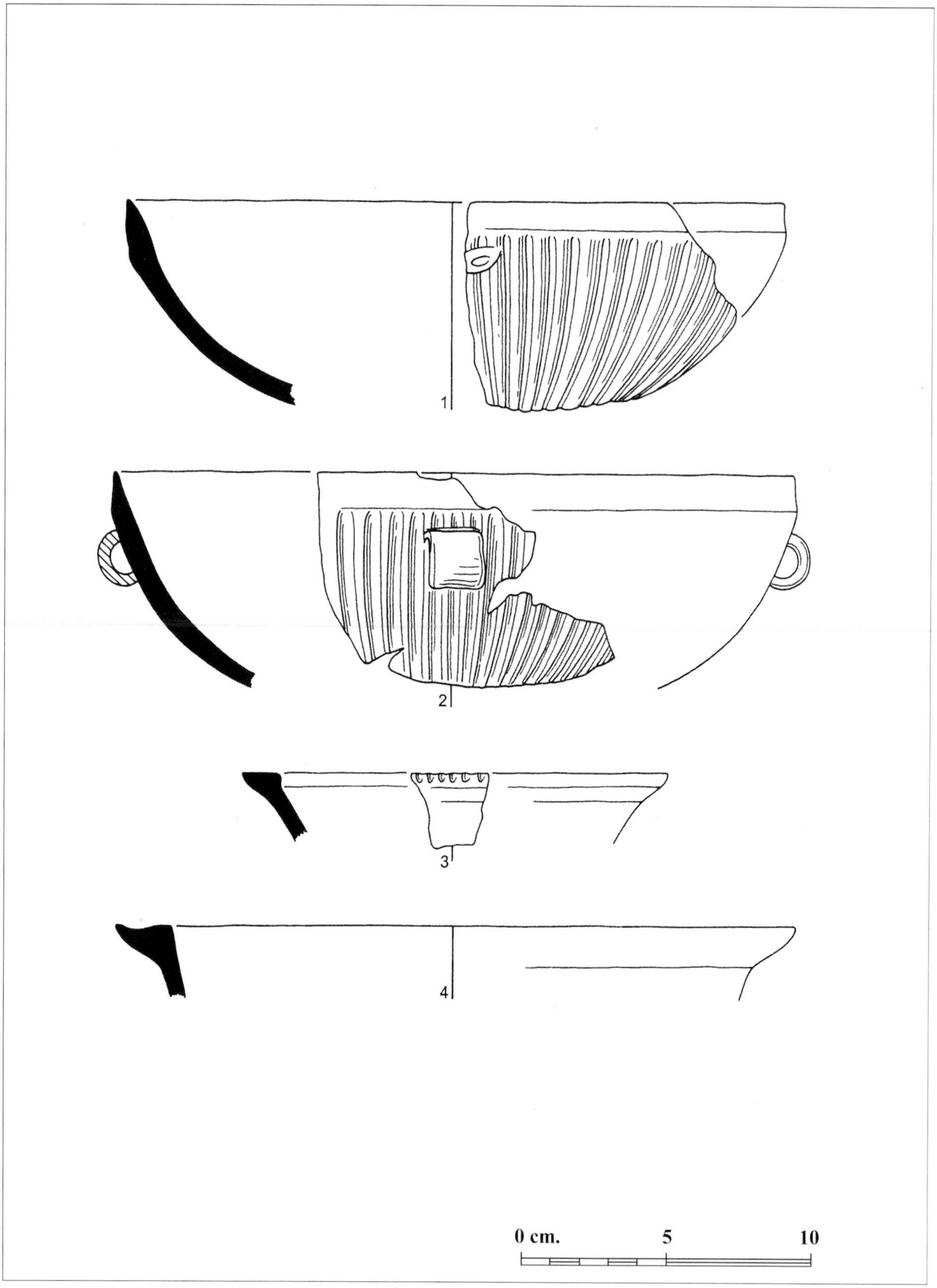

Figure 6–1 Catalogue numbers 1–4. Drawings by G. Pyke and G. Reed.

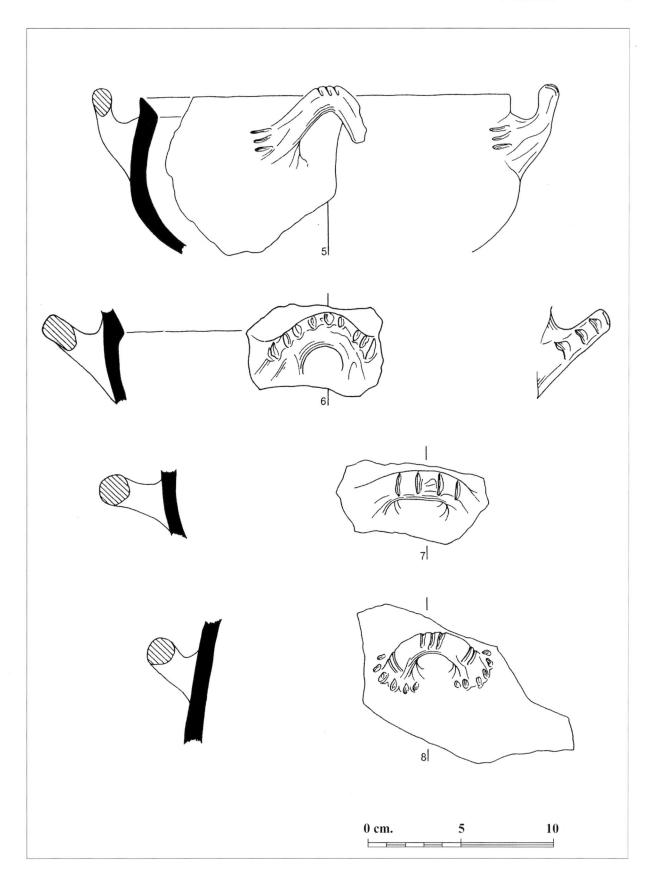

Figure 6–2   Catalogue numbers 5–8. Drawings by G. Pyke and G. Reed.

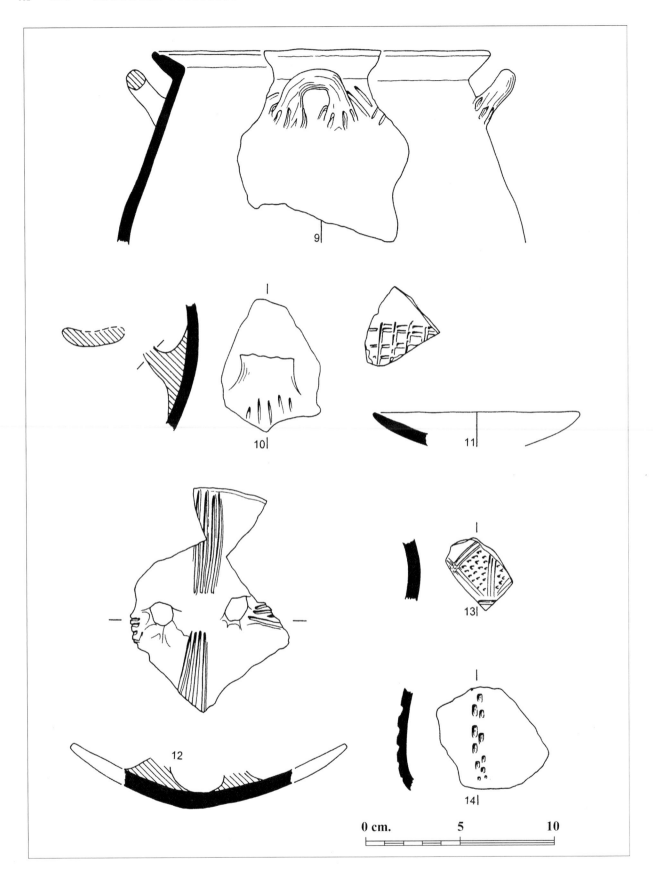

Figure 6–3   Catalogue numbers 9–14. Drawings by G. Pyke and G. Reed.

CHAPTER 7

EASTERN DESERT WARE FROM BERENIKE AND KAB MARFU'A

H. BARNARD AND P. J. ROSE[1]

Eastern Desert Ware (EDW) refers to a rather recently identified corpus of relatively small, handmade vessels with a remarkable surface treatment, dating from the fourth–fifth centuries AD and found in the Eastern Desert, between the Nile and the Red Sea, in southern Egypt, and northern Sudan. It is assumed that these vessels were produced and used by the indigenous, nomadic inhabitants of the desert at the time.

7.1   HISTORICAL BACKGROUND

During the ongoing excavation of Berenike and analysis of the material recovered there, as well as along the desert routes to the Nile Valley, numerous previously unknown observations could be made concerning the inhabitants of Berenike and their partners in the long-distance trade. These were not only based on the recovered pottery, coins, and ostraka, but also on the study of the organic remains, which were relatively well preserved (Sidebotham and Wendrich 1996c, 441–452 and Sidebotham and Wendrich 2000b, 413–420). Berenike appears to have been occupied until the mid-sixth century AD. Three periods of increased activity have been identified: the early Ptolemaic period (directly following the foundation of the town), the early Roman period (first century BC–first century AD) and the late Roman period (mid-fourth century AD–fifth century AD). During each peak the center of activity shifted to the east, following the changing coastline. The exact reasons for the fluctuations in activity are still largely unclear.

The composition of the population of Berenike also must have changed. Little is known about the Ptolemaic era as the remains thereof are not only covered by later debris but also have been mostly reused in later periods. Given the military nature of the operations, at least initially, and the general tendency of the Ptolemaic rulers toward centralized control, it is likely that during this period the population of Berenike consisted mainly of representatives of the military and the state bureaucracy. They would all have come from the Nile Valley, bringing or importing all their supplies. This is certainly true for the early Roman period as indicated, for instance, by the large number of pig, chicken, and catfish bones, as well as firm indications that cattle came on the hoof from the Nile Valley, to be slaughtered on site.[2] Next to these Greco-Roman Egyptians, other groups from even farther afield were present on site. Among these were a number of Palmyrene soldiers, who left a shrine and several inscriptions, and possibly representatives of traders in Rome, Aksum, and India.

Also in the late Roman period there was a strong Roman Egyptian presence at Berenike. This is reflected in the majority of the potsherds and also, for instance, by the find of a jar of *garum* (fish sauce), which was an important element of Roman cuisine, and the unearthing of a Christian church.[3] But from this period there were also finds of a much different nature, such as a large number of ovicaprid bones, as well as rope and textiles made of their hair.[4] Combined with a significant drop in the proportion of fish remains and commodities imported from the Nile Valley, this suggests a more-desert-oriented population. The most likely explanation for this would be that another group joined the already multiethnic population of Berenike (Sidebotham and Wendrich 1999b: 452–453), an explanation that seems supported by the contemporary historical sources, like Procopius and Olympiodorus, which mention the presence of a nomadic people in the area (Sidebotham 1994:8-10; Updegraff 1988; Eide, *et al.* 1998). Even though this group has at Berenike been tentatively linked with a corpus of pottery, its identity has so far escaped definition (Sidebotham and Wendrich 1996b: 17; Sidebotham and Wendrich 2001:256–267).

7.2   POTTERY FINDS IN BERENIKE

Already during the first excavation season, the variety in the origin of the potsherds found in Berenike became apparent, even though the number of types seemed limited (Hayes 1995:33–40; Hayes 1996:147–178) This pattern, concurrent with the function of the site as a harbor, was consistent during further

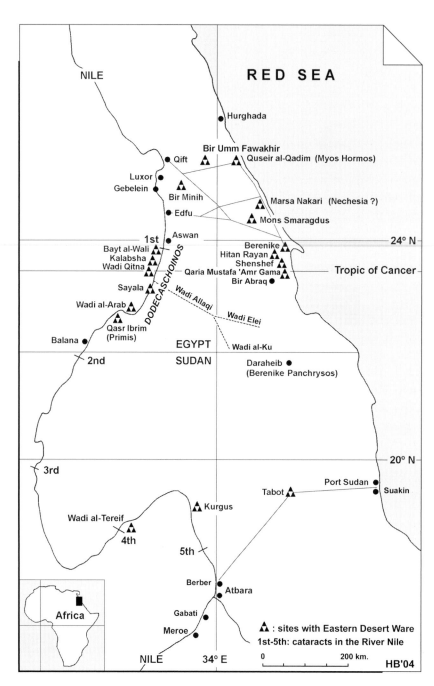

Figure 7–1   Map of the Eastern Desert, between the Nile and the Red Sea, showing the location of the place names mentioned in the text. Drawing by H. Barnard.

excavation and study of remains of pottery (Tomber 1998:163–180; Tomber 1999:123–159). Most of the sherds are from vessels made in the Egyptian Nile Valley. Comparable remains have been found at other, relatively nearby sites (Quseir al-Qadim and Balana), as well as associated with the numerous way stations along the desert routes. Trade, and maybe also traders, coming through Berenike from the west are attested by the remains of vessels produced in present-day Turkey, Italy, Tunisia, Spain, and France, among others. Vessels from the east to be expected include those from East Africa, Arabia Felix, and India. Of these, both Aksum and India have now been firmly identified (Begley and Tomber 1999:161–181; Tomber and Begley 2000:149–167; Tomber, Chapter 6 in this book).

Apart from these three large, more or less distinct groups from the Nile Valley, the Mediterranean, and the East, there is a heterogeneous group of sherds, mostly of handmade vessels, of unknown origin. These may originate from anywhere along the ancient trade routes, including Arabia Felix, which so far has escaped recognition in most of the find groups present in Berenike. A portion of these sherds, however, shows striking similarities with some of the sherds from other sites in the Eastern Desert and Lower Nubia. They are united by a very characteristic repertoire of vessel forms and decorative motifs, as well as technological features (Rose 1995:41–43). The most comprehensive description of these sherds derives from the excavation of the fourth–fifth-century AD cemeteries in Wadi Qitna and Kalabsha South (Strouhal 1984:157–177; 195–200; Tables 31–34; Plates 66–70). Comparable sherds, among much larger quantities of wheel-thrown Egyptian or (post) Meroitic sherds, have also been found in Kalabsha North (Ricke 1976:46–70, Tafel 23–28), Sayala (Bedawi 1976:29–31, Abb. 12, Fig. 2; Kromer 1967:19, 34, 96–99, Tafel 2, Tafel 32-2, Tafel 34-3, Tafel 37-5), Wadi al-Arab (Emery and Kirwan 1935:108–122), Qasr Ibrim (P. J. Rose, personal observation) and, much further south in the Nile Valley, in Kurgus (R. F. Friedman and G. Pyke, personal communication). Places in the Eastern Desert where similar sherds have been found include a number of tombs scattered in the Wadi Alaqi area, most notably in Wadi Elei and Wadi al-Ku (Sadr, Castiglioni, and Castiglioni 1995:210–222, Fig. 10-11, Fig. 25); several sites with an unknown function in the vicinity of Berenike: Hitan Rayan (Sidebotham, *et al.* 2002: 210–221), Shenshef (Tomber 1998:170; Tomber 1999,

152, Figure 5-15/75) and Qaria Mustafa 'Amr Gama (Sidebotham *et al.* 2002:210–221); sites associated with the beryl mines in the Mons Smaragdus area: Sikait (S. E. Sidebotham, personal communication), Gebel Zabara (I. M. E. Shaw, personal communication) and Kab Marfu'a (Barnard 2002); and, again much farther to the south, Tabot (Magid, Pierce, and Krzywinski 1995:165–170, Plate V).[5] Based upon the study of sherds associated with them, and in some cases on C^{14} analysis of associated finds, (Sadr, Castiglioni, and Castiglioni 1995:227), their production seems limited to the fourth–sixth centuries AD, and certainly to the second–eighth centuries AD.

Given the distribution of this ware and its homogenous physical characteristics, very sandy fabric without much organic temper, it has been labeled Eastern Desert Ware (EDW). It is remarkable that no EDW has been found in Daraheib, which is halfway between its northernmost and southernmost occurrence and has been tentatively identified as the ancient goldmine Berenike Panchrysos or the "desert capital of the Blemmyean kingdom," or in settlements west of there, in Wadi Alaqi (Sadr, *et al.* 1994; Sadr, Castiglioni, and Castiglioni 1995; Castiglioni, Castiglioni, and Vercoutter 1995). Because of the current lack of archaeological data and the confusing labeling in the historical sources, the people that must have produced and used EDW are prudently labeled Eastern Desert Dwellers. They are supposed to have lived a nomadic life, much like their present-day counterparts,[6] in the region enclosed by the areas in which EDW has been found (Figure 7-2). The sherds of the pottery produced and used by them are thinly scattered over a large area, which makes detection difficult. But in places where outsiders provided an infrastructure allowing for them to settle, probably temporarily assisting the newcomers in some way, sherds could accumulate and are now found in small quantities among pottery produced elsewhere. Other places of accumulation are graves and several of these, both in the Nile Valley and in the desert, have yielded EDW (Ricke 1967; Bedawi 1976; Strouhal 1984; Sadr, Castiglioni and Castiglioni 1995). The cemeteries in Sayala were close to desert settlements that were proposed to have been temporary settlements of nomads helping out with the harvest in the Nile Valley (Ricke 1967:33–35). Since then a number of very similar settlements of unknown function have been described far from the Nile Valley, making this interpretation doubtful (Sidebotham et al.: 210–221). As the retrieved pottery may be the only source of information about the Eastern Desert Dwellers, a research group has been formed to extract as much information from this as is possible.[7] The preliminary results of a pilot study of 52 sherds from Berenike and 14 from Kab Marfu'a (in the Mons Smaragdus area) are presented next.

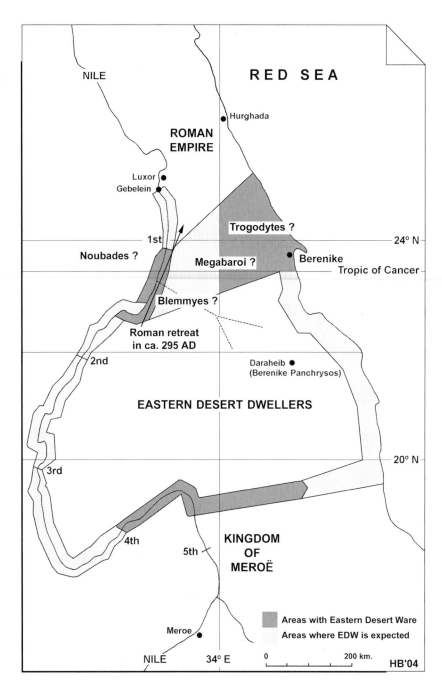

Figure 7–2 Map of the Eastern Desert, between the Nile and the Red Sea, showing, in darker gray, the areas in which Eastern Desert Ware has been found, as well as, in lighter gray, areas where it can be expected that the concentration of EDW is noticeable but not yet described. Also indicated are some of the traditional names for the inhabitants of the area as well as the region of the "Eastern Desert Dwellers" proposed here. Drawing by H. Barnard.

7.3 CLASSIFICATION OF EASTERN DESERT WARE

EDW can be described macroscopically using a slightly adapted version of the classification put forward by Strouhal on the basis of his finds in Wadi Qitna and Kalabsha South (Strouhal 1984:162, 165–168). In this classification there are eleven forms of the vessels, as well as eleven different layouts of the decoration. The most significant difference with the original classification is the addition of the form "jar/pot" (absent in the original system as almost all of the sherds are from relatively small cups and bowls), which replaces the "footed bowl" as form H 3. Together with the "suspending bowl" (which has holes just below the rim presumably to be suspended or carried) footed bowls are now classified as H 2d. The classes H 0, D 0, H 10, and D 10 have been added but do not fundamentally alter the system. Some of the H classes are further divided into several subforms, indicated by "a," "b," "c" or "d."

Classification of EDW according to vessel form (after Strouhal 1984):

H 0	Unknown
H 1	Cup
H 1a	Cup with S-shaped profile
H 1b	Carinated cup
H 1c	Cylindrical cup
H 1d	Conical cup
H 2	Bowl
H 2a	Globular bowl
H 2b	Hemispherical bowl
H 2c	Conical bowl
H 2d	Footed or suspending bowl
H 3	Jar/pot
H 4	Goblet
H 5	Miniature
H 5a	Miniature cup
H 5b	Miniature bowl
H 5c	Miniature jar/pot
H 5d	Miniature goblet
H 6	Beak-spouted vessel
H 6a	Beak-spouted cup
H 6b	Beak-spouted globular bowl
H 6c	Beak-spouted hemispherical bowl
H 6d	Beak-spouted vessel with handle
H 7	Tubular-spouted vessel
H 8	Ladle
H 9	Dish
H 10	Other

Classification of EDW According to Decorative Pattern (After Strouhal 1984):

D 0	Unknown/no decoration
D 1	Exclusively on rim
D 2	Narrow, single band
D 3	Multiple, horizontal bands
D 4	Vertical with metopes
D 5	Vertical without metopes
D 6	Horizontal and vertical
D 7	Continuous diagonal
D 8	Unarticulated/asymmetric
D 9	Zoomorphic
D 10	Other

Other characteristics that were recorded include the decorative motifs, the method and direction of the decoration (mostly incised or impressed with a chisel or a triangular point working from left to right), as well as more usual characteristics as the color and the treatment of the surface (often wiped, smoothed, or burnished with the decoration filled in with a white substance or emphasized with a red slip), and the (estimated) dimensions of the vessel (aperture, height, and weight).

Prevalent EDW Decorative Motifs (After Strouhal 1984):

Birds
Circles
Fishes
Grille
Indented rim
Lines
Maltese cross
Plants/trees
Rhomboids
Round brackets
Running dog
Sun-motif
Triangles
X-motif
Waves
Zigzag

The macroscopic description of the sherds is completed with a (digital) photograph and a drawing. As most of the published drawings of EDW follow the convention of having a section of the vessel on the right, we have chosen to do the same.

7.4 RESULTS AND CATALOGUE

After low-magnification study of the fabrics, three and possibly four fabrics could be identified. Two of these, labeled EDW-1 and EDW-2, are relatively hard with no (EDW-1) or very few (EDW-2) organic inclusions and an abundance of poorly sorted, coarse, white-transparent and blue-black quartz particles (sand). Other very similar fabrics could not readily be assigned to either EDW-1 or EDW-2, but are likely to belong to the same ware type. The reason for this diversity must be that although all vessels are from a similar environment and are probably produced by a limited number of potters, each of them is produced individually rather than to a standardized recipe. One body sherd, EDW 44 from Kab Marfu'a, was made from a much softer gray silt, most probably from the Nile Valley, with hardly any inclusions. The typical decoration (D 8, sun-motif), however, makes it very likely that it belongs to the same tradition. A few other sherds, among them EDW 53, had small shiny flakes of golden-yellow mica, best visible on the surfaces. The fabric of these has been tentatively labeled EDW-3. All data are entered into a relational database (using FileMaker Pro 5.5), which will eventually be made available on the Internet.[8]

The printed catalogue presented here has the following format: EDW number; context and date; weight and average thickness; color and treatment of the inside; color and treatment of the outside; method and direction of the decoration; reconstructed rim diameter and estimated vessel equivalent; color of break; fabric; classification; remarks; and possible parallels.

EDW 1   Berenike, BE98-21, late Roman trash dump, fifth century AD. Weight 80 g. Average thickness 5.4 mm. Inside 5YR 4/3, compacted, smoothed. Outside 5YR 4/2, burnished. Decoration impressed, punctuated with chisel (working left to right). Rim diameter 12 cm. (18 percent preserved). Break 2.5YR 2.5/1. Fabric EDW-1. Form H 2a. Decoration D 3 (round brackets). Parallel EDW 8.

EDW 2   Berenike, BE00-39 (003), Christian ecclesiastic complex, fifth century AD. Weight 22 g. Average thickness 5.5 cm. Inside 10R 3/1, treatment unknown. Outside 2.5YR 5/1, treatment unknown. Decoration impressed, incised with chisel (direction unclear). Rim diameter 9 cm. (10 percent preserved). Break 5YR 5/1. Fabric EDW-2. Form H 1c. Decoration D 7 (rhomboids). Surfaces very worn, treatment and original color uncertain.

EDW 3   Berenike, BE98-21, late Roman trash dump, fifth century AD. Weight 15 g. Average thickness 4.7 mm. Inside 2.5YR 4/4, burnished. Outside 2.5YR 4/4, burnished. Decoration colored, incised with triangular point (direction unclear). Rim diameter 8 cm. (8 percent preserved). Break 2.5YR 4/4. Fabric EDW-1. Form H 1b. Decoration D 6 (lines).

EDW 4   Berenike, BE98-21, late Roman trash dump, fifth century AD. Weight 150 g. Average thickness 7.1 mm. Inside 2.5YR 4/3, treatment unknown. Outside 2.5YR 2.5/1, burnt. Decoration impressed, incised, punctuated with round point (direction unclear). Rim diameter 16 cm. (18 percent preserved). Break 2.5YR 5/3. Fabric EDW-1. Form H 2a. Decoration D 3 (X-motif). Parallel Sayala 76.827 (Kromer 1967:96–99, Tafel 32-2); Bir Abraq (Sadr 1994: fig. 3)?

EDW 5   Berenike, BE98-21, late Roman trash dump, fifth century AD. Weight 25 g. Average thickness 6.9 mm. Inside 10YR 3/1, untreated. Outside 10YR 3/1, burnt. Decoration incised with chisel (working left to right). Rim diameter 18 cm. (15 percent preserved). Break 10YR 3/1. Fabric unclassified. Form H 3. Decoration D 2 (running dog). Might not be EDW but an import.

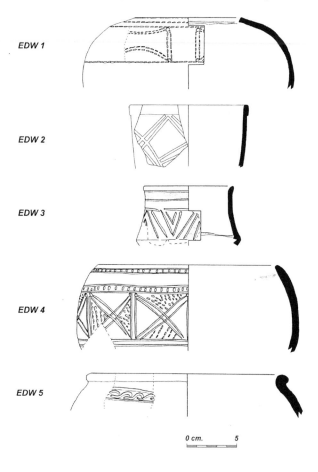

Figure 7–3   Eastern Desert Ware, catalogue numbers 1–5. Drawings by P. J. Rose and H. Barnard.

EDW 6   Berenike, BE98-21, late Roman trash dump, fifth century AD. Weight 35 g. Average thickness 5.6 mm. Inside 5YR 5/4, compacted, smoothed. Outside 7.5YR 4/2, burnished, smoothed. Decoration plastic and incised with triangular point (direction unclear). Rim diameter 17 cm. (15 percent preserved). Break 2.5YR 5/6. Fabric EDW-1. Form H 2b. Decoration D 3 (triangles). Note indented rim. Parallel EDW 22.

EDW 7   Berenike, BE98-21, late Roman trash dump, fifth century AD. Weight 25 g. Average thickness 4.9 mm. Inside 10YR 4/2, burnished, burnt. Outside 10YR 3/3, burnished, burnt. Decoration impressed, incised with chisel and filled in with white (direction unclear). Rim diameter 12 cm. (5 percent preserved). Break 10YR 4/1. Fabric EDW-2. Form H 1a. Decoration D 3 (lines). Parallel Beit al-Wali B73h (Ricke 1967:62, Abb. 74).

EDW 8   Berenike, BE98-21, late Roman trash dump, fifth century AD. Weight 25 g. Average thickness 4.6 mm. Inside 5YR 4/2, burnished, compacted. Outside 2.5YR 3/2, burnt. Decoration impressed with triangular point (working left to right). Rim diameter 14 cm. (16 percent preserved). Break 5YR 4/1. Fabric EDW-1. Form H 2a. Decoration D 3 (round brackets). Parallel EDW 1.

EDW 9   Berenike, BE98-21, late Roman trash dump, fifth century AD. Weight 22 g. Average thickness 5.2 mm. Inside 2.5YR 3/2, compacted, smoothed. Outside 2.5YR 2.5/1, burnished, burnt. Decoration plastic and impressed, punctuated with chisel and round point (direction unclear). Rim diameter 16 cm. (5 percent preserved). Break 2.5YR 5/1. Fabric EDW-1. Form H 3. Decoration D 2 (round brackets). Parallel Bir Abraq (Sadr 1994: Figure3)?

EDW 10   Berenike, BE98-21, late Roman trash dump, fifth century AD. Weight 120 g. Average thickness 4.4 mm. Inside 7.5YR 3/1, burnished. Outside 2.5YR 4/2, burnished. Decoration colored, incised, punctuated, and filled in with white (direction unclear). Rim diameter 12 cm. (31 percent preserved). Break 7.5YR 5/1. Fabric EDW-1. Form H 1a. Decoration D 8 (waves).

EDW 11   Berenike, BE98-21, late Roman trash dump, fifth century AD. Weight 14 g. Average thickness 5.4 mm. Inside 7.5YR 5/4, burnished. Outside 7.5YR 4/4, burnished. Decoration incised with triangular point (working left to right). Rim diameter 19 cm. (8 percent preserved). Break 7.5YR 5/1. Fabric EDW-1. Form H 2b. Decoration D 3 (running dog, triangles).

EDW 12   Berenike, BE98-21, late Roman trash dump, fifth century AD. Weight 12 g. Average thick-

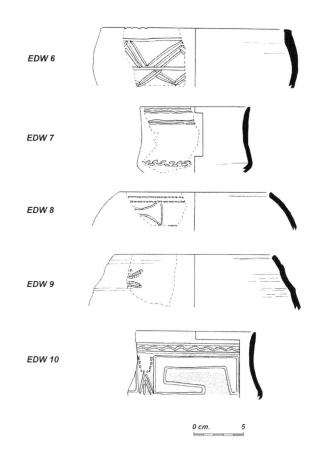

Figure 7–4   Eastern Desert Ware, catalogue numbers 6–10. Drawings by P. J. Rose.

ness 3.1 mm. Inside 10YR 2/1, burnished. Outside 10YR 2/1, burnished, smoothed. Decoration plastic and impressed with round point and filled in with white (direction unclear). Rim diameter 10 cm. (17 percent preserved). Break 10YR 5/2. Fabric EDW-1. Form H 1a. Decoration D 6 (running dog) Parallel Kalabsha P 1394a (Strouhal 1984: fig. 128).

EDW 13   Berenike, BE99-10.*365, 370, 378*, center of town, first–second century AD. Weight 180 g. Average thickness 5.1 mm. Inside 10R 5/8, burnished. Outside 10R 4/8, burnished, red slip. Decoration impressed, incised with triangular point (working left to right). Rim diameter 15 cm. (20% preserved). Break 2.5YR 5/2. Fabric unclassified. Form H 3. Decoration D 3 (lines, triangles). Note carefully squared rim, red slip spills over on inside rim. Parallel EDW 18.

EDW 14   Berenike, BE99-10.*374, 395, 396*, center of town, fourth-fifth century AD. Weight 57 g. Average thickness 5.1 mm. Inside 10R 5/6, burnished. Outside

10R 5/6, red slip. Decoration impressed, incised with chisel and filled in with white (working left to right). Rim diameter 10 cm. (35 percent preserved). Break 10R 5/6. Fabric unclassified. Form H 1a. Decoration D 2 (zig-zag). Note carefully squared rim, red slip spills over on inside rim.

EDW 15　Berenike, BE99-10.*365*, *378*, center of town, first–second century AD. Weight 45 g. Average thickness 4.2 mm. Inside 7.5YR 5/4, smoothed. Outside 2.5YR 5/8, burnished, red slip. Undecorated. Rim diameter 16 cm. (16 percent preserved). Break 5YR 3/2. Fabric unclassified. Form H 2b. Unusual type without decoration but with four pair of "lug-handles" instead;

note carefully squared rim, red slip spills over on inside rim. Parallels EDW 59, Kalabsha P 834 (Strouhal 1984: fig. 129); Hitan Rayan 51 (Sidebotham, *et al.* 2002:210, fig. 20/51).

EDW 16　Berenike, BE99-10.*374*, center of town, fourth–fifth century AD. Weight 50 g. Average thickness 4.8 mm. Inside 5YR 5/4, burnished. Outside 5YR 5/8, burnished, red slip. Decoration impressed with triangular point (working left to right). Rim diameter 17 cm. (17 percent preserved). Break 5YR 5/3. Fabric unclassified. Form H 2a. Decoration D 5 (waves). Might be from the same vessel as EDW 19; note carefully squared rim, red slip spills over on inside rim. Parallel EDW 19.

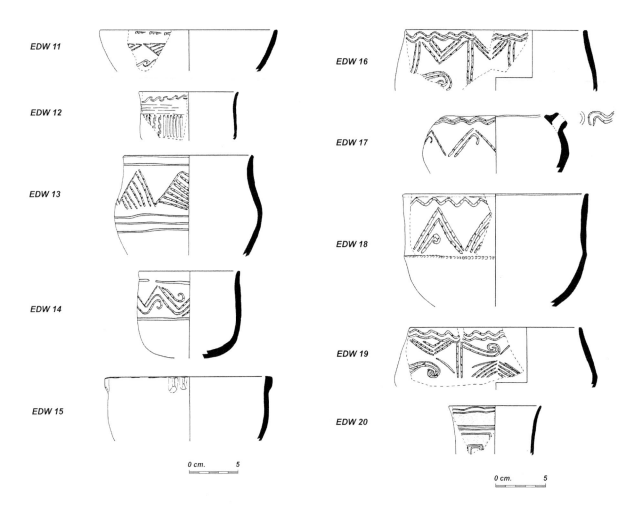

Figure 7–5　Eastern Desert Ware, catalogue numbers 11–15. Drawings by P. J. Rose.

Figure 7–6　Eastern Desert Ware, catalogue numbers 16–20. Drawings by P. J. Rose.

EDW 17 Berenike. BE99-10.*374, trench clean* (pb# 735 and 763), center of town, fourth–fifth c. AD. Weight 100 g. Average thickness 5 mm. Inside 2.5YR 5/8, smoothed. Outside 2.5YR 5/6, red slip. Decoration impressed with chisel (direction unclear). Rim diameter 11 cm. (45 percent preserved). Break 2.5YR 5/1. Fabric unclassified. Form H 7. Decoration D 3 (waves, zig-zag).

EDW 18 Berenike, BE99-10.*374, 396*, center of town, third–fourth century AD. Weight 75 g. Average thickness 5.9 mm. Inside 10R 5/6, smoothed. Outside 10R 4/8, burnished, red slip. Decoration impressed with chisel and filled in with white (direction unclear). Rim diameter 18 cm. (11 percent preserved). Break 10R 6/6. Fabric unclassified. Form H 3. Decoration D 3 (waves, zig-zag). Red slip spills over on inside rim. Parallel EDW 13.

EDW 19 Berenike, BE99-10.*345*, center of town, late second century AD. Weight 125 g. Average thickness 5.4 mm. Inside 10R 5/6, smoothed. Outside 10R 4/6, red slip. Decoration impressed, incised with chisel (direction unclear). Rim diameter 17 cm. (20 percent preserved). Break 10R 6/6. Fabric unclassified. Form H 2a. Decoration D 5 (waves, triangles). Note carefully squared rim, red slip spills over on inside rim. Parallel EDW 16.

EDW 20 Berenike, BE99-10.*393*, center of town, first c. BC–first century AD. Inside burnished, red slip. Outside burnished. Decoration colored, incised. Fabric unclassified. Form H 1b. Decoration D 6 (lines). This sherd may well be intrusive. Parallel EDW 48.

EDW 21 Berenike, BE98-21, late Roman trash dump, fifth century AD. Weight 18 g. Average thickness 7.8 mm. Inside 7.5YR 4/2, burnished. Outside 7.5YR 4/2, untreated. Decoration incised, punctuated with round point (direction unclear). Rim diameter 21 cm. (5 percent preserved). Break 7.5YR 5/3. Fabric unclassified. Form H 2b. Decoration D 2 (lines, running dog). May not be EDW but an import.

EDW 22 Berenike, BE98-21, late Roman trash dump, fifth century AD. Weight 24 g. Average thickness 7.3 mm. Inside 2.5YR 4/3, smoothed. Outside 10R 4/6, red slip. Decoration impressed, incised with chisel (direction unclear). Rim diameter 12 cm. (3 percent preserved). Break 2.5YR 4/3. Fabric EDW-1. Form H 2a. Decoration D 3 (rhomboids). Note indented rim. Parallel EDW 6.

EDW 23 Berenike, BE98-21, late Roman trash dump, fifth century AD. Weight 20 g. Average thickness 6.9 mm. Inside 2.5YR 6/6, smoothed. Outside 10YR 6/3, burnt. Decoration impressed, incised with round point (direction unclear). Rim diameter 15 cm. (10 percent preserved). Break 2.5YR 4/6. Fabric EDW-1. Form H 2a. Decoration D 2 (lines). Parallel Qaria Mustafa 'Amr Gama 70 (Sidebotham, *et al.* 2002:217, fig. 23/70).

EDW 24 Berenike, BE98-21, late Roman trash dump, fifth century AD. Weight 11 g. Average thickness 4.8 mm. Inside 2.5YR 5/4, smoothed. Outside 2.5YR 5/6, burnished, red slip. Decoration colored, incised with triangular point and filled in with white (direction unclear). Rim diameter 8 cm. (10 percent preserved). Break 2.5YR 4/1. Fabric EDW-1. Form H 2a. Decoration D 3 (waves).

EDW 25 Berenike, BE98-21, late Roman trash dump, fifth century AD. Weight 21 g. Average thickness 7.5 mm. Inside 10R 2.5/1, treatment unknown. Outside 10R 2.5/1, treatment unknown. Decoration impressed, punctuated with triangular point (direction

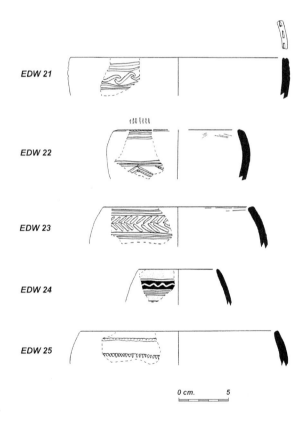

Figure 7–7   Eastern Desert Ware, catalogue numbers 21–25. Drawings by P. J. Rose.

unclear). Rim diameter 20 cm. (5 percent preserved). Break 10R 3/1. Fabric EDW-1. Form H 2a. Decoration D 2. Surfaces very worn, treatment and original color uncertain.

EDW 26 Berenike, BE98-21, late Roman trash dump, fifth century AD. Weight 17 g. Average thickness 5.8. Inside 7.5R 3/1, treatment unknown. Outside 7.5R 2.5/1, treatment unknown. Decoration plastic and impressed with chisel and filled in with white (direction unclear). Rim diameter 11 cm. (8 percent preserved). Break 7.5R 2.5/1. Fabric unclassified. Form H 3. Decoration D 2 (running dog).

EDW 27 Berenike, BE00-38.*017*, house/workshop in the center of town, fifth–sixth century AD. Weight 9 g. Average thickness 7.3 mm. Inside wiped. Outside mottled. Rim diameter 18 cm. (6 percent preserved). Fabric EDW-1. Form H 2a. Undecorated, may not be EDW.

EDW 28 Berenike, BE01-41.*027*, house/workshop in the center of town, fifth–sixth century AD. Weight 14 g. Average thickness 6.8 mm. Inside wiped. Outside burnt, smoothed. Rim diameter 16 cm. (4 percent preserved). Fabric unclassified. Form H 2a. Undecorated, may not be EDW.

EDW 29 Berenike, BE98-21, late Roman trash dump, fifth century AD. Weight 9 g. Average thickness 4.9 mm. Inside 10R 4/6, red slip. Outside 10R 4/4, red slip. Decoration impressed, punctuated with triangular point and filled in with white (direction unclear). Rim diameter 9 cm. (9 percent preserved). Break 10R 2.5/1. Fabric EDW-2. Form H 1a. Decoration D 6 (lines, triangles).

EDW 30 Berenike, BE98-21, late Roman trash dump, fifth century AD. Weight 16 g. Average thickness 5.6 mm. Inside 10R 2.5/1, burnished. Outside 10R 4/4, burnished, red slip. Decoration incised and filled in with white (direction unclear). Rim diameter 16 cm. (9 percent preserved). Break 10R 4/6. Fabric EDW-1. Form H 9. Decoration D 6 (lines, X-motif).

EDW 31 Berenike, BE98-10.*159, 166, 196*, center of town. Inside smoothed. Outside smoothed. Decoration incised. Fabric unclassified. Form H 3. Decoration D 2 (grille).

EDW 32 Kab Marfu'a, desert settlement in Mons Smaragdus area, first–fourth century AD. Weight 8 g. Average thickness 4.7 mm. Inside 7.5R 4/6, burnished. Outside 7.5R 5/4, burnished. Decoration incised with chisel (direction unclear). Rim diameter 17 cm. (5 percent preserved). Break 7.5R 2.5/1. Fabric EDW-2. Form H 2d. Decoration D 2 (running dog).

EDW 33 Kab Marfu'a, desert settlement in Mons Smaragdus area, first–fourth century AD. Weight 12 g. Average thickness 7.5 mm. Inside 5YR 5/6, smoothed. Outside 5YR 6/4, burnished. Decoration incised with triangular point (direction unclear). Rim diameter 19 cm. (5 percent preserved). Break 5YR 5/6. Fabric EDW-1. Form H 2b. Decoration D 2 (grille). Parallel EDW 35.

EDW 34 Kab Marfu'a, desert settlement in Mons Smaragdus area, first–fourth century AD. Weight 19 g. Average thickness 5.5 mm. Inside 10R 5/6, burnished. Outside 10R 5/4, burnished. Decoration impressed, incised with knife, triangular point (direction unclear). Rim diameter 19 cm. (7 percent preserved). Break 10R 5/4. Fabric EDW-1. Form H 3. Decoration D 7 (grille, rhomboids). Parallel EDW 49.

EDW 35 Kab Marfu'a, desert settlement in Mons Smaragdus area, first–fourth century AD. Weight 10 g.

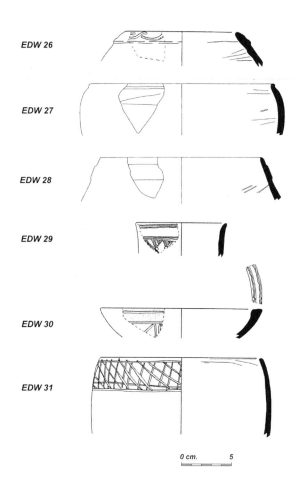

0 cm.   5

Figure 7–8 Eastern Desert Ware, catalogue numbers 26–31.
Drawings by H. Barnard and P. J. Rose.

Average thickness 6.1 mm. Inside burnished. Outside smoothed. Decoration incised with triangular point (direction unclear). Rim diameter 18 cm. (6 percent preserved). Fabric EDW-1. Form H 2a. Decoration D 2 (grille). Note carefully squared rim. Parallel EDW 33.

EDW 36   Kab Marfu'a, desert settlement in Mons Smaragdus area, first–fourth century AD. Weight 11 g. Average thickness 5.9 mm. Inside 7.5YR 6/6, burnished. Outside 7.5YR 6/6, burnished. Decoration incised with chisel (direction unclear). Rim diameter 20 cm. (4 percent preserved). Break 7.5YR 6/4. Fabric unclassified. Form H 2c. Decoration D 2 (lines). Parallel EDW 39.

EDW 37   Kab Marfu' a, desert settlement in Mons Smaragdus area, first–fourth century AD. Weight 11 g. Average thickness 5.4 mm. Inside 5YR 5/6, smoothed. Outside 2.5YR 4/6, smoothed. Decoration impressed with chisel (working left to right). Rim diameter 16 cm. (8 percent preserved). Break 5YR 4/1. Fabric EDW-2. Form H 2b. Decoration D 2 (waves). Note carefully squared rim. Parallel BE95-1.*080* (Hayes 1996: 174, Figure 6-19/5).

EDW 38   Kab Marfu'a, desert settlement in Mons Smaragdus area, first–fourth century AD. Weight 6 g. Average thickness 4.4 mm. Inside 10R 5/6, burnished. Outside 10R 5/6, burnished. Decoration plastic and incised with chisel (direction unknown). Rim diameter 13 cm. (9 percent preserved). Break 10R 3/1. Fabric EDW-2. Form H 1c. Decoration D 3 (spirals). Parallel Bir Abraq (Sadr 1994: fig. 3)?

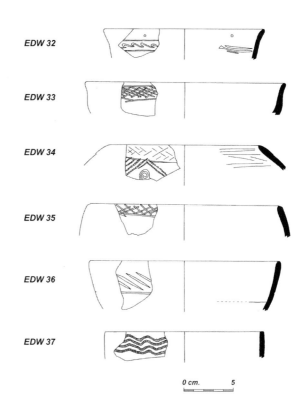

Figure 7-9   Eastern Desert Ware, catalogue numbers 32–37. Drawings by H. Barnard.

Plate 7–10   EDW 38. Photograph by H. Barnard

Plate 7–11   EDW 48, Photograph by H. Barnard

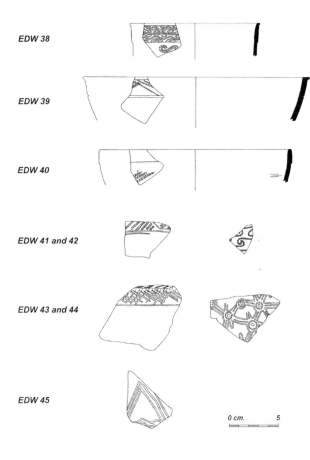

EDW 38

EDW 39

EDW 40

EDW 41 and 42

EDW 43 and 44

EDW 45

0 cm.   5

Figure 7–12   Eastern Desert Ware, catalogue numbers 38–45.
              Drawings by H. Barnard.

EDW 39   Kab Marfu'a, desert settlement in Mons Smaragdus area, first–fourth century AD. Weight 15 g. Average thickness 6.4 mm. Inside 10R 2.5/1, burnt, smoothed. Outside 10R 6/6, smoothed. Decoration incised with triangular point (direction unclear). Rim diameter 23 cm. (1 percent preserved). Break 2.5YR 6/6. Fabric EDW-1. Form H 2c. Decoration D 2 (lines). Parallel EDW 36.

EDW 40   Kab Marfu'a, desert settlement in Mons Smaragdus area, first–fourth century AD. Weight 8 g. Average thickness 6.1 mm. Inside 5YR 5/6, smoothed, wiped. Outside 2.5YR 6/6, smoothed. Decoration plastic and impressed with chisel (direction unclear). Rim diameter 20 cm. (3 percent preserved). Break 7.5YR 4/1. Fabric unclassified. Form H 2b. Decoration D 0 (lines). Too little remains for certain classification.

EDW 41   Kab Marfu'a, desert settlement in Mons Smaragdus area, first–fourth century AD. Weight 13 g.

Average thickness 5.8 mm. Inside 2.5YR 3/1, smoothed. Outside 2.5YR 4/6, smoothed. Decoration impressed, incised with chisel (direction unclear). Break 2.5YR 2.5/1. Fabric EDW-2. Form H 2d. Decoration D 0 (lines). Not a rim but judging by the preserved hole probably a suspending bowl.

EDW 42   Kab Marfu'a, desert settlement in Mons Smaragdus area, first–fourth century AD. Weight 2 g. Average thickness 3.9 mm. Inside 7.5YR 3/1, burnished, burnt. Outside 10R 4/8, burnished, red slip. Decoration impressed with triangular point (direction unclear). Break 10YR 4/1. Fabric EDW-1. Form H 0. Decoration D 0 (spirals). Too little remains for certain classification.

EDW 43   Kab Marfu'a, desert settlement in Mons Smaragdus area, first–fourth century AD. Weight 31 g. Average thickness 5.8 mm. Inside 10R 4/6, burnished. Outside 10R 5/8, wiped. Decoration impressed, incised with chisel, knife (direction unclear). Break 10R 6/8. Fabric unclassified. Form H 0. Decoration D 0 (grille, lines). Too little remains for certain classification.

EDW 44   Kab Marfu'a, desert settlement in Mons Smaragdus area, first–fourth century AD. Weight 17 g. Average thickness 4.8 mm. Inside 10R 6/6, wiped. Outside 10R 5/6, burnished. Decoration incised with triangular point (direction unclear). Break 10R 4/1. Silt. Form H 0. Decoration D 8 (sun-motif). Surfaces very worn, too little remains for certain classification.

EDW 45   Kab Marfu'a, desert settlement in Mons Smaragdus area, first–fourth century AD. Weight 13 g. Average thickness 5.3 mm. Inside 7.5YR 6/4, wiped. Outside 2.5YR 5/6, burnished. Decoration incised with triangular point (direction unclear). Break 5YR 6/1. Fabric unclassified. Form H 0. Decoration D 0 (triangles). Too little remains for certain classification.

EDW 46   Berenike, BE97-10.*090*, center of town. Weight 16 g. Outside 10R 5/6, burnished, red slip. Decoration punctuated with round point (direction unclear). Break 10R 2.5/1. Fabric unclassified. Form H 10. Decoration D 10. Handle (54.6 mm long; diameter 19.5 mm.), may not be EDW (Berenike ID: 3025-G; DN 581).

EDW 47   Berenike, BE00-10.*444*, center of town. Weight 27 g. Average thickness 5.9 mm. Inside 5YR 2.5/1, burnished, burnt. Outside 5YR 5/6, burnished, red slip. Decoration impressed, incised with triangular point (direction unclear). Break 10YR 4/1. Fabric unclassified. Form H 0. Decoration D 8 (lines). Two atypical body sherds with unusual decoration, may not be EDW (DN 586). Parallel BE97-13 (004)&(005) (Tomber 1999: 152, fig. 5-15/75).

EDW 48 Berenike, BE01-41.*062*, house/workshop in the center of town, late fourth century AD. Weight 19 g. Average thickness 3.9 mm. Inside 2.5YR 4/2, smoothed. Outside 2.5YR 4/6, burnished, red slip, smoothed. Decoration colored and impressed, incised with chisel and filled in with white (direction unclear). Rim diameter 10 cm. (22 percent preserved). Break 2.5YR 2.5/1. Fabric EDW-2. Form H 1c. Decoration D 6 (lines). Red slip spills over on inside rim. Parallels EDW 20, BE94/95-1 (cbe) pb# 115 (Hayes 1996:166, fig. 6-15/2).

EDW 49 Berenike, BE98-21, late Roman trash dump, fifth century AD. Weight 25 g. Average thickness 5.7 mm. Inside 7.5YR 3/1, compacted. Outside 2.5YR 4/2, smoothed. Decoration colored and incised, punctuated with triangular point and filled in with white (working left to right). Rim diameter 10 cm. (15 percent preserved). Break 2.5YR 4/3. Fabric EDW-1. Form H 3. Decoration D 7 (lines, rhomboids). Parallel EDW 34.

EDW 50 Berenike, BE00-37.*008*, house/workshop in the center of town, fifth century AD. Weight 12 g. Average thickness 3.9 mm. Inside 7.5YR 3/1, smoothed. Outside 10R 4/3, smoothed. Decoration incised with chisel (direction unclear). Vessel diameter 7 cm. (25 percent preserved). Break 10YR 5/4. Fabric unclassified. Form H 1c. Decoration D 0 (lines). Base of cylindrical cup with trace of incised lines.

EDW 51 Berenike, BE00-37.*028*, house/workshop in the center of town, fifth century AD. Weight 34 g. Average thickness 6.3 mm. Inside 10R 2.5/1, smoothed. Outside 10R 4/6, burnished, mottled, red slip. Decoration impressed, incised with chisel and filled in with white (direction unclear). Rim diameter 25 cm. (4 percent preserved). Break 10R 4/2. Fabric unclassified. Form H 3. Decoration D 0 (waves).

EDW 52 Berenike, BE00-37 *balk trim* (pb# 28), house/workshop in the center of town, fifth century AD. Weight 11 g. Average thickness 5.8 mm. Inside 2.5YR 4/3, burnished. Outside 7.5YR 4/2, burnished, burnt. Decoration incised with triangular point (direction unclear). Rim diameter 17 cm. (5 percent preserved). Break 5YR 5/4. Fabric EDW-1. Form H 2b. Decoration D 2 (X-motif). Note indented rim, rim toward the top much thicker than the wall of the vessel.

EDW 53 Berenike, BE00-41.*027*, house/workshop in the center of town, fifth century AD. Weight 42 g. Average thickness 7.2 mm. Inside 2.5YR 5/4, wiped. Outside 2.5YR 5/4, wiped. Decoration incised with round point (direction unclear). Rim diameter 19 cm. (21 percent preserved). Break 2.5YR 4/4. Fabric unclas-

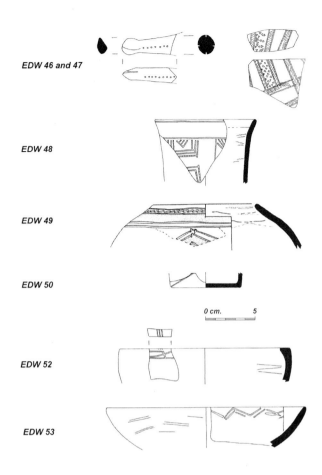

Figure 7–13 Eastern Desert Ware, catalogue numbers 46–53. Drawings by H. Barnard and P. J. Rose.

sified. Form H 9. Decoration D 2 (lines). Surfaces micaceous, outside surface very irregular. Parallel Sayala (Kromer 1967:96–99, Abb. 31-6).

EDW 54 Berenike, BE00-41.*048*, house/workshop in the center of town, late fourth century AD. Weight 24 g. Average thickness 6.0 mm. Inside 2.5YR 5/6, untreated. Outside 5YR 5/6, untreated. Decoration impressed with chisel and filled in with white (direction unclear). Vessel diameter 9 cm. (20 percent preserved). Break 2.5YR 5/6. Fabric EDW-1. Form H 1. Decoration D 0 (triangles). Base of a cup with traces of impressed, filled in decoration. Parallel Kalabsha P 792 (Strouhal 1984: fig. 127).

EDW 55 Berenike, BE01-41.*038*, house/workshop in the center of town, late fourth century AD. Weight 66 g. Average thickness 5.4 mm. Inside 2.5YR 4/6, burnt, wiped. Outside 2.5YR 4/2, burnt, wiped. Decoration incised with round point (direction unclear).

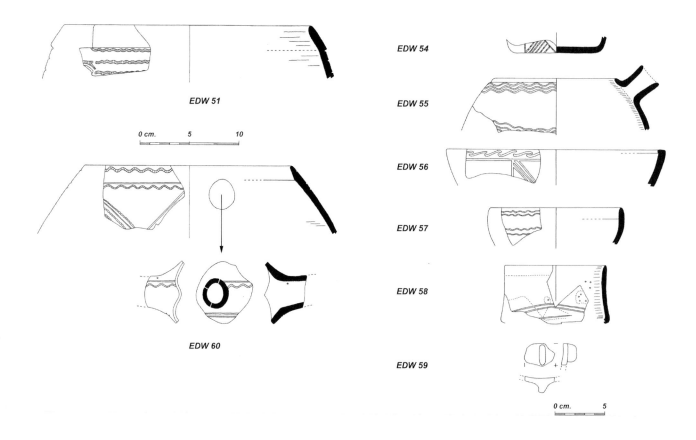

Figure 7–14   Eastern Desert Ware, catalogue numbers 51 and 60. Drawings by H. Barnard.

Figure 7–15   Eastern Desert Ware, catalogue numbers 54–59. Drawings by H. Barnard.

Rim diameter 13 cm. (19 percent preserved). Break 5YR 5/4. Fabric unclassified. Form H 7. Decoration D 3 (waves).

EDW 56   Berenike, BE01-41.*048*, house/workshop in the center of town, late fourth century AD. Weight 22 g. Average thickness 6.9 mm. Inside 10R 5/6, smoothed. Outside 10R 4/4, mottled, red slip, smoothed. Decoration punctuated with triangular point and filled in with white (direction unclear). Rim diameter 20 cm. (15 percent preserved). Break 2.5YR 5/4. Fabric unclassified. Form H 2b. Decoration D 6 (lines, running dog). Parallel Sayala (Kromer 1967:96–99, Abb. 30-1).

EDW 57   Berenike, BE0030.*154*, Christian ecclesiastic complex, fifth century AD. Weight 9 g. Average thickness 5 mm. Inside 10R 5/4, smoothed. Outside 10R 5/4, burnished, mottled, red slip. Decoration incised with triangular point (direction unclear). Rim diameter 13 cm. (8 percent preserved). Break 10R

6/1. Fabric unclassified. Form H 2b. Decoration D 3 (waves). Red slip spills over on inside rim. Parallels Sayala (Kromer 1967:96–99, Abb. 31-2), Sayala 76.251 (Bedawi 1976:29–30, Abb. 12-2, Tafel 28-2).

EDW 58   Berenike, BE00-37.*026*, house/workshop in the center of town, fifth century AD. Weight 44 g. Average thickness 4.1. Inside 2.5YR 2.5/1, burnished. Outside 10R 5/6, burnished, mottled, red slip. Decoration colored and incised, punctuated with triangular point and filled in with white (direction unclear). Rim diameter 10 cm. (20 percent preserved). Break 10R 2.5/1. Fabric unclassified. Form H 1b. Decoration D 3 (lines). Several sherds of carinated cup with incised, filled-in lines and remains of red and possibly black slip. Parallel EDW 7.

EDW 59   Berenike, BE98-20 *trench clean* (pb# 88), house/work-shop in center of town, fifth century AD. Weight 9 g. Inside 5YR 6/4. Outside 10R 4/6. Break

10R 4/6. Fabric EDW-1. Form H 0. Decoration D 0. Lug-handle (22.4 x 30.1 mm.) with possible fragment of the rim of the vessel (Berenike ID: 7570-G). Parallels EDW 15; Kalabsha P 834 (Strouhal 1984: Figure 129); Hitan Rayan 51 (Sidebotham, *et al.* 2002:210, fig. 20/51).

EDW 60 Berenike, BE00-37.*026*, house/workshop in the center of town, fifth century AD. Weight 88 g. Average thickness 6.4 mm. Inside 10R 5/6, smoothed. Outside 10R 5/4, red slip, smoothed. Decoration impressed, incised with triangular point (direction unclear). Rim diameter 21 cm. (10 percent preserved). Break 10R 4/2. Fabric unclassified. Form H 7. Decoration D 3 (triangles, waves). Two, nonjoining sherds of the same tubular spouted vessel. Note the multiple piercing of the spout.

EDW 61 Berenike, BE98-16.*082*, pagan shrine, fourth century AD. Weight 63 g. Average thickness 4.6 mm. Inside 2.5YR 5/6, smoothed. Outside 10R 5/6, red slip, smoothed. Decoration incised with round point and filled in with white (direction unclear). Rim diameter 19 cm. (20 percent preserved). Break 2.5YR 5/1. Fabric unclassified. Form H 2a. Decoration D 8 (waves). Red slip spills over on inside rim. Parallel Kalabsha P 1303a (Strouhal 1984: fig. 128).

EDW 62 Berenike, BE00-30.*162*, Christian ecclesiastic complex, fourth–fifth century AD. Weight 6 g. Average thickness 3 mm. Inside 2.5YR 6/6, burnished. Outside 2.5YR 6/6, burnished, mottled. Decoration incised with triangular point (direction unclear). Rim diameter 23 cm. (5 percent preserved). Break 2.5YR 4/1. Fabric EDW-2. Form H 2a. Decoration D 2 (lines). Note carefully squared rim.

EDW 63 Berenike, BE98-16.*080*, pagan shrine, fourth–fifth century AD. Weight 11 g. Average thickness 5.2 mm. Inside 5YR 5/6, wiped. Outside 10R 5/4, red slip, smoothed. Decoration impressed, incised with triangular point and filled in with white (working left to right). Rim diameter 19 cm. (5 percent preserved). Break 2.5YR 4/1. Fabric EDW-1. Form H 2b. Decoration D 8. Red slip spills over on inside rim. Parallel Sayala (Kromer 1967:96-99, Abb. 30-5).

EDW 64 Berenike, BE01-44.*048*, house/workshop in the center of town, fourth century AD. Weight 29 g. Average thickness 6.6 mm. Inside wiped. Outside wiped. Rim diameter 21 cm. (12 percent preserved). Fabric unclassified. Form H 3. Undecorated, may not be EDW.

EDW 65 Berenike, BE01-41.*041*, house/workshop in the center of town, early fifth century AD. Weight

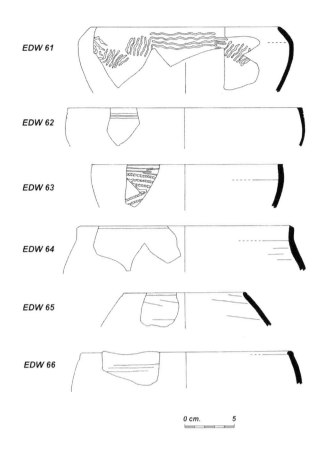

Figure 7-16   Eastern Desert Ware, catalogue numbers 61–66. Drawings by H. Barnard.

11 g. Average thickness 5.5 mm. Inside wiped. Outside smoothed. Rim diameter 12 cm. (7 percent preserved). Fabric unclassified. Form H 2a. Undecorated, may not be EDW.

EDW 66 Berenike, BE0141.*048*, house/workshop in the center of town, late fourth century AD. Weight 16 g. Average thickness 5.9 mm. Inside wiped. Outside wiped. Rim diameter 21 cm. (9 percent preserved). Fabric EDW-1. Form H 2a. Undecorated, may not be EDW. Parallel Hitan Rayan 50 (Sidebotham, *et al.* 2002:210, fig. 20/50).

7.5   DISCUSSION

The handmade, decorated pottery, here referred to as Eastern Desert Ware (EDW), appears to be a fringe phenomenon that can only be identified where the inhabitants of the Eastern Desert at the time, here referred to as Eastern Desert Dwellers, were living together with temporary settlers from elsewhere. Possible exceptions to this are chance discoveries of graves in which EDW has been (re-)used as grave goods, like in the Wadi Alaqi area, and maybe encampments that have been used for a longer time, but which have yet to be discovered.

The occurrence of EDW in the Mons Smaragdus area is noteworthy as Olympiodorus (writing in the fifth century AD) states that in his day one needed permission of the king of the Blemmyes, who seemed to have used the title *Basiliskos* (little king, Eide, *et al.* 1998:777), to visit the beryl mines in the desert. In Berenike the occurrence of EDW can be demonstrated to coincide with the presence of a desert-oriented group. The thin aeolian clay deposits on the surface at Berenike have proven to be suitable for the production of pottery (Van As and Jacobs 1995:45). This does not prove that production actually took place there, especially as the water and fuel necessary to do so would have had to be brought in from at least 10 km inland. Most likely EDW found in Berenike, and elsewhere, was produced somewhere in the Eastern Desert proper, either in a few specialized areas as a trade object or anywhere whenever the need occurred. The pottery was almost certainly used throughout the area, but it is not clear if its use was limited to a certain group or if any group limited itself to EDW exclusively.

Questions yet to be answered include the sources and uses of EDW. To address these questions it was decided to subject some of the sherds to additional, destructive research techniques including: petrologic thin-sectioning (Kempe and Harvey 1983:302–305; Schubert 1986; Rice 1987:375–382; Bourriau and Nicholson 1992:31–36; Herz and Garrison 1998:263–276), to establish more firmly the different fabrics; gas chromatography coupled with mass spectrometry (GC-MS), to identify fatty acid residues on the sherds (Condamin, *et al.* 1976; Patrick, *et al.* 1985; Gerhardt, *et al.* 1990; Morgan, Edwards, and Pepper 1992; Herz and Garrison 1998:268); and inductively coupled plasma mass spectrometry (ICP-MS), which will produce trace-element fingerprints of the different fabrics and may give indications as to whether pottery was only produced in a few areas or in many different places in the desert (Hart and Adams 1983; Rice 1987:413–426; Porat, *et al.* 1991; Herz and Garrison 1998:225, 269; Mallory-Greenough and Greenough 1998). As soon as a significant number of samples, from various sites, has been recorded, the analysis of the data will reveal

some of the culture of the people who produced and used EDW (Arnold 1985; Hair, *et al.* 1987; Rosen 1987; Shanks and Tilley 1987; Mommsen, *et al.* 1988; Rosen 1988; Bishop, *et al.* 1990; Cribb 1991; Bar-Yosef and Khazanov 1992; Rosen 1992; Jones 1997; Hodder, *et al.* 2001). This may well turn out not to be a homogenous group, as is suggested by the tentative, macroscopic examination of their pottery, or to coincide with any of the groups mentioned in the historical sources (Figure 7-2). That those texts should be taken with a grain of salt was already clear from the remark of Pliny the Elder stating that *Blemmyis traduntur capita abesse ore et oculis pectori adfixis*" ("the Blemmyes are reported to have no heads, their mouths and eyes being attached to their chests," *Natural History* 5, 46).

Notes

1. H. Barnard is Research Associate with the Cotsen Institute of Archaeology at UCLA (USA), P. J. Rose is Research Fellow with the McDonald Institute for Archaeological Research, University of Cambridge (UK). We would like to thank Dr. Steve A. Rosen, Dr. Roberta S. Tomber and Dr. Willeke Z. Wendrich for their comments.

2. Catfish is a freshwater fish that was common in the Nile at this time. Four taxa were found in Berenike, mostly in early Roman contexts. Similar contexts also yielded skeletal elements with a low meat weight (like metapodals and phalanges) of otherwise well-fed cattle, indicating that these animals most likely arrived from the Nile Valley alive (Van Neer and Ervynck 1999:339–340).

3. Christianity was the only religion officially allowed in Egypt after the decree of Theodosianus in AD 391 (*Codex Theodosianus* 16.10.11) with the exception of Lower Nubia where the cult of Isis (at Philae near Aswan) would have been legal until 100 years after the treaty of AD 453, even though the temple was closed by Justinian in *ca.* AD 540.

4. Including goat hair and not yet fully developed wool, which points toward local production (Wild and Wild 1998:234–236).

5. Some of the sherds from Bir Abraq may also belong to this corpus. They have been tentatively identified as representing the Pan-Grave culture (Sadr 1994:9) but their appearance, as judged from drawings, and especially their occurrence in association with Greco-Roman remains renders an interpretation as EDW also possible.

6. Most of the supposed region of the ancient Eastern Desert Dwellers is now inhabited by the Ababda, who are part of the larger nomadic group of the Beja (Murray 1935; Hobbs 1989; Barnard 2000).

7. The EDW research group currently consists of Dr. Anwar Abdel-Magid Osman, Dr. R. H. Pierce (University of Bergen, Norway), Dr. J. L. Bintliff, Dr. J. F. Borghouts, Dr. J. van der Vliet (all Leiden University, The Netherlands), Dr. S. M. Burstein, Dr. H. Neff (California State University Los Angeles and Long Beach, USA), Dr. J. H. F. Dijkstra (Groningen University, The Netherlands), Dr. J. W. Eerkens, Dr. S. T. Smith, Dr. W. Z. Wendrich (University of California Davis, Santa Barbara and Los Angeles, USA), Dr. A. Manzo (Istituto Universitario Orientale, Italy), Dr. P. T. Nicholson (University of Wales, Cardiff, UK), Dr. S. A. Rosen (Ben Gurion University, Israel), Dr. M. Serpico (University College London, UK) Dr. S. E. Sidebotham (University of Delaware, USA), Dr. E. Strouhal (Charles University, Czech Republic), Dr. R. S. Tomber (University of Southampton, UK), Dr. C. L. A. Willemse (Erasmus University, The Netherlands), Dr. G. Pyke, and the authors.

8. The material is made accessible at the password-protected site http://www.archbase.org/data/. An example of the format can be found at the publicly accessible site http://www.barnard.nl/EDWdata/, which also gives an introduction to the project.

CHAPTER 8 ∽

COINS

S. E. SIDEBOTHAM

The catalogue of coin finds from the Berenike 1999 and 2000 seasons (section 8.3) is preceded by a tabular presentation of the identifiable coins for 1999 and 2000 (section 8.1) and a similar overview of the coins found between 1994 and 2000 followed by a discussion of their distribution, date, and provenance (section 8.2).

8.1 QUANTIFICATION OF COINS FROM 1999–2000

During the 1999 and 2000 seasons 143 coins and one bronze medallion were recovered (Figure 8-1); 134 were from excavated contexts in 15 trenches and ten were surface finds; four were silver specimens; the remainder were *aes* or billon issues. Nine coins disintegrated upon cleaning (two from trench BE96/97/98/99-10, three from trench BE99-28, three from trench BE00-33, and one from trench BE00-38; the latter disintegrated after initial identification due to additional cleaning). The bulk of the coins was Roman, dating from the late first century BC/first century AD to the late fourth to fifth century AD (Table 8-2). Other issues included five Ptolemaic: two *aes* and three silver, one apparently barbarous copy of a small late Roman *aes*, an *aes* coin from the Kingdom of Aksum of the late third to early fourth century AD, a silver coin from western India of the fourth century AD (Table 8-3) and perhaps a small *aes* issue from Southern Arabia (from trench BE00-38, registry number 5824-C; disintegrated on second cleaning).

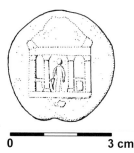

Figure 8-1   Obverse of a copper-alloy medallion (catalogue number 37, Plate 8–11). Drawing by A. M. Hense.

Period	Number of Coins
Ptolemaic	5
pre-AD 294/296 reform	1
1st century BC/1st century AD	4
1st century AD	5
1st/2nd century AD	1
2nd–3rd century AD	1
3rd century AD	2
1st–3rd century AD	3
4th century AD	21
4th–5th century AD	1
Total	44

Table 8-2   Chronological distribution of attributable coins found at Berenike during the 1999–2000 seasons.

Ruler/Dynasty	Number of Coins
Ptolemaic	5
Augustus	2
Tiberius	2
Julio-Claudian (?)	1
Claudius, Nero or Vitellius	1
Philip I or II	1
Aphilas (Aksumite)	1
House of Constantine	2
Theodosius I	1
Valentinian II	1
Rudrasena III (Kshatrapas of W. India)	1
Total	18

Table 8-3   Coins found at Berenike during the 1999–2000 seasons

8.2   QUANTIFICATION OF COINS FROM 1994-2000

Seven seasons of excavation at Berenike have produced 522 coins, one medallion plus 19 coins from one season of excavation at Shenshef and one coin from two seasons of excavation in the large fort (*praesidium*) in Wadi Kalalat.

The percentages in the chronological distribution and attributable categories show a peak in the early Roman period (late first century BC to first century AD), a relative dearth in the second through early–mid fourth centuries AD, with a second peak starting in the mid-fourth century AD (Table 8-4). This reflects data gleaned especially from epigraphic and ceramic evidence at Berenike about the periods of relative prosperity (or lack of it) at the port throughout its history. Few Ptolemaic levels have been excavated on site thus far, but one expects when more such early strata are reached that the relative percentage of Ptolemaic to Roman coins will increase.

Only two coins of the fourth–fifth century AD recovered these two seasons preserved mint marks: catalogue number 66, a small *aes* of Theodosius I from the Nicomedia mint, and catalogue number 130, a small *aes* of Valentinian II minted at Antioch. Both coins were struck between AD 383–392.

Category	Number of Coins	% of Total
Ptolemaic	13	2 %
Roman pre-AD 294/296 reform	156	30 %
Late 3rd/early 4th century AD	2	1 %
4th/5th century AD	112	21 %
Unattributable	240	46 %
Total	523	100 %

Table 8-4   Chronological distribution of 522 coins and one medallion (included in the 156 coins dated to the Roman pre-AD 294/296 reform) recovered at Berenike during the 1994–2000 seasons.

Mint Mark	Number of Coins
Alexandria	5
Antioch	3
Aquileia	1
Constantinople	1
Cyzicus	2
Nicomedia	1
Total	13

Table 8-5   Thirteen coins found at Berenike (1994–2000) with mint marks (does not include one coin found at Shenshef from the Antioch mint).

Thus far during seven seasons of excavation at Berenike only 13 coins have preserved mint marks (Table 8-5), all but one of these from mints in the eastern Mediterranean.

The abundance of ceramic finds suggests, and the limited numismatic data tend to corroborate, the conclusion that in the mid- to late fourth and fifth centuries, the bulk of the contacts that Berenike had with the Roman world occurred in the Eastern Mediterranean; contact with the Western Mediterranean seems to have diminished substantially since the early Roman period.

An *aes* coin of King Aphilas, the last pre-Christian ruler of Aksum (catalogue number 114), and a silver coin of Rudrasena III of the Kshatrapas of Western India (catalogue number 115) are the first numismatic evidence of contact between Berenike and regions beyond Rome's imperial frontiers (Table 8-6).

Ruler/Dynasty	Number of Coins	% of Total
Ptolemaic	13	
Subtotal Ptolemaic Period		13 = 15%
Augustus	6	
Livia	1	
Tiberius	4	
Julio Claudian/Flavian/Vitellius	3	
Claudius	10	
Nero	4	
Vespasian	3	
Domitian	3	
Flavian (unid.)	1	
Subtotal 1st century AD		35=41%
Hadrian	2	
Antoninus Pius	1	
Subtotal 2nd century AD		3=>4%
Philip I	1	
Philip II	1	
Philip I or II	1	
Diocletian	1	
Subtotal 3rd century AD		4=>5%
Aphilas (Aksum)	1	1=<1%
House of Constantine	10	
Constantius II	2	
Constantius II/Julian II	1	
Theodosius I/Valentinian II	1	
Theodosius I	2	
Arcadius	2	
Gratian	1	
Theodosius I/Valentinian I/Val. II	1	
Valentinian II	1	
Theodosius I/Gratian/Arcadius/Val. II	2	
Theodosius II/Valentinian III	5	
Rudrasena III	1	
Subtotal 4th-5th century AD		29=34 %
Total	85	85=100%

Table 8-6   Identifiable coins from Berenike from the past seven seasons (1994–2000).

Both coins were found in trench BE99-30 inside the putative church at the eastern end of the site. A third one, which disintegrated after photography during a second cleaning, appeared to be an *aes* issue from Southern Arabia (catalogue number 82), but that could not be confirmed. It was recovered in a building in the late Roman commercial-residential quarter between the church and the Serapis temple.

One would expect, given the volume of finds excavated at Berenike especially from South Asia (India and Sri Lanka) and, to a lesser extent from the Persian Gulf and Aksum, that more coins from those regions and from southern Arabia would appear in future excavations. That they have not thus far may reveal something of the nature of this trade between the Roman Empire and those regions: that is, that it was one based more upon barter than upon purchase/sale in coined money.

Another small group of coins is also worthy of discussion: possible barbarous imitations of late period Roman bronzes. This comprises only two *aes* issues identified thus far from the coins excavated at the site. One is a surface find from the 1995 season (Sidebotham and Seeger 1996: 192, Plates 7–11b; 193, Plates 7–12b; 196, catalogue number 113) and the other was recovered in the 1999 season (catalogue number 67, from BE99-27.*024* Pb 51). Both appear to be imitations of regular mid- to late fourth-century Roman *aes* issues. While such "barbarous" issues are common in north Europe in this period and later, they are unusual in Egypt; a Hungarian expedition recovered a similar coin at Bir Mineh in the Eastern Desert (personal communication from Lassányi Gábor).

The apparent dearth of "official" fifth-century Roman coinage circulating at Berenike and throughout the region in general may have prompted some "local" imitation of fourth-century issues, the circulation of which continued at Berenike late in the life of the port. If so, the source of these issues is uncertain; one might speculate that the Blemmyes, who were the political hegemons in the region in the fifth century, hinted at in the contemporary literary sources, might possibly have been the source of these issues.

8.3   CATALOGUE

The catalogue of coins has the following format:
(1) catalogue number, (2) Berenike registration number, not available for surface finds from the 2000 season, (3) locus and pottery bucket number, (4) denomination and/or diameter in mm, (5) identification and date of issue where possible, (6) mint if discernable, (7) obverse, (8) reverse, (9) die positions, if determinable, (10) published parallels, where available. The black and white increments in all the photographic scales are 10 mm.

Abbreviations:

AE	copper alloy
AR	silver alloy
c.	century
ex.	exergue
fig.	figure
l.	left
Obv.	obverse
r.	right
Rv.	reverse
stg.	standing
unid.	unidentifiable
*	coins marked with an * are illustrated

THE PTOLEMAIC AREA
Trench BE00–36

1   BE00 5825-C-001; 36.*068* Pb 123; AE 24.0; Obv. lost; Rv. one or two indistinct figs. stg.; unid.

THE EARLY ROMAN TRASH DUMP
Trench BE99–29

2   BE99 4389-C-002; 29.*017* Pb 26; AE 22.6 (broken in two parts); unid.

3   BE99 4697-C-003; 29.*016* Pb 24; AE 25.1; unid.

4   BE99 4391-C-004; 29.*002* Pb 4; AE 27.2; unid.

Trench BE99–31

5*   BE99 4585-C-005; 31.*016* Pb 26; billon tetradrachm 26.9; Tiberius 20/21 AD; Alexandria mint; Obv. laureate bust r., TIB[ΕΡΙΟΥΣ ΚΑΙΣ] ΣΕΒΑΣΤΟΣ, to r. LZ (= year 7); Rv. bust of Augustus r. with radiate crown, ΘΕΟΣ ΣΕΒΑΣΤΟΣ; ↑↑; Poole 1964: 6, nos. 36–38; Geißen 1974:26, no. 48; Milne 1982: cf. 2, nos. 38–52; Förschner 1987:31, no. 33; Sidebotham 1999:194, no. 2; following, catalogue no. 6, BE99 2905-C-006 (Plate 8-7).

Plate 8-7   Obverse and reverse of a billon tetradrachm 26.9 of Tiberius of AD 20/21 from trench BE99-31 (catalogue number 5). Photograph by S. E. Sidebotham.

Plate 8-8   Obverse and reverse of an AE 23.7 diobol of Augustus of AD 10/11 from trench BE00-33 (catalogue number19). Photograph by S. E. Sidebotham.

6   BE99 2905-C-006; 31.*007* Pb 9; billon tetradrachm 27.0; Tiberius AD 20/21. See above, catalogue no. 5 (BE99 4585-C-005) for description and parallels.

7   BE99 2239-C-007; 31.*007* Pb 2; diobol AE 26.0; first c. AD (probably Claudius AD 41–54); Alexandria mint; Obv. laureate bust r. CεB[—-]; Rv. AYTO[KRA] winged caduceus and ears of grain, tied together; ↑↖.

8   BE99 4589-C-008; 31.*020* Pb 32; AE 22.3; unid.

9   BE99 4740-C-009; 31.*018* Pb 29; AE 25.4; unid.

10   BE99 4693-C-010; 31.*018* Pb 29; AE 23.7; Obv. bust r., legend lost; Rv. lost; unid.

11   BE99 4390-C-011; 31.*017* Pb 27; AE 22.6; unid.

12   BE99 4396-C-012; 31.*013* Pb 21; AE 19.8; Obv. bust r., legend lost; Rv. lost; unid.

13   BE99 3481-C-013; 31.*007* Pb 9; AE 22.6; unid.

14   BE99 4695-C-014; 31.*cbe* Pb 38; AE 19.5; unid.

15   BE99 4587-C-015; 31.*cbw* Pb 36; AE 24.3; unid.

16   BE99 4588-C-016; 31.*cbs* no Pb; AE 23.9; unid.

Trench BE00–33

17   BE00 2348-C-017; 33.*005* Pb 10; AR 24.3 tetradrachm; unid. late Ptolemaic; unid. mint; Obv. bare or laureate bust r., no legend visible; Rv. eagle stg.1., legend very faint and illegible [ΠΤΟΛΕΜΑΙΟΥ ΒΑΣΙΛΕΩΣ]; ↑↖.

18   BE00 6675-C-018; *33.east balk trim* Pb 73; AR 27.8 tetradrachm; unid. late Ptolemaic; unid. mint; Obv. laureate bust r.; Rv. eagle stg.1., [ΠΤΟΛΕΜΑΙΟΥ ΒΑΣΙΛΕΩΣ]; ↑↑.

19*   BE00 2347-C-019; 33.*018* Pb 26; AE 23.7 diobol; Augustus AD 10/11; Alexandria mint; Obv. laureate bust of Augustus r., Rv. Nike advancing1., carries palm branch in1. hand, M (= year 40) to r.; ↑↗; Geißen 1974:20, nos. 22–23 (Plate 8-8).

20   BE00 2346-C-020; 33.*008* Pb 13; AE 19.7; Roman pre-AD 296 reform issue; Alexandria mint; Obv. bust r. legend not visible; Rv. eagle (?) stg. r. legend faint; ↑←.

21   BE00 5637-C-021; 33.*038* Pb 63; AE 26.9; Obv. bust r.; Rv. lost; unid.

22   BE00 2348-C-022; 33.*005* Pb 10; AE 16.7; Obv. bust r.; Rv. lost; unid.

23   BE00 6676-C-023; 33.*038* Pb 61; AE 26.2; unid.

Plate 8-9
Obverse and reverse of an unidentifiable late Ptolemaic AR 25.0 tetradrachm from trench BE96/97/98/99 /00-10 (catalogue number 32). Photograph by S. E. Sidebotham.

Plate 8-10
Obverse and reverse of an AE 29.4 80 *drachmai* of Augustus (reigned 30 BC–AD 14) from trench BE96/97/98/99/00-10 (catalogue number 33). Photograph by S. E. Sidebotham.

Plate 8-11
Obverse and reverse of AE 34.6 medallion probably of the first or second century AD from trench BE00-10 (catalogue number 37). Photograph by S. E. Sidebotham.

24 BE00 6676-C-024; 33.*038* Pb 61; AE 27.7; unid.

25 BE00 5822-C-025; 33.*025* Pb 49; AE 21.8; unid.

26 BE00 6673-C-026; 33.*025* Pb 48; AE 23.3; unid.

27 BE00 5821-C-027; 33.*025* Pb 45; AE 15.2; unid.

28 BE00 5636-C-028; 33.*025* Pb 44; AE 20.2; unid.

29 BE00 2348-C-029; 33.*005* Pb 10; AE 24.1; unid.

30 BE00 6675-C-030; 33.*east balk trim* Pb 73; AE 21.3; unid.

31 BE00 6674-C-031; 33.*south balk trim* Pb 75; AE 24.6; unid.

THE LEVELED AREA
Trench BE96/97/98/99/00-10

32* BE00 6763-C-032; 10.*587* Pb 1120; AR 25.0 tetradrachm; Ptolemaic, no earlier than Ptolemy VI Philometor (180–145 BC) to Ptolemy XII Neos Dionysus/Cleopatra VII (80–51 BC); mint unknown; Obv. laureate bust of a Ptolemaic ruler r., no legend; Rv. eagle stg.1, ΠΤΟΛΕΜΑΙΟΥ ΒΑΣΙΛΕΩΣ, LI (= regnal year 10) to l. of eagle, ΠΑ to r. of eagle; ↑↑ (Plate 8-9).

33* BE00 3405-C-033; 10.*236* Pb 924; AE 29.4, 80 drachmai; Augustus (reigned 30 BC–AD 14, no regnal year indicated); Alexandria mint; Obv. bare headed bust r., legend faint [CEBACTOC]; Rv. round temple of Mars Ultor (in Rome) with legionary standard inside, other figs. and legend indistinct [KAICAP]; ↑↗; Förschner 1987:25, nos. 4–5; Geißen 1974:16, nos. 5–6 (Plate 8-10).

34 BE00 2341-C-034; 10.*405* Pb 831; diobol AE 22.7; early Roman, probably first AD; Alexandria mint; obv. bare headed bust r., no legend visible; Rv. indistinct fig. stg.; ↑↖.

35 BE00 2767-C-035; 10.*345* Pb 665; AE 23.7; probably first c. AD; Alexandria mint; Obv. faint; Rv. eagle stg.1. AVTO [KPA—]; ↑↑.

36 BE00 4694-C-036; 10.*trench clean* Pb 581; billion tetradrachm, 26.6; probably first c. AD; Alexandria mint; Obv. bust r., legend lost; Rv. Fig. stg.1. crowned by Nike stg. r, no extant legend; ↑↖.

37* BE00 0793-D C-037; 10.*445* Pb 828; AE 34.6; medallion, first to second c. AD; Obv. bearded bust r. no legend visible; Rv. tetrastyle temple with large cult statue in center (between columns 2–3) and two smaller statues flanking (between columns 1–2 and 3–4), pediment with indistinct sculpture, indistinct symbol beneath temple; ↑↗; Dr. Peter van Alfen of the American Numismatic Society suggests a parallel in the collection of the American Numismatic Society: a drachm of Antoninus Pius from the Alexandria mint of AD 151/152 AD (Figure 8-1, Plate 8-11).

38 BE00 4388-C-38; 350 Pb 685; AE 22.3; pre-AD 296 reform issue; Alexandria mint; Obv. bust r., legend faint; Rv. bust r., legend faint; ↑↗.

39 BE00 3406-C-039; 10.*463* Pb 859; billon tetradrachm 26.9; Philip I or II (AD 244–249); Alexandria mint; Obv. laureate bust r., AKM IOV ΦΙΛΠ[ΠΟC EVC]; Rv. eagle stg.1., faces r. [wreath in beak], regnal year illegible; ↑↖; cf. Sidebotham and Seeger 1996:190–191, Pl. 7–9e–f and 7–10e–f; 194, catalogue nos. 68–69.

40 BE00 5646-C-040; 10.*513* Pb 987; billon tetradrachm 23.6; mid to late third c. AD; Alexandria mint; Obv. laureate bust r., [—]OC CEB; Rv. indistinct fig. stg., L to left (regnal year illegible); ↑↖.

41 BE00 5647-C-041; 10.*502* Pb 979; AE 21.5; Obv. bust r., legend lost; Rv. lost; unid.

42 BE00 6661-C-042; 10.*517* Pb 1001; AE 21.2; unid.

43 BE00 5648-C-043; 10.*504* Pb 999; AE 32.3; unid.

44 BE00 5645-C-044; 10.*462* PB 963; AE 28.6; unid.

45 BE00 2344-C-045; 10.*462* Pb 860; AE 26.5; unid.

46 BE00 2343-C-046; 10.*443* Pb 838; AE 25.3; unid.

47 BE00 2342-C-047; 10.*423* Pb 825; AE 26.0; unid.

48 BE00 2345-C-048; 10.*423* Pb 821; AE 30.0; unid.

49 BE00 5644-C-049; 10.*269* Pb 961; AE 27.5; unid.

50 BE00 3407-C-050; 10.*236* Pb 903; AE 21.8; unid.

51 BE99 3326-C-051; 10.*175* Pb 627; AE 21.5; unid.

52 BE99 4696-C-052; 10.*293* Pb 597; AE 27.3; unid.

53 BE99 4696-C-053; 10.*293* Pb 597; AE 27.6; unid.

54 BE99 4809-C-054; 10.*334* Pb 649; AE 23.5; unid.

55   BE99 4809-C-055; 10.*334* Pb 649; AE 23.5; unid.

56   BE99 4809-C-056; 10.*334* Pb 649; AE 22.4; unid.

57   BE99 4809-C-057; 10.*334* Pb 649; AE 25.4; unid.

58   BE99 4739-C-058; 10.*388* Pb 734; AE 26.2; unid.

59   BE99 4804-C-059; 10.*393* Pb 741; AE 26.2; unid.

60   BE99 4694-C-060; 10.*trench clean* Pb 581; AE 24.5; unid.

THE NORTHERN QUARTER
Trench BE98/99-23

61   BE99 2788-C-061; 23.*055* Pb 132; AE 25.9, broken, about half the coin is missing; unid.

THE CENTRAL QUARTER
Trench BE99–27

62   BE99 3325-C-062; 27.*018* Pb 31; AE 15.1; house of Constantine AD 335–341; Obv. helmeted head of Constantinople 1 with scepter, CONSTANTINO-POLIS; Rv. two soldiers stg. either side of one (or two ?) standards, GLORIA EXERCITVS, mint mark not legible; ↑↗; Hill, Kent, and Carson 1978:21, no. 858 (if Thessalonica; AD 337–341), 23, no. 942 (if Heraclea; AD 335–337), 25, nos. 1039–1040 (if Constantinople; AD 335–337), 27, no. 1131 (if Nicomedia; AD 335–337), 29, no. 1272 (if Cyzicus; AD 335–337), 31, nos. 1371 or 1373 (if Antioch; AD 335–341).

63   BE99 4803-C-063; 27 *north balk clean* Pb 69; AE 17.0; house of Constantine AD 346–361; Obv. laureate bust r., legend faint; Rv. Roman spearing fallen barbarian horseman [FEL TEMP REPARATIO], mint mark not legible; ↑↗.

64   BE99 4586-C-064; 27.*035* Pb 66; AE 18.4; mid–late fourth c. AD; Obv. bust r., legend lost; Rv. indistinct.

65   BE99 4394-C-065; 27.*026* Pb 55; AE 11.7; mid–late fourth c. AD; Obv. laureate bust r, legend faint; Rv. fig. stg., legend lost; ↑↖.

66*   BE99 1866-C-066; 27.*006* Pb 16; AE 14.7; Theodosius I (AD 383–392); Nicomedia mint; Obv. laureate bust r. DN THEODOSIVS PF AVG; Rv. Victory to l., trophy on shoulder, dragging captive r. SALVS REIPVBLICAE, in ex. SMNA (Nicomedia); ↑↗; Hill, Kent, Carson 1978:94, no. 2404 (Plate 8-12).

67*   BE99 4393-C-067; 27.*024* Pb 51; AE 10.9; barbarous? imitation of mid–late fourth c. Roman issue; Obv. laureate bust r., dots for letters in legend; Rv. uncertain (Plate 8-13).

68   BE99 4584-C-068; 27.*023* Pb 48; mid–late fourth c. AD; Obv. lost; Rv. indistinct fig. stg.

Trench BE99–28

69   BE99 4590-C-069; 28.*018* Pb 25; AE 13.5; mid–late fourth c. AD; Obv. bust r. legend lost; Rv. indistinct.

70   BE99 4810-C-070; 28.*038* Pb 76; AE 16.3; unid. fourth c. AD.

71   BE99 4810-C-071; 28.*038* Pb 76; AE 21.5; unid.; Obv. bust r.; Rv. fig. stg.; ↑↘.

72   BE99 4698-C-072; 28.*038* Pb 74; AE 21.4; unid.

73   BE99 4808-C-073; 28.*038* Pb 72; AE 9.2; unid.

74   BE99 4808-C-074; 28.*038* Pb 72; AE 28.5; unid.

75   BE99 4699-C-075; 28.*037* Pb 51; AE 20.3; unid.

76   BE99 4699-C-076; 28.*037* Pb 51; AE 20.3; unid.

77   BE99 4692-C-077; 28.*036* Pb 50; AE 17.3; unid.

78   BE99 4692-C-078; 28.*036* Pb 50; broken fragments, largest=AE 10.3; unid.

79   BE99 4692-C-079; 28.*036* Pb 50; AE 12.6; unid.

80   BE99 4395-C-080; 28.*036* Pb 49; AE 20.2; broken in two parts and joined; unid.

81   BE99 4811-C-081; 28.*036* Pb 48; AE 12.7; unid.

Trench BE00–38

82   BE00 5824-C-082; 38.*023* Pb 45; highly concave/convex AE 11.5, possibly from South Arabia; Obv. (convex) series of joined circles; Rv. (concave) sailing ship (?); disintegrated with additional cleaning.

83   BE00 6662-C-083; 38.*028* Pb 55; AE 12.6; unid. late fourth c. AD.

84   BE00 6662-C-084; 38.*028* Pb 55; AE 14.6; unid.

85   BE00 6663-C-085; 38.*024* Pb 53; AE 16.5; unid.

86   BE00 6663-C-086; 38.*024* Pb 53; AE 18.6; unid.

87   BE00 6665-C-087; 38.*024* Pb 52; AE 15.4; unid.

88   BE00 6665-C-088; 38.*024* Pb 52; AE 16.5; unid.

Plate 8-12
Obverse and reverse of an AE 14.7
of Theodosius I of AD 383–392
from trench BE99-27 (catalogue
number 66). Photograph by S. E.
Sidebotham.

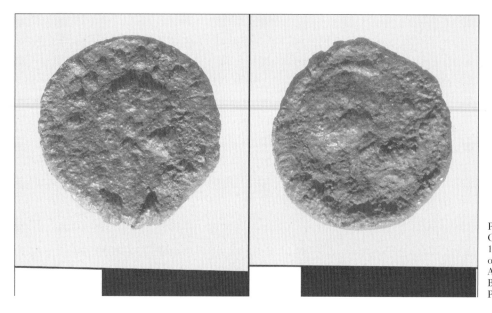

Plate 8-13
Obverse and reverse of an AE
10.9. Possible barbarous imitation
of a mid–late fourth-century
AD Roman issue from trench
BE99-27 (catalogue number 67).
Photograph by S. E. Sidebotham.

89   BE00 6665-C-089; 38.*024* Pb 52; fragment AE
13.6; unid.

90   BE00 6665-C-090; 38.*024* Pb 52; fragment AE
16.5; unid.

91   BE00 6145-C-091; 38.*018* Pb 26; 3 AE fragments of a single coin; unid.

92   BE00 6664-C-092; 38.*east balk trim* Pb 48; AE
14.2; unid.

93   BE00 6664-C-093; 38.*east balk trim* Pb 48; AE
14.2; unid.

Trench BE00-34:

94   BE00 5823-C-094/D-5136; 34.*027* Pb 63;
broken AE 14.1; unid.

95   BE00 6680-C-095; 34.*019* Pb 47; half coin AE
21.3; unid.

96   BE00 6680-C-096; 34.*019* Pb 47; AE 10.7;
unid.

Trench BE00-37:

97   BE00 5638-C-097; 37.*018* Pb 49; AE 21.1; first
c. AD either Claudius (AD 41–54) or Nero (AD 54–68)
or, less likely, Vitellius (AD 69); Alexandria mint; Obv.
laureate bust r. [—-]OY[—-]ΓΕΡΜΑΥΤ[?]; Rv. fig. stg.,
legend faint; ↑↙.

98   BE00 6667-C-098; 37.*008* Pb 114; broken AE
11.5; unid. late fourth c. AD.

99   BE00 6670-C-099; 37.*026* Pb 116; AE 25.0;
unid.

100   BE00 6669-C-100; 37.*026* Pb 110; AE 13.9;
unid.

101 BE00 6668-C-101; 37.*006* Pb 88; AE 21.7 halved in antiquity; unid.

Trench BE00-41

102 5640-C-102; 41.*009* Pb 17; AE 24.0; Roman pre-AD 296 reform issue, badly worn from circulation; Alexandria mint; Obv. lost; Rv. indistinct.

103 BE00 5642-C-102; 41.*009* Pb 21; AE 13.9; ca. 383–392 AD; Obv. bust r., legend very faint; Rv. Victory to l. trophy on shoulder, dragging captive to r., staurogram in field to l., SALVS REIPVBLICAE.

104 BE00 5641-C-104; 41.*009* Pb 14; AE 11.9; ca. AD 383–392; Obv. very faint; Rv. fig. faint [SA]LVS REI[PVBLICE/AE].

105 BE00 6672-C-105; 41.*027* Pb 39; AE 12.5, broken in two parts; late fourth c. AD unid.

106 BE00 5639-C-106; 41.*031* Pb 50; AE 11.1; unid.

107 BE00 6671-C-107; 41.*025* Pb 35; AE 20.8; unid.

108 BE00 5643; 41.*trench clean* Pb 22; AE 12.4; unid.

THE NORTHEAST QUARTER

Trench BE99-26

109 BE99 4807-C-109; 26.*033* Pb 59; AE 14.3, broken; fourth c. AD, unid.

110 BE99 4392-C-110; 26.*044* Pb 66; AE 17.4, broken and partly missing; mid–late fourth c. AD; Obv. laureate bust r., legend indistinct; Rv. fig. stg., legend faint; ↑↘.

111 BE99 3787-C-111; 26.*022* Pb 34; AE 14.3, badly worn; late fourth c. AD; Obv. laureate bust r., legend faint; Rv. lost.

112 BE99 3785-C-112; 26.*004* Pb 50; AE 12.9, badly worn; late fourth c. AD; Obv. laureate bust r., legend lost; Rv. lost.

113 BE99 4806-C-113; 26.*022* Pb 34; AE 10.6; late fourth to early fifth c. AD; Obv. lost; Rv. indistinct legend.

Trench BE99/00-30

114* BE99 4615-C-114; 30.*064* Pb 92; AE 17.3; Aksumite King Aphilas (reigned *ca.* AD 270–290, before AD 330); Obv. head and shoulders profile bust r., draped in garment with folds shown as lines curving from shoulder to shoulder and with the V-neck double collar, wearing head cloth with triangular ribbon behind. The bust descends to the base of the coin. Disc and crescent at top. Greek legend AΦIΛACBA᷅ CIΛЄYCAξW (King Aphilas of the Aksu . . .); some

examples read . . . CIΛYξC; Rv. Wheat stalk center field, stalk reaching the edge. Greek legend all around: MITWNBI CIΔIMHΛH (. . . mites, man of Dimele). A variant shows the legend written as . . . IMIΛH, and there are other variants as well. e.g. CIΔMIΛH, etc.; ↑↑. (Munro-Hay and Juel-Jensen 1995:95–96, copper type 13) (Plate 8-14).

115* BE00 5649-C-115; 30.*159* Pb 221; AR 15.2; Obv. Rudrasena III (reigned AD 348–390)(coin minted in Saka year AD 285? =AD 362) of the Kshatrapas of Western India, bust r., illegible date behind head; Rv. Caitya and legend (transliterated): Rājña Mahākṣatrapasa Suāmi-Rudradāmaputrasa Rājña Mahākṣatrapasa Suāmi-Rudrasenasa.↑?; cf. Rapson 1967:179–188 and Pl. XVII in general; Zeymal 1975:7 fig. 2,41, 10 (Sedov and Bates, personal communication) (Plate 8-15).

116 BE00 5653-C-116; 30.*136* Pb 188; AE 12.3; unid. late fourth c. AD.

117 BE00 6677-C-117; 30.*176* Pb 255; AE three fragments, largest 24.1; unid.

118 BE00 5652-C-118; 30.*173* Pb 239; AE 14.5; unid.

119 BE00 5652-C-119; 30.*173* Pb 239; AE 14.0; unid.

120 BE00 5651-C-120; 30.*163* Pb 230; AE 12.5; unid.

121 BE00 5649-C-121; 30.*159* Pb 221; AE 15.0; unid.

122 BE00 5653-C-122; 30.*136* Pb 188; AE 12.3; unid.

123 BE00 5650-C-123; 30.*117* Pb 187; AE 18.8; unid.

124 BE00 6678-C-124; 30.*104* Pb 169; AE 16.8; unid.

Trench BE00-39

125 BE00 6666-C-125; 39.*007* Pb 18; AE 11.2; unid. late fourth c. AD.

126 BE00 5654-C-126; 39.*007* Pb 15; AE 12.4; unid.

SURFACE FINDS

127 BE99 3786-C-127; surface *ca.* 50 m southeast of trench BE96-11; AE 24.1; unid. Ptolemaic; unid. mint; Obv. lost [bearded bust of Zeus Ammon r.]; Rv. eagle stg. r., legend lost [ΠΤΟΛΕΜΑΙΟΥ ΒΑΣΙΛΕΩΣ]; very worn.

128 BE99 2768-C-128; surface *ca.* 80 m south of trench BE96-11; AE 22.1 (very worn and broken in

Plate 8-14
Obverse and reverse of an AE
17.3. Aksumite King Aphilas
of *ca*. 270/290–before AD 330
from trench BE99-30 (catalogue
number 114). Photograph by S.
E. Sidebotham.

Plate 8-15
Obverse and reverse of an AR
15.2 of Kshatrapa (western Indian)
King Rudrasena III of AD 362
from trench BE99-30 (catalogue
number 115). Photograph by S.
E. Sidebotham.

two parts); unid. Ptolemaic; unid. mint; Obv. bearded
bust of Zeus Ammon r.; Rv. eagle stg.1., legend lost
[ΠΤΟΛΕΜΑΙΟΥ ΒΑΣΙΛΕΩΣ]; ↑↑.

129 BE00 surf-C-129; between early Roman trash
dump and camp; AE 24.2; Roman pre-AD 296 reform
issue; Obv. bust r., legend lost; Rv. indistinct.

130 BE00 surf-C-130; *ca*. 30 m northwest of
trench 10; AE 13.0 (AE 4); Valentinian II (AD
383–392); Antioch mint; Obv. laureate bust r. DN
VALENTINIANVS PF AVG; Rv. Victory advancing
1., trophy on shoulder, dragging captive, staurogram to
1., SALVS [REIPVBLICAE], in ex. ANTA; ↑↓; Hill,
Kent and Carson 1978:102, no. 2768.

131 BE99 3482-C-131; surface in camp; AE 26.3;
unid.

132 BE00 surf-C-132; from sieve pile from trench
BE99-22; AE 25.5; unid.

133 BE00 surf-C-133; near trench BE00-36;
broken AE 15.3; unid.

134 BE00 surf-C-134; west of trenches 6/16; AE
25.2; unid.

135 BE00 surf-C-135; AE 18.0; unid.

136 BE00 surf-C-136; AE 21.2; unid.

CHAPTER 9 ～

METAL FINDS

A. M. HENSE

During the 1999 and 2000 seasons more than 9,000 metal fragments were excavated. Lead comprised 52.3 percent of the total volume of unearthed metal, 95 kg alone found in trench BE00-36. Trench BE99/00-10 produced one quarter of all metal fragments (2,600) found. During the 2000 season over 2,400 slag fragments were also recovered. The following tables (9-1, 9-2, and 9-3) record the division of iron, lead, and copper alloys found during the 1999 and 2000 seasons.

Season	Cu-alloy frag.	Cu-alloy gr.	Fe frag.	Fe gr.	Pb fr.	Pb gr.
BE99	1,300 (35.1%)	6,350 (20.0%)	2,400 (64.8%)	25,050 (79.2%)	5 (0.1%)	240 (0.8%)
BE00	2,300 (43.4%)	9,900 (7.9%)	2,200 (41.5%)	21,000 (16.7%)	800 (15.1%)	95,000 (75.4%)
BE99/00	3,600 (40.0%)	16,250 (10.3%)	4,600 (51.1%)	46,050 (29.2%)	805 (8.9%)	95,240 (60.5%)

Table 9-1.   Excavated number of fragments and weights of copper alloy, iron, and lead.

Season	Cu-alloy, volume in cm³	Fe, volume in cm³	Pb, volume in cm³
BE99	725 (18.5%)	3,185 (81.0%)	21 (0.5%)
BE00	1,130 (9.3%)	2,670 (21.9%)	8,370 (68.8%)
BE99/00	1,855 (11.5%)	5,855 (36.4%)	8,391 (51.1%)

Table 9-2.   Volume of excavated metal.

Trench	A (Cu/Fe)	B (Cu/Fe)	C (B/A)	Date
BE98-10*	0.67	0.30	0.45	LR-ER
BE99-10*	0.44	0.18	0.41	ER
BE00-10*	0.37	0.18	0.49	ER
BE99-22	0.16	0.25	(1.56)	LR
BE98-23	0.36	0.20	(0.55)	LR
BE99-23	0.66	0.51	(0.84)	LR
BE99-26	1.31	0.81	(0.62)	LR
BE99-27*	0.89	0.37	0.42	LR
BE99-28*	1.15	0.58	0.50	LR
BE99-29*	0.51	0.17	0.33	ER
BE99-30	0.54	0.16	(0.30)	LR
BE99-31*	0.56	0.26	0.46	LR
BE99-32	0.68	0.82	(1.21)	LR
BE00-32	0.78	0.22	(0.28)	LR
BE00-34	0.52	0.60	(1.15)	LR
BE00-40*	3.29	1.53	0.47	Ptol

Table 9-3.   Relative size of metal fragments; trenches marked with an asterisk (*) produced a considerable amount of metal.

9.1   TRENCH BE96/97/98/99/00-10

Excavations in loci directly atop the two storage jar pits (loci *358* and *359*) produced concentrations of iron tools, mainly knives and chisels (loci *315, 313, 295*) (Figure 9-4). Mounting fragments were unearthed in several layers in, directly above, and under the storage jar pits. Iron edge protectors emerged in loci *313* and *290*, copper-alloy edge protectors in *354*. Most of the tools were unearthed in *290*, a locus that seems to be the start of a new building phase. The large quantity of iron nails may be an indication of the demolition of a large structure in this area. After construction of walls *175, 276*, and *102*, activities of a slightly different character were carried out in this area. Tools were discarded in loci *285/292* and *140/323*. And, as before demolition of the wooden structure, bowl-shaped slag with a diameter of 90 to 110 mm came to light in loci *308* and *279/283*. In addition to the bowl-shaped slag, iron-slag fragments were found in loci *304/291, 301, 302, 285/292*, and *287*. These industrial activities in the latest phase of BE99-10 can be directly connected to the early fourth-century AD tool concentrations, also accompanied with iron slag, bowl-shaped slag, and furniture fragments, in BE98-10 (see Hense 2000:192–195).

9.1.1 TRASH DUMP IN TRENCH 10

In trench 10 the early Roman period had successive trash layers, small fireplaces and installations,

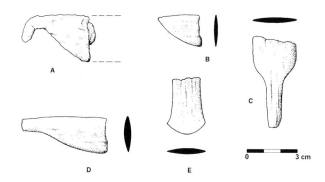

Figure 9-4.   Iron tools from trench 10. Drawings by A. M. Hense.
A=BE00 0787-D-6450 10.*313*
B=BE00 0346-D-6412 10.*290*
C=BE00 0790-D-6454 10.*315*
D=BE00 0477-D-6466 10.*295*
E=BE00 0346-D-6412 10.*290*

both in courtyards and on top of leveled buildings. Pottery sherds, some loci containing up to 40 percent, dominated the large pottery/trash dump (10.*423/44 3/453/464/465/468/482/469/473/474/483/486/490*). Another remarkable feature of these trash layers was the presence of tiny amounts of copper alloy; only 25 small fragments were excavated, whereas the same layers produced more than 190 iron fragments. Over 76 percent of these iron finds consisted of nail fragments. This huge early Roman trash/pottery dump showed a remarkable distribution of nails as noted in Table 9.5.

Locus	Copper-Alloy Fragments	Number of Copper-Alloy Nails	Iron Fragments	Number of Iron Nails
10.*423*	4	2 (50%)	35	33 (94%)
10.*443*	5	1 (20%)	12	11 (92%)
10.*453*	4	-	13	10 (77%)
10.*464*	-	-	4	4 (100%)
10.*465*	-	-	19	13 (68%)
10.*468/482*	5	3 (60%)	78	40 (51%)
10.*469*	1	-	10	5 (50%)
10.*473*	1	-	2	2 (100%)
10.*474*	-	-	4	4 (100%)
10.*483*	-	-	-	-
10.*486*	2	2 (100%)	2	1 (50%)
10.*490*	5	3 (60%)	4	4 (100%)

Table 9-5   Total number of metal fragments found and number/percentage of nails in total number of fragments.

Copper-alloy nails were almost nonexistent in these loci, which is remarkable for trash layers. The few copper-alloy nails found in these trash and pottery dumps were all large and used, like the iron nails, for large wooden constructions such as floors and roofs. Most of these construction nails emerged in the upper loci of the trash dump. Over 38 percent of the nails of the lower trash layers were small and would have been used, most likely, for furniture or other light construction. These trash and pottery dumps were not intended to be leveling and foundation for the later courtyard on this spot. There was no apparent effort made to level the height differences of over 0.80 m in this area. This makes these loci "natural" trash dumps, and provides, probably, a reliable view of the trash-disposal habits of residents in the Serapis temple area in the early Roman period.

Loci 10.*423* and 10.*443*, both with concentrations of large nails, represent the clearing of the floor level of an abandoned building, with the nails left after removal, most likely, of wooden floors and roof. Producing mainly small nails, locus 10.*465* and, to a lesser extent, 10.*468/482* represent the remnants of some interior objects of a building.

A normal sequence inside an abandoned building would have shown the greatest concentration of large construction nails in the lowest layers of the trash dump. There is a possibility that the original sequence of these layers was reversed when a nearby abandoned building, which had served as a trash dump for some time, was cleaned out. This would explain why the concentrations of large nails were found in the topmost trash layers (10.*423, 443*) and halfway through the buildup of dump layers (10.*468/482*).

9.1.2   HYDRAULIC INSTALLATION IN TRENCH 10

Some sort of hydraulic installation was built in the early first century AD in trench BE00-10. The still-unidentified structure of locus 10.*614* was dug into water deposit 10.*622/625*. These loci contained over 10 copper-alloy nails and several other metal fragments and objects, such as an iron ring and a bronze edge protector of a small box. The nails all had shaft diameters of 3 x 3 mm, and lengths of 21 to 22 mm. Locus 10.*614* contained five bronze nails, one of which was 72 mm long; the others were of the same type as those found in 10.*622/625*. The four iron nails also found in 10.*614* were of a larger type, with lengths varying from 86 to at least 96 mm. Another four copper-alloy nails from

10.*619/643* were also of the same dimensions as those found in 10.*622/625*. All these nails seem to have been part of the hydraulic installation; neighboring loci did not contain any nails, most of them not even a single fragment of metal.

9.1.3   CULT OBJECTS

Excavations recovered a medallion in locus 10.*445* (BE00 0793-D/C-037: see Chapter 8, Figure 8-1, Plate 8-11, catalogue number 37). The obverse of the copper-alloy disk, measuring 34.6 mm in diameter, depicted a bearded bust facing right; on the reverse was a tetrastyle (four-columned) temple or shrine. In the center was a figure, probably a cult statue. The spaces between the outer columns appear to be blocked by low screen walls or contain other cult statues.

A 30 mm high iron *uraeus* (BE00 6555-D-7237) from locus 10.*621* was probably one of a series of cobras adorning the upper edge of a small wooden shrine. The *uraeus* had two fastening pins with a diameter of 2 mm (Figure 9-6). The notch on the head of the cobra was probably a fastening point for a solar disk. This metal decoration and the small baboon-like figurine from locus 10.*423*—a depiction of the god Hapy or Thoth—offer some insight into the nature of activities in this area near the temple in the early Roman period.

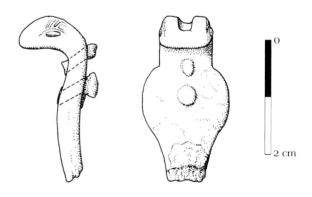

Figure 9-6   *Uraeus* of iron (BE00 6555-D-7237). Drawing by A. M. Hense.

9.2 PUTATIVE ECCLESIASTICAL STRUCTURE

9.2.1 TRENCH BE98/99-22

In trench BE98/99-22, a room paved with reused ashlars, the majority of metal fragments consisted of iron; 7.9 times as much iron as copper-alloy fragments were found (87 percent of the excavated volume). This can be explained, most likely, as the result of the collapse of the roof. The large room had functioned and been cleaned until the abandonment of the site. This room did not serve as a trash area, so there was never a buildup of rubbish layers with fragments of discarded copper-alloy objects before collapse of the structure. Most of the iron found, with a high percentage of nails, must have been part of the (roof) construction.

9.2.2 TRENCHES BE00-30 AND 39

The early Roman pottery dump beneath the walls of trench BE99/00-30 produced a few copper-alloy fragments. Except for two fishhooks, all of them were large nails. On the earliest floor (*011*) of the large room in BE00-39, excavations recovered a damaged bronze oil lamp (Figure 9-7). The molded lamp was decorated with an elaborate garland of lotus flowers. The garland wound around the 120 mm long body of the lamp. On the underside it was folded in a U-shape, forming a stable foot for the lamp. More fragments of this lamp, or a similar one, were found in loci 39.*011* and *002*.

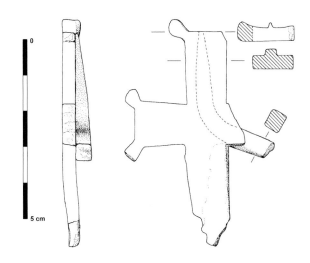

Figure 9-8   Copper-alloy cross BE00 4532-D-7695. Drawing by A. M. Hense.

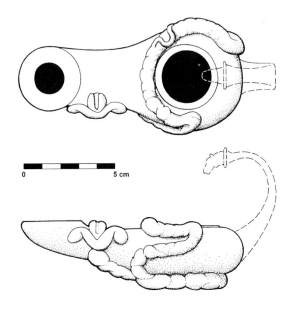

Figure 9-7   Oil lamp BE00 5818-gg/D-7857. Drawing by A. M. Hense

Another remarkable find was the small bronze cross, unearthed in tumble 39.*007* (Figure 9-8). This tumble layer was deposited directly atop floor 39.*011*, so lamp and cross were probably contemporary and the cross may have been part of the lamp handle. The cross was at least 60 mm high and 40 mm wide. It was backed with a bronze rod with a diameter of 9 to 10 mm. More indications for the furnishing of this room were the copper-alloy mounting fragments found in loci 39.*006*, *007*, and *003*.

9.3 THE NORTH SHRINE

TRENCHES BE98/99-23, BE99/00-32

This shrine was a small cult center with benches or platforms along the north and south walls and a focal point with altar and offering basins near the west wall. The discovery in BE98-23.*011* of a small copper-alloy statuette, a female figurine possibly depicting Isis, is one of the few indications to which cult this shrine may have been dedicated. A small *situla* was discovered in debris layer BE99-32.*013* (Figure 9-9*)*. It can be safely assumed that this *situla* belonged to the equipment of the sanctuary. A long iron rod with a hook, found in the same locus, probably functioned as a suspension point for a lamp or incense burner.

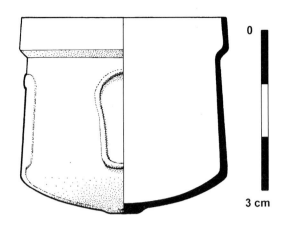

Figure 9-9   *Situla* (BE99 3584-D-6010). Drawing by A. M. Hense.

Wall tumble loci (BE98/99-23.*012* and BE99-32.*013*) contained considerable quantities of iron nails. Bent nails in these loci suggest a wood thickness of 60-65 mm. Two iron nails with a shaft diameter of 4 x 3.5 mm were found *in situ* in the wooden threshold of BE99/00-32.*023*.

9.4   SHOPS AND OFFICES

9.4.1   TRENCHES BE98-20/99-27, BE99-28/00-38
These trenches in two adjacent buildings along a side street off what may be Berenike's *decumanus maximus* furnished remarkably similar metal assemblages. Both trenches produced metal objects indicating commercial or official governmental activities. Fragments of balances were unearthed in BE99-27.*023* and BE99-28.*037* (Figure 9-10), weights in BE99-27.*026* and BE99-28.*038* (Figure 9-11).

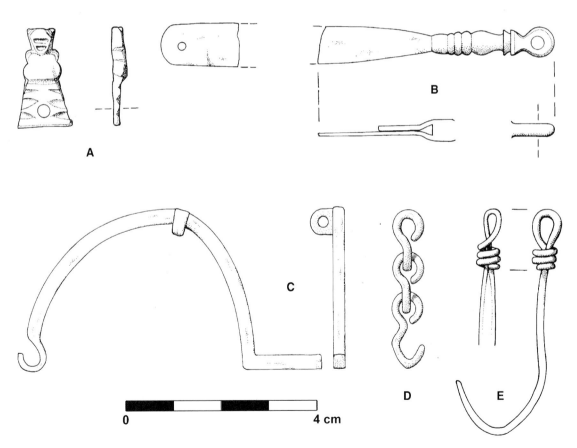

Figure 9-10   Balance and hook fragments from BE99-27/28. Drawings by A. M. Hense
          A=copper-alloy balance fragment BE99 3753-D-6007 (locus 27.*023*)
          B=copper-alloy balance fragment BE99 3582-D-6004 (locus 28.*037*)
          C=iron hook BE99 4078-D-6355 (locus 27.*026*)
          D=copper-alloy chain BE99 3909-D-6070 (locus 27.*024*)
          E=copper-alloy hook 3582-D-6004 (locus 28.*037*)

Locus BE99 28.*037* produced two pieces of a small copper-alloy balance. Fragments of a possible small balance were discovered in BE99-27.*023*. Five chain segments from BE99-27.*024* probably also belong to a small balance, all the more because one of the segments ends in a hook. A complicated iron hook (BE99 27.*026* 4078-D-6355) could have been used for suspending a medium-sized balance to the wall.

The copper-alloy weight BE99 4091-D-6285 from locus 27.*026* had an octagonal shape and was filled with lead. The thickness of the copper-alloy mantle varied from 2.0 mm at the walls to 1.5 mm on top and bottom. The filling hole was closed with a copper-alloy disk 5 mm in diameter. The weight of nearly 28 grams approximates the *uncia*. Shape and weight are identical to the weight found in BE99-28.*038*. The north balk of trench BE99-27 produced a mantle fragment of a larger weight, with an estimated diameter of 30 mm and a weight of 170 grams (=6 *uncia*). Locus BE99-28.*042* produced a fragment of a rectangular weight. A small copper-alloy weight of 4 to 5 grams found in BE99-27.*026* equals the weight of 6 *oboloi* and the gold solidus during the reign of Constantine I (AD 306–337), when the weight of this coin was 1/72 of a Roman pound.

In BE99-28 (*028, 038*) as well as BE99-27 (*023, 026*) debris loci of the collapsed buildings had a concentration of iron nails. This is only possible if the site was already mainly abandoned and reuse of wooden structures was reduced to a minimum.

9.4.2 TRENCH BE00-34

The courtyard of the building partially exposed in trench BE00-34 along the main east-west street produced only a handful of nails, which is not unusual in a large open area. Some iron nails were found in a large wooden beam with a length of at least 2.25 m. The iron nails were driven into this beam at intervals of 0.32 to 0.35 m. The beam was found in front of the entrance to the house and may have comprised part of a roof or some sort of gallery/balcony. A similar beam, without nails, was found in front of the main entrance of the building in BE00-37.

No industrial activities took place in the courtyard; the installations seem to have had purely a storage function. Although excavations found a few slag fragments in this area, there was no evidence of metal-smelting ovens. Similar slag fragments have been found in and around all late Roman buildings in the town center. It is likely that this material was scattered throughout the town during or shortly after the abandonment of most of the buildings.

On the *de facto* surface in the courtyard were a *situla* handle and a bracelet. The copper-alloy handle was adorned with a cobra. The copper-alloy bracelet had an estimated interior diameter of 60 mm. Locus 34.*014*, windblown sand deposited directly after abandonment, produced a copper-alloy vessel handle and two small decorated bronze fragments.

9.5 THE PTOLEMAIC AREA

9.5.1 TRENCH BE00-36

The second largest group of finds in this trench was the copper-alloy nails. Fragments of more than 75 copper-alloy nails were found, in sharp contrast to the handful of iron nails unearthed. The bronze nails were predominantly short, which makes them unfit for the use in building constructions. Surprisingly, in this industrial area, the other bronze finds consisted solely of jewelry and small utensils like spatulas and a tweezers.

Trench BE00-36 also produced a considerable amount of lead; 95 kg was unearthed from the Ptolemaic loci. Most of it consisted of fragments of lead sheets. Impressions of the surface they once covered are visible on some of the lead sheets from locus 36.*079*. Some preserve holes with a size varying from 4 x 4 mm to 3.5 x 3.5 mm, a common diameter for nails with a length varying from 30 to 80 mm. The thickness of the lead sheets varied from 1.0 to 2.5 mm.

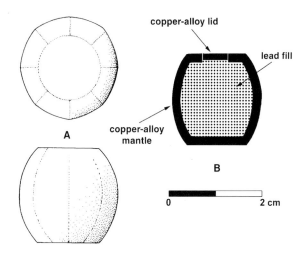

Figure 9-11 Weights of BE99-27/28. Drawing by A. M. Hense.

Locus 36.*066* (Phase II) alone produced over 40 kg of lead; another 30 kg were found in other loci of this phase. During Phase II, installation 36.*022* was used as a dump for charcoal, lead, shells, and pottery. In the area east of this installation some lead processing seems to have taken place. Hearth-like features in loci 36.*071* and *074* contained slag, lead, charcoal, and ash. Because of the low melting temperature of lead, its production did not need large installations. It is likely that small-scale lead smelting was conducted here, perhaps a combination of extracting new metal from ore and reuse of old lead.

There are several possibilities for the function of these lead fragments. They could have been used for lining hydraulic tanks like the *castellum plumbeum* (Adam 1994:255) or the water basins of bathhouses (Adam 1994:268). It is also possible that the lead once protected the hulls of merchant ships. Several wrecks of merchant ships, excavated in the Mediterranean area and dating from the third century BC to the first century AD, had lead-covered hulls (Meijer 1976:134; Hausen 1979: Tafel II; Casson 1994:35, 106, 121, 140).

9.5.2 TRENCH BE00-40

Similar to BE00-36, the large number of bronze nails (225) in trench BE00-40 exceeded by far the number of iron nails (70). Although not many complete copper-alloy nails were recovered from this trench, these nails seem to be predominantly short. The iron nails were much bigger, and most of them must have been part of some building.

As in trench BE00-36, delicate bronze utensils and jewelry were also found in trench BE00-40. These finds consisted of fragments of at least six small tweezers, eight spatulas, and three pins shaped like coiling snakes. An object, which looks like a tiny bronze temple door, was perhaps part of a miniature shrine (locus 40.*054*, Figure 9-12c). Small shrines like these were probably used and carried as amulets. Examples of small bronze shrines were already known in the New Kingdom (Andrews 1994:23).

The large quantity of slag fragments, in trench BE00-40 over 12,000 cm³, is an indication of the industrial activities in the third and mid-second century BC in this area. Some pieces of bowl-shaped slag, varying in diameter from 50 to 100 mm, indicate that at least some work involved smelting small amounts of copper (loci 40.*002, 059, 079*). Of the fragments of iron tools from trench BE00-40, knives (40.*003, 089, 094*), a pair

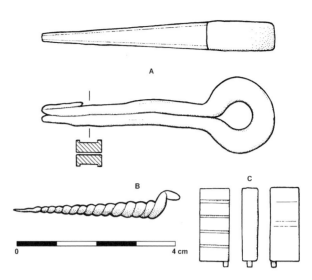

Figure 9-12   Bronze objects from BE00-40.*054*. Drawings by A. M. Hense.
A=tweezers (BE00 4011-D-7214c)
B=snake pin (BE00 4011-D-7214a)
C=miniature door (BE00 4011-D-7214b)

of tongs (40.*002*), and three small ax or chisel blades (40.*013*) could be identified.

Activities in the third and second century BC in this area seem to have consisted of smelting copper ore and producing bronze jewelry, utensils, and nails. Larger objects were probably also made here, but were less likely to become lost among the waste materials of the workshop. Lead was probably processed here, too. The stock of lead from locus *079* was probably collected for reuse.

9.6   KALALAT, SMALL FORT (TRENCH KL00-1)

Post-abandonment loci from trench KL00-1, the main gate on the eastern wall of the small fort in Wadi Kalalat, produced most of the metal finds (see Chapter 19); these comprised mainly knives, arrowheads, and tweezers. This is in sharp contrast with the loci representing depositions before abandonment of the large *praesidium* in Kalalat and the smaller one in Siket. It seems that the gate area was kept clean up to the moment of abandonment, as expected in a military installation. The abundance of material in the post-abandonment loci of gate KL00-1 suggests disturbance of the interior of the fort, or habitation of some sort in the fort after official withdrawal of the garrison.

One of the rare finds in the occupation phase loci was a piece of iron, which seems to be a fragment of a leaf-shaped arrowhead. Excavation recovered more fragments of putative arrowheads in KL00-1.*004*, *009*, and *010*. Locus 1.*004* also produced fragments of a bronze arrowhead. This slender, barbed arrowhead was a type common in both Berenike (BE94-1, Hense 1995:56; BE96-9.*053*; BE97-10.*113*; BE00-37.*008*) and Shenshef (SH97-4.*001*; SH97-2.*005*). Surprising is the find of fragments of at least three fragile copper-alloy tweezers. These instruments seem atypical for squatters and are more likely to have belonged to the Roman garrison. This idea is supported by the fact that one of these tweezers was found on floor KL00-1.*020*, a surface belonging to the first occupation phase. Excavations unearthed other fragments of identical tweezers in KL00-1.*009* and *011*, loci representing two different stages of decay of the deserted fort. Probably, the metal finds in the post-abandonment layers were a result of disturbance.

The only concentration of iron nails was found directly in front of the threshold in loci KL00-1.*014* and *018*, both representing the dismantling phase of the gate. These nails were remnants of the double wooden gate. Removing the gates was one way to reduce the defensive effectiveness of forts, so that any possible invaders of the area could not take full advantage of these structures. The wood from these gates could also be recycled elsewhere by the departing garrison. A few more nails were found on floors KL01-1.*022* and *023* (the first occupational phase), and in the post-abandonment loci, but never more than two or three in each locus. Most likely, these nails served as fastenings for iron plating or hinges of the large wooden gates. The length of these nails, over 110 mm, provides some indication of the thickness of these doors.

Excavations recovered only four copper-alloy nails—with remarkable rectangular heads—in this trench. A handful of nails of this type was also found in Berenike, but never concentrated in a single area or phase. Excavations in the small fort in Wadi Kalalat produced copper-alloy nails in loci KL01-1.*007*, *011*, *012*, and *025*. One of these nails was found in the first construction phase (*025*), the others in post-abandonment loci. With lengths ranging from 16 to 29 mm, they were too short to have served as fastening nails for the iron plating of the wooden gate.

9.7   *PRAESIDIUM* AT SIKET (TRENCH SK00-1)

Like the small fort in Wadi Kalalat, the gate of the *praesidium* at Siket produced only a few metal finds (see Chapter 20). Except for two fragments of an iron knife, found in locus SK00-1.*018*, the occupation phase of the gate produced only iron nails. Like locus KL00-1.*014* in the gate of the small fort in Wadi Kalalat, excavations in the locus associated with the abandonment of the *praesidium* at Siket also unearthed iron nails in front of the threshold. Although no complete nails were found, a length of at least 80 mm can be discerned from the fragments. As in the gate of the small Kalalat fort, these nails from Siket probably served as fastening nails for the iron armor plating or hinges of the wooden gate. Besides a few more iron nails, only a few pieces of metal were unearthed in the post-abandonment loci. Among those fragments was part of another iron knife.

9.8   DISCUSSION

The similarity in both architecture and metal assemblages of the two adjacent buildings in trenches BE98-20/99-27 and BE99-28/00-38 suggests a row of shops or government buildings north of the main east-west thoroughfare. In these buildings quantities of certain expensive mercantile goods, perhaps precious or semiprecious stones, were sold or inspected. Other metal finds in these buildings, such as fragments of vessels, *fibulae*, and furniture, give the impression of a fair degree of wealth.

Trench BE96/97/98/99/00-10 exhibits a long series of industrial activities in which the character of the products or production methods changed when small-scale metal smelting was introduced in this area during the early fourth century AD. Excavations in the Ptolemaic area seem to have uncovered an extensive industrial quarter in which, besides other materials, both copper alloy and lead were processed for building materials, luxury objects, and, possibly, ship repair. Increasingly, a picture arises of a town experiencing periods of intense industrial and commercial activities.

As in previous seasons, excavations unearthed evidence for the presence of Roman military units near Berenike. A somewhat improvised bronze lance head emerged in locus *002* in the early Roman trash dump in trench BE99-31. An iron arrowhead with a rectangular cross section was similar to the arrow points found in previous seasons (see Hense 1998:216, Figure. 9-21). A large iron arrow or lance head BE99

3011-D-6638 from locus *28.035* was of a type not previously encountered in Berenike.

The early Roman loci in BE00-10 produced several types of arrowheads. Excavations unearthed a four-bladed iron arrowhead in locus *482*; a three-bladed arrowhead and a tip of another were discovered in locus *514*. The connected loci produced a bullet-shaped iron arrowhead, a fragment of a lance head or arrowhead (*516*) and a leaf-shaped head (*517*). Another arrowhead was discovered in *551* and, possibly, a lance head or arrowhead in *550*. The three-bladed arrowhead from locus *514* was of a slightly different type than the one found in BE99-31.*006* (Figure 9-13A). The pottery of this locus dated mid–late first century AD. The BE00-10 loci containing arrowheads are also dated (early to middle) first century AD.

It is tempting to connect the three- and four-bladed arrowheads with one of the *cohors Ituraeorum* garrisoned in Egypt in the second half of the first century to well in to the second century AD. So far, a *cohors Ituraeorum* is the only unit whose presence near Berenike during the first century AD has been archaeologically attested. A fragmentary papyrus dated to the reign of Nero (AD 54–68), and found in Berenike, records an official contract or dispute in which one of the parties is serving in one of these cohorts. These people, originating from northeast Palestine, are known to have served in various military units in Egypt and the Roman East (personal communication from R. S. Bagnall and C. C. Helms). Comparable arrowheads, with three or four blades, were fairly common in the Roman arsenal and have been found on Roman military sites throughout the empire. Similar arrowheads were unearthed, for instance, near the limes in Scotland (MacDowall 1995:58).

The *cohors II Ituraeorum* was stationed in Syene (inscription of AD 98/99, *CIL* III 14147.2=*ILS* 8907), and a group of these was also dispatched to the Wadi Hammamat in AD 98 (*ILS* 8907). The *cohors III Ituraeorum*, already present in Egypt in AD 103, was stationed in Wadi Semna from AD 150 onward. The main body of these cohorts, which counted as independent units numbering 600 to 1,000 men, was most likely stationed in the southern Nile Valley where the most

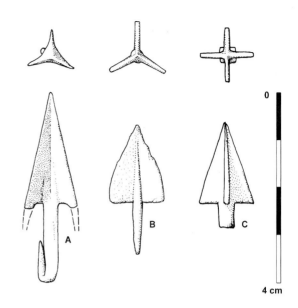

Figure 9-13   Roman arrowheads. Drawings by A. M. Hense.
A=BE99 3001-D-6001 (BE99-31.*006*)
B=BE00 3777-D-7496 (BE00-10.*514*)
C=BE00 2973-D-7466 (BE00 10.*482*)

serious threats from invading armies was expected (cf. Maxfield 2000:411, 422, 423, 429–430).

Although Palmyrene soldiers are also attested in Berenike and were serving in the Roman army from the first century AD onward, no proof of the presence of any Palmyrene unit in the Berenike area before the second century AD has been found thus far. The main body of the *ala Thracum Herculiana*, consisting of Palmyrene archers, was based in Koptos from AD 185 onward (Dijkstra and Verhoogt 1999:214). A stele found in Berenike, mentioning two officers belonging to this *ala*, is dated paleographically to AD 180/185–212 (Dijkstra and Verhoogt 1999:207). Another Berenike inscription, dedicated by the Palmyrene archer Marcus Aurelius Mocimus, is dated to the year AD 215 (Verhoogt 1998:193). The *Notitia Dignitatum* mentions the *ala VIII Palmyrenorum* in Lakeita, but the *Notitia* was compiled only at the end of the fourth century AD at the earliest. Therefore, a connection between the late first-century AD arrowheads and the Palmyrene archers cannot be made.

CHAPTER 10

GLASS FISH VESSEL

P. T. NICHOLSON AND J. PRICE[1]

During the 1999 season at Berenike, Jennifer Price joined Paul Nicholson in the field to help identify many of the pieces from that season and examine some of those from previous years. We intend to publish a selection of these in a forthcoming report. Nicholson also began the recording of the glass onto the ACCESS database, which was created by Ilka Schacht, whose assistance is gratefully acknowledged.

This report details the find of a large painted bowl decorated with a marine scene. It is hoped that this will be published in more detail elsewhere, but the authors felt that the preliminary description of it should be given in this volume. Numbers refer to individual sherds of the vessel. We provide only those numbers necessary for the description.

10.1 DESCRIPTION

From the rubbish deposits dating from the third quarter of the first century AD excavated in trench BE99-31 came more than 24 fragments, many joining in two principal groups, of a transparent colorless glass bowl with slight greenish tinge. Small bubbles are present in the glass throughout the profile but are so small and dispersed as to have no effect on the vessel's transparency. Some of the fragments show no visible weathering, while others have flaking deposits.

The bowl is convex in profile, with a vertical rim produced by cracking off the lid moil and then grinding the edge to leave it smooth and rounded, and a small concave base. As reconstructed it is approximately 63 mm high x 170 mm in rim diameter x 35 mm in base diameter x 1.5 to 4.8 mm thick. There is a narrow hori- zontal abraded band 2.6 mm below the rim edge; the surviving painted decoration does not overlap the rim.

The body is decorated with scenes of marine life in two registers, interspersed with vegetation and shells, and the base shows a roundel enclosing a dolphin. The upper register contains at least two fish swimming to the right that are noticeably spiny and heavy bodied, while the lower register contains at least two fish swimming to the left that are longer and sleeker. A wide variety of colors has been used in the composition, including red, browns, green, yellow, light blue, and black. Dr. W. van Neer of the Royal Museum of Central Africa in Tervuren, Belgium, provisionally identified the fish and shells on the vessel. Van Neer has studied the fish remains from Berenike, and the authors are indebted to him for his examination and interpretation of the representations.

The rim is preserved as three fragments, two of which join (2206 and 2270), and also join five of the body fragments (2208, 2207, 2029x2, and 2212, see left side of Figure 10-1).

The profile of the vessel is preserved in the two groups of joined fragments, and the decoration will be described working from the rim toward the base. Rim fragments 2206 and 2270 show the abraded band already described, and parts of two patches of three green blobs, presumably marine vegetation and the tips of yellow and brown dorsal spines. The next two pieces, which attach to 2206, show more of one patch of green blobs and further parts of a fish. The upper piece is preserved as a row of yellow and brown dorsal spines attached to a brown line along its back. Below this is a row of brown dots leading to downward-facing brown

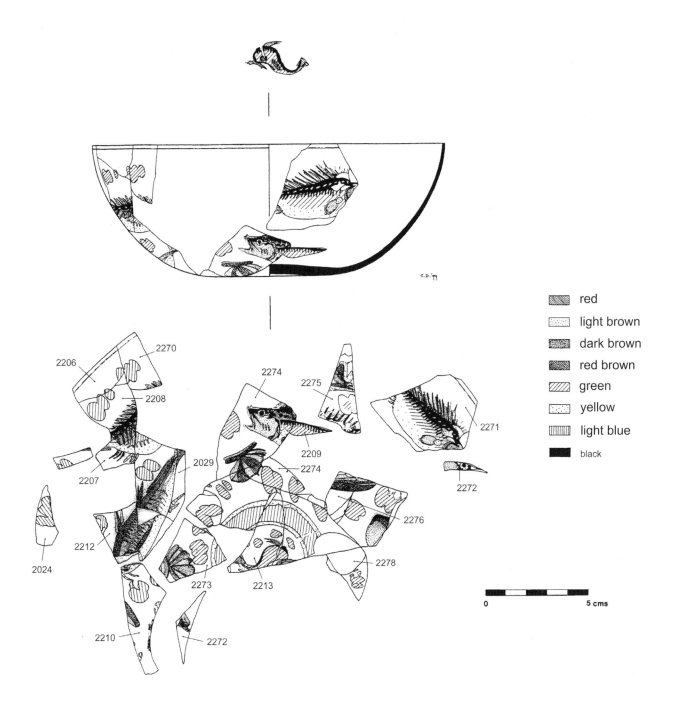

Figure 10-1. Fragments of the fish vessel found in the early Roman trash dump. The dolphin at the top of the drawing represents the inside view of the base of the vessel, where the figure, painted on the outside, is visible through the clear glass. Drawing by R. C. Dijkstra.

spines between which is a blob of pinkish red and a blob of pale blue, so that the effect is one of herringbone pattern overlying pink and blue (2208, 2207, 2029). The underbody is green with yellow ventral fins and has three brown fins or spines toward the tail. The tail is slightly raised, suggesting that the fish is diving downward to the right.

Below this fish (on 2029, see Plate 10-2) are two green blobs, again presumably some kind of marine vegetation, and below them is another fish, diving steeply to the left toward the base of the vessel at an angle of about 45 degrees. This fish is represented by three joining pieces (2029 [two fragments] and 2212) and a fourth (2210) that is surely part of the same creature. The fish has a brown dorsal surface with two dorsal fins. The rear of these is pale-brown/pink and the foremost brown outlined with yellow. The brown ventral surface is painted with toothlike projections running into the pale-brown/pink, which then runs into the yellow underbelly of the animal. Toward the tail of the fish on this ventral surface are two yellow fins. A darker red stripe appears to come from the outline of the gills, behind where the (now missing) eye would have been, and run back halfway along the fish, making up a sort of red flash. The fourth fragment showing this fish (2210; lowermost fragment on Figure 10-1) does not join firmly, but its colors and detail are very similar. It depicts the underside of the head with two yellow fins projecting downward; above that is an area of light-brown/pink. Below the foremost small fins is another piece of marine vegetation in green outlined with yellow. There are remains of three other pieces of green, presumably from plants, on the same piece, as well as a projection in the same brown and pink as the fish, but it is not clear how this is related to it. The right-hand edge of the fragment has the remains of a black line, but its purpose is also unclear. However, the glass at the lowest point is 2.7 mm thick, and must be very close to joining with the first of the base fragments.

The third rim fragment (2271) does not join the other fragments (right side of Figure 10-1). It shows a fish swimming toward the right, with its head slightly raised toward the rim. The underside of the body of the fish is painted in yellow and green with a large brown dot behind the gills. This dot may be intended to depict a fin on the right side of the fish. The upper body is painted black with toothlike projections running into the yellow and green area. The back of the fish has long spines painted in red and brown. The gill is outlined

Plate 10-2   Sherds 2210, 2212, 2029. Photograph by N.M. Blackamore.

Plate 10-3   Sherds 2274, 2209 and 2275. Photograph by N.M. Blackamore.

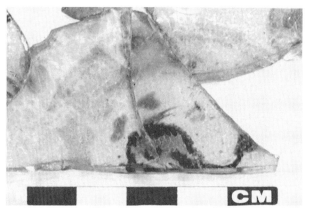

Plate 10-4   Sherd 2213 (center of base with dolphin). Photograph by N.M. Blackamore.

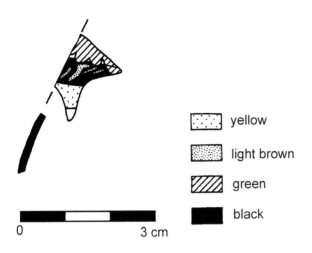

::::::::	yellow
▒▒▒▒	light brown
▨▨▨	green
■■■	black

0   3 cm

Figure 10-5   Sherd 2809 of the fish vessel found in 2000 in the adjacent trench (BE00-33.*025*). Drawing by Z. Green.

in red and the rear of the head by a black line. What remains of the face is shown in pinkish brown. A tiny sliver of glass (2272) showing a yellow eye with black pupil on a pink background may belong to the same fish, but it cannot presently be joined with it.

The second principal group of 10 joining fragments shows part of the scheme of decoration on the lower body and the base (center Figure 10-1). The top piece, (2274, Plate 10-3) is made of two joined fragments and shows the head of a fish, facing left, with its mouth open. The head is light brown and the eye is black and outlined by a white line. The body is a pale creamy yellow and part of a reddish dot remains. Below the head of the fish is a scallop shell (*Pectinidae*), painted in shades of brown. To its left are the remains of two green leaves, while a further one is immediately in front of the fish's mouth. These fragments are joined to four pieces of the lowest part of the body and the base, which show four patches of green blobs above a broad, circular, blue band with both edges outlined in yellow, enclosing a small stylized dolphin facing right (Plate 10-4). The body of the dolphin is green edged in black, with a red beak, dorsal fin, and tail. Above the dolphin there are four small green leaves. At the right of 2274 two joining pieces (2276 and 2280) show the remains of two yellow-green leaves of a marine plant, and traces of what may be a third are preserved at the very edge of the fragment. An elliptical object in reddish brown and pink similar to the feature already noted in 2210 may be a shell seen edge on, while another in the same colors

may also be a shell of some kind. Below these pieces, 2278 has a fracture on the surface so that only a part of a green leafy object is preserved.

Another piece of the lower body (2273) shows a green and yellow patch of the same type as the other pieces of marine vegetation, part of a second one, and above them the remains of a second scallop shell in shades of brown. Several other small fragments also preserve details of the decoration. Fragment 2275 preserves part of what is probably another scallop in the same colors, and below it the spines of a further fish painted in black and red. Two patches of greenish-blue opalescence probably represent the positions of now-lost leaves of vegetation. Fragment 2277 has the end of what may be one of these shells in shades of brown, but with two yellowish lines coming from it, suggesting that it may be part of a fish, or that some other object was approaching it, and a very small fragment (2279) has what is probably the edge of another leaf, plus a pinkish-red line. Other unattached fragments show areas of leaf and of what is probably scallop shell.

When examining more material during the 2000 season, a further small fragment (2809) was discovered in trench BE00-33.*025* (Plate 10-5). Although it does not join with any of the other pieces, it is almost certainly from the same vessel. It shows a green leaf and part of a fish body in yellow with mauve/brown with red details almost identical with those on 2212 and 2029. At least five fish are, therefore, depicted on the vessel, representing a busy scene of marine life.

The team's archaeozoologist, Dr. W. Van Neer identified the fish as *scombrids* because they have two dorsal fins (2212 and 2209) and a rather long pectoral fin (seen on 2212). Long anal and dorsal fins are also visible on 2271 and 2207. It may be possible to identify them more closely with further research.

10.2   TECHNIQUES AND PARALLELS

Painted glass of this kind is more correctly described as enameled, the colors being powdered glass mixed with a binding agent that was painted onto the surface of the vessel after it had been annealed. The vessel was then reheated to fuse the enamel to the surface (Mark Taylor and David Hill, personal communication). This operation demands considerable skill in order to fuse the colors to the underlying glass without reaching a temperature so great as to melt the vessel or cause the colors to run. The bowl in question here shows excellent control of the technique.

Enameled glass is said to have developed in the East, probably in Syria or Egypt, and then spread to the West (Rütti 1991:133–134) where it reached a peak during the first century AD, to which period the Berenike fish dish is very probably to be dated. Evidence for the supposed eastern origin of enameled glass is somewhat uncertain, however, and the question must remain open for the moment.

This Berenike example is unusual in several respects. First, the form is neither of those most commonly found with enameled decoration, which are Isings Form 12, the small hemispherical bowl or cup, and Form 15, amphorisk (Isings 1957; see also Rütti 1991:123). This example is from a bowl of larger dimensions and with a more convex profile. Second, the glass of the vessel is very nearly colorless, rather than brightly colored or pale bluish green, which is the norm in the Isings Forms 12 and 15. In addition, the pictorial subject is relatively unusual. The best-known example of a marine scene is from a small hemispherical bowl or cup of Isings Form 12. It comes from Oberwinterthur (*Vitudurum*) in northern Switzerland (see Rütti 1991:129 and Plate XXXIII). A second example with fish decoration is known from Oberwinterthur, and others have been noted at Vindonissa (Switzerland) (Rütti 1991:129) and Xanten (Germany; Charlesworth 1984).

The decoration on the Berenike vessel is much more accomplished than any of the pieces mentioned previously. There is greater detail in the presentation of the motifs, a wider range of color, and was painted without the use of guidelines. It has also been very fortunate; thanks to the favorable preservation conditions encountered in trench BE99-31 at Berenike, most of the glass fragments have not become badly weathered and very little of the paint has flaked off.

NOTE

1. Nicholson wishes to thank the School of History and Archaeology, Cardiff University, for allowing him time to undertake fieldwork at Berenike. The assistance of Jennifer Price in the field and subsequently is also gratefully acknowledged. Price is grateful both to Nicholson for inviting her to look through the glass at Berenike, and to the University for Durham for permission to visit the site in January 1999. Ms. Christine Dijkstra made the drawing of the fish vessel, and we wish to thank her for her patient work and attention to detail. Ms. Zadia Green drew the additional fragment and the material from the 2000 season.

CHAPTER 11 ～

TEXTILES

J. P. WILD AND F. C. WILD[1]

The textiles studied during February and March 2000 were recovered almost exclusively from a group of related early Roman midden deposits at the north end of town and west of the later Roman town center. Trench BE96-13, cut initially to secure an impeccably stratified botanical sample, yielded a limited number of early Roman textile fragments. Trenches BE97/98-19, BE99-29, BE99-31, and BE00-33 were opened subsequently and sectioned well-stratified rubbish deposits rich in organic and artifactual material including ostraka. The associated pottery indicates that deposition had ceased by about AD 70. Whether the underlying layers date to the Ptolemaic period remains to be seen; if there are residual Ptolemaic textiles in the early Roman midden, they could not be recognized as such.

The textile content of each finds registration number (all textile finds from a specific trench, locus, and "pottery bucket") was treated as a group, and the individual fabrics represented separated out for study. Identifying scraps that belonged to the same fabric was generally not difficult; for as well as sharing the same visible structural characteristics, they had reacted in the same way to the common post-depositional environment, which had affected both color and "soapiness," that is, the degree of degradation. Time could not be spent searching for all links between fragments from different loci; but, given the predictability and uniformity of most groups, this should not invalidate the statistical conclusions to be drawn. Approximately 900 textile items were analyzed and recorded.

While standardization was the hallmark of these early Roman assemblages, some differences in locus content were observed and will ultimately be explored further. Some were characterized by textile fragments with a probable utilitarian function, in linen, cotton, and goat hair, but very little wool. Others presented a more balanced spectrum of cloth types with much more wool. In at least one locus, however, low down in the depositional sequence (so far as it has been explored to date), the rags were almost entirely of Z/Z-spun—presumed Indian—cotton.

11.1 FIBERS

All yarns, which could not be immediately assigned to a fiber type under low-power magnification, were examined at higher power, and usually identified successfully. A dull beige-yellow yarn incorporated in coarse textiles woven from very dark brown and some orange-yellow goat-hair yarns were, after initial hesitation, identified as of goat hair, too. Inefficiently hackled flax was commonly encountered, particularly in the coarser basket weaves (some S/S, some Z/Z-spun); it was not obviously shives (the by-product of hackling), but was nonetheless, probably what the Romans called *stuppa* tow. (The bast fiber of the coarse Z/Z fragment BE00 1500-I-2406 is probably tow rather than an Indian exotic.) Yarn and fiber degradation was uniform throughout the corpus. Only the brown (probably once red-dyed) cotton in the selvedge of BE00 1989-I-2338 had disintegrated more speedily.

11.2 FABRICS

The remarks made about the general characteristics of the pre-Flavian textiles at Berenike set out in the 1998 interim report hold good for the present collection (Wild and Wild 2000). Only selected features will be discussed in the following pages.

11.2.1　Wool Fabrics

The largest surviving textile artifact (BE00 1081-I-2048) was an item—not necessarily a garment—composed of three pieces of at least two different tunics with red *clavi*, sewn edge to edge and backed by a disintegrating fine open tabby with dark "purple" weft and undyed warp, apparently serving as its lining. Measuring 650 mm x 410 mm, it had evidently reached the end of its recyclable life.

There were six scraps of fine 2/1 twill in strong colors (red, purple, chocolate brown, and green), four of them S/S, 2 Z/Z-spun. There were a number of Z/Z fine tabbies, two, again dyed, and four in Z/Z half-basket weave; but most tabbies were S/S, except for a few with Z-spun weft.

This season more tabbies were discovered with multicolored stripes, but the colors, particularly the narrow registers of green and yellow, were hard to define; none amounted to a shaded band. Narrow tapestry-woven bands—mostly of "purple" or blue yarn—inserted into fine wool fabrics abounded, but were rarely satisfactorily preserved. Warp was regularly grouped in the bands, and shadows of the grouping were visible at the interface with the ground weft. Warp elimination was more commonly practiced than warp crossing to achieve the grouping: in one case a few eliminated warp threads still floated on the back of the textile. Other decorative techniques included fine check patterns (two fragments) and pile: a half-basket weave fabric carried tufted pile, and blue weft loops covered a dark blue tabby.

Selvedges on wool cloth were almost invariably reinforced, the weft passing and repassing between three outer bundles of four to six warp threads. Corded transverse borders were noted on seven wool textiles, and there was one simple twisted fringe.

11.2.2　Linen Fabrics

Where a hint of original purpose could be glimpsed among the linen fragments, more of them seemed to have belonged to items of utilitarian function than to clothing. Several lengths of webbing in half-basket weave (paired warp) or basket weave, measuring 30–35 mm wide were recorded; this was the standard width used for sail reinforcing strips, as noted in 1998. Much coarser basket weaves in a yarn described previously as tow may have been from strapping or sacking.

Pieces of basket weave with overall decorative ribbing in the weft direction were more eye-catching than the modest pairs of self-bands that were a regular feature of Berenike's linen cloth. One example was highlighted by extra shots of red weft in the sheds opened for the self-bands. Blue check (four fragments this season) was the only other form of decoration.

Selvedges were plain, with the exception of an example incorporating two reinforcing warp bundles. The one starting border was a simple twined-cord variety, badly preserved. There was also a transverse-corded edge, a feature more familiar on wools, and a plain looped fringe.

Fragment BE00 5802-H-2161 appeared at first glance to be a piece of "Coptic knitting," a technique so far not found at Berenike. But on closer inspection its structure was seen to be a simpler type of looping.

11.2.3　Cotton Fabrics
Z/Z Cottons

Warp-faced cotton fabrics woven from Z-spun yarns and arguably of Indian origin dominated the find assemblage recorded this season. Most were tiny scraps of medium-weight tabby with no distinguishing features; but the expected repertoire of cloth types was extended by some remarkable new finds.

Five pieces from five different heavy cotton fabrics were immediately recognized as remains of carpets—though their role on shipboard and at Berenike was not necessarily as floor coverings. Number BE99 0688-I-1527 had symmetrical (Ghiordes) knots (At-Tar type A1) on both sides (but not overall); its warp was plied and its weft shots of six yarns, and it had a wrapped reinforced selvedge. Number BE99 0699-I-1514 (plied warp, four weft yarns in each shed) had symmetrical pile tufts laid round two warp-threads. Number BE99 0698-I-1537 (plied warp, 6-fold weft) had no surviving knots. Number BE00 1989-I-2338 was just a stout-wrapped reinforced selvedge including brown cotton yarns in an advanced state of disintegration. Number BE00 1142-I-2134 (pairs in both systems) carried rows of long loops.

A second surprise was two fragments of 2/1 cotton twill with plied warp and paired weft. The same combination of plied warp and paired weft was recorded in a length of webbing. Other examples of webbing, however, had plied warp, but single weft-threads—in one case with blue cotton pinstripes close to each selvedge. There was no direct indication this season that the webbing had been sail reinforcement; but one strip of plain tabby with edges folded under had the width (35 mm) characteristic of the 1998 finds of unequivocal sail attachments. A couple of detached patches might once have repaired sails, too.

Decorative styles found in previous years recurred in this collection. There were blue checks, both block checks and more complex tartans, and three pieces of fine cloth bearing rows of tufts, blue on an undyed ground in one case. Self-bands appeared in cotton, too, and in a thick ribbed fabric reminiscent of the ribbed linen already mentioned.

Structural features included a transverse border of short loops, preceded by three shots of weft in bundles. Fringes were composed of longer loops formed from adjacent warp-threads, only one showing any sign of having been locked at its base.

The finest cloth at Berenike normally proved to be of cotton under the microscope. Some fragments were balanced tabby (35–30/30 per cm), others warp-faced (40/20, 60/22 per cm). It was obvious how Indian cottons had earned their reputation in the Roman world.

S/S Cottons

While there were only six to eight fragments of S/S cotton tabby in the early Roman midden layers, it was noticeable that their yarns were consistently, evenly, spun like the linen yarns of Roman Egypt. By contrast the yarns in the Z/Z (Indian) cottons, even in the finest fabrics, varied considerably in diameter.

The source of the S/S cottons is probably local to the Nile Valley; already by the Flavian period Pliny the Elder (*NH* 19.1[3]) comments on its cultivation in Egypt, although most of the documentary evidence is later in date.

11.2.4   HAIR FABRICS

Straps and containers were woven from dark, plied goat-hair yarn, occasionally enlivened with extra stitching in orange-yellow goat-hair thread.

11.3   CONCLUSION

The focus of interest this season lay undoubtedly with the Indian cottons, particularly the newcomers to the attested repertoire. While fabrics of carpet character occur in the material recovered by Aurel Stein from later Han sites around the Tarim basin, they are not closely dated (Eiland 1979:110–112, 230–233). Those from Berenike have a fair claim to be the earliest so far known. The wide spectrum of cotton-fabric types at Berenike represents not just trade goods in transit to the Mediterranean, but seafaring textiles, sails and sacking, and the everyday garments and furnishings of the port's resident Indian community.

NOTE

1.   Financial support for traveling expenses was provided by the British Academy, to whom we are indebted.

CHAPTER 12 〜

BASKETRY AND MATTING

W.Z. WENDRICH

During the 1999 and 2000 excavation seasons, seven trenches at Berenike produced 242 fragments of basketry, belonging to 155 basketry objects (Tables 12-1 and 12-2). Three early Roman trash-dump trenches in the northwest part of the site (trenches BE99-29 and 31, trench BE00-33) produced most of the basketry remains. Although the preservational circumstances in these trenches were approximately the same, trenches BE99-31 and BE00-33 yielded considerably more basketry than BE99-29. This can be taken to reflect a difference in the nature of the deposition in the two trenches, which are not that far apart. A balk collapse in trench BE96/97-13, in the same general trash-dump area, showed two fragments of basketry that were recorded because they represent an interesting augmentation to the types of techniques recorded at Berenike.

The basketry finds in the other trenches (BE98/99-23 and BE99-32, the "northern shrine," and trenches BE99-28 and 29 in the central quarter of town) were exclusively remains of woven matting, used as floor matting or as structural stabilizers within the walls.

The recording method was the same as in previous seasons (cf. Wendrich 1991 for terminology and shorthand symbols used in this chapter). The basketry was in general consistent with trends of previous seasons, with exception of the occurrence of a large quantity of reed matting, in a continuous plait pattern that may be considered foreign to Egypt (see following).

12.1 MATERIALS

Among the raw materials used in Berenike were the well-attested leaf of the doam palm (*Hyphaene thebaica*), leaf and leaf-sheath fiber of the date palm (*Phoenix dactylifera*), as well as grass (both *Desmostachya bipinnata* and *Imperata cylindrica*). The as yet unidentified "material A," which was encountered in previous seasons (Wendrich 2000:227–228) has been found among the massive quantities of basketry from trench BE99-31. The most striking material in this trench, however, was quite stiff split culms of a reedlike plant (Plate 12-4), possibly *Phragmites communis*, but from the size and appearance, they could also represent split culms of the bamboo (*Bambusa species*, like *Phragmites* one of the *Graminae*). Microscopic identification has not been performed.

Table 12-2 shows the correlation between the techniques and the materials. Doam palm leaf was by far the most widely used material. It was the preferred material for coiling, sewn plait baskets and continuous plaiting. The reed culms and "material A" were only used for one type of basketry, respectively twill and tabby continuous plaiting. Miscellaneous techniques and materials were knotless netting with flax, a stake-and-strand basket made of a *Juncus* species, coiling with cotton string, and the handle of a sewn plait basket from date palm leaf. The "fiber" category refers to decayed fibrous grass, palm leaf, or a combination of both.

Year	Context	PB	Material	Technique	No.	ID number	Remarks
00	10.*015*	869	palm leaf	?	1	BE00 1638-H-131	decayed
	10.*cbw*	1220	doam palm/grass	coiling	1	BE00 6833-H-150	base of large basket
99	13.*bfs*	-	doam palm leaf	sewn plait	1	BE99 0869-H-055	fine
		-	date palm leaf	continuous plaiting	2	BE99 0869-H-056	balk fall: collapse of sw corner
99	23.*016*	67	grass	weaving	1	BE99 0405-H-061	fibers, soil colorations
99	27.*002*	2	grass	weaving	1	BE99 4625-H-200	fibers
	27.*006*	15	grass	weaving	1	BE99 1485-H-059	fibers
	27.*008*	12	grass	weaving	1	BE99 1484-H-058	fibers
	27.*016*	21	grass	weaving	1	BE99 1496-H-060	fibers
	27.*016*	22	grass	weaving	1	BE99 1590-H-057	fibers
99	28.*034*	53	grass	weaving	1	BE99 3802-H-072	fibers, soil colorations
	28.*042*	54	grass	weaving	1	BE99 3803-H-073	fibers, soil colorations
99	29.*002*	4	doam palm leaf	sewn plait	2	BE99 0412-H-062	
			doam palm leaf	continuous plaiting	2	BE99 0412-H-063	
			grass	weaving	1	BE99 0412-H-064	
	29.*006*	7	doam palm leaf	sewn plait	1	BE99 0539-H-065	
	29.*006*	8	date palm leaf	sewn plait	1	BE99 0696-H-066	
	29.*cbw*	34	*Juncus* stems	stake-and-strand	1	BE99 1873-H-067	base of basket
	29.*cbw*	34	doam palm leaf	continuous plaiting	1	BE99 1973-H-068	edge
99	31.*006*	16	doam palm leaf	sewn plait?	1	BE99 3056-H-160	small fragment
			date palm leaf	sewn plait	1	BE99 3056-H-161	
			doam palm leaf	continuous plaiting	1	BE99 3056-H-162	no edge
			doam palm leaf	continuous plaiting	1	BE99 3056-H-163	wear on one side
			doam palm leaf	sewn plait	1	BE99 3056-H-164	flat sewing strip
	31.*006*	23	doam palm leaf	sewn plait	3	BE99 3304-H-167	top edge present
			"material A"	continuous plaiting	1	BE99 3304-H-168	no edges
			doam palm leaf	cont. plaiting?	1	BE99 3304-H-169	insect damage
			doam palm leaf	sewn plait	1	BE99 3304-H-170	
	31.*007*	2	doam palm leaf	sewn plait	1	BE99 2282-H-074	sewn with twisted leaf, same as H-078
			"material A"	continuous plaiting	8	BE99 2282-H-075	
			"material A"	continuous plaiting	3	BE99 2282-H-076	coarser than H-075, same as H-079
			doam palm leaf	sewn plait	2	BE99 2282-H-077	
	31.*007*	3	doam palm leaf	sewn plait	1	BE99 2283-H-078	same as H-074
			"material A"	continuous plaiting	1	BE99 2283-H-079	same as H-076
			doam palm leaf	sewn plait	4	BE99 2283-H-080	
			doam palm leaf	sewn plait	5	BE99 2283-H-081	
			"material A"	continuous plaiting	2	BE99 2283-H-082	papyrus cover
	31.*007*	4	date palm leaf	sewn plait	7	BE99 2466-H-085	sewn with string
			date palm leaf	sewn plait	1	BE99 2466-H-086	sewn with string, finer than H-085
			date palm leaf	sewn plait	2	BE99 2466-H-087	sewn with string, coarser than H-085

Table 12–1   Catalogue of the Berenike 99/00 basketry and matting finds.

Year	Context	PB	Material	Technique	No.	ID number	Remarks
			date palm leaf	sewn plait	2	BE99 2466-H-088	dark, deteriorated
			date palm leaf	sewn plait	1	BE99 2466-H-089	rim fragment, sewn with string
			doam palm leaf	continuous plaiting	2	BE99 2466-H-090	sewn edge, cf. H-055
	31.007	9	grass	twining	1	BE99 2605-H-104	Z open twined strap
			"material A"	continuous plaiting	1	BE99 2605-H-151	small fragment
			doam palm leaf	continuous plaiting	1	BE99 2605-H-152	edge and wear marks
			date palm leaf	sewn plait	5	BE99 2605-H-153	fragments of base
			doam palm leaf	sewn plait	4	BE99 2605-H-154	
	31.007	10	reed	continuous plaiting	1	BE99 2526-H-091	coarsest fragment
			reed	continuous plaiting	1	BE99 2526-H-092	irregular, deteriorated, not retrieved, on top of H-101
			reed	continuous plaiting	1	BE99 2526-H-093	on top of H-098, 099 and 100
			reed	continuous plaiting	1	BE99 2526-H-094	edge fragment, not retrieved
			reed	continuous plaiting	1	BE99 2526-H-095	good condition
			reed	continuous plaiting	1	BE99 2526-H-096	small fragment, not retrieved
			reed	continuous plaiting	1	BE99 2526-H-097	small fragment
			reed	continuous plaiting	1	BE99 2526-H-098	small fragment with edge, part of H-099?
			reed	continuous plaiting	1	BE99 2526-H-099	part of H-098?
			reed	continuous plaiting	1	BE99 2526-H-100	folded fragment, edge
			grass	weaving	1	BE99 2526-H-101	folded, no edges
			doam palm leaf	sewn plait	5	BE99 2526-H-102	
			cotton	coiled	1	BE99 2526-H-103	complete ring-shaped obj.
			grass?	sewn plait	1	BE99 3303-H-166	badly decayed
	31.007	12	date palm leaf	sewn plait	2	BE99 3799-H-196	not retrieved
			date palm leaf?	sewn plait	1	BE99 3799-H-197	smooth appearance, not retrieved
			grass	sewn plait	1	BE99 3799-H-198	coarse, not retrieved
	31.007	13	date palm leaf	sewn plait	1	BE99 2888-H-155	half bag, start present
			date palm leaf	cord	1	BE99 2888-H-156	isolated handle of sewn plait basket
			date palm leaf	sewn plait?	1	BE99 2888-H-157	3 layers, insect damage
	31.007	18	reed	continuous plaiting	1	BE99 3055-H-159	not retrieved
	31.012	19	reed	continuous plaiting	1	BE99 3305-H-171	not retrieved
			grass?	sewn plait	3	BE99 3305-H-172	
			grass?	sewn plait	1	BE99 3305-H-173	coarser than H-172
	31.012	20	grass?	twined	1	BE99 3306-H-105	fine open matting, no edge
			date palm fiber	unworked	1	BE99 3306-H-174	quantity of dark-brown fine fiber
			reed	continuous plaiting	1	BE99 3306-H-175	not retrieved
			date palm fiber	twined	1	BE99 3306-H-176	ZS open twined strap
			palm leaf	twined	1	BE99 3306-H-177	S twined mat
			doam palm leaf	coiled	1	BE99 3306-H-178	coiled mat with repair
			grass	sewn plait	1	BE99 3306-H-179	base of sewn plait basket
			reed	continuous plaiting	1	BE99 3306-H-180	corner of reed mat
			grass	sewn plait	2	BE99 3306-H-181	

Table 12–1   Catalogue of the Berenike 99/00 basketry and matting finds. (continued)

Year	Context	PB	Material	Technique	No.	ID number	Remarks
			grass	sewn plait	2	BE99 3306-H-182	
			grass	sewn plait	1	BE99 3306-H-183	pronounced ridges, not retrieved
			grass	sewn plait	4	BE99 3306-H-184	not retrieved.
			grass	sewn plait	3	BE99 3306-H-185	pronounced ridges, not retrieved
			doam palm leaf	sewn plait	1	BE99 3306-H-186	sewn plait with 3-plait
			date palm leaf	sewn plait	7	BE99 3306-H-187	not retrieved
			date palm leaf	sewn plait	1	BE99 3306-H-188	stitches sewn across fabric
			doam palm leaf	sewn plait	1	BE99 3306-H-189	Z-slanted top edge, not retrieved
			doam palm leaf	sewn plait	1	BE99 3306-H-190	sewn with flat strand
			doam palm leaf	sewn plait	1	BE99 3306-H-191	not retrieved
			doam palm leaf	sewn plait	1	BE99 3306-H-192	not retrieved
			doam palm leaf	sewn plait?	1	BE99 3306-H-193	coarse, not retrieved
			reed	continuous plaiting	1	BE99 3306-H-194	not retrieved
			"material A"	continuous plaiting	1	BE99 3306-H-195	not retrieved
	31.cbs	33	div.	div.	-	BE99 3958-H	not recorded, not retrieved
	31.cbn	35	doam palm leaf	sewn plait	1	BE99 4204-H-199	top edge
	31.cbw	36	doam palm leaf	sewn plait	1	BE99 4213-H-106	sewn plait with 3-plait
			div.	div.	-	BE99 4213-H	not recorded, not retrieved
	31.cbw	37	div.	div.	-	BE99 4215-H	not recorded, not retrieved
	31.cbe	38	div.	div.	-	BE99 4220-H	not recorded, not retrieved
	31.bfw		div.	div.	-	BE99 4521-H	west balk fall, not recorded, not retrieved
99	32.013	15	grass	weaving	1	BE99 3302-H-165	fibers
			grass	weaving	1	BE99 3503-H-069	
	32.017	39	grass	weaving	1	BE99 4222-H-201	fibers
	32.018	34	grass	weaving	1	BE99 3800-H-070	matting, partly in E. balk, not retrieved
	32.019	36	grass	weaving	1	BE99 3801-H-071	soil colorations, not retrieved
00	33.003	4	doam palm leaf	sewn plait	2	BE00 1069-H-107	sewn with leaf strip
	33.004	5	doam palm leaf	sewn plait	1	BE00 1083-H-108	sewn with leaf strip
	33.005	9	doam palm leaf	continuous plaiting	5	BE00 1113-H-109	part of H-111
			doam palm leaf	sewn plait	1	BE00 1113-H-110	coarse but regular
	33.005	10	doam palm leaf	continuous plaiting	1	BE00 1154-H-111	part of H-109
	33.008	13	date palm leaf	continuous plaiting	1	BE00 1161-H-112	papyrus clung to it
			doam palm leaf	sewn plait	4	BE00 1161-H-113	sewn with leaf strip
			doam palm leaf	continuous plaiting	1	BE00 1161-H-114	coarse
	33.008	15	doam palm leaf	sewn plait	7	BE00 1320-H-120	sewn with leaf strip, covered with resin
			date palm leaf	sewn plait	1	BE00 1320-H-121	sewn with string
	33.008	19	doam palm leaf	continuous plaiting	2	BE00 1477-H-123	tabby, decorated?
			doam palm leaf	sewn plait	1	BE00 1477-H-124	flat wide seam
	33.008	23	doam palm/grass	coiling	1	BE00 1290-H-115	one coil preserved
			doam palm leaf	twining	1	BE00 1290-H-116	sieve grid, S-twined
			doam palm leaf	sewn plait?	1	BE00 1290-H-117	not preserved
			doam palm leaf	continuous plaiting	1	BE00 1290-H-118	
			doam palm leaf	sewn plait	4	BE00 1290-H-119	sewn with leaf strip

Table 12–1　Catalogue of the Berenike 99/00 basketry and matting finds. (continued)

Year	Context	PB	Material	Technique	No.	ID number	Remarks
	33.011	32	date palm leaf	continuous plaiting	1	BE00 2295-H-125	plait in Indian textile rim
	33.013	29	doam palm leaf	sewn plait	1	BE00 1998-H-143	top edge present
			doam palm leaf	sewn plait	1	BE00 1998-H-144	Z-slanted top edge
	33.013	31	"material A"	continuous plaiting	2	BE00 2151-H-128	
	33.017	22	date palm leaf	continuous plaiting	2	BE00 1506-H-127	no edges
	33.017	25	doam palm leaf	continuous plaiting	2	BE00 1666-H-132	
			doam palm leaf	sewn plait	1	BE00 1666-H-133	start of plait?
	33.018	26	doam palm / grass	coiling	1	BE00 1670-H-136	fine, colored decoration
			doam palm leaf	sewn plait	2	BE00 1670-H-137	insertions visible
			doam palm leaf	continuous plaiting	1	BE00 1670-H-138	
			doam palm leaf	continuous plaiting	1	BE00 1670-H-139	
			doam palm leaf	continuous plaiting	1	BE00 1670-H-140	
			doam palm leaf	sewn plait	1	BE00 1670-H-141	sewn with leaf strip
	33.018	27	doam palm leaf	sewn plait	1	BE00 1810-H-134	almost complete bag
			doam palm leaf	twining	2	BE00 1810-H-135	edge of matting
	33.018	28	doam palm leaf	sewn plait	3	BE00 1815-H-142	fine regular matting
	33.019	21	doam palm leaf	continuous plaiting	1	BE00 1505-H-126	coarse
	33.024	40	doam palm leaf	sewn plait	3	BE00 2843-H-129	
	33.025	45	date palm leaf	coiling	1	BE00 3350-H-130	
	33.cbn	71	doam palm leaf	sewn plait	1	BE00 5327-H-145	
	33.cbe	73	doam palm leaf	sewn plait	1	BE00 5488-H-146	
			coarse fiber	knotless netting	2	BE00 5488-H-147	coarse flax?
	33.cbw	77	coarse fiber	knotless netting	3	BE00 5893-H-148	of same object as H-147?
00	34.008	12	grass	weaving	1	BE00 1368-H-122	matting in tumble
	34.014		grass	weaving	1	BE00 H-202	matting in tumble
	34.019		grass	weaving	1	BE00 H-203	on occupation surface
			grass	weaving	1	BE00 H-204	southeast corner of trench
			grass	weaving	1	BE00 H-205	south under wooden beam
00	37.006		grass	weaving	1	BE00 H-206	doorway area
	37.008		grass	weaving	1	BE00 H-207	courtyard near staircase
	37.026		grass	weaving	1	BE00 H-208	courtyard near staircase
	37.036		grass	weaving	1	BE00 H-209	over installation 37.041
00	41.009		grass	weaving	1	BE00 H-210	south of wall 41.004
	41.009		grass	weaving	1	BE00 H-211	north of wall 41.004

Table 12–1   Catalogue of the Berenike 99/00 basketry and matting finds. (continued)

Technique	Date Palm Leaf	Doam Palm Leaf	Grass	Mat. A	Reed/ Bamboo	Fiber	Misc.	Total	Frags.
coiling	1	4					1	6	6
continuous plaiting	4	17		8	15			44	65
sewn plait	15	42				10		67	131
twining	2	2	1				1	6	7
weaving			26					26	26
miscellaneous	1						3	4	7
raw material	2							2	N/A
TOTAL	25	65	27	8	15	10	5	155	242

Table 12-2   Correlation between materials and techniques for the objects and number of fragments of Table 12-1. The "fiber" is a dark-brown deteriorated fibrous material consisting of grass leaves, palm leaves, and a combination of both.

12.2   EARLY ROMAN TRASH DUMP

By far the largest part of the basketry and matting, 55 fragments, were found in the Roman trash dump in trenches BE99-29, 31 and BE00-33. They represented a mixture of remains of carrying bags and plaited and woven mats in deposits which have been dated to the first century AD.

12.2.1   REED MATS

The continuously plaited matting with split culms of large reeds, resulted in a sturdy type of mat that could well have been used as walls or roofs of temporary light structures. This type of matting has been found in only one trench and two different loci (31.*007* and 31.*012*). The mats were discarded at the same time, or perhaps in two different events. In total 15 large fragments were found, made in a variety of continuous plaiting patterns (see Table 12-3). It is, therefore, likely that these matting fragments came from several different objects or structures. The size of the reed culms, the tightness of the plaiting and, therefore, the flexibility of the mats were very similar. All 15 fragments were clearly used for the same general purpose. This combination of a twill continuous-plaiting technique with

material that is hardly flexible does not occur elsewhere in Egypt. Continuous-plaiting techniques were not entirely unknown in the Egyptian basketry tradition, the sun roofs of the Old Kingdom funerary ship that was found in the boat pit next to Khufu's (Cheops') pyramid, for instance, were made in a regular twill continuous-plaiting technique. In the Greco-Roman period, continuous plaiting with fine strips of palm leaf was found in fans. It was, however, not a common technique in Egypt and certainly continuous plaiting with the large asymmetrical intervals that were used in several of the mats found in trench BE99-31 was unusual. Egyptian continuous plaiting occurred in a \2/2\\1 pattern or a \3/3\\1 pattern, but never in a \3/5\\1 combined with a \5/3\\1 or in combination with a \3/6\\1 and \6/3\\1 pattern, such as was found here.

Because many of the fragments were decayed, loosened, salt encrusted or too small, the plait pattern was not always clear, but from the larger fragments, especially H-95 and H-100 (Figure 12-5) it was apparent that the plait pattern varied along the two axes and that the pattern at the center of the mat was probably different from that at the edges. The best-preserved matting fragment measured 770 x 710 mm and showed a basic plait pattern of under 3, over 5' in one direction (the x-axes); under 5, over 3' in the other (the y-axes). Toward the edges, the pattern changed, however, and was different for each strand. Figure 12-5 provides an overview of the patterning. The general pattern along the x-axes of \3/5\\1 (under 3, over 5 with a shift of 1 strand) was as follows:

at a: /1\4/4\3/4\3/5\ repeating \3/5\\1
at b: /1\4/4\4/5\3/5\ repeating \3/5\\1
at c: /1\5/3\2/1\3/5\ repeating \3/5\\1
at d: /1\4/4\2/3\3/5\ repeating \3/5\\1

The general pattern along the y-axis is \5/3\\1, but at the edge the pattern ran equally irregular:

at 1: \1/4\4/2\5/3\ repeating \5/3\\1
at 2: \1/4\4/2\3/3\5/3 repeating \5/3\\1
at 3: \1/5\3/6\5/3\ repeating \5/3\\1
at 4: \1/4\4/4\5/3\ repeating \5/3\\1

The number of plait strips that were crossed before getting to the steady regular pattern varied considerably too. On the x-axis it was 12, 14, 16, and 18 (respectively at c, d, a, and b), on the y-axis it was 11, 13, 15, and 17 (respectively at 1, 4, 3, and 2).

Plait Pattern	Width of Strands	Size of Frag.	Remarks	ID	Context
\2/2\\1	22 mm	300 x 300 mm	coarsest fragment, salt encrusted	H-091	31.007
\2/2\\1?	15–20 mm	250-390 mm	decayed remains of reed matting	H-175	31.012
\3/3\\1	14–18 mm	400 x 300 mm	deteriorated and irregular	H-092	31.007
\3/3\\1	4–10 mm	200 x 250 mm	small fragment, narrow plait strips	H-097	31.007
\3/3\\1	9–15 mm	700 x 270 mm	large loosened fragment with edge	H-098	31.007
\3/3\\1	9–15 mm	670 x 160 mm	probably part of same mat as H-98	H-099	31.007
\4/4\\1?	7.5–10 mm	300 x 300 mm	decayed remains of reed matting	H-171	31.012
\4/4\\1	13 mm	190-200 mm	loosened remains of reed matting	H-194	31.012
\2/3\\1 and \3/2\\1	7–10 mm	70 x 80 mm	deteriorated and irregular, edge of \3/3\\1 matting?	H-094	31.007
\3/4\\1 and \4/3\\1	7–12 mm	620 x 680 mm	plait pattern differs: two directions	H-093	31.007
\3/5\\1 and \5/3//1 separate edge pattern	9–15 mm, 21.5 mm	770 x 710 mm	plait pattern differs: two directions see Figure 12-5 and description	H-100	31.007
\3/6\\1 to \3/5\\1 and \6/3\\1 to \5/3\\1	8–17 mm	800 x 560 mm	in good condition, variable plait pattern, different in both directions	H-095	31.007
unclear	8.5–14.5 mm	230 x 300 mm	small loosened fragment	H-096	31.007
unclear	8 mm	isolated reeds	split reeds from continuous plaiting, no pattern preserved	H-159	31.007
unclear	6.5–8.5	115 x 95 mm	corner of mat	H-180	31.012

Table 12-3   Overview of the coarse, continuously plaited matting out of the split culms of reeds (probably a bamboo species) found exclusively in trench BE99-31, a section of the early Roman trash deposit.

Plate 12-4
Continuously plaited fragment made of the split culm of a reed species (H-095, with H-097 on top). Scale=10 cm. Photograph by B. J. Seldenthuis.

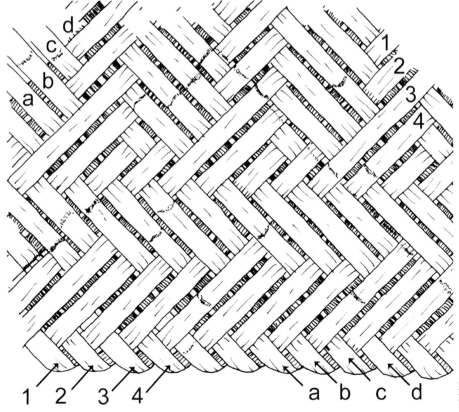

Figure 12-5
Drawing of the plait pattern of H-100. Not to scale. Drawing by W. Z. Wendrich.

The fact that such irregular plait patterns over such large intervals has not been attested in the Egyptian material provokes the suggestion that these mats were imported into Berenike, as attested for many other items. The material macroscopically resembled bamboo.

Even the coarsest of these reed mats was only 3–3.5 mm thick. They formed an excellent screen against sun and wind. Presumably these matting fragments came from shelters on ships. The deposit was concentrated in one locus, with some stray remains in a nearby locus in the same trench, but the variety in plait patterns makes it likely that the matting came from several shelters. The matting was probably discarded when the ships were refurbished or demolished and reused. The "foreign" origin of the matting is in keeping with the ample evidence of contacts between Berenike and the Indian Ocean basin (cf. Wendrich, *et al.* 2003). These mats probably originated in India, perhaps northern India, rather than the south, if we would draw a parallel with today's centers of bamboo basketry and matting production (Ranjan, *et al.* 1986). Bamboo matting very similar to the ones found in Berenike are nowadays also found in other regions of Asia, such as Indonesia (Jasper and Pirngadie 1912). This does not link the Berenike matting necessarily to a provenance that far east, but it does firmly link it to an Asian origin.

12.2.2 CONTINUOUS PLAITING

Apart from the reed matting discussed in the previous section, continuous plaiting was found both in tabby and twill patterns in three different materials, doam palm leaf, date palm leaf, and the as yet unidentified "material A" (cf. Wendrich 2000:230). Table 12-6 gives an overview of the plait patterns and fineness of the plaited fragments. It is immediately apparent that within the tabby plaits (under one, over one with a shift of one) there were two groups: the finer plaits, with plaiting strands ranging from 5 to 10.5 mm in width were made mostly from doam palm leaf and in two cases from date palm leaf. The coarser plaits, with 9–19.5 mm wide plaiting strands of the as yet unidentified "material A" made up the second group. Of the 19 fragments 15 were found in locus 31.*007*, the same locus where the reed continuous matting was found. One fragment was found in locus 31.*012*, the other area where the reed matting was found, the seventeenth fragment from trench 31 came from locus *006*, bordering locus *007*. Two small fragments were found in the following year in trench 33 in the same general area of the site. The unfamiliar material, unknown in Egypt, and its close association with the coarse reed matting, suggests that "material A" also had a foreign origin.

Pattern	Width Strands	Thickn.	Size Fragment	Mat.	Remark	ID	Context
\1/1\\1	5	3.5	30 x 60	doam		H-162	31.*006*
\1/1\\1	6	3	260 x 220 160 x 150	date	trench 13, balk fall	H-056	13.*bfs*
\1/1\\1	7–9	3-5	170 x 105	doam	oblique side edge, wear marks	H-152	31.*007*
\1/1\\1	6.5–10	4	55 x 35 45 x 35	doam	insertions? or decorations with 3.5 mm wide strip over 10 mm wide strip.	H-123	33.*008*
\1/1\\1	8	2.3	80 x 90	doam	slightly finer than H-138	H-139	33.*018*
\1/1\\1	8–8.5	2.5	180 x 350 130 x 330	date	plaiting with 2 or 3 strands on top of each other	H-127	33.*017*
\1/1\\1	8–9	2.0	180 x 50	doam		H-140	33.*018*
\1/1\\1	10	3.5	140 x 75 180 x 70	doam		H-063	29.*002*
\1/1\\1	10.5	2.6	70 x 70	doam		H-138	33.*018*

Table 12-6 Plait patterns of continuous-plaited fragments, in order of the width of the plaiting strands. Listed are: the plait pattern and the width of the plaiting strands; the thickness of the plaited fabric and the size of the fragment; the material used; remarks, basketry ID number, and the context. All sizes are indicated in mm.

Pattern	Width Strands	Thickn.	Size Fragment	Mat.	Remark	ID	Context
\1/1\\1	9–13	2.3	60 x 50 to 160 x 140	A	8 brittle fragments, all strands are double (insertions)	H-075	31.007
\1/1\\1	6–18.5	3.5	135 x 200 130 x 150	A	in both directions great variation in width of strands	H-128	33.013
\1/1\\1	11–13.5	3.5	100 x 60	A		H-151	31.007
\1/1\\1	10-14.5	3.5	215 x 80 190 x 65	A	two parts of a cover around papyrus 2284-uu	H-082	31.007
\1/1\\1	13.5	4	60 x 70	A		H-168	31.006
\1/1\\1	14–16	4	180 x 140 to 70 x 80	A	3 fragments. Part of H-079 from same locus.	H-076	31.007
\1/1\\1	14–16	4	30 x 40	A	part of H-76	H-079	31.007
\1/1\\1	15–19.5	3	90 x 80	A	small, deteriorated fragment	H-195	31.012
\2/2\\1	3.5	2	420 x 420 300 x 240	doam	very fine continuous plaiting	H-132	33.017
\2/2\\1	3.5	2.4	30 x 60	doam	very fine continuous plaiting	H-118	33.008
\2/2\\1	5	2.5	70 x 80	doam	wear traces on one side	H-163	31.006
\2/2\\1	5	3.5	100 x 90 to 30 x 40	doam	5 fragments, double fabric, one dark strand as decoration	H-109	33.005
\2/2\\1	5	3.5	60 x 80	doam	1 fragment, double fabric, one dark strand as decoration	H-111	33.005
\2/2\\1	5	4	70 x 50	doam	7.5 mm Z-slanted edge, balk trim	H-068	29.cbw
\2/2\\1	8.2	3	60 x 60 60 x 110	doam	twill plaiting with sewn Z-slanted edge, cf. H-068, 055	H-090	31.007
\2/2\\1	8.5		110 x 70	doam	insect damage	H-169	31.006
\2/2\\1	8–13	4	190 x 140	doam	knot at edge to insert strand	H-114	33.008
\2/2\\1	7.5–18	8	85 x 60	doam	coarse irregular matting	H-126	33.019
\2/2\\1?	3	3		date?	inside Indian cotton rim	H-125	33.011
\3/3\\1	3	3	110 x 120	date	see Plate 12-7	H-112	33.008

Table 12-6 Plait patterns of continuous-plaited fragments, in order of the width of the plaiting strands. Listed are: the plait pattern and the width of the plaiting strands; the thickness of the plaited fabric and the size of the fragment; the material used; remarks, basketry ID number, and the context. All sizes are indicated in mm. (continued)

All matting fragments made of "material A" found at Berenike were made in the same plaiting pattern and with the same range of width of the plaiting strips. In the eight small fragments of H-075, all strands were double: a broad strip with a narrow one underneath it. These are the ends of the strips that were exhausted or the beginnings of new plaiting strands that were laid in. Because the strands of material were approximately of the same length, the insertions were added roughly in one line. This strengthened the fabric at that point, which may explain why this particular part of the mat has been preserved.

The other types of continuous plaiting were found in all trenches of the early Roman trash deposit. Tabby continuous plaiting with date and doam palm leaf was finer than that made of "material A." In addition the two types of palm leaf were also used for twill plaiting, mostly in a twill pattern of under two, over two, but H-112 was an under-three, over-three twill plait, with a double-under-two, over-two twill edge (see Plate 12-7).

The nature of the deposit, a trash dump, explains why all the remains were very fragmentary. It was difficult to determine the function of the pieces. There were some indications of the original function. One papyrus was flanked on two sides by the two fragments of tabby plaited "material A" (H-082). They presumably formed a basketry envelope and it is interesting that the packing material was non-Egyptian. This papyrus was not composed in India, or somewhere along the route. From the text it is clear that the papyrus was written in Berenike (Bagnall, *et al.* 2005). Perhaps it was brought out of Egypt, packed for protection during the travels and discarded, envelope and all, upon arrival back in the harbor of origin. Another fragment, H-112, had papyrus stuck to its surface. The fine plaiting was made with strips of date palm leaf and if this was another envelope-type cover for papyrus then it was certainly produced in Egypt. The other fragments of fine twill plaiting could have been parts of fans. Parallels for fans are found on other Egyptian sites, for instance at Qasr Ibrim.

A curious object was H-125, a cotton textile from Indian origin (see Chapter 11) that was sewn with crude stitches around the rim of a finely plaited mat. The fragments were too small to determine the material from which the mat was made, but the plaiting strands were fine (only 3 mm wide) and protruded at an oblique angle, which makes it likely that this was a \2/2\\1 or perhaps \3/3\\1 plaited mat. The size and technique are consistent with Egyptian tradition, but that makes the addition of strips of Indian cotton fabric as repair of the rim remarkable.

Plate 12-7   Papyrus 2284-uu and the remains of a tabby plaited cover (H-082) made of "material A." Scale is 5 cm. Photograph by B. J. Seldenthuis.

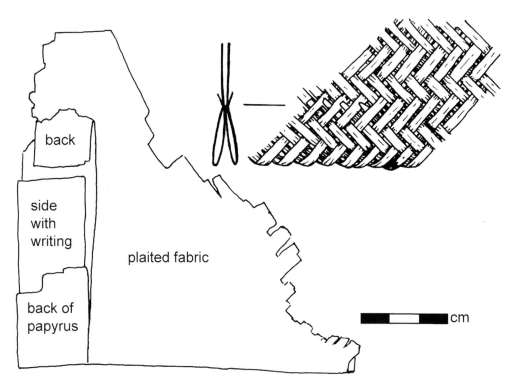

Figure 12-8
Edge and double fabric of twill plaited date palm leaf matting H-112 with four layers of very fragmentary papyrus attached. Note the insertions on two sides of the double fabric at the edge. Drawing by W. Z. Wendrich.

No.	Pattern	Width Str.	Width Plait	Mat.	Size Frag.	Size of Sewing Strip or String and Remarks	ID	Context
3	\1/1\\1	20	60	doam	245 x 560	3-plait with 3 parallel strands	H-106	31.*cbw*
3	\1/1\\1	26	75	doam	200 x 75	3-plait with 4 parallel strands	H-186	31.*012*
5	\1/1\\1	5	28	date	40 x 170 40 x 120	sewn with zS2 string 6/3.5	H-196	31.*007*
5	\1/1\\1	5	30.5	date	80 x 80	sewn with zS2 string 5/3	H-121	33.*008*
5	\1/1\\1	6-9	50	date	50 x 150	sewn with zS2 string	H-161	31.*006*
5	\1/1\\1	10	40	doam	100 x 60	sewn with Z-twisted doam 3.5	H-074	31.*007*
5	\1/1\\1	10	37.5	doam	40 x 85	sewn with Z-twisted doam 3.5	H-078	31.*007*
9	\2/2\\1	5	?	date	-	deteriorated remains of plait	H-157	31.*007*
9	\2/2\\1	5	26.5	date	65 x 100 60 x 65	sewn with zS2 string 4.5/2.0	H-087	31.*007*
9	\2/2\\1	5	30.8	grass?	245 x 210 50 x 150	3 frags. sewn with zS2 string 5/2.5. Dark brown.	H-172	31.*012*
9	\2/2\\1	5	35.5	date	135 x 130	sewn with zS2 string 5.5/2.5	H-086	31.*007*
9	\2/2\\1	5	37	doam	150 x 160	sewn with untwisted doam 3.5	H-102	31.*007*
9	\2/2\\1	5.5	33.5	date	70 x 120 60 x 160	sewn with zS2 string 6/2.5 7 fragments	H-187	31.*012*
9	\2/2\\1	5.5	33.5	date	110 x 270	sewn with zS2 string 4/2.5	H-188	31.*012*
9	\2/2\\1	5.5	36.5	grass	60 x 160 35 x 100	sewn with zS2 string 4.5/2.5, thickness 8–10 mm	H-185	31.*012*
9	\2/2\\1	6	35.8	date	270 x 270	sewn with zS2 string 5/3.5, base of basket, repair	H-153	31.*007*
9	\2/2\\1	6.5	35.5	date	60 x 100	sewn with zS2 string 4/2.5 largest of 7 fragments	H-085	31.*007*
9	\2/2\\1	6.5	26.5	grass	110 x 160	salt encrusted, thick ridges	H-183	31.*012*
9	\2/2\\1	8	48.5	date	70 x 70 40 x 50	sewn with zS2 string 4.5/3.5	H-088	31.*007*
9	\2/2\\1	8.5	46	grass	130 x 210 90 x 140	sewn with zS2 string thickness of mat 7 mm.	H-184	31.*012*
9	\2/2\\1	8.5	62	grass?	150 x 350	sewn with zS2 string 5.5/3.5	H-198	31.*007*
9	\2/2\\1	9	51	grass?	320 x 240	part of bag	H-155	31.*007*
9	\2/2\\1	9	44	grass?	120 x 210 90 x 120	sewn with zS2 string 4.5/3 dark brown deteriorated	H-182	31.*012*
9	\2/2\\1	9.5	47.5	grass?	175 x 215	base of basket, see description	H-179	31.*012*
9	\2/2\\1	10.5	66	grass?	90 x 70	sewn with zS2 string 2.5/4.5	H-166	31.*007*
9	\2/2\\1	10.7	49	grass?	150 x 110	sewn with zS2 string 5/3.5	H-173	31.*012*
9 +	\2/2\\1	4	41	doam	41 x 27	sewn with untwisted doam	H-146	33.*cbe*
9 +	\2/2\\1	5.5	-	doam	70 x 50	sewing strip untwisted doam 2	H-108	33.*004*
9 +	\2/2\\1	6	59.5	doam	120 x 90 60 x 55	sewn with untwisted doam 2.7 very fine regular matting	H-142	33.*018*

Table 12–9   Sewn plait baskets and mats.

No.	Pattern	Width Str.	Width Plait	Mat.	Size Frag.	Size of Sewing Strip or String and Remarks	ID	Context
13	\2/2\\1	5.5	42.5	date?	110 x 180	sewn with zS2 string 3/1.5	H-197	31.007
13	\2/2\\1	6.5	52	grass	230 x 240 180 x 180	sewn with zS2 string 4/2 thick matting (9–12.5 mm)	H-181	31.012
13	\2/2\\1	6–12	87.5	doam	320 x 95	sewn with untwisted doam 5.5 reuse of mat, stitched over with grass zS2 string 4/2.7	H-141	33.018
13 +	\2/2\\1	4	-	doam	60 x 35 to 30 x 20	sewn with untwisted doam 1.8 mm	H-119	33.008
13 +	\2/2\\1	7.5	-	doam	130 x 100 120 x 80	sewn with untwisted doam 2	H-107	33.003
13 +	\2/2\\1	4-9	-	doam	120 x 80	sewn with untwisted doam	H-164	31.006
17	\2/2\\1	7	-	doam	-	3 layers stuck in salt	H-191	31.012
17	\2/2\\1	8	80	doam	140 x 80	sewn with untwisted doam	H-189	31.012
17	\2/2\\1	7-9	87.5	doam	290 x 250 160 x 80	sewn with untwisted doam 3.5 insertions: see Figure 13-10	H-137	33.018
17	\2/2\\1	8.5	85	doam	110 x 90 40 x 50	sewn with untwisted doam 4 top edge sewn with doam 7	H-167	31.006
17	\2/2\\1	9	100	doam	100 x 150	sewn with untwisted doam 6.5	H-190	31.012
17	\2/2\\1	9	87	doam	330 x 190	sewn with untwisted doam 7	H-062	29.002
17	\2/2\\1	9	89	doam	370 x 170	sewn with untwisted doam 7 flat wide seam	H-124	33.008
17 +	\2/2\\1	4-5	30	doam	80 x 130 40 x 40	sewn with untwisted doam, 4 fragments	H-080	31.007
17 +	\2/2\\1	6	85	doam	85 x 120	sewn with untwisted doam 3.5 top edge S-slanted, balk trim	H-199	31.cbn
17 +	\2/2\\1	6-9	86.5	doam	100 x 120	sewn with untwisted doam 4	H-145	33.cbn
17 +	\2/2\\1	8.5	80	doam	80 x 65	sewn with untwisted doam 5	H-065	29.006
17 +	\2/2\\1	9.5	90	doam	100 x 80	no trace of sewing strip	H-160	31.006
21 +	\2/2\\1	3-4	70	doam	100 x 70	sewn with untwisted doam 3	H-170	31.006
21 +	\2/2\\1	6.5	79	doam	4 frags	sewn with untwisted doam 3	H-154	31.007
25	\2/2\\1	4	64	doam	79 x 57	sewn with s-twisted doam 3	H-143	33.013
25	\2/2\\1	7	150	doam	170 x 150 70 x 70	sewn with untwisted doam 5.5	H-077	31.007
25	\2/2\\1	7	120	doam	150 x 140	sewn with untwisted doam 6.5	H-192	31.012
25	\2/2\1	7-8	133.5	doam	140 x 250 190 x 140 100 x 210	sewn with untwisted doam 3.5 edge present	H-129	33.024
25	\2/2\\1	7.5	117	doam	210 x 160	sewn with untwisted doam 4	H-110	33.005
29	\2/2\\1	6.5	120	doam	150 x 150 to 90 x 60	sewn with untwisted doam 3.5	H-113	33.008

Table 12–9   Sewn plait baskets and mats. (continued)

No.	Pattern	Width Str.	Width Plait	Mat.	Size Frag.	Size of Sewing Strip or String and Remarks	ID	Context
33	\2/2\\1	4	79	doam	420 x 115	sewn with untwisted doam	H-055	13.*bfs*
33	\2/2\\1	4-7	108	doam		200 x 335 mm bag, made of four different plaited strips (A-D)	H-134 A	33.*018*
37	\2/2\\1	4.5	98.5	doam		see Figure 12-11	B	
37	\2/2\\1	4-5	125	doam			C	
37	\2/2\\1	3-5	105	doam			D	
?	\2/2\\1	5	-	date	deterior.	sewn with fine zS2 string	H-066	29.*006*
?	\2/2\\1	5.5	-	date	120 x 40	edge with zZ3 string sewn on	H-089	31.*007*
?	\2/2\\1	6.5	-	doam	51 x 39	edge with Z-slanted stitching	H-144	33.*013*
?	\2/2\\1	8.5	-	doam	53 x 35	start of plait? but deteriorated	H-133	33.*017*
?	\2/2\\1	10	-	doam	1 fragm.	coarse, fell apart	H-117	33.*008*
?	\2/2\\1	11	-	doam	5 frags	sewn with untwisted doam	H-081	31.*007*
?	\2/2\\1	13.5	-	doam	7 frags	sewn with untwisted doam 6	H-120	33.*008*
?	\2/2\\1	16	-	doam	140 x 190	coarse, thickness only 3mm	H-193	31.*012*

Table 12-9   Sewn plait basketry from the early Roman trash dump trenches excavated during the 1999 and 2000 seasons, in order of number and size of plait strands. Listed are the number of plaiting strands with which the strip is made, the plait pattern, the size in mm of the plaiting strands, the width in mm of the plaited strip, the size of the fragment(s), remarks, the basketry ID number, and the context (trench and locus number). The + sign means that only one edge is present and the plait could be wider.

13.2.3   SEWN PLAIT BASKETS AND MATS

Sewn plait was the most common technique found at Berenike. In total 54 percent of the fragments recorded in 1999 and 2000 (131 of 242) were remains of sewn plait basketry or matting. Long plaits were sewn either parallel to each other to form mats, or spirally to form flexible baskets. The five-strand plaits were solely used for baskets and made in an under 1/over 1' tabby pattern. The nine-strand plaits were made in a twill pattern (under 2/over 2 with a shift of 1) and were used for baskets. The wider plaits were used to produce mats. Because the objective of sewing the plaits was to form a fabric that seemed to be continuous, the edges of the plaits were pulled inside each other by the sewing strip. This means the edges had to be oriented in opposite directions, as illustrated in Figure 12-10. In a \2/2\\1 twill this can only be done with a specific number of plaiting strands: 9, 13, 17, 21, 25, 29, 33 and 37 were the ones found this season.

The sewing strip varied in size and with the material used. Date palm leaf plaits were, without exception, sewn with string, while doam palm leaf plaits were sewn with fine untwisted strips of doam palm leaf, ranging from 1.8 to 5 mm. In rare cases slightly broader sewing strips have been used, but they were never wider than 7 mm and only 1 mm thick. The result was that the sewing edges were very flat, only slightly thicker than the plaited strips. Even the coarsest plaited mats of doam palm leaf were only about 3 mm thick and approximately 4 mm at the edges. This was an enormous difference when compared to the date palm leaf basketry, which was sewn with zS2 string (two z spun yarns made of grass or date palm leaf, S-twisted into twine). The diameter of the string varied from basket to basket (see Table 12-9), but generally ranged between 4 to 5 mm in diameter. The result was that the area where the edges of the plait strip were sewn together formed an easily traceable ridge in the fabric. For matting this would not be suitable, but the string made for a strong connection in vertical direction: the nine-strand date palm plaits were mostly employed in large baglike carrying baskets.

Insertions of new material were important to notice, because they revealed the tradition in which the basket maker worked. A skilled basket maker, who works in a steady rhythm usually also has a regular inlay of new material. An excellent example is H-137, where new strips of doam palm leaf were laid in at every plaiting row. The insertions of the plait with 17 strands were done both from the left and the right. Figure 12-10 shows how the insertions appeared at the back of the fabric. The 89 mm wide strips were sewn together with a strip of doam palm leaf 3.5 mm wide.

Apart from the sewn plait basket made of strands of palm leaf, also bundles of a fibrous material were used, either grass or shredded palm leaf or, in some cases, a combination of both. Mostly this type of basketry was very badly preserved, and it would be logical to conclude that the fibrous appearance was the result of deterioration of the palm leaf after deposition. Fragment H-179, however, showed these plaits were made of a fibrous material, grass, and shredded palm leaf and that they probably had been put into water for a considerable time to soften and become more flexible. The shredded and deteriorated appearance was the result of a process that started before production. The start of the plait in H-179 was a bundle of fiber with a diameter of 28 mm, tied together with zS2 string. The bundle was divided into nine smaller bundles 9.5 mm in diameter, which were plaited in a twill \2/2\\1 pattern, resulting in a 47.5 mm wide plait with a thickness of 6.5 mm. This plait was sewn spirally into a basket with zS2 string. On the inside of the basket the inserts of new grass bundles were clearly visible.

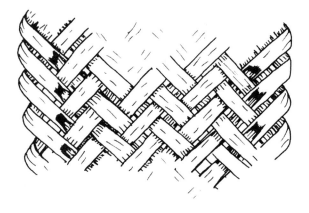

Figure 12-10   A 17-strand plait with insertions on two sides (H-137). Note the orientation of the edges and the regularity of the inserts. Not to scale. Drawing by W. Z. Wendrich

Two fragments were found of curious plaiting with three bundles of either three (H-106) or four (H-186) parallel strands of S-twisted doam palm leaf. A crude fabric was made by stitching several of these three-strand plaits together. Both fragments, one from locus 31.012, the other from the balk trim of the west balk of trench 31, were in extremely bad condition.

Object H-141 was a pad made by sewing three strips of broken-up sewn plait matting on top of each other with string. The strips were originally part of a doam palm mat, made out of 13-strand plaits and sewn with untwisted doam palm leaf. The sewing string was a deteriorated fibrous material, probably grass and the diameter was 4 mm (twined in S-direction out of two Z-spun yarns each with a diameter of 2.7 mm). The pad's function was unclear. Although the size and shape were reminiscent of a sandal, there were no traces of straps or wear patterns that are consistent with such use.

Part of a conical bag with pronounced sewing ridges was found in locus 31.007. The center and eight of the spiraling coils of the plait were left. The nine-strand plait was made out of bundles of fibrous grass, mixed with shredded palm leaf. The original diameter of the basket at the last extant coil was 220 mm with a height of 325 mm, but possibly we have just the tip of the basket, which may have been much larger. There were no traces of a handle or handle anchor. The basket was sewn in "inside E-direction", that is, when looking at the inside of the basket the start of the plait forms a letter E; the spiral turns counterclockwise. The object was heavily salt encrusted and it was difficult to make out how the center of the basket was sewn exactly.

The deposits in trench 31 were much more mangled, deteriorated, battered, and used than the ones found in trench 33. Clearly there was a different deposition behavior for the two areas of the trash dump. One find from the latter trench was, for instance, an almost complete bag made of sewn plaits (H-134). The bag showed a very different tradition than that of most of the basketry from Berenike. As explained above, most of the carrying bags were made of date palm leaf with a spirally sewn plait forming the bottom and sides of the bags. Bag H-134 seemed to be a bag formed out of re-used existing matting. The bag was 200 mm wide and 335 mm high. Four lengths of very wide plaits were sewn parallel to each other to form a tube, which was closed at the bottom (see Figure 12-11). The plaits used were among the widest found at Berenike: 33 strands and 37 strands were used to make the matting (H-134 A–D in Table 12-9). The sewing of the sides was invisible, as the edges of the plaiting strips were pulled inside each other. The sewing seems to have been done with a thin strip of untwisted doam palm leaf, as the seams were very flat.

Plate 12-12   A *beyt bursh* (mat house) of the day Ababda nomads who live in the Berenike region. The mats are purchased from Sudanese traders. Photograph by B. J. Seldenthuis.

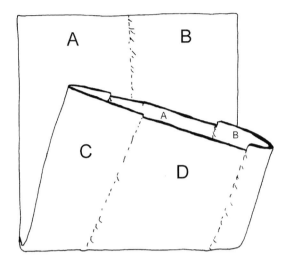

Figure 12-11   Sewn plait bag H-134. Not to scale. Drawing by W.Z. Wendrich

Plate 12-13   Detail of the modern Ababda mat house. The mats are made with 17 strands of doam palm leaf in a \2/2\\1 pattern. Photograph by B .J. Seldenthuis

The bottom of the bag was sewn very precisely; the top of the bag was probably repaired at some point. Unlike at the bottom, the sewing of the top edge disregarded the seam lines of the edges of the plaits: the bag was folded askew and then stitched. The bag has been treated by the project conservator, J. Trosper.

The mats made out of doam palm leaf were multipurpose. They could be used as floor mats, sun screens, but also as walls for temporary dwellings. Ethnographic parallels in the same region are the present mat houses of the Ababda nomads who live near Berenike, in the area between the Nile Valley and the Red Sea from the Sudanese border to the road between Quseir and Quft. The Ababda use a frame of acacia or tamarisk branches, lined on the outside with woven sheep's-wool carpets and covered with several large doam palm leaf sewn plait mats (Plates 12-12 and 12-13).

A description by Linant de Bellefonds from 1833 of the houses of the Bisharin, a tribe to which the Ababda are considered to be closely related, mentioned similar mat houses. This type of dwelling was common in the Etbai region to which Berenike belongs. This does not mean that there is a proven continuity in the region for the use of this type of matting for houses, but it does show that the mats are eminently suitable for building shelters and have been used at least from 1833 to the present in this function. Considering the amount of this type of matting that has been found at Berenike, it seems likely that it was used extensively in Berenike, possibly for similar purposes.

12.2.4 COILED BASKETRY

Only six fragments of coiled basketry were found during the 1999 and 2000 seasons. One was made of date palm leaf, four of doam palm leaf, and one of cotton string. The bundle material in most of the fragments was grass, with the exception of H-103 (material uncertain) and

H-178, which had a doam palm leaf bundle. All but one fragment was found in the early Roman trash dump. Most of the fragments were very small.

Locus 31.*007*, which preserved most of the foreign basketry, also yielded a small coiled ring, which seemed to be complete. It was probably a small pot stand (H-103, Figure 12-14). The choice of material is curious: not doam palm leaf, as used for most coiled basketry, but a fine cotton string wrapped around a bundle of striped culms. The bundle material was hardly visible, but consisted of 1 mm wide culms with lengthwise stripes, possibly a fine *Juncus* species. The diameter of the bundle was 8 mm. The cotton string (identification by A. Veldmeijer) used for the winders originally had a light color, but has weathered to a very dark brown and resembled goat hair. The zS4 string was 1.5 mm in diameter (consisting of 4 z-spun yarns each with a diameter of 0.6 mm, twined in S-direction). Spinning in Z-direction was a marker for an Indian origin for cotton textiles (see Chapter 11) and probably should be interpreted here in a similar way. Although coiling was a widespread and ancient technique in Egypt, both the material and the coiling pattern, alternately around one and two bundles, were very unusual. The irregular ring-shaped object flared out at the bottom. The diameter at the top was 64.1 x 61.9 mm at the outside and 46.5 x 45.6 mm at the inside (with a wall thickness that varied between 17.6 and 16.3 mm). The diameter at the base was 51 x 51.2 mm on the outside and 38 x 38.4 mm on the inside (wall thickness of 13 mm).

In locus 31.*012* an irregular-shaped, flat, coiled fragment was found amid large quantities of mostly plaited basketry (H-178, Plate 12-15). The fragment, which seemed to be part of a mat, rather than a container, was 350 x 220 x 12 mm thick. The coiling was very irregular, coarse on the outside and fine in the middle. The diameter of the bundle varied from 4 mm of an inserted repair to 12 mm for the outer bundles. The center part was isolated, a round fragment of 80 mm in diameter, the upper side coiled in E-direction (counterclockwise). The bundle diameter was 5 mm; the doam palm leaf winding strands were 3 mm wide. The fragment clearly had been repaired: an irregularly formed insert was tacked on to the center, made of 13 very fine coils with a diameter of 4 mm and a winding strand of 2 mm. The winding was strongly Z-slanted. The outer eight rows of extant coiling had a bundle diameter of 12 mm and a winder width of 4.5 mm. In all three parts the stitch with which the winding strands were fastened picked up part of the bundle material of the previous coil.

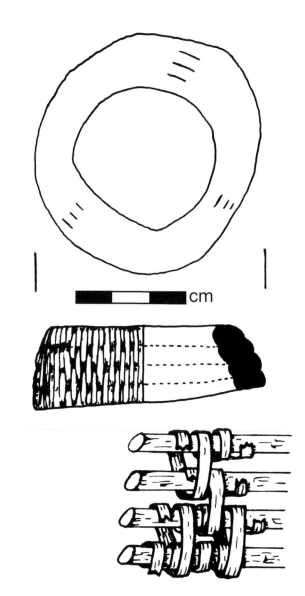

Figure 12-14   Appearance, shape, diameter and coiling pattern (not to scale) of the small ring-shaped coiled object H-103. Drawing by W. Z. Wendrich.

Plate 12-15   H-178 coiled mat of doam palm leaf: coiled repair inserted to one side of the center. Scale = 10 cm. Photograph by W. Z. Wendrich.

H-115 from locus 33.*008* was a small fragment: just one 30 mm long coil, consisting of a grass bundle 7 mm in diameter wound with 2.5 mm wide doam palm leaf. The stitch passed through the previous bundle.

From locus 33.*018* came a finely coiled basket with traces of a polychrome decoration (H-136). The object was 60.1 x 73.3 x 25.4 mm high. The thickness of the wall was 3.3 mm, and the center of this small basket was missing. The coiling, as viewed from the outside, was in E-direction (counterclockwise). The bundle, which probably consisted of doam palm leaf, was 2.2 mm in diameter and the winding strand, also doam palm leaf was only 1.2 mm wide. The stitch picked up a little bit of the bundle of the previous coil. On one side, 14 rows of coiling were extant, on the other side 12, so the basket looked lopsided. The winders showed traces of three different colors: natural, red brown, and dark brown or black. The surface of the winders was too deteriorated to make out a specific color pattern.

Fragment H-130 was a tiny part of a very fine and probably quite large coiled basket. The fragment measured only 46 x 11.1 x 4.7 mm thick. It consisted of two rows of coiling and the remains of two more. The grass bundle had a diameter of 3.7 mm and the date palm leaf winder was 1.7 mm wide. This choice of material was quite exceptional. Most of the ancient coiled basketry was made of doam, rather than date palm leaf. Judging from the present curve of the fragment, the diameter of the basket would have been 400 mm, which was large for such extremely fine coiling. The fragment could have easily flattened, however, so the basket may in fact have been smaller.

The only coiled object that was not found in the trash dump area was H-150, discovered during balk trimming in trench 10. The basket came from a fifth-century AD layer, approximately 0.75 m below the surface, south of wall 10.*032* from a mixed layer of trash and windblown sand. It was of interest, because the coiling patterns were decorative and ran over multiple bundles. The center was missing. The basket, which had an extant diameter of 315 mm, had a hole in the middle with a 100 mm diameter. The coil was made of a bundle of grass with a diameter of 8 mm, while the doam palm leaf winders were 2.5–3.5 mm wide. The stitch pattern from the inside out was: nine coils where the winder runs over two bundles, one coil of ordinary stitching (over one bundle), five coils of stitching over two bundles, one coil stitching over one bundle (see Figure 12-16).

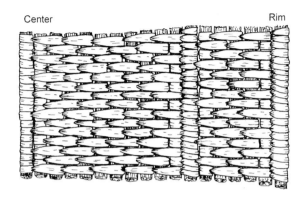

Figure 12-16   Coiling pattern of H-150. Not to scale. Drawing by W. . Wendrich

12.2.5   TWINED BASKETRY

Seven twined fragments were retrieved from the early Roman trash dump, two of which were part of the same object. The most spectacular twined basketry find was an open-twined band of a type found in previous seasons (Wendrich 1999a: 282; Wendrich 1995:71). The 1999 fragment, H-104, represented the complete width of such a strap, which in this case was 370 mm. The fragment had two side edges and part of the top edge. The latter had a looped feature, similar to the handles on sewn plait baskets (Plate 12-17). The fragment was 500 x 730 x 17.5 mm thick. It consisted of 21 rows of "passive" zS3 rope made of grass (diameter 10.2/6.3) and had five double rows of "active" twining in Z-orientation with zS2 string (diameter 6.5/5.0). The space between the passive ropes, which form loops at the side edges of the strap, was 11 mm, the space between the rows of twining was 50 mm. The inside width of the small side loops was 16.5 mm; the inside width of the large "handle" loop at the "top" edge was 45 mm.

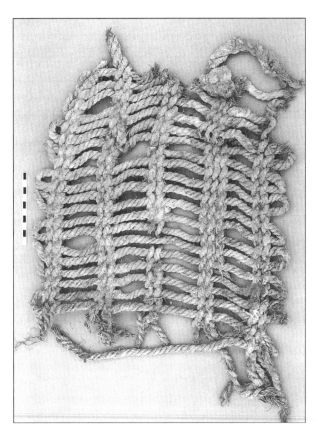

Plate 12-17   twined strap H-104 with two side edges and part of the top edge extant. Scale = 10 cm. Photograph by B .J. Seldenthuis.

One of the twining rows consisted of three rather than two parallel rows of Z-twining. This clearly represented a later repair. This type of open-work strap has been found both in early and late contexts in Berenike. Trench BE94-01.*012* yielded a large fragment of a very similar strap, or rather two of these next to each other, linked with a string, which hooked through the small side loops (Wendrich 1995:71 fig. 36). This one was dated to the fifth century AD. The strap found in the early Roman context of locus 31.*007* was not made of palm leaf, as the 1994 example, but of grass.

H-176 was a small fragment (190 x 110 x 16.5 mm thick) of a similar strap, but made of yet a different material. Both the passive and active strands were made of the hard leaf sheath fiber of the date palm. The passive strands were zS3 string (diameter 8/4.5), the composition of the active strands was zS2 (diameter 8.5/5). In this fragment the two rows of twining were oriented in ZS direction, which gave the effect of reversed V-shapes in the fabric. The strands twined around two parallel passive strands at a time. The width

of one row of ZS-twining was 22.5 mm and the space between the rows was 30 mm. There were no side edges present, but the fragment had the remains of a "top" edge loop.

The 1999 finds still did not give a secure answer to what the function of such straps was. Could they be belts for strapping down ship cargo? Were they a type of carrying sling? Were they part of camel trappings? The most logical explanation seems to be that they were related to securing cargo or merchandise. The lashings that connected the two straps found in 1994 suggest that the individual straps were fastened and then connected and tightened. The handles at the "top" edge may have had a function in lifting the loads or in fastening the belts. The material of the small fragment H-176, the rough date palm leaf sheath fiber, would not be suitable for securing goods on a camel, as it would damage their skin. From the context of the 1999 finds it also seems more probable that these straps were related to maritime rather than terrestrial loads.

From the same trench, BE99-31.*01, 2* came a small fragment of twined matting (H-105, 400 x 160 mm x 2.5 mm thick). The work was widely spaced in two directions. The passive elements were narrow bundles of very fine material, which had a leaf structure and may have been grass, but were much finer than either *Desmostachya bipinnata* or *Imperata cylindrica*. The bundles had a diameter of 3 mm and were spaced 2 mm apart. They were held together by S-twined zS2 string (1.5/2.0). The space between the rows of twining was 3.5 mm. The insertions of new twining strands were clearly visible: they were inserted parallel to the passive bundle and fastened by the next row of twining.

Locus 31.*012* also yielded a fragment of twined matting made of palm leaf string. H-177 was extremely deteriorated, which made it impossible to determine which type of palm leaf was used. The passive strands were zS2 string (diameter 9/5.5) and the active strands were S-twined zS2 strands with a diameter of 6/4. The passive strands were closely spaced, but the active strands were 32.5 mm apart.

The twined basketry from trench 33 was slightly different in character. Piece H-116 was a small fragment of sieve grid (28 x 17.5 x 2.6 mm thick). The sieve was made of the vein of the doam palm leaf. The fragment preserved four passive stakes, 2.1 mm wide and 1.5 mm apart. Of the S-oriented twining that held the fabric together, six rows survived. The twining rows were 2 mm apart and the S-twining was done with two 1.5 mm wide strips of doam palm leaf.

Lot H-135 represented two fragments of tightly twined matting. The fragment sizes were 99 x 17 and 100 x 23 mm, and the mat was 13 mm thick. The passive elements were strips of doam palm leaf from 4.8 to 8 mm wide, and the active elements were two strands of 3.5 mm wide doam palm leaf, S-twined around the passive strands. This made a very regular, closely spaced fabric. A small part of the edge was preserved: a bundle of S-twisted doam palm leaf was tied to the top of the mat, parallel to the twining rows, with sZ2 string of doam palm leaf (diameter 4.5/2.5).

12.2.6 STAKE AND STRAND BASKETRY

In locus 29.006 the base of a stake-and-strand basket was found (H-067). The center of the basket consisted of a cross of five horizontal bundles of three parallel culms, with four vertical bundles of six parallel culms, which were sandwiched by a second layer of five horizontal bundles of three parallel stems (see Figure 12-18). Thus the base of the basket started with 18 bundles of six parallel stems, held into place with twining. The fragment was in extremely bad condition, but it was possible to discern 18 rows of twining in Z-direction with single *Juncus* stems 2.5 mm in diameter.

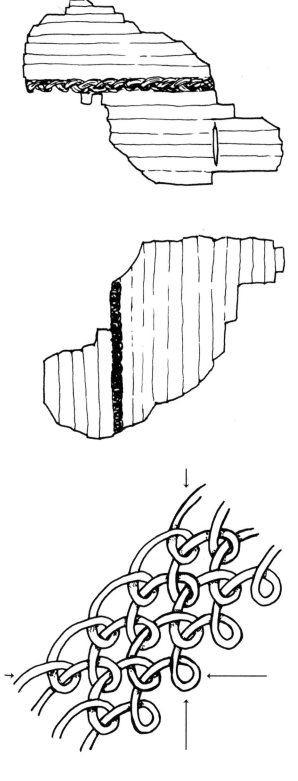

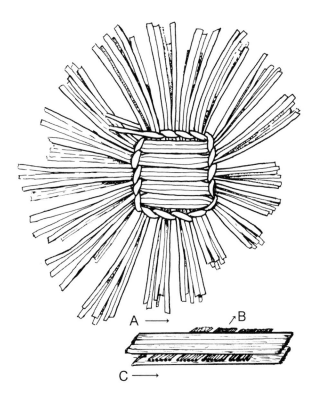

Figure 12-18 Schematic rendering of the center of stake-and-strand basket H-067. Not to scale. Drawing by W. Z. Wendrich.

Figure 12-19 Appearance of the knotless netting (H-147): one side (top) seems to consist of horizontal lines, the other side (middle) seems to consist of vertical lines, while the fabric in actuality is built up diagonally (bottom). Scale 1:1 for fragments, not to scale for detail. Drawing by W. Z. Wendrich.

12.2.7　KNOTLESS NETTING

Five fragments of knotless netting were retrieved from the east and west balk trim of trench 33 (H-147 and H-148). Although this seems improbable, given that they were found on opposite sides of the trench, they probably were part of the same object. Their context cannot be linked to a specific locus, but they can be firmly dated to the first or second century AD. The knotless netting was made with a coarse fiber, presumably a coarse type of flax. This type of fabric is built up of interlinking loops (Figure 12-19). The appearance of the knotless netting (H-147) is misleading. On one side of the fabric it seems to consist of horizontal lines, while the other side shows vertical lines. In fact the fabric is built up diagonally to both orientations.

This knotless netting differs from the type found in 1996 in trench 10 (Wendrich1998: 262-263), but is consistent with knotless netting found at other Egyptian sites (Wendrich 1999b: 176).

12.3　WOVEN MATTING AND ARCHITECTURE

As illustrated clearly by Table 12-1, most of the basketry was found in the early Roman trash dump, where the preservational circumstances are favorable for organic materials. In other trenches, textiles, leather, wood, basketry, and matting rarely survived. In some cases, however, impressions, soil color, and even the survival of some of the fibers, indicate that these materials were once present. In 1995, the coloration pattern of the soil provided information on the base of a large, oval, coiled basket that once stood in front of the bronze statue of a goddess in the Western Shrine (Wendrich and Veldmeijer 1996:292). Similarly, in 1999 and 2000, impressions and soil colorations of matting showed that woven matting was used as extensively in the earlier periods of occupation, as we knew to be true for the latest phases. In 1996 large quantities of grass matting, woven on a grass string warp were found in several fifth-century AD contexts at the highest parts of the site (Wendrich 1998a: 253–258).

In 1999 and 2000, while excavating several buildings that were located nearer to the sea, at lower elevations, the soil colorations proved that fourth- and fifth-century occupation layers all once had an abundance of woven matting. In many cases the soil colorations provided information, not only on the type of matting, but also on the spacing of the warp threads and the size of the weft bundles (Plate 12-20, Table 12-21).

Plate 12-20　Detail of woven matting impression H-072 from trench BE99-28 (cf. Figure 4.77). Scale = 20 cm. Photograph by W. Z. Wendrich.

Warp Size	Space	Weft Size	Remark	Size Fragment	ID	Context
-	-	-	within tumble, originally used in wall	-	H-057	27.016
-	-	-	within tumble, originally used in wall	-	H-058	27.008
-	-	-	within tumble, originally used in wall	-	H-059	27.006
-	-	-	within tumble, originally used in wall	-	H-060	27.016
-	28	10	floor mat, warp orientation: E-W	1080 x 870	H-061 A	23.016
-	28	10	floor mat, warp orientation: E-W, trace of edge	1200 x 1130	H-061 B	23.016
-	30	10	floor mat, warp orientation: SW-NE	700 x 660	H-061 C	23.016
-	28	10	floor mat, warp orientation: SW-NE	280 x 280	H-061 D	23.016
-	28	10	floor mat, warp orientation: SW-NE	140 x 240	H-061 E	23.016
8/5	18.5	8.5	4 zS2 warp strings, 10 weft grass bundle extant	110 x 130 x 9.5 th.	H-064	29.002
-	30	10	within tumble, used in wall	180 x 300	H-069	32.013
-	-	10	matting in E balk, on tumble in windblown sand. orientation N-S, part of awning or floor mat	1000 x ?	H-070	32.018
-	35.7	10	floor mat, irregular patch with some white gypsum specks, same level as the H-061 mats	600 x 440	H-071	32.019
6	40	10	floor mat, warp orientation: SW-NE, approx. 28 warp strings and 54 weft bundles. White gypsum specks. On surface 28.038 (Figures 4-77 and 12-15)	1270 x 520	H-072	28.034
5	34	11.5	floor mat, warp orientation E-W, approx. 18 warp strings and 186 weft bundles. Fraying at edges, white gypsum specks and dark line and spot (ancient termite activity?). On surface 28.038	840 x 1390	H-073	28.042
-	-	-	fibers indicating presence of grass matting	-	H-122	34.008
-	-	10	fibers in which some bundles can be recognized	-	H-165	32.013
-	-	-	only grass fibers	-	H-200	27.002
-	-	-	only grass fibers	-	H-201	32.017
-	-	-	only grass fibers from matting in tumble, under ashlar 34.010, originally used in wall		H-202	34.014
5.5	28.5	8	on occupation surface 34.019, N of wooden beam	360 x 220	H-203	34.019
-	-	-	on occupation surface 34.019, SE corner of trench	350 x 430	H-204	34.019
-	-	-	on occupation surface 34.019, under wooden beam	360 x 280	H-205	34.019
-	-	-	grass fibers, on top of doorway area, used in wall only in the southern trench extension	-	H-206	37.006
-	-	-	traces in the entire courtyard space, used in wall	-	H-207	37.008
-	-	-	fibers, in front of staircase 37.035, used in wall	-	H-208	37.026
-	-	-	fibers, covering installation 37.041	-	H-209	37.041
-	-	-	fibers, collapse of wall 41.004 or perhaps the matting was part of the roof construction	160 x 42	H-210	41.009
-	-	-	fibers, some traces of bundles, N of wall 41.004	150 x 70	H-211	41.009

Table 12-20   Woven matting recorded from soil colorations, impressions, and grass fibers, in order of basketry ID number. The weft space is by definition 0 and has, therefore, not been listed in the table.

The grass mats were thick and quite heavy, so they were used mostly on the floor or low benches for sitting and sleeping. Table 12-20 illustrates that the function of these woven mats was not only floor matting, but in many cases the thick fabric was also used in the architecture at Berenike. In some cases (as in H-210) the context gives rise to the suggestion that the mats were sometimes used in the construction of the roof. In order to improve the horizontal integration of the rows of coral heads, layers of matting were sometimes incorporated into the walls. This has been attested extensively in the fourth- and fifth-century AD buildings. We found remains of woven matting within the wall tumble and reused matting *in situ* in walls (for instance in trenches BE98-20 and BE99-27), as well as dark lines of decayed matting visible in between the rows of coral in several trenches excavated in the fourth-century ring east of the town's center and the fifth-century areas at the eastern edge of the city.

12.4   Conclusion

The abundance of basketry and matting found in the 1999 and 2000 seasons has provided important new insights into the lives and occupations of the occupants of Berenike. It is, for instance, possible to discern differences in the pattern of trash disposal in different areas of the early Roman trash dump. If we compare the finds from trenches BE99-31 and BE00-33 then it is clear that the trash deposited in the area of trench BE00-33 is less worn and battered than that deposited in trench BE99-31. The basketry found in trench BE00-33 is more the household type, with matting from shelters and windbreaks, small coiled containers, and a sieve that broke and was thrown out.

By contrast, the basketry from trench 31 looks as if it has been used, reused, repaired, and used once more. Furthermore, this trench produced most of the "foreign," apparently northern-Indian made, basketry: bamboo shelters, that are very different from the indigenous sewn plait matting made of doam palm leaf; the Indian cotton ring-shaped pot stand and the coarse matting made of the smoothly glossy "material A." Then there is the evidence of shipping: twined straps probably used to tie down cargo, a convenient type of strong strips of twined netting that can be adapted to the size of the load, interconnected, and pulled to fit, precisely the type of equipment needed to make ready a merchant ship for immediate departure.

CHAPTER 13 ⌒

PERSONAL ADORNMENTS

P. FRANCIS, JR.

The human adornments recovered from excavations at Berenike fall into three classes. One consists of beads, small objects meant to be strung and usually, though not exclusively, employed as personal ornaments. The second is bangles, rigid, open rings worn on the wrist. The third is a miscellaneous group, including cabochons (gems or glass to be mounted into jewelry), rings, and other types of jewelry. Due to the classification of artifacts used at Berenike, the author has been able to examine only some of these latter objects. Other specialists have identified ornaments in their reports.

This chapter will discuss some issues of the first two groups: beads and bangles. Details and the consideration of all the ornaments will be presented in a separate publication. Here an attempt will be made to put these objects into context, including their role at Berenike, and the importance the Berenike assemblage has in wider spheres.

13.1 MIDDLE EASTERN GLASS BEADS

Glass beads in the Middle East and those presumed exported from there are rather common. Yet, there is little information on them. This may seem ironic given the enormous archaeological efforts in this region, but it is a manifestation of the general scholastic disinterest in beads. Whether this happened because most early archaeologists were men and regarded beads as "women's trifles" or because of the sheer complexity of nearly any bead assemblage is difficult to say. Fortunately, the old prejudice is quickly changing.

Middle Eastern glass beads were once thought to be Phoenician (Francis 1985). Later writers generally called them "Roman," while some modern commentators label them "Early Islamic." None of this is enlightening. In 1994, the author embarked on a program to sort out the glass beads of the region. The archaeological literature was of limited help. Provenances and dates were useful, but the beads were usually poorly described and rarely well illustrated. It was difficult to know which bead was being discussed. The growing corpus of popular bead literature has many good color photographs and sometimes discussions of technical matters. These help identify the beads, but as all were obtained from the antiquities market, no provenances were available.

The most useful information came from excavated assemblages that the author had personally catalogued. In these cases provenance, date, and an adequate description of a particular bead was obtainable. The author has catalogued or closely examined beads from Fustat, Quseir al-Qadim, and Nubian cemeteries in Egypt; Aqaba, Jordan; Siraf and Nishapur, Iran; and importing sites in south, southeast, and east Asia.

The bead assemblages of none of these sites come close to that of Berenike. Not only are the estimated 4,200 beads the largest such group, but Berenike is also the most carefully excavated of these sites. Moreover, personal participation in the campaigns has allowed for contact with and feedback from the excavators and other specialists, which have proven most helpful. Berenike did not span the entire period of glass beadmaking in the Middle East, but the Hellenistic and Roman periods covered by its occupation are a critical time in the history of these beads. The author formed an outline of the development of Middle Eastern glass beads at Berenike during the 1998 season (Francis 1999).

Glass was invented in Mesopotamia approximately 4,500 years ago. Egypt began making it about a millennium later. However, dynastic Egypt rarely made glass beads, using faience, stones, and other materials for that purpose. Egypt stopped making glass altogether a few centuries before the invasion of Alexander (Harden 1987:3).

Soon after the founding of Alexandria, glassmakers, probably from Syria (herein used in the sense of the Roman province of that name), moved there to ply their craft, and Alexandria became celebrated for its glass. Although we have little direct evidence for Alexandrine glassmaking, its products were extolled in their day. Strabo (*Geography* 16.2.25) commented on "many-colored [polychrome in the Greek] and costly designs" made by workers in Alexandria. Diocletian listed Alexandrine glass at a higher price than other glassware (Kurinsky 1991:146). It is widely assumed that most fine glass vessels of the period, including wheel cut, cameo, millefiori, cage cups, gold-glass, and other luxury wares, were made in Alexandria (Nicholson 1993:67–69).

There was, however, a problem. Glassmaking requires a high temperature for which wood was the only viable fuel. Wood is scarce in modern Egypt as it was in antiquity. This is attested by imports (Bagnall 1993:42) and the high price put on even a single tree (Lewis 1986:145). At Berenike virtually all wood used in construction and a considerable amount used for charcoal was teak, obtained, most likely, from dismantled ships (Vermeeren 2000). The luxury products made at Alexandrine glasshouses no doubt gave the industry enough influence and wealth to import wood for their furnaces. Beadmakers, however, were not so well positioned.

The traditional way to make beads was to have molten glass held in crucibles in a furnace. The worker took an iron rod (a mandrel) and twisted some glass around it to build up a wound bead. This method, still practiced in what was once Syria as well as elsewhere, requires the constant burning of wood for the entire workday. From early in the Hellenistic era, new styles of beadmaking emerged in Egypt that (with one exception) did not require large amounts of wood. Rather, glass made at Alexandria, either as mosaic rods, flat plates, or even scrap glass, was formed into beads by methods never previously employed. Most of these "new" techniques persisted in Egypt until the collapse of the glass industry with the coming of the Crusades in the twelfth century.

The beads were made by a variety of means, which can be classified as "manipulated glass beads." Three or more pieces were fused together around a wire (fused bead). A flat mosaic chip was pierced through the sides (pierced bead). A similar chip might be pierced through the center and the ends folded up the wire (pierced-and-folded bead). A strip of glass could be folded around a wire and the two ends fused (single-strip folded bead). Two strips of glass could be folded around a wire and the four ends fused (double-strip folded bead). Pioneer bead researcher, Horace C. Beck (1928:61–62), described some of these methods including single- and double-strip folding and piercing-and-folding, though he did not assign names to all of them.

Mosaic chips and striped-glass plaques were formed into beads by different methods. At Berenike a striped white and blue plaque was found made into beads by single-strip folding, double-strip folding, piercing, and piercing-and-folding. "Eye canes" were made into beads by double-strip folding, piercing-and-folding, and piercing through the side (the latter is not yet attested at Berenike). These different methods of treating the same glass element suggest that the beads were made in more than one small workshop (Francis 2000:220).

The most remarkable of these beads were so well made that when the author looked at them in the 1998 season he thought they were simple wound beads. They are short bi-cones (two cones joined at their bases) of monochrome glass and are rather common at Berenike. It was not until the 2000 season that microscopic examination of these beads revealed that they were not wound beads and had some unusual characteristics:

1. The perforations were always conical. This happens when beads are wound on the tip of a tapered mandrel, but it is rare that all beads of the same size and shape would be wound at the mandrel's tip.

2. Around one aperture was one, often two, small "folds." Experiments revealed that such irregularities could occur on beads made at a lamp (a concentrated heat source outside a furnace, using prepared canes of glass), because of the force exerted to pull the bead off the mandrel. Furnace-wound beads are slipped off the mandrel more easily because iron contracts slightly faster than glass and for a short time the bead is loose and can be knocked off the mandrel. It is conceivable that such a pattern could be made on a furnace-wound bead, but it would be rare.

3. The glass appeared to encircle the perforation, a sure sign of a wound bead. However, under a microscope it was evident that only the glass at the surface swirled around the perforation. Under the surface, it had a different orientation, along the axis of the perforation.

After a little experimenting with local clay, it appeared that a complex form of the pierced-and-folded method made these beads. A square of glass was heated and pierced in the center. It was then folded up the wire. The distal end (farthest from the worker) was then marvered (rolled along a heat-resistant surface) to form into a cone. Then the proximal end, with two "flaps" of glass, was marvered into a cone (perhaps after the "flaps" were pushed together). The result was a bi-cone with a small aperture at the distal end where the glass had been pierced and a larger one at the proximal end, indicating that the mandrel was tapered. At the risk of an unwieldy term, the author calls these "pierced-folded-and-marvered beads."

We do not know where these manipulated beads were made. There is slight evidence that glassworking was carried out in villages outside of Alexandria (Nicholson 1993:70). The limited Polish excavations at Kôm el-Dikka in Alexandria have uncovered nothing to suggest that these beads were made there. These beads may not have been made in the city, but in its suburbs or in villages in the Delta. Glassmaking necessitates a high temperature, but once made, glass will soften with much lower heat. Annealed soda-lime glass (the type we are dealing with here) softens at 460° C (860° F). Special products of the Alexandrine glassmakers (such as mosaic canes or striped plaques) or scrap glass from their workshops could have gone to private homes to be turned into beads on a fire no more intense than that used for cooking.

Conversely, the other unique glass beads made in Egypt may have had much closer connections to the principal Alexandrine industry. These are segmented beads, made by rolling a warm tube of glass over a grooved stone to form constrictions along its length. The tube was cut up into individual or multiple beads. A special type of segmented bead was the gold-glass bead, made from a thin tube coated with gold foil that was slipped into a wider tube before the segmenting process began. There is evidence that segmented beads were made in Alexandria, in the form of a number of the stone molds and some glass wasters found at Kôm el-Dikka (Rodziewicz 1984:241–243, pl. 72). An important element of this production is the manufacture of the tubes. That would have required molten glass, rather than simply softened glass.

A further difference between manipulated glass beads and segmented beads is seen in the structure of their industries when the varieties of beads made by each group are plotted. The seeming "families" of the manipulated group are an artifact of bead nomenclature. Pierced, pierced- and-folded, pierced-folded-and-marvered, or single- and double-strip folded beads do not really represent a development or an evolution in beadmaking. Rather, they are distinct techniques.

On the other hand, the large variety of segmented beads at Berenike (the greatest variety ever recorded) was the result of a single process. All such beads began with the production of tubes, were constricted by the stone molds, were cut apart, and were either reheated or left as is. Compound glass (two layers of different colors), gold-glass, striped, and twisted striped segmented beads underwent operations to the tube before being molded. Beads with added balls or bosses and those with collars (extra glass around the apertures) were created with special molds. Flattened, decorated (added glass elements), and grooved segmented beads were treated after being molded. Each of these types is only a variation on a theme and could presumably be made by any beadmaker(s) when desired.

In sum, the manipulated glass beads with their variety of techniques, the use of cast-off or especially purchased (mosaic canes, striped plaques) glass elements, and employment of low-temperature fires likely represent an amorphous group of individuals or households producing beads. On the other hand, the industry producing segmented beads appears to have been more organized, needed access to a glass furnace, and was located in the center of Alexandria, at least in late Roman times. They were probably closely allied to the glassmakers of Alexandria and perhaps even enrolled in a glassworking guild.

Finally, there are two other tentative observations that need to be tested more rigorously. One is that some elements of glass beadmaking appear to precede similar developments in glass vessels. This seems especially true of gold-glass beads, which may predate blowing (if that is how the tubes were made), the use of clear glass, and perhaps the use of sandwich gold-glass. The other is that while segmented beads in general, and especially gold-glass beads, were widely traded from Berenike to South, Southeast, and even East Asia, the same cannot be said of the various manipulated beads, which are not found in the same numbers, if at all, in Asian littoral sites.

13.2 CARNELIAN BEADS

Carnelian was by far the most common semiprecious gemstone used for beads at Berenike. It is much more difficult to source stone beads than glass ones because they exhibit less diagnostic variations and stone bead-making is more conservative than its glass counterpart (Francis 2001:12). There are, however, some characteristics of the process that have permitted identification of lapidaries, especially those of western and south India (Francis 2001:103–125). Here the same criteria will be applied in an attempt to distinguish between carnelians made in Egypt and those imported from one of the Indian industries.

The first step in making stone beads is to chip the raw material into a crude shape called a "rough-out." The rough-out is then refined either by grinding it into a blank or removing tiny chips by a percussion technique known as "pecking." The remaining steps are polishing, dimpling, and drilling. Stone beads may be polished by abrasion (fine-grained stones, emery embedded in lac, teak, copper, and bamboo have all been recorded for this process) or by being tumbled (traditionally by putting the beads with water and agate dust in a leather bag and agitating it).

Drilling may be done with any stone harder or tougher than the one being drilled or with a softer drill and abrasion. By the late centuries BC, Indians had developed double-tipped diamond drills (Pliny, *Natural History* 37.15.60–61) and that technology probably reached Egypt by the time Berenike was a functional port. Before drilling, the stone is "dimpled," given a rough place for the drill to "bite." Chipping, pecking, grinding, and a drill bit larger than the final one are used for this process. Drilling may be done from one or both sides (with the perforations meeting in the interior of the bead). The second method is preferable, because drilling from one side causes the bead's distal end to break out, leaving an unsightly scar.

In the western Indian stone-bead industry, rough-outs are ground, dimpled, and drilled, and then polished. Oblates and other simple forms have been tumble-polished for a long time; faceted beads were not routinely tumbled until the tenth century. In the south, rough-outs were pecked, then polished by abrasion, and only then dimpled and drilled. Both areas principally used chip dimpling or a larger drill bit, and both drilled beads from both sides. It is not always possible to discern all steps used in stone beadmaking. Whether rough-outs were ground or pecked can only be decided by looking at beadmaking waste. However, the order of polishing and drilling, the method of polishing, the type of dimple, and whether a bead was drilled from one or both sides is usually capable of interpretation.

As noted above, there were some unfinished carnelian beads at Berenike, and a few that had been drilled from only one side, suggesting that these might have been locally made (Francis 2000:213). Study of additional specimens and reexamination of ones from previous seasons strongly suggest that a group of carnelian beads is almost certainly Egyptian. They tend to be small, rarely more than 6 mm in length or diameter and often less. The stone is often darker than the imported beads. Carnelian shades vary, but some of these beads are so dark that they are listed as sard (brown carnelian). There is not much variety in shape. There are oblates, suboblates, and barrels, but most are bi-cones, including hexagonal bi-cones.

The technical details best set these carnelian beads apart from those imported from India. Many of them are rather crude and drilled from one side only, an old Egyptian practice (Lucas and Harris 1962:42). They were polished by abrasion and then drilled, the dimpling done by grinding or using a larger drill bit. Abrasion polishing before drilling was (and still is) practiced in south India, but dimpling by grinding is never recorded there, and beads were drilled from both sides. While these technical differences cannot categorize every carnelian bead at Berenike into western Indian, southern Indian, or Egyptian, it accounts for the great majority of them.

13.3   AN EXTRAORDINARY SURFACE FIND

During the 1999 season a relatively large (20.0 mm in diameter and 17.0 mm in length) decorated bead was recovered on the surface (see Plate 13-1). It is the most extraordinary bead found to date at Berenike. It belongs to the class known as "East Javanese mosaics" (Francis 2001:134–136), also called *Jatim* beads (Adhyatman and Arifin 1993:62–65; 1996:64–67); *Jatim* is the Bahasa Indonesian abbreviation for East Java.

These beads were made on apparently older cores of wound and perhaps drawn or sintered glass. They are covered with one or more types of mosaic chips, sliced very thinly, suggesting that they were imports, likely from Egypt. The one at Berenike is coated all over with thin chips of a yellow surrounding red "bulls-eye." There is no precise parallel from Adhyatman and Arifin (1993; 1996), but several are comparable. The upper left bead in Plate 50 (Adhyatman and Arifin 1993:47; 1996:49) has similar yellow-over-red cane slices as well as more-complex cane slices. The last bead in the second row in Plate 56 (Adhyatman and Arifin 1993:50;

1996:52) and several in the upper left of Plate 64 (Adhyatman and Arifin 1993:57; 1996:59) have similar canes with different color combinations.

The dating of these beads is still imprecise. The Dutch excavated a few during the colonial period. Their dates relied heavily on ceramics, which were principally Tang Chinese (AD 618–906). They are so popular on the antiquities market (where they are mistakenly called "Majapahit beads"), and Indonesian archaeology is so poorly funded that they have never been found in excavated contexts in Indonesia. All those in Adhyatman and Arafin (1993; 1996) are from unexcavated contexts.

Adhyatman and Arafin (1993:67; 1996:69) note the connections with Tang ceramics, gold-glass beads, and collar beads and suggest a date of manufacture from about 300 to 900. Tang ceramics are no older than the early seventh century. Gold-glass beads were made for a long period, about 1,500 years in Egypt, and cannot be used for dating purposes. Collar beads, mostly a product of Arikamedu, India, did disappear around AD 300 (Francis 1986:117).

Plate 13-1   East Javanese mosaic bead. Scale = 4 cm. Photograph by S. E. Sidebotham.

The discovery of one of these beads at Berenike, especially since it is a surface find, suggests a date of the mid-sixth century AD, when the port was abandoned. There is always the possibility of an intrusion, but except for one brass-coated plastic bead (BE94-01.*007*) there are no intrusions at the site. It is one of the "cleanest" bead assemblages that the author has ever encountered. We are safe to assume that the bead was lost or abandoned close to the end of occupation of Berenike.

East Javanese beads are scarce anywhere beyond Java, though they have been found elsewhere in Indonesia in Sumatra and Kalimantan (southern Borneo). They are among the "bead money" on the island of Palau and have been found in the Philippines and Malaysia (Francis 2001:135). They have never before been identified west of the Malay Peninsula.

The question arises as to how the bead arrived at Berenike. Rome had no direct knowledge of Java. While the succeeding Arabs traded with Srivijaya, centered on Sumatra, the first Western geographer to refer to East Java ("Mul-Java") was Wassaf around 1300 (Tibbetts 1989:151–152). A traveler from South Asia could have brought it to Berenike, but these beads are not known in either India or Sri Lanka.

There is another possibility: the Cinnamon Route (Miller 1969). Cinnamon and the similar but distinct cassia (the ancients made the distinction) were known in Egypt and the Levant for a long time. Classical writers said they came from Arabia or East Africa. Casson (1989:122–124) suggested they were trans-shipped from India to East Africa, though Casson does not explain why the Indians did not bring them to Egypt. Pliny (*Natural History* 12.52.88) said that the spices were brought to East Africa from a great distance on "rafts" that took (an undoubtedly exaggerated) almost five years to make the round trip voyage (cf. Miller 1969:156). This sounds like Malays (in the broadest ethnic sense), who, after all, colonized Madagascar at an early date.

They would have been part of an extensive maritime system that included what is now southern Vietnam. This may help explain why there are so many more Roman beads and medallions at Oc Eo, Vietnam, than at the much-closer emporium of Arikamedu, on the Coromandel (southeastern) coast of India (Francis 2001:224 n. 12). Pliny said that in exchange for the spices, the traders returned with "brooches, armlets, and necklaces. And that trade depends chiefly on women's fidelity to fashion." (Pliny, *Natural History* 12.52.88, quoted in Miller 1969:156) This is not the forum to solve this problem, but this anomaly of a bead does raise the possibility.

13.4 CONUS SHELL BEADS

Mollusk shell has been widely employed for beads, especially in prehistoric times and by people living far from the sea. Numbers of beads at Berenike were made from whole or cut shells. By far most common were beads made from small conus shells. This large genus consists of about 400 species with a global distribution, though especially in the Indo-Pacific faunal zone (Eisenberg 1981: 133–147, 192).

Conus shells are favored for beads because the usual thick columella of univalves (the central supporting structure) is absent or reduced. That makes it possible to grind away the apex (protoconch) and string the whole shell. It is also common to smash the base, grind the apex and the jagged edge of the remaining spire, and form a discoidal bead. This process is fairly simple and speedy (Francis 1982a; 1988:28–30).

Oddly, there were no beads made from cowry (*Cypreaidae*) at Berenike. There was an excavated example with a crushed dorsal. It may have been a bead in the process of being made, but it was more likely accidentally broken. This is surprising, not only because of the global use of cowries, but also because of their status throughout the dynastic period, especially as "cowroids" (Shaw and Nicholson 1995:73), cowry-shaped amulets of faience, semiprecious stones, and gold. The modern Ababda nomads employ cowries and *Atyidae* (paper or little bubble) shells for decoration. Both are available in the Red Sea; inquiries should be made as to where the Ababda obtain them, but cowries, at least, are marketed worldwide.

Who used the conus beads? Greeks in the Neolithic and Bronze Ages used the small local *Conus mediterraneus*, but their function is not clear. Some were pierced through the large whorl and could have served as beads, but gaming pieces, toys, and garment and fishing weights are considered as likely. Many were not pierced, and none was worked as they are at Berenike (Reese 1983:356).

If either the Egyptian or Greek populations of Berenike used these shell beads or if they were regular articles of export, one would expect them to be distributed rather evenly in chronological terms. That is not the case. Of the 10 conus shell beads, one was from a surface clean of a trench and can, therefore, be assumed to be late; five were from late Roman deposits, one from a fifth–sixth-century AD context, and two from at the earliest a fourth-century AD context. Only one earlier example (a spire disc) was from a locus dated by the ceramics as Flavian (AD 69–96).

This suggests that the Eastern Desert dwellers used these beads. There is a consensus that beginning in the fourth century AD some of these desert nomads became a substantial element in the revitalized port, based on ceramics (Sidebotham and Wendrich 1998:452) and food refuse (Van Neer and Ervynck 1998:378). As noted at the beginning of this section, inland people especially favor shell beads. While the Eastern Desert dwellers at Berenike were not "inland," they probably thought of themselves that way, evidenced by their shunning of abundant marine food resources. There may be other explanations for this phenomenon; perhaps we shall learn more with additional excavations. It would be particularly interesting to learn who was making these shell beads.

13.5 GLASS BANGLES

Bangles are solid rings worn on the wrist (or less often the ankle). The literature usually refers to them as bracelets, but this term encompasses many other sorts of jewelry. The word *bangle* (from the Hindi) makes a useful distinction. There are bangles of glass, shell, horn, clay, and possibly cuttlebone (the interior shell of squids) at Berenike, but those considered here are the largest group: made of dark, usually black, glass.

These bangles are substantial pieces, ranging from 5.8 mm to 14.1 mm in width and from 3.2 mm to 6.6 mm in thickness. The interior diameters are from 30 mm to 100 mm; all pieces recovered were fragments, so this was estimated with the help of a chart. Most have plano-convex sections. Most of the thinner ones are plain, but the wider and thicker ones have decorations, principally of incised grooves and/or dots. A few decorative patterns are different from those reported by Spaer (1988); these will be detailed in a forthcoming monograph. None of the stamped figurative decorations on Palestinian bangles (Spaer 1988:58) was found at Berenike.

Making seamless bangles can be done in several ways. Spaer (1988:52) explains the technique in this manner: "A small bit of hot glass was pierced with a metal rod and in a fast motion (with or without the aid of an additional tool) detached from the rod, to which it tends to stick. It was then rotated on the rod, while frequently reheated, until it acquired the desired ring form."

While this may be possible, piercing a piece of glass (that has to be sitting on something) is not found in first-hand descriptions of this operation. These are: Theophilus' twelfth-century explanation of making finger rings (Hawthorne and Smith 1979:72–73); Gardi's (1969:99) description of banglemaking at Bida, Nigeria; this author's own account of traditional banglemaking at Purdalpur, India (Francis 1982b: 21); and a similar one of the same place by Kock and Sode (1995:15–16). Theophilus and traditional Indians wind a bead in the furnace. Indians expand it between two rods and then pull it up a large clay cone to the proper size. Theophilus tells his readers to jab the mandrel into a wooden post and continue to heat the glass and spin the mandrel, so that the glass expands and moves up the mandrel until it is the right size. In Nigeria, a worker removes glass from its crucible; the glass is then held over the crucible. Other workers take large drips from this glass onto their mandrels, wind them into beads, and enlarge them by heating and rotating the glass. Exactly how the Romans accomplished this process remains unknown.

No site has yet been identified as making these bangles. Given the heat necessary to produce them, Spaer (1988:60–61) is probably correct to assert that they were most likely made in one or more localities in Syria-Palestine and were imports to Egypt. There is no evidence in Asia for their export from Berenike.

The bangles at Berenike fall into the range of dates suggested by Spaer (1988:51–52). They appear initially in the third century AD and become increasingly common over the next three centuries. Spaer had trouble with the chronology because much of her evidence came from tombs rather than closely dated levels or loci. She also had to wrestle with the problem of the Roman-early Islamic transition (Spaer 1988:53), which does not concern us at Berenike. Bangles became even more important and colorful in the early Islamic period (Spaer 1992). Though it is hard to believe, bangles are even less studied than beads and Spaer's pioneering work is to be commended.

Aside from these technical details, a major question is, Who wore these bangles at Berenike? Since they were not exports, they might tell us something about the demographics of the site. To this end, a search of the literature and the Internet and queries of colleagues as to who may have worn them is revealing.

All professional students in the region agree that men would not have worn them. Hence, girls wore the small ones and adult women the larger ones.

These bangles are chunky and not particularly attractive suggesting a low social status for their owners. A. Bülow-Jacobsen, moderator of the online *The Papyrological Bulletin*, replied to the author's query. Bülow-Jacobsen's experience of these bangle fragments at Mons Claudianus and four small Roman forts along the road to Quseir suggested that camp followers or prostitutes wore them. Bangles were not necessarily, of course, a mark of prostitutes, but prostitutes were women and women wore bangles. Wives accompanied some of the higher officers, while common soldiers were allowed slaves as concubines (Starr 1982:113–114).

However, in the Palestinian context, Spaer (personal communication) noted that these bangles were found in the graves of at least middle-class women. Beginning as something of a novelty, they became part of many women's attires. She also suggests that they may have been a substitute for jet, which along with "a general vogue favoring the black color," was evident in late Roman times (Spaer 1988:52).

The bangles at Berenike are a mark of the female gender and were likely worn by all but the highest social strata. Further excavation will help determine if one class of women preferred them to another.

13.6   CONCLUSION

In the chapter on human ornaments published in the 1998 Berenike volume (Francis 2000), several aspects of the life of the site were revealed, including the Asian trading partners of the port, local ornament making, and the religious affiliation of some of its inhabitants. This chapter expands on some of these themes and has added new ones. These include: Egyptian beadmaking in both glass and carnelian; long-distance trade as far away as eastern Java, though probably indirect; and some demographic insights into the presence of the Eastern Desert dwellers and women. An understanding of beads is not yet in the tool kit of all archaeologists, but perhaps this report will suggest why it should be.

CHAPTER 14

JAR STOPPERS, SEALS, AND LIDS, 1999 SEASON

J. E. M. F. BOS

During the 1999 season, excavations unearthed 127 jar stoppers or fragments of stoppers from 10 trenches. The recording system and forms used last year were slightly modified for use this season. This season's study noted several techniques previously unrecorded at Berenike for the manufacture of stoppers; there was also evidence that stoppers were made along the Red Sea coast, perhaps at Berenike itself. These new types were added to the classification started last season (Bos 2000:277–281). This chapter presents a catalogue of the complete or nearly complete stoppers and unusual or previously unrecorded manufacturing techniques and decorations. The closing methods of the vessels varied depending upon the types of stoppers used: in most cases lids were employed, in two cases in the 1999 material in the form of flat wooden plates covering the vessel. Once the use of a seal was encountered. Because stoppers were most common, all fragments of stoppers, lids, and seals studied here are termed *stoppers* unless a more specific description is required. The distribution of stoppers across the site and manufacturing techniques will be discussed, as well as the prominent role these objects played in commercial activities at Berenike.

14.2 DISTRIBUTION

Table 14-1 represents the spatial distribution of the total number of stoppers across the site, which was relatively even. In this table, both small fragments and (nearly) complete stoppers are presented for the 10 contexts in which they were found. As seen last year, stoppers occur all across the site, in areas high above sea level as well as areas closer to the sea or at sea level, although stoppers made with organic material were not present in the lower areas of the site where the ground has a higher humidity due to the groundwater table. Again this year, stoppers came from trash deposits as well as from areas of occupation. Trenches BE99-26, BE99-29, and BE99-31 produced most of the stoppers. Plaster stoppers were recovered from balk collapse inside trench BE98-19 and from the sieve piles of trench BE95-4 (Building F). They were collected from the surface, but the sieve piles were not examined systematically. When BE95-4 was excavated, large quantities of gypsum plaster were found. The high groundwater table in that trench made it impossible to discern stoppers from the wet plaster surrounding them. After a few years of drying at the surface, however, the plaster that was dumped in unworked state became powdery, while the denser stoppers dried and were discernable in the white powdery mass.

Table 14-2 presents a list of loci of the 10 different trenches producing stoppers this season. All plaster plugs found in the region of Building F date to the fourth or fifth century AD and were only found in this area of the site in such great numbers. Trash dump contexts (trenches BE99-29 and BE99-31) produced the largest number and variety of types and sizes (cf. Bos 2000:276, Table 12-1) of stoppers. A type that appears thus far only in the trash dumps is the cork stopper. These stoppers all date to the first century AD. Stoppers preserving writing in black ink on top and made from coarse gray- or white-colored plaster (excavated from trenches BE99-10 and BE99-31) also came from early Roman contexts.

Context	Fragments	Nearly Complete	Total
BE99-10	6	4	10
BE98-19	1	1	2
BE99-22	2	0	2
BE99-23	1	2	3
BE99-26	23	4	27
BE99-27	6	1	7
BE99-28	0	2	2
BE99-29	11	4	15
BE99-30	0	1	1
BE99-31	40	11	51
surface	1	6	7
Total	91	36	127

Table 14-1   Spatial distribution of the stoppers found during the Berenike 1999 season.

Trench	Loci
BE99-10	*401, 344, 375*, trench clean
BE98-19	balk collapse
BE99-22	*104, 112*
BE99-23	*019, 022*
BE99-26	*022, 038, 035, 037, 041, 043, 049, south balk trim*
BE99-27	*006, 019, 020*
BE99-28	*036*
BE99-29	*001, 002, 012, 014, 016*
BE99-30	*005*
BE99-31	*002, 006, 007, 012, 014, 016, 017, 018, east and west balk trim, west balk collapse*
surface	1 m west of trench 10; sieve pile of BE95-04

Table 14-2   Loci of 10 trenches producing stoppers.

Context	Plaster	Mud	Pottery	Pottery round cut	Stone	Shell	Wood	Cork	Rope	Bitu-men	Unid.	Total
BE99-10	2	-	-	1	-	-	2	5	-	-	-	10
BE98-19	1	-	-	-	-	-	-	-	-	-	1	2
BE99-22	-	-	-	2	-	-	-	-	-	-	-	2
BE99-23	-	3	-	-	-	-	-	-	-	-	-	3
BE99-26	22	-	-	2	1	2	-	-	-	-	-	27
BE99-27	1	-	-	6	-	-	-	-	-	-	-	7
BE99-28	-	-	1	-	-	-	-	-	-	1	-	2
BE99-29	3	-	-	-	-	-	-	11	-	-	1	15
BE99-30	-	-	1	-	-	-	-	-	-	-	-	1
BE99-31	7	-	-	1	-	-	-	43	-	-	-	51
surface	6	1	-	-	-	-	-	-	-	-	-	7
Total	42	4	2	12	1	2	2	59	-	1	2	127

Table 14-3   Materials used for production of the stoppers found during the 1999 season.

14.2 MATERIALS AND TECHNIQUES

Nine different materials were attested this year: plaster, cork, an unidentified material, shell, bitumen, pottery, mud, stone and wood (Table 14-3). Some materials, which were attested last year to be used for entire stoppers, were not found this season, such as clay and the unidentified black material that was mostly found in trench BE98-10. Materials used for the production of stoppers recorded for the first time this season include shells, an unidentified material and bitumen. Again, following the pattern seen in previous seasons, plaster and cork were the materials most frequently used to make stoppers found at Berenike.

Several new types of plaster stoppers may be added to the typology that was started last season (Bos 2000:277–281) they are presented in Figure 14-4. The typology is based on the manufacturing technique of the stoppers, which obviously has a correlation with the material the stoppers were made from. Figure 14-4 shows the general shape of the newly added stopper types and outlines the material of the bung and other materials used. The new types are all different forms of plaster stoppers. Only in this stopper category could manufacturing techniques be distinguished and the largest variety of shapes and materials be found. Of stoppers that were made mainly of other materials the original shape, decoration and bungs were often not recovered and could not be reconstructed.

Excavations this season recovered no lids made of pottery, but two covers made of wood were excavated from trench BE99-10. They closed off two large early Roman storage vessels (loci 10.*361* and *362*) embedded in a floor or surface. Storage vessel 10.*361* contained 7.55 kg of black pepper (see Chapter 4, Plates 4-38, 39, 40). A new type of seal was found in trench BE99-10 (catalogue number 14), a bung made of plant material that closed off the neck of the jar. This jar neck was then covered by a piece of textile on which a black binding material was smeared to keep the seal in place. A piece of papyrus was stuck on top of that, probably onto the wet material (Figure 14-5). No traces of writing were found on the papyrus.

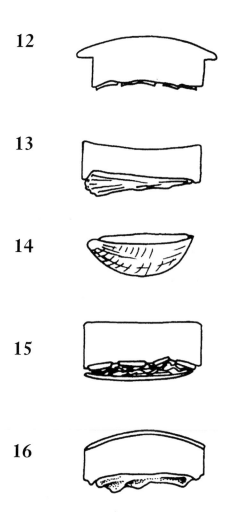

12

13

14

15

16

Figure 14-4   Addition to typology of stopper manufacture (for previously defined types number 1–11 see Bos 2000:277, fig. 12-3). Not to scale. Drawings by J. E. M. F. Bos.
12=plaster stopper with papyrus bung
13=plaster stopper with coral bung
14=plaster stopper with shell bung
15=plaster stopper with compound bung
16=plaster stopper with textile bung and mud slip

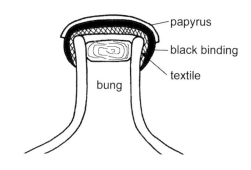

papyrus

black binding

textile

bung

Figure 14-5   Schematic drawing of a sealed jar (cf. catalogue number 14). Not to scale. Drawing by J. E. M. F. Bos.

Again this season many round-cut pottery sherds were found, some of which preserved traces of plaster or black binding material. Only when these sherds had some trace, indicating that they were used as the bung in connection with a stopper, were they recorded as part of the corpus of jar-sealing objects. These sherds were also collected, measured, and described. Round-cut sherds were found 12 times as isolated finds. In 10 of those cases, traces of plaster indicated that they had been parts of plugs, and, in three instances, black binding material was still visible, used to seal off the cavities between the vessel and the sherd. Only one time a round-cut sherd was found *in situ*, still part of a plaster stopper. Other types of bungs were small sherds (used in nine cases), textile (one case), plant fiber or leaves (nine cases), round-cut stone (one time), shell (two times, see Figure 14-4, type 14), coral (one time, Figure 14-4, type 13), and papyrus (one time Figure 14-4, type 12). Of the 127 stoppers and stopper fragments found, 35 preserved remains of a bung. This year no bowls or lids used as bungs were found. The textile bung discovered this season did not stretch out over the jar opening under the stopper, as found in examples previously recorded, but the textile found this year was bunched up (Figure 14-4, type 16). Coral and shell used as bungs were new this season and are a good indication that at least some of the vessels were sealed somewhere along the Red Sea coast and probably at Berenike. This season an example of the use of pieces of papyrus as bungs was found. Apparently, all kinds of discarded materials could be used in the stopper-making process. The enormous variety in materials used (especially in the plaster stoppers) suggests that whatever material came to hand that would serve the purpose of preventing the plaster from mixing with the vessel contents could be used to seal a container. This is best illustrated by a compound bung in which small sherds, palm leaf and a black binding material were used to close the vessel before plaster was poured onto the bung (catalogue number 13 and Figure 14-4, type 15).

Pop-top devices attested for the plaster stoppers this year ranged from one hole in the stopper (one time), impressions of small pieces of string at the side of the stopper (one time), to new kinds of pop-top devices, such as two holes in the center of the stopper (one time), shell serving as bung and as pop-top device (two times), and sherds at the side of the stopper. This last type is not new at Berenike and was attested in previous seasons (Dieleman 1998:266, catalogue number 1). In eight examples, a pop-top device could be reconstructed.

Thirteen specimens had extant traces of decoration. On the plaster stoppers, a red wash and a stamp were visible six times; an impression without wash was found in three cases. In two instances, stoppers preserved writing in black ink; one time red ink could still be seen. In one case, a piece of papyrus was stuck to the top of a seal as mentioned previously, and in one case two white stripes were visible on top of a mud stopper.

14.3 CATALOGUE

In the following catalogue, 21 of the 127 stopper fragments have been listed. Only those stoppers that were (nearly) complete and attested new fabrication methods or preserved traces of writing, have been incorporated.

1	*BE99 0564-Y-001*
Context:	surface southwest of trench BE95-04 (sieve heap, Building F)
Material:	plaster
Color:	*10YR 8/2* (very pale brown)
Dimensions:	diameter 90 mm; thickness 16.5 mm
Date:	unknown

The preservation of the stopper is very good, especially considering that the damp plaster has been exposed to the sun for a few years. Three-quarters of the stopper is still intact, and although the decoration is no longer clear, the outlines of a stamp are still visible. The diameter of the stamp is 80 mm and there is no wash discernable. The bottom of the stopper is very flat; a bung is also no longer discernable. These kinds of stoppers are very typical for this part of the site, and although they were found elsewhere in Berenike, they were less numerous than in this area inside and around Building F. This stopper came from the same context as catalogue numbers 2, 3, and 4.

2	*BE99 0564-Y-002*
Context:	surface southwest of trench BE95-04 (sieve heap, Building F)
Material:	plaster
Color:	*10YR 8/1* (white)
Dimensions:	diameter 100 mm; thickness 20.1 mm; length 100 mm; width 46.5 mm
Date:	unknown

About 50 percent of the original diameter of the stopper is extant. The material is very dry, but a stamp can still be seen. The center of the stamp probably contained decoration of some kind, but that can no longer be discerned. The letters around the edge cannot be read because the surface of the stopper has been heavily eroded. There still is a red wash (10YR 4/6 red) visible on the top of the stamp. This stopper came from the same context as catalogue numbers 1, 3, and 4.

3   *BE99 0564-Y-003*
Context: surface southwest of trench BE95-4 (sieve heap, Building F)
Material: plaster
Color: *7.5YR 8/1* (white)
Dimensions: diameter 140 mm; thickness 44.5 mm; length 120 mm; width 91 mm
Date: unknown
Bung: small sherds

There is still a very clear wash visible on the stopper (10YR 6/6, light red). The object originally had an *uraeus* (cobra) stamp; the tail of the *uraeus* is still visible. The stopper is very dry and numerous cracks preclude decipherment of letters around the edge. The diameter of the vessel this stopper originally sealed can still be discerned from the side and bottom of the stopper: 90 mm. Diameter of the stamp is 81.5 mm. The stopper came from the same context as catalogue numbers 1, 2, and 4. Comparable stoppers were found in Berenike (Dieleman 1998:273; Sundelin 1996:300-302) and at Myos Hormos/Quseir al-Qadim (Whitcomb and Johnson 1979:233).

4   *BE99 0564-Y-006* (Plate 14-6)
Context: surface southwest of trench BE95-4 (sieve heap, Building F)
Material: plaster
Color: *7.5YR 8/1* (white)
Dimensions: diameter 110 mm; thickness 65 mm; width 87 mm
Date: unknown
Bung: impression of coral. Pop-top device: impressions of a small string at the side of the stopper are extant.

The top of the stopper is very much decayed by the wet conditions in which it was preserved and the heat of the sun to which it was exposed after excavation. The bottom, however, was very well preserved in the sand and showed an impression of a new kind of material in Berenike used as a bung: coral. The stopper came from the same context as catalogue numbers 1, 2, and 3.

Plate 14-6   Catalogue number 4, bottom. Plaster stopper with impression of coral bung. Scale=5 cm. Photograph by B. J. Seldenthuis.

5   *BE99 0413-Y-007* (Plates 14-7 and 8)
Context: trench 29.002 PB 04
Material: could not be determined (perhaps plaster), very hard and preserving air bubbles. The color of the material is darker than plaster, however, and the substance is much harder.
Color: *10YR 5/4* (yellowish brown)
Dimensions: diameter 70 mm; thickness 10–21 mm
Date: first century AD
Bung: papyrus

Plate 14-7   Catalogue number 5, top. Scale=5 cm. Photograph by B. J. Seldenthuis.

Plate 14-8   Catalogue number 5, bottom. Impression of papyrus bung. Scale=5 cm. Photograph by B. J. Seldenthuis

This stopper shows another new material used as a bung at the site: papyrus. The object was found in the upper layers of the trash dump and was colored dark by the brown matrix that surrounded it.

6   *BE99 0413-Y-014*
Context: trench 29.*002* PB 04
Material: plaster
Color: *2.5Y 7.2* (light gray)
Dimensions: diameter 60 mm; thickness 18.8 mm
Date: first century AD (from AD 70 onward)
Bung: date palm fiber

No decoration at the top of the stopper is visible, but there is a large amount of fiber serving as a bung. Usually only the impression of the fiber rather than the fiber itself survives on the bottom of the stopper. The diameter of the vessel it originally sealed was 60 mm, judging from the shape and dimensions of the side of the stopper.

7   *BE99 3310-Y-015* (Plate 14-9)
Context: trench 31.*012* PB 19
Material: plaster
Color: *10YR 7/3* (very pale brown)

Dimensions: diameter could not be measured, thickness 26 mm; length 50 mm; width 40 mm
Date: mid- to late-first century AD
Bung: small sherds

The stopper is very fragmentary due to salt concretion. The top, however, is decorated with black ink, possibly representing a capital *alpha* or *delta*. No text is discernable.

Plate 14-9   Catalogue number 7, top. Plaster stopper fragment with remains of writing with black ink. Scale=5 cm. Photograph by B. J. Seldenthuis.

8   *BE99 1149-Y-024* (Plate 14-10)
Context: trench 29.*012* PB 17
Material: plaster
Color: *10YR 8/1* (white), 10YR 6/4 (light yellowish brown)
Dimensions: diameter 120 mm; thickness 22 mm; length 100 mm; width 75 mm
Date: mid- to late first century AD
Bung: impression of round-cut sherd

The stopper is concreted with salt, but a stamp remains visible on the top. The diameter of the stamp is 80 mm and no wash is left. The impression is most likely an *uraeus;* extant letters around the edge of the stopper are not legible.

9   *BE99 2754-Y-030* (Plate 14-11)
Context: trench 10.*401* PB 750
Material: plaster
Color: *10YR 7/2* (light gray)
Dimensions: diameter 90 mm; thickness 21 mm; width 80 mm
Date: early Roman, probably first century AD
Bung: small sherds

Plate 14-10   Catalogue number 8, top. Plaster stopper with remains of stamp. Scale=5 cm. Photograph by B .J. Seldenthuis.

Very well preserved stopper with illegible markings in black ink at the top. The stopper is not completely intact; about 60 percent of the original diameter is left. The diameter of the vessel is about 90 mm.

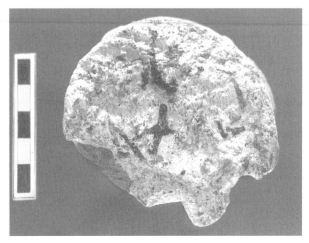

Plate 14-11   Catalogue number 9 top. Plaster stopper with ink markings. Scale=5 cm. Photograph by B. J. Seldenthuis.

10   *BE99 2755-Y-031*
Context: trench 31.*002* PB 11
Material: cork
Color: *10YR 5/3* (brown)
Dimensions: diameter 80 mm; thickness 20 mm; width 60 m
Date: poorly dated, early Roman

Very salt concreted, some black binding material visible at the sides of the stopper and some remnants of plaster

at the top. Most of the cork stoppers at Berenike have such traces, which make it likely that cork stoppers in general had a thin layer of plaster and binding material on the surface. The diameter of the jar neck was approximately 80 mm.

11   *BE99 3319-Y-033* (Plate 14-12)
Context: trench 26.*037* PB 60
Material: plaster and shell
Color: *10YR 8/1* (white)
Dimensions: diameter 40 mm; thickness 27 mm
Date: fifth century AD

The stopper was uncovered from the dump layers associated with the earliest building in the area. Plaster was pasted inside the shell that served probably as bung and pop-top device. This is the first appearance of this type of stopper in Berenike. A similar stopper was found this year (catalogue number 17) from the same area.

Plate 14-12   Catalogue number 11. Shell bung for plaster stopper. Scale=5 cm. Photograph by B. J. Seldenthuis

12   *BE99 2599-Y-035* (Plate 14-13)
Context: trench 31.*007* PB 09
Material: plaster
Color: *10YR 8/1* (white)
Dimensions: diameter 110 mm; thickness 34 mm
Date: mid- to late first century AD

The stopper preserves traces of red ink around the perimeter of the top. The plaster is coarser than the plaster used in the stoppers with the stamps and washes. The two kinds are very different both in decoration and material texture. The underside of this stopper has salt damage. The diameter of the neck of the vessel it sealed was 100 mm.

Plate 14-13   Catalogue number 12, top. Coarse plaster stopper. Scale=10 cm. Photograph by B. J. Seldenthuis.

Plate 14-15   Catalogue number 13, side. Scale=5 cm. Photograph by B. J. Seldenthuis.

13   BE99 1150-Y-037 (Plates 14-14 to 16)
Context: trench 19, middle trash deposit
Material: plaster
Color: *10YR 8/1* (white)
Dimensions: diameter 110 mm; thickness 74 mm
Date: early Roman, probably first century AD
Bung: compound bung

This stopper has a bung made of small sherds sticking into the plaster, palm leaf underneath and black binding material sealing off the vessel contents and keeping the leaves in place. The faint stamp (possibly *uraeus*) on the top of the vessel has a diameter of 78 mm. The wash over it is red (*2.5YR 4/4* dusky red).

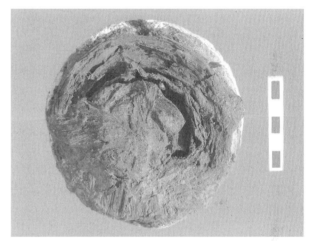

Plate 14-16   Catalogue number 13, bottom. Scale=5 cm. Photograph by B. J. Seldenthuis.

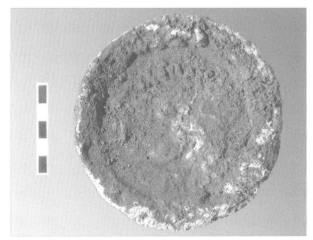

Plate 14-14   Catalogue number 13, top. Faint remains of stamp. Scale=5 cm. Photograph by B. J. Seldenthuis.

14   *BE99 2501-Y-039* (Plates 14-17 to 19)
Context: surface one meter west of trench 10
Material: mud with fiber temper, black binding material, and papyrus
Color: *10YR 6/3* (pale brown)
Dimensions: diameter 40 mm; thickness 20 mm
Date: fourth to fifth century AD
Bung: fiber

This seal covered a late Roman Amphora 3 rim that is 40 mm in diameter. The bung inserted into the neck of the jar is made of mud; a piece of textile was put over the bung and the jar neck; and black binding material was smeared over the textile and covered the entire jar neck. On top of the binding material is a piece of papyrus, probably stuck onto the wet material. The vessel has a hanging string extant around the jar neck.

15   *BE99 4270-Y-053*
Context: trench 10.*TC* PB 799
Material: plaster
Color: *10YR 8/2* (very pale brown)
Dimensions: diameter 90 mm; thickness 28mm
Date: fourth to fifth century AD

The stopper is well preserved, the plaster still hard. On the top of the stopper, a thin mud slip was applied over the smooth surface. The bung of the stopper left an impression of crumpled textile at the bottom. Textile was previously found serving as part of the stopper, but stretched over the neck of the vessel rather than bunched up.

16   BE99 3280-QQ/Y-086
Context: trench 28.*036* PB 48
Material: probably bitumen
Color: *10YR 3/2* (very dark grayish brown)
Dimensions: extant diameter 40 mm
Date: late fifth century AD on

The stopper, the first one made of bitumen, shows considerable decay. A source of bitumen is found at Gebel el-Zeit, 600 km north of Berenike on the Red Sea coast. This type of bitumen, however, most likely comes from the Dead Sea (see Chapter 5, section 5.2).

17   *BE99 3639-Y-089*
Context: trench 26.*022* PB 37
Material: plaster and shell
Color: *10YR 8/2* (very pale brown)
Dimensions: diameter 30 mm; thickness 23 mm
Date: fifth century AD on
Bung: shell

Very similar to catalogue no. 11. Both halves of the shell were used with some plaster between them serving as a bung and as pop-top device. The diameter of the vessel was *ca.* 24 mm. This is the first appearance of this type of stopper at Berenike. It was uncovered from use layers of the second building phase (dated to the fifth century AD) in the area.

18   *BE99 3471-Y-091* (Plate 14-20)
Context: trench 31.*014* PB 24
Bung: string
Date: second half first century AD

This stopper was excavated from the trash-dump area. It consists only of a piece of string inserted into the neck of a small Aswan trifoil flagon. This is the first appearance of string as a bung or a stopper at Berenike.

Plate 14-17   Catalogue number 14, top. Scale=1 cm. Photograph by B. J. Seldenthuis.

Plate 14-18   Catalogue number 14, side. Scale=1 cm. Photograph by B. J. Seldenthuis.

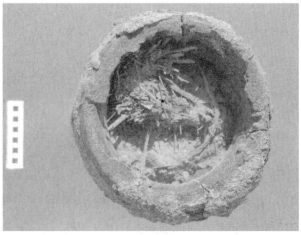

Plate 14-19   Catalogue number 14, bottom. Scale=1 cm. Photograph by B. J. Seldenthuis.

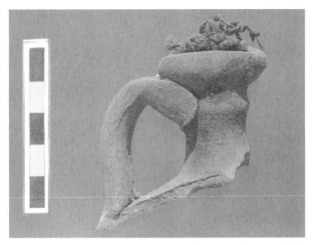

Plate 14-20 Catalogue number 18. Scale=5 cm. Photograph by B. J. Seldenthuis.

Plate 14-21 Catalogue number 20. Round-cut sherd with holes to create a pop-top device or children's game. Scale=5 cm. Photograph by B. J. Seldenthuis.

19 *BE99 4285-Y-092*
Context: trench 31-*BTE* PB 38
Material: plaster
Color: *10YR 7/2* (light gray)
Dimensions: diameter 120 mm; thickness 43 mm; length 100 mm; width 50 mm
Bung: small sherds
Date: early first century AD on

The stopper preserves a stamp on top that has the same diameter as the stopper itself. Some indeterminable letters survive. The wash is red (10YR 4/4, weak red) and the vessel and stamp diameter are 120 mm. The stopper is not very well preserved; the sides and edges are broken off, but the stamp is in good condition.

20 *BE99 1479-Y-105* (Plate 14-21, Figure 14-22)
Context: trench 30.*005* PB 08
Material: pottery
Color: *10YR 7/2* (light gray)
Dimensions: diameter 35.4 mm; thickness 6.3 mm
Date: fifth century AD

In the center of the stopper, two holes served as part of the pop-top device. A string could be passed through both in order to facilitate lifting the stopper from the vessel. This is also one of the few pottery stoppers found at the site; it came from wall tumble layers of one of the big buildings near the sea. The diameter of the vessel could be reconstructed at 35.4 mm. Alternatively this object could be interpreted as a game (van Beek 1989).

Figure 14-22 Pottery stopper with a reconstruction of a pop-top device. Not to scale. Drawing by J. E. M. F. Bos.

21 *BE99 0044-Y-106*
Context: trench 23.*019bis* PB 51
Material: tempered mud, organic temper
Color: *10YR 4/4* (dark yellowish brown)
Dimensions: diameter 38.3 mm; thickness 22.5 mm
Date: late fourth to fifth century AD

This stopper was found as part of the contents of an amphora that was embedded into a surface and the dump layer above (surface 23.*016* and layer 23.*022*). The stopper is in poor condition. The stopper is dry and powdery, but it is one of the very few mud stoppers that has been found more or less intact. On the top surface of the stopper there are three stripes of plaster; perhaps the original surface of the stopper was covered with plaster.

14.4   DISCUSSION

14.4.1   THE CONTEXT

The contexts in which the stoppers, lids and seals were found vary. An overview of the loci from which stoppers were uncovered, listed in Table 14-2, shows that very few came from occupation layers; most of the stoppers were found in trash dumps (BE97/98-19, BE99-29, BE99-31) or other dump areas of the site. Trench BE99-22 was a pottery-dumping area and the same is true for most of the loci in trench BE99-26 that produced stoppers. Similarly, the ones uncovered from trench BE99-10 mostly came from dump or fill strata between layers of occupation, as did stoppers from trenches BE99-27 and BE99-28. In addition to stoppers, BE98/99-23 also produced several amphora toes. Only in trenches BE99-26, BE99-28 and BE99-10 were stoppers found in occupational debris.

Based on the finds of the past two seasons, an attempt was made to interpret the association of stoppers in their specific contexts in order to draw conclusions on the use of stoppers, lids, and seals at Berenike. A careful consideration of the stoppers in some cases provided us with information on the activities in a certain area of the town related to loading and (re-) packaging. An example was Building F in trenches BE95-4 and BE97/98-17, where the stoppers and related finds suggest that the area in a late phase of its occupation perhaps functioned as a transshipment area (see following).

The intensity and type of use of an area where stoppers were found can be defined as follows. Occasional use of the contents of vessels closed with stoppers is characterized by a relatively small number of stoppers in the occupation layers. The types of stoppers would vary, and sometimes the jar neck, which was usually cut off in order to open the jar, would be retrieved. Most of the occupation layers that yield stoppers were of this kind. In 1999 the stopper finds from trenches BE99-27 and BE99-28 and some layers of trench BE99-10 could be interpreted this way.

Second, large numbers of one particular type of stoppers, in combination with broken-up jar necks, are an indication of an intense use of one specific type of content. In 1999 no occupational layers with this specific composition were found, but in 1998 the occupation layers in trench BE98-10 could be characterized thus. Unlike the 1998 season, trench BE99-10 did not produce small stoppers made of black binding material or plaster. Also the total number of stoppers from that trench differed considerably from the 1998 excavations, when a total of 59 stoppers was uncovered in trench 10. In contrast, BE99-10 yielded only 10 stoppers. Clearly, the activity in the later layers of trench 10, excavated in 1998, increased in comparison to the earlier occupation period, excavated in 1999. In addition, 1999 material does not represent large numbers of one specific type.

A third type of context identified, based on an analysis of the stoppers from 1998 and 1999, concerns areas where vessels were sealed. These occupation layers are characterized by the occurrence of one specific material, a relatively large number of stoppers and the raw material for making the stoppers. From the half-finished stoppers found in these contexts, it is clear that for vessels sealed in this area of Berenike mostly plaster was used. This activity was best represented in and around the area of Building F, where trenches BE95-04, BE95/96-07, and BE97/98-17 were excavated. In 1999 several of these stoppers were retrieved from that area.

14.4.2   STOPPERS, JAR TYPES, AND CONTENTS

An interesting question is how to define the relation between stopper type, stopper material, jar type and the contents that were sealed in the jar. Apart from the plaster stoppers, the excavations of 1999 yielded, for instance, 59 fragments of cork stoppers. Although some of these fragments were only a few centimeters in diameter, this is the largest material group for stoppers found this year. All cork dates to the first century AD and was found in the early Roman trash dumps in the northwestern part of the site. This can partly be explained by the fact that the preservation in that area is much better than in other parts of the site. Cork originated from the western part of the Roman Empire and is, on one level, an indication for specific trade activity in Berenike. On another level, this type of stopper may at some point provide an indication of the contents it once sealed. At the moment such a correlation cannot be made, because there is simply not enough information available. The cork-stopper fragments were not found in relation to a specific vessel type. In Berenike only in one case (the wooden cover of the storage jar found in trench BE99-10) was a clear relation between cover and content found.

Other cases, such as the black-stopper finds from trench BE98-10, the cork stoppers from trenches BE99-29 and 31 and the plaster finds from the Building F area may have been chosen to seal off a specific commodity type (wine, oil, pickled fruit, dry foodstuffs), but a relation to the original content of the vessel could not be determined. By studying the stoppers, in many of which the impression of the rim is clearly discernable, in combination with the neck diameters of known vessel types, perhaps a pattern will emerge. At the moment, however, the corpus of well-studied stoppers and stopper fragments is not large enough to do so.

The texts stamped into some of the stoppers and the ink writing on the surfaces of others may provide another important set of clues to original contents in relation to stopper type.

14.4.3 SUMMARY AND CONCLUSION

This season excavations revealed several new methods of stopper manufacture in Berenike. The variety of materials used to make stoppers was largely the same as encountered in previous seasons, now providing us with some general idea of what to expect at the site. The newly attested materials that were found were different bungs closing off the neck of the vessel prior to sealing with plaster. From the large variety of materials used as bungs found in past seasons it appears that any material at hand was used in making plaster stoppers, the only requirement being that the material should not crumble into the contents of the vessel and would be dense enough to stop the gypsum from running into the vessel before it could set.

Once more evidence was found to support the contention that vessels were sealed at Berenike because of the coral that was used as bung and also because of the finds uncovered in the area of Building F. As merchandise was transported to and from the harbor of Berenike, the seals of vessels may have been inspected at a harbor checkpoint or customs station before (trans) shipment. Vessels may have been opened to check their contents and would have needed to be resealed. Or perhaps the seals were checked in the merchants' warehouse to make sure that they had survived during the long transport overseas or through the desert and would hold for the remainder of the journey. A regular practice of resealing would explain the amount of complete and used stoppers in the area of Building F, an area near the coast.

From the evidence of the past seasons, a means to define contexts in which stoppers were found has been developed. Although the quantity of stoppers at Berenike was not always enough to provide a solid base for conclusions, in some cases an identification could be made. During the few years this find category has been studied at Berenike, it has become evident that these objects were a much more prominent feature of trade than has been assumed previously. The amount of stoppers uncovered at Berenike and the variety of materials and contexts in which they were found show that this group of objects yield important information on the commercial activity in this part of the Roman Empire.

CHAPTER 15 ～

JAR STOPPERS, SEALS, AND LIDS, 2000 SEASON

S. F. MULDER

Excavations during the 2000 season recovered 83 complete stoppers, lids, and stopper fragments from five trenches. In addition to recording types catalogued previously, a new variety of rope stopper was added to the typology (Bos 2000:277–280; Chapter 15 in this volume). Several new ceramic types were also recorded. Furthermore, the 2000 season produced a larger variety of clay and mud stoppers, one of which was stamped. It has been suggested that these stamps belong to *negotiatores*, merchants, who filled the amphorae and were responsible for their shipment (Sundelin 1996:299). However, these stamps have previously been recorded only on plaster stoppers, making this season the first time a stamp has been recorded on a mud stopper. In addition to plaster, clay, and mud stoppers, stone lids and round- or square-cut sherds were examined. Such round- or square-cut sherds and lids separated the contents of the amphora or jar from the plaster seal, which was usually applied over them. Although many of these objects were found, the criterion for their inclusion in the catalog was the presence of plaster on their surfaces. This chapter presents a catalogue of 44 complete stoppers, as well as stoppers that were stamped, decorated, or otherwise noteworthy; the remainder found this season were too fragmentary and are not included here. The distribution of the stoppers across the site will be discussed following, as well as new types and manufacturing techniques.

15.1 DISTRIBUTION

Unlike previous seasons, the 83 specimens recovered in the 2000 season were not evenly distributed over the site. The great majority of stoppers came from two trenches, BE00-33 and BE00-10. In conjunction with this narrow distribution was an overall decrease in the number of trenches producing stoppers and stopper fragments. In the 2000 season, five trenches produced the total number of stoppers, down from 10 trenches in 1999 (see Chapter 14 in this book). Table 15-1 represents the spatial distribution of all stoppers and stopper fragments across the site. The majority of stoppers, 52 of 83, were from trench BE00-33, with trench BE00-10 producing 26. Table 15-2 presents a list of loci in each of the five different trenches that produced stoppers. This table also indicates the number of stoppers recovered from these loci.

Seven different materials were isolated among the stoppers recovered this season. Table 15-3 presents the distribution of these materials by trench. "Material" here refers to the predominant medium used in each stopper's manufacture, and not to any other minor components that often comprise a stopper. A plaster stopper having a sherd-jammed bung, for example, is categorized as plaster despite the inclusion of ceramic as a secondary component. Most of the stoppers recovered were made of plaster, in keeping with the findings of previous seasons.

Context	Fragments	Nearly Complete	Total
BE00-10	5	21	26
BE00-30	1	2	3
BE00-33	31	21	52
BE00-38	1	0	1
BE00-40	1	0	1
Total	39	44	83

Table 15-1   Spatial distribution of the stoppers found during the Berenike 2000 season.

Trench	Loci
BE00-10	*238, 423 (2), 445, 465 (2), 468 (2), 473 (2), 482 (2), 495, 503, 513, 516, 520, 537, 548, 558, 564, 565, 573 (2), west balk trim and trench clean*
BE00-30	*163 (2), 117*
BE00-33	*003, 005, 008 (4), 017, 018, 022, 035 (6), 029, 033 (2), 034 (3), 036 (2), 038 (13), 039 (5), 041 (2), balk* trim of the north, west (2), south(2) and east (4) balks
BE00-38	*024*
BE00-40	*006*

Table 15-2   Loci of the five trenches producing stoppers. The quantity of fragments is 1 or indicated in parentheses.

Context	Plaster	Mud	Pottery	Pottery round cut	Stone	Shell	Wood	Cork	Rope	Bitu-men	Unid.	Total
BE00-10	20	-	6	-	-	-	-	-	-	-	-	26
BE00-30	1	-	1	-	1	-	-	-	-	-	-	3
BE00-33	28	6	-	-	-	-	2	15	1	-	-	52
BE00-38	-	-	1	-	-	-	-	-	-	-	-	1
BE00-40	1	-	-	-	-	-	-	-	-	-	-	1
Total	50	6	8	-	1	-	2	15	1	-	-	83

Table 15-3   Materials used for production of the stoppers found during the 2000 season.

Second in overall frequency was cork, and all cork came from trench BE00-33. This trench, which was excavated in the early Roman trash dump, showed the greatest overall variety of material types. Indeed, BE00-33 was the only trench to preserve stoppers made of fragile or organic materials such as wood, cork, or mud. The location of this trash dump, far from the sea in a relatively dry area on the northern perimeter of the site, likely encouraged the preservation of organic matter.

15.2   MATERIALS AND TECHNIQUES

Only one new type was added to the typology created in 1998 and 1999 (Bos 2000:277–280 and Chapter 14). This was a rope stopper (catalogue number 44, Figure 15-4) found *in situ* in the neck of a small, handmade, burnished Nubian-ware pitcher with a square rim. This unusual stopper was apparently made of rope tightly coiled around some sort of ring, with another rope protruding from the center, presumably to facilitate opening the pitcher. Resin or bitumen covered the entire stopper after insertion, and the pitcher is likely to have been opened by breaking the neck below the handle. Several thin strips of leather wrapped around the neck of the pitcher.

Figure 15-4   Rope stopper (catalogue no. 44).

A greater variety of ceramic stopper types was identified this season, and several types of lids or stoppers were recorded. Four of these (catalogue numbers 29–31, 33) were lids with small knobs or handles at their centers (Bos 2000:277, figures 12-3, 4, and 5). As these ceramic lids were later sealed in the neck of the amphora with plaster, completely burying the knobs or handles, it seems likely that these handles served only to help lower the lid into place. One of these lids was decorated with raised ridges radiating from its central handle (catalogue number 30). Another type was an inverted bowl-shaped stopper with a double rim, which presumably fit directly onto the rim of an amphora, and then sealed over the entire stopper and neck of the amphora with plaster. Finally, excavations recovered a type of ceramic plug, which might have been a reused amphora base as attested at Quseir al-Qadim (Whitcomb and Johnson 1979:234a, 235a).

Two wooden stoppers were found this season; both types had been recorded previously. Cork stoppers were of the usual variety, approximately 90 mm in diameter. Once again, these date to the first century AD. Cork likely originates somewhere in the Western Roman Empire (the Iberian Peninsula, western Tunisia), making its presence at Berenike somewhat remarkable (Bos 2000:280). Excavations recovered two complete cork stoppers, along with a large number of fragments. Typically, cork stoppers preserve traces of bitumen or another sealant on their surfaces.

Several unfired mud stoppers were found this season, two of which appear to display characteristics not previously seen at Berenike. One (catalogue number 40) is of a variety common in plaster stoppers but never before recorded for mud, and was manufactured by the application of wet mud to the jar mouth so that it completely covered the rim and neck of the vessel. Another mud stopper (catalogue number 41) had a flat upper surface with a stamp, apparently an *ankh* symbol, at its center. Previously, only plaster stoppers had been found bearing stamps at Berenike. Both of these mud stoppers seem to imitate common plaster-stopper techniques, but do so in the cheaper, more readily available medium of mud.

Period	ER1	ER2	LR	Total
pottery, lid	2	7	1	10
pottery, sherds	2	4	-	6
pottery, cut	3	2	-	5
stone, cut	-	-	1	1
textile	-	1	-	1
palm fiber/grass	2	6	-	8
"over-mouth"	1	3	-	4
Total	10	23	2	35

Table 15-5   Characteristics of plaster stoppers, divided by period. Listed are the composition of the bung (pottery, sherds, cut sherds, textile, fiber) and the shape of the stopper ("over-mouth," see Bos 2000:281, Figure 12-5c) divided by period. Early Roman (ER) 1 is the first century BC to first century AD; early Roman 2 is just the first century AD; late Roman (LR) is fourth to fifth century AD.

Period:	ER1	ER2	LR	Total
pop-top device	1	-	-	1
string	2	5	-	7
Total	3	5	-	8

Table 15-6   Characteristics of plaster stoppers: devices to remove the bung (pop-top or string) divided by period. Early Roman (ER) 1 is the first century BC to first century AD; early Roman 2 is just the first century AD; late Roman (LR) is fourth to fifth century AD.

Plaster stoppers consistently show the greatest diversity in bung material and other components. Tables 15-5 and 15-6 present the variety of plaster stoppers found in the 2000 season and their dates, sorted by type, as well as the frequency of occurrence of various technological components. Plaster stoppers found this season displayed the now-common variation in manufacturing materials and techniques, including those using a sherd-jammed bung, round-cut sherds, wadded textile, and palm fiber or grass. Several stoppers preserved their grass bung, and cordage specialist A. J. Veldmeijer identified this as a species of *halfa* grass, common throughout the Middle East. Several other stoppers preserved rope or string, which was used to remove the stopper from the mouth of its jar, and many more preserved string impressions on their edges or undersides. In addition, several stoppers preserved evidence of pop-top devices made from wood or ceramic. A number of plaster stoppers was of the variety that sealed over the neck and mouth of the amphora.

15.3 CATALOGUE

15.3.1   PLASTER STOPPERS

1   *BE00 4117-Y-8* (Plate 15-7)
Context: trench 10 *west balk trim* PB 994
Material: plaster
Color: *2.5Y 8/1* (white)
Dimensions: diameter 77 mm; thickness 3.5 mm
Date: late first century BC–early first century AD

Plaster stopper with clear impressions of wood or pottery pop-top devices which were inserted into the wet plaster at an angle of approximately 25–30 degrees, between the lip of the jar and edge of stopper, likely with end protruding over edge of jar rim. In this way the device could have served to pry the stopper from the jar neck. Impression of round-cut sherd on lower surface of stopper.

2   *BE00 4951-Y-9*
Context: trench 10.*537* PB 1041
Material: plaster
Color: *10YR 8/1* (white)
Dimensions: diameter 80.5 mm; thickness 21.5 mm
Date: first century BC–first century AD
Plaster stopper with impression of grass bung and finger-smoothed upper surface.

Plate 15-7   Catalogue number 1. Impression in the plaster stopper of a wooden pop-top device. Scale=10 cm. Photograph by R. Bakker.

3   *BE00 2276-Y-10*
Context: trench 10.*238* PB 918
Material: Plaster
Color: *10YR 8/1* (white)
Dimensions: diameter 74.5 mm; thickness 16 mm
Date: early Roman, possibly first century AD
Very hard plaster stopper that was sealed over rim of jar, with impressions of square-cut sherd in bottom as well as impression of 2 mm rope, which extended under lip, tied in knot at end, likely used as an opening device.

4   *BE00 5632-Y-11* (Figure 15-8)
Context: trench 33.*west balk trim* PB 76
Material: plaster
Color: plaster *10YR 7/4* (very pale brown)
              paint *10YR 4/6* (dark red)
Dimensions: diameter 14.5 mm; thickness 32 mm
Date: mid–late first century AD
One-quarter of large plaster stopper with repeating Greek stamp around periphery and figure (unclear) at center. Two stripes of red paint on surface and possible traces of clear sealing agent. Impression of wadded textile bung on underside.

Figure 15-8   Catalogue number 4. Large plaster stopper with repeating Greek stamp. Drawing by A. M. Hense.

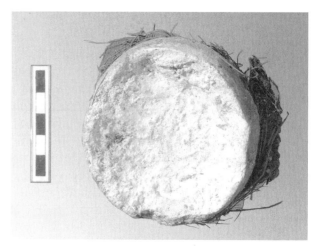

Plate 15-9   Catalogue number 6, top. Plaster stopper with palm fiber bung. Scale=5 cm. Photograph by R. Bakker.

5   *BE00 2514-Y-12*
Context: trench 33.*022* PB 35
Material: plaster, grass
Color: plaster *7.5YR 8/2* (pinkish white)
               grass *7.5YR 4/4* (brown)
Dimensions: diameter 78.5 mm; thickness 30.5 mm
Date: mid–late first century AD

Partial plaster stopper with grass bung *in situ* on underside. Cordage specialist A. J. Veldmeijer identified grass as one of two species of *halfa* grass, a common variety throughout the Nile Valley—perhaps indicating the stopper is of local origin.

6   *BE00 1674-Y-13* (Plates 15-9, 10, 11)
Context: trench 33.*017* PB 25
Material: plaster, palm fiber, rope
Color: plaster *7.5YR 8/2* (pinkish white)
               palm fiber *7.5YR 4/4* (brown)
Dimensions: diameter 91.5 mm; thickness 51.5mm
Date: mid–late first century AD

Complete plaster stopper with intact palm-fiber bung and several pieces of grass rope (4 mm in diameter.) Top of stopper is concave and roughly finished. Sides of stopper show marked variation in color: in places light brown (7.5YR 6/4) and in others, dark red (2.5YR 4/6), perhaps a result of the jar's contents having seeped around the edges. Also adhered to bung is a black resin with seeds and a leaf attached.

Plate 15-10   Catalogue number 6, side view. Plaster stopper with palm-fiber bung (toward top of figure). Scale=5 cm. Photograph by R. Bakker

Plate 15-11   Catalogue number 6, bottom Plaster stopper with palm-fiber bung. Scale=5 cm. Photograph by R. Bakker.

7   *BE00 1051-Y-14* (Plate 15-12)
Context: trench 10.*473* PB 874
Material: plaster
Color: *7.5YR 8/2* (pinkish white)
Dimensions: diameter 67 mm; thickness 7.5 mm
Date: early first century AD
Thin fragment of plaster stopper with inscription in black paint.

Plate 15-12   Catalogue number 7, top. Plaster stopper fragment with inscription. Scale=5 cm. Photograph by R. Bakker.

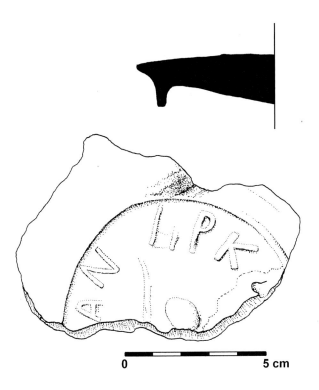

0   5 cm

Figure 15-13   Catalogue number 9, top. Plaster stopper with stamp. Drawing by A. M. Hense.

8   *BE00 4116-Y-15*
Context: trench 10.*420* PB 993
Material: plaster
Color: *7.5YR 8/3* (pink)
Dimensions: diameter 84 mm; thickness 16.5 mm
Date: late first century BC–first century AD
Fragment of plaster stopper inscribed (letter "A"?) in black paint. Top very roughly finished, bottom shows brown staining and impressions of sherds used as bung.

9   *BE00 3854-Y-16* (Figure 15-13)
Context: trench 33.*034* PB 51
Material: plaster, pottery
Color: *7.5YR 8/2* (pinkish white)
Dimensions: diameter 104 mm; thickness 38.5 mm
Date: mid–late first century AD
Fragment of large plaster stopper with stamped inscription, figure (unclear) and dark red (10R 3/6) paint. Bung made of sherds jammed into neck of jar, two still present in plaster. Stamp appears much smaller than stopper itself, perhaps intended for stamping the stopper of a smaller vessel.

10   *BE00 5920-Y-17*
Context: trench 10.*573* PB 1089
Material: plaster, pottery
Color: plaster *2.5Y 8/1* (white)
            pottery *7.5YR 6/4* (light brown)
Dimensions: diameter 99 mm; thickness 28.9 mm
Date: late first century BC–first century AD
Plaster stopper with round-cut sherd used as bung, still *in situ* on bottom of stopper. Plaster applied over mouth of jar, impression of rim visible on underside of stopper near edge of sherd.

11   *BE00 5287-Y-18*
Context: trench 10.*558* PB1087
Material: plaster, pottery
Color: plaster *10YR 8/2* (very pale brown)
            pottery *7.5YR 5/4* (brown)
Dimensions: diameter 122.5 mm; thickness 46 mm
Date: first century BC–first century AD
Large, thick, complete plaster stopper with impression of convex (protruding into jar) pottery lid on underside, impression of rim around edge of plaster with pottery flakes in rim impression. Small amount of black paint on surface. 10.3 mm of damage of the plaster near one edge reveals the way the jar was opened: a small tool was inserted between plaster and lid and the plaster was

pried loose, removing a bit of the rim of the lid with it, and the lid was then lifted from the jar.

12   *BE00 2854-Y-19*
Context: trench 33.*029* PB 40
Material: plaster, pottery
Color: plaster *10YR 8/2* (very pale brown)
           pottery *7.5YR 3/1* (very dark gray)
Dimensions: diameter 82.5 mm; thickness 23 mm
Date: mid–late first century AD
Plaster stopper with small amount of black paint on surface, round-cut sherd *in situ* on underside. Encrusted with dirt and salt around edges, but possibly two small rope impressions on one edge.

13   *BE00 4329-Y-26*
Context: trench 33.*039* PB59
Material: plaster
Color: *10YR 8/1* (white)
Dimensions: diameter 91 mm; thickness 22.5 mm
Date: mid–late first century AD
Plaster stopper that was sealed over neck of jar. Jar rim impression visible on underside of stopper, concave upper surface.

14   *BE00 5632-Y-27*
Context: trench 33 *west balk trim* PB 76
Material: plaster
Color: *10YR 8/2* (very pale brown)
Dimensions: diameter 102.5 mm; thickness 22.4 mm
Date: mid–late first century AD
Plaster stopper that was sealed over the neck of jar, with jar lip impression visible on underside. Concave upper surface with traces of dark red (2.5 YR 4/6) paint. Bung unclear due to heavy salt encrustation on underside.

15   *BE00 5493-Y-29*
Context: trench 33 *east balk trim* PB 73
Material: plaster
Color: *10YR 8/2* (very pale brown)
Dimensions: diameter 101.8 mm; thickness 29 mm
Date: mid–late first century AD
Plaster stopper with impression of grass bung on underside. A 12 mm wide rectangular area of damage of the plaster at one edge may indicate the use of a tool used to pry stopper from the mouth of the jar.

16   *BE00 5493-Y-30*
Context: trench 33 *east balk trim* PB 73
Material: plaster

Color: *10YR 8/2* (very pale brown)
Dimensions: diameter 85.2 mm; thickness 25 mm
Date: mid–late first century AD
Near-complete plaster stopper with impression of grass bung on underside, slightly concave upper surface.

17   *BE00 3794-Y-34* (Figure 15-14)
          BE00 4115-Y-44
Context: trench 10.*503* PB 983
          trench 10.*516* PB 990
Material: plaster
Color: *10YR 8/1* (white)
Dimensions: joint diameter 108.7 mm; thickness 25 mm
Date: late first century BC–first century AD
These two quarter-fragments of a plaster stopper of the over-the-neck variety were found to join after excavation, and share the impression of a concave pottery lid on their undersides. Both have remains of text on their surface, the only readable letter being a possible *lambda* on fragment 3794-Y-34, as well as some decorative elements, in black paint.

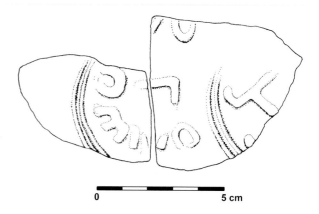

Figure 15-14   Catalogue number 17, top. Two fragments found in different loci of trench BE00-10. Drawing by A. M. Hense.

18   *BE00 3854-Y-35*
Context: trench 33.*034* PB 51
Material: plaster
Color: *10YR 8/3* (very pale brown)
Dimensions: diameter 95.4 mm; thickness 26.7 mm
Date: mid–late first century AD
Complete, medium-sized plaster stopper with impression of palm-fiber bung on underside. Plaster on underside has also dried in a swirling pattern, perhaps indicating the plaster was partially dried and somewhat

viscous when it was placed in jar neck. Impression of 4-mm-wide string on one side, reddish-yellow (*7.5YR 6/6*) paint on upper surface.

19   *BE00 5920-Y-36* (Plate 15-15)
Context: trench 10.*573* PB 1089
Material: plaster, pottery
Color: plaster *10YR 8/2* (white)
                 pottery *7.5YR 4/4* (brown)
Dimensions: diameter 89.2 mm; thickness 23.22 mm
Date: late first century BC–first century AD
Complete plaster stopper with square-cut sherd still *in situ* on underside. Two 2.5 mm wide string impressions visible on opposite sides of stopper edge.

Plate 15-15   Catalogue number 19, bottom. Pottery sherd bung in plaster stopper. Scale=10 cm. Photograph by R. Bakker.

20   *BE00 5792-Y-37*
Context: trench 10.*565* PB 1080
Material: plaster
Color: 2.5Y 8/1 (white)
Dimensions: diameter 106 mm; thickness 79 mm
Date: early Roman-Augustan
Large, thick, complete plaster stopper with impression of bung made of a wad of twigs on underside. A 4 mm wide rope impression is also visible on one edge.

21   *BE00 2983-Y-38*
Context: trench 10.*482* PB 938
Material: plaster
Color: *10YR 8/2* (very pale brown)
Dimensions: diameter 114.5 mm; thickness 34 mm
Date: early first century AD
Complete plaster stopper with impression on underside of concave pottery lid.

22   *BE00 1051-Y-39*
Context: trench 10.*473* PB 874
Material: plaster, pottery
Color: plaster *10YR 8/1* (white)
                 pottery *7.5YR 6/4* (light brown)
Dimensions: diameter 79.5 mm; thickness 34 mm
Date: early first century AD
Worn but complete plaster stopper with concave sherd or pottery lid *in situ*. As the edges of the sherd were broken, probably before insertion into the jar neck, it is difficult to ascertain whether it was originally a lid or simply a sherd cut to fit the diameter of the jar neck. Traces of black paint are still visible on the upper surface of this plaster stopper, though a pattern or text is not discernable.

23   *BE00 5069-Y-40*
Context: trench 33 *north balk trim* PB 68
Material: plaster, grass
Color: plaster *10YR 8/1* (white)
                 grass *7.5YR 3/3* (dark brown)
Dimensions: diameter 96.5 mm; thickness 28.6 mm
Date: mid–late first century AD
Nearly complete plaster stopper with a flat top and *halfa* grass bung partially remaining on underside. There is a rim impression from a jar with an inverted mouth on the sides of this stopper.

24   *BE00 685-Y-41*
Context: trench 10.*445* PB 828
Material: plaster, pottery
Color: plaster *10YR 7/4* (very pale brown)
                 pottery various colors
Dimensions: diameter 110 mm; thickness 23.7 mm
Date: late first century BC–first century AD
Near-complete plaster stopper with sherd-jammed bung. Six sherds still extant in plaster on underside of stopper, arranged vertically. Stopper also has impressions of three tiny (1.5 mm wide) strings on edges of jar, though because this stopper appears to be of the over-the-mouth variety it is unclear what purpose these strings may have served in terms of facilitating its removal from the jar mouth.

25   *BE00 2983-Y-42*
Context: trench 10.*482* PB 938
Material: plaster, pottery
Color: plaster *10YR 8/1* (white)
                 pottery *7.5YR 5/3* (brown)
Dimensions: diameter 82.4 mm; thickness 98 mm

Date: early first century AD
Half of extremely thick plaster stopper with vertically arranged sherd-jammed bung. Though only a single, large sherd remains *in situ*, impressions of several more are visible on the underside of the stopper. The shape of this stopper seems to indicate it once sealed the mouth of a straight-mouthed jar with a long, deep neck.

26   *BE00 1179-Y-43* (Plates 15-16 to 18)
Context: trench 33.*008* PB 13
Material: plaster, pottery
Color: plaster *10YR 8/1* (white)
             pottery various colors
Dimensions: diameter 85.2 mm; thickness 52.5 mm
Date: mid-first century AD

Nearly complete plaster stopper with sherd-jammed bung. Small sherds were arranged vertically in the mouth of the jar, of which six remain. In addition, this stopper shows the impressions of three very small strings (1.5 mm wide), one of which still has traces of string remaining. Resin or black sealing agent adheres to the sides of this stopper, perhaps indicating that this agent was applied to the interior of the jar mouth before plaster was applied.

27   *BE00 2646-Y-45*
Context: trench 10.*468* PB 931
Material: plaster, pottery
Color: plaster *10YR 8/1* (white)
             pottery *5YR 4/6* (red)
Dimensions: diameter 96 mm; thickness 36.5 mm
Date: first century AD

Thick, badly worn stopper with concave pottery lid on underside. The surface of this stopper also bears traces of red (5YR 4/6) paint.

Plate 15-16   Catalogue number 26, top. Plaster stopper with sherd-jammed bung. Scale=10 cm. Photograph by R. Bakker

Plate 15-17   Catalogue number 26, side. Plaster stopper with sherd-jammed bung (toward top of figure). Scale=10 cm. Photograph by R. Bakker.

Plate 15-18   Catalogue number 26, bottom. Plaster stopper with sherd-jammed bung. Scale=10 cm. Photograph by R. Bakker.

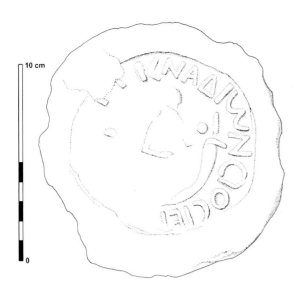

Figure 15-19   Catalogue number 28, top. Complete plaster stopper with intact stamp. Scale=10 cm. Drawing by A. M. Hense.

This concave pottery lid has a round, flattened knob or protrusion (diameter 50 mm) in the center of the upper surface. Traces of plaster on this surface indicate that the lid was lowered into the mouth of a jar, perhaps by means of this small handle, and had plaster poured on top of it to seal the closure. Thus the lid presented its concave underside to the interior of the jar, with its "handle" buried in plaster. This type has been catalogued previously at Berenike (Bos 2000:277, Figure 12-3).

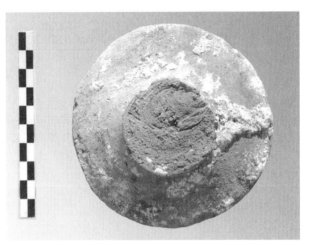

Plate 15-20   Catalogue number 29. Convex side of pottery lid. Scale=10 cm. Photograph by R. Bakker.

28	*BE00 4525-Y-82* (Figure 15-19)
Context:	trench 33.*038* PB 61
Material:	plaster, pottery
Color:	plaster *10YR 8/2* (very pale brown)
	pottery *7.5YR 6/4* (light brown)
Dimensions:	diameter 129.9 mm; thickness 107 mm
Date:	mid–late first century AD

This large, complete plaster stopper was found in trash deposits, still *in situ* in the mouth of an amphora that had been broken off below the neck, likely in the process of opening the vessel. The stopper was manufactured by pouring plaster over vertically arranged sherds jammed into the neck of the jar to prevent the contents from being contaminated. The upper surface was decorated with a clear, raised, stamped inscription around the outer edge and a central figure. In addition, this upper surface was given a wash of weak red (10R 4/4) paint over both inscriptions and figure. The amphora itself is likely imported, perhaps originating in Asia Minor or the Aegean.

15.3.2   POTTERY STOPPERS AND LIDS
29 *BE00 3318-Y-47*

	(Plates 16-20 and 21)
Context:	trench 10.*495* PB 957
Material:	pottery
Color:	pottery *2.5YR 5/4* (weak red)
	plaster traces *7.5YR 8/2*
Dimensions:	diameter 115 mm; thickness 34.5 mm
Date:	first century AD

Plate 15-21   Catalogue number 29. Concave side of pottery lid. Scale=10 cm. Photograph by R. Bakker.

30   *BE00 0788-Y-48* (Plate 15-22)
Context: trench 10.*465* PB 864
Material: pottery
Color: *7.5YR 6/4* (light brown)
Dimensions: diameter 59.2 mm; thickness 14.2 mm
Date: early first century AD

Partial flat pottery lid with round, 2.5 mm diameter knob protruding from top, and radiating; raised ridges around knob on upper surface. Pottery has coarse black sand temper. Traces of plaster remain along edge of lid, possibly indicating plaster was applied only at edges to make an impermeable seal.

Plate 15-22   Catalogue number 30. Pottery lid with knob and raised ridges. Scale=5 cm. Photograph by R. Bakker.

31   *BE00 0788-Y-49*
Context: trench 10.*465* PB 854
Material: pottery
Color: *10YR 7/3* (very pale brown)
Dimensions: diameter 93.9 mm; thickness 21.5 mm
Date: early first century AD

Partial, coarse-grained pottery lid with small (15 mm in diameter) knob at center of upper surface. This upper surface is otherwise completely flat, while the lower surface is convex and smoothly rounded. The stopper has the general appearance of a flattened ball, which has been halved. This stopper appears to be a type not previously attested at Berenike; however, because it lacks traces of plaster on its surface, its identification as a stopper must remain tentative.

32   *BE00 2172-Y-51*
Context: trench 10.*423* PB 851
Material: pottery
Color: *5YR 5/3* (reddish brown)
Dimensions: diameter 97.5 mm; thickness 41.5 mm
Date: early first century AD
              (late Augustan-Tiberian)

Thick, coarse-grained pottery lid with flat top and roughly broken lip, round trace of jar rim on edge. This lid was apparently placed directly on rim of jar, so that the edge of the jar rim fit within a groove in the rim of the lid, which was presumably then sealed with plaster. This lid represents a new type at Berenike.

33   *BE00 2940-Y-54*
Context: trench 30.*163* PB 229
Material: pottery
Color: *5YR 6/6* (reddish yellow)
Dimensions: diameter 44.6 mm; thickness 6.5 mm
Date: late fourth–early fifth century AD

Small, thin, concave pottery lid, wheel-turned, with wide, flat knob in the center of the upper surface. Broken along one edge, possibly from attempt to pry jar open.

34   *BE00 3812-Y-57*
Context: trench 10.*513* PB 987
Material: pottery
Color: *2.5Y 7/3* (pale yellow)
Dimensions: diameter 40.5 mm; thickness 39.6 mm
Date: late first century BC–first century AD

Small pottery plug, marl fabric, traces of plaster on upper surface. This plug is possibly a recut amphora toe, reused as bung for a plaster stopper (Whitcomb and Johnson1979: 234a, 235a). Wider at top, the cylindrical plug tapers toward the bottom. This type has not previously been recorded at Berenike.

15.3.3   STONE LIDS

35   *BE00 1908-Y-56*
Context: trench 30.*117* PB187
Material: stone
Color: surface *10YR 8/1* (white)
              interior *10YR 4/1* (dark gray)
Dimensions: diameter 85.2 mm; thickness 16.6 mm
Date: fourth–fifth century AD

Flat, round-cut stone stopper lid made of hard, dark-gray stone with clear, glittering inclusions. Traces of plaster on upper surface. This stopper clearly functioned as many of the ceramic lids did: resting on the neck, it served as a barrier between the wet plaster and the jar's contents.

15.3.4　Wood Stoppers

36　　　*BE00 1451-Y-58* (Plate 15-23)
Context:　　trench 33.*005* PB 10
Material:　　wood
Color:　　　exterior *10YR 5/3* (brown)
　　　　　　interior *7.5YR 3/3* (dark brown)
Dimensions:　diameter 18.5 mm (top); 12.9 mm
　　　　　　(bottom); thickness 34 mm
Date:　　　mid–late first century AD

Wood stopper plug, lathe-turned with three concentric ridges on upper surface and small hole in center. The wood is a very hard, dark variety. The stopper has precisely the appearance of a modern wine cork and presumably sealed the mouth of a very narrow-necked bottle or jar. (see Bos 2000:298 catalogue number 25, Plate 12–21).

37　　　*BE00 5631-Y-59* (Plate 15-24)
Context:　　trench 33 *south baulk trim* PB 75
Material:　　wood
Color:　　　*5YR 3/4* (dark reddish brown)
Dimensions:　diameter 43.3 mm (top); 16.9 mm
　　　　　　(bottom); thickness 37.2 mm
Date:　　　mid–late first century AD

This wood-stopper plug is narrow and cylindrical at bottom and has a flat-topped upper surface, giving the stopper a T-shape profile. Its upper surface would have protruded over the lip of the jar, sealing not only the opening, but also the entire mouth of a jar with its flat, wide rim. Alternatively, if the plug was used to seal a narrow-mouthed jar or bottle, its wide, flat top would have provided a secure grip when extracting the plug from the bottle opening. The interior of the cylindrical portion of the stopper has been hollowed out, perhaps as a result of turning on the lathe, but also possibly to give the wooden stopper greater flexibility as it was inserted into the neck of the jar or bottle (see Bos 2000:297, catalogue number 24, Plate 12-20).

Plate 15-23　Catalogue number 36. Wooden stopper plug. Scale=5 cm. Photograph by R. Bakker.

Plate 15-24　Catalogue number 37. Wooden stopper plugs. Scale=5 cm. Photograph by R. Bakker.

15.3.5　Mud and Clay Stoppers

38　　　*BE00 4707-Y-60* (Plates 15-25 and 26)
Context:　　trench 33.*038* PB 62
Material:　　mud
Color:　　　*7.5YR 4/3* (brown)
Dimensions:　diameter 85.2 mm; thickness 35.5 mm
Date:　　　mid–late first century AD

Mud stopper with rounded lower surface and flat top. Unfired mud has a large quantity of organic inclusions and one edge has a bit of pottery from the mouth of the jar attached. This stopper may have been sealed with a textile bung, as indicated by its smoothly rounded lower surface (Bos 2000:277, Figure 12-3 type 10).

Plate 15-25   Catalogue number 38, bottom. Mud stopper; note organic inclusions. Scale=10 cm. Photograph by R. Bakker.

Plate 15-27   Catalogue number 39, top. Mud stopper with piece of string. Scale=10 cm. Photograph by R. Bakker.

Plate 15-26   Catalogue number 38, top. Mud stopper; note smooth surface. Scale=10 cm. Photograph by R. Bakker.

40   *BE00 1469-Y-65*
Context: trench 33.*008* PB 19
Material: mud
Color: *10YR 6/3* (pale brown)
Dimensions: diameter 110.9 mm; thickness 35.3 mm
Date: mid-first century AD

Large, thick, straw-tempered mud stopper, rounded top, imprint of vessel rim on flat underside. The way the lower edges of this stopper are broken suggests that it sealed the opening of a vessel by completely covering the top and coating the sides with the wet mud, a technique previously known for plaster stoppers (Bos 2000: 281 fig. 12- 5).

41   *BE00 1453-Y-66* (Plate 15-28)
Context: trench 33.008.16
Material: mud
Color: 10YR 6/2 (light brownish gray)
Dimensions: diameter 105.6 mm; thickness 51.1 mm
Date: mid-first century AD

Large, thick, straw-tempered mud stopper. Rounded upper surface is stamped with what seems to be an ankh symbol, making it perhaps the first occurrence of a stamped or decorated mud stopper at Berenike. The presence of this typically Egyptian symbol suggests a local origin for the jar's contents, or a local mediator in its trade. Several leaves are attached to the lower surface.

39   *BE00 4330-Y-61* (Plate 15-27)
Context: trench 33.*036* PB 58
Material: clay
Color: *7.5YR 3/2* (dark brown)
Dimensions: diameter 103.8 mm; thickness 44.4 mm
Date: mid–late first century AD

Large, thick, unfired clay stopper with organic inclusions: small bits of wood, grass, and a bit of soft fiber rope, possibly flax. Stopper is flat on both upper and lower surfaces. Sides of stopper are quite smooth and were perhaps coated with resin.

Plate 15-28   Catalogue number 41. Mud stopper with seal impression. Scale=10 cm. Photograph by R. Bakker.

Plate 15-29   Catalogue number 42. Cork stopper. Scale=10 cm. Photograph by R. Bakker.

15.3.6   CORK STOPPERS

42   *BE00 5091-Y-67* (Plate 15-29)
Context: trench 33.*041* PB 67
Material: cork
Color: cork *10YR 5/6* (yellowish brown)
              resin *10YR 2/1* (black)
Dimensions: diameter 99.7 mm; thickness 16.9 mm
Date: mid–late first century AD

Large, flat, and quite thin, this cork stopper of which the complete diameter is extant, had resin on its lower surface and sides. The cork is very fine and compact and has decayed to a soft, powdery surface consistency.

43   *BE00 1101-Y-68*
Context: trench 33.*003* PB 4
Material: cork
Color: surface *10YR 6/4* (light yellowish brown)
              interior *7.5YR 5/6* (strong brown)
Dimensions: diameter 96 mm; thickness 32.3 mm
Date: mid–late first century AD

Large, thick, complete cork stopper. Cork is very woody and dry in consistency, in contrast with catalogue number 42, suggesting different origins for the cork used in these two stoppers. The stopper also displays a difference in texture between its upper and lower surfaces, perhaps a result of contact of the lower surface with the contents of the jar.

15.3.7.   ROPE STOPPERS

44   *BE00 1671-Y-83* (Figure 15-4)
Context: trench 33.*018* PB 26
Material: rope
Color: resin *10YR 2/1* (black)
Dimensions: diameter approximately 28 mm
Date: mid–late first century AD

This stopper represents a completely new type at Berenike and appears to have been made of rope coiled around some sort of ring, with a single rope protruding from the center of this coil to aid in removal of the stopper. The stopper was found *in situ* in the neck of a small, square-rimmed ceramic bottle or pitcher and was completely sealed with resin after insertion. The pitcher is probably a type of handmade Nubian burnished ware, weak red in color (10R 3/4); the neck of this pitcher was broken off below the handle. The neck was also wrapped with several thin strips of leather.

15.4   DISCUSSION

As mentioned previously, the spatial distribution of stoppers found during the 2000 season differs from that of previous seasons in that the vast majority came from early Roman loci (first century BC–first century AD) in two trenches, BE00-10 and BE00-33 (Tables 15-1 and 2). Within these trenches, however, the contexts in which they were found varied little. Trench 33, in the early Roman trash dump, produced 62 percent of all stoppers found this season. Trench 10, which consisted of occupation levels interspersed with thick trash layers, produced 31 percent of the total. As with trench 33, most of the stoppers from trench 10 came from dump or fill layers between occupation levels from the first century BC to the first century AD.

Only five stoppers came from occupation levels in other areas of Berenike, one each from trenches BE00-40 and 38 (not catalogued), and three from trench BE00-30: two of which, catalogue numbers 33 and 35, were from the fourth–fifth century AD). Thus, the findings from this season strongly reinforce those of previous seasons, in which the majority of stoppers were found in fill or debris levels or in trash-dump areas. In 2000 no contexts were found that indicated areas in which amphorae were filled, such as discerned during the 1998 and 1999 seasons, by the occurrence of raw material for making plaster and half-finished products or discards (see Chapter 14).

Because of the variety of materials used in their manufacture, plaster stoppers lend themselves to the creation of a clearly defined typology. Table 15-5 represents the temporal distribution of all plaster stoppers that have sufficient bung material remaining to make such typological distinctions. For drawings of these plaster stopper types, see Bos 2000:277, Figure 12-3 (types 1–11) and Chapter 14, Figures 14-4 (types 12–16). None of these stoppers falls clearly into the period of the first century BC, while the majority is from the first century AD.

The most common plaster type used a pottery lid as bung, followed closely in frequency by the use of grass or palm fiber. Also common were stoppers using sherd-jammed bungs or round- or square-cut sherds. Textile and round-cut stone were very uncommon, and the only occurrence of the use of a round-cut stone as bung belongs to the fourth–fifth century AD (catalogue number 35). Table 15-6 represents the distribution of the variety of stopper-opening technologies. A total of eight stoppers had string or the evidence of pop-top devices remaining in the plaster. These are relatively evenly distributed throughout the first century BC to the first century AD. No stoppers with pop-top devices were found from later periods.

A number of stoppers preserved decoration or inscriptions on their surfaces. In addition to the mud stopper discussed previously, possibly decorated with a stamped *ankh* symbol, 10 were plaster stoppers. In general, the decoration of these plaster stoppers consisted of abstract designs (stripes, etc.) in red or black paint. It was not discernable whether these stoppers ever had writing (catalogue numbers 4, 11, 12, 14, 22 and 27). Others, however, preserved traces of painted text (catalogue numbers 8 and 17). Two stoppers had stamped decoration consisting of an inscription and central figure (catalogue numbers 9 and 28). The stamped decoration on these two stoppers was covered in a wash of red paint. Future publication will include readings of these inscriptions, in the hope of perhaps isolating the names or origins of various *negotiatores* operating in this part of the Roman world.

15.5 CONCLUSION

Excavation at Berenike this season revealed the presence of a new stopper type, made of rope, sealing the mouth of a burnished Nubian-ware jug (catalogue number 44, Figure 15-4). Otherwise finds from this season conformed largely to the typology for plaster stoppers created during previous seasons. Bung materials not found this season included shell and coral, but other materials, such as broken sherds jammed into the necks of jars, round- or square-cut sherds, textile, palm fiber or grass, and pottery lids, were common with the pottery lids being encountered most frequently. The majority of plaster stoppers belonged to the first century AD.

In addition to plaster stoppers, two types of wood stopper were found, as well as a large number of cork stoppers and fragments, many sealed by bitumen. Remarkable also this season was the discovery of a stamped mud stopper. These types were distributed narrowly across the site, with the majority of stoppers coming from two trenches, BE00-33, an area of early Roman trash deposition, and BE00-10, where most stoppers came from debris or fill layers between levels of occupation. The context of these stoppers is similar to that of previous seasons and serves as an indication of the industrial and mercantile nature of this find category, which played a prominent role in trade throughout the Roman period.

CHAPTER 16 ～

SOUTH ASIAN PERSPECTIVE

S. A. ABRAHAM

Trade between Rome and India has received considerable attention over the past half century from scholars, first because of the notice the ancient commerce attracted in classical western documents, such as the *Periplus Maris Erythraei* and the accounts of Strabo, Pliny, Claudius Ptolemy, and others. Interest then intensified with the recovery of corroborating material finds on the Indian subcontinent, including Roman ceramics (e.g., Wheeler, *et al.* 1946, Begley and De Puma 1991, Begley 1996), coins (Turner 1989), jewelry (Devasahayam 1985), and other artifacts. Early Indian texts also express familiarity with overseas trade with the *Yavanas* (or foreigners) and, more recently, the body of data has been enriched by the discovery of materials of Indian origin within the Roman Empire, especially from Roman Egypt.

The recovery of objects from Quseir al-Qadim and Berenike is now adding an important new dimension to Indo-Roman trade studies. Over the course of six seasons (1994–1999), the Berenike project has amassed a large and diverse collection of artifacts whose origins can be traced to the Indian subcontinent, providing ample material evidence for contact between the Roman port and early South Asia in the centuries surrounding the turn of the Christian era. The collection has now grown to a point where it becomes useful to discuss those finds—and Indo-Roman trade in general—from a South Asian perspective.

Berenike's active contact with South Asia corresponds roughly to what is termed the *Early Historic* period in the South Asian subcontinent, which is currently one of the most active areas of research in South Asian archaeology and history (Morrison 1997:91). One topic of particular interest is the nature of internal and external trade networks that linked various parts of the subcontinent with one another and with the rest of the world—making the discoveries from Berenike a critical new element for the consideration of South Asian archaeologists and historians. This chapter will attempt to situate the South Asian artifacts from Berenike within the context of South Asia's society and economy from roughly the third century BC to about fourth to fifth century AD and to introduce recent South Asian interpretations of the subcontinent's maritime trade.

Among South Asian scholars, reconstructions of ancient South Asian mercantile activity heavily favored the long-distance maritime trade networks of which India was a member at this time, particularly its trade relations with the Roman Empire (Begley 1996). Incorporating a number of regions along the Indian Ocean littoral, South Asia acted as a major node in the interregional transmittal of merchandise during Hellenistic and Roman times. South Asian trade studies in India have, therefore, focused on issues such as the presence of non-Indians on the subcontinent (Laeuchli 1981–84; Ray 1988), the identification of imports and import-influenced objects (Ardika, *et al.* 1993; Begley and De Puma 1991; Comfort 1991; Gogte 1997; Parker 2002), and the search for and examination of coastal trading ports, inland urban sites (Begley 1996; Deloche 1983; Gokhale 1987; Gupta 1994; Gurrukal and Whittaker 2001; Howell and Sinha 1994; Raman 1988; Rao 1969; Ray 2003; Reddy 2001; Shajan, *et al.* 2004). More recently, greater efforts have been made to integrate the various lines of material, textual, epigraphic, and numismatic evidence in order to generate more comprehensive reconstructions of South Asian trade (see, for example, Champakalakshmi 1996; Gurukkal 1995; Mahadevan 2003; Ray 1994).

16.1 REGIONAL VARIABILITY IN SOUTH ASIA

The first point to be made about South Asia is that, in addition to flourishing exchange networks, the Early Historic period marks the onset of a series of important cultural developments: the emergence of urban centers, the first appearance of indigenous texts, a noticeable increase in the number of coins and coin types, and the burgeoning impact of religious and political institutions on Indian society. One finds broad regional similarities in some of the technological and cultural changes occurring across the subcontinent—improved agricultural techniques, the introduction of iron, and increased population and settlements (Allchin 1995:151). The second—and more important— point is that rather than being a widespread and comprehensive transformation of the South Asian social landscape, the evidence now suggests a degree of regional variability in the areas of political and economic development (Allchin 1995:139), especially in the organization of trade. Following the decline of the Mauryan empire in the third century BC, various dynasties and chiefs arose and consolidated their hold on different portions of the Indian subcontinent—among them, the Kusanas in northwest India, the Kalingas in the northeast, the Saka Ksatrapas in the west, the Satavahanas in the Deccan plateau, and the Tamil chiefs in the deep south (Allchin 1995:274–277).

South Asian documentary texts and various foreign records, together with a large body of archaeological, numismatic, and epigraphic data, form the foundation for the portrayal of South Asian society during the time of Berenike's contact with the subcontinent. The Early Historic period, in fact, marks the large-scale onset of written documents (Morrison 1995:206). The indigenous historical literature is made up of several largely separate bodies of texts, associated with different regions of the subcontinent, which vary in their usefulness for interpreting early social patterns. The documents relevant to the Deccan, for example, are comparatively insubstantial and include Puranic literature, Buddhist religious texts, and political tracts such as the *Arthasastra* (Margabandhu 1985:316; Morrison 1995:206–207). For the Tamil south, there exists a large, sophisticated corpus of works known as *Sangam* literature, an anthology that includes bardic and epic poems compiled over a long span of time by multiple authors (Champakalakshmi 1996:175). Associated with early Sri Lanka are the ancient Buddhist chronicles known as the *Mahavamsa* and *Dipavamsa*.

It was the coasts of peninsular India that were best known to western classical writers, and those appeared to have been the main targets of Mediterranean traders. "Peninsular" India refers to the land south of the Vindhya Mountains, that is, the triangular portion of the subcontinent that juts out into the Indian Ocean between the Arabian Sea and the Bay of Bengal (Figure 16-1). From its southern tip, the coastline extends for about 2,000 km, along the western Malabar and Konkan coasts and the eastern Coromandel coast. The peninsula is located about halfway along the sea route between the Mediterranean and China and played an important role in the early Indian Ocean trade. The northern part of the peninsula is referred to as the "Deccan" region of south India, and the southern part as "Tamilakam."

The ports along both coastlines of the Indian peninsula have been charted and discussed in various western texts, the most significant being the *Periplus Maris Erythraei* (Casson 1989; Schoff 1995 [1912]). Roman trade with South Asia covered many regions accessed by these coasts (Figure 16-2). Initially, the trade contact seems to have concentrated on the southwestern coasts of Tamilakam in the second and first century BC, where goods were exchanged and then conveyed overland to the east coast. Later, western traders circumnavigated the peninsula themselves and contributed to an intensification of east-coast trade activity during the first and second centuries AD. The distribution of Roman coin finds in south India seems to corroborate the transition.

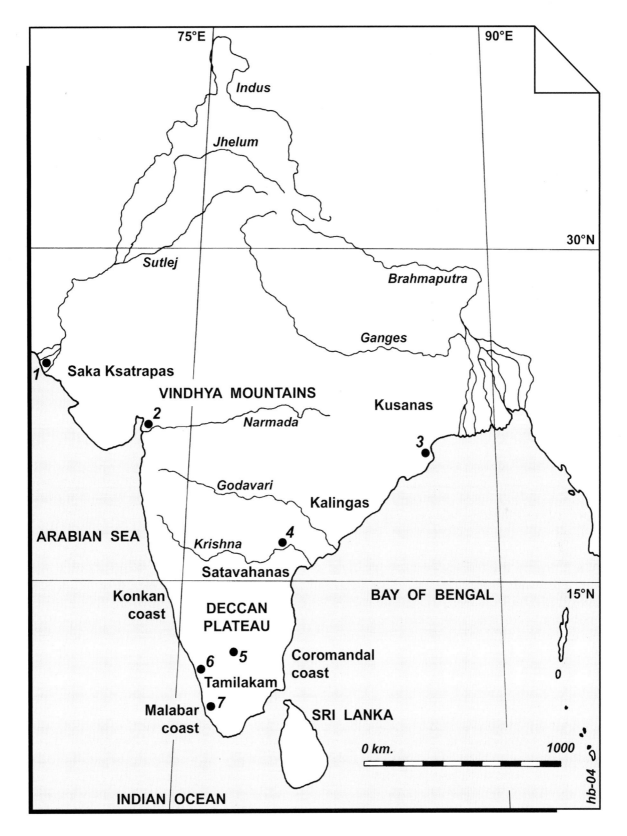

Figure 16-1   Map of Early Historic South Asia (circa 300 BC–AD 300). Sites, regions, and polities mentioned in the text. Drawing by S. A. Abraham and H. Barnard.

Key:
1—Barbarikon   4—Nagarjunakonda
2—Barygaza   5—Kodumanal
3—Sisupalgarh   6—Muziris
                    7—Nelkynda

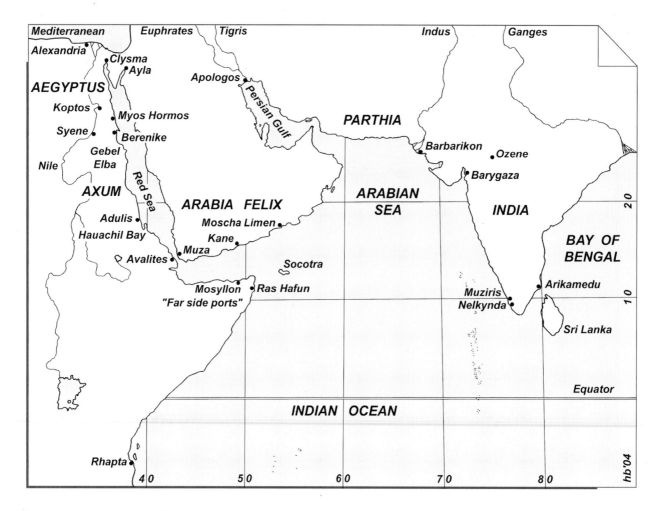

Figure 16-2   Map of the Indian Ocean basin. Drawing by H. Barnard.

Early first century BC Roman coins were found on the west coast, while more first to second century AD coins were retrieved on the east coast, and, finally, third to fourth century AD coins were encountered mainly on the east coast and Sri Lanka (Champakalakshmi 1996:113–115).

Archaeological reconstructions make it clear that each region underwent different experiences that varied in political organization, level of social complexity, and religious influences. By the first century BC in the Deccan, for instance, urban settlements began to be established along overland trade routes and, under Satavahana rule, there was a growth in monumental architecture. Nearly 800 Buddhist rock-cut caves, for example, are known in the western Deccan, and many of them are located at strategic points along trade routes (Ray 1989:444). At the same time in the Tamil south, on the other hand, the principal chiefdoms of the region left little in the way of material evidence for

state development (Ray 1995:106); the most significant architectural remnants in Tamilakam consist of rock-hewn burial/commemorative structures, popularly called *megaliths*. The recent discovery, however, of an Early Historic urban settlement on Kerala's Malabar coast (Abraham 2005; Shajan, *et al.* 2004), will certainly lead to a reevaluation of these and related early features. Historical reconstructions of social, political, and economic life in each of these regions of peninsular India also demonstrate regional distinctions (see, for example, Parasher 1992; Gurukkal 1995).

Generalizations, then, about the nature and impact of transoceanic trade activities in India as a whole, would be rather misleading (Thapar 1992:7), and it is this point that must be stressed during any examination of "Indo-Roman" trade. These regional distinctions are apparent also in trade-related activities. As Ray has pointed out, it would seem that Early Historical trade networks were not monolithic in nature, but are better described as smaller circuits linked to one another over a large area (Ray 1989: 456–457). Without a unified political authority, the structure of trade on the subcontinent would have been built largely on interregional trade networks and local power structures (Ray 1989:453). Indian historical documents reflect diversity among the regions in trade organization, trade goods, the structure of internal and external exchange patterns, and the impact of religious and political influence on trade activities. Thapar points out that western India, which includes the ports of Barbarikon and Barygaza, was involved not only in overseas maritime trade, but was also an extension of the overland trade from West Asia (Thapar 1992:8). Casson (1983) discusses evidence from the *Periplus* that indicates the level of hostilities between the Satavahanas and the Kshatrapas as these polities vied for access to maritime trade goods along the western Deccan coast. Tchernia (1995:153) has remarked on several differences in trade activity that can be identified between the Deccan and Tamilakam. A brief look at the *Periplus,* for example, shows that manufactured items, such as silk and cotton, were more often sought from the northern ports of Barbarikon and Barygaza; the southern Tamil ports of Muziris and Nelkynda, by contrast, tended to offer raw materials such as spices and pearls. There is variability in the distribution of Roman coin finds as well: the relative abundance of high-value Roman silver and gold coins in south India is in stark contrast to the paucity of similar finds in north India, perhaps indicating different ways of carrying out and negotiating trade (Turner 1989). The distribution of Mediterranean artifacts in South Asia is also skewed: relatively few are to be found in the Tamil south, for example, compared to the large number of clay seals, terracotta figurines, bronze statuettes, Roman glass, and other items that have recovered from sites in the western Deccan (Thapar 1992:11). It has been suggested that the presence of Roman artifacts in the Deccan is an indication of the strength of the overland trade routes, rather than coastal activity (Thapar 1992:11), or else an emphasis on barter rather than currency-based exchange. There was a well-formed system of economic exchange in the Deccan, including the widespread use of local punch-marked coins, and the lack of Roman coins in this region may reflect a practice of melting down the metals in order to mint local coins. And, during the period in question, it has been established that Buddhist monasteries played an integral role in both trade and politics in the Deccan plateau under Satavahana rule (Heitzman 1984;

Morrison 1995; Ray 1995). The presence of monasteries in the Deccan, as well as fortified settlements such as Nagarjunakonda and Sisupalgarh (Seneviratne 1981:66), can be contrasted with the situation farther south in the Tamil part of south India, where no such architectural investments have been found and where there is little clear evidence of sophisticated economic participation by religious sects. The regional distribution of certain local ceramics—including rouletted ware, one of the Indian fine wares found at Berenike—further supports the argument for a clearer separation between the various regions of India (Begley 1991).

16.2 SOUTH ASIAN FINDS FROM BERENIKE

The South Asian artifacts from Berenike cover a wide range of materials and include ceramics, archaeobotanical remains, semiprecious stones and beads, a Tamil-Brahmi graffito, a western Indian coin, cotton textiles, and matting (see Chapter 12).

16.2.1 ARCHAEOBOTANICAL REMAINS

The botanical remains of possible South Asian origin recovered thus far from Berenike include black pepper, coconut, indigo, rice, Job's tear (*Croix lacryma-jobi*) and abrus cf. *precatorius* from the Barygaza region (Cappers 1995, 1996, 1997).

The presence of black pepper in several contexts at Berenike is not surprising given the extensive references to the spice in classical Mediterranean sources of the trade between Rome and India. Classical Tamil accounts also mention pepper and its position as a valued trade item—references are made to "sacks of black pepper"— reaching a south Indian port by carts (Champakalakshmi 1996:186). Black pepper (*Piper nigrum*) grows abundantly along the Malabar coast of southwest India (Ramachandra Nair 1986:151) and was traded at the southern Tamil ports of Muziris and Nelkynda. Of all the articles of trade from India, the classical texts, both western and eastern, emphasize the western obsession for pepper, called by the ancient Tamils the "passion of the Greeks." Pepper has not been reported from archaeological deposits in any part of India, including the southwest coast, but this may be due to the relative lack of research or poor preservational circumstances in many parts of the subcontinent.

Cappers reports at least four different specimens of coconut (*Coco nuciferas*) from Berenike, and he concludes that these discoveries cannot be attributed solely to accidental sea drifting (Cappers 1998:316). The *Periplus*, however, does not mention coconut as an article of trade, except perhaps indirectly in the reference to palm oil (Schoff 1995:94), or are there any other firm references in the western texts. It is known, however—according to a classic Tamil source called the *Shilappadikaram*—that by the second century AD, coconut trees were being cultivated by some of the south Indian mountain tribes (Adigal 1965:72). By the sixth century AD, Cosmas Indicopleustes (McCrindle 1897:362) commented on the presence of coconut in south India.

Much of the India's west coast is well suited to the cultivation of plantation crops like coconut and there is indirect historical evidence of its cultivation and use in early historic times. Buddhist monastic sites in the Deccan carry inscriptions referring to gifts of coconut groves (Morrison 1995:212). Like today, in antiquity the coconut plant had a number of uses beyond the food value of the nut and the oil—its timber was used for houses and ships and its palm leaves for thatch and fiber for binding and weaving (Schoff 1995:99). Recent research by Ray on ancient Indian maritime industry reminds us about the use of coir (coconut husk) threads by Indian shipbuilders (Ray 1995:1266). The earliest mention of these Indian vessels occurs in the *Periplus* (Schoff 1995:36) with the reference to *mada-rata*—vessels built in the Persian Gulf, whose wooden planks were secured with fiber taken from the husks of the coconut (Schoff 1995:154).

The discovery of a present-day colony of indigo plants in the vicinity of Berenike by Cappers (Wild 1998:235–36; Cappers 1996:320) has led to speculation about a South Asian origin for the plant. This is a possibility, since Zarins has suggested that the likeliest origins for indigo cultivation and dye extraction are either India or Africa (Zarins 1992:471). Although the widest variety of wild forms of indigo are found in Africa (over 700 species and subspecies, compared to around 40 for India), there are a number of arguments for a South Asian origin; indigo is mentioned as one of the export products from India by both the *Periplus* (39) and Pliny (*Natural History* 35.27.46), obtainable from the northern port of Barbarikon, at the mouth of the Indus River. Furthermore, India has since classical times dominated the world indigo market; and the common name for indigo in the Middle East and Africa originates from Sanskrit. Nevertheless, it should be noted that the particular species found at Berenike—*Indigofera articulata*—apparently has a wide distribution within sub-Saharan Africa (Zarins 1992:471), and an African

origin for the Berenike sample cannot be ruled out.

Relatively large amounts of teak (*Tectona grandis*) were recovered both from Berenike and Shenshef, in the shape of pins, planks, a doorpost, and even in charcoal form (Vermeeren 1998:343; 1999:315–16, 318). Teak is found at regular intervals in the Deccan portion of the Indian peninsula (Sastri 1966:39), as well as in Tamilakam; it is cited in the *Periplus* (36) as a product from the Deccan port of Barygaza, along with sandalwood, blackwood, and ebony. Teak was also very likely used in shipbuilding and repair because of its strength and durability, and this explanation may better account for its presence at Berenike. Some of the teak remnants recovered in excavations at Berenike were in the form of waste wood, pointing to the idea that the wood came from reuse (Vermeeren 1999:319). An interesting line of research would be to discover, if possible, whether the dismantled ships from which the discarded teak was taken were of Indian origin.

Little can be said at this point about the remaining archaeobotanical finds of possible South Asian origin recovered from Berenike. There appears to be no firm archaeological or textual reference in the Indian sources about the inclusion of Job's tear (either as a raw material or in bead form, as it was found at Berenike) as an article of trade between Rome and India. The plant (*Coix lacryma-jobi*) is native to South Asia and its seeds have been known to be used to fashion beads (Francis 1984); one has been found in the Berenike excavations.

Rice (*Oriza sativa*) was certainly a cultivar throughout peninsular India, though probably not to the extent that it is today, since wetland agriculture, according to the Tamil poems, was relatively limited during Early Historic times (Gurukkal 1995:244). Rice has been present in the subcontinent since the third millennium BC, and, during the Early Historic period, the number of sites in India containing rice increased (Morrison 1995:212). Rice was not known to be an article of trade to Egypt, although it was exported to Arabia and East Africa (Schoff 1995:176). It was also a staple item in the local coastal and overland trade networks of peninsular India (Champakalakshmi 1995:102), and its presence at Berenike is, therefore, interesting. If it indeed is of Indian and not Palestinian origin (see Cappers 1998:305), it may have been imported as a food item for Indian traders in Egypt, in much the same way that wheat may have been exported to South Asia for western traders.

16.2.2 SEMIPRECIOUS STONES AND BEADS

Remnants of a number of semiprecious stones have been recovered from excavations at Berenike that could have South Asian origins (Harrell 1998:143–144; 1999:110, 114), including a small piece of lapis lazuli (Afghanistan) and several partially worked cameo blanks of onyx and sardonyx. Worked pieces of blue sapphire (one from Berenike and one from Shenshef) and corundum are also among the artifacts, as are fragments of carnelian, sard, and agate.

There are numerous references in classical Tamil literature to gem stones such as sapphire, ruby, crystal, coral, but the allusions are too vague to identify their origins (Champakalakshmi 1996:183). Nearly all of these materials, however, are found in abundance throughout South Asia (Lahiri 1992), and could conceivably have been traded at many points along the subcontinent's coast. Agate and carnelian, for example, are found in the central Indian hills, in the western part of India, and along the eastern side of the peninsular region; these sources have been exploited since Mesolithic times (Allchin 1979:92)

The gemstone industry of Early Historic South Asia is well known—beads made from sapphire, beryl, agate, carnelian, amethyst, lapis lazuli, jasper, soapstone, quartz, and onyx have been recovered from numerous burial and settlement sites. Recent evidence for a gem-working industry was found at the site of Kodumanal, an Early Historic urban center in Tamil Nadu (Rajan 1994:102), a region known for its beryl mines. What is of interest here is that many of the pieces found at Berenike are those of partially worked stones, for example, sapphire cabochons and onyx cameo disks (Harrell 1998:144), and it would be worth investigating whether the materials were worked in India or in Egypt. At the major south Indian port site of Arikamedu, for instance, onyx was found made into thick oval cabochons, perhaps for export as cameos (Francis 1991:38).

The beads of South Asian origin found at Berenike and Shenshef are made of garnet, quartz crystal, milky quartz, banded agate, onyx, and carnelian/sard. Also found were Indo-Pacific beads made of glass, which are known from south India, Sri Lanka, and Southeast Asia (Francis 2000:221–223). Bead manufacturing sites are found in South Asia (e.g., Banerjee 1959, Rajan 1994), and beads are a principal artifact category from many Early Historic sites on the subcontinent. The occurrence of stone beads at almost every excavated site on the subcontinent points to their popularity as an indigenous trade item as well as an object for overseas export (Allchin 1965:98).

16.2.3 POTTERY

Begley and Tomber (Begley and Tomber 1999, Tomber 2000) have already discussed in some detail the South Asian ceramics from Berenike. Besides the course wares, which have been difficult to source precisely in India, the most distinctive Indian pottery to come from Berenike is rouletted ware, a fine ware with a wide distribution in the southeastern portion of the Indian peninsula, which dates at least to the last centuries BC and has been sourced to India's northeast coastal region (Begley 1996; Gogte 1997). Begley and Tomber (1999) have examined in detail the implications of its discovery in Egypt, but one point that may be mentioned here is the considerable benefit that will be derived from having securely datable contexts for the several early South Asian wares recovered from Berenike. Chronological resolution for Early Historic South Asia has been a vexing problem for decades, and it is only in recent years that excavations have been undertaken that are supplementing and refining sequences developed over half a century ago (e.g., Begley 1996; Shajan, et al. 2004).

16.2.4 A TAMIL-BRAHMI GRAFFITO

In a context dating to AD 40–70, a small shoulder fragment of a Dressel 2–type amphora fragment was recovered on which were scratched five characters of the Tamil-Brahmi script, a script associated with early south India. According to Mahadevan, the translation refers to "Korran, the Chieftain" (Mahadevan 1996). This find complements the earlier discovery at the Red Sea site of Quseir al-Qadim of two sherds inscribed in the Tamil-Brahmi script and bearing the names of Kanan and Catan (Johnson 1982:263–64). Like Kanan and Catan, Korran was a common name during the Sangam era of the Tamilakam (Mahadevan 1996). These three finds are the only known instances of Tamil-Brahmi writing in the Roman world, although several finds have come to light elsewhere in Sri Lanka and southeast Asia (Mahadevan 1994). Another ostrakon was found earlier from Quseir al-Qadim bearing an inscription in the Prakrit-Brahmi script of the Deccan (Salomon 1991).

16.2.5 INDIAN COIN

Following the decline of Mauryan influence in the third century BC, political power in the northern peninsular region fell principally in the hands of the Satavahanas, a clan or dynasty originating in the eastern part of India. From there, the Satavahanas extended the territory of their control in the Deccan to include the western part of the peninsula, particularly the coastal regions. In the west, the Satavahanas faced competition from a western Indian dynasty of the same period, known as the Kshatrapas or Saka-Kshatrapas.

The Kshatrapa rulers belonged to about six families and are known principally from their coins and inscriptions, many of which have been found in the Deccan. The coins date from the beginning of the second half of the first century AD to the beginning of the fifth century AD, and it has been through the coins that the much of Kshatrapa history has been reconstructed (Jha and Rajgor 1992:21). This dynasty produced a predominantly silver currency with inscriptions in Brahmi and in northern Karosthi (Allchin 1995:312). Satavahana coins, in contrast, were predominantly in copper, lead, or potin (an alloy of lead and copper). The Kshatrapas are thought to have displaced Satavahana power in the west sometime in the first and second centuries AD (Margabandhu 1995:4), and coins of both polities have been recovered in most sites of the Deccan, including both the eastern and western coastlines. While Satavahana coins are known from the second to first centuries BC up to the middle of the third century AD, the coins of the Kshatrapas continue to occur well into the fourth to fifth centuries AD in parts of central and western India (Margabandhu 1995:71).

The coin recovered during the 2000 season at Berenike has been identified as a late silver issue of Rudrasena III of the western Kshatrapas, dating to the latter half of the fourth century AD (see Chapter 8, catalogue number 115, Plate 8-15). Most Kshatrapa coins were issued in silver, although some of the ruling families also issued coins in base metals like copper and lead (Jha and Rajgor 1992:21).

16.2.6   COTTON TEXTILES

Among the textiles found at Berenike are a high proportion of cotton-made artifacts. Some of these materials are described as South Asian and include Z/Z cottons that represent sailcloth and resist-dyed pieces (Wild and Wild 2000:264–270, 271–273; 2001 and Chapter 11). Although the cotton plant and cotton manufacture has long been associated with the South Asian subcontinent, the archaeological and literary evidence is sketchy and rather piecemeal. The origin of Old World

cotton plants is still debated, but it has been argued that both varieties of cotton—*Gossypium arboreum* L. and *Gossypium herbaceum* L.—are descended from wild cottons from South Asia (Watson 1977:355). The first evidence for the cultivation of cotton in South Asia comes from pre-Indus Period II phase from the site of Mehrgarh, which dates roughly 2500 BC (Allchin and Allchin 1982:109). One of the earliest identified pieces of cotton comes from the Harappan site of Mohenjo-daro: a fragment of woven cloth found sticking to the side of a silver vase, dating to 1760 BC (Gopal 1961:60). Bits of cotton fluff were also found spun into silk and flax threads in mid-second millennium BC burials at the western Deccan sites of Nevasa and Chandoli (Allchin and Allchin 1982:276; Watson 1977:357).

Classical Indian literature contains numerous references to cotton cloth, although there is a surprising lack of commentary on the plant itself or the process of cotton manufacture (Schlingloff 1974:85). The technique of resist-dying cotton cloth—achieved by binding individual areas of the cloth to prevent those portions from absorbing dye—is known in India as *bandhani* or *bandhej* (Murphy and Crill 1991:9). The origins of this technique are obscure, but the earliest depiction of the practice in India is found on the walls of a western Deccan cave dating to the sixth century AD, and the earliest written Indian reference is contemporary to the cave paintings (Watson 1977:357). Wild and Wild (2000:271–273) speculate that the fragments of resist-dyed cotton found in late fourth to fifth centuries AD at Berenike may be seen as forerunners to the abundant examples of Indian cottons that were traded with Egypt during the medieval period. The fourth- to fifth-centuries AD dates for the Berenike artifacts are somewhat earlier than other similar finds in Egypt, which date to the fifth to sixth centuries—although resist-dyed wool materials were recovered from an early-second-century context at Mons Claudianus (Vogelsang-Eastwood 1990:10).

Unfortunately, from the South Asian side, there seem to be no published citations for archaeological discoveries of cotton during the Early Historical period, although the importation of cotton goods from India to the Mediterranean world is mentioned in western classical texts. The *Periplus Maris Erythraei* (6, 14, 31, 32, 41, 48, 51, 62, 63) of the first century AD, for instance, describes cotton cloth as an export item from the Indian port of Barbarikon, although Wild and Wild believe that some of the fabric recovered from Berenike represents repair materials for sailcloth from trading ships and personal items brought back by participants in the Indian trade (Wild and Wild 2000:264–270, 271–273; 2001).

16.2.7 MATTING

The plaited reed matting found in large quantities during the 1999 season seems to have an Indian origin. The material and technique point to the northern region of the Indian West coast, as outlined in Chapter 12, section 12.2.1.

16.3 RELEVANCE OF BERENIKE FINDS

Any conclusions drawn from the South Asian materials at Berenike would be speculative at this point, but it is undeniable that these discoveries will very likely lead to productive lines of inquiry for scholars working on Early Historic South Asia. One line of research will certainly center on attempts to source more securely the various artifacts and ecofacts found on the subcontinent. Although many finds will be hard to source precisely, some of them can be narrowed down substantially. Rouletted ware, for example, occurs principally on the east coast of peninsular India, but there are numerous inland finds as well. The Kshatrapa coin points to a central Indian origin, and the pepper and the Tamil-Brahmi graffito indicate a Tamilakam origin.

But, as important as it is to try to trace the specific origins of the South Asian artifacts, it may be more useful to discuss the Indo-Roman interactions with reference to recent scholarly research on Early Historic South Asia. There are a number of issues that bear attention. As mentioned already, one must keep in mind that India's transoceanic trade was essentially an extension of internal trade networks already in existence (Ray 1995:98). Localized trade circuits that linked ports and hinterlands were in use prior to the onset of Roman trade (Thapar 1992:3). In Tamilakam, the *Sangam* texts indicate the presence of different levels of local exchange—including the person-to-person barter of daily goods like honey, meat, fish, etc., and a larger exchange network in the region that incorporated goods like rice and salt.

It has been argued that spices, pearls, some gemstones, wood, and textiles may have been produced principally for overseas consumption (Champakalakshmi 1996:102–103), but it is not clear to what extent each region supported an established surplus economy. It may be that the impact of maritime trade during this period was felt primarily in the formation and consolidation of urban centers and coastal trading stations.

The growth of the port sites listed in the *Periplus* may well have been a phenomenon peripheral to the central local networks that were continuously active before and during the integration of oceanic trade. This point is reinforced by the fact that the Indian coast has few natural harbors. A closer examination of the location of port sites described by the *Periplus* suggests that their position and usefulness probably had less to do with their geographic location and more to do with the resources of their hinterlands (Ray 1995:98).

Another area that warrants further investigation is the extent to which indigenous Indian communities were involved in the transoceanic leg of the overseas trade. Earlier studies on the subject assumed that it was the outsiders—Romans, Arabs, and others—who dominated the transoceanic portion of the networks, while local peoples focused on the coastal and overland segments (Thapar 1992:3; Ray 1995:100). But, as Ray and others have pointed out, this assumption ignores the indigenous evidence of maritime activity from textual, epigraphic, and iconographic sources (Gupta 1994:222; Ray 1995:100). Images of seacraft, for instance, can be found on Satavahana coins and in Deccan cave reliefs. And, although the Sangam poetry of Tamilakam seems to indicate little knowledge of or interest in the world beyond its immediate borders, one can find in the texts a measure of familiarity with seafaring practices and descriptions of sea adventures (Champakalakshmi 1996:180). Whether these seafaring references pertain only to coastal maritime activity, or whether there were systematic ventures farther abroad, is still unclear. Although the material evidence for South Asian seafaring vessels is rare, there is a growing collection of possible South Asian finds all along the Indian ocean littoral, from East Africa to Egypt to Arabia to the Persian Gulf to Southeast Asia (Gupta 1994:222), and a badly needed comprehensive analysis of these finds could offer insights about this issue.

The impact of overseas trade on the various segments of early South Asian society is another area of research that may benefit from the current data coming from excavations at Berenike. South Asian scholars have differed when assessing the consequences of participating in the interregional networks of the Indian Ocean region. Although most scholars agree that trade originating in the Mediterranean provided an increased economic stimulus for South Asian development (Allchin 1995:151), the extent of its impact remains poorly understood. Some believe the impact was substantial, acting as the trigger for "civilization" (Maloney 1970).

Others have minimized its influence, citing the long-standing existence of traditional exchange patterns in the subcontinent (Gurukkal 1995).

Also unclear is the complex relationship among merchants, markets, religious institutions, upland foraging communities, and the state (Morrison 2002; 1997). Given the regional variability revealed by the documentary records and the archaeological data, it is unlikely that a single explanation will apply to the entire subcontinent. As with the structure of trade, the impact of overseas trade very likely differed in various parts of the subcontinent. Changes over time must also be considered; it is noteworthy that later portions of the Tamil Sangam literature express familiarity with *Yavanas*, or foreigners, who have settled in some urban centers in south India, which is in contrast to earlier texts, where there is little mention of these people (Thapar 1992:16).

Certainly work remains to be done, especially in the areas of sourcing raw materials, identifying manufacturing sites, and understanding the range of material production, distribution, and consumption. The relative lack of problem-oriented archaeological research and proper documentation at many excavated South Asian sites has left researchers with large masses of data, but little context and interpretation.

16.4 CONCLUSION

The conclusions drawn here are of course preliminary. As excavations at Berenike continue, the number and variety of South Asian artifacts could increase considerably, requiring an updated analysis. The current collection is just the introduction of what will, hopefully, develop into a growing assemblage of comparable materials, both from the Red Sea and other parts of the Indian Ocean littoral. Also, as reconstructions of Early Historic South Asia become better focused and integrative, it will be possible to appreciate its role as a principal player in maritime exchanges of the ancient world. As mentioned earlier, what is needed now, from a South Asian perspective, is a synthetic analysis of the South Asian artifacts found outside of South Asia. As the quantity and significance of such materials increase, it will doubtless result in a growing dialogue among all the archaeologists and historians interested in the subject of early Indian Ocean maritime networks.

CHAPTER 17 〜

SURVEY OF THE HINTERLAND

S. E. SIDEBOTHAM

There was no survey in 1999. The survey conducted during the 2000 season continued locating and plotting roads and settlements in the vicinity of Berenike and farther afield. The results included the identification of seven previously unrecorded sites comprising two gold mines, an emerald mine, three road stations/stops, and another site of unknown function. The survey also located previously unrecorded structures in the vicinity of Hill Top Fort Number 5 at Wadi Abu Greiya (Vetus Hydreuma). In addition, a survey team visited Siqdit and Abu Murewa and collected pottery for dating activities at these sites (see Figures 17-1 and 3).

A survey, conducted by H. Barnard, V. M. Selvakumar, B. J. M. Tratsaert, and the author, also drew a measured plan of the late Roman settlement in Wadi Umm Atlee called Qaria Mustafa 'Amr Gama (at 23° 36.72' N/35° 23.40' E) first recorded in 1998 (Sidebotham 2000:367–372). A separate survey team comprising J.-L. Rivard and B. C. Foster spent almost six weeks drawing a detailed plan and elevations of buildings at the emerald-mining settlement of Sikait (at 24° 37.95' N/34° 47.73' E). Publication of the site in Wadi Umm Atlee has appeared elsewhere (Sidebotham, *et al.* 2002); an initial report on the survey at Sikait appears in this book (Chapter 18). A survey conducted by R. E. Zitterkopf and the author also continued plotting the route of the Via Hadriana and of stations and wells on and immediately off and associated with that highway. Final publication of the results of this survey will appear elsewhere (in Sidebotham, *et al.* in preparation; cf. Sidebotham and Zitterkopf 1997, 1998; Sidebotham, *et al.* 2000).

17.1 NEWLY RECORDED SITES

17.1.1 GOLD MINES

Gebel Abu Arta/Bir Handosi gold mine
Local Ababda nomads alerted the surveyors to the existence of ruins in the vicinity of Gebel Abu Arta and Bir Handosi. Small circular- to rectangular-shaped huts scattered at the bases of several low mountains here included a main settlement (located at 23° 41.45' N/34° 58.35' E) of approximately 46 structures; three of these were larger than the others and square in plan. Nearby were several other smaller groups of buildings associated with the main camp. One, south of the main camp at 23° 41.21' N/34° 58.30'E, comprised about eight structures, while a third building complex had six small circular structures and one larger rectangular one at 23° 41.28' N/34° 58.40' E. Though there may be other mines, the only mining shaft noted by the survey cut west and down a hill immediately south of the main camp. Grinding stones littered the main site and were of the circular type typically found at Roman period gold-mining settlements throughout the Eastern Desert. The survey found very few sherds; these were poorly dated first to third century AD.

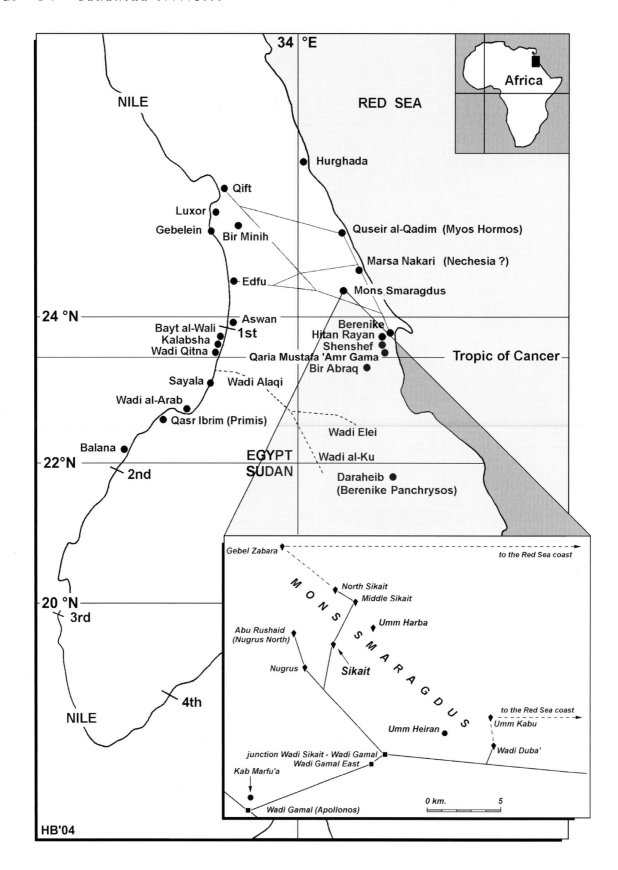

Figure 17-1   Mons Smaragdus/Sikait region, with the sites mentioned in Table 17-2. Drawing by H. Barnard.

Gold mine at Abu Samra in Wadi Howeitat

Ababda nomads led the survey to a second gold-mining settlement, which they called Abu Samra in Wadi Howeitat. The approximate center of the site was at 23° 22.21' N/35° 11.86' E. Comprising several dozen structures, this camp stretched approximately 75 m N-S x 400 m E-W along the bottom and edges of a wadi. There were few sherds here, and project pottery specialists were unable to date these; they were, however, neither Ptolemaic nor Roman. The survey recovered deliberately cut "T-" and "Y-" shaped sherds at this gold-mining camp. The survey has recovered close parallels for these worked sherds at a number of sites in the Eastern Desert. These include the first- to third-century-AD *praesidium* at Siket (cf. Sidebotham, *et al.* 2000:363 and 365, Pl. 16-10) 7.2 km northwest of Berenike; at the fifth- to sixth-century AD site of Hitan Rayan (Sidebotham, *et al.* 2002); from the large fifth- to sixth-century AD site of Tala'at al-Farraj (25° 19.83' N/33° 14.61' E); from the second to late fourth/early fifth-century AD site of Kab Marfu'a (24° 32.62' N/34° 44.20' E) about 1 km north of the large fort in Wadi Gemal (Apollonos), just off the Berenike-Nile road; and from the late classical and Hellenistic, to early Roman station of Rod al-Buram (25° 05.12' N/34° 08.19' E) on the Berenike-Koptos and Marsa Nakari-Edfu roads. The function of these "T-" and "Y-" shaped sherds—found at sites of various functions and a wide range of dates—has not been determined; perhaps they were gaming pieces. The grinding stones found at Abu Samra in some numbers had shapes similar to those seen at other Roman period gold-mining settlements in the Eastern Desert.

17.1.2 EMERALD MINES

Mine and settlement in Wadi Duba'

An Ababda guide alerted the survey to the existence of an ancient emerald-mining complex (at 24° 34.65' N/34° 53.93' E) and settlement (at 24° 34.53' N/34° 53.58' E) in Wadi Duba'. Hume (1934:113–114) records a Wadi Um Deba'a, which debouches into Wadi Gemal, but his description does not mention any ancient remains, which suggests that his location and the sites noted by our survey in Wadi Duba' are not the same. Thus, it appears that this site was previously unrecorded. The mines are small open-pit features resembling those first to second and fourth- or fifth-century-AD mines at Umm Kabu (at 24° 35.44' N/34° 53.54' E to 24° 35.25' N/34° 53.60' E; cf. Murray 1925:144; Hume 1934:113).

The Wadi Duba' site has cairns atop the hills adjacent to the mines and at least one *skopelos* (watchtower). The presence of modern structures and discarded metal cans here is evidence of mining activity in relatively recent times. The survey found little surface pottery here—dated late first century BC to early first century AD—or at the nearby, apparently associated, settlement somewhat to the southwest of the mines at 24° 24.53' N/34° 53.58' E. The settlement preserves approximately 16 structures on the northern side of a small hill that forms a hairpin turn in the wadi. These were too small for human habitation or for use as animal pens; perhaps they were for storage purposes. An additional small structure survives atop the low hill separating these putative storage units and approximately 10 to 12 badly robbed structures, most likely for habitation, on the southern side of the hill.

Site	GPS Coordinates	Date
Nugrus	24° 37.15' N 34° 46.36' E	early Roman and 5th c. AD on
Abu Rushaid/ Nugrus North	24° 38.33' N 34° 45.88' E	1st–2nd c. AD
Sikait	24° 37.95' N 34° 47.73' E	1st–5th c. AD
Middle Sikait	24° 39.45' N 34° 48.30' E	1st–2nd and 4th c. AD
North Sikait	24° 39.84' N 34° 47.50' E	5th-6th c. AD
Wadi Duba' mines	24° 34.65' N 34° 53.93' E	late 1st c. BC– early 1st c. AD
Wadi Duba' settlement	24° 34.53' N 34° 53.58' E	late 1st c. BC– early 1st c. AD
Gebel Zabara	24° 46.27' N 34° 43.08' E	1st–2nd/3rd c. AD and Islamic
Umm Kabu	24° 35.44' N 34° 53.54' E to 24° 35.25' N 34° 53.60' E	1st–2nd and 4th or 5th c. AD

Table 17-2 Known emerald-mining settlements in the Mons Smaragdus area. Dates are based on surface pottery.

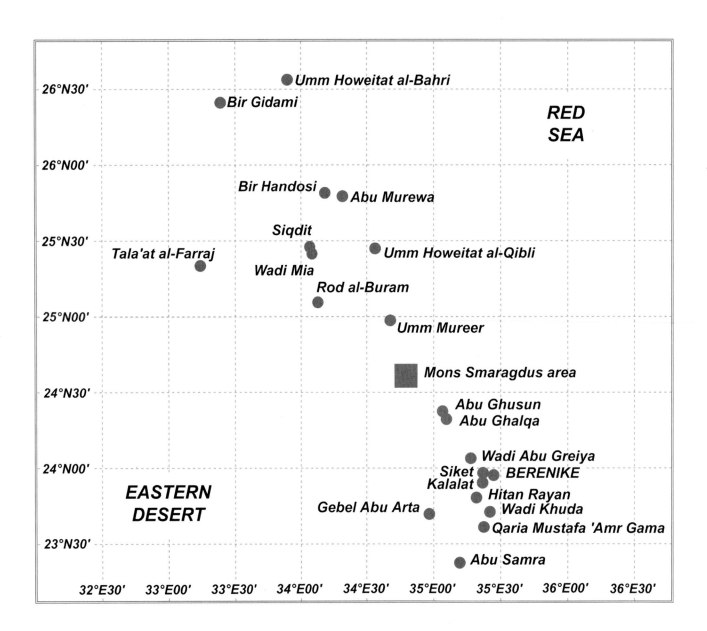

Figure 17-3   Distribution of sites recorded during the 2000 survey. Also indicated are the locations of the Wadi Kalalat and Siket *praesidia* (see Chapters 19 and 20). For a detailed map of the Mons Smaragdus/Sikait area see Figure 17-1. Drawing by H. Barnard.

Mons Smaragdus/Sikait area

With the one in Wadi Duba', the number of recorded ancient emerald-mining settlements in the Gebel Sikait (Mons Smaragdus) region now totals nine, listed in Table 17-2. That Mons Smaragdus was the only known source of low-grade emeralds (actually beryls) in the ancient Mediterranean world and only one of three or four known sources for the gem anywhere in the Eastern Hemisphere in antiquity—the others being in Austria, the Swat Valley in Pakistan (Stokstad 2000; Giuliani, *et al.* 2000), and southern India (Sinkankas 1989:445)—one would expect that other mining sites remain to be recorded in this remote and rugged region of the Eastern Desert (cf. Hume 1934:109–125; Sidebotham 1995:8; Shaw 1999; Shaw, *et al.* 1999; Rivard, *et al.* 2002; Sidebotham, *et al.* 2004).

17.1.3   ROAD STATIONS/STOPS

Two road stations/stops in Wadi Khuda

The same Ababda who showed the survey the gold-mining settlement in the Gebel Abu Arta–Bir Handosi region also revealed what appeared to be, in one instance, a road station and in another a major camping site along a road south of Berenike.

At the very eastern end of Wadi Khuda as it debouches onto the coastal plain of the Red Sea (at 23° 41.97' N/35° 27.16' E) was a large area with a substantial scatter of Ptolemaic- to at least Augustan-period pottery, a series of graves, windbreaks, and animal-tethering lines covering an area approximately 174 m N-S and 34 m E-W. This seems to have been a *de facto* rest and camping spot for travelers proceeding along a generally north-northwest/south-southeast route parallel to the Red Sea. Ababda nomads in the region have long claimed that the ancient road running from the mouth of Wadi Kansisrub north, immediately west of the large *praesidium* in Wadi Kalalat, and on to the forts in Wadi Abu Greiya (Vetus Hydreuma, cf. Sidebotham 1998:415–421) continued south for many kilometers. This campsite, clearly used by a substantial number of people over time, probably represents one stop on this putative road.

The survey found evidence of another area where this putative route would have passed immediately east of Wadi Umm Atlee where it debouched into the coastal plain. Here (at 23° 37.73' N/35° 27.16' E), the route passed numerous cairns and graves scattered in a hilly area called Gebel Rungab and on lower ground adjacent to it. One goal of future seasons of survey work will be to search for, identify, and plot the course of this coastal track south of Wadi Kansisrub.

At a distance of 3.5 km farther up Wadi Khuda, west of the stop discussed previously, was a small settlement on the north side of the wadi. Its purpose is not entirely clear, but it may have been a road station between the north–south-running coastal track described above the an east-west communication route to the gold-mining settlement described above in the Gebel Abu Arta–Bir Handosi region. Here at 23° 42.09' N//35° 25.12' E, the survey located approximately 10 structures built of large cobbles and dry-laid small boulders dry laid (Figure 17-4).

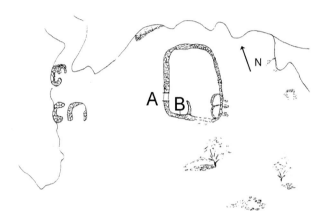

Figure 17-4   Unmeasured sketch plan of stop in Wadi Khuda. A= doorway; B=niche. Not to scale. Drawing by S. F. Mulder.

Three were in fairly ruinous condition; five others were huts of the circular to rectangular type commonly seen throughout the Eastern Desert (three of which abutted adjacent wadi walls); one was more of a straight wall abutting a wadi wall. The most significant was a large, freestanding, rectangular- to oval-shaped structure built of locally available fieldstones. It had interior dimensions of 11.40 m N-S and 8.5 m E-W. The wall had a maximum extant height of 1.25 m and was about 1 m wide. This comparatively impressive building had a niche with a shelf on the southwestern interior wall, a door at the southern end of the western wall, and at least two smaller interior rooms at the southeastern interior corner. The southern wall at the eastern end had collapsed; small spur walls abutted the exterior face of the eastern wall at its southern end. Pottery collected here was mainly late fourth to fifth century AD with some residual early Roman material.

Road station/settlement in Wadi Gemal

The survey made the serendipitous find of a site located in Wadi Gemal and up one of its small side wadis toward the north. The survey named this site Wadi Gemal East. This small, scattered, but well-built settlement lay between the large fort in Wadi Gemal (Apollonos: at 24° 32.11' N/34° 44.15' E) and the turnoff for the emerald mines in the Sikait/Nugrus area (at approximately 24° 34.47' N/34° 49.45' E). Parts of Wadi Gemal East lay on both the southern and northern sides of Wadi Gemal, with the larger concentration of structures on the northern side at 24° 33.98' N/34° 48.98' E. Other edifices stretched up a side wadi north-northwest of the larger wadi site where the main concentration of buildings was located at 24° 34.12' N/34° 48.92' E. In this part of the site, up the side wadi, structures preserved door lintels and windows and walls with niches. Animal-tethering lines were also extant on the northern side of Wadi Gemal (cf. Sidebotham forthcoming), south of the main settlement. Surface pottery collected here dated early Roman to at least the second half of the second century AD. The survey drew a plan of this site during the winter 2001 season; full publication will appear elsewhere. The site may have facilitated traffic between the Nile and the emerald mines in Wadis Sikait and Nugrus; animal lines also occur at the juncture of Wadi Gemal with Wadis Sikait/Nugrus (at 24° 34.47' N/34° 49.45' E, cf. Sidebotham, *et al.* 2004). That such animal-tethering lines do not occur at other sites along the Berenike-Koptos road except in this area suggests that these accommodations were designed especially for traffic to and from the mines.

17.1.4   SITE OF UNKNOWN FUNCTION

An Ababda guide showed another site to the survey in Wadi Mia. Hume (1934:213–214) reported ruins in this general vicinity, but his description is vague and it is uncertain if those he noted are the ones recorded here. The site comprised several concentrations of buildings on both the western and eastern sides of the wadi.

Plate 17-5   Wadi Mia, large building on the eastern side of the Wadi looking west. Photograph by S. E. Sidebotham.

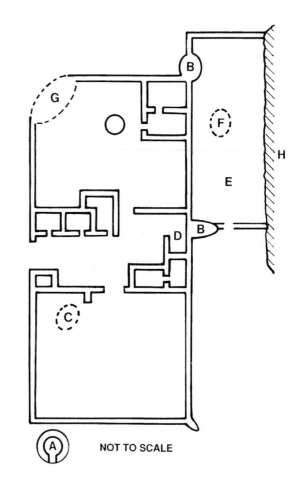

Figure 17-6   Unmeasured sketch of Wadi Mia, large building on the eastern side of the Wadi.
A=external watchtower with raised base
B=tower; C=stone scatter
D=bases of two saddle-grind stones on surface
E=putative animal pen; F=boulder pile
G=building corner removed by wadi flood
H=steep natural rock face
Drawing by R. E. Zitterkopf.

The larger concentration was on the eastern side at 25° 24.86' N/34° 05.14' E and included one massive multi-roomed structure at the northern end of the building concentration; this seemed to have been used for gold ore grinding and processing (Plate 17-5 and Figure 17-6). The pounders and quartz fragments found here are similar to those noted by the survey several years ago at a gold–ore-working platform in the Ptolemaic mining settlement at Umm Howeitat el-Qibli (south side of wadi at 25° 26.58' N/34° 34.16' E, north side of wadi at 25° 26.66' N/34° 34.22' E). Also on the eastern side of the wadi were a nine-room building and a seven-room building. Additional small structures abutted the eastern stone face of the wadi, with at least one large installation on the slope above.

The smaller concentration on the western side of Wadi Mia at 25° 25.00' N/34° 05.03' E comprised two large buildings each atop a small hill and each with a number of internal rooms. One toward the north appeared to be almost square in plan, measuring approximately 12 m x 12 m; it comprised six or seven rooms (Figure 17-7). The second larger building towards the south had at least 11 rooms (Figure 17-8). Both structures had large amounts of wall tumble in and around them obscuring precise demarcation of doors and internal rooms.

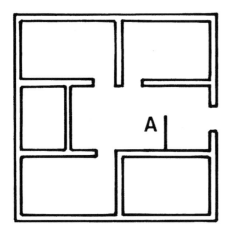

Figure 17-7 Unmeasured sketch of Wadi Mia, northern building on the western side of the wadi. A is step in bedrock. Not to scale. Drawing by R.E. Zitterkopf.

Surface pottery collected by the survey from the site on the western side of Wadi Mia comprised a good collection of table and cookwares that were likely early Roman (probably first or early second century AD in date: personal communication R. S. Tomber). Ceramics collected from the eastern side of Wadi

Mia included an amphora rim and coarse wares that appeared to be Ptolemaic in date (personal communication R. S. Tomber). A saddle-type gold-grinding stone appeared on the eastern side of the wadi very similar in appearance to those found in such abundance at the Ptolemaic period site of Umm Howeitat el-Qibli (cf. Sidebotham and Zitterkopf 1997: 224 table, 225, 233, fig. 5; Sidebotham 1999:368–369; separate publication planned).

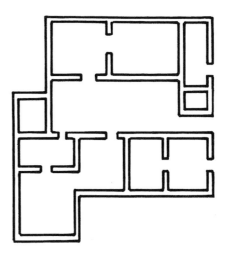

Figure 17-8 Unmeasured sketch of Wadi Mia, southern building on the western side of the wadi. The large amount of fallen rubble obscures the doorways. Not to scale. Drawing by R. E. Zitterkopf.

The survey team was able to spend only approximately two hours at the Wadi Mia site and did not have adequate time to examine in detail all the important aspects of the settlement. There was some evidence that this was a gold–ore-processing center; the surveyors, however, did not establish the location of the mines that this site in Wadi Mia might have served.

17.1.5 STRUCTURES AT WADI ABU GREIYA

A return visit to the forts at Wadi Abu Greiya resulted in recording additional structures on the other side of the steep wadi east of Hill Top Fort Number 5 (at 24° 03.44' N/35° 17.02' E). These included a *skopelos* at 24° 03.47' N/35° 17.10' E, from which all five forts in the Wadi Abu Greiya area were visible. The southern and western walls of the *skopelos* survived but were partly collapsed; there was no sign of a northern wall, and this may have been the entrance to the structure. A large boulder formed the eastern wall. A badly preserved stone staircase led from the bottom of the wadi to the *skopelos*.

Additionally, there was a large retaining platform; its artificial wall faced south at 24° 03.41' N/35° 17.05' E. The survey recorded parts of a second staircase leading up from the bottom of the wadi at 24° 03.43' N/35° 17.10' E. These comprised eight intact steps made of cut stone.

Clearly, there was some degree of activity relating to observation, security and other unknown functions on the higher parts of the mountain across the wadi opposite Hill Top Forts Numbers 4 and 5. The dates of that activity, however, could not be determined from the remains themselves. Their proximity to Hill Top Forts Numbers 4 and 5, however, suggests that they operated in association with and at the same time as those installations, that is, Ptolemaic/early Roman through the fourth century AD.

17.2 OTHER SURVEY WORK

17.2.1 THE VIA HADRIANA

The project spent two weeks continuing the survey of the Via Hadriana, which began in the summer of 1996. During this period an additional 217 km of the route was traced. This comprised road sections that were both of the cleared type with windrows defining its edges, occasionally with cairns on or outside the windrows, and segments lacking cleared portions and having only route-marking cairns.

The survey recorded several additional stops on the Via Hadriana and the existence of a branch road toward the southern end of the Via Hadriana that linked it to the Berenike-Nile road immediately to the west.

The results of previous seasons of survey of the Via Hadriana have been published elsewhere, as noted in the opening paragraph of this chapter, and a final publication is in preparation (Sidebotham, Zitterkopf and Tomber).

17.2.2 SIKAIT

Figure 17-1 and Table 17-2 give an overview of the sites located in the general Mons Smaragdus/Sikait area. J.-L. G. Rivard and B. C. Foster began and made excellent progress toward completing the drawing of a detailed plan of the Roman beryl-mining community of Sikait (ancient Senskis or Senskete) and also produced elevation drawings of some of the more important structures (see Chapter 18 in this volume). Numerous ancient authors from the turn of the Christian era until the mid-sixth century AD commented upon this settlement, located at 24° 37.95' N/34° 47.73' E. (Strabo, *Geography* 17.1.45; Pliny, *Natural History* 37.17.65, 37.18.69; Aelian, *De Natura Animalium* 7.18; Ptolemy, *Geography* 4.5.8; Epiphanius *De Gemmis* in Blake and De Vis 1934:244–247=Fol. V[b] & 88R[a]; Olympiodorus, *History* in Blockley 1983:200–201=Frag. 35.2; Cosmas Indicopleustes, *Christian Topography* in McCrindle 1897:371=11.339) A number of Muslim writers and European travelers and scholars over the past two hundred years or so also commented upon or visited the site (cf. Hume 1934:120–125; Sidebotham 1995:8). Surprisingly, the remains at Sikait had never been drawn in plan prior to our project.

17.2.3 SIQDIT

The *Tabula Imperii Romani* (Meredith 1958: map sheet) lists Siqdit (at 25° 27.44' N/34° 04.65' E) as a gold mine though Hume (1937:689–824) does not mention it. The survey found no evidence of gold-mining activity here; no mining shafts, tailings, or grinding stones were seen. The site resembled a number of other late Roman sites noted by the survey at Umm Howeitat al-Bahri (26° 33.48' N/33° 54.33' E to 26° 33.12' N/33° 54.42' E), Bir Gidami (26° 24.53' N/33° 24.07' E, 26° 24.21' N/33° 24.30' E and 26° 24.70' N/33° 24.40' E), Bir Handosi (25° 48.44' N/34° 11.00' E), Hitan Rayan (23° 47.82' N/35° 19.57' E), Qaria Mustafa 'Amr Gama in Wadi Umm Atlee (23° 36.77' N/35° 23.43' E, 23° 36.70' N/35° 23.40' E and 23° 36.71' N/35° 23.29' E) and Umm Mureer (24° 58.08' N/34° 40.71' E and 24° 57.98' N/34° 40.80' E). There were numerous structures of the circular-oval-rectangular type with low walls. Some comprised single while others had multiple rooms. Pottery collected at Siqdit was fifth century AD with some modern.

17.2.4 ABU MUREWA

Bedouin guides showed the surveyors several small concentrations of buildings in Abu Murewa (at 25° 47.67' N/34° 19.04' E and 25° 47.82' N/34° 19.06' E). The few surface sherds collected here could not be dated. The function of this small site remains enigmatic.

17.3 CONCLUSION

The survey continued to document route networks and settlement patterns in the region around Berenike. It is clear that there were many more routes and a greater population density in the Eastern Desert in the environs of Berenike in the early and late Roman periods than had heretofore been believed. Future survey work will concentrate on recording additional sites and roads, drawing plans of the more important of these, and conducting limited excavations to understand better how these disparate sites and routes related to one another and to Berenike.

CHAPTER 18

SURVEY OF THE EMERALD MINES AT WADI SIKAIT 2000/2001 SEASONS

B. C. FOSTER, J.-L. G. RIVARD, S. E. SIDEBOTHAM, H. CUVIGNY

"It is curious that, with all the maps which had been examined before starting on this journey, we had no notion that we were close upon the houses and temples of perhaps the oldest and most extensive emerald mines in the world. . . ." (Floyer 1893:417).

While Floyer, the leader of the scientific expedition dispatched by the Khedive, recognized the historical significance of the emerald mines at Wadi Sikait, he and other modern travelers who followed never recorded a detailed archaeological plan of the site (cf. MacAlister 1900:538). Located in one of the most important mining settlements in the region, known as Mons Smaragdus, Sikait lay in proximity to a major stretch of the trans-desert road system connecting Berenike to the Nile. This fact added to its significance. By far the largest and most densely built of the mining settlements surveyed in the region; it was part of a much larger network of traffic and activity. Historical references emphasize its importance, extensive routes in the Eastern Desert connected it far afield, and the complexity of the site itself now provokes many questions about similar settlements in the area. Despite these facts, a detailed survey had never been undertaken prior to our project.

Located approximately 45 km inland from the Red Sea coast, Sikait, even now, presents significant difficulties for access and communication. (Figure 18-1). Until recently this isolation provided a degree of protection

for the site, but regrettably it no longer enjoys such solitude. Rapidly encroaching development along the Red Sea coast has placed Sikait within easy reach of tourists, vandals, and treasure hunters, whose depredations have accelerated natural erosion and the destruction of the site and irreparably damaged this valuable archaeological document. It is, thus, not only the historical significance of Sikait that prompted the survey team to begin documenting the site and assessing the possibility for future excavation, but in addition, the developing threats to the integrity of the site which underlined the urgency of the project.

The initial detailed survey of the emerald-mining settlement in Wadi Sikait took place in winter 2000 as a component of the Berenike Project. A two-man team consisting of Foster and Rivard completed a map of Sikait proper and the approach to it from the south, and began a series of exploratory surveys to ascertain the ancient extent of Middle and North Sikait. (Figure 18-2) The survey continued in summer 2001 under the aegis of the University of Delaware. It consisted of five team members, adding J. E. Gates, B. Tratsaert, and S. E. Sidebotham. This second season revised the original map of Sikait and produced initial plans of both Middle and North Sikait, while further extending the radius of the known structures scattered around all of these sites.

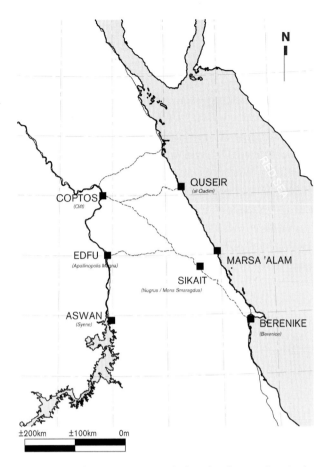

Figure 18-1   The Eastern Desert and selected settlements. Drawing by
J.-L. G. Rivard.

18.1   POSITION IN THE REGION

Located on a branch road from Wadi Gemal, northwest
of Berenike, the center of ancient Sikait (by the acacia
tree in the middle of the wadi) is 24° 37.95' N/34°
47.73' E as measured on July 18, 2001. This location
reference represents an average of multiple readings
taken with a Magellan NAV 5000 D GPS receiver
rounded off to the nearest one hundredth of a second.
The handheld GPS receiver was set to the Old Egypt
Helmert 1906 ellipsoid.

The greater region surrounding Sikait was known
in antiquity as Mons Smaragdus. It includes a portion
of the Eastern Desert some 30 km N-S x 20 km E-W
located northwest of Berenike and immediately southwest of Marsa 'Alam, part of what the Berenike Project
refers to as the surrounding hinterlands. Previous
surveys, conducted throughout the 1990s in conjunction with the Berenike Project, documented other
hinterland sites including the emerald-mining camp
at Wadi Abu Rashid/Nugrus North (24° 38.33' N/34°

45.88' E) and the settlements at Shenshef (23° 44.25'
N/35° 22.72' E) and Hitan Ryan (23° 47.82' N/35°
19.57' E). Sikait, however, presents a more involved
subject of study due to the size of the settlement, the
apparent nature and intensity of the ancient mining
activities conducted here, and the topographical character of the site.

The current project initiates the long-term survey
and excavation of Sikait and aims to answer a number
of questions. These include: the relationship of the
site to other settlements and stations that appear on
or near the caravan route between Berenike and the
Nile, understanding the system of extraction and organization of the operations, determining the ethnic and
socioeconomic composition of the population and how
that changed over time, and studying the environmental
impact ancient mining activities had on the region. In
general, little is known or has been written about the
ancient mining of precious stones. Where developing
scholarly interest in ancient mining and quarrying in
Egypt emphasizes the importance of the study of Sikait,
further excavations at the site promise useful information concerning this important industry. Coupled
with recently published work of other ancient mining
sites in Egypt, it will add to our overall knowledge of
Roman-period mining.

18.2   ANCIENT AND HISTORICAL SOURCES

Repeated mention of Mons Smaragdus in ancient texts
indicates its importance to the Romans. Sikait and
the mines located around it were the sole source of
emeralds (actually beryl: beryllium aluminium silicate
or $Be_3Al_2 (SiO_3)_6$ in the classical Mediterranean world
(Stokstad 2000; Giuliani et al. 2000; cf. Lucas and Harris
1989:389–390). In the Augustan era, Strabo (*Geography*
17.1.45) writes that the Arabs dug deep tunnels to
extract the emeralds. In the first century AD, Pliny the
Elder (*NH* 37.17.65, 37.18.69) mentions Sikait, saying
that emeralds were dug near Coptos from mines in
the hills. In the fifth century AD, Olympiodorus states
(frag. 35.2 in Blockley 1983:200–201) that one needed
permission from the king of the Blemmyes, a nomadic
desert tribe then controlling the area, to visit the mines.
A number of other ancient authors mention the emerald
mines including the mid-second century AD geographer
Claudius Ptolemy (*Geography* 4.5.8), the fourth-century
monk and bishop Epiphanius, *De Gemmis* (40V[b] and
88R[a] in Blake and De Vis 1934:244–247) and the
sixth-century monk Cosmas Indicopleustes (*Christian*

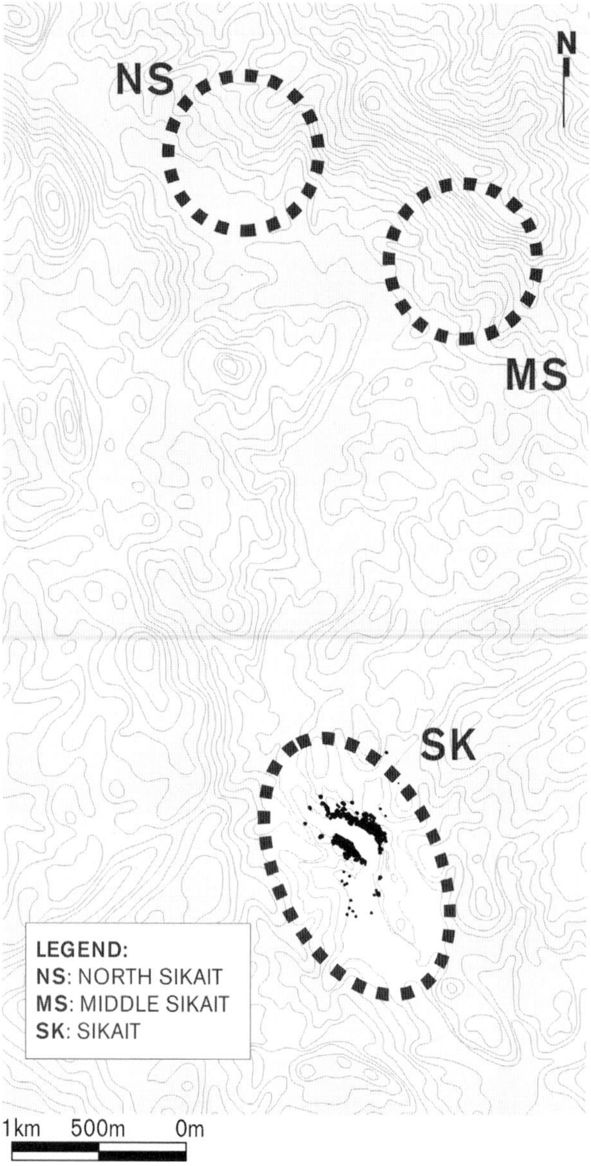

Figure 18-2 Wadi Sikait sites. 20 m contours based on Egyptian geological survey topographic maps. Drawing by J.-L. G. Rivard.

Topography 11.339 in McCrindle 1897:371). An inscription dated AD May 26, 11, from the quarry settlement in Wadi Umm Wikala/Semna (ancient Ophiates) also mentions Mons Smaragdus (cf. Bernand 1977:118–123, no. 51; Sidebotham, *et al.* 2001:138–139).

Preliminary studies of the pottery sherds found at Sikait suggest occupation from the first to the fifth century AD; thereafter, the mines seem to have been lost from collective memory. Sikait remained unknown to "westerners" until "rediscovered" by European explorers in the nineteenth century, when Mohammed Ali Pasha came to power as viceroy of Egypt. Determined to exploit the mineral wealth of his domain, in 1816 Ali sent out Frédéric Cailliaud, a French goldsmith, mineralogist, and adventurer from Nantes to locate the mines.

Cailliaud conducted extensive investigations of the subterranean caverns at Gebel Zabara north of Sikait, exploring "immense excavations that could hold three hundred workers at a time" (Cailliaud 1821:62; translation by J.-L. G. Rivard). He then "discovered" the settlement at Sikait in November 1817 on his second expedition into Mons Smaragdus (Cailliaud 1821:71–73). Although Cailliaud successfully located the mines, they were never reopened. Attempts proved too costly and the conditions too severe.

In the second half of the eighteenth century, J. Bruce (1812:95–96) claimed to have visited the mines at "Zumrud" (Zabara?) (before Cailliaud), and while Bruce's itinerary took him as close to Sikait as Quseir on the Red Sea Coast, there is little evidence that his report is based on firsthand knowledge of Sikait itself. It is more likely that he recorded secondhand reports. Later nineteenth-century writers dealing with Sikait include G. B. Brocchi (1841:61–83), J.G. Wilkinson (1847:403), O. Schneider (1892:41–100), and E. A. Floyer (1893a: 26–27, 97–109; 1893b: 417–418, 424–426). These were followed by numerous visits throughout the twentieth century and later, including those of D. A. MacAlister (1900), E. S. Thomas (1909), F. W. Hume (1907:33, 40–41, 59–61; 1934:107–125), K. Fitzler (1910:8, 48, 99, 100, 118–119), J. Ball (1912:29–31, 99–100, 106), A. Stella (1934), M. Ismalun (1943), A. F. Weheba, M. Riad and M. M. A. Seteha (1974:7–24), I. Shaw, J. Bunbury, and Jameson (1999), I. Shaw (1999), and J.-L. G. Rivard, B. C. Foster, and S. E. Sidebotham (2002).

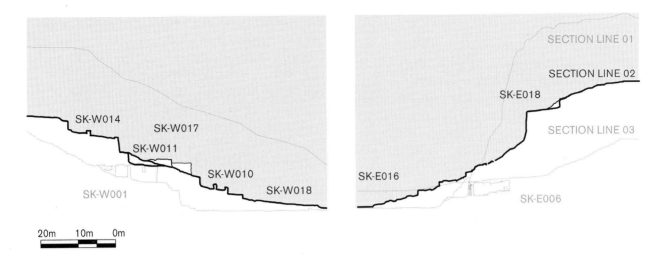

Figure 18-3.   Overlaid sections through Wadi Sikait. Drawing by J.-L. G. Rivard.

Figure 18-4.   Digital terrain modeling of the Sikait site. Drawing by J.-L. G. Rivard.

18.3　The Site

Surveys undertaken to date document settlements scattered over an area measuring about 12 km N-S x 6 km E-W around Gebel Sikait. Numerous satellite buildings and groupings surround three main concentrations of structures. Sikait is the first and largest of the three settlements. Middle Sikait is approximately 3.5 km farther north, while North Sikait is another cluster of buildings and mines located approximately 1 km farther northwest of Middle Sikait (see Figure 18-2).

Sikait is cradled in a deep wadi with extant structures lining the slopes on both sides. The remains indicate that, at its zenith, the settlement was extensive, with architectural features encompassing multiple terrains and landscapes (see foldout map at back of this volume).

18.4　Documentation

The present study focuses on the architectural remains at Sikait. Both Middle and North Sikait will be discussed in future publications.

Due to the extremely varied nature of the topography at the site, a conventional two-dimensional plan conveys very little of Sikait's true character and situation. The difference in elevation from the bottom of the wadi to the surrounding peaks varies approximately 70 m or more, with structures scattered at all elevations within this range. Because of the steepness of the wadi slopes on which these buildings were constructed, structures were not only built upward on various terrains, but also cut downward into that same ground plane. This presents numerous difficulties in recording the remains, complications compounded by the difficulty of coordinating the field notes of multiple observers. Conventional section drawings through the site provide a reference only for structures falling on the line of the section, and completing sections of every location is an impractical way of recording the standing architecture at this stage of study (Figure 18-3). Thus, a three-dimensional computerized plan of the site is a first step toward anticipating the difficulties to come in later excavation and provides a powerful tool for analysis and documentation (Figure 18-4).

While the computer has become a common tool in the process of post-excavation reconstruction and in the assembly of registry data, it has remained underemployed as a tool of spatial analysis. One aim of the Sikait survey is to exploit the capacity of the three-dimensional visualization capabilities of the computer as a tool for analysis during the course of archaeological investigation. The plan then becomes a tool, not just for the realistic rendering or reconstruction of structures, but also as an instrument for the manipulation of and interface with data. Thus, the survey data become a tool for understanding the spatial relationships of a site with varied topography in addition to mapping the complex spatial correlations of artifacts and stratigraphy typically encountered in a scientific excavation. The complex three-dimensional situation of the Sikait sites presents a good candidate for such an investigation, and these tools will be more fully explored in a forthcoming publication.

18.5　Equipment and Methods

The survey during the 2000 season used a Leica Distomat Wild DI 1001. The team made a roughly drawn map using a walking scale and compass. Coordinates were then taken using the Distomat and recorded in a notebook. These three- dimensional coordinates were then downloaded into AutoCAD 14 to create an overall map of the site, indicating relative orientations and positioning of structures. The hand-drawn map was used as a key to create a plan of each structure and as a base for numbered points surveyed by the Distomat. These hand-drawn maps were extremely accurate and proved to be an invaluable tool during the 2001 season.

Selected individual buildings of importance were then measured manually using line levels and a plumb bob for elevation and sectional information. This information was then inserted into the overall model. Numerical correction and conventional scanning combined and correlated field drawings, site photographs, measured dimensions, and surveyed coordinates.

The summer 2001 season used a Nikon "Top-Gun" Model DTM-A10 Total Station powered by a portable solar panel to corroborate the accuracy of the 2000 season coordinates by reshooting key points on all structures to verify their positions. Again, this set of points was inserted into the same CAD model. Additional detailed drawings of other buildings were input in the same manner.

A hierarchy of controls was employed to correlate the data. Total station coordinates were taken as most accurate in assessing overall orientations and relative position in plan (X, Y) and at a baseline (Z) for each structure. Earlier and more finely measured Distomat readings were set within this framework to increase the level of detail. Hand-drawn elevations and sections were then correlated in CAD according to positions described by the surveyed points. At each stage, a preliminary plan printout of a given structure (comprising some 20–100 surveyed points) was taken on site and used as a base drawing for measuring with tape and line levels between known points. In this way the survey continually refined architectural as well as topographical data. Layering the input of data in these stages attempted to limit the field of error by positioning the next level of detail within a "known" quantity of diminishing radius. Aberrant points were discarded.

The original CAD files consisted of 3-dimensionally positioned vector drawings. A rough massing model of solid modeling was then generated to overlap. Each modeled structure was progressively revised as new and more fully measured data became available.

18.6 APPROACH TO THE SITE

A branch road approximately 7.9 km long leads from Wadi Gemal to Wadi Sikait via Wadi Nugrus. Animal-tethering lines and outbuildings that mark this juncture were documented in the summer of 2002 and will be discussed in a forthcoming publication. The route north from this point is littered with indications of the settlement beyond. Cairns mark the way, while outbuildings and graves sporadically dot the sides of the wadi. Prior to entering the main basin of Sikait proper, structures SK-W039 to SK-W049 identify the southern limits of the site on the west side of the wadi, while to the east, SK-E001 to SK-E004 mark the east side of the wadi. Structure SK-E002 is a small temple, close to the wadi floor that is discussed in the following pages. Structure SK-E004 is a small, rock-cut cavern facing north, on the peak of a cliff above the site at this point. The interior of SK-E004 is dominated by three interior niches on the rear wall (Plate 18-5). Finally, approximately 200 m farther north, perched upon a terraced outcrop on the western side of the wadi slope, is one of the largest and most completely preserved buildings, SK-W001 (also discussed in the following pages). Structure SKW-001 and SKW-078 delimit the southern and northern extents respectively of the most densely built area of the site.

18.7 PRELIMINARY ARCHITECTURAL AREAS

Ostensibly the first "westerner" to visit Sikait, Cailliaud described "Environ cinq cents maisons baties en pierre sèche sont encore sur pied; trois temples ont été

Plate 18-5.   Sikait. Interior of SK-E004. Scale=1 m. Photograph by S. . Sidebotham.

creusés dans le roc, ou construits en pierre du lieu." (Cailliaud 1821: 71) Spending two days at the site after investigations at Gebel Zabara (Cailliaud 1821: 73), Cailliaud took notes and drew plans of a small number of buildings on the site. The text cited suggests that Cailliaud did not venture beyond Sikait to the areas here designated as Middle and North Sikait; Floyer, however, does mention using Cailliaud's map to find the mines "3 miles along the wadi." (Floyer 1893b: 418; Figure 18-2). The wadi runs roughly to the northwest, where numerous swells and recesses push into and pull back from the basin of the wadi floor (Figures 18-6 and 18-7). Structures remain on both sides of the wadi, on what have been termed the East and the West Slopes. The undulating pattern of the wadi sides provides a convenient topographic basis for dividing the site into zones. This system partitions the site into planimetric "areas" that will be revised after excavation and stratigraphic phasing.

There are well over 100 identifiable clusters of structures, individual buildings, and complexes. A great number of these are relatively well preserved: walls as high as 4.5 m, extant doors, windows, niches, shelves, and what are best described as storage areas. Many other buildings, however, are severely deteriorated, leaving little standing evidence of their original form. These have either collapsed and have subsequently been washed away, or lay beneath tumbled debris.

The survey loosely categorized the structures on the West Slope into five areas; these appear in Figure 18.7. Seen in plan, the undulating edge of the wadi can be read as a wave, with crests closest to the wadi floor and furrows receding from it. (Figures 18-7 and 18-8).

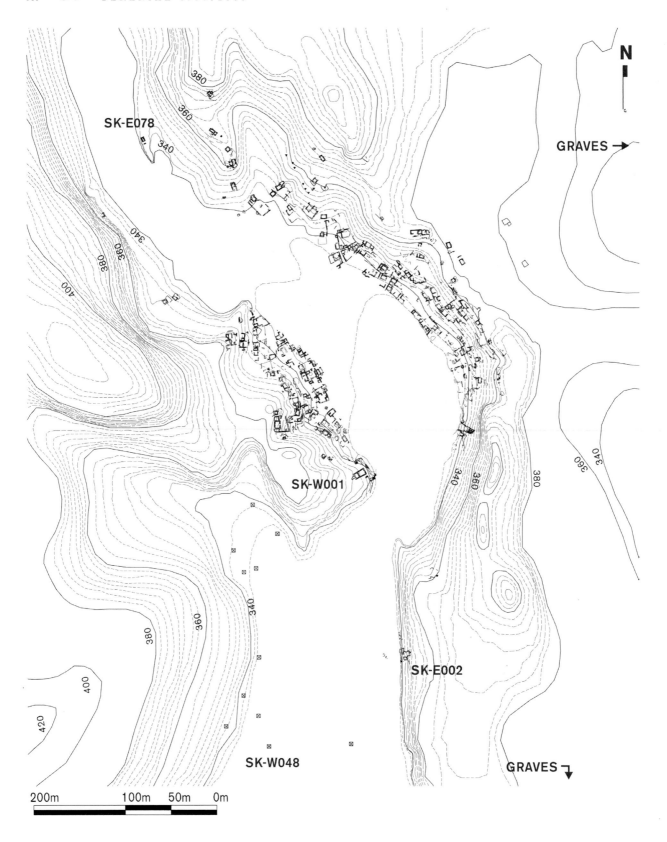

Figure 18-6   Plan of Sikait. Drawing by J.-L. G. Rivard and B. C. Foster.

Structures located at the crest occur in a much more open and ordered arrangement, while those in the furrow cluster more tightly and are less likely to be geometrically aligned. The areas on the West Slope are numbered: W1, W2, W3, W4, and W5. Structures occur throughout. On the East Slope, major structures can be found from the extreme south of Areas E1 to E3, while obvious evidence of mining survives on one of the slopes above Area E3.

Of the furrows with significant architecture, one (E1) is so expansive that the building area is not restricted and proximity to the wadi basin not impeded in any significant way. At its northern edge (E1'), this furrow coincides with a major low-lying pass that allows access up and over the ridgeline of the valley, affording it additional topographical importance. On the West Slope,

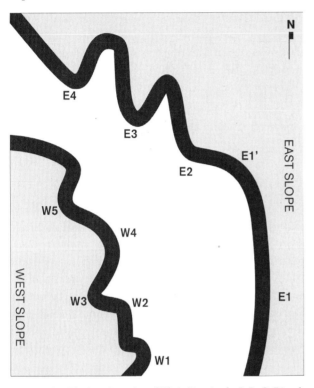

Figure 18-7.   Planimetric zoning of Sikait. Drawing by J.-L. G. Rivard.

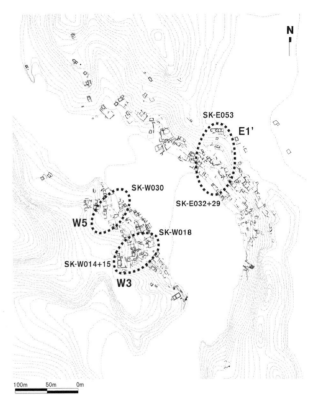

Figure 18-8.   Plan of structures in Wadi Sikait, the furrow areas. Drawing by J.-L. G. Rivard and B. C. Foster.

In comparing the crest/furrow diagrams of both the East and West Slopes, we observed that structures tend to occur more frequently at the crest of the wave (toward the wadi floor) and less frequently in the furrow. Of the seven crests and six furrows, all seven crests are relatively densely built, while only three of the furrows exhibit similar densities. This pattern may have been due to the natural wash on the wadi walls, where hollows on the slope of the wadi would naturally channel water and rock debris down the slope, making building in this area impractical. These natural depressions may also have been a logical area in which to place stairways, ramps and other means of accessing buildings farther up the slope, though most routes occur in closer proximity to the structures themselves. Whatever the reason, the three furrows with significant construction require further examination.

the second furrow (W5), actually has the greater part of its architecture concentrated toward its northern end. This extensive architecture effectively "jumps" onto the next crest. The deeper zone of the furrow preserves no visible evidence of significant structures.

The final furrow, and the only one that has considerable architectural remains, is W3. The question of why this and only this true furrow should have been densely developed is significant, and the answer may lie in the nature of the structures found there (cf. SK-W014 discussed in the following pages).

18.8   ORIENTATION

The general orientation of the majority of buildings is toward the wadi floor, with doorways facing in that direction. It is possible that some doors existed on the sidewalls of a few buildings (i.e., SK-E015, SK-E026). This remains conjectural until clearing of tumble and debris in and around these structures is undertaken.

18.9 GEOLOGY, CONSTRUCTION AND MINING

Discussions with J. A. Harrell regarding the geology of the site have revealed that the most common general rock types found throughout Sikait are varicolored schists and white-veined quartz. In addition to these are varicolored metadiorite to metagabbro and metagranite to metagranodiorite. Schist is the single-most abundant and perhaps most important rock type found, for it is from this stone that the inhabitants derived both building materials and mining resources. At higher elevations, yellowish-green serpentinite also occurs, and cutting through all the rock types are occasional veins of black dolerite. On the west side of the wadi there are also occurrences of light-grayish garnetiferous granite gneiss.

Most of the structures at Sikait are constructed of locally quarried or scavenged gray- to brown-quartz mica schist. While most buildings appear to have been dry-laid, close examination of some structures reveals what may be a mud mortar. Three structures in particular (SK-W001, SK-E032, and SK-E060 discussed in greater detail following) display evidence of this mortar used in their construction. This suggests the possibility that other structures throughout the site may also have used a similar bonding agent that may have eroded over time due to weathering. Dry-laid construction has, however, been observed at other Eastern Desert sites (cf. Zitterkopf 1998). A number of later structures, presumably early twentieth-century dry-laid British buildings near North Sikait, mirror these ancient edifices.

Numerous major rock-cut structures at Sikait are carved into deposits of talc schist, and these are discussed following (SK-E002, SK-E006, SK-E004, and others).

Talc schist is also the most common rock type found in the mining areas, followed by phlogopite schist and vein quartz. Mining activity on the site focused on deposits of a blackish phlogopite (also know as biotite mica) schist, the rock type that contained most of the beryl. Beryl also occurs in the vein quartz, and this may have been mined despite the difficulty of separating the beryl from the quartz. Closely associated with the phlogopite schist are green chlorite schist, green actinolite schist, black schoralite tourmaline schist, and gray- to brown-quartz mica schist.

18.10 CLASSIFICATION OF STRUCTURES

The norm for surveys of sites with standing architecture has been to propose a typology for recorded structures (cf. Hitan Rayan [Aldsworth and Barnard 1996], Shenshef [Aldsworth and Barnard 1996; Aldsworth 1999]). Prior to clearing tumbled rock, however, any attempt to categorize the buildings at Sikait would be forced and artificial and would add little to our understanding of the site. The only buildings that appear to fall into a general "type" are the relatively small, single room structures that perch high along the wadi slopes; these have been identified as *skopeloi* or watchtowers (SK-E012, SK-E037, SK-E054, and others). Other architectural remains at Sikait significantly reflect the constraints of topography and this suggests an alternate "typology" of zone-based architecture for analyzing the preserved buildings and the larger settlement plan.

18.11 SECTIONAL ZONES

Because Sikait covers a wide range of topographical elevations, it is natural that these conditions should dictate the grouping of structures and their architectural character. It is possible to identify topographic zones based on this observation, where terrain influenced visible architectural remains. The following four sectional zones present a simple method of classifying the architectural remains based on topography. Subsequent clearing, excavation, and stratigraphic analysis will allow a clearer organization. These zones are: (1) wadi floor, (2) stage, (3) slope, and (4) apex. Although not mutually exclusive, these topographical categories are telling in relation to the construction methods that occur within each zone.

The buildings discussed in the following sections have been chosen because in each case they exhibit characteristics common to the construction techniques in the respective zone dictated by the topography of the wadi, are well preserved and are some of the most interesting buildings/complexes preserved at the site.

18.11.1 THE WADI FLOOR ZONE

The majority of the extant buildings at Sikait were constructed well above the wadi floor. At present, no discernable structures can be observed on the wadi floor. Any that may once have stood here have since been washed away by the periodic *seyl* (plural: *seyal*) that occurs "once every five or six years, of water so deep and rapid that though a camel may, a man may not cross it; such *'seyl'* last for two days" (Floyer 1893b: 413). Naturally formed lines of erosion along the wadi's edge have undermined structures between the wadi floor and the higher elevation of the stage. This line indicates that structures continued further into the space of the wadi floor, but at what level is still unclear.

18.11.2 THE STAGE ZONE

The stage is a relatively flat, raised shelf-like zone that surrounds the lowest level of the wadi floor (Figure 18-9, Plate 18-10). This location would have provided natural protection from *seyal*. The visible structures in this zone possess no significant retaining works to level the ground plane artificially. The rear edges of structures sometimes intersect with the rising wadi slope behind and cut into the incline itself. These represent minor features in proportion to the size of the structures.

There is evidence that parts of some of the buildings on the stage were washed away over the centuries by *seyal*. One need only look at the natural cuts created along the base of the eastern slope (SK-E029, SK-E032, SK-E044, SK-E045, SK-E052; Plate 18-11, Figures 18-12 and 18-13) to see evidence of former walls continuing into the area of the modern wadi floor. Similarly, portions of some of the buildings that line the stage on the western side of the wadi have also been washed away (SK-W033, SK-W032, SK-W030, SK-W027, SK-W029, SK-W023). It is not evident if these structures continued at the lower level of the wadi floor or if the edge of the stage itself has receded. Excavation will shed light on this question.

The area of the stage creates a semicomplete ring around the wadi floor. Structures found here occur in more uniform arrangements along the line of the contours. These configurations form a more open and contiguous pattern than within the slope, where structures are more closely built. This pattern is found elsewhere in the region at sites such as Shenshef.

Figure 18-9   Sikait, diagrammatic rendering of the stage zone. Drawing by J.-L. G. Rivard.

Plate 18-10   Sikait, composite showing buildings in the relatively flat stage zone on the eastern side of the wadi, looking N-NW. Photographs by J.-L. G. Rivard.

Plate 18-11.   Composite photos of the eastern side of Wadi Sikait showing balk between the wadi floor and the stage zone. Photographs by J.-L. G. Rivard.

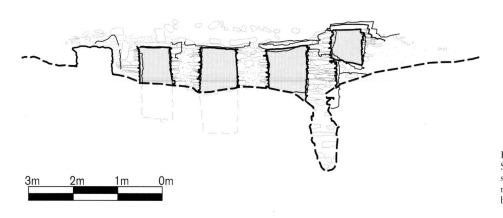

3m   2m   1m   0m

Figure 18-12
Sikait structure SK-E044, N-S section looking east at partially rock-cut storage area. Drawing by J.-L. G. Rivard.

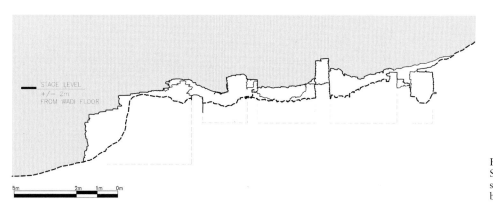

STAGE LEVEL
+/− 2m
FROM WADI FLOOR

5m   2m   1m   0m

Figure 18-13
Sikait structure SK-E044, E-W section looking north. Drawing by J.-L. G. Rivard.

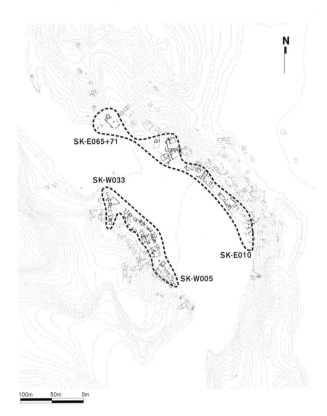

The more-uniform arrangement of structures on the stage often includes open areas, termed "courtyards" for the present, that are larger than those found on the slope. These courtyards tend to be surrounded with a larger number of rooms at the same elevation as the courtyard itself than those on the slope. In the structures at the stage level, the courtyard area is a clearly recognizable feature, immediately establishing a hierarchy in the disposition of surrounding rooms in the structure. In the slope zone, the courtyard either takes the form of a long terrace-like feature running parallel to the slope in front of a "row" of rooms against the slope, or in many cases a possible courtyard area seems indistinguishable from other "rooms" in the structure on the basis of size and proportion (See Figure 18-14).

Figure 18-14   Plan of structures in the stage zone. Drawing by J.-L. G. Rivard and B. C. Foster.

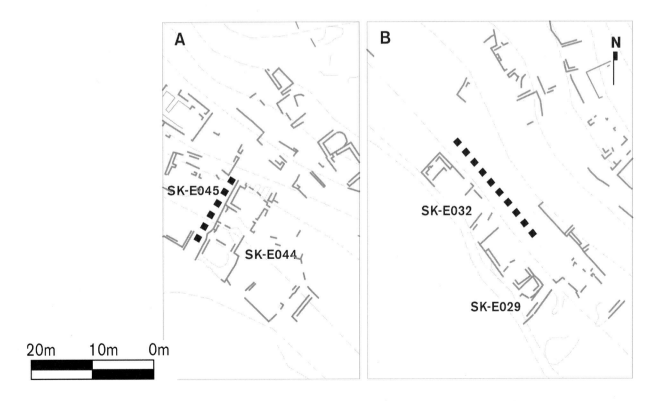

Figure 18-15   Diagram of circulation routes in the stage zone at the Wadi Sikait settlement. A. Typical route perpendicular to contours; B. possible route parallel to contours. (cf. Figure 18-85). Drawings by J.-L.G. Rivard.

Lacking excavation evidence, it is not yet possible to determine what occupation patterns accompanied these architectural and topographic details. Table 18-16 lists selected structures comparing average dimensions of plannimetric features of this type.

Occasionally, the aligned features of structures on the stage imply circulation routes. Structures SK-E029 and SK-E032 and the immediately adjacent tumble suggest a linear organization together with a route parallel to the slope, which rises behind. This reading must be contrasted with the more typical pattern of routes at this elevation. These paths tend to be perpendicular to the slope and occur between buildings facing the wadi floor at the "front" and intersecting the rising slope at the "rear" (SK-E044 and others; see Figures 18-15 and 18-85).

Notable Structure in the Stage Zone
"Three windows" building SK-E060

Referred to as "three windows," SK-E060 derives its name from three prominent windows on the western wall of the main chamber of the structure. SK-E060, together with SK-E032, preserves evidence of a bonding material used in the construction of the primary room of the building. This main wall faces the wadi floor: its three windows from south to north measure 0.50 m wide x 0.53 m high x 0.75 m deep; 0. 45 m wide x 0.59 m high x 0.78 m deep; 0.40 m wide x 0.47 m high x 0.80 m deep. While the wall survives to about 3.4 m at its greatest height, the mortar or bonding agent used on the building could be clearly seen up to approximately 2.5 m. The size of the stones above this point becomes noticeably smaller. This type construction break and change in stone size also occur in SK-E019. The rear of this room was cut from the wadi slope in an irregular semicircular shape and was possibly entered from the southwest. The smaller rooms on the northwest and south sides of the complex occur on a relatively flat ground plane with no retaining structure.

Structure (by zone)	Courtyard Dimensions			No. of Adjacent Rooms
	N-S in m	x	E-W in m	
STAGE ZONE				
SK-E024	7	x	8.5	5
SK-E044	11	x	9	4
SK-E058	8	x	8	3
SK-E059	4.5	x	12	3
SK-E060	8	x	16	6
SK-E065	16	x	11	3
SK-W050	15	x	8	4
SK-W023	9	x	9.5	5
SLOPE ZONE				
SK-E011	8	x	5	3
SK-E034	12	x	3.5	2
SK-E056	4	x	11	3
SK-E063	8.5	x	8	2
SK-E066	9	x	9	2
SK-W034	5.5	x	5.5	2
SK-W025	7	x	10	1
SK-W035	7	x	5	3

Table 18-16   Sikait, selected statistics on structures with courtyards and adjacent rooms.

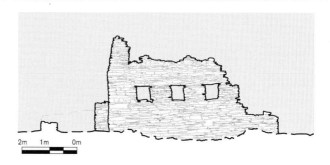

Figure 18-17   Sikait structure SK-E060 ("three windows") west elevation. Drawing by J.-L. G. Rivard.

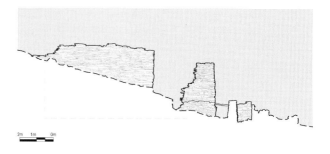

Figure 18-18   Sikait structure SKE060 ("three windows") north elevation. Drawing by J.-L. G. Rivard

Plate 18-19   Sikait structure SK-E060 ("three windows") looking east-southeast. Photograph by S. E. Sidebotham

Plate 18-20   Sikait structure SK-E060 ("three windows") looking north-northwest. Photograph by S. E. Sidebotham.

The construction of the edifice suggests multiple phases of building. The east-west wall that defines the northern edge of the main chamber has a second wall running parallel to it on its northern side. This second wall abuts directly onto the first, creating a wall of doubled thickness. It stands 1.4 m high x 3.8 m long (see Figure 18-17, bottom left; Figure 18-18, bottom center). A small room (with which this large wall may have been associated) sits northwest of the primary room. What appears to be a lintel across the 1 m opening into this room rises only 0.75 m from ground level. While the width and position in plan of the opening suggests a doorway, the height of the lintel would not have allowed entry as such. A second small room added onto the first extends the complex farther to the west. This later room utilizes the western wall of the earlier chamber as its eastern limit. All that can be suggested regarding

construction phases is the relative order of building. The larger primary room is earliest, with additions made extending westward. The complex was clearly larger, but much of it has been washed away.

18.11.3 THE SLOPE ZONE

Adjoining the relatively flat stage, the sides of the wadi rise steeply in the zone termed the slope. This zone contains the largest number of structures at Sikait (Plate 18-21 and Figure 18-22) and also the most remarkable due to their architectural complexity and state of preservation. The acuteness of the incline necessitates that they almost invariably sit atop significant retaining substructures. (SK-W001, SK-W014, SK-W035, SK-E011, SK-E018, and others). In addition to this, many buildings were carved into the phlogopite schist and talc schist incline, the most common type of bedrock on the wadi slopes, forming the rear walls and in some instances portions of the sidewalls of their structures (SK-W001, SK-W014, SK-W015, SK-E018, SK-E019, SK-W031, and others). In some structures, it appears as though the natural rock surfaces were quarried to provide stone for the freestanding walls, and it is the quarried area that has been incorporated as the rear wall of the building (SK-E047, SK-E060). In other instances, it appears as if the natural stone face was cut and used as wall surfaces without contributing to the building materials used in the freestanding walls. Moreover, many buildings retain rock-cut "storage areas" (SK-W018, SK-E049, SK-044, SK-E058, and others) and, in at least one example (SK-E011), a complete room, that were carved into the schist bedrock. (Plates 18-23 and 18-24, also Figures 18-12 and 13). These rock-cut features may have been created deliberately as cool, dry areas for storage. They could not originally have been small mining operations, as the beryls and emeralds at Sikait are not found in this type of stone.

Of the 40 structures/complexes along the western incline of the wadi, the survey identified 25 as constructed on the slope. Of the 78 structures/complexes along the eastern incline along the wadi, at least 48 were constructed on the slope. All mines found thus far at Sikait occur on the slope, concentrated in the northern end of the site. These are discussed further in the following pages.

Plate 18-21 Composite photograph of Sikait slope zone on east side of wadi looking south. Photographs by J.-L. G. Rivard.

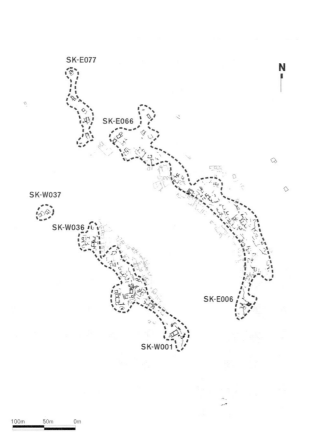

Figure 18-22 Sikait, plan of structures in the slope zone. Drawing by J.-L. G. Rivard and B. C. Foster.

Plate 18-23 Sikait structure SK-E011 looking northeast. Scale=1 m. Photograph by S. E. Sidebotham.

Plate 18-24 Sikait structure SK-E011 rock-cut storage area looking east. Scale-=-50 cm. Photograph by S. E. Sidebotham.

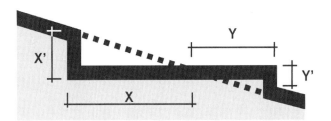

Figure 18-25   Sikait, diagram of typical structures in the slope zone. Drawing by J.-L. G. Rivard.

Figure 18-25 defines structures found on the slope. A retaining platform bisects the line of the slope. A portion projects beyond the incline atop a terrace wall, and a portion cuts into the slope itself. The dimensions of the values x and x', y and y' vary according to the steepness of the slope. One or more values occasionally reduce to zero. The condition of x' being a negative value and y' being positive describes the majority of the structures in this zone.

Notable Structures in the Slope Zone
"Administration" building SK-W001

The most imposing structure at Sikait is SK-W001 (Area W1). While Cailliaud (1821:73) referred to SK-W001 as a temple, the survey applied the nomenclature of the "administration" building. Structure SK-W001 sits on the southern end of the western slope atop a large retaining terrace accessed from three directions. A ramp climbs along the incline from the southwest (Plate 18-32), a large and steeper stair cuts into the southeastern corner of the retaining structure, and a more relaxed stair provides access from the north.

Plate 18-26   Sikait, southwest side of wadi with SK-W001 ("administration" building) to lower left and SK-W014 ("tripartite" building to upper right) looking west northwest. Photograph by S. E. Sidebotham.

The ramp from the southwest runs along the top of a retaining wall and intersects the larger stair at the southeastern corner of the retaining structure. The two then climb three additional steps to the level of the terrace that precedes the building. If this ramp existed in antiquity, or if there were steps along its length, remains a question to be answered by excavation. The larger stair at the southeastern corner of the retaining structure begins near the wadi floor. A total of 18 steps are immediately visible: four at the bottom, 2.3 m wide, that seem to have been much wider; what appear to be four more above this that were badly damaged, and finally 10 well-defined steps at the top, 1.5m wide and framed by retaining walls. (Figure 18-28 and Plate 18-30) The stair then intersects the ramp as described previously.

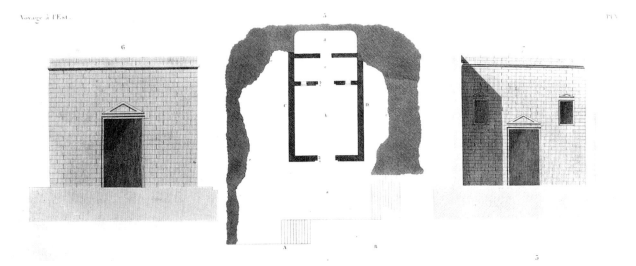

Figure 18-27   Sikait, Cailliauds drawings of SKW001 "administration" building).

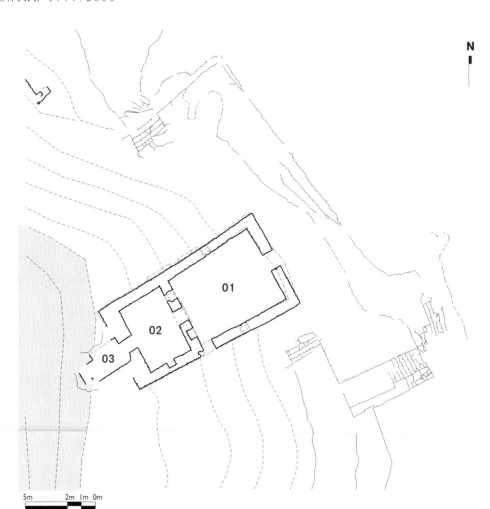

N

Figure 18-28
Sikait, plan of SK-
W001 ("administration"
building). Drawing by
J.-L. G. Rivard.

5m   2m 1m 0m

A third set of 10 stairs can be seen amid the debris on the northern side of the building and terraced platform. From the top of the platform, these stairs descend northward and then curve eastward. The largest of the stones used for the treads measures approximately 1.3 m long x 0.7 m wide.

The "administration" building consists of three rooms along a central axis of doorways (Figure 18-28). Entering from the center of the terrace on the eastern side, the rooms become progressively smaller and the last (westernmost) and smallest is cut from the incline. Two doors provide access into the first room (room 01) of the building: a monumental entrance in the eastern façade (Figure 18-28 and Plates 18-29 to 31, 33 and 39) and a smaller entrance along the southern wall (Plates 18-29 to 33 and 38). The monumental eastern entrance is approximately 3.75 m high x 1.35 m wide. Single stones, both still *in situ*, comprise both the threshold and lintel. The lintel of the smaller southern entrance remains *in situ*, approximately 2.0 m from

Plate 18-29   Sikait, SK-W001 ("administration" building) looking west-northwest. Photograph by S. E. Sidebotham.

modern ground level while the door is approximately 0.85 m wide.

Room 01 is roughly rectangular, 6.8 m deep E-W x 5.3 m wide N-S. The room is paved with large, flat, irregularly shaped stones measuring up to +/- 0.7 m at their greatest size. Two small, roughly cantered windows survive, one in the northern and another in the southern wall about 2.5 m from modern ground level (Plates 18-29, 32–34 and 38). Double shelves topped by projecting pediments measuring 0.7 m wide x 1.7 m high decorate the rear (western) wall of room 01; these flank a central door. These pediments add a decorative aspect to the room and are the only such examples found thus far on the site. Moreover, the lintel above the door on the rear wall extends approximately 0.10 m beyond the face of the wall, further adding to the room's ornamentation (Plates 18-38, 40 to 42). It is interesting to note that Cailliaud's drawing (Figure 18-27) only records a single shelf recess on either side of the door, corresponding to the higher of the two that actually exist. The floor level of the room slopes up toward the rear of the building. Modern ground level at the rear of the room is approximately 0.50 m higher than at the front where one enters the building. The remaining stone and tumble suggests the presence of a floor of stone pavers, yet this cannot be determined for certain without clearing the area.

Room 02 (Figure 18-28) is also rectangular (3.2 m deep E-W x 4.8 m wide N-S). The door into this chamber from room 01 is 1.1 m wide and elevated roughly 0.25 m above the floor level of the rear of room 01. Two projecting, decorative lintels protrude from the surface of the wall above this doorway on both the east and west faces of the dividing wall between rooms 01 and 02. (Plate 18-38 and Figure 18-43). What seems to be a double shelf is almost completely destroyed on the southern wall of chamber two. A second door, 1.90 m high from modern ground level x 1.05 m wide, pierces the west wall and provides access to the third chamber. It is possible that room 02 may have also been paved. This would likely have required a stepped floor to follow the natural incline that rises through the structure (Figure 18-41).

Room 03 (Figure 18-28) is rock-cut, approximately 2 m N--S x 3.5 m E-W and was originally roofed by at least six massive stone slabs. Two of these remain *in situ*, while debris and two other collapsed ceiling stones fill the room (Plates 18-36 and 37). Due to the tremendous amount of tumble, debris and wash, little else can be discerned of the space.

Not only does the building's position on the site, upon a high terrace overlooking the whole of the eastern slope, speak of its importance, but so, too, does the ornamentation of both its exterior and interior.

Plate 18-30   Sikait, SK-W001 ("administration" building) looking west. Photograph by S. E. Sidebotham.

Plate 18-31   (detail of Plate 18-30) Sikait, SK-W001 ("administration" building) east façade looking west. Photograph by S. E. Sidebotham.

Plate 18-32   Sikait, SK-W001 ("administration" building) ramp and building looking north from wadi floor. Photograph by S. E. Sidebotham.

Plate 18-33   Sikait, SKW001 ("administration" building) looking north-northwest from terrace in front of building. Photograph by S.E. Sidebotham.

Plate 18-36   Sikait, SK-W001 ("administration" building) looking east-southeast from above "administration" building. Note SK-E006 (large rock-cut temple) across wadi to the left. Photograph by S. E. Sidebotham.

Plate 18-34   Sikait, SKW001 ("administration" building) detail of south façade looking north. Note sagging of upper portion of east façade. Photograph by S. E. Sidebotham.

Plate 18-37   Sikait, SK-W001 ("administration" building) looking east from above the "administration" building. Note both *in situ* and fallen stone roof beams in room 03 (see Figure 19-28). Photograph by S. E. Sidebotham.

Figure 18-35   Sikait, SK-W001 ("administration" building) east elevation. Drawing by J.-L. G. Rivard.

Plate 18-38   Sikait, SK-W001 ("administration" building) interior of room 01 (see Figure 19-28), looking west-southwest toward room 02. Photograph by B. C. Foster.

Plate 18-39   Sikait, SK-W001 ("administration" building) interior, looking east from room 02 into room 01 (see Figure 18-28). Photograph by S. E. Sidebotham.

Plate 18-40   Sikait, SK-W001 ("administration" building) interior west wall of first room, south of door into second room: double shelves topped by pediment, looking east. Scale=1 m. Photograph by S. E. Sidebotham

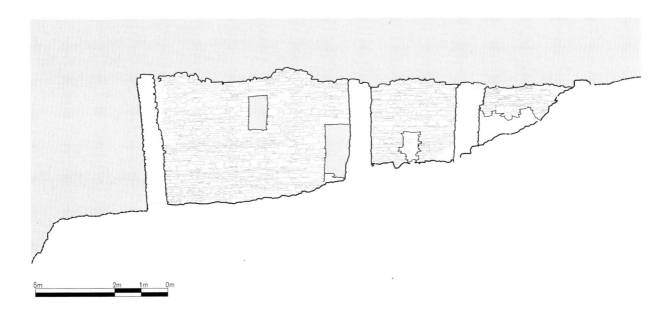

Figure 18-41   Sikait, SK-W001 ("administration" building) east-west section through structure looking south. Drawing by J.-L. G. Rivard.

Plate 18-42   Sikait, SK-W001 ("administration" building) interior west wall of first room, north of door into second room: double shelves topped by pediment looking northwest. Scale=1 m. Photograph by S. E. Sidebotham.

The tops of the exterior walls include a continuous, undecorated frieze course approximately 0.20 m wide (Plates 18-33 and 34). Parallel bands of local stone protrude from the face of the wall, approximately 0.15–0.20 m at the top and about 0.05–0.10 m at the bottom. The building appears to have used a type of mortar, which is much eroded toward the wall faces, suggesting falsely on an initial cursory inspection that the masonry was dry-laid.

Rock-cut temple SK-E006

Immediately opposite SK-W001 on the eastern slope is the most dramatic example of the rock-cut-type structure that occurs within the slope zone. SK-E006 (Area E1) is a monumental temple structure almost entirely cut from the talc schist of the steep wall of the wadi.

This type of rock-cut temple can be compared to others in the region including that at Bir Abu Safa, (23° 18.07' N/34° 47.84' E), about 170 km south of Sikait, discussed by Floyer (1893b: 411), who says, "Here, at the foot of a lofty cliff, walling on the north the valley formed by the junction of Hothein and the 'Anid', is a carved portal with an obliterated Greek inscription. The sockets are seen of beams, which roofed in a spring of sweet water still maintaining two or three palm trees. A good engraving of this picturesque well is given by Linant de Bellefonds. . . ." (cf. Linant de Bellefonds 1833: 164 and pl. 13).

While SK-E006 does not occur in relation to a well as Floyer describes the temple at Wadi Hodein ([sic] actually Bir Abu Safa), the occurrence of carved sockets and a Greek inscription perfectly describes Sikait's largest temple, also found at the base of a high cliff. Linant de Bellefonds dates the Bir Abu Safa temple to the Ptolemaic period (Linant de Bellefonds 1833: 164). If this is true, it may suggest that SK-E006 also originally dated to the Ptolemaic period and was reused with the later Roman occupation of the site.

Cailliaud's drawing of 1817 indicates that the temple was approached directly from the wadi floor (Figure 18-44), though modern ground level is more than 2 m below the base of the façade. Today one must climb a large amount of tumble to reach it.

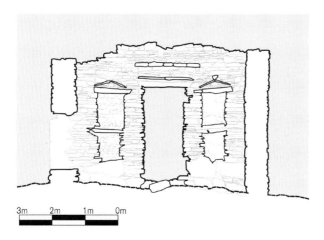

3m   2m   1m   0m

Figure 18-43   Sikait, SK-W001 ("administration" building) north-south section looking east through structure, view from first (01) into second room (02); (see Figure 18-28). Drawing by J.-L. G. Rivard.

Figure 18-44
Sikait, SK-E006 (large rock-cut temple)
Cailliaud's fanciful west elevation.

Figure 18-45
Sikait, SK-E006 (large rock-cut temple) west
elevation. Drawing by J.-L. G. Rivard.

Plate 18-46
Sikait, SK-E006 (large rock-cut temple) west
elevation looking east. Photograph by S. E.
Sidebotham.

Plate 18-47 Sikait, SK-E006 (large rock-cut temple) looking east. Photograph by S. E. Sidebotham.

Plate 18-49 Sikait, SK-E006 (large rock-cut temple) northern interior wall looking northeast. Scale=1 m. Photograph by S. E. Sidebotham.

Plate 18-48 Sikait, SK-E006 (large rock-cut temple) top portion of façade (including pediment) looking east. Photograph by S. E. Sidebotham.

Plate 18-50 Sikait, SK-E006 (large rock-cut temple) interior northern wall at western end looking north. Scale=20 cm. Photograph by S. E. Sidebotham.

The entire façade measures about 18 m wide N-S; a pair of small shrines flanks a main portal (Plates 18-56 to 58). How these shrines were related is not immediately clear, as they are separated from the central chamber by massive masonry walls projecting perpendicular to the face of the cliff. Each shrine consists of a single portal defined by two engaged columns. The interiors comprise a small chamber measuring roughly 1.4 m wide (N-S) by 0.6 m deep (E-W), while the southern shrine also contains an additional shelf extending the rear wall back an additional 0.3 m. The northern shrine has a niche in the center of the rear wall (Plate 18-56). The southern shrine has three interior niches (Plate 18-58). Cailliaud describes a disc and pair of serpents atop each door, but they are no longer preserved.

An unroofed porch, approximately 6.3 m x 5.7 m, fronts the central entrance. (Figures 18-59, 60) The sidewalls of this porch were cut into the cliff face and left flat. They were extended with the massive masonry walls that separate the main portal from the shrines on either side. On the western end of the northern rock-cut sidewall, three ornamented niches mark the upper area. Below these are two roughly rectangular openings, which allow access into a small, irregularly shaped chamber cut deeper into the slope (Plates 18-49 to 51). Inside the main chamber, are four square holes carved into the northern side wall near the floor (Plate 18-55); their purpose is uncertain. There are no rock-cut niches anywhere on the southern rock-cut sidewall (Plates 18-52, 53) although there are a number of dipinti and

Plate 18-51   Sikait, SK-E006 (large rock-cut temple) interior northern wall with small shrine at western end looking north. See also Figure 19.60. Each black and white increment on the scale=20 cm. Photograph by S. E. Sidebotham.

Plate 18-52   Sikait, SK-E006 (large rock-cut temple) interior looking southeast from main cella into two southern innermost chambers. Scale=1 m. Photograph by S. E. Sidebotham.

graffiti (see following). At present it appears that the masonry portions of the sidewalls were dry-laid, but this remains to be determined. The level of the base of these walls suggests, contrary to Cailliaud's sketch, that there was, indeed, a difference in the level of the wadi floor and the portal entry in antiquity (Figure 18-45 and Plate 18-46). This would further suggest the presence of a larger retaining structure than what is now immediately evident. If this was the case, it has eroded and been lost.

The main portal is 4.5 m wide and extends about 10 m into the mountainside. Two engaged three-quarter Doric/Tuscan columns, each topped by a square abacus, flank the main portal (Plates 18-46 and 47). Portions of three lines of a Greek inscription remain immediately beside the northernmost of the column capitals. Cailliaud commented that the text was traced in red.

Extant letters at the beginning of the first two lines read ΕΠΙ/ΤΥ (Plate 18-61). At least six regular cuts in the cliff face above the portal suggest a treatment topping the arrangement, but neither the remains nor Cailliaud's drawings give any clues to whether or not more existed (Plate 18-48).

The interior of the main temple chamber (see Figure 18-59, Levels 1-3) measures 5 m wide (N-S) x 10 m deep (E-W). It consists of three levels, each rising as it delves deeper into the hillside. Two massive columns, each topped by a square abacus, were cut in the round in level 1 (Figure 18-59, 1) and divided the space. These large columns undoubtedly supported the weight of the hillside. The northern one has largely collapsed (Plates 18-46, 47, 52, 53 and 54). Structural cracks appear in the walls of this first chamber.

Plate 18-53   Sikait, SK-E006 (large rock-cut temple) interior southern wall looking southeast. Scale=1 m. Photograph by S. E. Sidebotham.

Plate 18-56   Sikait, SK-E006 (large rock-cut temple) exterior of northern side chamber, not physically connected to main temple, looking east southeast. Scale=1 m. Photograph by S. E. Sidebotham.

Plate 18-54   Sikait, SK-E006 (large rock-cut temple) interior looking southeast from main cella into three innermost chambers. Scale-=1 m. Photograph by S. E. Sidebotham.

Plate 18-57   Sikait, SK-E006 (large rock-cut temple) exterior of southern side chamber, not physically connected to main temple, looking east. Scale-=1 m. Photograph by S. E. Sidebotham.

Plate 18-55   Sikait, SK-E006 (large rock-cut temple) northern interior wall toward eastern end shows four square holes of unknown function looking north-northeast. Scale=1 m. Photograph by S. E. Sidebotham.

Plate 18-58   Sikait, SK-E006 (large rock-cut temple) interior of southern side chamber looking east. Scale-=50 cm. Photograph by S. E. Sidebotham.

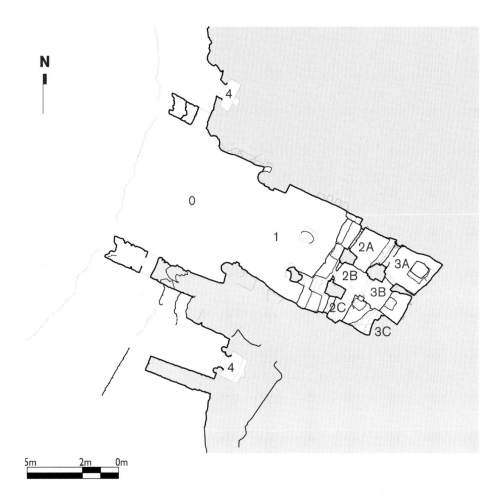

N

0

1

2A

2B

3A

2C

3B

3C

4

4

5m   2m   0m

Figure 18-59
Sikait, SK-E006 (large rock-cut temple) plan. Drawing by J.-L. G. Rivard.
0=uncovered porch
1=main chamber
2=second level
3=third level/inner sanctuary
4=shrine

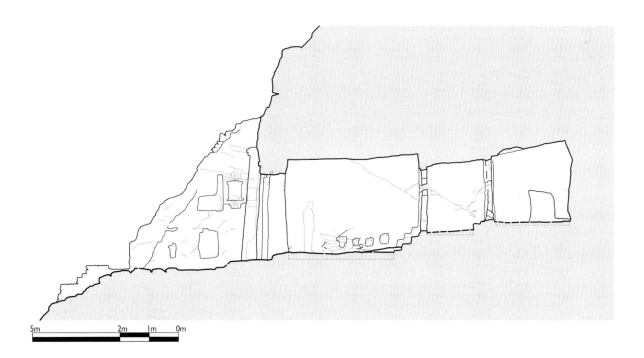

5m   2m   1m   0m

Figure 18-60   Sikait, SK-E006 (large rock-cut temple) east-west section looking north. Drawing by J.-L. G. Rivard.

Plate 18-61   Sikait, SK-E006 (large rock-cut temple) location and detail of remnants of Greek inscription *in situ* on temple façade. Photographs by J.-L. G. Rivard.

The four small, roughly rectangular holes (mentioned previously; Plate 18-55) line the lower portion of the north wall of this first room. Dipinti and graffiti from antiquity to modern times emblazon the walls and columns (see appendix by H. Cuvigny). One from the nineteenth century located on the southern interior face of the main temple chamber records Leonidas de Crete 1844 juin 5 (or 6). The floor is carefully paved with flat stones varying from about 0.4–0.7m in dimension.

A flight of three stairs rises to level 2 of the temple (Plates 18-52 and 54 and Figure 18-59, 2). The stairway itself is divided horizontally into three bays and each flight culminates in a rectangular threshold and portal. These doorways increase in size from south to north. Level 2 consists of three small, unadorned "rooms" that measure approximately 1.1 m x 1.1 m on the south (Figure 18-59, 2C), 1.2 x 1.4 m in the center (Figure 18-59, 2B), and 1.4 m x 1.4 m on the north (Figure 18-59, 2A), each separated by roughly rectangular piers (Plates 18-52 and 54). Both round and square holes were cut into the thresholds, jamb, and header between level 1 and level 2. This detail also occurs in the threshold between levels 2 and 3, and suggests an assembly of screens or pivoting doors closing the deeper recesses of the temple from open view.

Level 3, (Figure 18-59, 3) chamber 3C appears unfinished, where the back wall of the temple protrudes forward to fill the space. Chamber 3B consists of a roughly square space, with a large niche cut into the back wall at a height of 0.9 m. A small raised square on the horizontal surface of the niche (0.55 m x 0.49 m) suggests a rough altar. The northern room (Figure 18-59, 3A) contains an irregularly shaped freestanding altar, approximately 0.9 m x 0.8 m x 1.05 m high.

Smaller Temple SK-E002

SK-E002 is a second example of a rock-cut temple occurring in the talc schist of the wadi slope. Found at the extreme southern end of the site, SK-E002 marks the approach to Sikait just before the wadi opens into the densely built basin.

SK-E002 appears in Cailliaud's text with a somewhat fanciful drawing (Figure 18-62); "a smaller temple, in the form of a room with niches cut from the talc mountain; its entrance is decorated by four well-preserved columns surmounted by arches. Above the doors, as in the other temple, one saw a disc accompanied by two serpents. The construction was not well preserved, and the workmanship more crude when compared with that of the ancient Egyptians. In truth, the nature of the stone did not always permit the workers to do as they would wish. Above the portals and on the façade . . . were numerous inscriptions carved in Greek." (Cailliaud, 1821:72, translated by J.-L. G. Rivard) There was, in fact, only a single 14-line-long inscription, first transcribed by Cailliaud and followed by G. Belzoni and J. G. Wilkinson. Portions of the text remain *in situ*, but it is now much damaged with portions missing. One of the authors (Sidebotham) saw portions of some of the inscription broken and lying on the ground in front of the temple in summer 1991; these had disappeared by winter 2000. The inscription (cf. Plates 18-66 to 68) records that the temple was dedicated to the deities "Sarapis, Isis [of Senskis/Senske, the ancient name of Sikait], Apollo and all the gods sharing their temple" (cf. Bernand 1977:167–177, no. 69). Meredith (1953:105) wrote that "The end name of Gallienus was still legible in the early nineteenth century and the inscription includes a dedication to Isis, Apollo (preceded probably by Serapis)." Other graffiti include Leonidas de Crete (as appeared in the larger temple) and G. Forni/di Milano/1819 E 1888.

Figure 18-62
Sikait, SK-E002 (small rock-cut temple of Serapis, Isis, and Apollo). Cailliaud's west elevation.

Figure 18-63
Sikait, SK-E002 (small rock-cut temple of Serapis, Isis, and Apollo), west elevation. Drawing by J.-L. G. Rivard.

2.0m 1.0m 0m

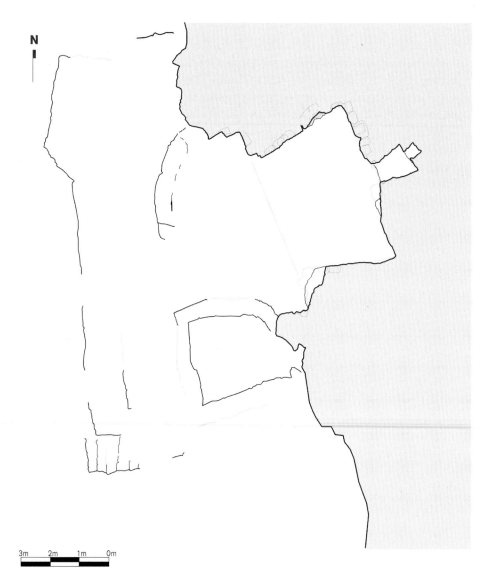

Figure 18-64
Sikait, SK-E002 (small rock-cut
temple of Serapis, Isis, and Apollo)
plan. Drawing by J.-L. G. Rivard.

3m 2m 1m 0m

Plate 18-65   Sikait, SK-E002 (small rock-cut temple of Serapis, Isis, and Apollo) west elevation looking east. Photograph by S. E. Sidebotham.

Plate 18-66   Sikait, SK-E002 (small rock-cut temple of Serapis, Isis, and Apollo) southern chamber looking east. Photograph by S. E. Sidebotham.

As in the case of SK-E006, Cailliaud's drawing of SK-E002 (Figure 18-62) suggests that the temple was approached from the wadi floor. Evidence of a retaining wall and stairs indicates that this was not the case, where modern ground level is considerably lower. (Figures 18-63 and 64).

"Tripartite" building SK-W014

SK-W014 is a three-room building with a large court-yard that sits atop one of the largest retaining terraces at Sikait. It is located north of SK-W001 in the plan area W3. The building sits at the point farthest recessed from the wadi floor and, together with SK-W015, is the highest structure on the western slope. The survey noted a large pottery dump on the other side of the ridge behind the building.

A wall defines the extent of the retaining structure supporting SK-W014, surrounding a courtyard in front of the building. A door on the southern side of the wall leads into the court. This wall abuts the southern wall of the building itself. A construction break suggests multiple phases of construction or perhaps repair. The eastern façade of the edifice is stepped, with the central chamber projecting forward of the two side chambers to the north and south respectively. (Plates 18-69, 71–73 and Figures 18-70, 74–76).

Three doors provide access into the central room through this wall, one larger door flanked by two smaller portals. Although only the southern door

Plate 18-67   Sikait, SK-E002 (small rock-cut temple of Serapis, Isis, and Apollo) remains of Greek inscription from reign of Gallienus *in situ* over entrance of southern chamber (in Plate 18-66). Photograph by S. E. Sidebotham, 1998.

remains fully intact, there are gaps in the partially preserved doorjamb of the central door, where a lintel likely stood at a height of 2.05 m. This central lintel would have spanned 1.3 m. The fully intact southern door measures 1.66 m high and tapers, measuring 0.76 m wide at the threshold and 0.70 m at the lintel.

Plate 18-68   Sikait, SK-E002 (small rock-cut temple of Serapis, Isis, and Apollo) remains of Greek inscription from reign of Gallienus, fallen on ground. Scale=10 cm. Photograph by S. E. Sidebotham, 1991. This fragment has since disappeared.

Plate 18-69
Sikait, SK-W014 ("tripartite" building)
looking north-northwest. Photograph by
S. E. Sidebotham.

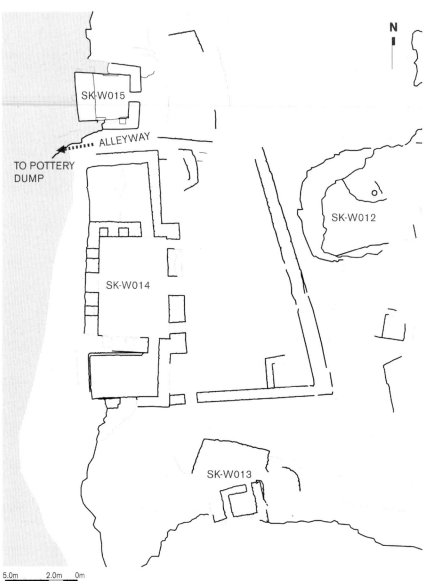

Figure 18-70   Sikait, SK-W014 ("tripartite"
building) plan. Drawing by
J.-L. G. Rivard.

hewn stone. Upon entering the central chamber of the building (6.8m wide [N-S] x 5m deep [E-W] interior), the viewer faces a series of niches carved from the western (rear) wall together with shelves and pedestals built along and protruding from it. A pair of double shelves 0.60 m wide remains on the northern wall of the main room. The upper shelf measures 0.38 m high x 0.37 m deep while the bottom shelf is 0.42 m high x 0.55 m deep. The southern wall is damaged, but it seems likely that there was also a similar pair of double shelves here.

A door in the northern wall of the room 1.36 m high from modern ground level (debris) x 0.80 m wide along the lowest measurable point leads to the northern room. A transom window 0.50 m high x 0.74 m wide along its top sits above the door. Opposite this, a similar door in the southern wall of the room ,1.41 m high x 0.77 m along its lowest measurable width, accesses the southern room. A transom window (0.53 m high x 0.61 m wide along its top) survives above the door. Two flat stones (0.08–0.12 m thick) serve as the lintels of each door and the bottom stone of each light window.

The northern room measures approximately 4.0 m wide (N-S) x 4.2 m deep (E-W). Debris or modern disturbance and robbing covers almost the entire floor. The southern room (2.9 m wide (N-S) x 4.8 m deep (E-W) interior) has largely collapsed, but it seems to have resembled the northern room. Both rooms have a small window centered in the eastern wall.

Plate 18-71   Sikait, SK-W014 ("tripartite" building) looking north northeast. Photograph by S. E. Sidebotham.

Plate 18-72   Sikait, SK-W014 ("tripartite" building) interior of southern-most room, northern wall, looking northwest. Note shelves and door. Photograph by S .E. Sidebotham.

Three lintel stones spanning the thickness of the wall remain *in situ* at the top of this door. Only the lower portion of the northern door remains, and it is too damaged to suggest any dimensions. A transom window remains *in situ* over the southern door and measures 0.70 m wide x 0.91 m high. It seems very probable that a similar construction existed above both the central and northern doors.

The building utilizes the soft stone of the wadi slope as its western (rear) wall, as well as part of its northern and southern walls. In all cases the natural stone was cut so that stone walls could be built on top of the

Plate 18-73   Sikait, SK-W014 interior north wall of central room with shelves. Photograph by J.-L. G. Rivard.

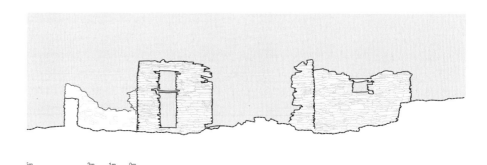

Figure 18-74
Sikait, SK-W014 ("tripartite"
building) east elevation.Drawing by
J.-L. G. Rivard.

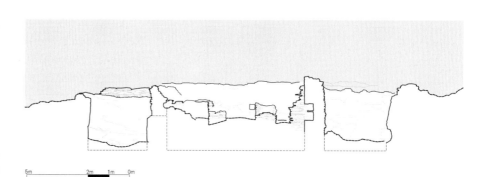

Figure 18-75
Sikait, SK-W014 ("tripartite"
building) north-south section looking
west. Drawing by J.-L. G. Rivard.

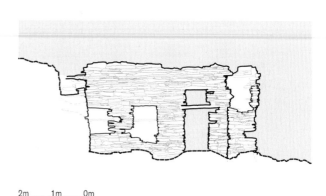

Figure 18-76
Sikait, SK-W014 ("tripartite"
building) west-east section looking
north. Drawing by J.-L. G. Rivard.

Plate 18-77
Sikait, SK-W015, interior north wall
looking north. Scale=1 m. Composite
photographs by J.-L. G. Rivard.

The single room structure SK-W015 just north of SK-W014 frames an alleyway and a possible stair between the two buildings, leading in the direction of the large pottery dump immediately over the ridgeline of the western slope. A single door in the eastern wall leads from a retained terrace in front of the building into the one chamber of SK-W015. A low bench-like installation, which filled the entire width of the west wall, dominates the rear of the room. The interior of the room also preserves a relief decoration that was carved on the northern wall, where a large portion of plastered wall surface remains. Looking out from the doorway is a clear view of SK-W006 on the opposite side of the wadi.

The group of structures SK-W013, SK-W014, and SK-W015 clustered in the furrow of Area W3 suggesting a programmatic relationship due to their proximity and similar orientation. The relief decoration of SK-W015 (Plate 18-77) also suggests a possible religious use for this structure. If this is true, then the entire group may have been used in a similar manner. Furthermore, the stucco or plaster surfacing that remains on the lower half of the north wall of SK-W15 may provide further evidence of similar treatments elsewhere on the site that have been lost due to erosion.

"Six Windows" building SK-E066

SK-E066 is a prominent building at the northern end of the site referred to as "six windows," which clearly faces the wadi floor (Plates 18-78 and 80 and Figures 18-79 and 81). It sits at the base of a small zone of wash that separates Area E4 from Area E3, atop a retaining platform. The means of access to the top of the platform is not clear, though there may have been a stair assembly on the southwestern side.

Plate 18-78
Sikait, SK-E066 ("six windows") looking north-northwest. Photograph by S. E. Sidebotham.

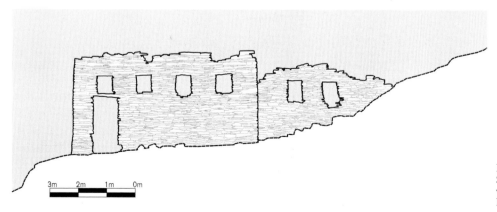

3m 2m 1m 0m

Figure 18-79
Sikait, SK-E066 ("six windows") south elevation. Drawing by J.-L. G. Rivard.

Plate 18-80   Sikait, SK-E066 ("six windows" westernmost part of structure looking north. Photograph by S. E. Sidebotham.

The building consists of two roughly rectangular rooms (west and east respectively) and appears to have had a small third room attached later, southwest of the platform (SK-E067). The building preserves six windows high up on the southern wall of the two main rooms, ranging between 0.45–0.56 m wide x 0.53–0.64 m high. Four are located in the western room (hereafter referred to as "room 1"), one of which rests directly above a door in the same wall. The remaining two are in the eastern room (hereafter referred to as "room 2"). Wholly preserved, the door stands 1.9 m above modern ground level x 0.87 m wide. At its greatest height, the wall of room 1 stands 3.25 m above modern ground level. There is no evidence to suggest a second storey, though niches, quite probably for roofing beams, are extant in the interior of the wall.

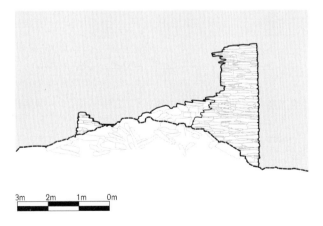

3m   2m   1m   0m

Figure 18-81   Sikait, SK-E066 ("six windows") west elevation. Drawing by J.-L. G. Rivard.

Room 1 contains a partially preserved double shelf in the northern wall (there was quite probably a second; the wall, however, has collapsed). A door, only 0.75 m wide, leads through the eastern wall of the chamber. Room 2 is partially hewn from the wadi slope. Along the eastern wall are the remains of what may have been a storage closet that runs parallel to the wadi slope. The walls vary between 0.55–0.70 m thick.

Mining Shafts SK-E068 and SK-E070

These two structures are significant less for their architectural character than for their proximity to the clearest evidence for mining at Sikait. It is noteworthy, however, that SK-E068 was constructed of stones with a much higher concentration of white quartz and is the only such building on the site. The stone is much harder and is evidently found in and around the area in which this building was constructed.

N

100m   50m   0m

Figure 18-82   Sikait plan locating general area of large mine shafts at northern end of the site. Drawing by J.-L. G. Rivard and B. C. Foster.

Numerous shafts delve into the eastern slope at this point (Figure 18-82). The immediate vicinity around and below the shafts is dominated by tailings of the blackish phlogopite/biotite mica schist and other stone fragments that indicate the intensity of activity that once took place here. Worn steps survive carved into the steep sides of the largest shaft, which was about 7.7 m in diameter and at least 10 m deep (Plate 18-83); another nearby shaft is about 1.5–2 m wide x 4.5 m deep.

Plate 18-83   Sikait, one of the large mine shafts at the northern end of the site. This example is about 7.7 m in diameter x at least 10 m deep. View looking south southeast. Photograph by S. E. Sidebotham.

Many of the structures on the slope are complex aggregations of terraced platforms and chambers at various levels. Some indicate multistorey constructions following the incline of the steep topography (SK-E028, SK-E046). A more detailed study of several of these buildings is forthcoming.

18.11.4 STAIRS, RAMPS, ALLEYS, AND RETAINING WALLS

The buildings of Sikait interact with a traceable pattern of circulation routes comprising stairways, alleys, and ramped constructions that predominantly traverse the slope zone. Prior to clearing and more in-depth investigation, the detailed nature of each axis of movement remains unclear because of the large amount of tumbled stone covering the site. It is not always possible to differentiate between interior and exterior routes. Larger, better-preserved clusters of rooms often very clearly define paths of apparently exterior circulation running either perpendicular to the slope in stairways or parallel to it in gently ramped configurations. In most cases, severe erosion and tumble make definite classification very difficult. All routes noted are above the wadi floor, although many lead down to this elevation. Together with the buildings found here, they terminate in a line of evident and drastic erosion.

The low-lying pass in Area E1' (indicated in Figure 18-7) preserves numerous architectural and retaining

structures at its lower elevations, while the area above it seems to remain naturally defined. The route climbs over the eastern ridgeline and leads toward structures SK-E053, SK-E054, and SK-E038, SK-E39, SK-E040 and SK-E041.

Figure 18-84   Sikait, diagrammatic analysis of circulation routes. Drawing by J.-L. G. Rivard.

Both masonry and rock-cut stairways and ramps identify major structures at Sikait. As noted in section 18.9, the use of mortar in the construction of the masonry stairs cannot yet be adequately determined. At present they appear to have been dry-laid. Discernable routes run above SK-E018 (rock-cut), beside the multileveled SK-E027 and SK-E028 (masonry), and lead up to SK-E074 (masonry). Some stairways are likely internal (SK-E033, SK-E045, and SK-E51). They occasionally suggest multistoried structures together with other architectural features such as door and window positions. Major retaining walls and platforms support many buildings. At its most ambitious, the retaining structure of SK-E018 creates a platform nearly 10 m above the steep inclines at its base, and SK-W001 crowns a monumental platform 7 m above the wadi floor that was cut with three stairways/ramps

as discussed previously. A cluster of stairs, alleys, and
routes traverses the ascent into Area W3 (Figure 18-7).
Well-preserved examples remain between SK-W016
and SK-W017 (masonry), clearly visible paths and
alleys divide SK-W011 and SK-W013, SK-W014 and
15 (rock-cut) and indicate a link to the pottery dump
behind SK-W014. Countless smaller but more complex
assemblies of terraced walls render the natural slopes
entirely architectural in many areas.

18.11.5 THE APEX ZONE

Structures found at the apex of the slope typically sit
atop minor retaining constructions (Figures 18-85 and
86). Located at the crest of the slope, these are not
carved into the incline to complete enclosing walls at
the rear or sides. With the exception of SK-E053, their
configuration tends to be much simpler than structures
on the slope below (SK-E038, SK-E039, SK-E078).

Figure 18-86   Sikait, diagram of typical structure found in the apex zone.
Drawing by J.-L. G. Rivard.

Notable buildings in the Apex Zone
Skopeloi
A number of lone structures, termed *skopeloi* (watchtowers) for the purpose of the survey, lay scattered
about the site at or near the ridgelines of the slopes and
in visually advantageous locations (Figures 18-87 and
88). Between the eastern and western ridgelines, the
structures are intervisible. Most occur in the apex zone.
The majority are small single-chamber constructions
measuring an average of 3–4 m x 3–4 m.

In some instances, these structures are indicative
of important satellite groupings in proximity to the
main wadi at Sikait. On the ridge of the eastern slope
a number of these structures cluster around the low-
lying pass in area E1' (SK-E037, SK-E04, SK-E054,
see Figure 18.7). Two others occur farther east in a
neighboring wadi where one overlooks a group of
graves on a nearby slope, and another sits in the wadi
below this location.

These structures may have served as watch points
over access to and from the area, for defense, for the
regulation of the movement of resources in the area,
and as signal relay points as indicated by Floyer (1893b:
418) who described "Watch-towers and magazines
. . . posted on prominent peaks." They would have
offered protection to watchmen from the hot wind and,
minimally, from the sun. A closer examination of the
interrelationships of these *skopeloi* is forthcoming. Until
that time, however, a distinction cannot be made among
skopeloi types, which may have served, for example, as
watchtowers versus those that may have functioned in
other capacities.

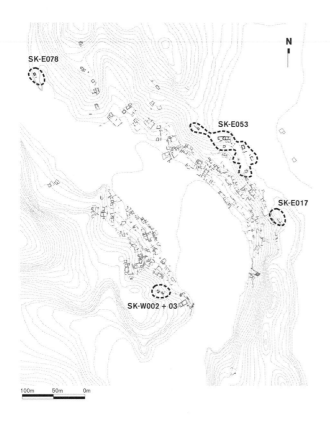

Figure 18-85   Sikait, plan of site showing the apex zone. Drawing by J.-L.
G. Rivard and B. C. Foster.

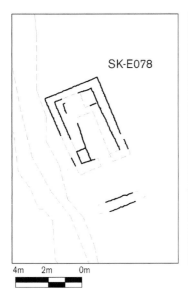

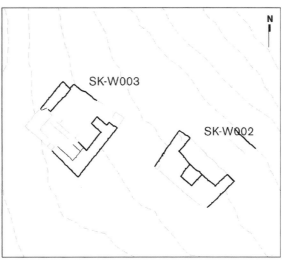

Figure 18-87
Sikait, detail plan of typical apex structures, SK-E078, and *skopeloi* SK-W002, SK-W003. Drawings by J.-L. G. Rivard.

Plate 18-88 Sikait, *skopelos* above and within cluster of robbed graves east of main site, looking east-northeast. Photograph by S. E. Sidebotham.

Plate 18-89 Sikait, robbed grave looking southeast. Scale=50 cm. Photograph by S. E. Sidebotham.

18.12 NECROPOLIS

The low-lying pass at Area E1' (Figure 18-7) leads in the direction of the largest cluster of robbed tombs found so far in proximity to Sikait. One group lay on the eastern side of a tall peak that overlooks the main wadi of Sikait. A second group encircles a smaller hill north of the first. A *skopelos* also appears on the same slope, whose walls are built around a jutting cleft of natural stone (Plate 18-88). All of the tombs have been robbed (Plate 18-89) and are in various states of preservation, while abundant pottery litters the slopes over the immediate area.

Numbering only about 100 graves, it is doubtful that this was the only such necropolis used over the life of Sikait. Other smaller clusters of graves, such as a group found in South Sikait, add to the total, yet the number remains small.

18.13 FUTURE AGENDA AND WORK UNDERWAY

Following the completion of the survey of Sikait, the team proceeded to Middle and North Sikait to begin documentation. This work will continue in future seasons. These investigations will map the significant architectural remains preserved at these sites together with the surrounding evidence of mining activity.

The 2002 season began small-scale excavations, architectural restoration, and conservation at Sikait. It also continued surveying at Middle and North Sikait as well as farther afield. The summer 2002 season cleared debris currently obscuring some structures at Sikait and allowed a fuller analysis and elaboration of the current text. A forthcoming publication of the results of the summer 2002 season will include a typological analysis of the architectural remains and reconstruction analysis.

18.14 CONCLUSION

Initial surveys of the standing architecture at Sikait reveal an intense locus of mining and building activity in this area of ancient Mons Smaragdus. It suggests the presence of a sizable population requiring a dependable system for the provision of food and water, either produced on site, obtained from without, or a combination of the two. It further implies a dependable human network for the distribution of the material resources exploited at the site.

The mining activity justified an ambitious building program that included elaborate multistoried architecture with modest decoration. The complexity of building was perhaps augmented by the mining industries it served, resulting in significant subterranean "construction." The visible phasing suggests a decline in the skill of construction, but it is not yet possible to develop an accurate chronology. The surface pottery suggests a Roman date of first through fifth century AD for the site, but the possibility remains of a Ptolemaic or earlier Egyptian and later Islamic settlement here. The size of the site and its state of preservation, as well as the large number of mines that surround the area, beg further work and undoubtedly will provide unique information about mining of precious and semiprecious stones in the Eastern Desert.

The architectural evidence suggests a significant religious infrastructure serving the population, but the true extent of this remains to be determined. It is not yet possible to estimate the size and fluctuations of the population and the phases of occupation of the site, but the preliminary results of the excavations conducted in summer 2002 better documented these. The evidence of the mine shafts themselves, however, suggests that the population based in Sikait gradually extended its mining activities over time to sites farther north before ceasing altogether.

18.15 APPENDIX (H. CUVIGNY)

Dipinto rouge dans le *pronaos* du grande temple rupestre de Sikait

Le village de mineurs de Sikait n'a livré jusqu'à présent que deux inscriptions grecques.

L'un (*I.Pan 69*, Bernand 1977), de loin la plus importante, était gravée au linteau des portes d'un petit temple rupestre (*speos*) qui se trouve à l'entrée du site. Le texts, aujourd'hui largement vandalisé, n'a malheureusement jamais été vu par des épigraphistes avant sa destruction. Ceux-ci se sont appuyés sur des transcriptions réalisées par des voyageurs: le premier fut Frédéric Cailliaud, l'inventeur du site (Cailliaud 1821: Pl. VIII.3), bientôt suivi be Belzoni (Belzoni 1821:90); plus tard, de meilleurs dessins furent réalisés par Wilkinson ainsi que par Nestor L'Hôte, qui visita Sikait en 1841. Le texte a été établi successivement par Letronne (Letronne 1842:453-463), Franz (*CIG III 4839*) et Dittenberger (*OGIS II 717*) don't l'édition a été reprise à peu de détails près dans *IGRR* I 1274 et *SB* V 8384; enfin, A. Bernand a proposé une nouvelle edition dans *Pan du désert* (*I. Pan 69*). L'inscription est datée du règne de Gallien seul (260-268), d'après une conjecture de Letronne fondée sur le dessin de Wilkinson.

L'autre inscription grecque Sikait est un *dipinto* à l'encre rouge. Letronne ne s'est pas aperçu que Cailliaud le mentionne, le reproduit et signale qu'il se trouvait dans *un autre* temple rupestre que le petit *speos* aménagé: Cailliaud le localise en effet "dans le temple principal" (Belzoni 1821:11 and 72). En revanche, Belzoni situe le dipinto au même endroit que la grande inscription (Belzoni 1821:91).

Letronne n'a pris connaissance du *dipinto* que par le dessin de Wilkinson d'après lequel il le publie (Letronne 1848:228); croyant à tort qu'il est "sur une des parois" du même *speos* que *I.Pan 69*, il le date en conséquence, par analogie, de Gallien: on voit que cette datation n'a aucune valeur. Franz republie le *dipinto* (*CIG* III 4840) en reproduisant la mauvaise transcription de Cailliaud (Cailliaud 1821: Pl. VIII.4); dans un *addendum*, Franz

(1217 sq.) reproduit la transcription de Wilkinson et, en modifiant un peu la présentation, l'édition de Letronne. Si Franz n'ignore pas que la transcription de Cailliaud a échappé à Letronne, il suit Letronne en situant le *dipinto* dans le même temple que l'inscription. Le *dipinto* n'a été repris, d'après Letronne *apud* Franz, qu'en *SB* V 8650; son existence semble avoir échappé à A. Bernand, qui ne l'a pas intégré dans *Pan du désert*.

Lors d'une visite à Sikait le 6 janvier 2001 en compagnie de M. Hussein el Afiouny, alors directeur des antiquités de Qena et de la mer Rouge, j'ai pu, avec Adam Bülow-Jacobsen, constater l'état désespéré de l'inscription du petit *speos* à l'entrée du site. En revanche, le *dipinto* dans le temple principal est resté très frais, ce qui nous permet d'en lever une photographie et une nouvelle édition.

Sur la paroi à droite en entrant, au fond du pronaos du temple rupestre principal 54 x 69 cm haut. Lettres ca. 3.5 cm; κθ: 8 cm.

La fin des lignes 1 et 2 est effacée au point d'être presque imperceptible.

Édition de Letronne (Letronne 1848:2)

Πακύβης ου Πάκυβις
Πετοςιρις . . . ἐπιφὶ
προφήτης   κθ
της Ιςιδ[ος καὶ Cαράπι-]
τος Lια
μ. παυνι κθ

Édition SB V 8650 (d'après Letronne *apud* Franz, *CIG* III: 1218) :

Πακύβη[ς—(ἔτουσ)-], Ἐπῖφι κθ .
Πετοσῖ ρις ,
προ[φ]ήτης
τῆς }Ἰσιδ[ος καὶ Cαρὶπι] -
τος (ἔτους) ια ,
Πα[ῦ]ν[ι] κθ .

Il convient en fait de présenter l'inscription ainsi:

Πάκυβις *c.* 4?
        της *c.* 7?
        ς ι ι ο Φαμεντ^ω
                κθ

5   Πετόςιρις
     προ[φ]ήτης
     τῆς Ιςιδί-
     τος *vac.* (ἔτους) ια
     Φαμαντ κθ

3 et 9 1. Φαμενωθ || 7-8 1.Ιςιδος

"Pakybis Y le 29 Phamenôth.
Petosiris, prophète d'Isis.
L'an 11, le 29 Phamenôth."

1.   Du *iota* de détache une ligne courbe qui devait à l'origine séparer les deux *dipinti*. On en verrait l'autre extrémité (le milieu ayant été effacé) à droite de κθ (1.9). C'est cette courbe qui a donné à Wilkinson et Letronne l'impression que le nom était peut-être Πακυβης.

2.   της. Peut-être l'article τῆς ou la fin de προφητῆς

3.   φα ou φλ. Letronne écrit à propos de ce mot: "le nom du mois paraît été ΕΠΙΦΙ à moins que ce ne soit παωφι. Le mois de la seconde date doit être ΠΑΥΝΙ" (Letronne 1848:229).

7-8.   Je n'ai pas trouvé d'autre exemple de ce génitif aberrant. La conjecture de Letronne me paraît devoir être écartée, car il n'y a pas la moindre trace d'écriture à droite de ιςιδι.

8.   Sachant que le *dipinto* n'a rien à voir avec l'inscription de *speos*, nous n'avons aucune raison particulière d'attribuer cet an 11 à Gallien (dont le nom en *I.Pan 69*, rappelons-le, n'est qu'une conjecture). L'absence de titulature plaide peut-être pour un règne qui n'est pas antérieur au dernier tiers du IIe s. p.C.

9.   Dans cette ligne, l'encre n'a pas disparu mais s'est mélangée et forme une sorte de long pâté. Les lettres sont à peine reconnaissables, sauf le *mu* et le *tau* final. Encore ce *tau* pourrait-il être une croix (+), mais c'est sans doute une illusion créée par le fait que son jambage est dans le prolongement de celui du *alpha* du quantième de l'année. *Phi* apparaît comme un vague rond; je le déduis du Φ très clair de la ligne 3. Il est en effet très vraisemblable que les deux signatures ont été écrites au même moment (et peut-être par la même main) : il faut donc que le quantième κθ soit précédé du même nom de mois.

CHAPTER 19 ～

EXCAVATIONS AT THE SMALLER *PRAESIDIUM* IN WADI KALALAT

A. E. HAECKL

During the 2000 season, excavations were conducted at two ancillary military sites in the immediate vicinity of Berenike proper: the *hydreuma, praesidium et lacus* at Siket (see Chapter 20), and the smaller of two garrisons in Wadi Kalalat, which is the subject of this report (Figure 19-1 and Chapter 17, Figure 17-3). The Siket and Kalalat *praesidia* were roughly equidistant from the main settlement site of Berenike. The fortified water source at Siket was located 7.2 km west northwest of Berenike at 23° 55.88' N/35° 24.46' E, while the two forts in Wadi Kalalat lay approximately 8 and 8.5 km southwest of Berenike. The smaller Kalalat fortification, located at 23° 52.54' N/35° 24.97' E, stood only 1 km northeast of its neighbor. The excavations at Siket and Kalalat were part of an ongoing archaeological effort to clarify the relationship of outlying "forts to port," integrating the Red Sea entrepôt of Berenike into the wider network of Roman roads, water sources, and military outposts in the Eastern Desert. This regional aspect of the Berenike project has acquired increasing urgency over the years, as development sparked by the Red Sea tourist industry and commercial mining in the Eastern Desert continues to accelerate, threatening the integrity of ancient sites previously protected by remoteness and inaccessibility.

A systematic campaign of documentation through survey, photography, and drawing, all published in prior Berenike excavation reports, preceded this season's excavations at the satellite sites of Siket and Kalalat. The *praesidium* at Siket was identified, surveyed, and drawn in 1998 (Sidebotham 2000:359–366). The large *hydreuma* in Wadi Kalalat was surveyed in 1994 (Sidebotham 1995:91–93), planned in 1995 (Sidebotham and Zitterkopf 1996:384–391) and excavated in 1997 and 1998 (Sidebotham and Barnard 2000; Bagnall 2000). The smaller garrison at Kalalat, which measured approximately 26 m E-W x 32 m N-S in external dimensions, was surveyed and planned in 1994 (Sidebotham 1995:87–91; Figures 19-1, 3, 5 and 6, Plates 19-2 and 4).

20.1 GOALS AND STRATEGY

Excavation in the smaller Kalalat fortification had four interconnected goals:
1. To date its foundation, occupational sequence, and abandonment;
2. To identify its purpose;
3. To relate it both chronologically and functionally to surrounding civilian settlements and military outposts;
4. To understand its individual history within the larger framework of Roman involvement in the Red Sea trade.

The question of chronology was particularly important, as survey and excavation in the large *praesidium* at Kalalat had left certain aspects of its occupational history unresolved. Archaeological survey at that site suggested activity in both the first/second and fifth/sixth centuries AD (Sidebotham 1995:86), while excavation produced stratigraphic evidence for only a single phase of occupation in the earlier period (Sidebotham and Barnard 2000:395–397). Survey of the smaller Kalalat garrison likewise pointed to two periods of occupation. Pottery collected at the site dated to "the second–third centuries and, possibly, later" (Sidebotham 1995:91). The architecture of the fort also exhibited two building phases, with "at least two of the earlier rounded towers . . . remodelled later on . . . into rectilinear–shaped features" and a postern gate in the rear wall deliberately blocked shut (Sidebotham 1995:87).

The unusually close proximity of the two Roman fortifications in Wadi Kalalat raised additional questions to be addressed by excavation. Were the two Kalalat garrisons contemporary or consecutive? Did they share the same functions or were they erected for different purposes? The 1997 and 1998 excavations in the larger fortification at Kalalat produced convincing archaeological and epigraphic evidence that it operated as a *praesidium* and *hydreuma*, or fortified water source, into the reign of Trajan (Sidebotham and Barnard 2000; Bagnall 2000). The dedicatory inscription discovered in the gateway of the *praesidium* at Siket attested that it was established as an *hydreuma et lacus*, a fortified well and cistern, under Vespasian (see Chapter 20; Bagnall, Bülow-Jacobsen, and Cuvigny 2001). Since the larger garrison at Kalalat and the small *praesidium* at Siket were apparently built principally to supply Berenike with potable water, we began excavations at the smaller Kalalat garrison with the working hypothesis that it also served as a water source administered by the Roman army.

In hopes of finding epigraphic evidence for the date and purpose of the smaller garrison at Kalalat, we followed an excavation strategy that had proven successful at three other forts in the Eastern Desert (Abu Sha'ar, the large fort at Kalalat, and the *praesidium* at Siket). Since trenches located in the main gateways of each of these buildings produced complete or fragmentary dedicatory inscriptions, trench KL00-1 was duly laid out in the gateway of the smaller fortification in Wadi Kalalat (Figure 19-3 and Plate 19-4). Unfortunately, no official building inscription came to light in the KL00-1 gateway trench.

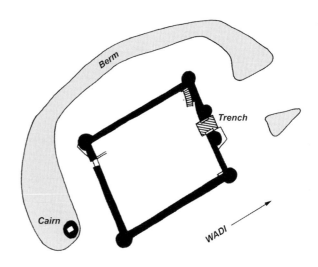

Figure 19-1   Plan of smaller *praesidium* in Wadi Kalalat and location of trench KL00-1. Drawing by H. Barnard.

Plate 19-2   View of smaller *praesidium* in Wadi Kalalat looking southeast. Photograph by S.E. Sidebotham.

Trench KL00-1 was intended to span the entire main (east) gateway of the smaller fort in Wadi Kalalat. It was situated between the two gate towers of the fort, a semicircular tower on the north and a rectilinear, possibly remodeled tower on the south. The trench measured 4.00 m N-S x 6.00 m E-W. As it turned out, trench KL00-1 encompassed only the northern side of the gateway, where the architecture proved to belong to a single period of construction. The possibly two-phase south tower of the gateway lay outside the borders of the trench.

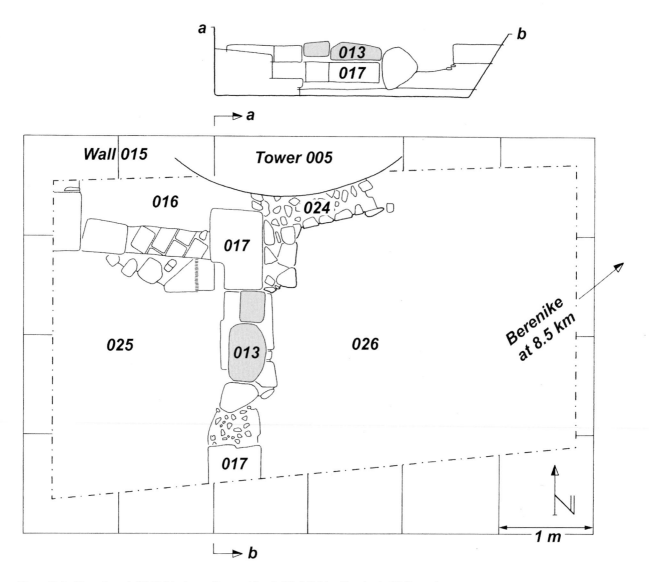

Figure 19-3　Plan of trench KL00-1 in the smaller *praesidium* in Wadi Kalalat. Drawing by H. Barnard.

19.2　ARCHITECTURAL DESCRIPTION

The architectural plan of the northern side of the gateway of the smaller fort at Kalalat emerged clearly from excavations in trench KL00-1 (Figures 19-1, 3 and 5; Plate 19-4). Along the northern balk in the western half of the trench, the eastern enclosure wall of the fort and its projecting gate tower *005* extended 0.80 m N-S into the trench. A construction break marked the juncture of wall and tower, with each component of the enceinte measuring approximately 2.00 m in E-W width.

The architectural features of the gateway were built against the enclosure wall. The *015* E-W northern wall of the gateway was 0.60 m wide N-S x about 2m long E-W. It extended from the presumed interior corner of the enclosure wall on the west to the gateway threshold *017* on the east. Threshold installation *017* was 0.60 m wide E-W and extended 3.20 m N-S across the trench; it continued into the southern balk.

Threshold *017* divided the gateway into a western, interior section and an eastern, exterior section. The threshold was aligned with the construction break between enceinte and gate tower *005*, so that wall *015* defined the interior of the gateway and tower *005* framed its exterior. Threshold *017* was structurally bonded into gateway wall *015* on the west, while it abutted gate tower *005* on the east. The L-shaped curb *024* of foundation cobblestones sealed and buttressed the structural intersection between threshold and gate tower. As defined by these architectural features, trench KL00-1 encompassed a 2.60 m N-S x 2-m E-W area inside the gateway and a 4-m N-S x 3.40 m E-W area outside the gateway.

Plate 19-4 Main (eastern) gate of the smaller *praesidium* in Wadi Kalalat. Threshold *013/017* looking west. Scale=1 m. Photo by S. E. Sidebotham.

19.3 STRATIGRAPHIC SUMMARY

Excavation in the main gateway of the smaller fortification in Wadi Kalalat produced a straightforward stratigraphic profile of five subphases within a single period of occupation (Figure 19-5). A primary sub-phase of construction was followed by two subphases of occupation by the Roman army. Stratigraphic evidence for a hiatus of indeterminate length separated the two successive subphases of flooring in the gateway. Military presence at the site ended with a fourth and final subphase of orderly military withdrawal that seems to have involved the systematic dismantling and removal of parts of the gateway. Abandonment by the Roman army initiated a long, uninterrupted fifth subphase, a period of progressive architectural erosion and collapse that continued until the present day.

The chronology of the smaller garrison at Kalalat derived solely from pottery dates; neither inscriptions nor coins were excavated in trench KL00-1. Pottery from KL00-1 contexts was very poorly dated, with costrel sherds providing the best dating evidence. In 2000, the costrel loci were initially dated from the mid-second through third centuries AD. During the subsequent 2001 excavation season, however, ceramicist Roberta Tomber (personal communication) identified a new, albeit very poorly dated, ceramic horizon in trench BE01-43 at Berenike. Tomber's new horizon seemed to date from the third to mid-fourth century AD, filling a previous chronological gap in the ceramic sequence at Berenike. With this new dating possibility in mind, Tomber reexamined the KL00-1 assemblage and determined that its costrel loci could also fit into the newly identified ceramic horizon of third through mid-fourth century AD.

Stratigraphic excavation in the KL00-1 gateway has, therefore, modified the results of the 1994 survey, which dated Roman occupation at the site to the second or third century AD. However, as was the case for the large *praesidium* in Wadi Kalalat, excavation in its smaller neighbor produced no evidence for a second, fifth-century AD phase of occupation, despite indications to that effect from surface sherding of the site.

19.3.1 SUBPHASE IA: GATEWAY CONSTRUCTION.
Excavation in trench KL00-1 indicated that the smaller fortification in Wadi Kalalat was erected on sterile wadi sediments in a previously unoccupied site. Tomber noted, however, that rare residual sherds of Italian *sigillata* and Dressel 2 to 4 amphorae did appear

in the KL00-1 ceramic assemblage, suggesting some Roman presence on-site prior to the second century AD. The architectural features of the gateway were founded upon a compact, fine-grained sedimentary sand *030*. In the western half of the trench, a 2.60 m N-S x 2 -m E-W probe below the structural foundations of the gateway revealed that layer *030* overlay two further stratified wadi sediments, the *031* layer of coarse-grained sand and gravel, and the *032* layer of compact, orange, clayey sand. The *030*, *031*, and *032* sediments were semi-sterile, producing only a few tiny, abraded potsherds.

The principal architectural features of the gateway, north gateway wall *015* and threshold *017* (Figure 19-3 and Plate 19-4), were erected in conjunction with the deposition of a series of construction fill layers. These fills, composed primarily of redeposited natural wadi sediments, simultaneously stabilized structural foundations and leveled the gateway area. In the interior section of the gateway, the loose, gravelly *029* sand layer was the first fill deposited along foundations of wall and threshold. Igneous cobbles, the predominant inclusions in *029*, were deliberately concentrated along these architectural foundations, apparently to buttress and support them. Locus *028*, a level, 0.04 m thick temporary working surface, overlay *029*. Surface *028* was hard-packed and composed of a distinctive, clayey orange sand. The same type of sand appeared throughout the architecture of the gateway, where it was utilized as mortar matrix in wall cores and courses. Clayey orange sand mortar was the bonding agent of choice in both unworked igneous stone and ashlar gypsum masonry in the gateway.

A thick (up to 0.14 m), dense, hard-packed fill of igneous cobbles set in orange sand was then deposited across the entire interior section of the gateway. This *025* layer served a double purpose: as a leveling fill in the gateway proper and as foundation packing along wall *015* and in threshold *017*. Since locus *025* sloped down markedly from west to east, a final construction fill was required to level the gateway area along the interior face of threshold *017*. To this end, *027*, a loose, gravelly sand fill was deposited over *025* in a depression (1.70 m long N-S x 0.40 m wide E-W x 0.10 m deep) along the northern end of the threshold. The porous *027* fill may also have been intended as a drainage sump along the threshold's interior face.

In the exterior portion of the gateway, excavation halted at the level of *026*, the final leveling/construction fill deposited in preparation for *020*, the earliest floor at the entrance to the fort. The loose, gray, gravelly *026* sand layer ran under the *025* foundations of threshold *017*. Locus *026* also underlay *024*, an independent L-shaped foundation installation that lined the structural intersection of threshold *017* and gate tower *005*. The *024* curb of foundation cobbles lay at the northern end of the threshold, where it was two rows wide and up to two courses high. Along the exterior face of the threshold, it measured 0.90 m long N-S x 0.30 m wide E-W; along gate tower *005*, it measured 0.35 m wide N-S x 1.40 m long E-W. The *024* cobble curb seems to have been the structural and stratigraphic equivalent to the *025* construction fill on the interior side of the gateway.

The military architects of the gateway employed a hierarchy of building materials that privileged the interior of the entrance over the exterior. Therefore, although all the architectural features of the gateway belonged to a single phase of construction, one could still identify construction breaks that recorded three successive steps in the overall building campaign. The gateway comprised three architectural elements, each constructed of different building materials. The first component to be erected was the eastern enclosure wall of the fort and its *005* semicircular gate tower. Both were built of unworked igneous cobbles and boulders, laid in courses and bonded with sand mortar. The excavated portion of gate tower *005* was preserved to a maximum height of 1.60 m (eight courses). Preliminary calculations by architect J.-L. Rivard suggested that the tower had a diameter of 2.50 m and a radius of 1.50 m, which he considered proportionate to the size of the fort as a whole.

The second architectural element of the entrance, gateway wall *015*, was constructed of higher quality materials. Its white gypsum ashlar masonry (now largely robbed out) would originally have made a striking contrast with the somber black, gray, and dark-red hues of the igneous-stone enceinte. This interior gateway wall employed one row of *015* ashlar blocks to face an inner core of *016* olive-green sand bricks (*jeluse*). The *016* sand bricks were set in rough courses with the same orange sand mortar used in the adjacent igneous cobble architecture. Only three gypsum ashlar blocks remained *in situ* at the western end of wall *015*, which rose to the height of 0.63 m (two courses). The largest preserved ashlar measured 0.60 m long x 0.26 m wide x 0.13 m high.

The olive-green sand bricks of wall *015/016* were noteworthy in their own right, and samples were collected for geological analysis. The bricks were composed of coarse-grained, salt-concreted, sun-dried olive-green sand. They ranged in size from 0.15 m square to rectangular blocks of 0.10 m x 0.25 m. Prior to their appearance in Roman military architecture at Wadi Kalalat, sun-dried sand bricks had been archaeologically attested only in Ptolemaic contexts at Berenike (Sidebotham 1999:48–57; Schijns, Kila, and Harrell 1999:96–101). Experiments in the production of sand bricks during the 1997 season concluded that "Ptolemaic bricks did not come from the *sabkha* but rather from a nearby wadi. Clay-rich, fine-grained sands should occur in the wadis near Berenike in what are called "slack-water" deposits" (Schijns, Kila, and Harrell 1999:100). These results point to Wadi Kalalat itself as the most likely source of the olive-colored sand used to make the *016* sand bricks. The construction technique of wall *015/016* proves that the Roman army, as well as Ptolemaic pioneers at Berenike, occasionally found unfired sand bricks a convenient building material. In the Eastern Desert, military sand/mud-brick construction has also been attested in the late Roman fort at Abu Sha'ar (Sidebotham 1993:5; Sidebotham 1994:269).

The northern elevation of the gateway revealed a sharp construction break between gate tower *005* and gateway wall *015*. A clear vertical line marked the point at which the *016* core of ashlar-faced wall *015* was built up against the igneous stone masonry of the enceinte. Although the circuit and gateway walls functioned together as parts of a single complex, the heavier, stronger *005* igneous stone architecture was obviously erected first. Ashlar wall *015* and its *016* sand-brick fill comprised a final, essentially decorative flourish.

Threshold *017* formed the third architectural feature of the tripartite gateway. It was structurally bonded into gateway wall *015*. Both features shared the same 0.60 m width and utilized gypsum ashlar blocks. Primary threshold *017* was apparently altered twice. First, the *013* secondary rebuild course raised the level of the threshold. Subsequently, at least one primary threshold block was robbed from the central portion of the installation (see the following). Despite these later repairs and disturbances, four of the original *017* threshold blocks survived *in situ*.

In contrast to the monolithic SK00-1.*011* gypsum threshold installation in the gateway of the *praesidium* at Siket (see Chapter 20), primary threshold *017* in the smaller fort at Kalalat was constructed of several gypsum ashlars and one igneous boulder. At least three

ashlar blocks (measuring 0.80 m long x 0.54 m wide x 0.16 m high; 0.78 m long x 0.56 m wide x 0.18 m high; and [partially revealed under *013*] 0.50 m long x 0.56 m wide x 0.19 m high) and one igneous boulder (0.35 m long x 0.40 m wide x 0.36 m high) can be attributed to primary installation *017*. One additional ashlar block (0.53 m long x 0.35 m wide x 0.15 m high) was positioned in the interior northwestern corner of the threshold to form part of the entrance. This interior corner block functioned in tandem with two contiguous *017* blocks to create a pivot socket at the northern end of the threshold. Aligned rectilinear notches cut into the three blocks matched up to define a socket measuring 0.25 m x 0.20 m x 0.08 m deep.

Pottery from Subphase Ia construction strata, such as working surface *028*, included costrel sherds whose dates could range from the mid-second to the mid-fourth century AD. The same was true for Phase II architectural debris layers (see the following). Ironically, these strata, which represented the collapse of gateway structures long after the Romans withdrew from Wadi Kalalat, can still be used to date construction of the fort. Architectural tumble layers *010* and *011* comprised primarily fallen masonry, sand bricks, mortar, and render, the original structural material of the gateway. These loci also produced nothing later than mid-second to mid-fourth century costrel fragments. Ceramic evidence, therefore, opens a fairly wide chronological window— from AD 150 to 350—for the construction of the gateway.

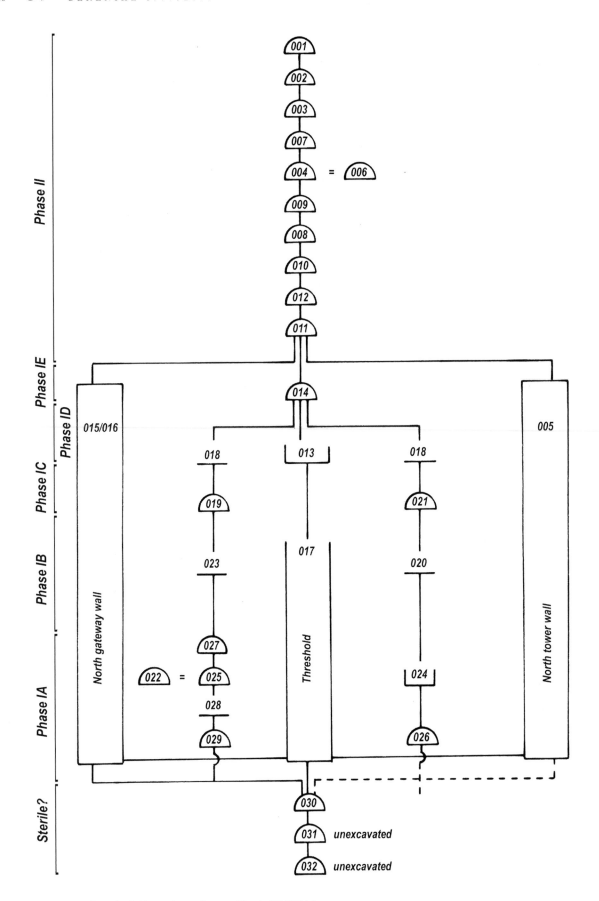

Figure 19-5 Matrix of trench KL00-1 in the smaller *praesidium* in Wadi Kalalat.

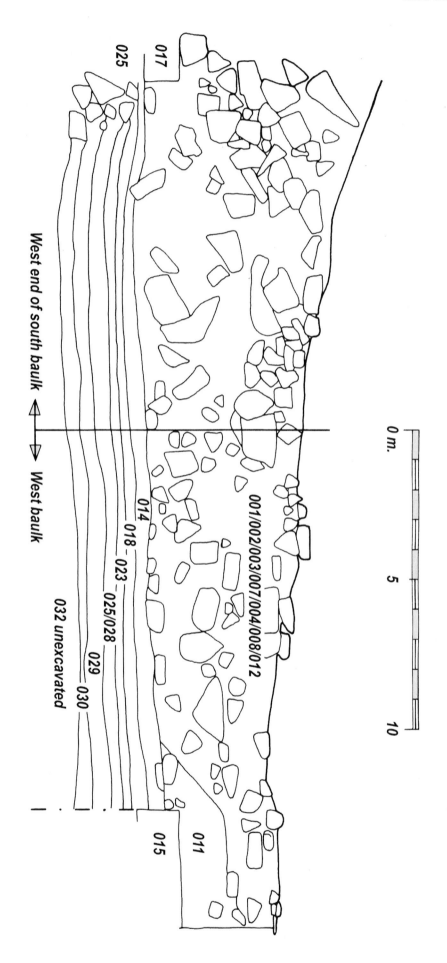

Figure 19-6   Trench KL00-1 western balk and western end of southern balk. Drawing by A. E. Haeckl and H. Barnard.

Although these ceramic parameters permit the gateway of the smaller garrison at Kalalat to postdate its neighboring *praesidium* by as much as 200 years, the two military gateways paralleled each other closely in design and building materials. Both confined the use of gypsum ashlar masonry exclusively to interior gateway features, so that official entrances of gleaming white-dressed stone stood out impressively from the rough, dun-colored *jebel*-stone courses of enceinte and towers. Like the *015* ashlar wall of the KL00-1 gateway, the northern (*005*) and southern (*006*) side walls of the large *praesidium*'s eastern entrance were also built of dressed gypsum blocks. A similar combination of *jebel*-stone and gypsum-ashlar masonry appeared in the fourth-century and later fort at Abu Sha'ar (Sidebotham 1993:4–5; 1994:268–269), suggesting that this distinctive construction style was employed in Roman military installations throughout the Eastern Desert.

The entire threshold of the larger fort in Wadi Kalalat (abbreviated as KA) was excavated (Sidebotham and Barnard 2000:381–387), giving a more complete picture of that installation than is possible for its partially exposed KL00-1.*017* counterpart. The comparable sections of the two thresholds seem almost identical in construction. Both forts were fitted with thresholds constructed of several ashlar blocks, rather than with monolithic installations like the SK00-1.*011* threshold in the *praesidium* at Siket. Both Kalalat thresholds had door-pivot blocks in their interior corners (north KA97-1.*026* and south KA97-1.*027* in the large *praesidium*; the KL00-1.*017* north ashlar pivot block in the smaller fort). Although pivot block KA97-1.*026* in the larger garrison contained fragments of a teak gatepost (Sidebotham and Barnard 2000:381), not a single trace of wood appeared in its KL00-1 counterpart.

The only major difference between the two Kalalat thresholds was the presence of a central ashlar locking block (KA97-1.*017*) in the larger installation. The absence of a locking block in the KL00-1 gateway is surprising, as such features seem to have been standard components of military gateways in the vicinity of Berenike. The threshold of the fort at Siket was also equipped with an example (SK00-1.*017*). An intriguing gap, in fact, existed in threshold KL00-1.*017*. Located about 1.30 m from the northern end of the installation, a gap measuring approximately 0.70 m long N-S x 0.60 m wide E-W could well mark the spot where a central locking block once stood (see the following for discussion of the Subphase Id remodeling of the primary KL00-1.*017* threshold).

The two military thresholds in Wadi Kalalat exhibited one final similarity in construction technique. Both utilized L-shaped curbs of igneous cobbles to seal and buttress threshold foundations at intersections with adjacent gateway features. In the larger gateway, KA97-1.*021*, an L-shaped cobble foundation curb lined the intersection of the KA97-1.*017* locking block and the northern end of threshold KA97-1.*014*. In the KL00-1 gateway, a virtually identical cobble installation (KL00-1.*024*) formed an L-shaped juncture between gate tower KL00-1.*005* and the northern end of threshold KL00-1.*017*.

The gateways of the two fortifications in Wadi Kalalat share such striking similarities in plan, building materials, and construction technique that, from a purely typological standpoint, one would tend to consider them contemporary. Excavation in the large *praesidium*, however, produced no evidence of military occupation after the reign of Trajan, while construction of the smaller fort apparently did not begin until the mid-second century at the earliest. It appears, therefore, that the two garrisons in Wadi Kalalat were constructed consecutively rather than simultaneously. Their close architectural affinities, however, suggest that the smaller fort was erected not long after its larger predecessor was abandoned.

In addition to their close physical proximity and marked architectural resemblance, the two fortifications in Wadi Kalalat were apparently erected in rapid chronological succession. An obvious question occurs: what motivated the Roman army to expend such efforts in Wadi Kalalat, establishing, within a comparatively short period of time, two separate garrisons in what was effectively a single location? The most likely answer involves water. As noted previously, there is solid archaeological and epigraphic evidence that both the larger fort at Kalalat and the Flavian *praesidium* at Siket functioned as *praesidium et hydreumata*, fortified water sources. Precedent and chronology argue that the smaller garrison at Kalalat probably served the same purposes. Since the smaller fort was apparently erected only after its larger neighbor ceased to operate, it is logical to assume that this new outpost, located a mere one kilometer away from its predecessor, replaced the earlier garrison in function as well as strategic position. If the original *hydreuma* in Wadi Kalalat failed as a source of fresh water, identification of another well nearby might have prompted the expeditious foundation of a second, smaller fort.

The composition of certain Subphase Ia fills and building materials suggests that excavation of a substantial well may have been part of the primary construction activity at the new garrison in Wadi Kalalat. Development of potable water sources in the *praesidium et lacus* at Siket and the large fort at Kalalat required excavation of wells. In the smaller fort at Kalalat, it appears that wadi sediments dug up during similar hydraulic excavations were recycled as foundation leveling fills and as matrix for the sand bricks and sand mortar used in wall construction. For example, the earliest *032* wadi sediment exposed in trench KL00-1 seemed identical to the clayey orange sand encountered in the *024* and *025* foundation fills and the mortar of walls *005* and *015*. In addition, the *026* and *029* leveling fills comprised a coarse-grained, gravelly, grayish-brown sand that closely resembled the *030* and *031* wadi sediments upon which the gateway was founded. Sediments excavated within the fort could also have been reworked into the *016* sand bricks found in the core of gateway wall *015*. Finally, the berms that encircled the northern and eastern enceinte of the fort (described and drawn during the 1994 survey; see Sidebotham 1995:87–91) probably represented mounded debris from the initial excavation and subsequent cleanouts of a well or cistern housed within the walls.

These observations admittedly do not prove that the smaller garrison at Kalalat contained a *hydreuma* or *lacus*. Nevertheless, the simplest and most logical explanation for the foundation of a new fort virtually in the shadow of a "decommissioned" predecessor remains that the former was intended to replace the latter. Since archaeological excavation has identified the larger fort at Kalalat as housing a *hydreuma*, it seems reasonable to assume that its smaller neighbor also functioned primarily to develop and defend a source of potable water for Berenike.

19.3.2 SUBPHASE IB. MILITARY OCCUPATION
The earliest subphase of military occupation in the gateway directly overlaid Subphase Ia construction and leveling fills and was contemporary with primary threshold *017*. The threshold physically separated two outdoor gateway surfaces that functioned in phase with each other. Floor *020* was laid against the eastern face of the threshold and paved the exterior section of the gateway. Surface *023* was the interior counterpart of *020*, compacted up against the western face of the threshold.

The top levels of the contemporary surfaces *020* and *023* were quite consistent, varying by only a few centimeters across the entire 6 m N-S excavated area of the gateway. The two hard-packed floors were also similar in thickness (0.10 m) and composition, a soil matrix of salty to clayey sand with wadi wash gravel as the predominant inclusion. Both *020* exterior and *023* interior gateway surfaces exhibited signs of weathering and wear. Each was broken in several places, worn down to uneven, shelving layers, and cut by water-runoff rivulets. Such marks of heavy traffic and exposure to the elements are only to be expected in the outdoor gateway of a putative fort containing a *hydreuma* that would have been frequented by donkey or camel trains hauling water to Berenike.

Unfortunately, primary gateway pavements *020* and *023* were poor in occupational material. They produced little pottery and no identifiable imports that could narrow the mid-second- to mid-fourth-century dating parameters of the construction subphase. Small finds were limited to a few fragments of metal. Floor *023* yielded two tiny pieces of iron; *020* contained nine iron fragments, including nails, and a minute piece of bronze wire.

19.3.3 SUBPHASE IC. HIATUS
Several stratigraphic indices recorded a brief hiatus between the two subphases of flooring in the gateway. In the interior section of the gateway, a layer of loose windblown sand (*019*) separated earlier floor *023* from its later *018* replacement. Layer *019* was localized in the northwestern corner of the gateway, where it had mounded against wall *015*. Since windblown sand tended to accumulate in that corner of the gateway even during the course of excavation, the presence of such a layer between two floors need not reflect a long-term interruption in military occupation of the fort. A single windstorm in Wadi Kalalat could easily deposit the amount of sand excavated in locus *019*.

A stratigraphic horizon also existed between two successive floors in the exterior section of the gateway. Along gate tower *005*, *de facto* weathering surface *021* formed above earlier surface *020*, stratigraphically separating it from overlying gateway floor *018*. Locus *021* was an orange crust of sun-dried sand mortar, washed down from the wall face of the adjacent gate tower. Washdown layer *021* extended 1.50 m N-S from tower *005* and was thickest (up to 0.09 m) along the wall face.

Disuse layers *019* and *021* yielded no diagnostic pottery. With no ceramic evidence to the contrary, Subphase Ic is probably best interpreted as a hiatus of short duration, lasting only long enough for windblown sand layer *019* to accumulate inside the gateway and sand mortar washdown *021* to pool and dry alongside the northern gate tower.

19.3.4 SUBPHASE ID: MILITARY OCCUPATION

The hiatus between subphases of flooring in the gateway could represent nothing more than a prolonged construction break, a temporary interruption in normal usage while the gateway was remodeled. The second subphase of military occupation in the small fort at Kalalat did, in fact, involve a major refitting of the gateway; primary threshold *017* was repaired and raised, and a new gateway pavement created.

Remodeling began with the threshold. One of the primary *017* threshold blocks was pried out down to its *025* foundations, leaving a gap that measured approximately 0.70 m long N-S x about 0.60 m wide E-W in the center of the installation. As mentioned above, this gap could mark the original placement of a central locking block, a gateway feature that, if rebuilt during Sub-phase Id alterations, was ultimately robbed out completely (see following Subphase Ie for evidence of wood and stone robbing in the gateway). The missing block of threshold *017* was clearly removed after the creation of Subphase Ib gateway surfaces *020* and *023* and prior to the laying of the Subphase Id floor *018*. The earlier *020* and *023* floors respected the line of this missing block, being compacted against, but not over, its *025* foundation cobbles. Later floor *018*, on the other hand, entirely covered the reexposed *025* foundations, extending through the gap and raising it about 0.15 m to the height of a new secondary threshold.

Only the northern end of secondary threshold *013* survived (Figure 19-3 and Plate 19-4); it consisted of two worn gypsum ashlars (0.55 m long x 0.40 m wide and 0.30 m long x 0.28 m wide, respectively) and measured approximately 0.80 m NS x 0.50 m EW in overall dimensions. These *013* ashlars effectively formed a second course of threshold blocks; they were laid directly atop primary *017* ashlars to raise the height of the threshold 0.20 m.

Floor *018*, the second and final occupational surface in the gateway, was laid in conjunction, and functioned in phase with, secondary threshold *013*. The original *020* and *023* surfaces treated the interior and exterior sections of the gateway as distinct spaces, paving each one separately. Floor *018*, in contrast, extended across the entire excavated area of the gateway, partially covering primary *017* threshold blocks in the process.

Locus *018* was a good quality gateway floor, appropriate to official military occupation. Even, hard-packed, and up to 0.11 m thick, *018* was compositionally similar to the underlying surfaces *020* and *023*. Its matrix was a gravelly grayish-brown sand intermixed with orange sand and scattered chunks of olive-green sand bricks.

As was the case for the *020* and *023* gateway floors, *018* produced little pottery. Small finds from floor *018* also paralleled those from *020* and *023*; the sum total of occupational inclusions in *018* was 10 iron fragments, including nails. To judge from the poverty of cultural material in the three floors of the gateway, Roman military discipline must have enforced cleanliness. Since gateway floors excavated in the larger fort at Kalalat and the *praesidium* at Siket were equally devoid of occupational debris, a Roman version of the "white-glove" standard was apparently imposed at other garrisons as well. Although floor *018* can be interpreted as the final subphase of military occupation in the fort, its dates cannot be distinguished from those of earlier subphases. According to ceramic evidence, the entire *floruit* of the smaller garrison in Wadi Kalalat fell within a broadly dated period from the mid-second to the mid-fourth century AD.

19.3.5 SUBPHASE IE. SYSTEMATIC DISMANTLING

The earliest abandonment-period stratum in trench KL00-1 was *014*, a layer of loose, gravelly, tracked-in, and windblown sand up to 0.08 m thick. Locus *014* directly overlay floor *018* and extended across the entire excavated area of the gateway. Layer *014* also lay immediately below the earliest architectural tumble strata in the trench (*011*, *012*, and *010*). Gravelly sand layer *014*, therefore, accumulated during an interval between the end of official military occupation at the site and the first episodes of structural collapse in the abandoned gateway.

An exact stratigraphic equivalent to *014* appeared in the gateway of the *praesidium* at Siket. The SK00-1.*013* abandonment-period debris layer also postdated military occupation, but predated architectural tumble. Not only were these two layers comparable stratigraphically, but they also contained the same types of metal finds, distributed in identical patterns. In both strata, numerous iron nail fragments were concentrated along the exterior edges of gateway thresholds.

Parallel stratigraphies of abandonment in the smaller fort at Kalalat and the one at Siket argue that the two garrisons were evacuated in the same manner. Each seems to have experienced an organized military withdrawal that included partial dismantling of gateway features. Wooden gates were carefully removed, presumably for reuse elsewhere in the wood-poor desert environment, leaving behind only a scatter of iron fittings along the thresholds. At Berenike, wood is frequently preserved in walls and architectural features. The fact that not a single trace of decayed wood came to light in either of these two military gateways suggests that their wooden fixtures were systematically salvaged for recycling, most probably by the departing army itself. Archaeological evidence for the deliberate removal of gates from abandoned fortifications has also been identified in the milecastles of Hadrian's Wall in Britain, at the opposite end of the Roman Empire (Breeze 1982:112; Johnson 1989:73).

Evidence for the robbing of gypsum ashlar masonry as well as wood came to light in both fortifications in Wadi Kalalat. In the smaller garrison, stone-robbing seems to have occurred at the same stratigraphic level as the dismantling of the wooden gate, that is, the KL00-1.*014* abandonment debris layer. For example, only three blocks of the *015* ashlar gateway wall remained *in situ*. The rest were missing down to the wall's *016* sand-brick foundations, which were contiguous with *014*. The same was true for the *013* secondary threshold, whose southern ashlars and hypothetical central locking block disappeared at the level of *014*. Not a single ashlar block was recovered from the cubic meters of architectural tumble excavated in trench KL00-1, nor were robber trenches cut through abandonment-period strata deposited above *014*. Therefore, decamping soldiers remain the most likely suspects in the dismantling of the gateway, breaking down and hauling away its ashlar and wooden features as the *014* gravelly sand layer accumulated around their detritus.

Military stone robbers may even have chopped up and carted off the dedicatory inscription of the fort. Such epigraphic destruction did indeed occur at Kalalat's large fort, which also suffered the depredations of stone and wood robbers. In its case, however, the culprits were less than thorough in their efforts, leaving behind in the gateway 33 fragments of two inscriptions and portions of a teak doorpost (Sidebotham and Barnard 2000:383; Bagnall 2000). Ironically, it is quite possible that the foundation of the smaller garrison at Kalalat precipitated the despoiling of its earlier neighbor. Since the large fort was apparently unoccupied at the time its smaller successor was erected, the idea of exploiting this conveniently located, empty fortification as a quarry

must have occurred to practical Roman military minds. One can easily envision such a desert "army ecology" evolving over the centuries of Roman military occupation in the Eastern Desert, with new garrisons in an inhospitable, resource-poor environment inevitably forced to recycle as well as to replace their predecessors. Removing the gate from the earlier fort would also have been a practical security measure, intended to prevent hostile forces from occupying and defending the empty garrison.

The stratigraphically crucial *014* abandonment layer produced no pottery later than the poorly dated mid-second- to mid-fourth-century AD horizon established for the KL00-1 ceramic assemblage as a whole, indicating that the smaller fort at Kalalat was abandoned within two centuries (at most) of its initial construction and occupation.

19.3.6   PHASE II: ABANDONMENT AND COLLAPSE

The robbing of ashlar blocks from gateway wall *015* triggered a sequence of progressive architectural collapses that continued uninterrupted until the present day. Deprived of its *015* ashlar facing, the wall's *016* sand-brick core was the first structural unit in the gateway to fall. It toppled directly upon abandonment/robbing stratum *014*, creating sand-brick debris layer *011* in the northwestern quadrant of the trench.

A major collapse of igneous cobble and boulder masonry followed, depositing heavy tumble layer *012* over *011* and *014*. Locus *012* extended across all but the eastern end of the trench and consisted of unworked *jebel* stones embedded in a compact matrix of orange sand mortar. The third stratum of architectural debris to accumulate was *010*, a massive pile of igneous cobbles and boulders up to three layers and 0.50 m thick, that overlay *012* in the eastern half of the trench. The matrix of *010* was a loose, fine-grained windblown sand that had filtered between and mounded above the fallen stones.

Subsequent architectural collapse layers followed a similar pattern of accumulation, which was repeated three times after the site was abandoned. Episodes of sudden, catastrophic wall collapse produced strata of igneous tumble embedded in orange sand mortar (*012*, *008*, and *007*). These major events alternated with periods of gradual erosion and decay, when wall stones fell less violently and windblown sand had time to collect among them. Five stratified layers of igneous tumble and loose, windblown sand were excavated in the trench: *010* intervened between *012* and *008*; *004* separated *008* and *007*; successive *003*, *002*, and *001* were the latest strata.

Architectural debris loci excavated in trench KL00-1 produced a surprising amount of pottery for abandonment strata. Since sherds recovered from Phase II tumble strata derived from collapsed masonry, broken pottery was apparently incorporated as aggregate into the primary architecture of the gateway. As mentioned above, pottery dates from post-abandonment collapse layers were consistent with those of construction and occupation strata: mid-second to mid-fourth century AD.

19.4 DISCUSSION

Although the ceramic corpus from the gateway of the smaller garrison at Kalalat was poorly dated, it was at least consistent, from the earliest construction subphase to the latest abandonment stratum. Ceramic evidence indicates that the fort was erected, occupied, and abandoned within the span of 200 years, from the mid-second to the mid-fourth century AD. *Pace* survey results, no stratigraphic evidence of a "possibly later" phase of occupation was uncovered (Sidebotham 1995:91). In this sense, excavation in the smaller fort paralleled the results of excavation in its larger neighbor. Whereas survey pottery suggested that the large fort was occupied in both the early Roman period and the fifth to sixth centuries AD, excavation in three separate trenches recovered no dating evidence later than the reign of Trajan. Wadi Kalalat may have received transitory visitors during the fifth century efflorescence of Berenike, but it now seems clear that neither of its earlier fortifications was reoccupied at that time.

Although excavation found no conclusive proof that the smaller garrison at Kalalat ever functioned as a *hydreuma*, the development and protection of a potable water supply for Berenike remains the most compelling explanation for its existence. Wadi Kalalat, however, must ultimately have proved unreliable as a water source. Neither of its fortifications was maintained much longer than a century or two, and the wadi as a whole was apparently abandoned as a source of fresh water after the fourth century AD. Since Berenike itself experienced a surge of growth in the fourth and fifth centuries, it is likely that any viable well or spring in Wadi Kalalat would have been redeveloped in consequence. Perhaps the late Roman survey pottery collected at Kalalat was dropped during failed fifth-century prospecting for water.

One issue that excavation in trench KL00-1 did resolve successfully was the chronological relationship between the two fortifications in Wadi Kalalat. They were clearly not contemporary, although they followed each other in fairly quick succession. The larger was the earlier garrison, founded in the first century AD and abandoned sometime after 109/110. The smaller fort was not established before the midsecond century AD and occupied no later than the mid-fourth century AD.

Survey of the Berenike-Nile roads identified two examples of paired forts that were located in close proximity to each other and apparently functioned in succession. Both of these parallels to the garrisons in Wadi Kalalat occupied a stretch of the Berenike-Nile Valley route that was shared by roads to Edfu and Koptos. A distance of only 5.6 km separated two late-Roman forts located in the neighboring wadis of Abu Ghusun (24° 23.24' N/35° 02.87' E) and Abu Ghalqa (24° 20.95' N/35° 04.19' E). Surface pottery collected at these sites dated to the late fourth to fifth and fifth to sixth centuries AD, respectively. Another pair of successive fortified water sources stood eight km apart in Wadi Abu Hegilig. Here, an early Roman, perhaps first-century AD, garrison at Wadi Abu Hegilig South (that may have replaced an even earlier Ptolemaic garrison: 24° 23.94' N/34° 59.48' E) seems to have preceded a fourth- to fifth-century AD successor at Wadi Abu Hegilig North (24° 25.22' N/34° 55.46' E).

In each of these pairs, Sidebotham (personal communication) interprets the later installation as a replacement for its earlier counterpart, the same explanation proposed here for the successive fortifications in Wadi Kalalat. As was true at Kalalat, the Abu Ghusun and Abu Ghalqa forts seem to have been built in close succession, within the span of a century or so. On the other hand, a period of several hundred years apparently elapsed between the garrisons in Wadi Abu Hegilig. It is significant that both pairs of fortified water sources on the Berenike-Nile route were apparently redeveloped in the late Roman period. In view of the fifth-century "boom" in Red Sea commerce now attested archaeologically at Berenike, such earl Roman activity along caravan routes between Berenike and the Nile Valley makes good sense historically. It does, however, pose a perplexing question: why did the first- through fourth-century AD forts in the hinterland of Berenike not receive comparable attention in the same period?

The forts in Wadi Kalalat and Siket, all excavated stratigraphically and discussed in this book, are the only known fortified Roman water sources in the immediate vicinity of Berenike. None of these first- through fourth-century garrisons showed evidence of reoccupation in the fifth century AD. *Ergo*, the obvious question: If not from Wadi Kalalat or Siket, whence did thriving late Roman Berenike obtain its supply of fresh water? Was the water table already so depleted that one had to go as far afield as Wadi Shenshef to find a sustainable source of potable water?

Despite a series of 1997 sondages in trash middens at Shenshef, the purpose of this late Roman settlement remained problematic (Gould 1999:379–380). Subsequent excavations at Berenike, Kalalat, and Siket, however, have clarified Shenshef's regional and historical context to the point that it seems worthwhile to address the issue again.

Two contemporary unsolved archaeological mysteries—late Roman Berenike's unidentified water source and late Roman Shenshef's unidentified purpose—may have a single, simple explanation. When viewed contextually, Shenshef's main attraction suddenly emerges as its possession of late Roman Berenike's closest and, at this point, only identified perennial source of fresh water (Gould 1999:371). The prosperous and thirsty population of late Roman Berenike may have had no alternative but to solve the logistics of transporting water from Shenshef to Berenike, a formidable trek across 21.3 km of mountainous and desert terrain. The difficulties were probably not insurmountable; by the fifth century AD, the Romans had acquired centuries of experience in provisioning water to settlements throughout the Eastern Desert and Red Sea coast of Egypt.

It is also interesting that the first-century BC to first-century AD hilltop fort at Shenshef seems not to have been reoccupied during the late Roman heyday of the wadi settlement. If the hypothesis advanced here is correct, and Shenshef was the primary supplier of Berenike's potable water in the fourth and fifth centuries AD, one would expect the site to be garrisoned by the army. The absence of early Roman fortifications in Wadi Shenshef has two possible implications. First, Shenshef may have been founded as an economically motivated civilian venture by enterprising private citizens who hoped to profit from the upsurge in international trade at Berenike. Secondly, its inhabitants may have lived as *limitanei*, maintaining a local civilian militia with a personal stake in defending their own homes and families. Ancient watchtowers still line the rocky track to Shenshef. Manned by patriotic citizen soldiers, these guardposts might have provided adequate security to the naturally defended mountain defile.

When integrated into a larger contextual framework, the *lacuna* in late Roman occupation at the smaller fortification at Kalalat nevertheless contributes valuable insights into the regional dynamics of contemporary Berenike. The same holds true when one returns to the *floruit* of the garrison. No evidence for the identity of the Roman army unit stationed there emerged from excavation. The chronology of the fort, however, suggests an intriguing possibility. It was apparently founded during the late second or third century AD, concurrently with the Palmyrene military shrine at Berenike. This small temple, patronized by Palmyrene auxiliaries in the Antoninian Archers and *ala Herculiana*, also flourished during the Antonine and Severan periods (Dijkstra and Verhoogt 1999:208–218). It is tempting to attribute these two contemporary military foundations, the smaller fort in Wadi Kalalat and the Palmyrene shrine at Berenike, to the same army units. Since both Palmyrene detachments are attested in Koptos as well as Berenike, their personnel could have rotated between the Nile Valley, Berenike, and Kalalat, charged with responsibility for escorting caravans across the Eastern Desert, providing security at Berenike, and maintaining a precious water source in Wadi Kalalat.

Perhaps not coincidentally, military occupation in the smaller fort at Kalalat and the Palmyrene phase of the pagan shrine at Berenike ended around the same time, from the mid-third through the mid-fourth century AD. The disappearance of Palmyrene auxiliaries from Berenike, therefore, seems to coincide with Zenobia's invasion of Egypt in AD 270. This bold, if ultimately unsuccessful, military venture by the queen of Palmyra was motivated as much by economic exigencies as imperialistic ambitions, with Palmyra invading Egypt to secure its financial interests in the Red Sea trade when Roman control of the commerce broke down during the "crisis of the third century AD." In circumstances so fraught with the potential for divided loyalties, Roman army authorities may well have deemed it prudent to transfer Palmyrene auxiliary units away from Berenike. Whether or not it was initially garrisoned by Roman auxiliaries of Palmyrene origin, the smaller fort at Kalalat was apparently never reoccupied after Palmyra lost its standing as an international commercial power in late third century AD.

CHAPTER 20

EXCAVATIONS AT THE *PRAESIDIUM ET HYDREUMA* AT SIKET

L.A. PINTOZZI

Excavation commenced in 2000 at Siket, a small fort about 7 km west northwest of Berenike at 23° 55.88' N/35° 24.36' E (Figures 20-1 and 20-2, and Chapter 17, Figure 17-3). The excavation was a component of a larger project designed to survey systematically and to excavate selectively the Ptolemaic and Roman hinterland of Berenike. Siket, whose surface pottery dates first to third century AD, was part of an extensive network of well-maintained roads, way stations, forts, settlements, and mines that dotted the region between the port cities on the Red Sea and emporia on the Nile in the Roman period (cf. Aldsworth 1999; Aldsworth and Barnard 1996b, 1998b; Bagnall 2000; Cappers 1999; Gould 1999; Sidebotham 1995b, 1998, 1999c, 2000c; Sidebotham, *et al.* 2000; Sidebotham and Zitterkopf 1995, 1996; Van Neer and Ervynck 1999; Vermeeren 1999). In addition to Siket, excavations were also conducted at the small fort in Wadi Kalalat (see Chapter 19). It was expected that excavations at Siket would supply data regarding its relationship to Berenike, specifically its role in providing water and defense to the city.

Since 1994 the Berenike survey has documented 10 major fortifications within a 35 km radius of the city (Sidebotham, *et al.* 2000:400). Of these, three have now been recorded through limited excavations. The small fort at Siket, surveyed in 1998 (Sidebotham 2000c: 359–365), and the small fort at Wadi Kalalat, surveyed in 1994 (Sidebotham 1995b: 87–91), were excavated this season. The large fort at Wadi Kalalat, surveyed in 1995, was excavated during the 1997 and 1998 seasons. The two forts at Wadi Kalalat are approximately 8.5 km southwest of Berenike and lie about 1 km apart.

Various routes connected the ancient Red Sea ports with the cities on the Nile in the Ptolemaic and Roman periods. Two major roads joined Berenike with the Nile Valley, the Berenike-Edfu and Berenike-Koptos routes; a third, the Via Nova Hadriana, ran north parallel to the Red Sea coast before heading towards the Nile emporium of Antinoopolis in Middle Egypt. All three thoroughfares have been extensively surveyed and published in preliminary form (cf. Sidebotham and Zitterkopf 1995, 1996, 1997, 1998; Sidebotham, *et al.* 2000); they will be fully published elsewhere. All three routes passed by Vetus Hydreuma where three forts of varying ages guarded the mouth of a wadi and a water supply; two other forts lay close by, up a nearby wadi. Additional trunk routes off these major thoroughfares served other settlements in the interior. The fort at Siket lay approximately 1 km southwest of the major thoroughfare linking Berenike to Vetus Hydreuma. A minor route intermittently marked with cairns led from Siket farther west toward the mountains where it probably joined a secondary route coming up from the south, parallel to the coast en route to Vetus Hydreuma (Sidebotham 2000c: 365–366). Prior to excavation, it was clear that the fortress at Siket was not intended as a strategic military station. The garrison, positioned well off the major roadway, clearly did not function as a way station to protect commerce traveling along the major thoroughfares. This fact plus the proximity to Berenike suggested that Siket's main function was to supply potable water to the city.

20.1 GOALS AND STRATEGY

The goals of the excavation of the fort at Siket were to document occupational sequence of the installation and to determine its relationship to Berenike. Surface topography indicated a fort that enclosed a large circular depression reminiscent of that discovered at the large fort in Wadi Kalalat. The excavations of the large fort at Wadi Kalalat recorded that it was Trajanic in date (Sidebotham, *et al.* 2000; Bagnall 2000). Though nothing of its function was recorded on any of the inscription fragments found in the excavations, the huge size of the well and proximity to Berenike strongly suggest that the large fort in Wadi Kalalat served as both a defense for the city and a supplier of some of its potable water (Sidebotham and Zitterkopf 1996:384–392).

Plate 20-1   View of *praesidium et hydreuma* at Siket looking south-southeast. Photograph by S. E. Sidebotham.

An objective this season was to determine if the fortress at Siket also contributed to the supply of fresh water for the inhabitants of Berenike and to discover if the large circular depression functioned as a water reservoir. While the former function was confirmed, lack of time precluded excavation of the circular depression.

The general plan of the fort at Siket is rectilinear measuring 23.85–24.88 m E-W x 32.15–38.40 m N-S with six oval-shaped guard towers (Plate 20-1, Figure 20-2, see also Sidebotham 2000c: 359–365).

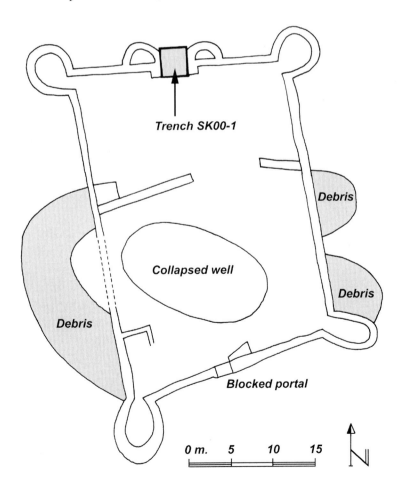

Trench SK00-1

Debris

Collapsed well

Debris

Debris

Blocked portal

0 m.   5   10   15

Figure 20-2
Plan of *praesidium et hydreuma* at Siket showing location of trench SK00-1. Drawing by H. Barnard

Two towers flank the main north gate and an additional four appear at each of the corners. The fort surrounds a circular depression approximately 19 x 10 m on the southern interior of the fort. This feature probably represents a sanded-up well. Piles of detritus outside the perimeter walls both to the east and west probably represent dredging from the well inside the fort. In addition, outside the perimeter of the fort lay five cairns or graves, four to the north and one to the south (Sidebotham 2000c: 363).

The large fort at Wadi Kalalat possessed similar features, enclosing a large well with the addition of reservoir tanks positioned immediately outside both east and west perimeter walls. The small fort at Wadi Kalalat also preserves a large berm of detritus wrapping around the exterior of the structure (Sidebotham 1995b: 87–91; see Chapter 19), which may represent cleaned-out debris from the well.

20.2　DESCRIPTION OF THE GATEWAY AT SIKET

Excavation in a 4 m x 4 m trench (Figure 20-3) placed at the north gate of the fort revealed a 2.80 m wide gateway approximately midway along the north wall. Both an eastern and western semicircular guard tower flanked the portal though excavation revealed only a section of each tower. Installations remaining *in situ* within the gateway included portions of the afore-mentioned guard towers, two step walls abutting each tower wall, a monolithic threshold block carved from white gypsum, and door-locking mechanism. Abutting both guard-tower walls and running the length of the exposed gateway were two additional low-lying step walls (Plates 20-4 and 5). The monolithic threshold block was set perpendicular to the step walls with the distal ends of the threshold incorporated within the low-lying walls. These step walls were of primary construction, serving as a bulwark and providing support and reinforcement to the doorjambs that rose from the distal ends of the threshold block. The step walls restricted the width of the interior of the gateway to 2.46 m. Also found within the architectural tumble were two monolithic doorjambs and a single triangular-shaped inscription once supported by the doorjambs (Plates 20-6 to 8). The inscription dated the founding of the *hydreuma*, *praesidium*, and *lacus* to AD 76/77, during the reign of the Emperor Vespasian. It reads:

"In the ninth year of Imperator Caesar Augustus Vespasianus, L. Julius Ursus, prefect of Egypt, returning from Berenike gave instructions for a well to be sought in this place. When it had been found, he ordered a fort and cisterns to be constructed, under the direction of M. Trebonius Valens, prefect of the desert region of Berenike."

Exposed western tower *004* was 1.13 m wide x 4.0 m long, x 0.87 m (five courses) extant height. Western step wall *009* abutted tower wall *004* and measured 0.25 wide x 4.0 m long with a fully exposed height of 0.31 m (two courses). Exposed eastern tower wall *006* measured 0.18 m wide x 4.0 m long x 0.90 m (five courses) extant height. Eastern step wall *010* abutted tower wall *006* and measured 0.40 wide x 4.0 m long x 0.34 m (two courses) exposed height. All exposed walls, guard towers, and steps were composed of local igneous cobblestones and small boulders set within a clay loam sediment matrix.

Threshold *011* (Plates 20-4 and 5) was a single block with two worked piers at either terminus. The mono-lithic block was set perpendicular to the low-lying step walls with the distal ends incorporated into those walls. The block measured 2.35 m long x 0.30 m wide x 0.27 m high, with the two terminal piers adding an additional 0.17 m in height and individually measuring 0.24 m in length at the distal ends.

Additionally, single-worked ashlar *017* abutted the southern interior face of the threshold block (Plates 20-4 and 5). The block measured 0.70 m x 0.33 m x 0.27 m deep and was placed slightly off center in relation to the threshold block. Carved into the top of block *017* were two sockets 0.11m apart. The western socket measured 0.08 m x 0.08 m x 0.05 m deep. The eastern socket measured 0.09 m x 0.09 m x 0.06 m deep. Installation *017* was part of the locking mechanism for the hinged wooden gate. The presence of such a locking mechanism indicates that double-entry doors secured the main gate, with the two doors pivoting to meet in the center of the gateway. Once closed, metal bars or wooden beams could lock down vertically, inserted into the sockets, to secure the gate in a closed and locked position. An additional horizontal bar must have braced the middle section of the door.

Installation KA97-1.*017* in the large fort at Wadi Kalalat was a similar type of locking block dating to the first to second century AD (Sidebotham, *et al.* 2000:381). As at Siket, the ashlar block in the large fort in Wadi Kalalat was placed slightly off center

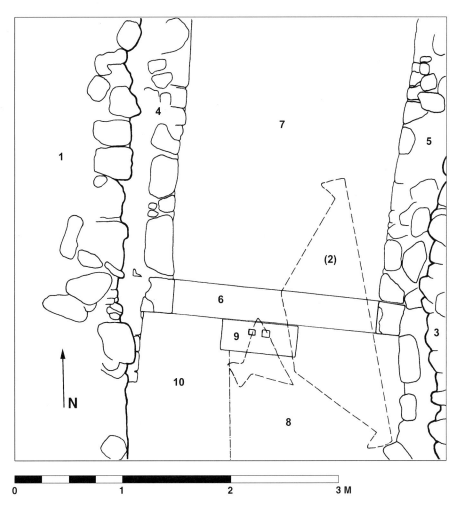

Figure 20-3
Plan of trench SK00-1 (north gate
of *praesidium et hydreuma* at Siket).
Drawing by A. M. Hense.

1 =tower wall *004*
2 =tumble locus *005* with inscription
3 =tower wall *006*
4 =stepped wall *009*
5 =stepped wall *010*
6 =threshold *011*
7 =surface *015*
8 =surface *016*
9 =locking mechanism block *017*
10=*sondage 019*

indicating that the entry doors overlapped to create an extremely secure and stable gate.

As already mentioned, rising from the piers of the threshold block were two doorjambs. Cut from single blocks of white gypsum, the monolithic doorjambs abutted each tower wall as they rose to support the inscription (Plate 20-6 and Figure 20-9). Although found within tumble locus *003*, it was clear that these jambs once sat upon the distal ends of the threshold, supporting the inscription block crowning the gateway. Mortar remained *in situ* on both threshold piers indicating that the ashlars once adhered to the ends of the block. This mortar rose on average 0.03 m above

the two piers. The two ashlar blocks found within the tumble measured 2.28 m long x 0.50 m high x 0.30 wide and 2.32 m long x 0.50 m high x 0.28 m wide.

Finally, a large triangular-shaped monolithic inscription, recovered from tumble locus *005*, crowned the gate (Plates 20-7 and 8). Although found broken in two pieces, the eight-line Latin inscription was fully intact. The main body of the inscription block was in the shape of an isosceles triangle with three additional smaller triangular forms adjoining each end; attached to the distal ends were two flanges, and a single decorative finial mounted the crest.

Plate 20-4   Siket *praesidium et hydreuma* trench SK00-1, threshold *011*, and locking block *017* looking east. Scale=1 m. Photograph by S. E. Sidebotham.

Plate 20-5   Siket *praesidium et hydreuma* trench SK00-1, detail of threshold *011*, and locking block *017* looking west. Scale=20 cm. Photograph by S. E. Sidebotham.

The end flanges were right triangles set with their hypotenuses facing the main isosceles triangle. The overlap of the main body of the inscription and right triangle generated a 0.14 m wedge. The height of the right triangles was 0.25 m. The crowning finial was simply an inverted isosceles triangle, measuring 0.22 m at its base x 0.16 m high. Furthermore, a 0.09 m wide molding extended along the main body of the inscription, creating two additional triangular forms: the frame for the inscription itself and the interior space in which the inscription was carved. Finally, occupying the empty space directly above the inscription was the only nontriangular decorative motif, a roughly hewn round boss 0.14 m in diameter. The full base of the inscription, including the two right triangle flanges, measured 2.46 m. The base of the inscription to the top of the crowning finial measured 1.12 m. The inscription block was 0.18 m thick.

20.3   STRATIGRAPHIC REPORT

Excavation of the main, northern, gate at Siket produced three phases. The stratigraphic sequence was quite simple with only a single phase of occupation (Figure 20-10). Well dated by the inscription, the construction and initial occupation of the fort dated to the reign of the Emperor Vespasian, AD 76/77. Excavations revealed little additional cultural material indicating that the gateway was, not surprisingly, kept clean and well maintained during its use. Although excavation provided a definitive founding date for the structure, excavations in the gate area this season did not produce the full occupational chronology of the fort; the abandonment date of the installation is uncertain.

Plate 20-6   Siket *praesidium et hydreuma* trench SK00-1, columns that once supported the inscription looking west. Scale=1 m. Photograph by S. E. Sidebotham.

Plate 20-7   Siket *praesidium et hydreuma* trench SK00-1 with threshold *011* and inscription looking west. Photograph by S. E. Sidebotham.

It must be surmised that once the water supply had dwindled, the fortress was abandoned sometime during the middle Roman period as surface pottery indicates a first- to third-century AD occupational period.

Final phasing for trench SK00-01 is as follows:

Phase I: Construction of gateway dating to the ninth year of the reign of the Emperor Vespasian (AD 76/77)

Phase II: Occupation— Flavian (AD 76/77–96) and later

Phase III: Decay and abandonment of the structure sometime between the first and third century AD

20.3.1   PHASE I: CONSTRUCTION

Excavation revealed a single phase of construction upon a large artificially leveled and tamped-down natural deposit of wadi wash. Extremely compact deposit 019 consisted of coarse sand intermixed with fine pebbles devoid of all cultural debris. Excavation removed 0.30 m of this material without providing evidence of earlier occupation.

Although not revealed in this trench, it is likely that the foundations were cut after leveling of the area and after large guard tower walls *004* and *006* were raised. In preparation for the construction of the gateway, a small pit was cut through wadi wash *019* for the placement of locking mechanism *017* (Figures 20-4 and 20-5) to anchor it deep within the sand. Installation *017* extended 0.27 m down into the wadi wash. Dug through sand, the pit revealed no cut. Concreted fills *015* and *016* were then deposited throughout the gateway, further anchoring the locking-block mechanism. The level of concretion of this fill suggests that sand and small pebbles were intermixed with gypsum powder to form a solid surface. The fill simultaneously created a stable foundation for the two-step walls *009* and *010*, threshold *011*, the *017* locking mechanism, and served as a surface for the gateway. Although a single deposit, threshold block *011* remained *in situ*, physically separating surface *015* to the north and *016* to the south. Surface *016* produced scant finds, only a few scrappy potsherds. Concreted surfaces *015* and *016* remained exposed throughout the entire occupational phase of the structure with little debris accumulating on them.

Constructed directly on these concreted leveling fills/surfaces were the step walls and threshold block. Situating block *011* (Figures 20-4 and 5) directly upon surfaces *015* and *016* created a raised threshold for the gateway. This feature contributed to the maintenance of the structure, not allowing debris to be carried easily into the interior of the fortress. Finally, the full gateway, including the doorjamb and monumental inscription, were raised.

20.3.2   PHASE II: OCCUPATION

Surfaces *015* and *016* defined the occupational phase of the structure. This floor of concreted sand and fine pebbles was well maintained with little occupational debris accumulating in the gateway. This minimized pollution of the water source (*hydreuma*) inside the *praesidium*.

De facto surface *012* lay north of threshold block *011*, outside the limits of the fort. Sloping uphill toward the installations, this tamped-down accumulation of debris consisted of compacted clay-loam sediments wrapping around the edge of the architecture, along the two-step walls and threshold block. Excavations recovered only a few scrappy early Roman sherds and igneous rocks in this deposit.

Plate 20-8   Siket *praesidium* and *hydreuma* trench SK00-1 with threshold 011, inscription, and interior of fort looking toward the south-southwest. Scale=50 cm. Photograph by S. E. Sidebotham.

Figure 20-9   Artist's reconstruction of front gate of the *praesidium* and *hydreuma* at Siket looking south. Drawing by A. M. Hense.

20.3.3   PHASE III: ABANDONMENT AND DECAY

The majority of the loci excavated in the trench were abandonment and decay. These loci exhibited a distinct pattern of the accumulation of windblown sand separating episodes of architectural tumble, indicating that collapse occurred over a period of time. It is within two important tumble loci that major architectural features were found: the inscription, within locus *005*, and the two monolithic gypsum doorjambs, within locus *003*.

South of threshold *011*, the earliest episode of abandonment debris had a small amount of collapse (*013*), extending over locking-mechanism block *017* and lapping over both step walls *009* and *010*.

Excavations recovered within this debris approximately 25 small iron nails weighing 120 g (see Chapter 9). In a similar context at the excavations of the small fort in Wadi Kalalat numerous small iron nails were also discovered, weighing 170 grams (see Chapters 9 and 19). Loci in both forts were located within the interiors up against the threshold blocks suggesting at the time of abandonment that wooden doors were dismantled with the intent of reusing them elsewhere. These nails are the only remains of those structures. Timber was a precious commodity in the desert, certainly reused whenever possible. At Berenike for instance, reused wooden planks—mainly of teak—have been found within the walls serving to level the courses (cf. BE96/97-10, BE97/98-16, BE98/99/00-23/32; Sidebotham 1999b: 26, 94; Vermeeren, 1999:315–317, 319). Thus, the presence of these nails is easily explained as the remnants from the wooden gate that once fortified the main entrance at Siket.

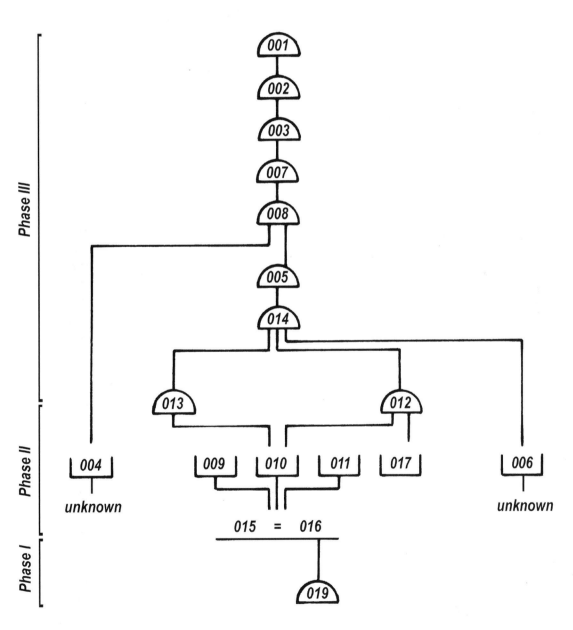

Figure 20-10   Matrix of trench KL00-1 in the *praesidium, hydreuma* and *lacus* of Siket.

Subsequent to the removal of the wooden gates, the abandoned *praesidium* lay dormant, at which time the first deposits of windblown sand swirled throughout the open portal. Sand locus *014* accumulated between the guard towers, measuring on average 0.12 m deep. After a period of time, decay began to wreak havoc on the structure and the fortress suffered considerable collapse. The first features to experience this deterioration were the inscription block and the upper sections of the guard towers. As the large inscription block swung away from its supports, a segment of the surrounding towers was also brought down. This episode is defined by architectural tumble *005*, which extended throughout the entire gateway. The inscription, embedded within this tumble, lay perpendicular to its original mount above the gate. This configuration indicates that the block initially pivoted at its eastern end, with the western flange swinging toward the north. As it pivoted, the weight of the inscription block caused it to fall face up at nearly a 90-degree angle from its original position above the gate. When the inscription fell, the main body broke into two pieces. Fortunately, the Latin inscription remained intact.

Following this episode of collapse, deposition of windblown sand continued within the gate. Sand *007* accumulated between the walls of the guard towers covering the earlier tumble to an average depth of 0.14 m. Subsequently, the *praesidium* suffered further decay. Although the inscription block and upper reaches of the guard towers sheared off during an earlier episode of collapse, the monolithic doorjambs remained in place up until this time when a final collapse occurred. With this event, the gypsum doorjambs and portions of the remaining guard tower walls cascaded into the gateway. The ensuing tumble, *003*, spanned the entire main entrance of the fort. Found within the tumble, the two doorjambs extended east-west across the gateway, lying roughly parallel to one another, indicating that each pillar simply broke away from its position against the guard-tower walls. The entire event was then covered by windblown sand, *002*, sealing off the history of the *praesidium* at Siket for centuries.

20.4   DISCUSSION

The excavation of the *praesidium* at Siket provided valuable data regarding its relationship to Berenike and the hinterland. Although *praesidia* have been identified throughout the Eastern Desert, most are located along major commercial thoroughfares (Sidebotham,

et al. 1991; Sidebotham 1995b, 1998, 1999c, 2000c; Sidebotham and Zitterkopf 1995, 1996). As neither the fort at Siket nor the two forts in Wadi Kalalat were associated with commercial infrastructure, it has long been presumed that these installations guarded sources of potable water available to Berenike. The inscription at Siket and the huge well and exterior hydraulic tanks at the large fort in Wadi Kalalat confirm this hypothesis. Although excavations recovered no inscription at the small *praesidium* in Wadi Kalalat, that facility also most likely existed to protect potable water supplies (see Chapter 19).

The inscription found at Siket is valuable as it records a precise date for the founding of the *praesidium*: the ninth year of the reign of Vespasian, AD 76/77. During his reign and that of his successor sons, many civil works projects were undertaken both in Rome and in the provinces. The inscription from Siket defines the role of the administration in the Roman hinterland. The Siket *praesidium* was constructed and maintained by order of L. Julius Ursus, an agent of Marcus Trebonius, *praefectus* of Mons Berenike. Clearly, the control of the water supply did not fall under local public works, nor was it the responsibility of a private individual. In the Eastern Desert, where potable water was the most precious commodity available, the government oversaw every aspect of its provision, holding sovereignty over the hinterland by controlling its most valuable asset.

A further indication that the central authority played a pivotal role in managing the potable water supply is the inscription itself. As Berenike is located in the Roman East, Greek was primarily used for written documents. The Siket inscription, however, is written in Latin, conveying its association with the Roman central administration and the Roman military. The *praesidium* was constructed on the orders of the *praefectus Aegypti*, a governor appointed by the emperor himself, an adjunct with close relationships to Rome. The status of the *praefectus Aegypti* denotes the relationship between Rome and this distant region. As control of the area was imperative due to the lucrative commerce passing through the district, the government did not take a lackadaisical approach to its security. The Latin text signifies the government's close monitoring of this barren land and indicates that the local administration was merely the custodian of the area.

The central government's administration of this region is apparent. Large-scale governmental projects in the Eastern Desert overseen by the prefect of Egypt and the prefect of Berenike have been attested elsewhere. Parallel texts inscribed during the tenures of M. Trebonius Valens and L. Julius Ursus have been found on the Berenike-Nile Road, both at Khawr ej-Jir (Aphrodito) and at Zeydun/Khashm al-Menih (Dydme/Didymoi). Wilkinson documented an inscription in 1826 at the Aphrodito station. The five-line text, dated to the reign of Titus (AD 79–81), recorded the repair of a cistern when M. Trebonius Valens was prefect of Berenike and L. Julius Ursus was prefect of Egypt (Bagnall, Bülow-Jacobsen, and Cuvigny 2001).

Other *praesidia* and *hydreumata* have been located in the Eastern Desert. From the epigraphic evidence, both the fort at Siket and the large fort in Wadi Kalalat have been substantially identified as *praesidia* enclosing circular depressions, the putative *hydreumata*, or wells. Other similar structures have been identified in the Eastern Desert and have long been interpreted as *hydreumata*. Numbers of *hydreumata* and *praesidia* occur on all the major transdesert routes between the Red Sea and the Nile further indicating the government's domination of the entire region by controlling and regulating water in this hostile environment.

The dates assigned to Siket and the two forts in Wadi Kalalat lend further understanding to the environs of Berenike and the constant need for water. The inscription at Siket records a Flavian date for the founding of the *praesidium*. Although surface pottery collected during the 1998 survey of Siket suggested a first- to third-century AD period of occupation, excavation did not ascertain the precise period of abandonment. The inscription found at the large fort Wadi Kalalat records a Trajanic date. And finally, the pottery dates from the small fort at Wadi Kalalat indicate a first or second- to fourth-century AD date. During the first centuries of Roman rule, the city of Berenike flourished and needed sizable quantities of potable water. Throughout Berenike's history, authorities were vigilant concerning these supplies. Although imposing fortresses guarded these provisions, the environment could not be tempered, generating constant monitoring of the potable water. As each source became exhausted, additional supplies were needed. Once another source was identified, it is clear that authorities immediately laid claim to the area, constructed a *praesidium* and excavated a *hydreuma*. With the strong government maintaining control of the water supplies, the routes along which these lay remained within its sphere of influence.

CHAPTER 21 ⌒

INTERPRETATIVE SUMMARY AND CONCLUSION

S. E. SIDEBOTHAM AND W. Z. WENDRICH

Excavations in 1999 and 2000 (the sixth and seventh seasons of fieldwork) greatly expanded our knowledge of Berenike's development, especially in relation to the mil370 on the provisioning of the town, especially the establishment and protection of the all important freshwater resources.

For a more complete picture of the region as a whole and Berenike's role in it, the project has conducted extensive and intensive site surveying within a 45 km radius of Berenike and additional surveying farther afield between 1990 and 2000. It is evident that an elaborate communication network linked Berenike to numerous desert sites and these sites to one another. Desert settlements include military installations, possible Christian monastic communities, civilian settlements of unknown function, gold and beryl mines, and hard-stone quarries. A number of early and late Roman cemeteries and numerous solitary graves, rock drawings, and pictographs attest the presence of travelers or residents of the region throughout antiquity. The linking road networks and similarity of finds indicate that some degree of cooperation and interdependence was clearly at work among the numerous settlements in the region. This is especially true in early and late Roman times that mirror peak periods of activity at Berenike itself.

21.1 TOPOGRAPHICAL SUMMARY

The division of the site of Berenike into different sectors, as outlined in Chapter 2, more or less coincides with discrete functional and temporal units of the town and reflects the town's development.

Approaching Berenike from the west, the first urban quarter one encounters is the Ptolemaic area (trenches 11, 35, 36, and 40[1]). On this part of the site, the earliest occupation is visible on the surface, while in the rest of the town the Ptolemaic layers are covered under a 2 to 5 m deep deposit of later occupation. The development pattern of the town, gradually expanding and shifting to the east, followed the retreating seashore.

The western quarter, where the only building excavated appears to have had a religious function (trenches 6 and 16, the Western Shrine), is divided from the Ptolemaic industrial area by what may have been a small lagoon . The fourth- to fifth-century building had several earlier phases and covered Ptolemaic remains, which were discovered too deep in the trench to be excavated safely. North of these western outskirts of the town proper was a large early Roman trash dump (trenches 3, 13, 19, 29, 31, and 33 as well as *sondages* 14, 24, and 25). Most of the trash was thrown out on a previously unoccupied area outside the town, but some remains of Ptolemaic habitation were uncovered under the eastern part of the dump.

The approach of the actual center of town, now a leveled area, climbs from the Western Shrine to the highest part of the site. In contrast to most of Berenike, where lines of coral indicate the outline of the latest phase buildings, this area does not have any surface features other than the protruding walls of the Serapis temple. The temple, "cleared" on several occasions in the nineteenth century and published by Meredith (Meredith 1957), was built after the founding of the city by Ptolemy II Philadelphus in approximately 275 BC. The founding date is unknown, but the temple existed at least in the early Roman period. During the latest phase of occupation of the town, before the middle of the sixth century AD, the temple, and the area that in earlier periods was part of its precinct, were closely surrounded with houses, some of which were filled with trash, a certain sign of abandonment, while the town still functioned. Excavations in trench 1 were initiated in this area in 1994 to provide a diachronic overview of the site. The depth of deposit required a much larger surface to be excavated, however. This was undertaken in trench 10 (excavation of which began in 1996). Excavations here were halted at the end of the 2000 season at late first-century BC levels, the top (latest) layers of Ptolemaic occupation.

West of the leveled area the site slopes sharply down toward the sea. The central quarter consisted of a combination of commercial and residential buildings (trenches 20/27, 28/38, 34, 37, and 41) and a trash dump (trench 21); the levels visible at the surface and throughout the excavations dated to the late fourth and early fifth centuries AD.

North of the central quarter, in an area bordering the shoreline where it curved inland, was the northern quarter. Only one building was excavated here, the so-called Northern Shrine (trenches 23 and 32), dated to the fourth and early fifth centuries AD. The area south of the central quarter preserves the outline of buildings, but no excavations have been undertaken here.

East of this area is the northeastern quarter with Building F (trenches 4, 7, and 17), the shallow remains of a multiphase building (trench 26) at the north side of the shoreline and the Christian ecclesiastical building (trenches 8, 12, 22, 30, and 39) at the eastern edge of town. This entire area had been uninhabited during the Ptolemaic period and was prepared for construction in the mid- to late fourth century AD as part of Berenike's third period of prosperity (after the early Ptolemaic and early Roman periods). Buildings in this area were all large and seemed mostly to have had public, that is, commercial, administrative, or religious, functions.

The purposes of most of the buildings in the southeastern quarter of the town, where trenches 2, 5, 9, and 18 were excavated, are still enigmatic. The southern part of the area borders the most likely location of the harbor, or ships' landing place (the other indication for a landing is in the northeastern quarter just west of Building F). It is not clear at the moment, however, whether most of the buildings in this quarter are mostly linked to commercial activities. Trench 5, however, appears in its late fourth/early fifth-century-AD phase to have been a warehouse.

21.2 LAYOUT AND FUNCTIONAL DISTRIBUTION

Berenike in its latest phase did not resemble a formally planned Greek or Roman city. Even though established in the early Ptolemaic period, the street grid, although vaguely orthogonal, lacks the rigid outline that characterized Alexandria, the Ptolemaic showcase city on the Mediterranean. This cannot be attributed only to eight centuries of construction cluttering the original organization of the town. If anything survives the ages, then it is a town's basic street plan. Perhaps the fledgling town once was built to a more Greek schema, but we cannot now detect that. The area that overlays most of the original Ptolemaic settlement, however, has been leveled and the street plan, discernable elsewhere from the surface remains of coral walls, has become invisible as a result. Most of the presently visible street plan was established in Berenike's third major period of development in the late fourth/early fifth centuries AD and is evident from excavations in the late Roman commercial-industrial quarter (Sidebotham 2002).

21.2.1 HARBOR AREA

There are two potential areas where Berenike's harbor could have been: to the north of the town (adjacent to the northeastern quarter, near Building F), or south of the town, where a protected inlet between the town and the peninsula to the south could have been used as such. Survey and excavation so far have produced tantalizing indications that both locations could have been harbors and, at the moment, the working hypothesis is that both areas, and probably the entire eastern part of the town, were both formal and informal landing places for boats.

The inlet south of Berenike is today almost completely silted up and has even at high tide not more than 1 m of muddy depth. The landscape at the western side of the inlet, however, has a fingered appearance: five dam-like stretches of land run into what once probably was a much deeper bay. Furthermore, the discovery on the surface of these "fingers" of piles of vesicular basalt strongly suggests that ships unloaded here. This material, not a local stone, but occurring in the Hauran area of southern Syria and northern Jordan and along the South Arabian and African coasts near the Bab el-Mandeb, was most probably put in the ships' holds as ballast.

Based on geological coring that took place in 1995 and excavation in several trenches, there is also evidence for ships' landing facilities in the northeastern quarter of the city. The discovery of large seawalls in trenches 2 and 17 and a possible seawall or pier in trench 22 supports this identification. Furthermore, trench 17 also produced decayed wooden poles that were found in a position that suggested a quay built to bypass the shallow mud flat that divides the shoreline from the reefs and deeper water. During the 1999 season, magnetic surveying of the area between trench 17 and the small peninsula-like feature to the west, on which trenches 23 and 32 are located, revealed no structures whatsoever. While the equipment used in the survey could not detect features more than approximately 1.5 m below ground surface, the dearth of structures suggests that this region may have been a lagoon or, more likely, an inlet at the northern end of the city at some point in the Roman period. If the tentative identification of the structure in trench 17 as a seawall is correct, then this northern part of the site may have been a protected bay or inlet at some point in early Roman times. Although this seawall was covered over by a later pottery dump, there is no way to determine, at present, if this putative bay or inlet continued to function in later Roman times. The discovery of evidence of resealing of jars in Building F, the structure built atop the pottery dump, suggests that in the late fourth and early fifth centuries this edifice may have had a function in controlling the trade. Such an administrative service would not be housed far from the entrance to the harbor, or the ships' access point. A religious function for Building F also remains a possibility (see the following).

21.2.2 RELIGIOUS STRUCTURES

The religious buildings in Berenike were distributed throughout the settlement. The ones known to date are the Serapis temple (and its courtyard, in the leveled area, trench 10), the Western Shrine (trenches 6 and 16), the Northern Shrine (trenches 23 and 32) and a Christian ecclesiastical complex in the northeastern quarter (trenches 8, 12, 22, 30, 39). Compared to the 41 trenches excavated at Berenike, the number of trenches that revealed religious structures is high (9=22%). Perhaps this is not surprising, considering the dangers of the sea route, the transdesert tracks and the mere feat of living in a desert town at the edge of the sea. Surviving in such circumstances may have been viewed by many as truly due to the favor of the gods and as such, they deserved commemoration.

The Serapis temple was dedicated to several well-established Egyptian gods including Serapis and Isis (Meredith 1957:60–70). The Western Shrine was dedicated to the Roman Imperial cult in the time of Caracalla and Julia Domna (AD 215), and to the Palmyrene god Hierobol/Yarhibol. Apart from these cults it is possible that Isis, Harpocrates, and other Hellenistic deities were worshipped here as well (Sidebotham 2000:52–73). Apart from the dedicatory inscriptions, the shrine yielded a small stone altar. Remnants of over 100 wooden bowls were also found here.

It is unclear which deity was worshipped in the Northern Shrine (trenches 23/32). Four temple pool offering tables, a partially painted ostrich egg, and a stone columnar-shaped altar with burn marks were found here, as well as soil colorations indicating that burning offerings in wooden bowls was part of the ritual. Although excavations recovered a broken relief reused as a seat, no images or texts were found that could clarify which deity was worshipped here. The presence of a number of terracotta oil lamps and amphora toes reused as torches suggests that the room in which the rituals took place was dark. Perhaps this was the venue of a mystery cult, in a windowless room, or a cult celebrated at night.

Building F in the northeastern quarter has a layout that is reminiscent of an Egyptian temple, but from the scarce excavated material, it seems more likely that its function was administrative rather than religious.

The latest and largest religious structure excavated thus far was the Christian ecclesiastical building in trenches 8, 12, 22, 30, and 39. From the relatively undisturbed situation found in the other shrines, it seems that Christianity and pagan cults were performed side by side until the end of Berenike's existence sometime before the middle of the sixth century AD.

The one feature that all shrines, with the exception of the church, have in common is the occurrence of wooden bowls with burnt offerings. These were even found in trench 10, which at that level was part of the precinct of the Serapis temple in the first century AD. The large Indian-made storage jar containing 7.55 kg of black peppercorns found embedded in the courtyard floor was probably also property of the temple, and its contents may have been destined as dedications.

Another common feature was the temple pool offering tables. Wilkinson found a double temple pool offering table in the Serapis temple and brought it back to Great Britain (British Museum, accession number EA 135). This type of offering table is a southern Egyptian or Nubian feature. A more extensive publication of these religious objects will appear in the report on the 2001 excavations.

Neronian and Trajanic inscriptions found in a late Roman context in trench 37 indicate the worship of Jupiter and Isis at Berenike and suggest that they derived from edifices dedicated to those deities that have not yet been located.

21.2.3 COMMERCIAL/GOVERNMENT BUILDINGS

Buildings with an apparent commercial or governmental function have been excavated in the northeastern, central, and southeastern quarters. Building F has been mentioned before as one such possible structure. At the southeastern part of the site, trench 5 was perhaps part of storage or commercial facility. The central quarter seems to have been dedicated to smaller shops in combination with residential areas on the upper floors (trenches 20/27, 28/38, 34, 37, and 41). Excavations have not uncovered any Roman-style *macellum* or *forum* or a Greek style *agora*.

While no public entertainment buildings, such as a stadium, theater, amphitheater, or a circus, have been identified at Berenike, there is circumstantial evidence for the presence of a bath in the city, possibly in the center not far from the Serapis temple. The discovery of a number of kiln-fired bricks—traditionally used in hydraulic installations in the Eastern Desert—in trench 10 reused as portions of walls for installations in the second and third centuries AD and the recovery of glass fragments identified as deriving from bath-oil vessels suggest the presence of a bathing facility near the Serapis temple that functioned sometime prior to the late second and third centuries AD.

21.2.4 INDUSTRIAL AND MANUFACTURING AREAS

In the Ptolemaic period large-scale manufacturing took place west of the main settlement, perhaps partly separated from it by a lagoon. Surface surveying in this area and excavations in trench BE96-11 in previous seasons showed industrial activity, especially manufacturing of fired bricks and metal products. Such manufacturing activities would have been segregated from other areas of the city for obvious fire-prevention reasons and to reduce the noxious fumes that would have engulfed the town. The magnetic survey in 1999 and excavations in 2000 confirmed this interpretation and recorded the presence of sizable structures and kilns in this quarter lying not more than 1–1.5 m below the present ground surface. Large quantities of lead sheeting and copper-

alloy nails found in this area seem to point at ship repair and refurbishment. Presumably, this part of the city also was used as a water station. Perhaps it was here, in the Ptolemaic period anyway, that drinking water arrived on pack animals and was stored and distributed to the settlement's residents and to the ships that needed freshwater supplies. The discovery of large quantities of lead in this region may have been destined to cover the merchant ships' hulls, but may also have been used to seal amphorae with water for shipping.

Small-scale manufacturing and processing activities are apparent in the eastern and central parts of the site in a number of trenches, including 10, 12, 18, possibly 28, and 30. Excavations in the latter trench, part of the fifth-century AD Christian ecclesiastical complex in the northeastern quarter, documented evidence of the production of fine shell inlays. Both raw materials, in the form of 36 bivalve shells and two partial shells and decoratively cut shell and bone inlays, were found here. Considering the scarcity of wood in the area, it is possible that this was the production site only for the inlays, rather than for complete end products, such as wooden inlay boxes or furniture. In the same building, trench 12 yielded evidence for large-scale food preparation, which included the use of *garum*. Evidence for manufacture and food preparation from the other trenches was much less than that found in trenches 10, 12, 18, and 28. Small, informal installations, some with, some without, traces of fire were found mostly in the courtyards of combined commercial/residential buildings of the late fourth to early fifth centuries AD.

The latest evidence for residential use, found in many trenches, occurred after abandonment of the site; this took the form of roughly built "banana-" shaped walls, which probably acted as windbreaks. Putative residential areas while the city still functioned have been more difficult to identify, but undoubtedly include the upper floors of the buildings in the central quarter (trenches 28/38 and 37, and, possibly, in trenches 20/27, 34, and 41). These, however, are all mid to late fourth to fifth century AD; no recognizable residential areas have been noted from the Ptolemaic or early or middle Roman periods.

Clearly, military units were stationed at Berenike. It is uncertain if these troops used Berenike as their home base or if that was somewhere on the Nile. It is also uncertain where Roman troops stationed in Berenike itself would have been billeted in the city. The ostraka from the early Roman trash deposits at the northern end of the city (trenches 13, 19, 29, 31, 33) and the late second- to early third-century inscriptions from the shrine of the Palmyrenes in trenches 6/16 indicate the presence of Roman and auxiliary troops at Berenike and, as was typical of Roman garrison practices in the eastern Roman Empire, troops were often stationed in cities (cf. Isaac 1992:269–282). Whether they would have been housed by units in barracks designed for them in specific quarters of the city or whether they would have lived scattered throughout various quarters of Berenike remains uncertain.

Architectural and epigraphic evidence confirms military presence at the large *praesidium* in Wadi Kalalat and at the *praesidium* at Siket; though lacking epigraphic evidence, there is little doubt that the smaller fort in Wadi Kalalat also housed a military unit.

21.2.5   CEMETERIES

Few human remains have been excavated at Berenike. Those of an adult female in trench 11 seem to have been a proper burial, as do those of an adult male in trench 36. Both were buried in this part of the site, the Ptolemaic industrial area, after it had been abandoned. Because neither of the bodies was associated with any dateable strata, they "float" in a temporal vacuum.

The finds of a human fetus in trench 7 and an adult male in trench 9 are, most likely, not proper burials. The latter seemed to be the victim of an accident, or had been deposited in an abandoned building after death. A few human bones found in the early Roman trash may represent amputations. A large number of graves line the tops of hills surrounding the city to the southwest and northwest; undoubtedly others existed to the west that have been destroyed by the military bunkers constructed in about 1973. Investigations of the ring-cairn graves dotted around Berenike indicate that they are late Roman in date; no identifiable Ptolemaic, early, or middle period Roman burials have been located. Thus, it is not clear whether there were cemeteries in the Ptolemaic and early and middle Roman periods. Although Berenike was not a run-off-the-mill town, it seems unlikely, however, that the bodies of everybody who died in Berenike were brought back to the Nile Valley. The long trip across the desert would make that all but impossible. Yet, the famous Coptos Tariff of AD 90, which records tolls on the passage of peoples and goods between the Nile city of that name and the Red Sea coast, lists a duty to be paid of one drachma and four obols levied on corpses, suggesting that those who died in the desert, and could afford it, were returned to the Nile Valley for burial (Young 2001:49–50).

Unfortunately, all late Roman period tombs in the region around Berenike have been badly robbed.

21.3   POPULATION

Excavations this season shed no dramatic new light on the size of the population of Berenike at different points in its history. With some augmentations, conclusions reached and described in the 1997 and 1998 reports remain valid for these two seasons. Periods of maximum population sizes appear to have been in the early Ptolemaic era, early Roman times, especially the first century AD, with a third peak in the late Roman period, between the middle of the fourth and into the fifth century AD. Little evidence has come to light regarding population sizes for the middle or very late Roman periods, but sufficient documentation of activity in Berenike in the third century AD survives to conclude that the city in its eight centuries of existence never seems to have been completely abandoned.

As outlined in previous Berenike volumes, it is clear that women and children resided in the city. New information obtained in 2000 indicates that some of these women had a relatively high social status as can be concluded from Philotera's dedications to Zeus during the reign of Nero found in a secondary, late Roman context in trench 37.

The names of individuals not known previously came to light in the early Roman trash deposit north of the city in these two excavation seasons. These appear on orders to pass written on ostraka and include the names of Alexandros; Theodoros, who is a military official—*quintanensis*, a rank attested in the ostraka in previous seasons—associated with the customs house at Berenike; and one Antonios. A Titus Flavius Potamon appears on one of the ostraka; his name pushes the latest dates for the ostraka from the Julio-Claudian into the Flavian period (not earlier than AD 69). This date is reinforced by the appearance of a man named Albius, who was a military official involved in the customs-house operations early in the reign of Vespasian (AD 69–79). The soldier, C. Cornelius, member of the century of Domitius, also appears for the first time. More certainly Egyptian names, such as Sarapion, son of Kasios, appear in the texts. Horus, son of Komaros; Nektharaus, son of Haryothes; and Kalleis, son of Harpochration, also appear on two Neronian-period papyrus bills of sale. On one of these papyri, the seller's name is lost, but he was a member of the *Cohors Equitata Ituraeorum*. The military rank of *decanos* also appears in the ostraka. Unlike some of the individuals with apparent Greek or

Latin names who were in the military, the status of the Egyptian-name–bearing men is not clear. Notable is the fact that the bulk of the early Roman period documents, where offices or status are recorded, are predominately military/governmental. Two duplicate inscriptions from the reign of Nero are dedications by Philotera, daughter of Patentais, to Zeus have already been noted previously. An interpreter and secretary whose name is lost, but whose father was Papiris, dedicated another inscription from the time of Trajan and the prefect of Egypt Marcus Rutilius Lupus to Isis. All three inscriptions appeared in secondary late Roman contexts in trench 37.

There was important new evidence recognized for the first time these seasons regarding the possible presence of ethnic groups at Berenike that had not been noted previously. The recovery of Aksumite pottery from several trenches and a single Aksumite coin of the late third to early fourth century suggest that individuals from that sub-Saharan East African Kingdom traded with and may have resided in Berenike, beginning probably at least as early as the fourth century AD.

The possible Aksumite presence in Berenike in the late Roman period mirrors the existence of Indian merchants in early Roman times. The evidence for the latter is stronger, however. A fourth-century AD West Indian coin attests merely that at that time there were still trade contacts with India. The discovery of Indian pottery, however, not only the decorative "rouletted" fine ware, but also Indian coarse ware, possibly should be interpreted differently. That evidence, in combination with the discovery of rice, may point to an Indian presence at Berenike for at least part of each year. Added to that is the puzzling occurrence in Berenike of a type of belt, made in local goat hair, in a technique that is not commonly found at other Roman sites. This technique, known as ply-split braiding, probably has an Indian origin. To find these belts made in Egyptian goat hair means either that Egyptian sailors had learned a new technique, but more likely, that Indian sailors used the time they had to wait in Berenike to return home making belts in the technique they learned at home, with material at hand in Berenike.

Both the early Roman evidence of Indian sailors or merchants, as well as the fourth-century evidence of an Aksumite presence leads us to review carefully our presumptions about the organization of the long-distance trade. Literary sources from the early Roman period, such as the *Periplus Maris Erythraei*, tell us that the initiative for the trade lay with Rome. While this may or may not have been true in early Roman times, archaeological evidence seems to give us a slightly different and perhaps more balanced view certainly for the late Roman period, in which the trade partners seem to show more initiative and play a larger role than ancient "western" literary sources suggest.

21.4 Providing Water and Security

Indians, Aksumites, Egyptians, Greeks, Romans and other ethnic groups, and military and civilians alike were dependent on water, the one important provision that was hard to come by in Berenike. The 1999 and 2000 seasons have provided great progress in understanding the water provision over time and the security measures that went hand in hand with it.

The water in wells dug near Berenike is too brackish to drink, so water had to be brought in either by pipeline or pack animals over a distance of at least 5 km to be out of the brackish zone. When the city was founded in about 275 BC, a water source must have been identified and exploited, not only for the inhabitants of the city, but also as provision for the ships that left the harbor. We do not know the source, but it seems that the site of trench 36 in the Ptolemaic area west of the town proper was the receiving end of the caravans of pack animals loaded with leather water sacks. A water tank lined with hydraulic plaster and a rimmed area with solidly Ptolemaic amphorae may represent a filling area where water was distributed for the town and the ships.

We have much more information for the early Roman period. Military patrols protected travelers using the roads between Berenike and the Nile and, as evidenced from the forts in Wadi Kalalat and Siket, the military provided potable water to the city at least in the early and middle Roman periods from nearby *hydreumata*. No evidence for pipelines, a feature well known from other Roman sites in Egypt, was found, so presumably early Roman Berenike was still dependent on water brought in by caravans.

Thus, the government not only took an active role in promoting the commerce passing through the city, but in providing protection (in the form of 10 forts surrounding the city, from south to north: the hilltop fort at Shenshef, the large *praesidium* in Wadi Kalalat, the small fort in Wadi Kalalat, the *praesidium* at Siket, the five forts in Wadi Abu Greiya, and the fort in Wadi Lahma) and vital water supplies as well. None of the nearby forts (those in Wadi Kalalat and Siket) operated in late Roman times. Thus, it remains uncertain where Berenike obtained its drinking water in that period. It is possible, though evidence is at present lacking, that water could have been shipped to

Berenike from the late Roman site of Shenshef, about 25 km to the southwest or from one of the forts in Wadi Abu Greiya (Vetus Hydreuma), 21.3 km northwest of the city. Wherever the city obtained its water then or at any time in its history, it will have been from multiple locations to ensure a steady, if not always adequate, supply.

21.5 DATING THE TRADE

All the datable evidence from surface finds and from excavated remains from trenches 11, 36, and 40 points to these facilities being early to middle Ptolemaic (third to second century BC) in date. The recovery of a Demotic ostrakon here and one from the early Roman trash dump, of late Ptolemaic date, expands our chronological knowledge of Ptolemaic activity at Berenike from the early and middle Ptolemaic periods, known from previous seasons, into probably the late second to first century BC.

Berenike's main *raison d'être*, of course, was as a conduit for merchandise and peoples traveling between the Mediterranean and Egypt on the one hand and other points in the Red Sea-Indian Ocean littorals on the other as part of a large long-distance trade network. As a result of this, Berenike was an important governmental administrative center where officials dealt with various aspects of the commerce (its regulation, taxation, and protection) passing through the city.

Interestingly, the so-called Eastern Desert Ware (EDW), which had been found previously only in late strata at the site, was, in 2000, also recovered from earlier Roman levels. While not in the quantities that it appears in later Roman contexts, this does indicate that this pottery was produced and used at Berenike in much earlier periods than had heretofore been believed. It may also suggest that a small element of a Lower Nubian or Upper Egyptian desert-dwelling population was in residence at or trading with Berenike at this time. The early Roman trash dump north-northwest of the Serapis temple provided additional information on early Roman customs-house activities and on private business transactions in the first century and pushed the period of this activity into the Flavian era (AD 69–96).

Previous seasons had produced very little evidence for activity at Berenike in the second and third centuries. Aside from the epigraphic evidence of late second- to early third-century date from the Western Shrine (trenches 6 and16), the hieroglyphic inscription from the Serapis temple of Marcus Aurelius and Lucius Verus reported by Meredith (1957:61), a very few recognizable second- and third-century coins, and a slight quantity of pottery, prior to this season there was simply too little evidence to say more than that some groups were in the city at that time. Now with the excavation of small-scale industrial activities from the second and third centuries in the region immediately north of the Serapis temple (trench 10), one can say with some confidence that the Serapis temple itself and its immediate environs to the north were operating in this period.

The relative dearth of data in the second through early to mid-fourth centuries changes dramatically beginning in the middle of the fourth through fifth centuries when additional evidence for a major renovation of the city was undertaken. Previous seasons noted this phenomenon, and this was reinforced during research in 1999 and 2000 in many of the trenches, in the Northern Shrine (trenches 23 and 32), the central quarter, east of the Serapis temple (trenches 26, 27, 28/38, 34, 37, and 41), and the northeastern quarter (trenches 22, 30, and 39). The recovery of a late third- to early fourth-century Aksumite coin in a fourth- or fifth-century context and a late fourth-century AD coin from western India attests long-distance commercial activity at this time. Berenike's trade network in this late period expanded to include at least India, Sri Lanka, the Persian Gulf, and the kingdom of Aksum in the Red Sea and Indian Ocean, while at the same time the emporium's contacts with the wider Mediterranean world shrank to the region of the eastern Mediterranean. There was in this period also a noticeable increase in the presence of a desert-dwelling population. As we now know from the discovery of the type of pottery, which seems to be one of the indicators of this group (EDW), in middle Roman levels at the site, this connection between Berenike and the indigenous inhabitants of both its immediate and more-distant desert hinterlands had been in existence for some time and merely increased in this late period.

NOTE

1. For the years of excavation for these trenches, see Chapter 2.

APPENDIX A ～

ERRATA BE94-98

It seems appropriate here in the sixth volume of the Berenike series to note errors and make corrections found in the previous five reports (Sidebotham and Wendrich 1995, 1996a, 1998a, 1999a, 2000a); some additions have also been made here. The errata cited here are only major ones; minor spelling mistakes are not noted. The editors hope that these earlier errata have not caused readers too much inconvenience.

BERENIKE 1994 PRELIMINARY REPORT

p. 18, Figure 5
Printed upside down, north is at the bottom.

p. 39, Figure 15
Numbers associated with drawings are missing. They should appear as 1-5. The upper row of three drawings should be numbered (from left to right) 1–3; the lower row of two drawings should be numbered (from left to right) 4–5.

p. 40, Figure 16
Numbers associated with drawings of glass are missing. They should appear as 1–10. The top row of two should be numbered 1–2 (from left to right). The next three drawings beneath 1 should be 3–5, that beneath 2 should be 6. Number 7 is beneath 6; 8–10 appear on the bottom row (from left to right).

p. 52, Figure 21
Letters associated with drawings are missing. They should appear as a–d. The top row of two should be lettered a-b (from left to right). The bottom row of two should be lettered c–d (from left to right).

p. 52, Figure 22
Letters associated with drawings are missing. They should appear as a–b (from left to right).

p. 53, Figure 23
Letters associated with drawings are missing. They should appear as a–b (from left to right).

p. 54, Figure 24
Letters associated with drawings are missing. They should appear as a–b (from left to right).

p. 55, Figure 25
Letters associated with drawings are missing. They should appear as a–d. The top two are a. The bottom row should read d-c-b (from left to right).

BERENIKE 1995 PRELIMINARY REPORT

p. 7
Following last line on page the following should be added: "this trench. The project completed excavations in trenches BE94/95-2, BE95-3, and BE95-4 this season. Trenches BE95-5 to 7 will be continued next season."

p. 206, Plate 9-1
Caption should indicate Korra as a south Indian chieftain, not a king.

p. 207, Figure 9-2
Caption should indicate Korra as a south Indian chieftain, not a king.

pp. 269–296
The formulae for cables noted in the 1995 and 1997

reports as (e.g.) $sZ_2[S]_2$ whereas these formulae were noted in the 1996 report as $sZ_2[S_2]$. The movement of the subscript within the square brackets was to clarify that the subscript belonged to the cabled stage and not to the total of the formula, a notation preferred by A. Veldmeijer.

p. 269
Table 15-1 under Trench BE94/95-1, read "294" fragments for "292" fragments.

p. 271
Under subsection "15.2.1 Cordage from trench BE94/95-1," sixth line down, read " . . . differed considerably: only 294 fragments . . ." for "292."

p. 276
Figure 15-8 was not excavated from trench BE94/95-1 as the position of the figure and the discussion of the fragments suggest. The fragment was recovered from trench BE95-6.

p. 276, Figure 15-7
Add to caption: "BE94/95-1.*007* 0431-h-0833."

p. 276, Figure 15-8
Add to caption: "BE95-6.*004* 1451-h-0456."

p. 277, Figure 15-9
Add to caption: "BE94/95-1.*012* 0435-h-0629."

p. 278, Figure 15-10
Add to caption: "BE94/95-1.*012* 0435-h-0614."

p. 279, Figure 15-11
Add to caption: "BE94/95-1.*037* 0469-h-0559."

p. 279, Figure 15-12
Add to caption: "BE94/95-1.*007* 0431-h-0835."

p. 280. Plate 15-13
Add to caption: "BE94/95-1.*007* 0431-h-0835."

p. 281, Figure 15-14
Add to caption: "BE94/95-1.*003* 0402-h-0685."

p. 282, Figure 15-15
Add to caption: "BE94/95-1.*012* 0435-h-0618."

p. 283, Figure 15-16
Add to caption: "BE94/95-1.*wbc* 1206-h-0386."

p. 284, Figure 15-17
Add to caption: "BE94/95-1.*007* 0431-h-0819."

p. 285, Figure 15-18
Add to caption: "BE94/95-1.*027* 0480-h-0950."

p. 286, Figure 15-19
Add to caption: "BE94/95-1.*nbc* 1221-h-0430."

p. 286, Figure 15-20
Add to caption: "BE94/95-1.*036* 0535-h-0296."

p. 287, Figure 15-21
Add to caption: ABE94/95-1.*003* 0401-h-0890."

p. 320, Lines 6–7
Read "Triraphis pumilo" for "Tiraraphis pumilo."
Read "Acacia tortilis s.1." for "Acacia Tortilis sp."

BERENIKE 1996 REPORT

p. 46, Line 1
Read "3.2.3 Trench BE95/96-7" for "3.2.3 Trench BE95/9-7."

p. 100, Plate 3-79
Plate is printed upside down.

p. 180, Figure 6-8
Read caption "catalogue no. 80" for "catalogue no. 90."

p. 238, Lines 10–11
Read "The term rope is used for cordage with a diameter of 10 mm or more, . . ." for "The term rope is used for cordage with a diameter larger than 10 mm . . ."

p. 240, Line 7 (beneath Table 11-5)
Read "The fragments had an sZ_3 orientation . . ." for "The fragments had an sZ^3 orientation . . ."

p. 249, Plate 11-21
Plate is printed upside down.

p. 252, Line 16
Read "The three small *sondages* . . ." (italicized).

p. 302, Table 15-5
Under "rachis nodes/Triticum dicoccum" add:

	Berenike				Shenshef	
13	14	15	29	10	7
D C	D C	D C	D C	D C	D C
12 1	10 -	19 -	4 -	- -	- -

p. 317, Figure 15-12, caption line 2
Read "does" for "soes."
The olive stone was perhaps not a bead, but its worked appearance should probably be attributed to gnawing by a rodent.

p. 327, second full paragraph, line 3
Read "(Table 15-5)" for "(Table 15-18)."

pp. 438–442
The following additional finds were made: Q12 in structure 2, Q13 in structure 116, Q14 in structure 65, Q15 in structure 186, a tower or grave on a hilltop close to the fort at 23° 44.22' N/35° 23.02' E, Q7 & Q8 were moved from the center of the wadi into structure 127 to protect them from future flash floods.

BERENIKE 1997 REPORT

Figure 1-1
Read "The Southeastern Part of the Roman Empire during the time of Trajan (AD 98–117)." for "The South-Eastern part of THE ROMAN EMPIRE under the Flavian emperor Trajan at the end of the first century AD."
Spell "Cyprus" for "Cypros."
Spell "Caesarea" for "Ceasarea."
Spell "Mare Erythraeum" for "Mare Erythreum."
Spell "Rhinocolura" for "Rhinocorura."

p. 123, Line 12
Read "5-18 to 5-21" for "5-9 to 5-12."

p. 124, Line 15
Read "middle to late Augustan" for Aearly Augustan."

p. 124, Line 29
Read " . . . third century. Berenike, therefore, provides firm stratigraphic evidence . . ." for " . . . third century Berenike. There is, therefore, firm evidence . . ."

p. 125, Table 5-1
Under "Other Egyptian forms," under "% RBH number," Read "1.6" for "1.8."

p. 126, Line 4
Read "(catalogue number 47)" for "(catalogue number 45)."

p. 126, Line 14
Read "The latter is associated with . . ." for "These are associated with . . ."

p. 127, Catalogue entry 4
Read "middle to late Augustan" for "early Augustan."

p. 130, Catalogue entry 26
Read "Not illustrated in Chapter 6. For illustrations of paddle-impressed sherds see BE98 Chapter 3, Plates 3-9 to 3-11" for "Not illustrated. For illustrations see Chapter 6, catalogue numbers 17–18."

p. 136
For missing catalogue entry no. 50* insert heading "Reworked objects" and see page 152.

p. 138
Note: Loci indicated with an asterisk all derive from BE97-13.*004* PB 29-39 which contained material likely to be Ptolemaic in date.

p. 138, Line 3
Read "black glazed" for "blue glazed."

p. 140
For missing catalogue entry no. 69* insert heading "Table wares, other" and see page 152.

p. 142
Insert heading "Handmade cooking wares" for catalogue entry nos. 74-75.

p. 142
For missing catalogue entry no. 75* see page 152.

p. 145, Line 3
For relevant catalogue nos. 96–97 see p. 150.

p. 145, Table 5-9
Vessel 5 is complete apart from one sherd.

p. 146, Table 5-10
For the date of ARS 31/50 read "3–late 4/early 5." For the date of ARS 73 read "late 4–late 5."

p. 146, Line 23
Read "BE97-Sh.7" for "BE95/96-7." See catalogue number 95.

p. 147, Plate 5-12 caption
Read "BE97-Sh.7" for "BE95/96-7." See catalogue number 95.

p. 148, Table 5-13,
Trench Sh.2 Aswan cups
Read "53.0–41.9" for "40.0-51.9."
Trench Sh.7
Read "33.3–22.1" for "52.1-74.3."

p. 150, Catalogue entry no. 95
Read "BE97-Sh.7" for "BE95/96-7." It has three, not two, lead rivets.

p. 152
Add an asterisk to catalogue entry nos. 61*, 62*, 69*, 75* (see p. 138).

p. 155, Plate 5-17, caption
Read "Nagari" for "Nagiri."

p. 163, Line 23,
Read "(Begley forthcoming: fig. 3.10)" for "(Begley, forthcoming)."

p. 163, Line 33
Read "catalogue number 5" for "catalogue number."

p. 171, Line 24
Read "Sedov refers to" for "refers to."

p. 171, Lines 27–28
Read "and it could be Egyptian in origin" for "and it could be a coarse silt, Egyptian in origin."

p. 171, Line 33
Read "(Begley forthcoming: fig. 3.224-228)" for "(Begley, forthcoming)."

p. 171, Lines 33–34
Read "at other medieval Cola sites, and at Gangaikondacholapuram it is firmly dated in the eleventh century AD."

p. 171, Line 37
Read "(Wheeler, *et al.* 1946: Types 28–29)" for "(Wheeler, *et al.* 1946: Type 29)."

p. 173, Line 16
Delete "Marks on the vessel wall may indicate that at least some were coil made."

p. 174, Line 10
Delete "93."

p. 174, Line 17
Read "Alagankulam" for "Alagankulma."

p. 174, Line 25
Read "(V. Selvakumar, Appendix B)."

p. 174, Line 31
Add "These sherds are not illustrated in the BE97 report. For illustrations of paddle-impressed sherds see BE98, Chapter 3, Plates 3-9–3-11."

p. 176, Catalogue no. 10, lines 4–6
Read "containing common ill-sorted quartz . . . possibly sandy limestone" for "containing some ill-sorted quartz . . . possibly of limestone."

p. 176, Catalogue no. 11, line 1
Read "poorly dated" for "poorly."

p. 178, Catalogue no. 17

For an illustration of this entry see BE98, Chapter 3, Plate 3-9.

p. 181, Line 1
Read "south" for "south-east."

pp. 257–276
For the notation on cabled cordage see remarks made under the Berenike 1995 report pp. 269–296.

p. 264, penultimate and last lines
Read " . . . that this fragment was used as a pot stand rather than a head ring." for " . . . that the fragment this fragment was used as a pot stand rather than a head ring."

p. 266, Line 3
Read ", . . . knotted to the ring (Wendrich 1989: 183–184)." for ", . . . knotted to the ring (Wendrich 1989: 183–4)."

p. 272, Figure 13-13
The construction shown in the figure is not two opposite hitches and, therefore, it is an unsuitable comparison to the construction depicted in the Berenike 1995 report p. 279, Figure 15-11.

p. 274, Line 5
A reexamination of the knot in Figure 13-15a indicates that the construction is a running loop and not a noose.

p. 274, under subsection 13.5 CORDAGE FROM TRENCH BE97-SH.5 lines 5–6,
Read " . . . shown by the high percentage of string made from goat hair rather than grass or palm leaf." for " . . . shown by the high percentage of string made form goat hair rather than grass of palm leaf."

p. 303, Table 16-1, *Citrus medica*
See remark below 3E98 report p. 308

BERENIKE 1998 REPORT

p. 45, Line 3
Read "with the indications of decay" for "with the traditions of decay."

p. 150, under *3.2.2. Wheeler Type 10/Begley Form 5*, Line 3
Read "(Catalogue number 5 on p. 152)" for "(Figure 3-1, catalogue number 5)."

p. 180, next to last line
Read "Neronian receipt" for "Tiberian receipt."

p. 289, Lines 7–8
The first of these "illegible" letters is certainly an alpha or A, the second a rho or P, depending on what language it is.

p. 296, Lines 4–5
Read "Ποπλίωι ῾Ρούφωι" for "Πόπλιωι ῾Ρούφωι" (acute accent on the first iota and rough breathing accent in front of the P).

p. 308, Table 13-1, *Citrus medica*
Prudence is called for. So far only one botanical record exists from a third century AD context (BE95-11.007 PB 12).

p. 308, Table 13-1, *Pisum sativum*
After publication the seeds were identified as the species *Pisum abyssinica*. This is a rare species originating from Ethiopia or Yemen.

pp. 308-310, *Terminalia chebula*
Species has been misidentified. The shriveled specimens are very similar in appearance to *Terminalia chebula*, but they have now been identified with certainty as the inner parts of cloves of garlic (*Allium sativum*).

p. 409, Line 19
Read "δακ" for "δαχ"

CONTEXT AND FIND REGISTRATION NUMBERS

Since one of the purposes of this volume is to present an overview of work performed in previous seasons, a brief explanation of the registration numbering system used at Berenike is presented here.

The context registration numbers are assigned on site and indicate the archaeological context: area, excavation season, trench number, locus number, and Pottery Bucket number.

The areas are indicated with two capital letters. Most trenches have been excavated in Berenike (BE), but the team also excavated in Shenshef (SH), the large fort in Wadi Kalalat (KA), the small fort in Wadi Kalalat (KL), Siket (SK), and, in the 2001 season, at Wadi Abu Greiya (AG).

The code for the area is followed by the excavation season and the trench number, e.g., BE94-01. If a trench is excavated during a number of years, then all these seasons are mentioned, separated by backslashes, while the trench is distinguished from the excavation season by a hyphen, e.g., BE96/97/98/99/00-10. This reference is used when discussing the trench as a whole. Reference to a particular locus is made by mentioning only the year in which that specific locus has been excavated, e.g., BE00-10.*649* (note that locus numbers are always printed in italics). A locus is a stratigraphic unit that can comprise a deposit, cut, or structural feature, such as a wall or threshold. Each locus represents an archaeological event, such as the cutting of a pit, the fill that was deposited in the pit, or the floor that was subsequently laid over the pit. Each trench has its own sequence of locus numbers, starting with *001* and continuing through all the years the trench was excavated.

The smallest stratigraphic unit is the Pottery Bucket number (PB#). Each trench has its own sequence of Pottery Bucket numbers, which runs parallel to the locus number sequence and forms a check on possible mistakes, such as, for instance, switching two numbers. All finds from one locus excavated on a given day are given the same Pottery Bucket number. If excavation of the locus is continued the following day, a new Pottery Bucket number is allocated. Pottery Bucket numbers can also be given to different parts of a locus if a trench supervisor is in doubt about the extent or borders of that locus. If a subtle change in soil composition turns out to be in fact a new context, a new locus number can be given, and the finds from that new locus can be traced in retrospect through their separate Pottery Bucket number. A full context number would be, for example, BE00-33.*038* PB# 61.

For each locus, a recording sheet is filled out with full details on the location, dimensions, stratigraphic relations, and a detailed description, which includes soil color, composition, and other relevant features. All finds from a locus are noted on the locus sheet, as well as the photograph and drawing numbers, and the notebook pages. A small plan of the position of the locus in the trench on each locus sheet complements the daily top plans.

Finds arrive at the registry with a full context number consisting of region, year, trench, locus, and Pottery Bucket number. For example: BE00-41.*0154* PB#230 (Excavations in Berenike in 2000, trench 41, locus *154* , Pottery Bucket number 230). The registrar then assigns a unique registry number to each group of finds from that area. This means that all objects of a certain

Code	Finds Category
A	ostraca
aa	dipinti or graffiti
B	beads
bb	personal ornaments (rings, bezels, bracelets, anklets, earrings, pendants)
C	coins
D	metal
dd	slag, crucibles
E	glass
F	faience
G	remarkable pottery: (nearly) complete vessels, important sherds (e.g. Indian or Aksumite)
gg	lamps
H	basketry, matting
hh	cordage, netting
I	textiles
J	leather
jj	skin, hide
K	hair
kk	feathers
L	bone, turtle shell, eggshell
ll	worked bone
M	shell
mm	worked shell
O	botanical (macro) remains
oo	botanical soil samples
P	wood
pp	worked wood
Q	charcoal
qq	resin
R	geological samples
rr	worked stone
S	architectural samples (building stone, mud brick, fired brick)
T	terracotta figurines
tt	sculpture, statues, reliefs
U	monumental inscriptions
uu	papyri or wooden tabulae
V	insects
W	dung
Y	amphora stoppers
yy	round-cut pottery sherds
Z	"show and tell," unknown

category found in one locus on the same day receive the same registry number. The only exception is the bulk of the pottery, which is identified by the full context number only. Because of the large numbers of finds that Berenike generates, the registry numbers start each year at 0001 and it is, therefore, important to always indicate the year with the finds registry number.

The registry number is followed by a code that indicates the finds category: The finds category is sometimes followed by a second number, the specialist's number. Thus BE00 6676-C-023 is a coin (finds category C) excavated in 2000, with the registry number 6676 and the coin specialist's number 023. BE00-6676-C-024 is a second coin from the same context (BE00 6676-C refers to all coins from context BE00-33.*038* PB# 61), with specialist's number 024. Thus 0001-A (or in our example 6676-C) is a registry number, while A-001 (in our example C-023 and C-024) is a specialist's number. The specialists design their numbering system according to their professional needs.

The find category indication is not meant to be a classification or taxonomy. The sole purpose of the registry is to keep track of what is found and of the routing and storage of each object. All finds from the same category are stored together in the Berenike storage room and are meant to be studied by one or several specific specialist(s).

The registrar gives a brief, standardized description of each find and records features such as dimensions, material, color, and weight. Striking features are briefly described in order to enable the project members to recognize objects in case a label is damaged or lost. A decision is made whether an object should be photographed and drawn. After this procedure the object is given to a conservator or a specialist who studies and analyzes the material in detail. The specialists' information, photographs, and drawings are added to the database.

BIBLIOGRAPHY

Abraham, S.
  2005   The Malabar Regional Archaeological Survey. *Journal for the Centre for Heritage Studies* 2:5–7.
Adam, J. P.
  1994   *Roman Building Materials & Techniques.* Indiana University Press, Bloomington-Indianapolis.
Adhyatman, S., and R. Arafin
  1996   *Manik-manik di Indonesia: Beads in Indonesia.* 2nd ed. Penerbit Djambatan, Jakarta.
Adigal, I.
  1965   *Shilappadikaram.* New Directions, New York.
Aldsworth, F. G.
  1999   The Buildings at Shenshef. In *Berenike 1997. Report of the 1997 Excavations at Berenike and the Survey of the Egyptian Eastern Desert, Including Excavations at Shenshef,* edited by S. E. Sidebotham and W. Z. Wendrich, pp. 385–418. Research School of Asian, African and Amerindian Studies (CNWS), Leiden, Netherlands.
Aldsworth, F. G., and H. Barnard
  1996a   Berenike Survey. In *Berenike 1995. Preliminary Report of the Excavations at Berenike (Egyptian Red Sea Coast) and the Survey of the Eastern Desert,* edited by S. E. Sidebotham and W. Z. Wendrich, pp. 5–6. Research School of Asian, African and Amerindian Studies (CNWS), Leiden, Netherlands.
  1996b   Survey of Hitan Rayan. In *Berenike 1995. Preliminary Report of the Excavations at Berenike (Egyptian Red Sea Coast) and the Survey of the Eastern Desert,* edited by S. E. Sidebotham and W. Z. Wendrich, pp. 411–440. Research School of Asian, African and Amerindian Studies (CNWS), Leiden, Netherlands.
  1998a   Berenike Survey. In *Berenike 1996. Report of the 1996 Excavations at Berenike (Egyptian Red Sea Coast) and the Survey of the Eastern Desert,* edited by S. E. Sidebotham and W. Z. Wendrich, pp. 3–10. Research School of Asian, African and Amerindian Studies (CNWS), Leiden, Netherlands.
  1998b   Survey of Shenshef. In *Berenike 1996. Report of the 1996 Excavations at Berenike (Egyptian Red Sea Coast) and the Survey of the Eastern Desert,* edited by S. E. Sidebotham and W. Z. Wendrich, pp. 427–443. Research School of Asian, African and Amerindian Studies (CNWS), Leiden, Netherlands.
Aldsworth, F. G., S. E. Sidebotham, and W. Z. Wendrich
  1995   The Town Site: Survey, Plan and Description. In *Berenike 1994. Preliminary Report of the 1994 Excavations at Berenike (Egyptian Red Sea Coast) and the Survey of the Eastern Desert,* edited by S. E. Sidebotham and W. Z. Wendrich, pp. 13-20. Research School of Asian, African and Amerindian Studies (CNWS), Leiden, Netherlands.
Allchin, B.
  1979   The Agate and Carnelian Industry of Western India and Pakistan. In *South Asian Archaeology 1975,* edited by J. E. v. Lohuizen-de Leeuw, pp. 91-105. E. J. Brill, Leiden, Netherlands.
Allchin, B., and F. R. Allchin
  1982   *The Rise of Civilization in India and Pakistan.* Cambridge University Press, Cambridge.
Allchin, F. R.
  1995   *The Archaeology of Early Historic South Asia: The Emergence of Cities and States.* Cambridge University Press, Cambridge.
Alston, R.
  1995   *Soldier and Society in Roman Egypt.* Routledge, London.
  2002   *The City in Roman and Byzantine Egypt.* Routledge, London, New York.
Altheim, F., and R. Stiehl (editors)
  1971   *Christentum am Roten Meer,* Erster Band Walter de Gruyter, Berlin, New York.

Andrews, C.
1994   *Amulets of Ancient Egypt*. British Museum, London.
Anfray, F.
1963   Première campagne de fouilles à Matara (Nov 1959–Janv 1960). *Annales d'Èthiopie* 5, pp. 87–166.
1965   La musée archéologique d'Asmara. *Rassegna di Studi Etiopici* 21, pp. 5–15.
1966   La poterie de Matara. *Rassegna di Studi Etiopici* 22, pp. 5–74.
1967   Matara. *Annales d'Èthiopie* 7, pp. 34–88.
Ardika, I. W., P. S. Bellwood, R. A. Eggleton, and D. J. Ellis
1993   A Single Source for South Asian Export-Quality Rouletted Ware? *Man and Environment* 18(1), pp. 101–109.
Arnold, D. E.
1985   *Ceramic Theory and Cultural Process*. Cambridge University Press, Cambridge.
As, A. v., and L. F. H. C. Jacobs
1995   Archaeo-Ceramological Survey. In *Berenike 1994. Preliminary Report of the 1994 Excavations at Berenike (Egyptian Red Sea Coast) and the Survey of the Eastern Desert*, edited by S. E. Sidebotham and W. Z. Wendrich, p. 45. Leiden, Netherlands University Research School of Asian, African and Amerindian Studies CNWS, Leiden, Netherlands.
Aston, B. G., J. A. Harrell, and I. Shaw
2000   Stones. In *Ancient Egyptian Materials and Technology*, edited by P. T. Nicholson and I. Shaw, pp. 5–77. Cambridge University Press, Cambridge.
Bagnall, R. S.
1993   *Egypt in Late Antiquity*. Princeton University Press, Princeton.
2000   Inscriptions from Wadi Kalalat. In *Berenike 1998. Report of the Excavations at Berenike and the Survey of the Egyptian Eastern Desert, Including Excavations in Wadi Kalalat*, edited by S. E. Sidebotham and W. Z. Wendrich, pp. 403–412. Research School of Asian, African and Amerindian Studies (CNWS), Leiden, Netherlands.
Bagnall, R. S., A. Bülow-Jacobsen, and H. Cuvigny
2001   Security and water on the Eastern Desert roads: the prefect Iulius Ursus and the construction of *praesidia* under Vespasian. *Journal of Roman Archaeology* 14, pp. 325–333.
Bagnall, R. S., C. C. Helms, and A. M. F. W. Verhoogt
2000   *Documents from Berenike, Volume 1. Greek Ostraka from the 1996–1998 Seasons. Papyrologica Bruxellensia:* 31. Fondation Égyptologique Reine Élisabeth, Brussels.
2005   *Documents from Berenike, Volume 2. Texts from the 1999–2001 Seasons. Papyrologica Bruxellensia :* 33. Fondation Égyptologique Reine Élisabeth, Brussels.

Ball, J.
1912   *The Geography and Geology of South-Eastern Egypt*. Government Press, Cairo.
Banerjee, N. R.
1959   The Technique of the Manufacture of Stone Beads in Ancient Ujjain. *Journal of the Asiatic Society* 1(2), pp. 189–196.
Bard, K. A., R. Fattovich, A. Manzo, and C. Perlingieri
1997   Archaeological Investigations at Bieta Giyorgis (Aksum), Ethiopia: 1993–1995 Field Seasons. *Journal of Field Archaeology* 24, pp. 387–403.
Barnard, H.
2000   Geneeskunst geïnspireerd door armoede [Medicine Inspired by Poverty]. *Nederlands Tijdschrift voor Geneeskunde* 144, pp. 39–41.
2002   Eastern Desert Ware, a first introduction. *Sudan & Nubia* 6, pp. 53–57.
Bar-Yosef, O., and A. M. Khazanov (editors)
1992   *Pastoralism in the Levant*. Prehistory Press, Madison, Wisconsin.
Beck, H. C.
1928   Classification and Nomenclature of Beads and Pendants. *Archaeologia* 77, pp. 1–76.
Bedawi, F. A.
1976   Die römische Grabfelder von Sayala-Nubien.
van Beek, G. W.
1989   The Buzz: A Simple Toy from Antiquity. In *Bulletin of the American Schools of Oriental Research* 275, pp. 53–58.
Begley, V.
1991   Ceramic Evidence for Pre-Periplus Trade on the Indian Coasts. In *Rome and India: The Ancient Sea Trade*, edited by V. Begley and R. D. De Puma, pp. 157–196. Oxford University Press, Delhi.
Begley, V. (editor)
1996   *The Ancient Port of Arikamedu: New Excavations and Researches 1989–1992* Volume 1. École Française d'Extrême Orient, Paris, Pondicherry.
Begley V., and R. D. De Puma
1991   *Rome and India: The Ancient Sea Trade*. University of Wisconsin Press, Madison, Wisconsin.
Begley, V., and R. S. Tomber
1999   Indian Pottery Sherds. In *Berenike 1997. Report of the 1997 Excavations at Berenike and the Survey of the Egyptian Eastern Desert, Including Excavations at Shenshef*, edited by S. E. Sidebotham and W. Z. Wendrich, pp. 161–181. Research School of Asian, African and Amerindian Studies (CNWS), Leiden, Netherlands.
Belzoni, G. B.
1821   *Voyages en Egypte et en Nubie suivis d'un voyage sur la côte de la mer Rouge et à l'oasis de Jupiter Ammôn, II.* Librairie française et étrangère, Paris.

Bernand, A.
1977 *Pan du désert*. E.J. Brill, Leiden, Netherlands.

Bingen, J.
1996 Dumping and the Ostraca at Mons Claudianus. In *Archaeological Research in Roman Egypt (Journal of Roman Archaeology, supplement 19)*, edited by D. M. Bailey, pp. 29–38.

Bishop, R. L., V. Canouts, P. L. Crown, and S. P. D. Atley
1990 Sensitivity, Precision and Accuracy: Their Roles in Ceramic Compositional Databases. *American Antiquity* 55, pp. 537–546.

Blake, R. P., and H. D. Vis
1934 *Epiphanius De Gemmis. The Old Georgian Version and the Fragments of the Armenian Version and Coptic–Sahidic Fragments.* Christophers, London.

Blockley, R. C. (editor)
1983 *The Fragmentary Classicising Historians of the Later Roman Empire: Eunapius, Olympiodorus, Priscus and Malchus. Text, Translation and Historiographical Notes. 2 Text.* Francis Cairns, Liverpool.

Boëthius, A., and J. B. Ward-Perkins
1970 *Etruscan and Roman Architecture.* Penguin Books, Harmondsworth, England.

Bopearachchi, O., and R. M. Wickremesinhe
1999 *Ruhuna, an Ancient Civilisation Re-visited; Numismatic and Archaeological Evidence on Inland and Maritime Trade.* R.M. Wickremesinhe, Nugegoda, Sri Lanka.

Bos, J. E. M. F.
2000 Jar Stoppers and Seals. In *Berenike 1998. Report of the 1998 Excavations at Berenike (Egyptian Red Sea Coast) and the Survey of the Eastern Desert, Including Excavations in Wadi Kalalat*, edited by S. E. Sidebotham and W. Z. Wendrich, pp. 275–303. Research School for Asian, African and Amerindian Studies (CNWS), Leiden, Netherlands.

Bourriau, J. D., and P. T. Nicholson
1992 Marl Clay Pottery Fabrics of the New Kingdom from Memphis, Saqqara and Amarna. *Journal of Egyptian Archaeology* 78, pp. 29–91.

Bradley, K. R.
1978 Claudius Athenodorus. *Historia* 27, pp. 336–342.

Breeze, D. J.
1982 *The Northern Frontiers of Roman Britain.* St. Martin's Press, New York.

Brocchi, G. B.
1841 *Giornale delle Osservazioni fatte ne' Viaggi in Egitto, nella Siria e nella Nubia*, Vol. 2. Presso A. Roberti Tip. Ed Editore, Bassano, Italy.

Bruce, J.
1812 *Travels, Between the Years 1765 and 1773, Through Part of Africa, Syria, Egypt, and Arabia, into Abyssinia, to Discover the Source of the Nile.* J. and J. Cundee, London.

Brun, J.-P., and M. Leguilloux
2003 Les objets en cuir. In *La route de Myos Hormos. L'armée romaine dans le désert oriental d'Égypte*, Fouilles de l'Institut français d'archéologie orientale 48/2, edited by H. Cuvigny, pp. 539-547. Institut Français d'Archéologie Orientale, Cairo.

Bureth, P.
1964 *Les titulatures impériales.* Fondation Égyptologique Reine Élisabeth, Brussels.

Cailliaud, F.
1821 *Voyage à l'oasis de Thèbes et dans les déserts situés à l'orient et à l'occident de la Thébaïd, fait pendant les années 1815, 1816, 1817 et 1818.* Imprimerie Royale, Paris.

Cappers, R. T. J.
1996 Archaeobotanical Remains. In *Berenike 1995: Preliminary Report of the Excavations at Berenike (Egyptian Red Sea Coast) and the Survey of the Eastern Desert*, edited by S. E. Sidebotham and W. Z. Wendrich, pp. 319–336. Research School of Asian, African and Amerindian Studies (CNWS), Leiden, Netherlands.

1998 Archaeobotanical Remains. In *Berenike 1996. Report of the 1996 Excavations at Berenike (Egyptian Red Sea Coast) and the Survey of the Eastern Desert*, edited by S. E. Sidebotham and W. Z. Wendrich, pp. 289–330. Research School of Asian, African and Amerindian Studies (CNWS), Leiden, Netherlands.

1999 The Archaeobotanical Remains. In *Berenike 1997: Report of the 1997 Excavations at Berenike and the Survey of the Egyptian Eastern Desert, Including Excavations at Shenshef*, edited by S. E. Sidebotham and W. Z. Wendrich, pp. 299–305. Research School of Asian, African and Amerindian Studies (CNWS), Leiden, Netherlands.

Casson, L.
1971 *Ships and Seamanship in the Ancient World.* Princeton University Press, Princeton.

1983 Sakas Versus Andhras in the "Periplus Maris Erythraei. *Journal of the Economic and Social History of the Orient* 26(2), pp. 164–177.

1989 *The Periplus Maris Erythraei: Text with Introduction, Translation, and Commentary.* Princeton University Press, Princeton, New Jersey.

1994 *Ships and Seafaring in Ancient Times.* University of Texas Press, Austin.

Castiglioni, A., A. Castiglioni, and J. Vercouter
1995 *Das Goldland der Pharaonen.* Verlag Philipp von Zabern, Mainz.

Champakalaksmi, R.
1996 *Trade, Ideology and Urbanization: South India 300 BC to AD 1300.* Oxford University Press, Delhi.

Charlesworth, D.
1984   The Xanten Glass. *Rheinische Ausgrabungen, Beiträge zur Archäologie des römischen Rheinlands* 4, pp. 283–300.

Comfort, H.
1991   Terra Sigillata at Arikamedu. In *Rome and India: The Ancient Sea Trade*, edited by V. Begley and R. D. De Puma, pp. 134–150. University of Wisconsin Press, Madison, Wisconsin.

Condamin, J., F. Formenti, M. O. Metais, M. Michel, and P. Blond
1976   The Application of Gas Chromatography to the Tracing of Oil in Ancient Amphorae. *Archaeometry* 18, pp. 195–201.

Cribb, R.
1991   *Nomads in Archaeology.* Cambridge University Press, Cambridge.

De Contenson, H.
1963   Les fouilles à Axoum en 1958, rapport préliminaire. *Annales d'Èthiopie* 5, pp. 1–52.

De Romanis, F.
1996   *Cassia, cinnamomo, ossidiana. Uomini e merci tra Oceano Indiano e Mediterraneo.* Bretschneider, Rome.

Deloche, J.
1983   Geographical Considerations in the Localisation of Ancient Sea-Ports of India. *The Indian Economic and Social History Review* 20(4), pp. 439–448.

Devasahayam, N.
1985   Roman Jewellery from Vellalore Site During the Sangam Period. *Lalit Kala* 21, p. 53.

Dieleman, J.
1998   Amphora Stoppers. In *Berenike 1996. Preliminary Report of the 1996 Excavations at Berenike and the Survey of the Eastern Desert,*, edited by S. E. Sidebotham and W. Z. Wendrich, pp. 265–277. Research School of Asian, African and Amerindian Studies (CNWS), Leiden, Netherlands.

Dijkstra, M., and A. M. F. W. Verhoogt
1999   The Greek-Palmyrene Inscription. In: *Berenike 1997. Report of the 1997 Excavations at Berenike and the Survey of the Egyptian Eastern Desert, Including Excavations at Shenshef*, edited by S. E. Sidebotham and W. Z. Wendrich, pp. 207–218. Research School of Asian, African and Amerindian Studies (CNWS), Leiden, Netherlands.

Dittenberger, W.
1903   *Orientis graeci inscriptiones selectae: supplementum sylloges inscriptionum graecarum.* S. Hirzel, Leipzig.

Egyptian Geological Survey and Mining Authority
1979   *Mineral Map of Egypt (with Explanatory Notes).* Egyptian Geological Survey and Mining Authority, Cairo.

Eide, T., T. Hägg, R. H. Pierce, and L. Török
1998   *Fontes Historiae Nubiorum, Textual Sources for the History of the Middle Nile Region Between the Eighth Century BC and the Sixth Century AD.* Vol. III. University of Bergen Press, Bergen.

Eiland, M. L.
1979   *Chinese and Exotic Rugs.* Zwemmer, London.

Eisenberg, J. M.
1981   *A Collector's Guide to Seashells of the World.* Crescent Books, New York.

Emery, W. B., and L. P. Kirwan
1935   *The Excavations and Survey Between Wadi es-Sebua and Adindan 1929–31.* Government Press Bulaq, Cairo.

Fattovich, R.
1980   *Materiali per lo studio della ceramica pre-Aksumita etiopica Suppl. 25 agli Annali* 40. Don Basco, Naples, Italy.
1990   Remarks on the Pre-Aksumite Period in Northern Ethiopia. *Journal of Ethiopian Studies* 23, pp. 3–33.

Fattovich, R., and K. A. Bard
1993   Scavi archeologici nella zona di Aksum. F. Ona Nagast (Bieta Giyorgis). *Rassegna di Studi Etiopici* 37, pp. 71–94.

Fitzler, K.
1910   *Steinbrüche und Bergwerke im ptolemäischen und römischen Ägypten ein Beitrag zur antiken Wirtschaftsgeschichte.* Verlag von Quelle & Meyer, Leipzig.

Floyer, E. A.
1893a   *Étude sur le Nord-Etbai entre le Nil et la Mer Rouge.* Imprimerie Nationale, Cairo.
1893b   Further Notes on the Eastern Desert of Egypt. *The Geographical Journal* 1, pp. 408–431.

Forbes, R. J.
1964   *Studies in Ancient Technology* 1. E.J. Brill, Leiden, Netherlands.

Förschner, G.
1987   *Die Münzen der römischer Kaiser in Alexandrien.* Historisches Museum, Frankfurt.

Francis, P., Jr.
1982a   Experiments with Early Techniques for Making Whole Shells into Beads. *Current Anthropology* 23(6), pp. 713–714.
1982b   *The Glass Beads of India: The World of Beads Monograph Series* 7. Lapis Route Books, Lake Placid, New York.
1984   Plants as Human Adornment in India." *Economic Botany* 38(2), pp. 194–209.
1985   Bead Report XIV: A Collection of "Phoenician" Beads. *Ornament* 8(4), pp. 42–45.
1986   Collar Beads: A New Typology and a New Perspective on Ancient Indian Beadmaking. *Bulletin*

of the Deccan College Postgraduate & Research Institute 45, pp. 117–121.

1989   The Manufacture of Beads from Shell. In *Proceedings of the 1986 Shell Bead Conference. Research Records No. 20*, edited by C. F. Hayes III, pp. 25–53. Rochester Museum and Science Center, Rochester, New York.

1991   Beadmaking at Arikamedu and Beyond. *World Archaeology* 23(1), pp. 28–43.

1999   Middle Eastern Glass Beads: A New Paradigm. *Margaretologist* 12(2), pp. 3–11.

2000   Human Adornments. In *Berenike 1998. Report of the 1998 Excavations at Berenike and the Survey of the Egyptian Eastern Desert, Including Excavations in Wadi Kalalat*, edited by S. E. Sidebotham and W. Z. Wendrich, pp. 212-225. Research School of Asian, African and Amerindian Studies (CNWS), Leiden, Netherlands.

2001   *Asia's Maritime Bead Trade from ca. 300 B.C. to the Present.* University of Hawai'i Press, Honolulu.

Franz, J. (editor)

1845–1853   *Corpus Inscriptionum Graecarum.* Berlin-Brandenburgischen Akademie der Wissenschaften, Berlin.

Gardi, R.

1969   *African Crafts and Craftsmen.* Van Nostrand Reinhold, New York.

Geißen, A.

1974   *Katalog Alexandrinischer Kaisermünzen der Sammlung des Instituts für Altertumskunde der Universität zu Köln (volume 5, band 1) (Nr. 1-740: Augustus-Trajan)Papyrologica Coloniensia.* Westdeutscher Verlag, Opladen, Germany.

Gerhardt, K. O., S. Searles, and W. R. Biers

1990   Corinthian Figure Vases: Non-Destructive Extraction and Gas Chromatography-Mass Spectrometry. *MASCA Research Papers in Science and Archaeology* 7, pp. 41–50.

Giuliani, G.

2000   Oxygen Isotopes and Emerald Trade Routes Since Antiquity. *Science* January 28, pp. 631–633.

Gogte, V.D.

1997   The Chandraketugarh-Tamluk Region of Bengal: Source of the Early Historic Rouletted Ware from India and Southeast Asia. *Man and Environment* 22, pp.69–85.

Gokhale, B. P.

1987   Bharukaccha/Barygaza. In *India and the Ancient World: History, Trade and Culture Before AD 650*, edited by G. Pollet, pp. 67–79. Departement Orientalistiek, Leuven, Belgium.

Gopal, L.

1961   Textiles in Ancient India. *Journal of the Economic and Social History of the Orient* 4(1), pp. 53–69.

Gould, D. A.

1999   The Excavations at Shenshef. In: *Berenike 1997. Report of the 1997 Excavations at Berenike and the Survey of the Egyptian Eastern Desert, Including Excavations at Shenshef*, edited by S. E. Sidebotham and W. Z. Wendrich, pp. 371–383. Research School of Asian, African and Amerindian Studies (CNWS) Leiden, Netherlands.

Gragg, G.

1996   "South Arabian/Axumite" Dipinto. In *Berenike 1995. Preliminary Report of the 1995 Excavations at Berenike (Egyptian Red Sea Coast) and the Survey of the Eastern Desert*, edited by S. E. Sidebotham and W. Z. Wendrich, pp. 209–211. Leiden University Research School of Asian, African and Amerindian Studies CNWS, Leiden, Netherlands.

Greer, R. M.

1962   *Diodorus of Sicily (Books XIX 66–110 and XX).* Harvard University Press, Cambridge.

Gupta, S.

1994   Archaeology of Maritime Traditions: The Early Historic Phase. *Man and Environment* 14(1-2), pp. 217–225.

Gurukkal, R.

1995   The Beginnings of the Historic Period: The Tamil South. In *Recent Perspectives of Early Indian History*, edited by R. Thapar, pp. 237–265. Popular Prakashan, Bombay.

Gurukkal, R., and D. Whittaker

2001   In Search of Muziris. In *Journal of Roman Archaeology* 14-1, pp. 335–350.

Hair, J. F., R. E. Anderson, and R. L. Tatham

1992   *Multivariate Data Analysis.* Macmillan Publishing, New York.

Harden, D. B.

1878   Introduction. In *Glass of the Caesars*, edited by D. B. Harden, H. Hellenkemper, K. Painter, and D. Whitehouse, pp. 1–8. Olivetti, Milan.

Harrell, J. A.

1996   Geology. In *Berenike 1995. Preliminary Report of the 1995 Excavations at Berenike (Egyptian Red Sea Coast) and the Survey of the Eastern Desert*, edited by S. E. Sidebotham and W. Z. Wendrich, pp. 99-126. Research School of Asian, African and Amerindian Studies (CNWS), Leiden, Netherlands.

1998   Geology. In *Berenike 1996. Report of the Excavations at Berenike (Egyptian Red Sea Coast) and the Survey of the Eastern Desert*, edited by S. E. Sidebotham and W. Z. Wendrich, pp. 121–148. Research School of Asian, African and Amerindian Studies (CNWS), Leiden, Netherlands.

1999   Geology. In *Berenike 1997. Report of the 1997 Excavations at Berenike and the Survey of the Egyptian Eastern Desert, Including Excavations at Shenshef,* edited by S. E. Sidebotham and W. Z. Wendrich, pp. 107–121. Research School of Asian, African and Amerindian Studies (CNWS), Leiden, Netherlands.

Harrell, J. A., V. M. Brown, and L. Lazzarini

2002   Breccia Verde Antica—Source, Petrology and Uses. In *ASMOSIA VI, Interdisciplinary Studies on Ancient Stone—Proceedings of the Sixth International Conference of the Association for the Study of Marble and Other Stones in Antiquity, Venice, June 15–18, 2000*, L. Lazzarini (Ed) pp. 207–218. Aldo Ausilio—Bottega d'Erasmo Editore, Padua, Italy.

Harrell, J. A., and M. D. Lewan

2002   Sources of Mummy Bitumen in Ancient Egypt and Palestine. *Archaeometry* 22(2), pp. 285–293.

Harrell, J. A., and S. E. Sidebotham

2004   Wadi Abu Diyeiba: an amethyst quarry in Egypt's Eastern Desert. *Minerva* 15(3), pp. 12–14.

Hart, F. A., and S. J. Adams

1983   The Chemical Analysis of Romano-British Pottery from the Alice Holt Forest, Hampshire, by means of inductively coupled plasma emission spectrometry. *Archaeometry* 25, pp. 179–185.

Hasek, V.

1999   *Methodology of Geophysical Research in Archaeology. British Archaeological Reports* issue 769. British Archaeological Reports International Series, Oxford.

Hausen, J.

1979   *Schiffbau in der Antike.* Koehlers Verlagsgesellschaft mbH, Herford, Germany.

Hawthorne, J. G., and C. S. Smith

1979   *Theophilus On Diverse Arts: The Foremost Medieval Treatise on Painting, Glassmaking and Metalwork.* Dover, New York.

Hayes, J. W.

1972   *Late Roman Pottery.* British School at Rome, Rome.

1995   Summary of Pottery and Glass Finds. In *Berenike 1994. Preliminary Report of the 1994 Excavations at Berenike (Egyptian Red Sea Coast) and the Survey of the Eastern Desert*, edited by S. E. Sidebotham and W. Z. Wendrich, pp. 33–40. Research School of Asian, African and Amerindian Studies (CNWS), Leiden, Netherlands.

1996   The Pottery. In *Berenike 1995. Preliminary Report of the 1995 Excavations at Berenike (Egyptian Red Sea Coast) and the Survey of the Eastern Desert*, edited by S. E. Sidebotham and W. Z. Wendrich, pp. 147–178. Research School of Asian, African and Amerindian Studies (CNWS), Leiden, Netherlands.

Heitzman, J.

1984   Early Buddhism, Trade and Empire. In *Studies in the Archaeology and Paleoanthropology of South Asia*, edited by G. L. Possehl and K. A. R. Kennedy, pp.

121–127. AIIS, Oxford and IBH Publishing, New Delhi.

Hense, A. M.

1995   Metal Finds. In *Berenike 1994. Preliminary Report of the Excavations at Berenike (Egyptian Red Sea Coast) and the Survey of the Eastern Desert*, edited by S. E. Sidebotham and W. Z. Wendrich, pp. 49–57. Research School of Asian, African and Amerindian Studies (CNWS), Leiden, Netherlands.

1998   The Metal Finds. In *Berenike 1996. Report of the 1996 Excavations at Berenike (Egyptian Red Sea Coast) and the Survey of the Eastern Desert*, edited by S. E. Sidebotham and W. Z. Wendrich, pp. 199–220. Research School of Asian, African and Amerindian Studies (CNWS), Leiden, Netherlands.

2000   Metal Finds. In *Berenike 1998. Report of the 1998 Excavations at Berenike and the Survey of the Egyptian Eastern Desert, Including Excavations in Wadi Kalalat*, edited by S. E. Sidebotham and W. Z. Wendrich, pp. 191–202. Research School of Asian, African and Amerindian Studies (CNWS), Leiden, Netherlands.

Herath, J. W.

1975   *Mineral Resources of Sri Lanka. Economic Bulletin Geological Survey Department 2.*

Herz, N., and E. G. Garrison

1998   *Geological Methods for Archaeology.* Oxford University Press, Oxford.

Hill, P. V., J. P. C. Kent, and R. A. G. Carson

1978   *Late Roman Bronze Coinage.* Spink & Son, London.

Hobbs, J.

1989   *Bedouin Life in the Egyptian Wilderness.* American University in Cairo Press, Cairo.

Hodder, I., M. Shanks, A. Alexandri, V. Buchli, J. Carman, J. Last, and G. Lucas

2001   *Interpreting Archaeology.* Routledge, New York.

Houston, G. W.

1988   Ports in Perspective: Some Comparative Materials on Roman Merchant Ships and Ports. *American Journal of Archaeology* 92, pp. 553–564.

Howell, J., and A. K. Sinha

1994   Preliminary Report on the Explorations Around Sopara, Surat, and Bharuch. *South Asian Studies* 10, pp. 1989–1999.

Hume, W. F. (editor)

1907   *A Preliminary Report on the Geology of the Eastern Desert of Egypt, between Latitudes 22° N and 25° N.* Survey Department, Cairo.

1934   *Geology of Egypt. Volume II. The Fundamental Pre-Cambrian Rocks of Egypt and the Sudan; their Distribution, Age, and Character. Part I. The Metamorphic Rocks.* Government Press, Cairo.

1937   *Geology of Egypt. Volume II. The Fundamental Pre-Cambrian Rocks of Egypt and the Sudan; their* distribution, Age and Character. Part III. The Minerals of Economic Value. Government Press, Cairo.

Hussein, A. A.
1990 Mineral deposits. In *The Geology of Egypt*, edited by R. Said, pp. 511–566. A. A. Balkema, Rotterdam.

Isaac, B.
1992 *The Limits of Empire. The Roman Army in the East.*, 2nd revised ed. Clarendon Press, Oxford.

Isings, C.
1957 *Roman Glass from Dated Finds.* Wolters, Groningen, Netherlands.

Ismalun, M.
1943 Émeraudes et Béryls. *Bulletin de la Société royale de Géographie d'Égypte* 21, pp. 51–60.

Jasper, J. J., and M. Pirngadie
1912 *De Inlandsche Kunstnijverheid in Nederlandsch Indië*, Facsimile Waringin, Monnickendam, 1998 edition. Mouton, The Hague.

Jha, A., and D. Rajgor
1992 *Studies in the Coinage of the Western Kshatrapas.* Indian Institute of Numismatic Studies, Anjaneri, India.

Johnson, J. H.
1982 Inscriptional Material. In *Quseir al-Qadim 1980 Preliminary Report*, edited by D. S. Whitcomb and J. H. Johnson, pp. 263–266. Undena Publications, Malibu, California.

Johnson, S.
1989 *Hadrian's Wall.* B. T. Batsford/English Heritage, London.

Jones, H. L.
1941 *The Geography of Strabo VII.* William Heinemann, Harvard University Press, London; Cambridge, Massachusetts.
1966 *The Geography of Strabo (Books XV–XVI).* Harvard University Press, Cambridge, Massachusetts.

Jones, S.
1997 *The Archaeology of Ethnicity.* Routledge, New York.

Jördens, A.
1995 Sozialstrukturen im Arbeitstierhandel des kaiser-zeitlichen Ägypten. *Tyche* 10, pp. 37–100.

Kayser, F.
1993 Nouveaux textes grecs du Ouadi Hammamat. *Zeitschrift für Papyrologie und Epigraphik* 98, pp. 111–156.

Kempe, D. R. C., and A. P. Harvey
1983 *The Petrology of Archaeological Artefacts.* Oxford University Press, Oxford.

Kobischanov, Y. M.
1979 *Axum.* Penn State University Press, University Park, Pennsylvania.

Kock, J., and T. Sode
1995 *Glass, Glassbeads and Glassmakers in Northern India.* THOT Print, Vanlose, Denmark.

Kromer, K.
1967 *Römische Weinstuben in Sayala (Unternubien).* Österreichischen Akademie der Wissenschaften, Vienna.

Kuenz, C.
1981 Bassins et Tables de Offrande. *Bulletin de l'Institut Français d'Archéologie Orientale, Bulletin de Centenaire,* pp. 243–383.

Kurinsky, S.
1991 *The Glassmakers: An Odyssey of the Jews, the First Three Thousand Years.* Hippocrene, New York.

Laeuchli, S. C.
1984 Yavana Inscriptions of Western India. *Journal of the Asiatic Society of Bombay* 56–59, pp. 207–221.

Lahiri, N.
1992 *The Archaeology of Indian Trade Routes Up to C. 200 BC.* Oxford University Press, Delhi.

Letronne, A.-J.
1842 *Recueil des inscriptions grecques et latines d'Égypte* I. Imprimerie royale, Paris.
1848 *Recueil des inscriptions grecques et latines d'Égypte* II. Imprimerie royale, Paris.

Lewis, N.
1977 *Notationes Legentis, 45. Bulletin of the American Society of Papyrologists* 14, pp. 149–150.
1986 *Greeks in Ptolemaic Egypt: Case Studies in the Social History of the Hellenistic World.* Clarendon Press, Oxford.

Linant de Bellefonds, L. M. A.
1833 *L'Etbaye ou pays habité pas les Arabes Bichariehs. Géographie, ethnologie, mines d'or.* Arthus Bertrand, Paris.

Lucas, A., and J. R. Harris
1962 *Ancient Egyptian Materials and Industries*, 4th ed. Edward Arnold, London.
1989 *Ancient Egyptian Materials and Industries*, 4th reprinted ed. Histories & Mysteries of Man, London. .

MacAlister, D. A.
1900 The Emerald Mines of North Etbai. *The Geographical Journal* 16, pp. 537–549.

Macdowall, S.
1995 *Late Roman Cavalryman.* Reed International Books, London.

Magid, A. A., R. H. Pierce, and K. Krzywinski
1995 Test Excavation in the Southern Red Sea Hills (Sudan): Culural Linkages to the North. *Archéologie du Nil Moyen* 7, pp. 163–190.

Mahadevan, I.
1994 Ancient Tamil Contacts Abroad: Recent Epigraphical Evidence. *Journal of the Institute of South Asian Studies* 12(1), pp. 136–155.
1996 Tamil-Brahmi Graffito. In *Berenike 1996: Report of the Excavations at Berenike (Egyptian Red Sea Coast)*

and the Survey of the Eastern Desert, edited by S. E. Sidebotham and W. Z. Wendrich, pp. 205–208. Research School of Asian, African and Amerindian Studies (CNWS), Leiden, Netherlands.

2003 *Early Tamil Epigraphy: From the Earliest Times to the Sixth Century AD.* Harvard Oriental Series, Cambridge.

Mallory-Greenough, L. M., and J. D. Greenough
1998 New data for old pots: trace-element characterization of ancient Egyptian pottery using ICP-MS. *Journal of Archaeological Science* 25, pp. 85–97.

Maloney, C.
1984 *The Effects of Early Coastal Sea Traffic on the Development of Civilization in South India.* PhD dissertation, University of Pennsylvania, Philadelphia, Pennsylvania.

Margabandhu, C.
1985 *Archaeology of the Satavahana Kshatrapa Times.* Sundeep Prakashan, Delhi.

Maxfield, V. A.
2000 The Deployment of the Roman Auxilia in Upper Egypt and the Eastern Desert During the Principate. In *Kaiser, Herr und Gesellschaft in der römischen Kaiserzeit*, edited by G. Alföldy, B. Dobson, and W. Eck, pp. 407–442. Franz Steiner Verlag, Stuttgart.

McCrindle, J. W.
1897 *The Christian Topography of Cosmas, an Egyptian Monk.* Burt Franklin, New York.

Meiggs, R.
1973 *Roman Ostia*, 2nd ed. Clarendon Press, Oxford.

Meijer, F.
1976 *Wrakken, ankers en amforen.* A.J.G. Strengholt's Boeken, Naarden, Netherlands.

Melkawi, A., K. 'Amr, and D. S. Whitcomb
1994 "The excavation of two seventh century pottery kilns at Aqaba," *Reports of the Department of Antiquities of Jordan* 38, pp. 447–468.

Meredith, D.
1953 The Roman Remains in the Eastern Desert Of Egypt (continued). *Journal of Roman Archaeology* 39, pp. 95–106.
1954 Inscriptions from the Berenice Road. *Chronique d' Égypte* 29, pp. 281–287.
1957 Berenice Troglodytica. *Journal of Egyptian Archaeology* 43, pp. 56–70.
1958 *Tabula Imperii Romani, Sheet N.G. 36, Coptos.* Society of Antiquaries of London, Oxford.

Miller, J. I.
1969 *The Spice Trade of the Roman Empire: 29 B. C. to A. D. 641.* Clarendon Press, Oxford.

Milne, J. G.
1982 *Catalogue of Alexandrian Coins.* Reprint edition. Sanford J. Durst, New York.

Mommsen, H., A. Keruser, and J. Weber
1988 A method for grouping pottery by chemical composition." *Archaeometry* 30, pp. 47–57.

Morgan, E. D., C. Edwards, and S. A. Pepper
1992 Analysis of the fatty debris from the wreck of a Basque whaling ship at Red Bay, Labrador. *Archaeometry* 34, pp. 129–133.

Morrison, K. D.
1995 Trade, Urbanism, and Agricultural Expansion: Buddhist Monastic Institutions and the State in Early Historic Western Deccan. *World Archaeology* 27(2), pp. 203–221.
1997 Commerce and Culture in South Asia: Perspectives from Archaeology and History. *Annual Review of Anthropology* 26, pp. 87–108.
2002 Pepper in the Hills: Upland-Lowland Exchange and the Intensification of the Spice Trade. In *Foragers-Traders in South and Southeast Asia*, pp. 105–128. Cambridge University Press, Cambridge.

Munro-Hay, S. C. H.
1989a The British Museum excavations at Adulis, 1968. *Antiquaries Journal* 69, pp. 43–52.
1989b *Excavations at Aksum. Memoirs of the British Institute in Eastern Africa* 10. British Institute in Eastern Africa, London.
1991 *Aksum. An African Civilisation of Late Antiquity.* Edinburgh University Press, Edinburgh.
1996 Aksumite Overseas Interests. In *The Indian Ocean in Antiquity*, edited by J. Reade, pp. 403–416. Kegan Paul International in Association with the British Museum, London; New York.

Munro-Hay, S. C. H., and B. Juel-Jensen
1995 *Aksumite Coinage.* Revised, enlarged ed. Spink, London.

Murphy, V., and R. Crill
1991 *Tie-Dyed Textiles of India: Tradition and Trade.* Rizzoli and Victoria and Albert Museum, New York.

Murray, G. W.
1914 Ancient workings of amethysts. *Cairo Scientific Journal* 8, pp. 179.
1925 The Roman Roads and Stations in the Eastern Desert of Egypt. *Journal of Egyptian Archaeology* 11, pp. 138–150.
1935 *Sons of Ishmael.* Routledge, London.

Nicholson, P. T.
1993 *Egyptian Faience and Glass.* Shire, Buckinghamshire, England.
2000 The Glass. In *Berenike 1998. Report of the 1998 Excavations at Berenike and the Survey of the Egyptian Eastern Desert, Including Excavations in Wadi Kalalat*, edited by S. E. Sidebotham and W. Z. Wendrich, pp. 203–209. Research School of Asian, African and Amerindian Studies (CNWS), Leiden, Netherlands.

Nissenbaum, A.
1978 Dead Sea Asphalts: Historical Aspects. *American Association of Petroleum Geologists Bulletin* 62, pp. 837–844.

Oleson, J. P.
1994 Non-Ceramic Finds: General Discussion of Types and Catalogues of Unstratified Examples. In *The Harbours of Caesarea Maritima. Results of the Caesarea Ancient Harbour Excavation Project 1980–85. Volume II: The Finds and the Ship. Center for Maritime Studies, University of Haifa* Publication No. 5, *British Archaeological Reports* International Series 594, edited by J. P. Oleson, M. A. Fitzgerald, A. N. Sherwood, S. E. Sidebotham, R. L. Hohlfelder, R. L. Vann, and A. Raban, pp. 65–86. Tempus Reparatum, Oxford.

Parasher, A.
1992 Nature of Society and Civilization in Early Deccan. *The Indian Economic Review and Social History Review* 29(4), pp. 437–477.

Paribeni, R.
1907 Richerche nel luogo dell'antica Adulis. *Monumenti Antichi, Reale Accademia dei Lincei* 18, pp. 438–572.

Parker, G.
2002 Ex Oriente Luxuria: Indian Commodities and the Roman Experience. *Journal of the Economic and Social History of the Orient* 45, pp. 40–95.

Patrick, M., A. J. Koning, and A. B. Smith
1985 Gas liquid chromatography analysis of fatty acids in food residues from ceramics found in the Southwestern Cape, South Africa. *Archaeometry* 27, pp. 231–236.

Pharr, C.
1952 *The Theodosian Code and Novels and the Sirmondian Constitutions. A Translation with Commentary, Glossary, and Bibliography.* Princeton University Press, Princeton.

Phillips, J.
2000a Appendix II Classical Aksumite pottery: surface treatment and decoration. In *Archaeology at Aksum, Ethiopia, 1993-7,* Memoirs of the British Institute in Eastern Africa 17, *Research Committee of the Society of Antiquaries of London Report* 65, edited by D. W. Phillipson, pp. 491–493. British Institute in Eastern Africa/Society of Antiquaries of London, London.
2000b Overview of pottery development. In *Archaeology at Aksum, Ethiopia, 1993–7, Memoirs of the British Institute in Eastern Africa* 17, *Research Committee of the Society of Antiquaries of London Report* 65, edited by D. W. Phillipson, pp. 453–458. British Institute in Eastern Africa/Society of Antiquaries of London, London.

Phillipson, D. W.
1995 Excavations at Aksum, Ethiopia, 1993–4. *Antiquaries Journal* 175, pp. 1–41.

2000 *Archaeology at Aksum, Ethiopia, 1993–7. Memoirs of the British Institute in Eastern Africa 17, Research Committee of the Society of Antiquaries of London Report* 65. British Institute in Eastern Africa/ Society of Antiquaries of London, London.

Phillipson, D. W., and A. Reynolds
1996 BIEA excavations at Aksum, Northern Ethiopia, 1995. *Azania* 31, pp. 99–147.

Piganiol, A.
1947 Le codicille impérial du Papyrus de Berlin 8334. *Comptes-rendus de l'Académie des inscriptions et belles-lettres,* pp. 376–386.

Poole, R. S.
1964 *Catalogue of the Coins of Alexandria and the Nomes.* Reprint. Arnaldo Forni, Bologna.

Porat, N., J. Yellin, L. Heller-Kallai, and L. Halicz
1991 Correlation between petrography, NAA and ICP analysis: application to early bronze Egyptian pottery from Canaan. *Geoarchaeology* 6, pp. 133–149.

Rajan, K.
1994 *Archaeology of Tamilnadu (Kongu Country).* Book India, Delhi.

Ramachandra Nair, A. K. K. (editor)
1986 *Kerala State Gazetteer, Volume 1,* Trivandrum: State Editor, Kerala Gazetteers.

Raman, K. V. (editor)
1988 *Excavations at Uraiyur (Tiruchirapalli) 1965–1969.* University of Madras, Madras.

Ranjan, M. P., N. Iyer, and G. Pandya
1986 *Bamboo and Cane Crafts of Northeast India.* Development Commissioner of Handicrafts, Govt. of India: Distributed by National Crafts Museum, New Delhi, India.

Rao, S. R.
1969 Kaveripattinam Excavations. In *Transactions of the Archaeological Society of South India,* edited by A. S. o. S. India, pp. 163–165. ASSI, Government Museum, Madras.

Rapson, E. J.
1967 *Catalogue of the Coins of the Andhra Dynasty, The Western Ksatrapas, the Traikutka Dynasty and the "Bodhi" Dynasty.* Reprint ed. Trustees of the British Museum, London.

Ray, H. P.
1988 The Yavana Presence in Ancient India. *Journal of the Economic and Social History Review of the Orient* 31, pp. 311–325.
1989 Early Historical Trade: An Overview. *The Indian Social and Economic Review* 26(4), pp. 437–457.
1994 *The Winds of Change: Buddhism and the Maritime Links of Early South India.* Oxford University Press, Delhi.

1995   Trade and Contacts. In *Recent Perspectives on Early Indian History*, edited by R. Thapar, pp. 142–167. Popular Prakashan, Bombay.

2003   *The Archaeology of Seafaring in Ancient South Asia.* Cambridge University Press, Cambridge.

Reddy Krishna Mohan, P.

2001   Maritime Trade of Early South India: New Archaeological Evidence from Motupalli, Andhra Pradesh. In *East and West* 51(1-2), pp.143–156.

Reese, D. S.

1883   The Use of Conus Shells in Neolithic and Bronze Age Greece. *The Annual of the British School of Archaeology at Athens* 78, pp. 353–357.

Rice, P. M.

1987   *Pottery Analysis: A Source-Book.* University of Chicago Press, Chicago.

Ricke, H.

1967   *Ausgrabungen von Khor-Dehmit bis Bet el-Wali.* University of Chicago Press, Chicago.

Rivard, J. L., B. C. Foster, and S. E. Sidebotham

2002   Emerald City. *Archaeology* 55(3), pp. 36–41.

Roby, T. C.

2000   Architectural Conservation. In: *Berenike 1998. Report of the 1998 Excavations at Berenike and the Survey of the Egyptian Eastern Desert, Including Excavations in Wadi Kalalat*, edited by S. E. Sidebotham and W. Z. Wendrich, pp. 343–354. Research School of Asian, African and Amerindian Studies (CNWS), Leiden, Netherlands.

Rodziewicz, M.

1984   *Alexandrie III: Les habitatons romains tardives d'Alexandrie à la lumiére des fouilles polonaises à Kôm el-Dikka.* Éditions Scientifiques de Pologne, Warsaw.

Rose, P. J.

1995   Report on the Handmade Sherds. In *Berenike 1994. Preliminary Report of the 1994 Excavations at Berenike (Egyptian Red Sea Coast) and the Survey of the Eastern Desert.*, edited by S. E. Sidebotham and W. Z. Wendrich, pp. 41–43. Research School of Asian, African and Amerindian Studies (CNWS), Leiden, Netherlands.

Rosen, S. A.

1987   Byzantine Nomadism in the Negev: Results from the Emergency Survey. *Journal of Field Archaeology* 14, pp. 29–42.

1988   Notes on the Origins of Pastoral Nomadism: A Case Study from the Negev And Sinai. *Current Anthropology* 29, pp. 498–506.

1992   Nomads in Archaeology: A Response to Finkelstein and Perevoletsky. *Bulletin of the American Schools of Oriental Research* 287, pp. 75–85.

Rullkötter, J., and A. Nissenbaum

1988   Dead Sea asphalt in Egyptian mummies—molecular evidence. *Naturwissenschaften* 75, pp. 618–621.

Rütti, B.

1991   Early enamelled glass. In *Roman Glass*, edited by M. Newby and K. Painter, pp. 122–136. Society of Antiquaries of London, London.

Sadr, K.

1994   Preliminary report on an archaeological reconnaissance in the Eastern Desert, southeast Egypt. In *Étude Nubiennes. Actes du VIIe congrès international d'études nubiennes, 3–8 septembre 1990*, II, Étude Nubiennes, edited by C. Bonnet, pp. 7–11. ,Geneva, Switzerland.

Sadr, K., A. Castiglioni, and A. Castiglioni

1995   Nubian Desert archaeology: a preliminary view. *Archéologie du Nil Moyen* 7, pp. 203–235.

Sadr, K., A. Castiglioni, A. Castiglioni, and G. Negro

1994   Archaeology in the Nubian Desert. *Sahara* 6, pp. 69–75.

Salomon, R.

1991   Epigraphic Remains of Indian Traders in Egypt. *Journal of the American Oriental Society* 111(4), pp. 731–736.

Sastri, N.

1966   *A History of South India.* 4th ed. Oxford University Press, Madras.

Schijns, W. H. M., J. D. Kila, and J. A. Harrell

1999   Architectural Observations. In *Berenike 1997. Report of the Excavations at Berenike and the Survey of the Egyptian Eastern Desert, Including Excavations at Shenshef*, edited by S. E. Sidebotham and W. Z. Wendrich, pp. 95–105. Research School of Asian, African and Amerindian Studies (CNWS), Leiden, Netherlands.

Schlingloff, D.

1974   Cotton-Manufacture in Ancient India. *Journal of the Economic and Social History of the Orient* 17(1), pp. 81–90.

Schneider, O.

1892   Der ägyptische Smaragd. *Zeitschrift für Ethnologie* 24, pp. 41–100.

Schoff, W.H.

1912   *The Periplus of the Erythraean Sea; Travel and Trade in the Indian Ocean.* Longmans Green, New York.

1974   *The Periplus of the Erythraean Sea: Travel and Trade in the Indian Ocean.* 2nd ed. Oriental Books Reprint Corp (exclusively distributed by Munshiram Manoharlal Publishers), New Delhi.

1995   *The Periplus of the Erythraean Sea.* Reprint ed. Munshiram Manoharlal Publishers, Delhi.

Schubert, P.

1986   Petrographic Model Analysis, a Necessary Complement to Chemical Analysis of Ceramic Coarse Ware. *Archaeometry* 28, pp. 163–178.

Scollar, I., A. Tabbagh, A. Hesse, and I. Herzog
  1990 *Archaeological Prospecting and Remote Sensing.* Cambridge University Press, Cambridge.

Seneviratne, S.
  1981 Kalinga and Andhra: The Process of Secondary State Formation in Early India. *Indian Historical Review* 7(1-2), pp. 54–69.

Serpico, M.
  2000 Resins, Amber and Bitumen. In *Ancient Egyptian Materials and Technology*, edited by P. T. Nicholson and I. Shaw, pp. 430–474. Cambridge University Press, Cambridge.

Shajan, K.P., R.S. Tomber, V. Selvakumar, and P.J. Cherian
  2004 Locating the Ancient Port of Muziris; Fresh Findings from Pattanam. In *Journal of Roman Archaeology* 17(1), pp. 312–320.

Shanks, M., and C. Tilley
  1987 *Social Theory and Archaeology.* Cambridge University Press, Cambridge.

Shaw, I.
  1999 Sikait-Zubara. in: *Encyclopedia of the Archaeology of Ancient Egypt*, edited by K. A. Bard, pp. 731–733. Routledge, London, New York.

Shaw, I., J. Bunbury, and R. Jameson
  1999 Emerald Mining in Roman and Byzantine Egypt. *Journal of Roman Archaeology* 12, pp. 203–215.

Shaw, I., and R. Jameson
  1993 Amethyst Mining in the Eastern Desert—a Preliminary Survey at Wadi el-Hudi. *Journal of Egyptian Archaeology* 79, pp. 81–97.

Shaw, I., and P. T. Nicholson
  1995 *British Museum Dictionary of Ancient Egypt.* Trustees of the British Museum, London.

Sidebotham, S. E.
  1986 *Roman Economic Policy in the Erythra Thalassa 30 B. C.–A. D. 217.* E. J. Brill, Leiden.
  1993 University of Delaware Archaeological Project at 'Abu Sha'ar: The 1992 Season. *Newsletter of the American Research Center in Egypt* 161/162, pp. 1–9.
  1994a Preliminary Report on the 1990–1991 Seasons of Fieldwork at 'Abu Sha'ar (Red Sea Coast). *Journal of the American Research Center in Egypt* 31, pp. 133–158.
  1994b University of Delaware Fieldwork in the Eastern Desert of Egypt, 1993. *Dumbarton Oaks Papers* 48, pp. 263–275.
  1995a Historical Sources. In *Berenike 1994. Preliminary Report of the 1994 Excavations at Berenike (Egyptian Red Sea Coast) and the Survey of the Eastern Desert*, edited by S. E. Sidebotham and W. Z. Wendrich, pp. 5–11. Research School of Asian, African and Amerindian Studies (CNWS), Leiden, Netherlands.
  1995b Survey of the Hinterland. In *Berenike 1994. Preliminary Report of the 1994 Excavations at Berenike (Egyptian Red Sea Coast) and the Survey of the Eastern Desert*, edited by S. E. Sidebotham and W. Z. Wendrich, pp. 85–101. Research School of Asian, African and Amerindian Studies (CNWS), Leiden, Netherlands.
  1996 The Excavations. In *Berenike 1995. Preliminary Report of the Excavations at Berenike (Egyptian Red Sea Coast) and the Survey of the Eastern Desert*, edited by S. E. Sidebotham and W. Z. Wendrich, pp. 7–97. Research School of Asian, African and Amerindian Studies (CNWS), Leiden, Netherlands.
  1998a The Excavations. In *Berenike 1996. Report of the 1996 Excavations at Berenike (Egyptian Red Sea Coast) and the Survey of the Eastern Desert*, edited by S. E. Sidebotham and W. Z. Wendrich, pp. 11–120. Research School of Asian, African and Amerindian Studies (CNWS), Leiden, Netherlands.
  1998b The Survey. In *Report of the 1996 Excavations at Berenike (Egyptian Red Sea Coast) and the Survey of the Eastern Desert*, edited by S. E. Sidebotham and W. Z. Wendrich, pp. 415–426. Research School of Asian, African and Amerindian Studies (CNWS), Leiden, Netherlands.
  1999a The Coins. In *Berenike 1997. Report of the 1997 Excavations at Berenike and the Survey of the Egyptian Eastern Desert, Including Excavations at Shenshef*, edited by S. E. Sidebotham and W. Z. Wendrich, pp. 183–199. Research School of Asian, African and Amerindian Studies (CNWS), Leiden, Netherlands.
  1999b The Excavations. In *Berenike 1997. Report of the 1997 Excavations at Berenike and the Survey of the Egyptian Eastern Desert, Including Excavations at Shenshef*, edited by S. E. Sidebotham and W. Z. Wendrich, pp. 3–94. Research School of Asian, African and Amerindian Studies (CNWS), Leiden, Netherlands.
  1999c Survey of the Hinterland. In *Berenike 1997. Report of the 1997 Excavations at Berenike and the Survey of the Eastern Desert, Including Excavations at Shenshef*, edited by S. E. Sidebotham and W. Z. Wendrich, pp. 349–369. Research School of Asian, African and Amerindian Studies (CNWS), Leiden, Netherlands.
  2000a Coins. In *Berenike 1998. Report of the 1998 Excavations at Berenike and the Survey of the Egyptian Eastern Desert, Including Excavations in Wadi Kalalat*, edited by S. E. Sidebotham and W. Z. Wendrich, pp. 169–178. Research School of Asian, African and Amerindian Studies (CNWS), Leiden, Netherlands.
  2000b The Excavations. In *Berenike 1998. Report of the 1998 Excavations at Berenike and the Survey of the*

Egyptian Eastern Desert, including Excavations in Wadi Kalalat, edited by S. E. Sidebotham and W. Z. Wendrich, pp. 3–147. Research School of Asian, African and Amerindian Studies (CNWS), Leiden, Netherlands.

2000c   Survey of the Hinterland. In *Berenike 1998. Report of the 1998 Excavations at Berenike and the Survey of the Egyptian Eastern Desert, Including Excavations in Wadi Kalalat*, edited by S. E. Sidebotham and W. Z. Wendrich, pp. 355–377. Research School of Asian, African and Amerindian Studies (CNWS), Leiden, Netherlands.

2002   Late Roman Berenike. *Journal of the American Research Center in Egypt* 39, pp. 217–240.

Sidebotham, S. E., H. Barnard, J. A. Harrell, and R. S. Tomber

2001   The Roman Quarry and Installations in Wadi Umm Wikala and Wadi Semna. *Journal of Egyptian Archaeology* 87, pp. 135–170.

Sidebotham, S. E., H. Barnard, D. K. Pearce, and A. J. Price

2000a   Excavations in Wadi Kalalat. In *Berenike 1998. Report of the 1998 Excavations at Berenike and the Survey of the Egyptian Eastern Desert, Including Excavations in Wadi Kalalat*, edited by S. E. Sidebotham and W. Z. Wendrich, pp. 379–402. Research School of Asian, African and Amerindian Studies (CNWS), Leiden, Netherlands.

Sidebotham, S. E., H. Barnard, and G. Pyke

2002   Five Enigmatic Late Roman Settlements in the Eastern Desert. *Journal of Egyptian Archaeology* 88, pp. 187–225.

Sidebotham, S. E., H. M. Nouwens, A. M. Hense, and J. A. Harrell

2004   Preliminary Report on Archaeological Fieldwork at Sikait (Eastern Desert of Egypt), and Environs: 2002–2003. *Sahara* 15, pp. 7–30.

Sidebotham and J. A. Seeger, S. E.

1996   The Coins. In *Berenike 1995. Preliminary Report of the 1995 Excavations at Berenike (Egyptian Red Sea Coast) and the Survey of the Eastern Desert*, edited by S. E. Sidebotham and W. Z. Wendrich, pp. 179–196. Research School of Asian, African and Amerindian Studies (CNWS), Leiden, Netherlands.

Sidebotham, S. E., and W. Z. Wendrich

1995   *Berenike 1994. Preliminary Report of the 1994 Excavations at Berenike (Egyptian Red Sea Coast) and the Survey of the Eastern Desert.* CNWS publications. Special series; no. 1. Research School of Asian, African and Amerindian Studies (CNWS), Leiden, Netherlands.

1996a   *Berenike 1995. Preliminary Report of the Excavations at Berenike (Egyptian Red Sea Coast) and the Survey of the Eastern Desert.* CNWS publications. Special

series; no. 2. Research School of Asian, African and Amerindian Studies (CNWS), Leiden, Netherlands.

1996b   Berenike: Roman Egypt's Maritime Gateway to Arabia and India. *Egyptian Archaeology* 8, pp. 15–18.

1996c   Interpretative Summary and Conclusion. In *Berenike 1995. Preliminary Report of the Excavations at Berenike (Egyptian Red Sea Coast) and the Survey of the Eastern Desert*, edited by S. E. Sidebotham and W. Z. Wendrich, pp. 441–452. Research School of Asian, African and Amerindian Studies (CNWS), Leiden, Netherlands.

1998a   *Berenike 1996. Report of the 1996 Excavations at Berenike (Egyptian Red Sea Coast) and the Survey of the Eastern Desert.* CNWS publications. Special series; no. 3. Research School of Asian, African and Amerindian Studies (CNWS), Leiden, Netherlands.

1998b   Berenike—Archaeological Fieldwork at a Ptolemaic-Roman Port on the Red Sea Coast of Egypt, 1994–1998. *Sahara* 10, pp. 85–96.

1998c   Interpretative Summary and Conclusion. In *Berenike 1996. Report of the 1996 Excavations at Berenike (Egyptian Red Sea Coast) and the Survey of the Eastern Desert*, edited by S. E. Sidebotham and W. Z. Wendrich, pp. 445–454. Research School for Asian, African and Amerindian Studies (CNWS), Leiden, Netherlands.

1999a   *Berenike 1997. Report of the 1997 Excavations at Berenike and the Survey of the Egyptian Eastern Desert, Including Excavations at Shenshef.* CNWS publications. Special series; no. 4. Research School of Asian, African and Amerindian Studies (CNWS), Leiden, Netherlands.

1999b   Interpretative Summary and Conclusion. In *Berenike 1997. Report of the 1997 Excavations at Berenike and the Survey of the Egyptian Eastern Desert, Including Excavations at Shenshef*, edited by S. E. Sidebotham and W. Z. Wendrich, pp. 445–456. Research School of Asian, African and Amerindian Studies (CNWS), Leiden, Netherlands.

2000a   *Berenike 1998. Report of the 1998 Excavations at Berenike and the Survey of the Egyptian Eastern Desert, Including Excavations in Wadi Kalalat.* CNWS publications. Special series; no. 4. Research School of Asian, African and Amerindian Studies (CNWS), Leiden, Netherlands.

2000b   Interpretative Summary and Conclusion. In *Berenike 1998. Report of the 1998 Excavations at Berenike (Egyptian Red Sea Coast) and the Survey of the Egyptian Eastern Desert, Including Excavations in Wadi Kalalat*, edited by S. E. Sidebotham and W. Z. Wendrich, pp. 413–420. Research School of Asian,

African and Amerindian Studies (CNWS), Leiden, Netherlands.

2001   Berenike, Roms Tor am Roten Meer nach Arabien und Indien. *Antike Welt* 32(3), pp. 251–263.

2002a   Berenike: A Ptolemaic-Roman Port on the Ancient Maritime Spice and Incense Route. *Minerva* 13, pp. 28-31.

2002b   Berenike: Archaeological Fieldwork at a Ptolemaic-Roman Port on the Red Sea Coast of Egypt 1999–2001. *Sahara* 13, pp. 23–50.

Sidebotham, S. E., and R. E. Zitterkopf

1995   Routes Through the Eastern Desert of Egypt. *Expedition* 37(2), pp. 39–52.

1996   Survey of the Hinterland. In *Berenike 1995. Preliminary Report of the 1995 Excavations at Berenike (Egyptian Red Sea Coast) and the Survey of the Eastern Desert*, edited by S. E. Sidebotham and W. Z. Wendrich, pp. 357–409. Research School of Asian, African and Amerindian Studies (CNWS), Leiden, Netherlands.

1997   Survey of the Via Hadriana by the University of Delaware: The 1996 Season. *Bulletin de l'Institut français d'archéologie orientale, Bulletin de Centenaire* 97, pp. 221–237.

1998   Survey of the Via Hadriana: The 1997 Season. *Bulletin de l'Institut français d'archéologie orientale, Bulletin de Centenaire*, pp. 353–365.

Sidebotham, S. E., R. E. Zitterkopf, and C. C. Helms

2000   Survey of the Via Hadriana: The 1998 Season. *Journal of the American Research Center in Egypt* 37, pp. 115–126.

Sidebotham, S. E., R. E. Zitterkopf, and J. A. Riley

1991   Survey of the 'Abu Sha'ar-Nile Road. *American Journal of Archaeology* 95(4), pp. 571–622.

Sidebotham, S. E., R. E. Zitterkopf ,and R. S. Tomber

        Survey of the Via Nova Hadriana: Final Report. Forthcoming.

Sinkankas, J.

1989   *Emerald and Other Beryls.* Geoscience Press, Prescott, Arizona.

Smith, G. F., and F. C. Phillips

1972   *Gemstones.* 14th ed. Pitman Publishing, New York.

Spaer, M.

1988   The Pre-Islamic Glass Bracelets of Palestine. *Journal of Glass Studies* 30, pp. 51–61.

1992   Islamic Glass Bracelets of Palestine: Preliminary Findings. *Journal of Glass Studies* 34, pp. 44–62.

Starr, C. G.

1982   *The Roman Empire 27 B. C.–A. D. 476: A Study in Survival.* Oxford University Press, New York, Oxford.

Stella, A.

1934   Contributo alla conoscenza dei giacimenti di berillo dell'alto Egitto. *Bollettino della Societá geologica italiana* 53, pp. 329–332.

Stokstad, E.

2000   Geology: Discovering the Original Emerald Cities. *Science*, January 28, pp. 562–563.

Strouhal, E.

1984   *Wadi Qitna and Kalabsha-South.* Charles University, Prague.

Sundelin, L. K. R.

1996   Plaster Jar Stoppers. In *Berenike 1995. Preliminary Report of the 1995 Excavations at Berenike (Egyptian Red Sea Coast) and the Survey of the Eastern Desert*, edited by S. E. Sidebotham and W. Z. Wendrich, pp. 297–308. Research School of Asian, African and Amerindian Studies (CNWS), Leiden, Netherlands.

Suter, C. E., and M. Gibson

1998   Diyala Objects Project. *Oriental Institute 1997–98, Annual Report*, pp. 50–56. University of Chicago, Oriental Institute, Chicago.

Syme, R.

1954   Review of A. Stein, Die Präfekten. *Journal of Roman Studies* 44, pp. 116–119.

Tchernia, A.

1995   Rome and India, Archaeology Alone? In *Athens, Aden, Arikamedu: Essays on the Interrelations Between India, Arabia, and the Eastern Mediterranean*, edited by M.-F. Boussac and J.-F. Salles, pp. 147–156. Manohar, Centre de Science Humaines, New Delhi.

Thapar, R.

1992   Black Gold: South Asia and the Roman Maritime Trade. *South Asian Studies* 15, pp. 1–27.

Thomas, E. S.

1909   The Mineral Industry of Egypt. Precious Stones: Emeralds. *Cairo Scientific Journal* 3, pp. 267–272.

Thomas, R., and J. Whitewright

2001   Roman Period Maritime Artefacts. In *Myos Hormos—Quseir al-Qadim: A Roman and Islamic Port Site. Interim Report 2001* (unpublished report), edited by D. Peacock, pp. 37–40. University of Southampton, Southampton.

Thomas, R., J. Whitewright, and L. Blue

2002   Maritime Artefacts. In *Myos Hormos-Quseir al-Qadim: A Roman and Islamic Port Site Interim Report 2002* (unpublished report), edited by D. Peacock, pp. 81–83. University of Southampton, Southampton.

Tibbets, G. R.

1979   *A Study of the Arabic Texts Containing Material on South-East Asia. Oriental Translation Fund* 44. E. J. Brill, Leiden, Netherlands.

Tomber, R. S.

1998   The Pottery. In *Berenike 1996. Report of the 1996 Excavations at Berenike (Egyptian Red Sea Coast) and the Survey of the Eastern Desert*, edited by S. E. Sidebotham and W. Z. Wendrich, pp. 163-180. Research School of Asian, African and Amerindian Studies (CNWS), Leiden, Netherlands.

1999   The Pottery. In *Berenike 1997. Report of the 1997 Excavations at Berenike and the Survey of the Egyptian Eastern Desert, Including Excavations at Shenshef*, edited by S. E. Sidebotham and W. Z. Wendrich, pp. 123-159. Research School of Asian, African and Amerindian Studies (CNWS), Leiden, Netherlands.

2000   Indo-Roman Trade: The Ceramic Evidence from Egypt. *Antiquity* 74, pp. 624–631.

Tomber, R. S., and V. Begley

2000   Indian Pottery Sherds. In *Berenike 1998. Report of the 1998 Excavations at Berenike and the Survey of the Egyptian Eastern Desert, Including Excavations in Wadi Kalalat*, edited by S. E. Sidebotham and W. Z. Wendrich, pp. 149–167. Research School of Asian, African and Amerindian Studies (CNWS) Leiden, Netherlands.

Turner, P.

1989   *Roman Coins from India*. Royal Numismatic Society, London.

Updegraff, R. T.

1988   The Blemmyes I, the Rise of the Blemmyes and the Roman Withdrawal from Nubia Under Diocletian (with Additional Remarks by L. Török). *Aufstieg und Niedergang der römischen Welt* 2.10.1, pp. 44–106.

Van Neer, W., and A. M. H. Ervynck

1998   The Faunal Remains. In *Berenike 1996. Report of the 1996 Excavations at Berenike (Egyptian Red Sea Coast) and the Survey of the Eastern Desert*, edited by S. E. Sidebotham and W. Z. Wendrich, pp. 349–388. Research School for Asian African and Amerindian Studies (CNWS), Leiden, Netherlands.

1999   The Faunal Remains. In *Berenike 1997. Report of the 1997 Excavations at Berenike and the Survey of the Egyptian Eastern Desert, Including Excavations at Shenshef*, edited by S. E. Sidebotham and W. Z. Wendrich, pp. 321–348. Research School of Asian African and Amerindian Studies (CNWS), Leiden, Netherlands.

Verhoogt, A. M. F. W.

1998   Greek and Latin Textual Material. In *Berenike 1996. Report of the Excavations at Berenike (Egyptian Red Sea Coast) and the Survey of the Eastern Desert*, edited by S. E. Sidebotham and W. Z. Wendrich, pp. 193–198. Research School of Asian, African and Amerindian Studies (CNWS), Leiden, Netherlands.

Vermeeren, C. E.

1998   Wood and Charcoal. In *Berenike 1996: Report of the Excavations at Berenike (Egyptian Red Sea Coast) and the Survey of the Eastern Desert*, edited by S. E. Sidebotham and W. Z. Wendrich, pp. 331–348. Research School of Asian, African and Amerindian Studies (CNWS) Leiden, Netherlands.

1999   Wood and Charcoal. In *Berenike 1997. Report of the 1997 Excavations at Berenike and the Survey of the Egyptian Eastern Desert, Including Excavations at Shenshef*, edited by S. E. Sidebotham and W. Z. Wendrich, pp. 307–324. Research School of Asian, African and Amerindian Studies (CNWS), Leiden, Netherlands.

2000   Wood and Charcoal. In *Berenike 1998. Report of the 1998 Excavations at Berenike and the Survey of the Egyptian Eastern Desert, Including Excavations in Wadi Kalalat*, edited by S. E. Sidebotham and W. Z. Wendrich, pp. 311–342. Research School of Asian, African and Amerindian Studies (CNWS) Leiden, Netherlands.

Vogelsang-Eastwood, G. M.

1990   *Resist-Dyed Textiles from Quseir al-Qadim, Egypt*. Association pour l'Étude et la Documentation des Textiles d'Asie (AEDTA), Paris.

Wadia, D. N.

1975   *Geology of India*, 4th ed. Tata McGraw-Hill, New Delhi.

Warmington, E. H.

1974   *The Commerce Between the Roman Empire and India*, 2nd ed. Curzon Press, London.

Watson, A. M.

1977   The Rise and Spread of Old World Cotton. In *Studies in Textile History*, edited by V. Gervers, pp. 355–368. Royal Ontario Museum, Toronto.

Weheba, A.-F., M. Riad, and M. M. A. Seteha

1974   *South-East Egypt (Geological Essays)*. Beirut Arab University, Beirut.

Wendrich, W. Z.

1995   Basketry and Cordage. In *Berenike 1994. Preliminary Report of the Excavations at Berenike (Egyptian Red Sea Coast) and the Survey of the Eastern Desert*, edited by S. E. Sidebotham and W. Z. Wendrich, pp. 69–84. Research School of Asian, African and Amerindian Studies (CNWS), Leiden, Netherlands.

1998a   Basketry and Matting. In *Berenike 1996. Report of the Excavations at Berenike (Egyptian Red Sea Coast) and the Survey of the Eastern Desert*, edited by S. E. Sidebotham and W. Z. Wendrich, pp. 253–264. Research School of Asian, African and Amerindian Studies (CNWS), Leiden, Netherlands.

1998b   Fringes Are Anchored in Warp and Weft: The Relations Between Berenike, Shenshef, and the Nile Valley. In *Life on the Fringe: Living in the*

Southern Egyptian Deserts During the Roman and Early Byzantine Periods, edited by O. E. Kaper, pp. 243-251. Research School CNWS School of Asian African and Amerindian Studies, Leiden, Netherlands.

1999a Basketry and Matting. In *Berenike 1997. Report of the 1997 Excavations at Berenike and the Survey of the Egyptian Eastern Desert, Including Excavations at Shenshef*, edited by S. E. Sidebotham and W. Z. Wendrich, pp. 277–284. Research School of Asian, African and Amerindian Studies (CNWS), Leiden, Netherlands.

1999b *The World According to Basketry: An Ethnoarchaeological Interpretation of Basketry Production in Egypt*. Research School for Asian, African and Amerindian Studies (CNWS), Leiden, Netherlands.

2000 Basketry and Matting. In *Berenike 1998. Report of the Excavations at Berenike and the Survey of the Egyptian Eastern Desert, Including Excavations in Wadi Kalalat*, edited by S. E. Sidebotham and W. Z. Wendrich, pp. 227–250. Research School of Asian, African and Amerindian Studies (CNWS), Leiden, Netherlands.

Wendrich, W. Z., and G. v. d. Kooij (Eds.)

2002 *Moving Matters, Ethnoarchaeology in the Near East*. Research School of Asian, African and Amerindian Studies CNWS at Leiden University, Leiden, Netherlands.

Wendrich, W. Z., R. S. Tomber, S. E. Sidebotham, J. A. Harrell, R. T. J. Cappers, and R. S. Bagnall

2003 Berenike Crossroads: The Integration of Information. *Journal of the Economic and Social History of the Orient* 46(1), pp. 46–87.

Wendrich, W. Z., and A. J. Veldmeijer

1996 Cordage and Basketry. In *Berenike 1995. Preliminary Report of the Excavations at Berenike (Egyptian Red Sea Coast) and the Survey of the Eastern Desert*, edited by S. E. Sidebotham and W. Z. Wendrich, pp. 269–296. Research School of Asian, African and Amerindian Studies (CNWS), Leiden, Netherlands.

Wessely, K.

1904 *Topographie des Faijum (Arsinoites nomus) in griechischer Zeit. Denkschriften der Kaiserlichen Akademie der Wissenschaften, Philosophisch-Historische Classe; 50 Bd., Abb. 1*. In Kommission bei C. Gerold's Sohn, Vienna.

Wheeler, R. E. M., A. Ghosh, and K. Deva

1946 Arikamedu: An Indo-Roman Trading Station on the East Coast of India. *Ancient India* 2, pp. 17–124.

Whitcomb, D. S., and J. H. Johnson

1979 *Quseir al-Qadim 1978 Preliminary Report*. American Research Center in Egypt, Princeton, New Jersey; Cairo.

Wild, J. P., and F. C. Wild

1998 The Textiles. In *Berenike 1996. Report of the 1996 Excavations at Berenike (Egyptian Red Sea Coast) and the Survey of the Eastern Desert*, edited by S. E.

Sidebotham and W. Z. Wendrich, pp. 221-236. Research School of Asian, African and Amerindian Studies (CNWS), Leiden, Netherlands.

2000 Textiles. In *Berenike 1998. Report of the 1998 Excavations at Berenike and the Survey of the Egyptian Eastern Desert, Including Excavations in Wadi Kalalat*, edited by S. E. Sidebotham and W. Z. Wendrich, pp. 251–274. Research School of Asian, African and Amerindian Studies (CNWS), Leiden, Netherlands.

2001 Sails from the Roman Port at Berenike, Egypt. *The International Journal of Nautical Archaeology* 30(2), pp. 211–220.

Wilding, R. F.

1989 The Pottery. In *Excavations at Aksum, Memoirs of the British Institute in Eastern Africa* 10, edited by S. C. H. Munro-Hay, pp. 235–316. British Institute of Eastern Africa, London.

Wilkinson, A.

1998 *The Garden in Ancient Egypt*. The Rubicon Press, London.

Wilkinson, J. G.

1847 *Hand-Book for Travellers in Egypt*. John Murray, London.

Williams, D.

2000 Appendix III. Petrology of Imported Amphorae. In *Archaeology in Aksum, Ethiopia, 1993–7, Memoirs of the British Institute in Eastern Africa* 17, *Research Committee of the Society of Antiquaries of London Report* 65, edited by D. W. Phillipson pp. 494–496. British Institute in Eastern Africa/Society of Antiquaries of London, London.

Young, G. K.

2001 *Rome's Eastern Trade International Commerce and Imperial Policy, 31 BC–AD 305*. Routledge, London; New York.

Zarins, J.

1992 The Early Utilization of Indigo Along the Northern Indian Ocean Rim. In *South Asian Archaeology 1989*, edited by C. Jarrige, pp. 469–483. Prehistory Press, Madison, Wisconsin.

Zeymal, E. V.

1975 Western Kshatrapa Coins in the Hermitage. *Kul'tura i iskusstvo Indii i stran Dal'nego Vostoka (Culture and Art of India and Far Eastern Countries)*, pp. 4–20. Avrora, Leningrad.

Zitterkopf, R. E.

1998 Roman Construction Techniques in the Eastern Desert. In *Life on the Fringe. Living in the Southern Egyptian Deserts During the Roman and Early Byzantine Periods. Proceedings of a Colloquium Held on the Occasion of the 25th Anniversary of the Netherlands Institute for Archaeology and Arabic Studies in Cairo 9–12 December 1996*, edited by O. E. Kaper, pp. 271–286. Research School of Asian, African and Amerindian Studies (CNWS), Leiden, Netherlands.

INDEX